HARWICH FERRIES

Parkeston Quay under Railway Ownership

Stephen Brown

Copyright © 2014 Ferry Publications. All rights reserved.

ISBN 978-1-906608-40-8

The right of Stephen Brown to be identified as the author of this work has been asserted in accordance with the Copyright Act 1991.

No part of this publication may be reproduced, stored in a retrieval system or transmitted in any form or by any means, electronic, mechanical, photocopying, recording or otherwise, without prior permission in writing from the publisher.

Produced in the Isle of Man by Lily Publications Ltd. Ferry Publications is a trading name of Lily Publications Ltd.

First published in the Isle of Man in 2011 by
Ferry Publications
PO Box 33
Ramsey
Isle of Man
IM99 4LP

CONTENTS

Foreword 3

Introduction 4

Early Days 5

The 1840s 10

The 1850s 13

The 1860s 16

The 1870s 23

The 1880s 27

The 1890s 36

The 1900s 41

The 1910s 49

The 1920s 59

The 1930s 71

The 1940s 81

The 1950s 93

The 1960s 109

The 1970s 141

The 1980s 163

The River and Harbour Services 193

Fleet List 196

Previous page: A view from the *Braemar* looking along No. 3 Berth with the *Dana Anglia* in the West Portal berth - 25th July 1989. (Stephen Brown)

FOREWORD

I am very pleased to write the foreword to this highly interesting account regarding the ferry activities at Harwich and Parkeston Quay.

Personally I have never ceased to be amazed at just how bold and enterprising the Great Eastern Railway (GER) was in the late 1870s in deciding to build a new port on Ray Island, an isolated area upstream of Harwich in the River Stour. By doing so they not only created what became known as Parkeston Quay but in the process also diverted the existing railway line that ran to Harwich.

My term of office there covered the last five years of nationalised ownership under the British Rail Board and the first five years of privatised ownership under Sea Containers. During those times I saw all the original land plans produced by the GER. These covered an area of mudflats stretching from west of Ray Island, across Bathside Bay and towards old Harwich and which, when all were collected together, gave the GER plenty of room for expansion. In subsequent years Parkeston Quay was twice extended in response to a growth in services and trade until when, during the late 1960s, it received a substantial capital investment towards providing a Harwich - Zeebrugge container service and the conversion of the Harwich - Hoek van Holland route into a roll-on/roll-off ferry service. A number of new ships and new berths all came into operation during 1968 and these were supplemented by a new passenger terminal and car bridge over the railway (known by the dockers as the Hurdy Gurdy!).

In due course ever larger ferries arrived on the Hook route such as the *St. Edmund* and the *Princess Beatrix*, the *St. Nicholas* and the *Koningin Beatrix* along with many other ships on other routes operated by Continental companies. In addition to the ferry operations I also saw the reclamation of about one third of Bathside Bay as a result of the pumping ashore of sand and gravel dredged from the estuary. The Centenary of the opening of Parkeston Quay took place in 1983 and the event allowed the occasion, recorded in this book, of myself and the four previous Shipping and Port Managers all being present together.

Since those days, sadly, the number of staff has reduced considerably as have the variety of services and sailings. Although the port nowadays hosts the *Stena Hollandica* and *Stena Britannica*, these being the largest ro-ro passenger ships in the world and which continue in the best traditions of the Harwich - Hook route, it is alas nowhere near as bustling or varied as it once was. This book is therefore a highly creditable work that reminds us all of what Harwich and Parkeston Quay were once like when the railways were in charge, their rise into becoming ports of national importance and the huge variety of ships that have visited in the past. Accordingly I commend it to its readers.

Colin Crawford,
formerly Shipping and Port Manager
(General Manager) of Harwich Parkeston Quay
1979-1989

Right: Early promotional poster for LNER ferry service featuring new ships *Amsterdam*, *Prague* and *Vienna*. (Stephen Brown)

INTRODUCTION

Harwich has long been associated with the sea and its port at Parkeston Quay has seen a worthy succession of ferries and other commercial vessels not only having been utilised in regular service across the North Sea but also in moving goods from around the world. Much of its acclaimed rise into being one of Britain's foremost ferry ports was due to the foresight and investment of the various railway companies that once owned it. What follows is an account of the many major developments that occurred up until the end of the 1980s when both ownership by the railways and the scope of this book ends.

Such an account might well start 'In the beginning...' but here there was practically nothing to begin with. There had for many centuries existed an established settlement at Harwich but there was no such place as Parkeston and certainly no quay there until the railways arrived in the late 19th century. Today Parkeston still hosts a very substantial and modern quay facility equipped to deal with all manner of sea going traffic. Sadly there are times now when not a single ship can be seen tied up alongside.

Parkeston Quay was renamed Harwich International Port in 1997 and its current state of activity makes it hard to imagine that what rose up from a wasteland of mudflats and tidal saltings was once a port of unrivalled versatility amongst all of Britain's cross channel ports. From the outset its railway owning managers had sought to open up more links and better facilities for trade between Britain, Holland and Belgium and for more than a century it thrived as a place of expansion, variety and innovation. Their efforts were as much influenced by social, economic and political events as they were aided by the many technological, entrepreneurial and business activities that occurred on both sides of an intervening North Sea.

Thus the Great Eastern Railway, the London & North Eastern Railway and British Railways in turn operated not only the cargo and passenger steamers of Victorian times that later developed into large scale passenger and ro-ro ferries, freight ships and container vessels out of Parkeston Quay but also train ferries and river boat services out of Harwich itself. In addition a number of other operators such as DFDS and Fred Olsen, RMT and SNCF were attracted into ultimately linking Parkeston Quay with all of the Continent's North Sea and Channel facing countries from as far north as Norway all the way down to Spain.

Practically all semblance of what could be termed 'the good old days' has now gone. The port, along with the ferry industry in general, has long suffered the effects of the loss of duty free, the increased competition from low cost airlines, the Channel Tunnel and the ever rising price of fuel. Nowadays it is further threatened by the introduction of 'green' regulations concerning fuel emissions, a factor that caused DFDS to close its historic link to Esbjerg on 29th September 2014. Doing so then left the port with just one remaining ferry route, a situation that hasn't existed at Harwich since 1854!

In between such times the history of Harwich's ferries may perhaps be best referenced against the comments of LNER Director Sir Hugh Bell who, in 1924 during the ceremony to mark the opening of the train ferry terminal at Harwich, remarked that such an enterprise might be regarded *'as the beginning of a long career of satisfactory usefulness to the world'*. Throughout those 'railway days' the port of Harwich Parkeston Quay was indeed a long serving place of usefulness to a great many people and highly deserving of its leading role in cross-channel ferry port history.

EARLY DAYS

Harwich, Herewiz or Herewych, is thought to have started as a modest seafaring community around the start of the 13th century. By 1253 it had grown large enough to be granted a weekly market and other privileges by the then Lord of the Manor of Dovercourt, Roger Bigod, 4th Earl of Norfolk. A primitive local government under a Bailiff, or Chief Burgess, then followed and in 1319 Parliamentary representation was secured when Edward II, influenced by his step-brother, Thomas de Botherton, Lord of the Manor of Dovercourt and Harwich, signed a Charter of privileges at Berwick.

Harwich faced out across the North Sea towards a Europe offering lucrative opportunities for both trading and commerce that were greatly enhanced by the arrival of the railways during the mid 19th century. The attraction for the railways was that from Harwich they could engage in the sea going trade between Britain and the Low Countries and access the ports of Rotterdam in Holland and Antwerp in Belgium. At the time both Holland and Belgium were relatively new as nation states with each then barely twenty years old. A brief historical background helps explain how these two important ports became significant to developments at Harwich.

The history of The Low Countries, ie the Netherlands, Belgium and Luxembourg, has been marked by various periods of forced integration, separation and rivalry with the Dutch being viewed as the more dominant throughout. Add to that the various monarchical ambitions, wars throughout Europe and a consequent assortment of treaties and alliances for the territories of these countries and it becomes clear that their emergence as independent entities was somewhat traumatic and complicated.

After years of individual principalities, bishoprics and inter-marriages it was the Holy Roman Emperor Charles V who in 1519 organised the area into the 'Seventeen Provinces of the Netherlands'. Charles V was Flemish by birth and during his tenure towns such as Bruges and Antwerp became prosperous through trade and manufacturing. His son, Philip II of Spain who inherited in 1556, had a cold and disdainful attitude towards his new subjects and installed his half sister, Margaret of Parma, as Governor of the Netherlands.

The imposition of high taxes and the cruelties of the Inquisition which followed were such that in 1566 some 500 nobles, both Catholic and Protestant, petitioned against this Spanish tyranny. The petitioners were referred to as 'beggars' and their requests were refused. In protest a small number of Protestant groups then vandalised and destroyed a number of Catholic buildings and artefacts and in doing so provoked a swift and brutal response from Spain inflicted by the Duke of Alva.

Having earlier fled to England, William the Silent, Prince of Orange, (a descendant of the German house of Nassau and 'Silent' because of his calm and patient manner when in danger), returned in 1568 to lead a resistance army against the Spanish ruler. In league with the 'sea beggars', a group of maritime based fugitives or privateers, he harried Spanish shipping and managed to capture the port of Brielle or Briel in 1572. This success marked the start of Dutch national history.

A ten percent transaction tax on trade, instigated by the Duke of Alva, then stirred southern Catholics and wealthy merchants into revolt as business ceased to be viable. In the events Antwerp was sacked. In 1576 all the northern and southern provinces except Royalist Luxembourg vowed to work together for victory over Spain but after William had triumphantly entered Brussels the nature of the Low Countries changed.

At the Union of Utrecht in 1579, the ten Catholic southern provinces, roughly today's Belgium, broke with those of the north and became known as the Spanish Netherlands having concluded a separate peace treaty with Spain. The seven Protestant provinces in the north then created the United Provinces of the Netherlands and declared full independence from Spain. The Rhine and Meuse or Maas rivers came under Dutch control and in 1585 the Dutch closed off the river Scheldt and the port of Antwerp in retaliation against its southern neighbours for having chosen to favour Spain.

At Harwich Queen Elizabeth I had been a visitor in 1561 and during her reign the port became established as one of 'exit and entry'. A Customs Officer, acting as a deputy to the Officer at Ipswich, was stationed there in 1577 for the 'examination of passengers'. A new Charter was granted in 1603 by James I and in July 1620 when the Pilgrim Fathers sailed onboard the *Mayflower* from London her Master was Christopher Jones, one time resident of Harwich.

The 17th century saw the Netherlands develop into a leading industrial and maritime power unlike their southern neighbour who had not the freedom to determine their own future. The Dutch sought to expand and colonise parts of the New World and Asia and in doing so formed The Dutch East India Company in 1602 to rival similar expansion by the British. The Peace of Westphalia in 1648, marking the end of the Thirty Years War, forced Spain to recognise the Netherlands as an independent entity with the Dutch being allowed to retain its control of the Scheldt river. Such control was important to the Dutch as it allowed them to both protect and develop its own port of Amsterdam as the Low Countries main port for trade and wealth. The southern provinces remained under the governorship of Spain.

Between 1652 and 1654 Britain and the Netherlands were at war, an event sparked off by the English Navigation Act of 1651 which decreed that goods coming to England must be carried either in English ships or ships of the country supplying the goods. This act severely interrupted Dutch trade.

It was not until after the Restoration of the British Monarchy in 1660, under Charles II, that Harwich was officially noted as being a 'packet-port'. An 'Act for erecting and establishing a Post Office' led to a Packet Service being brought into operation to which Colonel Henry Bishop, as Post Master General, undertook to reorganise the postal service. He contracted to pay the King £21,500 and as part of his proposed improvements he made an agreement with 'the Lord Ambassador Horne', on behalf of the city of Amsterdam, for a direct service to Holland starting in 1661.

Previously the mails to Holland had been sent via Folkestone and Flanders but this new service from

Harwich sailed to Hellevoetsluis, on the south west corner of Voorne Island, slightly inland from the Dutch coast on the river Old Maas. It exclusively employed English boats for the carrying both ways of all letters. In addition to carrying this 'common mayle', passengers such as bankers, diplomats, artisans and senior civil servants were also carried for the sum of 12 shillings First class and 6 shillings Second class.

The Postmaster's arrangements at Harwich required a resident deputy with the responsibility of seeing to the handling of the mails on shore, for the provision of horses and for the quick despatch of the mail bags after they came into his charge. A resident Agent, attending to all other shipping matters on shore, soon came to regard himself as 'a Commander of the packet service'. Three craft of unknown ownership, known as 'hoys', were used at the start but it quickly became the practice for the Agent to hire suitable vessels from private syndicates of owners.

Whilst the Packet agreement was initially said to have been well kept there were soon complaints that the Dutch were disregarding it. Amidst accusations of unjust practises and 'a hundred other evil artes' the Dutch brought in superior and faster vessels that sought to attract any passengers carrying letters that should have been paid for as public mail. In keeping with the times, there being a Second Dutch War between 1665 and 1667 when the packet service was suspended, all the English vessels were well armed. The Agent agreed to refund the value of the ships if any were lost and was also contracted to employ and pay the crew, usually numbering about twenty men per ship. They sailed irregularly as sources of information from the Continent, unless otherwise intercepted. The official packet service resumed in 1668 with sailings leaving Harwich on Wednesdays and Saturdays.

A new agreement was made in 1671 between officials in Amsterdam, the Postmaster Andrew Carr in Harwich and Thomas Langley as Agent. Langley undertook to 'equip fully and victual three galliot hoys, for £76, payable every 28 days, to transport the ordinary mails, letters and passengers to and from Harwich and Holland twice in every week'. The days of sailing from Harwich remained as Wednesdays and Saturdays leaving at around 2 o'clock in the afternoon. Despite a Third Dutch War between 1672 and 1674, in which Charles II and the French King Louis XIV invaded the United Provinces, this improved packet service lasted until 1676 after which the Dutch port was changed from Hellevoetsluis to Brielle, a little further to the north.

In 1686 a further new Post Office contract was agreed whereby £900 a year was paid to operate 3 boats on the Harwich to Brielle route. However problems with the shifting sandbars on the approach to Brielle saw the service returning to Hellevoetsluis where it remained throughout most of the 18th century.

In 1689 the three small hoys were replaced with four boats 'of force' armed primarily to defend themselves at a time when Britain was now at war with France. Any carriage of mails out of Dover was by then suspended making the route out of Harwich all the more important. However the 'boats of force' were quite liable to chase others they referred to as 'Captains Prizes'. Consequently the service became one of dubious reliability as 'packet boats were apt to disappear mysteriously for days at a time even when the wind was in the most favourable quarter'. Reports of smuggling, petty piracy and boats vanishing up a multitude of creeks and inlets were not uncommon. Furthermore the fare had risen to 20 shillings First class and 10 shillings Second class.

Patronage by Royalty occurred when King William III of Orange and Queen Mary, the niece of Charles II, crossed over to England in 1688 to accept the title of Monarch. In 1693 the royal pair again crossed over, on the vessel *Vine,* with the occasion being marked by a medal and chain of gold being presented to Captain Robert Stevens for his gallantry against a more heavily armed French privateer. However such gallantry was later considered as being unwise on a regular basis given the nature of the cargo at risk and so in 1694 the Post Office built four small packet boats of remarkable speed, the idea being to outrun rather then fight off any aggressors.

During a lull in hostilities with France the Dover service to Calais resumed in 1697 leaving just the four Post Office boats from Harwich running to Hellevoetsluis. However when war was resumed in 1702 the armed packets re-appeared at Harwich with the route to Holland being the only one linking the Continent. In 1710 the Post Office added an extra boat. In 1711 sailings were twice a week leaving Harwich each Thursday and Sunday at 2 o'clock. The ships were then of around 60 tons with a crew of 20 and would normally carry a total of 100 passengers onboard with room for up to 150 if needed.

In 1712 the war with France ceased and in 1713 came the end of the War of the Spanish Succession which ended Spain's governorship of Belgium. However Belgium was then ruled over by the Austrian Hapsburgs and was known as the Austrian Netherlands.

In 1728 H.R.H. Frederick, Prince of Wales, crossed on the *Dispatch* and showed his appreciation of the care and attention afforded him throughout the voyage by ordering the Mate, Mr. John Fuller, to receive 100 guineas and a gold medal. In addition five guineas went to each of the crew. In 1730 the packet service from Harwich remained at just the five Post Office boats, the *Dispatch, Dolphin, Eagle, Marlborough* and *Prince of Wales*. Few details of these early packets remain but of the *Eagle* it is said that 'of 77 tons, she was built at Arundel, Sussex, in 1703 and was a round sterned sloop 53 feet long and 18 and a half feet beam, with a large Cabin or State Room, good windlass, suit of masts and yards, caps and cross trees'.

By the 1760s the service between Harwich and Hellevoetsluis was up to four times a week, weather permitting. It was not unusual to be stormbound for days and the enforced delays in hostelries of dubious quality and 'sharp accounting of the bill' led many to heavily criticize the service suggesting that 'the captain is in league with the innkeeper!'.

Accommodation on board was quite crude in the earliest boats but improved as the years went by giving rise to experiences of varied account. In August 1763 Dr. Samuel Johnson, before seeing his friend Boswell off on the *Prince of Wales* to Hellevoetsluis, took those due to sail on her to St. Nicholas Church in Harwich where he then sent them to their knees saying, *'Now that you are going to leave your native country recommend yourselves to the protection of your Creator and Redeemer'.*

On a lighter note, in 1786 a young German lady passenger, Sophie la Roche, noted in her diary;- *'Two rooms and two cabins hold 26 berths for passengers: it is all very attractive. The outer room is panelled with mahogany and has a fine mirror and lamp brackets fastened to the wall. The berths are arranged along the side walls in two rows like theatre boxes, one above the other; they have thoroughly good mattresses, white quilted covers, neat curtains, and on a ledge in the corner is a chamber made of English china used in case of sickness. In order to lie down, the outer board of these boxes is removed and then fitted in again by the sailors to prevent people from falling out. It holds one person quite comfortably and the whole looks very neat!'.*

Since the early 1700s the Dutch, British and French had slowly squeezed the Belgian provinces out of any commercial competition. However the latter part of the 18th century saw a gradual decline in Dutch influence, trade and culture under a somewhat lack lustre House of Orange. Anti-Orange supporters led the Dutch to become involved in a widespread reforming movement and ultimately the American Revolution where its sea power was destroyed by the British.

A reduction in the movement of diplomats and senior figures through Harwich to the Netherlands coincided with a generally declining standard of efficiency and the honesty of certain local landlords. Furthermore the crews of the sailing packets were now allowed to carry personal goods for sale but the privilege was so much abused that it threatened the end of the service as the public lost confidence in it. Gradually Dutch commercial traffic drifted away from Harwich to be taken by London and wharves along the Thames.

Of the Captains it was said they were men of substance and of local account though there supposedly was a clause in their contract which permitted the Captain, provided he had good reason or excuse and got the consent of the Agent, to stay on shore and send the packet to sea in charge of the Mate or someone else. In support of this contention, in 1793, the Postmaster General was moved to draw attention to the fact that of the twelve packets at sea on a certain date no less than ten of their Captains were on shore. In 1798, one Captain had been absent for years, his last valid excuse being when he had lost his mother some six years before!. The packet ports concerned were not named but it seems likely to have included Harwich because a further war with France in 1793 had once again seen Dover's packet service closed.

Being 'men of substance and of local account' did not guarantee that Captains were all trustworthy, honest or of good character. Accusations were rife that they were making a fortune through bribery, deception, smuggling and swindling both passengers and the Post Office alike. Sums of £1,000 to £1,500 a year were spoken of which was an astonishing amount of money for the times.

In 1789 came the French Revolution and the Belgians took steps to form their own fledgling republic against the repressive Austrian Emperor, Joseph II. Unfortunately with Austria and Prussia declaring their support for the French monarchy France went to war and invaded Austrian controlled Belgium. The Republic of France was created in 1792 and during that year the French re-opened the river Scheldt after it having been closed for over 200 years, an event of obvious significance to Antwerp. The French revolutionary forces went on to invade the Netherlands in 1795, creating a Batavian Republic as a satellite of France, (the name Batavi being that of a first century A.D. Germanic tribe), whilst in the 1796 the Belgian provinces were fully incorporated into the French First Republic.

When the French were advancing towards the Netherlands some Harwich packets were still sailing to Hellevoetsluis but as the advance became ever more threatening alternative packet services were established with ports much further north at Cuxhaven and Husum in Germany and with Gothenburg in Sweden. The Dutch route from Harwich ended with the Napoleonic occupation and in 1795 most of the packet boats were moved up the coast to more safely sail out of Great Yarmouth to Hamburg. Services from Harwich to Hellevoetsluis and Cuxhaven resumed in 1801 this time using 9 packet boats, later increased to 10, each of which was around 70 to 100 tons.

A map of Harwich harbour and its approaches in 1804 showing the location of Ray Isle, the future site of Parkeston Quay.

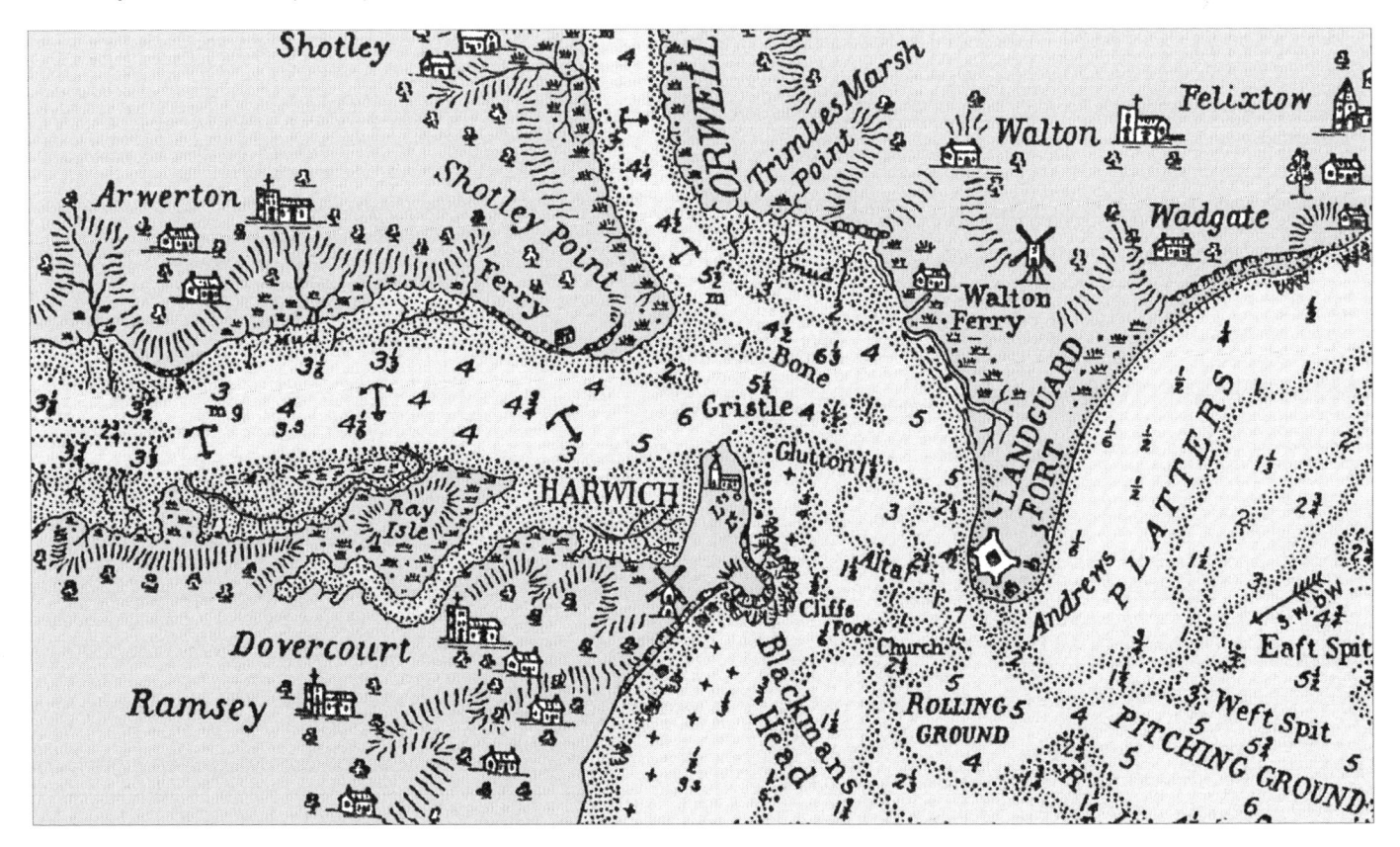

In 1806 the Emperor Napoleon abolished the Batavian Republic and created The Kingdom of Holland and installed his brother Louis as its King. Unfortunately for Louis, Napoleon forced his abdication after just four years during which British goods were being smuggled in and out of Dutch ports at will. From 1810 onwards Holland became a part of the French Empire.

Just prior to the Battle of Waterloo, which took place on 18th June 1815, the northern and southern provinces, ie the former Dutch Republic and the former Austrian Netherlands, were united via the Treaty of Vienna on 9th June 1815 into the Kingdom of the Netherlands under King William I of Orange-Nassau, the 'Merchant King' - the need for an independent Belgium being considered less important than a strong Netherlands that could act as a buffer against France.

The Battle of Waterloo not only ended an era of Napoleonic wars but also of what for Harwich had been 10 years of almost a monopoly of carrying mails to the Continent. In 1815 the Dover to Calais packet service re-opened as did one from Dover to Ostend in Belgium. Dover then quickly became the more important of the packet ports due to its shorter and more frequent crossings and thus a re-appraisal was needed as regards the role of Harwich. Attention turned to the port of Rotterdam on account of it being further inland and with access to waterways that reached deep into Germany.

Throughout this time Amsterdam had remained the principal Dutch port but it was Rotterdam, in 1816, that was to see the first arrival of a steamship. Unfortunately Rotterdam was only reachable via arduous routes along channels that were prone to silting up. The original way in from the North Sea was to use the old exit of the River Maas, past a large area of protective sandbanks and dunes, through the Brielsche Gat or Brielle Gap, onto Botlek and then up the Nieuwe Maas or New Maas. However ships were frequently grounding on what was known as the Brielle Bar. To avoid this hazard a longer and deeper channel to the south was used by small ships from 1830 onwards that went through the Goereesche Gat and then by way of Haring Vliet, Hollands Diep and Dordsche Kil to reach the Oude Maas or Old Maas and then Botlek from the south east. Further south was a route for larger ships that entered the estuary through the Brouwershavense Gat and on past Brouwershaven and the island of Overflakkee to join the middle route west of Haring Vliet. This lasted only until 1835 after which the larger ships were using an even more southerly route via the Oosterschelde or Eastern Scheldt and Stavenisse but whichever way was chosen the journey was slow and treacherous even at high tide when it was often impossible to distinguish the channel from the shore.

A more reliable and direct route was needed and so King William ordered and financed the construction of the Voorne Canal. This cut across the island of Voorne in a north easterly direction from Hellevoetsluis in the south, slightly upstream from the Goereesche Gat, to reach the old Maas at Nieuwesluis near to Botlek. Work began on the canal in 1827 and when it opened for traffic in 1829 it had locks at both ends capable of handling ships up to 270 feet long and with a maximum draught of 17 feet. If the locks were left open, at times of matching tide and water levels, then even longer ships could pass through but all were constrained by it being only 46 feet wide.

Whilst undoubtedly providing a safe and well used route into Rotterdam it eventually become used mainly for conveying cargoes that were transhipped into smaller vessels at Brouwershaven, often in accordance with Dutch insistence at the time that any foreign cargoes could only transit Holland and the Rhine in Dutch river vessels.

Elsewhere by 1826 steamers in general and in particular much larger and more powerful ones on the Dover to Calais route were causing severe competition to the Harwich packets whose Masters still retained their faith in sail to a port some 20 miles inland. The first steamer at Dover was introduced in 1821 and somewhat ironically during 1826 and 1827 the Dover to Calais Post Office Packet Service received 10 new steamers that were built by George Graham's works at the old Naval Yard in Harwich itself. These were the *Spitfire* 120 tons, *Fury* 120 t, *Watersprite* 180 t, *Escape* 237 t, *Wizard* 237 t, *Crusader* 120 t, *Thetis* 290 t, *Dolphin* 320 t, *Salamander* 237 t and *Dragon* 237 t.

The Kingdom of the Netherlands was never an easy situation and in August 1830 the Belgians revolted over issues such as religious intolerance, heavy taxation and unfair laws. They refused to be treated as a conquered province and declared their independence. After the Dutch failed to control the revolution the Belgians constituted a monarchy of their own in 1831 under King Leopold I, Prince of Saxe-Coburg.

That same year saw issues arise at Harwich when the Post Office put the mail service out to tender. This time the contract for the Holland and North German mails was won by the General Steam Navigation Company. (GSNCo.). This was a company formed in 1824 which was already operating paddle steamers out of Tilbury and crucially was a company free from the abuses often perpetrated on the Harwich route. The GSNCo. carried the mails to a number of ports including Antwerp, Rotterdam and Hamburg.

Meanwhile Belgium, which had laid claim to all provinces sympathetic to the 1830 revolution, was becoming as much concerned with its future commercial and economic plans for a direct trading route into Germany as it was in merely claiming territory. Having achieved a 'political peace' there still remained an 'economic battle' with both the Netherlands and Belgium harbouring a mutual suspicion over the development of each others ports.

The Napoleonic wars had seen much of the Anglo-North European trade bypass Belgium and divert to using safer Dutch or German ports. Since the ending of hostilities Antwerp had sought to regain a share of this traffic and since Waterloo the port had became an important link between Britain and the Rhineland. The Treaty of Vienna had included issues over the freedom of navigation on the Scheldt but Antwerp felt that with Rotterdam and Amsterdam having access to a superior inland waterways network the Dutch might yet again conspire to bring about the city's economic downfall. This the Dutch had done during the Belgian revolt when they severed the links between Antwerp and Germany that went via Dutch waterways. Further concerns were raised when the Dutch objected to the establishment of a joint Belgian-Dutch commission for the supervising of shipping on the Scheldt.

An agreement was reached in 1831 which gave most of the inland territories still under dispute to the Netherlands. The only real concession to Belgium was the right of transit through Dutch Limburg, and on into

Germany. Zeeland-Flanders and both banks of the Scheldt estuary were confirmed as belonging to the Netherlands though Belgium was given partial control of shipping on the Scheldt and a right to navigation on connecting waterways between the Scheldt and the Rhine.

With a freedom of navigation guaranteed and Antwerp's future as a commercial port thus safeguarded the Belgians considered that the ideal and long term choice of a future trade route into Germany should be a rail link from Antwerp to Cologne and into the Rhineland. Under the Treaty of XXIV Articles Belgium had the right of free transit up to the Dutch canton of Sittard. However the Dutch King William 1 considered all this to be a violation of his country's sovereignty as well as an unacceptable commercial threat to his own ports.

With the Dutch opposing the treaty and doing all they could to maximise their hold over the Rhine/Maas delta the Belgians set out to develop their newly favoured rail network. In 1834 The *Chemin de fer de l'Etat Belge or Belgian State Railway,* was granted the right to construct a railway from Antwerp to Germany or Prussia via Verviers. As this bypassed Limburg the Belgians did not need to exercise its right of transit. The line was opened through to Cologne, after many difficulties, in 1843 with the Dutch viewing it as 'an enormous threat to the trading position of Rotterdam', as it broke that port's dominant hold on transit trade and tariffs via the Rhine and Mainz rivers, and 'an even greater threat to the position of Amsterdam'. as the latter port had no adequate link with the river Rhine. The Belgians came to call their railway the 'Iron Rhine'. However the Dutch still retained an influence over the Scheldt even if they no longer controlled it. The Treaty of Separation of 1839 saw Holland officially, though grudgingly, accept the independent sovereignty of Belgium but still allowed Holland to levy tolls on all shipping using the Scheldt, regardless of flag, due to both banks of the river being in Dutch territory. These tolls were paid for by the Belgian Government.

Thereafter what was once an inter-national rivalry was now duplicated by inter-regional disputes within Holland at a time when the country was hugely in debt with a King, who ruled on determining economic policy, having little personal accountability for his decisions.

Contrary to the position in Belgium, where railway development was seen as being vitally important, Holland already possessed a well laid out rivers and canal system as well as a paved road network, especially within the provinces of Holland and Zeeland. The need for railways was not seen as being particularly vital except in Amsterdam which was desperate for a direct rail link with Germany. In 1836 a line was proposed from Amsterdam to Cologne and Prussia via Arnhem but was defeated over doubts as to whether the State could, or should, pay for it. It was then given a financial guarantee by King Willem in 1838 who ordered that this Rhine Railway be built.

His successor in 1840, King Willem II, honoured this arrangement but a commission of inquiry was drawn up to discuss future arrangements as to whether railways should be state or privately funded. In 1844 the commission favoured the state method but Parliament decided on the private route and the Amsterdam Rhine railway was transferred into the Dutch Rhine Railway Company or Nederlandsche Rhijn-Spoorweg-Maatschappij (NRS). By 1845 only this company and the Dutch Iron Railway Company or Hollandsche IJzeren Spoorweg Maatschappij (HIJSM) existed, there being no state railway company.

The line into Germany from Amsterdam was severely delayed by supporters of Rotterdam who were naturally advocating a greater use of inland navigation via the Rhine though here they had problems of their own. After about 1840 when trade began to develop and expand with the Dutch East Indies the Voorne Canal became increasingly inadequate in coping with the size of newer ships.

Such difficulties coincided with an era when the national debt of the Netherlands was so high that more than half its total income went on trying to pay it off. However a short while later the revenues from the East Indies were to vastly increase and in the 1850s, when Dutch agriculture was also much improved, money became available for the state itself, should it so wish, to develop rail links of its own in areas where private companies were showing little or no interest. These were usually at places such as river crossings and associated bridge works where high costs exceeded the likelihood of a return on their capital. Meanwhile Dutch and German boatmen agreed in 1851 to join forces to compete with the various new railway lines reaching into the Rhineland area as it was generally acknowledged that the river system was becoming increasingly inadequate.

The idea that the state might build railways but ought not to end up being responsible for them later on was one that raged throughout the Dutch Parliament between 1860, when state funded building works began, and 1863, when how to operate them was decided. A new private company, the State Railways, would run the new State owned lines though it was not until 1869 that the whole situation was agreed.

The situation in Britain as regards similar infrastructure developments was one of privately funded schemes appearing throughout the country with the Government concerning itself largely with regulatory and safety measures though it would also throw out those applications for schemes deemed too hopeless to succeed. Harwich was to find itself subjected to such methods and procedures when it embarked upon securing its own rail links and better port facilities.

Fragments of early accounts sheets – see synopsis in later chapter.
(Stephen Brown collection)

THE 1840s

The story of how the railway arrived at Harwich contains a mixture of rivalry and over ambition combined with times of reckless financing, and even attempted bribery, that ended in the eventual amalgamation of the competing companies. It was played out during what became known in Britain as the 'Railway Mania' where everybody jumped on the bandwagon of 'we want a railway'.

When the packet boat service left Harwich its hotel and other business interests suffered heavily for want of customers. Local industries such as fishing, shipbuilding and cement making were unable to compensate for the loss and it soon became apparent that any future revival or development would largely depend upon better transport links with London and many places inland and the faster those links were the better. The existing road system allowed for only slow and uncomfortable journeys and this led some to look towards a new means of transport, the railways, as a way forward.

At the time railways were a relative novelty though of undoubted worth when up and running with the Darlington to Stockton Railway of 1825 and the Liverpool to Manchester Railway of 1829 being the most notable to date. Any form of a planned nationwide system was a long way off and railways in general were very often opposed by the owners of canals and turnpike roads as well as by many landowners. Despite the objections, often vigorously expressed, it became ever more the case that local interests, businesses, towns and even very small villages were increasingly coming out in favour of linking themselves with major centres in order to distribute their goods and produce more easily and cheaply.

As such it fell upon the local communities themselves to both promote and finance their aspirations and this led to the proposing of a multitude of both large as well as often quite small scale lines and the creation of many grandiose sounding and imposing company titles. However the process was a long and costly one that required plans and any other information concerning them to be placed before Parliament as a Bill, and the process of seeing the Bill through all its stages to an Act ready for Royal Assent was so involved and lengthy that prospective railway companies would often have Members of Parliament or experienced politicians on their Board of Directors to assist its progress.

In 1834 a prospectus was issued to create a 'Grand Eastern Counties Railway' that proposed the construction of a railway line from London to Yarmouth via Colchester, Ipswich and Norwich. This was based mainly upon recommendations made by a prominent civil engineer, John Braithwaite. The London and Westminster Bank were asked to act for the projected company and that three directors of the Bank would lend their services. With terms between the two parties agreed and after due lengthy and protracted opposition, mainly from landowners, a Bill to construct the line received the Royal Assent on 4th July 1836. When the Company's first general meeting was held at the London Tavern on 26th September 1836, one of the bankers, Henry Bosenquet, was elected first Chairman of the 'Eastern Counties Railway', (ECR), the 'Grand' having long been dropped from its title.

That same year, 1836, the residents of Harwich attempted to promote a railway of their own, along land also surveyed by Braithwaite, but being such a small town they were unable to raise the money required and the project never got very far.

With an estimated cost of £1.6m work on the ECR line began in spring 1837 and on 18th June 1839 the line was declared open from London as far as Romford, though in actual fact 'London' was only a temporary halt at Devonshire Street in the Mile End Road. The line was built to a gauge of 5 feet and progress was hampered by many problems of a constructional and, more especially, a financial nature.

On 1st July 1840 two further stretches of line were opened. One went westwards from Mile End creating a new terminal at Webb's Square in Shoreditch whilst the line from Romford was extended out eastwards to Brentwood. The town of Colchester was later reached and opened to passenger traffic on 29th March 1843. From July 1843 the ECR started carrying mails between Shoreditch and Colchester. By this time the Company had already spent more than all the money, (close on £3m!) on these 51 miles from London than had been set aside for reaching Norwich. Work now ceased other than to survey the line a further 2½ miles north as far as Ardleigh.

With construction of the line to Norwich having now terminated at Colchester the townsfolk of Ipswich were rightly aggrieved at being isolated from an expanding railway system that could benefit its port. Since 1824, when the Ipswich Steam Navigation Company was formed, there had been both local and coastal steamer services to places such as London and Harwich plus longer distance ones, albeit on an irregular basis, to various ports in Holland and by 1842 Ipswich had developed its extensive dock system into being internally served by its own railway lines.

In 1840 Harwich made another attempt to promote a 'Harwich Railway' and here again nothing happened. In 1841 John Attwood, a railway speculator, was elected MP for Harwich after bribing voters with a promise to support and fund a railway. Upon his election he went lukewarm on the idea. Meanwhile Ipswich's demands were taken up by a member of the Suffolk brewing family of Cobbold and John Chevallier Cobbold was to become instrumental in obtaining an Act of 19th July 1844 that formed the 'Eastern Union Railway' (EUR) with a company head office in Ipswich. Cobbold had been aided in his efforts by Peter Bruff, an engineer who had previously been employed by the ECR between 1840 and 1842 but was then sacked for having neglected his railway responsibilities in favour of his developing a port at Colchester.

This EUR Act was intended to open up Suffolk to rail by building a line from Ipswich to Colchester where the EUR would build their own station. This was later amended, through a joint agreement with the ECR conditional upon that company extending their own line north, so that both companies would join up at Ardleigh and utilise just the one station in Colchester. This was all to be built to the standard gauge of 4ft. 8½in. and thus during September and October 1844 the ECR narrowed their existing 5ft. gauge line out of London.

The 17 miles of line from Ipswich to Colchester were built by Bruff under the guidance of Joseph Locke who was acting as the consulting engineer. The works cost £270,000 and were opened to goods traffic on 1st June 1846. Passenger traffic started on 15th June and was celebrated by a series of special trains and banquets hosted by Mr. Cobbold, now Chairman of the EUR. The day's events also included a trip down the River Orwell to Harwich and back on a small steamer, the *River Queen*.

A more adventurous trip was arranged for 17th June 1846 whereby Mr Cobbold and the directors of both the EUR and the ECR would attempt a practical experiment to demonstrate what could be done by combining a rail and steamer service to the Continent.

A party representing the ECR left London Shoreditch station at 5.30 am on board an excursion train and bringing with them bundles of the day's newspapers. They reached Ipswich at 7.20 am and there they were met by their EUR hosts. All were then conducted on board the *Orwell*, a specially chartered paddle steamer of the Orwell Steam Navigation Company built in 1838, which headed out at 7.35 am bound for Rotterdam under the command of Captain Rackham.

The route was to be via the Brielle Bar and on this occasion the Bar was reached at 6.30 pm with the *Orwell* having earlier been some 12 miles off course. Here the Dutch Customs boarded the ship, examined the stores, enjoyed a dinner and drank various toasts to the health of H.M. the King of the Netherlands, H.M. Queen Victoria and the eternal friendship between Britain and the Netherlands. The ship finally arrived in Rotterdam at 8.45 pm. Members of the party were then able to walk ashore and distribute copies of their English newspapers to various hotels and other establishments before midnight.

After a night spent at the Grand Hotel des Pays Bas the party assembled for a return journey which set off from Rotterdam at 10.30 am and arrived back at Ipswich at 10.30 pm. From there they left at 11.00 pm on board a special train which arrived in London at 1.00 am on the 19th. The journey showed that a new era of Continental travel was possible by train and ship and it became one that the EUR sought to consolidate throughout 1846. Unfortunately such a service from Ipswich lasted for just two round trips, a situation that was to further encourage supporters of a railway line to Harwich who thought that they had much the better location and much the better chance of successfully connecting with the Continent. Their idea of a through service, via Harwich, was one whereby travellers could leave London at 6.00 am, transfer to a steamer that left Harwich at 9.00 am, sail by daylight to arrive in Rotterdam and be in the Hague at 6.00 pm the same day. It was nothing if not ambitious but it was also hugely optimistic. Harwich was still no nearer to having a railway of its own though it was not for a lack of schemes.

Both the ECR and EUR were firmly committed to building a Harwich branch line of their own. Each believed that the port could further the development of Continental steamer services and their competing proposals were continually being laid before Parliament.

In 1843 Mr. Attwood MP was called upon to honour his earlier promise and he now backed a 'Harwich Railway and Pier' scheme via Ardleigh which was adopted by Joseph Locke. As an alternative there was Braithwaite's ECR scheme for the 'Colchester and Harwich Railway' extension. Both were rejected in 1844 on the grounds of there being thought 'an insufficiency of traffic'.

Attwood then proposed an alliance that had Braithwaite working on a new 'Harwich Railway and Pier' scheme based on Locke's ideas. The plans were resubmitted in 1845 and again rejected. In 1845 plans appeared for developing Bathside Bay, a marshy area to the west of Harwich, into a major quay and tidal basin, this being entered through lock gates leading to three docks, shipyards and various slipways. Together with ongoing hopes of developing a railway service, to such places as Birmingham or to operate 'The Great Western, Southern and Eastern Counties Railway', otherwise known as the 'Harwich and Southampton Railway', it was clear the town was not short of ideas. Such plans were indeed visionary but were equally abandoned due, not too unsurprisingly, to a lack of financial support.

By now Locke was Chief Engineer for the EUR and he had Bruff survey a new route to Harwich starting from Manningtree, midway along the line between Colchester and Ipswich. In February 1846 Locke's new line, a proposed 'Eastern Union & Harwich Junction Railway', would be 11 miles long and follow the south bank of the River Stour.

Attwood and Braithwaite's 'Harwich Railway and Pier' proposal became known as the 'Harwich & Eastern Counties Junction Railway & Pier' and was slightly longer at 13½ miles and would join the EUR near Ardleigh. Unfortunately for Atwood it was no longer supported by the ECR themselves. The ECR had, since September 1845, agreed instead to support the EUR's Manningtree route, lease it, work it and abandon proposals for their own Colchester to Harwich line in return for running rights over the EUR line between Colchester and Manningtree.

The Board of Trade initially objected to Locke's riverside line but were induced to withdraw. Then the Commons Committee rejected it and passed the 'Harwich & E.C. Junction Rly. & Pier' proposal instead. This was then rejected by the Lords in June 1846 on the grounds, it is alleged, that their Lordships considered that too many railway Bills had already been passed that session.

The idea that the ECR would lease and operate the proposed EUR line was on account of their having apparently made 'efficient arrangements to collect trade and traffic at the port'. However a proposal on 20th October 1846 that the ECR form and finance 'The Harwich Steam Packet Co.' (or 'The Harwich and Eastern Counties Steam Packet Company') was rejected by its own shareholders on 19th February 1847.

Compared to events elsewhere progress at Harwich on obtaining a railway line or developing a shipping service was falling ever further behind the times. By way of example sailings out of Dover were increased on 4th March 1846 when a daily steam packet service was started from Ostend using the mail boat *Chen de Fer*. This was inaugurated by the Belgian Government in co-operation with its State Railways and Marine Transport Authority.

The 'Harwich & E.C. Junction Rly. & Pier' proposals appeared again in 1847 as did those of the 'E.U. & Harwich Junction' but this time the latter was being promoted by the EUR as a branch of their own. The Borough Council petitioned the Prime Minister, Sir Robert Peel, to refer the competing plans to the Railway Commissioners as a matter of urgency pointing out that it was now over ten years since the railway was first projected. This the Parliamentary Committee did and a subsequent report from the

Railway Commissioners came out in favour of the Eastern Union's proposals. Their decision had a damaging effect on supporters of the 'Harwich & E.C. Junction Rly. & Pier' though they were later glad to withdraw their own Bill for a small pecuniary consideration. An Act of 22nd July 1847 in favour of the EUR then settled the issue such that railway access to Harwich and its port should be a line in from Manningtree and furthermore that the EUR be authorised to there construct a pier. Authority was granted to raise £200,000 capital and to lease the line to the ECR when completed. However there would be no provision for them to run their own shipping services.

Throughout these times the accounts of the ECR were, to say the least, somewhat strained. In 1845 the company's financial situation was so bad that the 'Railway King' George Hudson was invited by the shareholders to become its Chairman and restore the Company's fortunes, much as he had a reputation for doing with a number of other railway companies. Unfortunately one of his first decisions was to raise the Company's dividends from 2% to 6% with a view to attracting new investment but he chose to pay them out of capital, not revenue. His intention was to repay the capital account from increased business but a lot of his dealings were somewhat dubious. By 1849 this policy had proved disastrous and George Hudson resigned. When asked as to why the directors had gone along with his ideas, the answer was 'if they hadn't he would have resigned'.

On 30th March 1849 it was reported in Hamburg that the ECR had purchased six former Government owned steamers for £35,000 for the Harwich to Holland and Cuxhaven mails only for the scheme to fall through a fortnight later, on 13th April, on account of the Company being unable to raise sufficient finance.

Early view of the ticket office at Halfpenny Pier, Harwich. The pier opened on 2nd July 1853 and the office in 1854.
(NRM collection)

THE 1850s

By 1850 and with no building work having started on the line to Harwich the powers made available under the Act of 22nd July 1847 lapsed. The capital raised under this Act had however been appropriated by the EUR for use on their Ipswich to Norwich line and it needed a further Act of 5th July 1850 to restore the powers granted in 1847. In the meantime arguments and actions of self interest had arisen between the ECR and EUR. For example the ECR would run comparatively slow trains between London Bishopsgate, (the new name for Shoreditch since 27th July 1846), and Colchester because they did not want passengers changing there for faster EUR trains that would arrive in Norwich before those of their own via Cambridge. In 1847 the 51 mile run to Colchester took 1 hour 35 minutes. In 1849 it became a leisurely 2 hours. A pooling agreement whereby revenues were shared proportionate to the total mileage of the two routes between London and Norwich was scrapped by the EUR in 1851.

By now the lack of progress at Harwich, either for a railway or a pier, saw the Harwich Corporation separately obtain for themselves 'The Harwich Improvement, Quays and Pier Act' of 1851. This was 'despite strong and very unfair opposition from the corporation and certain ship-owners of Ipswich', who by then had come to regard themselves as being quite capable of acting as a focal port for steamer services to Holland.

The Harwich Corporation engaged Peter Bruff, now rising to become the company engineer and manager of the EUR, to construct a quay from the Naval Yard to King's Head Street and also to build a pier, the first pile for which was driven in on 2nd June 1852. Built of timber the main part of the pier was 243 feet long by 23 feet wide and extended out into the river in a roughly north westerly direction. About half way along this section a pier arm extended eastwards measuring 213 feet long by 22 feet wide. The structure would officially be referred to as the Corporation Pier, though it was also known as the Town Pier, and was opened on 2nd July 1853. Today it is known as the Halfpenny Pier from when, in the 1890s, it cost those who were not travelling one half penny to enter.

A second aspect of this development was to then extend the quay face westwards into Bathside and create a series of wharves. Behind the quay the seaward end of King's Head Street to West Street was to be extended by infill and the area built up on reclaimed land. These works took place between 1852 and 1853.

In 1853 arrangements were drawn up that allowed the ECR to take over the EUR and the Harwich line with effect from 1st January 1854. This was later ratified by an Agreement dated 6th February 1854. The agreement also included the transfer to the ECR of the EUR's fleet of local paddle steamers then sailing between Ipswich and Harwich. The ECR had previously taken over the Norfolk Railway on 8th May 1848 and control of the East Anglian Railway on 1st January 1852 though the latter was to remain an independent company. They then purchased the Newmarket Railway on 30th March 1854.

Work on constructing what was now Peter Bruff's Manningtree to Harwich line, to which only a minimal effort had been made in October 1848, was properly started in January 1853 and when finished had cost £177,000 to build. The line was single track and the railway station at Harwich was built about a quarter of a mile from Corporation Pier, close by the shore end of George Street, on dredged material and reclaimed land. The contractor was George Wythes.

The first train to run through to Harwich arrived on 29th July 1854 carrying Bruff (now the ECR's Chief Engineer until he resigned in 1857), a party of navvies and the town band. This was followed on 4th August by an inspection train conveying Major Wynne and representatives from the Board of Trade. The line was absorbed into the ECR by an Act of 7th August 1854. Officially opened to passenger traffic on 15th August 1854 the day was marked by the arrival of the first train from London amidst a series of festivities hosted by the Mayor and other official dignitaries.

Whilst the original railway Acts of 1847 and 1850 had allowed the EUR to construct their own pier at Harwich they chose instead to take control of the newly built Corporation Pier after the Harwich Corporation found themselves in some difficulty when the time came to pay for their completed works. In 1854 the railways, by now the ECR, lent the Corporation £7,000 with an option to buy the quay and pier, the arrangement being, with the approval of the three railway companies, ie the ECR, the Norfolk and the EUR, *'that the Eastern Counties should be at liberty to take over the land required and the Pier and works constructed by the Corporation at the actual cost thereof'*. In November nearly four thousand shareholders of the ECR came down from London in four special trains to attend a public dinner held on the Corporation Pier.

Although the quayside had railway lines extending along its length and the pier had rails upon its deck so that horses could draw trucks of coal used in the bunkering of ships there was no provision for passengers other than they walk between the station and the pier. Despite the inconvenience it was from here, the Corporation Pier complete with its own two storey ticket office, that the first sailing under the auspices of the Eastern Counties Railway took place. That was on 16th September 1854 when the paddle steamer *Aquila,* from the North of Europe Steam Navigation Company, set out for Antwerp. The N. of E.S.N. Co was promoted by Samuel Peto along with Mr. J. Cobbold, Chairman of the EUR, Mr. D. Waddington, Chairman of the ECR and several railway Directors.

The Illustrated London News dated 30th September 1854 describes the events: *'The North of Europe Steam Navigation Company, encouraged by the success which has attended their efforts to establish a regular system of communication with the countries north of the Scheldt, via Hull and Lowestoft, and further stimulated by the recent extension of the Eastern Counties branch railway to Harwich, determined on making an attempt to provide equal facilities at that port for the traffic between London on the one hand, and Antwerp on the other. At present the greater portion of this traffic is conveyed by steamers, which traverse the Thames and the Scheldt; the entire journey being performed by water, and usually occupying from eighteen to twenty hours. By adopting the Harwich route, the North of Europe Steam Navigation Company proposed to realise the following results: First, the avoidance of the long and tedious passage up and down the Thames; second, the increase and development of the local traffic between the Eastern Counties and Belgium; third, the accomplishment of the journey in twelve hours, thus effecting a saving in the distance, measured by time, of some eight or twelve hours and, lastly, the establishment of the new service as essentially a "day" service.*

The first trip on this service was taken, in the nature of an experiment, on Saturday week last, the ship selected being the Company's new steamer the Aquila, from the building-yard of Henderson, Glasgow and fitted with engines of 120-horse power, constructed upon the oscillating principle, by McNab, of Greenock. Her length is 200 feet, breadth of beam one-tenth of her length, or 20 feet, and her burden about 300 tons. Her engines, for new ones, work with much ease, whilst the unpleasant vibration we so often experience, even in crack steamers, is scarcely perceptible. Both out and home she gave the greatest satisfaction to all on board, and averaged a speed of thirteen knots; in returning, on the following Tuesday, she passed the buoy at the mouth of the Scheldt at eight o'clock in the evening, steamed gallantly through a tremendous sea, and arrived safely at Harwich at half-past two the next morning, accomplishing the distance from the Scheldt hither in exactly six hours and a half. In this part of the voyage the sea-going qualities of the Aquila, under the severest stress of weather, were capitally brought out.

The conclusions, to which this experimental trip lead us, are these: — For the purpose of the traffic between London and Antwerp, and certainly all the local traffic, the Harwich route has no real competitor in any of the other existing routes; that during the summer months the day service may be conducted with punctuality both ways, provided the railway arrangements are made compatible with the demands of the service, and, above all, that the Belgian Government can be induced to maintain additional lights, and erect a few more landmarks, in the Scheldt; that, in the existing state of the navigation of that river it presents insuperable obstacles to the project of ascending it at high water in the evenings of the short winter days; and that until these difficulties are removed, the steam-packet company have acted wisely in determining to dispatch their boat from Harwich, on the arrival of the night mail from London, so as to reach Antwerp early on the following morning'.

Despite the report's encouraging tone this once a week service was totally unsuccessful. A lack of passengers and cargo led to the route's closure on 10th December 1854 after just twelve sailings but the ECR's Annual Report for 1855 suggested there might still be a prosperous future stating '...*if steam boats are put upon the route of sufficient power and capacity for carrying cargo and making quick passages, a considerable revenue will be obtained for the Railway, experience having proved that Harwich Harbour can be entered at all states of the tide, and it being the nearest port in this country to Antwerp must, with the aid of powerful steam boats, become a valuable adjunct in promoting the prosperity of the Company'.*

With the ECR still restrained by the 1847 Act against establishing a steamship service of their own they created a subsidiary company in 1855 that assumed control of the North of Europe Steam Navigation Company. On 23rd April 1855 they chartered the *Aquila,* along with her sister ship *Cygnus,* and resurrected the service to Antwerp.

Both these iron paddle steamers were almost new having been built in 1854 by J. Henderson & Sons of Renfrew. Their 200 feet length consisted of a 180 feet long hull extended by a clipper bow and each was fitted with two masts and two tall funnels abaft the paddles.

The service started out as twice a week from 2nd May. It then became three times a week on 2nd July and during the summer season the ECR river steamer *Orion* was used on six occasions when acting as a relief ship. The summer schedule of departures from Harwich were on a Monday, Wednesday and Saturday with the ship sailing 'after the arrival of the 8.30 pm mail train from London'. As the train did not leave Colchester until 10.35 pm the sailings from Harwich would have been close on midnight. The return journey from Antwerp was also on a Monday, Wednesday and Saturday but at 9.00 am thus giving a daylight crossing back to Harwich and from where a connecting train was advertised as arriving in London at 10.40 pm. One stated attraction was that the sea passage would last only 4½ hours though in reality this only meant that part out in the open sea.

Single fares to Antwerp were:

	1st class and Saloon	2nd class and Saloon	2nd class and Fore cabin
from London	£1.7s.0d.	£1.4s.0d.	£1.0s.0d.
from Harwich	£1.1s.0d.		16s.0d.

whilst to Brussels the fares were:

	1st class and Saloon	2nd class and Saloon	2nd class and Fore cabin
from London	£1.10s.6d.	£1.6s.9d.	£1.2s.9d.
from Harwich	£1.4s.6d.		18s.9d.

The service quickly declined until only the *Aquila* was left in service and sailing just once a week from 20th October onwards until the route closed on 16th December 1855 having lost the Company £5,976.

Although this initial enterprise ended in failure the idea of travelling abroad for pleasure had attracted the attention of Mr. Thomas Cook who was later to become synonymous with the concept of a 'package tour'. The very first of his Continental tours took place during this 1855 period when he personally conducted two parties via the Harwich to Antwerp service taking in Brussels, Cologne, Frankfurt, Heidleberg and Strasbourg before finally arriving in Paris to view the International Exhibition.

As regards the shipping scene in general the 1850s were a time of great technological advances in marine engineering. Fewer vessels were being made with wooden hulls as larger ships with iron hulls became ever more common. The earlier problem of making iron plates watertight when using rivets had been solved as far back as 1840 but the method of generating steam power remained a problematical one. Early steam engines had condensed the steam by the injection of cold water and with small engines it was possible to make use of sea water. However this was not a suitable process for larger engines and it was not until 1855 that a condensing system appeared that was.

The 1850s were also a time when Holland's finances were much improved following a decade of financial mismanagement that had left the country with a national debt so high that more than half its total income went on trying to pay it off. Since the early 1840s the country had been increasing its trade with the Dutch East Indies and by the 1850s the vastly increased revenues from both this and Dutch agriculture meant that money was now available for the state itself, should it so wish, to develop rail links of its own in areas where private companies were showing little or no interest, these being at river crossings and associated bridge works where high costs exceeded the likelihood of a return on their capital. Such issues were still ongoing from the 1844 commission of inquiry though Amsterdam had since got its rail link to Cologne in 1849 despite the opposition from Rotterdam who naturally had been advocating a greater use of its inland navigation via the Rhine.

However, for Rotterdam, the Voorne Canal was becoming an ever increasing problem as larger ships were now unable to fit into its locks or to pass each other within its narrow channel. Furthermore there still remained the 'battle' between Holland and Belgium that had existed since the Treaty of Separation in 1839 over allowing Belgium to transit Dutch territory in its own pursuit of reaching Germany by rail and especially any new lines that gave Antwerp an advantage over Rotterdam. Despite this the two countries agreed in 1850 to linking Antwerp and Rotterdam via the construction of a railway from Antwerp to the Moerdijk in Hollands Diep and from there by ferry to Rotterdam. This later led, via the subsequent building of the Moerdijk railway bridge, to the eventual linking of Rotterdam to Germany by rail.

In 1856 this new route was opened by the Dutch Rhine Railway and the *Aquila* was chartered on 16th October in order that Directors of both the ECR and the EUR could attend the relevant ceremonies. As regards this leading to any new steamer service from Harwich two very short lived schemes were later promoted. The first was on 25th April 1857 when the paddle steamer *London* was chartered by the 'London, Harwich & Continental Steam Packet Company'. Originally built in 1853 for service at Newhaven she made just one journey to Rotterdam after which the Company went bankrupt. The second scheme was when the *London* was chartered by the 'Harwich Steam Packet Company' on 1st July 1857. This Company initially ran her twice a week to Rotterdam; then once a week in December until her last sailing on 26th December. The charter expired on 7th January 1858 and the service was discontinued. This was followed by the winding up of The North of Europe Steam Navigation Company on 26th February 1858.

Fresh attempts to reach Rotterdam were made by the ECR on 4th June 1858 in conjunction with the Dutch Rhenish Union Transit Co.. These again made use of the *London* and again the service soon closed due mainly to a lack of traffic.

This lack of trade was also affecting receipts on the Harwich branch line. During the first half of 1859 the figures were down by £1,609 and this raised the possibility that the Harwich end of the line might close leaving just a Manningtree to Mistley section which the ECR had double tracked in 1856. The ECR Traffic Committee were advised on 23rd November 1859 that Harwich had no foreign trade or local manufactures and its streets were deserted. There were hardly any receipts on the line at a time when *'persons who go to and from that place and London do go and will go by steamer at a third or quarter of the cost of carriage by railway'*.

Impression of the frontage outside the Harwich Hotel. (The Illustrated London News, August 1865)

THE 1860s

The 1860s saw a variety of schemes, developments and initiatives on both sides of the North Sea many of which, when implemented, would prove highly beneficial. Some however still fell by the wayside. In Holland the idea that the state might build railways but ought not to end up being responsible for them later on was one that raged throughout the Dutch Parliament between 1860, when state funded building works first began, and 1863, when how to operate them was decided. A new private company entitled Maatschappij tot Exploitatie van Staatsspoorwegen or Dutch State Railways (SS) was set up to run the new state owned lines though it was not until 1869 that the whole situation was finally agreed. At Harwich the railways there would soon be assuming a greater influence internationally.

In 1860 the Harwich Dock and Pier Company submitted plans, laid out by Peter Bruff, for the reclamation of land within Bathside Bay. It envisaged the formation of a new tidal basin whereby ships would pass through a lock to berth within a huge enclosed dock. The plans were a revision of the earlier ones of 1845 and they further set out a new frontage to the quays at Harwich, a new 'Continental Pier' and a rail line extending out into the harbour. Again nothing appeared of yet another highly ambitious project.

The ongoing control of five regional railway companies under the auspices of the Eastern Counties Railway (ECR) was formally acknowledged by the Act of 7th August 1862 that was 'to amalgamate the Eastern Counties, the East Anglian, the Newmarket, the Eastern Union and the Norfolk Railway Companies, and for other purposes'. The Act was back dated with effect from 1st July 1862 and through it was created the Great Eastern Railway (GER).

As regards the harbour itself matters were in need of some improvement. Whilst Harwich was long known for being a safe refuge for sailing ships, no matter what the condition of weather or tide might be, the advent of steam powered vessels was gradually reducing the need for such a haven. However the harbour constituted a position of strategic importance and this was recognised by the Admiralty, merchants and the railway alike.

By the mid 19th century its easy accessibility was being threatened. This was because Landguard Point, a sheltering spit of land on the Suffolk side of the Stour estuary, had been rapidly extending westwards and out into the channel approach. This movement was largely due to the removal of stone from both sides of the estuary for use in the making of Roman cement, an activity that dated back to 1812. The approach to the channel and on into Harwich harbour was at that time marked by two land based lighthouses erected in Harwich in 1817. These were a stone 'high lighthouse' and a wooden 'low lighthouse', the idea being to line up the lights one above the other for a safe approach. By 1829 natural forces and neglect were raising concerns about the subsequent erosion of a headland on the Harwich side of the Stour that was causing the estuary mouth to widen. As a consequence this widening was lessening the scouring effect of the tide which in turn was leading to the build up of shingle banks that threatened to close off the harbour altogether.

The Harwich Corporation informed the Admiralty and other parties of its concerns and eventually a report was produced by Captain John Washington, R.N., who surveyed the harbour on board the gunboat *H.M.S. Shearwater*. His report of 19th January 1843 led to the cessation of stone removal, a start on the dredging of deep water channels and the construction to the south of a stone breakwater between Harwich and Dovercourt known as Stone Pier. By 1850 some 520 yards of breakwater had been built at a cost of £68,000. A further £72,000 was spent on dredging the channel but the overall works still failed to halt the westward advance of Landguard Point.

In May 1862 Parliament appointed a Select Committee to look into a permanent solution. Their investigations revealed a conflict of responsibilities towards the harbour such that Harwich Corporation had no powers beyond its own foreshore, Ipswich Corporation had jurisdiction over a vague area from Shotley to Landguard whilst the greater part of the Orwell was in the hands of the Ipswich Dock Commission. This basically meant there was no one in overall charge of the Stour and enquiries suggested there was no likelihood of local interests combining for the general good.

A month later the Committee therefore proposed the creation of a single authority to control the Stour estuary, Harwich harbour and that part of the Orwell not under the jurisdiction of the Ipswich Dock Commission. An Act for the Preservation and Improvement of Harwich Harbour received the Royal Assent on 28th July 1863 and created the Harwich Harbour Conservancy Board (HHCB). This Board was made up of nine 'Conservators' of which two were appointed by the Board of Trade and one each by the Treasury, the Admiralty, Trinity House, Harwich Corporation, Ipswich Corporation and Ipswich Dock Commission with the ninth being elected by the ratepayers of Mistley and Manningtree. Peter Bruff was appointed engineer to the Board. The HHCB received powers to help curtail the growth of Landguard Point, carry out preservation and improvement works within the harbour, to dredge and make byelaws and to levy harbour dues of one penny per net registered ton on vessels of 30 tons and upwards.

As a result of the channel having since changed its course the two lighthouses of 1817 were abandoned in favour of two further lighthouses built by Trinity House in 1863 at nearby Dovercourt. These new lighthouses were made of iron and mounted on screw piles with the same idea as before, to line up two lights to steer clear of Landguard Point. The creation of the HHCB had one further local implication, that of ending an earlier ancient authority long claimed by the townsfolk of Ipswich whereby its Mayor would carry out a ceremony known as 'beating the bounds' of the estuarial waters with a silver oar whilst travelling in a row boat. Over one hundred and fifty years on the HHCB is still the Harbour Authority.

Prior to the amalgamation that created the Great Eastern Railway the ECR had received a letter in early 1862 from the vice-president of the Dutch Rhine Railway Company calling for the early establishment of a maritime route between Harwich and Rotterdam.

The Dutch port's rail links to Cologne since 1856 not only gave access to the German production centres of coal, iron and steel but also the means to distribute British machinery and colonial goods on the Continent. Since 1st May 1857 the agent of the Dutch Rhine Railway in Rotterdam had been Mr G. S. Pieters, a member of the firm that later became Hudig & Pieters in 1860, and who had been encouraging business and businessmen to use a potentially important sea and rail connection that the then ECR and Dutch Rhine Railway Company could offer.

On 28th March 1863 Directors from the recently constituted Great Eastern Railway visited Harwich to discuss plans on starting new shipping services to the Continent. Eventually they secured the Great Eastern Railway (Steamboats) Bill which, on its third reading, was passed by Parliament on 24th July and received the Royal Assent on 28th July 1863, the same day as the creation of HHCB! There had been strong opposition from other East coast ports to 'An Act to authorize the Great Eastern Railway Company to run Steam Vessels between Harwich and certain Foreign Ports'. Those foreign ports were listed at a shareholders meeting in August when the first Chairman of the GER, Mr. Horatio Love, announced, *'After strenuous opposition in both Houses a Bill authorising the running of steamships between the port of Harwich and those of Antwerp, Rotterdam and Flushing was passed by the Committee'*.

The significance of reaching Antwerp and Rotterdam has already been explained, ie both were developing and expanding transport links to the interior of Europe - mainly rail via Antwerp and river and rail via Rotterdam. Antwerp received a major boost in 1863 with the ending of the Dutch toll on shipping using the river Scheldt though rather than the Dutch simply abolishing this tax they were effectively bought off by the Belgians who paid over the sum of 17,141,640 Dutch florins. Its removal was almost a case for national rejoicing within Belgium as it represented a highly symbolic end to a much resented foreign interference.

The fortunes of Harwich as a port were considered capable of much improvement as political and economic developments in Europe were bringing increased opportunities for British trade and to any east coast port that was linked with those in Holland. Since 1862 Germany's Chancellor Bismarck had embarked upon uniting the various German states into a great political and industrial power, often provoking conflicts to achieve his ambition. The potential benefits to Harwich were that much of Germany's foreign trade was then passing through Rotterdam with up to 80% of Anglo-German traffic being handled by this one Dutch port. However it, and the Voorne Canal, were in endless struggle with the increasing size of new ships. What Rotterdam needed was a direct and more reliable route to the sea.

As far back as January 1858 a young Dutch engineer, Pieter Caland, had proposed an idea to the state appointed Council of Water that a cut, or channel, be built from Rotterdam directly westwards and out through coastal sand dunes into the North Sea. At the time these dunes curved southwards across what nowadays is known as the Hook of Holland or, in Dutch, Hoek van Holland or corner of Holland and extended south for about four miles. Caland reasoned that he need only provide for a narrow opening as the tide then flowing through it would scour the entrance away and over time it would widen itself. Although the idea was adopted in August 1858 the Dutch Government had earlier been inclined

Comments by the GER Traffic Committee April 1865 regarding the accommodation onboard the *Rotterdam*. (Stephen Brown collection)

to favour, on the basis of national interests and development, the construction of a shorter canal linking Amsterdam to the North Sea at Ijmuiden and leave Rotterdam to rely upon a rail line to the Moerdijk. This led to local business interests campaigning that they be allowed to construct the channel privately.

The estimated cost of the initial Caland plan was 5 million Guilders to which the Government was asked to guarantee a 4½% return on a 99 year concession lease. The Council of Water then argued that any waterway would only need to accommodate ships with dimensions of up to around 460 feet long, 60 feet wide and 23 feet deep as it was thought that not many ships any bigger than this would ever be built. By 1860 that argument had collapsed mainly on account on the increasing size of ocean going vessels such as Brunel's *Great Eastern* that had been launched in 1858 measuring 692 feet long and 82 feet wide Accordingly the waterway plans were in need of a serious revision. Progress remained slow and by April 1862 Hudig & Pieters were re-iterating the urgent need of a much better route to the North Sea. Eventually it was decided that the Dutch State would adopt the works and having revised the cost estimate upwards to 6.3 million Guilders, the Bill was passed in September 1862. The Royal consent was then given by King Willem III on 24th January 1863.

With the GER by now in the business of running its own steamship services the Traffic Committee was able to announce on 16th September 1863 the commencement of a once a week service between Harwich and Rotterdam, again in connection with the Dutch Rhine Railway, for the conveyance of cattle and goods at through rates as from 1st October 1863. New cattle sheds had been erected on the quay for just such a purpose and agents were appointed to act for the Company, these being Groom & Daniels in Harwich and the aforementioned Hudig & Pieters in Rotterdam.

With no ships of their own the GER set about chartering a number in quick succession. The paddle steamer *Blenheim* was chartered from Tod & McGregor of Glasgow on 24th September 1863 for a period of three months at £170 per week including insurance and part of the crew charges. Without any ceremony the vessel quietly left Harwich on the 1st October for Rotterdam and it was from there, on 3rd October 1863, that commenced the Great Eastern Railway Company's very first commercial steamboat service. She arrived back at Harwich at 8.00 am on the 4th October with 70 head of cattle which, after having been landed at the Corporation Pier, were then taken by special train to London where they arrived by 1.00 pm that afternoon.

Another ship, the *Norfolk*, soon followed after having been chartered from Cuncliff & Watson of Goole on 28th October at £300 per month including crew and stores. Despite some of the crew on board the *Blenheim* having deserted ship in October the entry into service of the *Norfolk* on 6th November saw sailings increased to twice a week. Such was the increase in demand that a third ship, the *Prince of Wales,* was chartered from F. Kemp & Co. of Fleetwood on 16th December for an initial period of three months at £70 per week.

In 1863 a total of 93,000 tons of shipping entered Harwich Harbour though not all of it went through the port at Harwich itself. The year, that had seen the creation of a new harbour authority, the go ahead given for a new waterway into Rotterdam and the start of steamer services to the Continent with the GER running three cargo and cattle ships, ended with the successful return of the Post Office Mail service. However all was not without mishap.

On 15th January 1864 the *Blenheim* suffered ice damage in the River Maas and was sent away for repairs. She was replaced by the screw steamer *Killarney* which, as from 19th January, had been chartered from H.T. Watson of Goole for £115 per week. The ice also damaged the *Prince of Wales* and this led to yet another charter, again from F. Kemp & Co., of the *Princess Alice* which commenced on 29th January at £80 per week. The *Blenheim* went off charter on 24th February followed by the *Killarney* on 6th March. That of the *Princess Alice* was extended on 30th March for a further six months at £101.10s per week and that of a repaired *Prince of Wales* was extended from 4th May upon her return to service. Between them the *Norfolk*, *Princess Alice* and the *Prince of Wales* would maintain a two or three sailings a week service to Rotterdam.

In the meantime there had been a shareholders half-yearly meeting, in February 1864, during which the new Chairman of the GER, Mr. James Goodson, drew attention to what he called, 'the modern institution of the service from Harwich'. Many though remained despondent as regards the results. Although there was support from the Chairman in its local Manager, Mr. R. Moseley, the poor situation was largely due to events outside the latter's control. November and December 1863 had been stormy months making navigation along the Dutch coast difficult with it being further mentioned that when ice set in the ships had often broken down. Whilst in general the vessels in use had proved tolerably suitable there were few any better to be had as those that were had been taken up by the American Civil War.

What was needed was not an assortment of chartered cargo and cattle carrying tonnage but some proper purpose built vessels and the good news was that soon there would be some. On order were brand new passenger vessels, from eminent London builders, and new cattle ships, leading the Manager to become confident that this experiment was bound to be successful. He went on to say '*When we get our own boats, which have been especially ordered to suit the peculiarities of the Rotterdam trade and the necessary facility for the transhipment of the traffic generally at Harwich, the advantages of the route will be even more apparent than now, and the result such as to equal the continental traffic of any railway in the Kingdom*'.

The promised new ships duly arrived in 1864 and all were paddle steamers initially intended for the Rotterdam route. The *Avalon* and the *Zealous*, each 230 feet long, were built for passenger service by J.&W. Dudgeon of Cubitts Town, Poplar (later to become the Thames Ironworks Company), and the *Harwich* and the *Rotterdam*, each 215 feet long, were built for livestock service by G. Simpson & Company.

The *Avalon* was launched in March 1864 followed by the *Zealous* some two months later. The *Harwich* was delivered in May and the *Rotterdam* in August 1864. All had a beam of 27 feet and engines in the region of 220 nominal horse power (nhp) which were capable of working separately in case of one breaking down. Service speed was around 10 knots though the *Avalon* managed to be a bit faster at nearer 12 knots. The GER advertised these new ships as being 'in all respects first class, the accommodation the best that can be supplied, the captains and officers are selected with the greatest possible care'.

The *Avalon* was the first purpose built Harwich based railway ship and could accommodate up to 150 passengers, their luggage and the mails. On 21st May 1864 a full compliment of Company Directors and invited guests went by special train from London Bishopsgate to Tilbury. There they boarded the *Avalon* to witness her trials during which, over the measured mile, she attained the impressive speed of 14 knots.

She was fitted with a hurricane deck for roughly one third of her length at the after end of which was a short bridge spanning the open space of the deck below where the passengers boarded. Across this bridge was a poop deck somewhat larger than the hurricane which made for a 'glorious promenade'. Port and starboard side steps led down to the open space of the deck. Here was a bar and pantry while adjacent to this a large open saloon contained wooden tables and comfortable seats. Around the outside of the saloon, curtained off from the main area, were alcoves in which were fitted twin bunks.

The *Avalon* left on her maiden voyage to Rotterdam on 13th June 1864 sailing overnight with, amongst others, Directors of the railway company and officials of the Royal Harwich Yacht Club on board. As she headed out to sea she was accompanied by various types of other craft witnessing the 'Thames - Harwich' yacht race. It was reported as being '..a great day for the port as it seemed to inaugurate a new era in its history. Rarely has any other harbour borne upon its bosom such splendid specimens of naval architecture and mechanical skill'. She was the first of a new type of packet ship being straight stemmed and fitted with two funnels. Her design became a standard for many a cross channel vessel, one which remained constant until the arrival of turbine steamers in the early 1900s.

The *Zealous* joined the *Avalon* on 8th July with the intention that one of these ships would leave Harwich on Mondays, Wednesdays and Fridays at 9.00 pm and arrive at Rotterdam the following morning at 8.00 am whilst returning passengers would leave Rotterdam, also at 9.00 pm, and reach Harwich by 8.00 am. Unfortunately such a regular timetable of sailings was far too optimistic and the service was only twice a week. Furthermore the process of actually travelling at all remained an altogether arduous experience.

The railway timetable showed that the departure of the boat train from London Bishopsgate for Rotterdam would be 'determined by the state of the Dutch tides' for the steamers still had to get across the Brielle Bar off the Dutch coast. This could only be done within one and a half hours either side of high water and passengers had to transfer to smaller ships in order to land if the tide was in an inappropriate state. Doing so meant they would often arrive four or five hours late thereby missing their onward connections.

The railway carriages of the GER were said to be specially 'adapted' for the Harwich service from which, somewhat interestingly, passengers 'could step direct from the train onto the steamer'. This was never the case in view of the walk required between the railway station and Corporation Pier. It would be at least four hours from leaving London that passengers would be clear of Harwich and then a further twelve hours before they reached Rotterdam. Passengers were however assured that 'no small boats are used' though once under way the noise of the heavy oscillating machinery would no doubt have kept many of them awake. When they finally arrived in Rotterdam the ship berthed at the Oosterkade, in the centre of town on the north bank of the New Maas, and close by the Dutch Rhine Railway's Maas station which had opened in 1858. Any train passengers could easily walk to and from the ships.

A few weeks later, on 1st August 1864, the *Zealous* opened a once a week service to Antwerp though later on most of this route's sailings were carried out by the *Prince of Wales*. However the timetabling was little more precise than it was to Rotterdam. Trains would leave London Bishopsgate at 4.45 pm but no expected time of arrival was given except to say that Antwerp passengers might complete their journey in 'about' 17 and a half hours depending on the ability to gauge the tides in the River Scheldt. Thus travelling on either of these continental routes under such vague timings and conditions, hauling luggage through the back streets of Harwich in all weathers, was certainly not for the faint hearted. The two new cattle boats, *Harwich* and *Rotterdam*, joined the Rotterdam route on 9th August and 14th November 1864 respectively.

The *Avalon* was not in service very long. She had grounded off what is now the Hook of Holland on 1st September 1864 and after getting off the sandbanks two days later was then laid up at Harwich. The GER were critical of her construction 'not being up to standard' and her future, or lack of it, was noted in the Marine Superintendents register. *7th December 1864. Laying up of 'Avalon'. This ship is now laid up in Harwich. The Engineer has had a good deal of work with her Engines and Boilers and I have permitted him to keep 3 Firemen with him until this work is finished. The vessel will be coaled and got ready for immediate service and as there is no Commander in her I should recommend that one be appointed - as in case of necessity the vessel could not proceed to sea. Captain Dorman of the 'Prince of Wales' has been most active and energetic in the execution of his duty and at all times most willing to further the views of the Company and as he has been in command of the 'Prince of Wales' since I have been here and with great credit to himself and advantage to the Company I would suggest he be appointed to Commander. The Committee Resolved that the consideration of the subject be deferred, it being probable that the vessel will be sold.*

The *Avalon* was indeed sold, having sailed just 41 trips to Rotterdam and 3 to Antwerp, and went back to her builders, J.&W. Dudgeon, on 21st December 1864 for £23,500. Her sister ship, the *Zealous,* was retained by the GER without criticism.

All in all 1864 was not a good year. The GER ships lost £7,238 and the route into Rotterdam, via Hellevoetsluis and the Voorne Canal, remained unpredictable at the best of times. Passengers considered themselves lucky if they arrived only 2 hours late. By now nearly all the chartered-in ships had been handed back, the last to leave being the *Norfolk* in February 1865.

Summary of ships chartered by the G.E.R.:
Blenheim
    24th September 1863 to 24th February 1864
    (21 trips to Rotterdam)
Norfolk
    28th October 1863 to 23rd November 1864 and 1st January 1865 to 26th February 1865
    (62 trips to Rotterdam and 1 to Antwerp)
Prince of Wales
    16th December 1863 to 15th January 1864 and 4th May 1864 to 5th January 1865
    (23 trips to Rotterdam and 24 to Antwerp)
Killarney

19th January 1864 to 6th March 1864
(9 trips to Rotterdam)
Princess Alice
29th January 1864 to 28th October 1864
(55 trips to Rotterdam)

In order to maintain the fleet's strength the 235 feet long *Pacific* was acquired from C. Lungley of Deptford on 23rd February 1865. Similar in design to the preceding quartet of new vessels her trials were recorded thus;- *8th March 1865. 'P.S. Pacific'. This ship was on her trial at the measured mile - made an average speed of 12¾ knots with and against the tide. Pressure of Steam 25lbs, Vacuum 25lbs, Revolutions 30. The engines worked well without the slightest indication of hot bearings and we never had occasion to ease them between Gravesend and Harwich. The consumption of fuel, full speed, will not exceed 1 ton and she answered her helm admirably, making the whole circle in 3 minutes. She left for Antwerp a few hours after her arrival and arrived there in 12 hours and returned again to Harwich at 2 pm loaded. She is plentifully supplied in the Engine Room, having about £200 spare gear on board, besides stores for Engine Room and deck. She was barquee rigged and fully equipped for sea, which, being of no possible use for our traffic, I would recommend it be subject to further enquiry as to disposal of it. Read - suitable for the traffic.* Later that month Mr Lungley offered £200 for the spare gear and also to re-rig the ship with 2 polemasts complete with fore and aft sails.

Since January 1865 sailings to Rotterdam had been running three times a week and soon after the *Pacific* entered service alongside the *Zealous* the GER Continental Traffic Manager proudly reported that no fewer than 581 passengers had been carried across the North Sea in a single week. Sailings to Antwerp ran twice a week.

The *Zealous* and the now discarded *Avalon* were originally built for passengers and cargo and as such carried no cattle. Conversely the *Harwich* and the *Rotterdam,* both now on the Antwerp service with the ending of the *Prince of Wales's* charter, were built as cattle carriers and carried much fewer passengers. However by reference to the Traffic Committee minutes passengers and cattle were somewhat interchangeable. The minutes also illustrate the diversity of considerations that the early days of running a shipping company entailed, some of which no doubt were very different to that of running a railway.

15th March 1865. 'Zealous'. The Manager suggested an alteration to 'Zealous' by converting the Ladies Saloon into a hold for Cattle and setting aside the lower suite of Cabins in the General Saloon for Ladies, the expense of which will not exceed £20.

11th April 1865. 'Rotterdam'. Great complaints having been made from passengers of the want of accommodation in the 'Rotterdam' I would suggest that part of the after hold be taken into the saloon we would only require the place of 20 cattle and 50 berths for passengers would be gained. The 'Rotterdam' is seldom if ever so filled that 20 cattle would make any difference. The ladies saloon of the 'Zealous' having been taken away all the fittings would do for the 'Rotterdam' which has now only cabins for 4 passengers, where by the alterations room for 40 will be made. The expense would be around £50

26th April 1865. 'Rotterdam'. The 'Rotterdam' is now laid up for accommodation to be made for each passenger in accordance with your resolution of the 11th inst. I would recommend that the 'Harwich' be similarly altered if it is not the intention of the directors to sell her.

Whilst all of these recommendations were agreed to there remained more important matters to discuss such as the dangers of safely navigating a way down the Maas river.

26th April 1865. The 'Pacific' in coming down the river at 3.30 am on the 15th inst ran on the mud turning the point near Brielle. The weather was thick at the time and the tide being very high the banks were not distinguishable. The vessel remained their until the morning of the 18th inst when I succeeded in getting her off making use of the 'Zealous' …(she being on her way to Rotterdam) I have recommended to Mr Moseley that our vessels should not start away now from Rotterdam during the night as it is impossible to avoid accidents if we continue to do so. Mr Moseley …quite agrees with me and the time table for this month has been amended. I have held an inquiry into the cause of the ship getting ashore and attribute it to the time of night and state of weather and do not blame either the commander or the pilot. - Resolved that no vessel leave Rotterdam at night in future

In July 1865 the GER opened the Great Eastern Hotel at Harwich to its wealthier passengers travelling to and from the Continent. Built right opposite the pier it was described by the Illustrated London News as *'a noble pile of buildings, the style is Italian with a handsome facade. The elevation to the first floor is handsomely carved and in the panels below the windows are life size heads of the various Kings and Queens associated with the town'.*

The hotel had excellent facilities for the period … *'with windows on each floor looking up and down the river in different directions to the main front. Fixed to the first-floor windows of these parts of the building, in the same line as the portico, are two very handsome circular balconies, with stone balustrades. The centre compartment of the building is crowned by a pediment, in which is an illuminated clock supported by stone dolphins. The hotel is entered by a flight of stone steps, ornamented on each side with globular lamps on massive bronze standards. The interior is most conveniently and handsomely arranged. On the ground floor is a large and elegant dining-room, with a coffee-room separated from it only by an ornamental screen, a smoking-room and public billiard-room; all spacious, commodious, and tastefully decorated. The tavern department, with a separate entrance, is at the other end of the building; and the kitchens, with other domestic offices, are behind. On the first floor which contains also seven large private sitting-rooms and four best bedrooms, are a large occasional dining-room, a private billiard-room, and two other rooms, which can be used as one when required, for the use of the Harwich Yacht Club; besides which there are six bedrooms, baths, and linen closets, at the back of the building, on the same floor. The second floor is very pleasantly situated, the rooms commanding extensive views of the harbour, the River Orwell and the Stour, with pleasant and varied scenery. At the north-west end of the corridor are two cheerful sitting-rooms; and on the second floor, fourteen bed-rooms, all fitted with stoves, marble mantelpieces, and other requisites, the same as on the first floor. On the third floor are fifteen bedrooms, bath-room, and closets, neatly furnished. The three corridors are all of stone; the stairs ascending to each floor maintain the same width throughout. The roof of the hotel is covered with lead,* giving a promenade about 70 ft. long by 10 ft. wide. This will be protected by neat iron railings, and seats will be provided for the accommodation of hotel visitors. From this point an extensive view is obtained. On the one side is the German Ocean, with Dovercourt in the distance; and on the other the River Orwell, the harbour and piers of Harwich, the Stour, Shotley, and Landguard Fort. At the back of the hotel lies the town of Harwich. The cellars, which are provided with a lift or hoist for raising heavy stores to the upper floors of the hotel, are very extensive, and include bonding warehouses for the storage of wine, spirits, or tobacco. An engine has been provided to pump salt water up to bath and washing rooms, from a well sunk by the company, This water runs through a bed of sand, and will always be found clean and cool. A courtyard surrounds the entire building.

The architect was Mr. Allom of London and the builders were Messrs. Lucas Brothers of London and Lowestoft. It cost over £5,000 with Mr. Lacey of the GER being in overall charge of its construction.

However comfortable the Hotel's interior there remained the matter of cattle being moved from close by the front door and residents must have felt decidedly uncomfortable when, in 1866, an imported cow was landed on the quayside suffering from cattle plague. '..the Government inspector directed the beast to be slaughtered and buried where it had landed. A hole was dug on the quay to receive the carcass, and the animal was just about to be slaughtered when the town authorities interfered, and refused to allow it to be killed or buried in Harwich'. The animal was instead taken away in a railway truck to be slaughtered and buried in the countryside. When the local farmers found out about this they were not at all pleased at the potential spread of disease and for their actions the GER were later fined.

Throughout 1865 J&W.Dudgeon were engaged in constructing another paddle steamer for the GER which was due to be named *Ravensbury*. This was changed before entering service and the company brought this ship in as a second *Avalon*. Her trial runs were described as follows

Avalon new ship trial. September 27th 1865. This ship left Tilbury for Harwich on Saturday the 16th last, having Mr. J. Dudgeon, Mr. Casey, Mr. Harrington, Mr. Duncan and myself on board, and we made four trials at the measured mile on the Maplin Sands, which gave us a mean speed, with and against tide, of 15.205 knots, Steam 31lbs, Vacuum 25lbs, Revolutions 41½. Engines worked well and with out the slightest indications of hot bearings. She answered her helm quickly making the circle in 5 minutes 40 seconds in about twice her own length. After landing Mr Dudgeon at Southend we proceeded on for Harwich, where we arrived in 3¼ hours from the pier. We left on her first trip on Friday morning at 5. Strong breeze with moderate sea on which she realised all that could be desired. Making the trip exclusive of detention at Bar in 9½ hours. The consumption of fuel will be as near as possible that of the 'Zealous' viz about 28 cwt. When working ... her draughts of water with 181 beasts, 115 calves, 660 sheep, 207 pigs, and 30 ton of goods are forward 7ft 10", aft 8ft 10".

In 1865 it was said that Harwich was 'an indescribable labyrinth of rails, with carriages and trucks of all kinds'. Such was the growth in traffic that a new pier was needed and work was already in hand on constructing one on land that the GER, in April 1865, had taken on a 60 year lease from the Crown Commissioners. When finished it was fully brought into use on 30th September 1866 and was variously known as either the New Pier or the GER Pier but was more commonly referred to as the Continental Pier.

Sited further to the west it was built of timber and being 490 feet long by 90 feet wide was substantially larger than the existing Corporation Pier. Berths were provided for three ships at a time and although railway tracks were similarly laid out upon its deck the shunting of wagons was still carried out either by hand or horse power. Close by were sheds, coal dumps and a small marshalling yard with around 2 miles of sidings built on reclaimed land. Along the pier were a number of one-ton steam travelling cranes and a ten-ton hand powered crane together with pens and water troughs for the cattle trade. It cost £6,490 and was built by Perry & Jackson.

Its construction and access to it required the demolition of the existing Harwich railway station. This closed on 1st December 1865 and a new one was built further inland and completed in the summer of 1866. Passengers for the ship still needed to make their own way there, again via George Street and West Street, with the distance in between now almost twice as far as before. The old Corporation Pier was no longer used for continental traffic and its use was later confined to excursion and local river boats. These new works brought a very small part of the earlier plan of 1860 into existence. The site of this Continental Pier is nowadays occupied by Trinity Pier.

A further new ship, the *Ravensbury*, arrived in November 1865 as a sister ship to the recently arrived *Avalon* and both these passenger and cargo carriers were put on the Rotterdam route. A somewhat unusual purchase was made in 1866 of the cargo vessel *Great Yarmouth*. She was built for the GER by Jones Bros. of London and entered service in August as what would later be described as a 'London coaster'. This basically meant that she ran as a feeder vessel for cargoes between London and Harwich that connected in with the Company's steamer services to the Continent though she would also sail along the East Anglian coast as far round as King's Lynn. She had very little passenger accommodation and was relatively slow at only 10 knots.

The number of passengers carried via the GER ships in 1866 was 9,350. Thereafter this rate of progress began to slow due to events that were both within and without the control of the Company. Many of the GER's growing financial problems were legacies of having been created from Companies that were not always in the best of financial health themselves but disaster arose in May 1866 with the crash of the broking firm of Overend, Gurney and Company. The resultant panic saw ten banks ruined and was accompanied by a recession.

As to how it affected the GER much of Overend's funds had been linked to various railway securities and advances to contractors and thus the firm's demise had curtailed the construction work of many a railway enterprise throughout the country. However the timing of the crash was doubly unfortunate for the GER as they themselves were financially over extended as regards the construction of a new railway terminal at Liverpool Street in London. This project, authorised in August 1864, had started out with dubious merit and viability but by 1866, due to reckless accounting, the cost of abandoning the works had risen to more than if they actually managed to complete it. Outstanding claims for land purchases, often agreed before the money was raised, had been calculated as exceeding the total sum set aside for the entire construction project raising similarities in (in)competence with the earlier construction of the ECR line from London to Yarmouth that was only to reach as far as Colchester. Attempts to raise new money were unsuccessful and holders of GER stock were told there would be no dividends due to the claims of creditors upon the new station works.

Despite a general lack of trade due in part to the banking crisis the Company obtained an Act on the 31st May 1867 that authorised them to own and operate steam boats between Harwich and Harlingen, situated north west of Amsterdam, and Geestemunde which was close to Bremerhaven in Germany. Quite why is unexplained as it seemed unnecessary to seek to expand services whilst there remained keen competition from other east coast ports.

A further event that year saw the GER decide that, as from 19th June 1867, all their ships would be registered at Harwich. The following month saw those they already had in the hands of others. In July 1867 an application to appoint a receiver was sent to the Court of Chancery. This resulted in the GER effectively being declared bankrupt and Company assets, including the trains and ships, being seized by creditors as security, The *Harwich, Avalon, Pacific* and *Great Yarmouth* were claimed by Mr. Tracy of Cambridge and the *Zealous, Rotterdam* and *Ravensbury* by Mr. Booth of Nottingham.

Eventually the Company underwent a financial reorganisation when the raising of £3 million was sanctioned by Parliament on 26th August 1867. This was used to pay the outstanding dividends, settle some debts and complete the Liverpool Street station land purchases. Together with the appointment of a new Chairman in February 1868 of Lord Cranborne, later to become the Marquis of Salisbury and eventually Prime Minister, this arrangement was to prove successful in realigning the Company's future and its fortunes. The GER came out of Chancery in early 1869 and the company resumed ownership of its fleet though the much under-utilised *Great Yarmouth* was chartered out for trading in the Mediterranean and the Black Sea.

In January 1868 the timetables had three GER services per week between London Bishopsgate and Rotterdam departing each Tuesday, Thursday and Saturday in both directions - 'unless prevented by unforeseen circumstances'. The service was still dependant upon the tides off the Dutch coast with departure times from Harwich varying between 4.00 pm and 3.00 am. The return trips variously left Rotterdam between 5.30 am and 1.30 pm. (ie no night time departures since determined in April 1865) with some correspondingly unsociable arrival times in London. Any pre-noon departure from Holland meant a 12.15 am train from Harwich that arrived in London at 4.30 am. Post-noon departures connected with the 7.55 am from Harwich which arrived in London at a more reasonable 10.30 am.

By comparison the Antwerp service was fairly straight forward with two sailings a week, these being each Wednesday and Saturday eastbound and Tuesday and Friday westbound. Departure time from London Bishopsgate was 4.25 pm and from Harwich it was 9.00 pm with the arrival time in Belgium being 'about' 9.00 am the next day. The return journey left Antwerp at 1.00 pm with the train to London leaving at 7.55 am next morning. As on the Rotterdam service the sea journey took 12 hours and so the night time waits in Harwich from around 1.00 am until the breakfast time departure of the train to London must have been an ordeal to be suffered or enjoyed depending upon ones character, temperament and the hostelry chosen in which to pass the time.

The arrangement dating from 1854 whereby the railway companies could take over the Harwich pier at cost price resurfaced in 1868 when the Harwich Corporation presented those costs for consideration by the Great Eastern Railway. In their summary from 1851 up until 31st August 1868 the Corporation showed it had received a total of £38,375.6s.5d. of which £31,547.7s.9d. had come from the railways. Against this the Corporation claimed costs and expenses of £48,644.14s.8d.. The balance shown as owing came to £10,269.8s.3d. Elements within the Corporation's claim were disputed by the GER Board who resolved on 10th June 1869 *'that unless such reduction be made in the accounts as may be deemed proper by the Committee, application be made to the Board of Trade to appoint an Arbitrator in accordance with Clause 262 of the Great Eastern Railway Act 1862'*. However the GER's Land and Construction Committee on the 13th July 1869 proposed a payment in cash of the agreed balance due the Corporation viz - £10,500 with a recommendation that the Company raise a mortgage equal to that already raised by the Harwich Corporation, namely £9,400. The Board approved the payment on 29th July 1869, whilst deferring the idea of a mortgage, and on 10th August 1869 the Board instructed the Law Clerk to see that the whole of the property was properly vested in the GER by Conveyance or otherwise.

In 1868 there were, by combining those of the GER and other Companies, a total of twelve weekly sailings from Britain to Rotterdam; ten to Antwerp and nine to Hamburg. With such a number already in existence it is not surprising that the additional routes granted to the GER in 1867 were never taken up.

Since October 1863 work had been ongoing in Holland on constructing the New Waterway. The process, which had begun with the requisitioning of any necessary land, did not progress to the stage of actual digging until 31st October 1866 when King Willem's son, the Prince of Orange, cut the first sod. Two years later, on 26th November 1868, the works had reached the North Sea. With the GER as a whole now more firmly financed and its shipping services having become profitable by late 1869 the prospect of this new waterway into Holland could only bring further trade and benefits to Harwich.

GER Timetable of Continental Crossings - January 1868. (Stephen Brown collection)

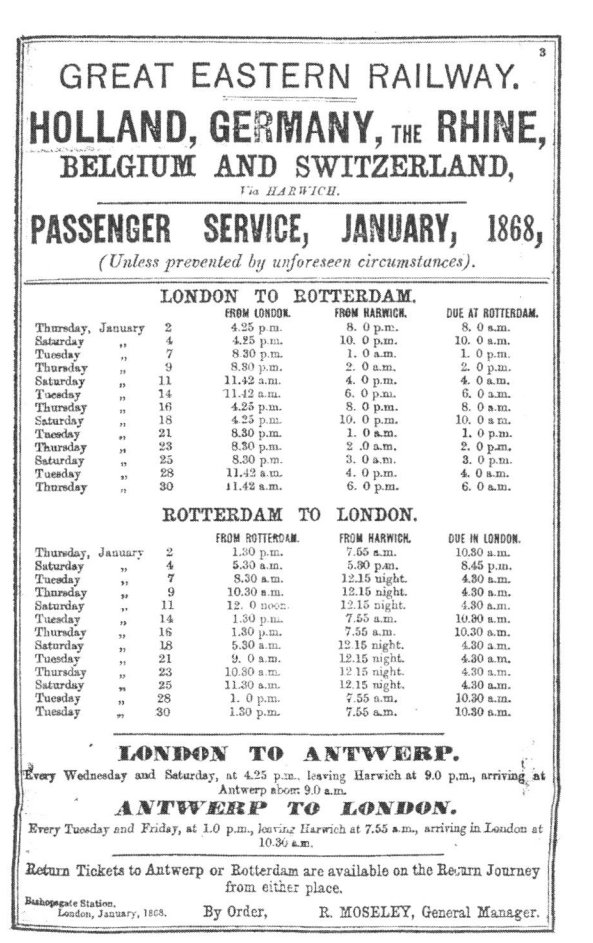

THE 1870s

On 5th March 1870 the *Ravensbury* ran aground as she was nearing Rotterdam. Her passengers and cargo were all safely evacuated but after the vessel later sprang a leak and flooded she was abandoned on the 8th and left to disappear into the mud and silt of the River Maas. As with many other vessels the *Ravensbury* had had a few minor groundings and collisions beforehand but this was the most serious event to date and she went down as the first ship lost to the GER. She lay there for over a century until 're-discovered' in 1971 during dredging work in the Maasvlakte. Part of the wreck was lifted and exposed as were her steam boilers, two oscillating engines and paddle wheels that still had their wooden blades. A china washbasin bearing the crest of the Great Eastern Railway Company's Marine Department was also found. The wreck was eventually reburied.

Two years on from the loss of the *Ravensbury* came the highly significant opening of the long awaited New Waterway leading into the River Maas and on up to Rotterdam. The fairway had already been in use for fishing boats and various small craft ever since 1870 but it was not opened officially until 9th March 1872 when the first steam boat to use it passed through. This was the GER vessel, *Richard Young*, which sailed up to Rotterdam with specially invited members of the Company on board. She had been delivered by J.&W. Dudgeon in 1871 with the same dimensions as the *Avalon* and was named after a former GER director. A fortnight later, on 24th March, the *Pacific* was to safely navigate her way through the new channel though she returned to sea via the Voorne Canal.

The advantage of the New Waterway and its deep water channel was that shipping could now reach the centre of Rotterdam at times irrespective of the tide and for the Harwich steamer service, and others, it offered the prospect of operating to a fixed timetable. With vessels no longer having to wait off the Dutch coast for sufficient water in order to cross the Brielle Bar the opening of the New Waterway heralded a new era of prosperity for Rotterdam.

Unfortunately it was not an immediate long term success. Although the channel was over 2½ miles long and had a width at bottom of around 33 feet its depth at low water was only a little over 6 feet. The *Richard Young* had only managed to navigate its way through at high water and enough time had not yet elapsed for the expected tidal scouring to do its work. Unfortunately the mud and sand that was expected to be carried out by the tide was instead starting to accumulate itself within the narrow seaward entrance and was now creating a new bar of its own.

A few months later an account of an uncomfortable crossing from Harwich to Rotterdam was reported in the New York Times dated August 1872. It mentions the steamer stopping to take soundings at the Bar and a somewhat overworked and harassed steward explaining that this meant measuring the depth of water. The writer then describes the steward's job as one not many would relish: *'The steamer was packed like a cattle van with most of the passengers on the cabin floor. It rained miserably all the way, and was very rough. My bed was a restless sofa-cushion in the extreme stern. I trust I may not again hear such sounds as broke upon that sleepless night. Amid it all toiled indefatigably the pink-cheeked little steward,.. picking his way with deft rapidity, bearing grisly burdens and answering insane questions. I wonder what he gets for it all! Precious little, I fancy; and I solemnly believe I was the only individual on board who gave him a shilling to insure attention at supper. He brought me the best cut of beef, and the choicest bottle of ale; and had I been sick, would no doubt have cared for me like a brother, and all because of a shilling. He must have been originally a good man, but his experience would subvert the profoundest faith in human nature. … .down in the ladies' cabin, all were sick, unmanageable and insanely interrogative'.*

Examination of the passengers luggage was done before the ship arrived in port. *'An hour or so before our arrival at Rotterdam, …..a boat appeared with a harsh-featured gentleman, in a laced cap and gold buttons, professionally severe of demeanour - the Custom-house officer. When the examination of the*

A map from 1881 showing the original route of the G.E.R. branch line to Harwich as it crossed the southern edge of Ray Island.

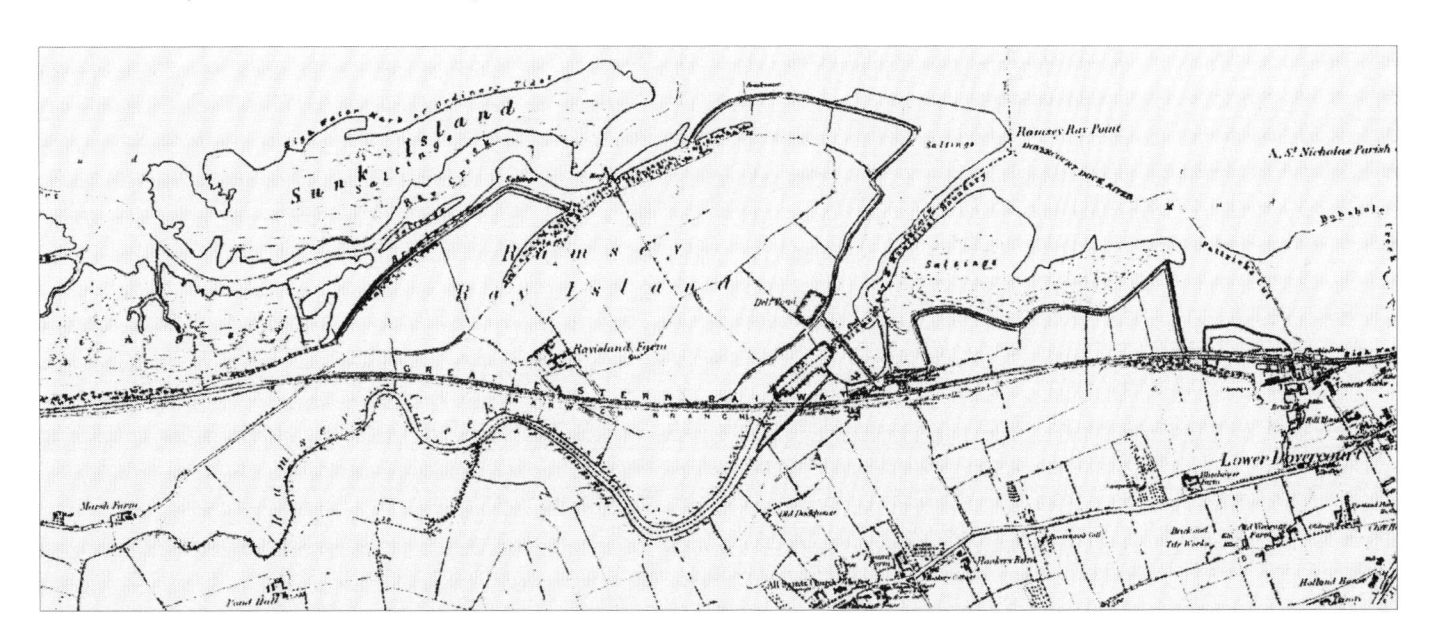

luggage began, many of the passengers approached this dignitary with a servile and cringing manner, evidently supposing that to promote good feeling was half the battle. I am inclined to think he liked it. But he had a row with the Captain, a dauntless, imperturbable and quietly scornful Englishman which showed him in quite another light. He hastened to and fro with rapid and feverish steps, talking sharply and overbearingly, evidently relying chiefly on bluster to gain his point - the moving of the luggage to a different part of the deck. "It must be moved here - it is my orders - No! I cannot have it there - that won't do me - here I say'" It was no use; the Captain, leaning on his elbows over the railing of his bridge, smilingly omitted to give any orders; if he wanted it done, he must do it himself. He quieted down at last, and was more complaisant, not only to the Captain, but to every one else thereafter'.

At low water vessels had little choice but to revert to using the old Voorne Canal despite its limitations in handling the larger ships that were bringing with them an associated increase in cargo and trade. It was almost a case of going back to square one. By the end of 1872 only 416 ships had used the New Waterway and Caland's estimate of 5 million Guilders for its construction was seeming woefully low. By 1873 the intended erosion of the seaway had stopped altogether and it was thought that an even deeper channel was needed to restart the process of scouring away this build up of sand.

Despite this problem Rotterdam was to see a general rise in its mercantile activities that gradually led to new banking and commercial districts being created along with residential areas complete with many fashionable shops and offices. A commercial house, the Pincoffs, were instrumental in much of this development throughout the 1870s and had themselves, in 1862, been involved in negotiations to privately construct the New Waterway itself.

The early 1870s also saw growing support for a railway line linking Rotterdam to the Dutch coast at Hoek van Holland where, if a quay were built nearby, steamers could then connect their passengers with waiting trains. This would save up to two hours on existing journey times by river and greatly aid the transport and export of perishable goods such as fruit, vegetables and fish as well as help to make the route from Harwich more popular and, more importantly, regular.

At the time Holland had three main competing railways companies. The Nederlandsche Rhijn-Spoorweg-Maatschappij (NRS or Dutch Rhine Railway Company), the Hollandsche IJzeren Spoorweg Maatschappij (HIJSM or Dutch Iron Railway Company), both of which were private, and the Maatschappij tot Exploitatie van Staatsspoorwegen (SS or Dutch State Railways), another private company more recently created to run those railways owned by the Dutch State.

In 1872 the Dutch Rhine Railway applied to build a line from Rotterdam to the Hoek. An alternative was proposed by the Pincoffs and their newly created Rotterdam Trading Company but this was opposed by the Rotterdam Chamber of Commerce who preferred that of the Dutch Rhine Railway. The GER maintained a close interest in the proceedings via their agents, Hudig & Pieters, who continued to represent the Dutch Rhine Railway.

By the summer of 1872 the service to Antwerp was sailing three days a week with departures from Harwich on a Monday, Wednesday and Friday and in the following year the GER took over control of the pier at Harwich. This occurred on 7th January 1873 following the GER's receipt of an updated summary of the Harwich Corporation Accounts showing that since 1868 their expenses had grown to £51,628.6s.0d. whilst receipts from items such as tolls, dues, rents and sales had come to £8,609.11s.1d. To a GER Board meeting on 12th February the Secretary reported that '*the Harwich Pier, Quays, &c. have now been handed over to the Company by the Corporation, the total amount paid by the Eastern Counties and Great Eastern Companies after deducting all credits to which they were entitled being £43,018.14.11d.*'

In September 1873 the GER examined the possibility of using a new Dutch port in Flushing given the problems they were experiencing with Rotterdam as regards the New Waterway. Since 1867 the Dutch had built new coastal barriers to link the isolated areas of Flushing, in the Province of Zeeland, with mainland Holland and from a newly constructed port at Vlissingen in Flushing, on the north bank of the River Scheldt, there now ran a railway line from Vlissingen-Stad directly into Germany via Roosendaal and Venlo. Despite this show of interest the GER decided against developing the idea any further even though others had already realised its potential. In various ways that decision would later influence developments at Harwich.

Such interest came at a time when the Dutch had become somewhat complacent as regards their communication links into Europe. This had allowed the industrious Belgian railways to gain the upper hand and the opening of their line to Cologne in 1843 had led to a great expansion of Antwerp. Furthermore Ostend had become the main focus for postal services between England and Europe with even the Dutch mails dependant upon the sailings of Belgian steamers.

Thus the use of Vlissingen was re-examined in 1874 only this time it was Prince Hendrik of the Netherlands, younger brother of King Willem III, who took the lead along with the Dutch Government and the Dutch State Railways. Together they proposed a steamer and mails service to England in competition to the Belgian State service from Ostend to Dover. Such a proposal had first been suggested in 1871 and with the new port at Vlissingen being much closer to the open sea these ongoing suggestions were of great concern to Antwerp. It was not exactly greeted with enthusiasm in Rotterdam either.

On 9th June 1874 the Rotterdam Chamber of Commerce and the Dutch Rhine Railway argued that this Flushing idea would be a mistake and that the Dutch Treasury should make a relatively small contribution towards the mails being carried by the GER Harwich to Rotterdam service in return for a large national and international benefit. For this they had the support of the Dutch Finance Minister but the Prime Minister favoured the Flushing route. Meanwhile Prince Hendrik persisted and gained the support of a friend and ally, the Koninklijke Nederlandsche Stoomboot Maatschappij (KNSM or Royal Dutch Steamship Company) of Amsterdam, a city which also favoured Flushing.

Despite all the protests there was formed, in October 1874, the 'Reederij Stoomvaart Vlissingen-Engeland' or Flushing England Steamship Co. with Prince Hendrik as Honorary President. Two former American Civil War blockade runners, the *Southern* and the *Northern*, had already been acquired and when the founding company was renamed, on 10th June 1875, as the 'N.V. Stoomvaart Maatschappij Zeeland' otherwise known as the Zeeland Steamship Company or SMZ, a third ship, the *Snaefell*, had been purchased from the Isle of Man Steam Packet Company. Prince Hendrik and the KNSM between them took up three quarters of SMZ's share issue. The rest were sold to private interests with the whole start up capital amounting to 2 million Guilders. The KNSM acted as managers having already secured a place on the Board.

From Flushing the SMZ was to sail to Queenborough on the Isle of Sheppey in Kent. From there trains would run into London through an agreement with the London, Chatham and Dover Railway (LC&DR) whereby the latter would construct a connecting railway line to the port. The three paddle steamers were renamed *Stad Middelburg*, *Stad Vlissingen* and *Stad Breda* respectively and would operate a nightly service, except Sunday. In later years, such had been the enthusiasm and close interest of Prince Hendrik and his proposed offer of guaranteeing interest payments to investors, the company SMZ would be accorded the privilege of naming their ships after members of the Dutch Royal family.

An inaugurating voyage took place on board the *Stad Middleburg* on 19th July 1875 with the service being opened for business on 26th July 1875. However the intended terminal at Queenborough was not yet fully completed and so services sailed instead to Sheerness. At Flushing the railway line had been extended from its original terminal station at Vlissingen-Stad to a new quayside station at Vlissingen-Haven in order to better serve passengers and traffic that would otherwise have needed to be 'omni-bussed' between ship and train.

These events at Flushing had already provoked a response from the GER. In 1874 there had been 35,390 passengers on their three times a week service to Rotterdam. In June 1875 they doubled their number of sailings into Holland by making the Rotterdam service run every night, except Sunday, in order to pressurise the new competition. The timetable now was to depart London Bishopgate at 7.00 pm and Harwich at 9.00 pm so as to arrive in Rotterdam at 9.00 am next morning. The return journey left Rotterdam at 5.00 pm to arrive Harwich at 5.00 am and London at 7.05 am. The passage fare, travelling First class, was £1.6s.0d single and £2.0s.0d. return at a time when the average wage was little more than £1 a week.

The pride of the Great Eastern fleet was now the *Claud Hamilton* and her arrival on the Rotterdam route on 14th August 1875 did much to improve the Company's prestige. Built on the Clyde by John Elder & Company of Govan, later known as Fairfield of Govan, she was launched on 3rd June 1875 and named after the Deputy Chairman of the GER. This 962 grt paddle steamer, measuring 251 feet by 30 feet, was both reliable and popular. She was the Company's first Clyde built ship and the first to be fitted with compound oscillating engines. She was also the largest ship in cross-channel service and carried her 558 passengers in new levels of on board comfort.

In September 1875 the GER Chairman, Mr. Parkes, met with Dutch Ministers in the Hague to welcome and further urge the idea of a rail link between Rotterdam and the Hook of Holland. Ideas for its funding were discussed with Mr. Parkes in anticipation of finding investors in Britain who were willing to back it. Unfortunately a degree of confusion arose as to who those investors might be as it certainly wasn't the case that they would include the GER themselves. As previously mentioned the GER had a history of financial predicaments and investors would be hard to find for a project that might bear its name.

The ongoing arguments over who should build the Hoek Line were eventually settled on 10th November 1875 when the Dutch Government agreed to state fund its construction with its operation being given over to the Dutch State Railways rather than the Dutch Rhine Railway. The Rotterdam Chamber of Commerce was disappointed that their preferred choice, the Dutch Rhine Railway, had lost out to the same Dutch State Railways that was threatening them with increased competition via Flushing. To some it seemed as if the old port rivalry with Amsterdam would never go away given that its Royal Dutch Steamship Company had played such a large part in helping create SMZ and the Flushing route.

It is arguable that the SMZ was not directly engaged in any aggressive competition with the GER steamers, merely that the Dutch only wanted a route of their own into England at the expense of the Belgians. However the two companies would become competitive in terms of service provision, technical innovations and ever more impressive additions to their fleets and as such its presence did not go unchecked at Harwich.

In those early days it was Harwich that clearly gained the upper hand as just four days after the announcement was made on the new railway line to the Hook of Holland the fledgling SMZ service was closed, on 14th November 1875, due to a lack of support. The route has been open for less than four months with the ships having proved to be less than ideal especially as regards their rates of coal consumption which was both higher and more costly than originally envisaged.

A further boost for Harwich had come just a fortnight earlier when the GER's new London Liverpool Street railway station was finally opened on 1st November 1875, this having followed a partial opening on 2nd February 1874. It was the part known as the West Train Shed and contained the platform numbers one to ten. It had cost £2m and was potentially a source of extra passengers travelling through Harwich. The former passenger terminal at Bishopsgate was then closed and converted into a goods depot that re-opened in 1881.

The SMZ service from Flushing re-opened on 15th May 1876 using the same three vessels as before but this time they were sailing to Queenborough. Again the service was overnight, departing Flushing at 9.00 pm, and with each ship making the 111 mile crossing in 9 hours it was possible, via a connecting boat train, to arrive in London at 7.55 am. This route was also responsible for now carrying all of the mail between Britain and Holland in return for a payment of 150,000 Dutch florins per year. As a result, on 3rd October 1876, the company's official name became 'De Stoomvaart Maatschappij Zeeland Koninklijke Nederlandsche Postvaart N.V.' by adding the suffix Royal Dutch Mail to its title.

Although the SMZ was still principally concerned with challenging the Belgian State run routes into Dover their re-emergence did heighten concerns within the GER about the competitiveness of the Harwich to Antwerp service as well as renewing their existing concerns about the state of the New Waterway into Rotterdam. By 1876 the need for dredging the channel had become an urgent priority and attempts at doing so had failed to solve the problem. Costs had since risen to 12.8 million Guilders as Caland fought not only the channel but also those who were now advocating a lock system. Together with leading interests in Rotterdam he argued for retaining an open channel, which they succeeded in securing, but the city's influence deteriorated when the Pincoff business went bankrupt in 1879 and its owner's fleeing to America.

By now the facilities at Harwich were regarded as being totally outdated whilst not only had the mails been lost but in 1877 the importation of livestock from Holland and Belgium had ceased due to outbreaks of disease. The adverse nature of comments directed at Harwich had been going on ever since 1876 when the SMZ had re-emerged with its new terminals. That year had also seen Amsterdam gain access to the open sea at Ijmuiden by the opening of the North Sea Canal and with the recent collapse of the Pincoff empire there had also gone any point in constructing a railway line linking the Hook of Holland to a now somewhat impoverished Rotterdam. As the port of Rotterdam went into decline and its shipping, trade and passenger numbers gradually fell away there was little money left to dredge an increasingly silted up river channel. Ships were increasingly having to use the now inadequate and congested Voorne Canal with the result that Rotterdam's scheduled arrival and departure times could no longer be guaranteed.

A further issue with Rotterdam was that in 1877 a railway bridge was opened that spanned the River Maas and its presence now prevented ships from passing underneath and reaching the Oosterkade berth. Accordingly the GER ships were moved to a new berth slightly down river at the Westerkade, opposite the offices of Hudig & Pieters, and later on the GER were to berth at the Parkkade. A major disadvantage to these moves was the loss of the easy walk to the railway station and passengers were now inconveniently forced into using horse drawn carriages or trams.

The SMZ route out of Flushing received new and more powerful paddle boats in March and April 1878. They were of roughly 1,550 grt with a speed of 16 knots and were now named after members of the Dutch royal family as the *Prinses Marie* and *Prinses Elizabeth*. A third vessel of similar size arrived in 1880, appropriately named as the *Prins Hendrik,* just as new connecting railways in Holland now enabled through trains to run between Flushing and Berlin. In 1880 the Flushing route carried 35,000 tons of cargo and the average number of passengers per voyage was said to be 96 which would equate to around 60,000 passengers per year.

For the GER a second Clyde built steamer arrived in the form of the 1,098 grt *Princess of Wales,* this being the first in their fleet to measure over 1,000 grt. On board was accommodation for 579 passengers with 110 cabin berths in First class and 77 in Second class. She first entered service on the Rotterdam route on 6th July 1878 though in later years she also sailed to Antwerp.

Throughout it remained the case that the route into Antwerp was still the GER's premier service and in 1879 the Belgian port became better linked to Europe after the opening of a new and more direct rail route into Germany. To enhance the route further special boat trains, made up of luxurious six wheel coaches, ran from London Liverpool Street station to Harwich though the overall timings were little changed from those of ten years earlier. The service was still three times a week with trains leaving Liverpool Street on Mondays, Wednesdays and Fridays at 4.45 pm to arrive at Harwich just after 7.00 pm. The steamer then left at 7.30 pm and arrived in Antwerp by 9.00 am the next day. Such quick transfers between train and ship were due to there being very few customs formalities and no passports though the walk between the two must have been a fairly brisk one. The return sailing from Antwerp would depart at 1.00 pm which usually meant an arrival time in Harwich at the unearthly hour of 2.00 am though passengers for London now benefited from a much earlier departure from Harwich via the 3.00 am boat train which was scheduled to arrive in the capital at 5.10 am.

Amidst all that had happened during the 1870s there had been the Act of 16th July 1874 which authorised the GER to construct a quay on the River Stour. By July 1879 plans were available to show what progress had been made in constructing what was called the 'Liverpool of the East'. It was to prove a hugely significant development.

The original Station Approach to Parkeston Quay. (Robert Clow collection)

THE 1880s

On 4th June 1880 the Danish vessel *Riberhuus* arrived at Harwich from Denmark loaded with cattle, sheep and pigs. The operator was the United Steamship Company Ltd., a company founded in Copenhagen on 11th December 1866 by the union of several Danish shipping companies. In Denmark it was known as Det Forende Dampskibs-Selskab A/S., or DFDS for short. At Harwich it would long remain known as the United Steamship Company Ltd and its services, timetables and literature would refer to either this or Det Forende Line. (However for the convenience of this narrative the shortened DFDS will be used throughout)

The formation of DFDS followed Denmark having lost a large part of southern Jutland after the 1864 war with Prussia and further losing access to its most important port for agricultural goods, this having been at Altona in Hamburg. The subsequent re-drawing of national boundaries further to the north also lost Denmark the North Sea port of Tonning in what had previously been Danish Schleswig and from where, up until 1847, Danish cattle had been exported to London. In 1848 such exports had moved further north up the Jutland coast to the port of Hjerting, close by the present day site of Esbjerg, and from where the Continental Cattle Conveyance Company once sent the *City of Norwich* on a run to Harwich in 1849. By the early 1850s other companies were competing on the route to London and these included the North of Europe Steam Packet Co., the General Steam Navigation Co. and a weekly passenger and goods service to Lowestoft which started in April 1851.

By 1860 Hjerting had closed in favour of a re-emergent Tonning but the latter's loss, and that of Altona, had prompted Denmark into re-assessing its maritime trading activities and especially its need for an alternative port on its North Sea coast. On 24th April 1868 there came Parliamentary approval to build a new one at Esbjerg which was then a place with nothing more than 2 farms, 3 houses and 23 inhabitants. Initial start up capital was set at Dkr 1.8m and its construction and purpose would alleviate the problems facing Danish shipping companies when trading with Britain. This included the recently formed DFDS who, having commenced operations on 1st January 1867, were exporting cattle and goods to London from a much more distant Copenhagen. Their destination at the time was Thameshaven, a small port located on the north bank of the lower reaches of the River Thames, just west of Canvey Island, and which had had a railway connection since 7th June 1855.

The new port of Esbjerg was first opened to traffic on 15th August 1874 when around 820 feet of quay was then available for use. Early developments saw a preference for the use of paddle steamers due to the presence of a number of shallow sandbanks at its harbour entrance but these were later dredged out to provide for a greater use of screw steamers by the time the port was completed in 1878.

DFDS had delayed a while from using the new port as their first sailing from there, to Thameshaven, was not until 24th June 1875. This was by the newly built 615 grt paddle steamer, *Riberhuus*, delivered from the Gourley Brothers yard in Dundee. Although principally a cattle carrier the *Riberhuus* did have some rudimentary cabin accommodation for up to 28 passengers. The First class fare was £1.10s.0d.,. meals extra, though the beer was free. Plush furnishings on board included mahogany furniture and red velvet upholstery. For those prepared to endure the rigours of a deck passage the fare was just 4s.0d. though anyone travelling on this first trip would have been in the company of 415 cattle, 500 sheep and 65 pigs. The service was once a week with departures from Esbjerg each Thursday.

The sailings to Thameshaven were later changed in favour of Harwich and for two reasons. Firstly Harwich had much better lairage facilities and secondly the DFDS ships had been further required to sail from Thameshaven and on up to Gravesend for the purposes of coaling. This was much easier to do at Harwich.

The redirected service to Harwich commenced on 2nd June 1880 when both the *Riberhuus* and the *Esbjerg* left Esbjerg. The *Riberhuus* arrived first, on 4th June, and was followed in on the 5th by the *Esbjerg*, she being a bit slower at 8½ knots compared with the *Riberhuus* which could do 9½ knots. On board the *Esbjerg* were the route's first passengers - all two of them. Both ships were used in maintaining a once a week sailing though it was mainly the *Riberhuus* in service. It is interesting to note that for such a long journey of 340 n. miles both these ships were not only much slower than those of the GER but also much shorter, the *Riberhuus* measuring 190 feet long overall and the *Esbjerg* just 182 feet. Also interesting is that the summer of 1880, the period during which DFDS changed ports, was the last year that 'boat trains' ran to Thameshaven, these being trains that connected with a regular steamer service to Margate. In 1881 such steamers were transferred to Tilbury as were the train connections.

For the GER 1880 was the year when its last new build paddle steamers arrived. The *Lady Tyler* was built at North Shields and entered service on 29th May. She was 261 feet long with accommodation for 709 passengers and was fitted with 2 sets of 3 cylinder tandem steeple engines which resulted in her single funnel appearing as though unusually set further aft of the paddle box. She was followed by the *Adelaide*, built at Barrow in Furness, and which entered service on 23rd July as not only the Company's very last paddle steamer but also their first ship in service constructed of steel. Both ships went into service to Rotterdam. The GER boats in 1880 carried 17,434 passengers and 48,753 tons of cargo. In 1881 these figures had jumped to 82,686 passengers and 193,187 tons of cargo.

About this time an issue had been raised in Parliament concerning the finances and the ongoing subsidizing of the Harwich Harbour Conservancy Board. In 1880 the HHCB owed the Treasury £32,372 for advances plus a further £7,400 to the Public Works Loan Commissioners. Total expenditure on works had so far amounted to £21,000 plus a further £11,817 on land, engineering costs and wages etc.. Total revenue had only been £19,000 and the Board's assets were put at just a boat and stores, £22.4s.0d. and some ballast worth £10.12s.6d.! The HHCB was described as being 'in an exceedingly bad way' with revenue very slight, liabilities immense and little prospect of paying back what it owed. In June 1881 it was suggested that the GER be allowed to take over the harbour for themselves and relieve the Government of having to forever fund the HHCB. One honourable member commented, *'After all, it was a very small undertaking'*. All that was to change dramatically.

As far back as 1872 larger ships were bringing ever more traffic through the piers at Harwich and such was the growth in trade that the GER was already proposing plans to further extend their facilities there. The timing was co-incident with the opening of the New Waterway in Holland but the proposals were strongly resisted by the Harwich Corporation on various grounds not least of which that they included the large scale destruction of much of the town. They would also have meant a huge disruption to services whilst the works were in progress and so the GER turned to ideas put forward earlier, namely that they might expand further west and into Bathside Bay. However it was soon decided that this would be too expensive an undertaking on account of the ground thereabouts being far too soft. Thereafter attention was turned to developing an area even further west at Ray Island or the Isle of Ray, a bleak isolated wilderness of mud banks, saltings and marshland, located two miles upstream the River Stour.

Ray Island itself was not a true island. At low water it was joined to the mainland at its western edge and was then being used for limited agricultural and grazing purposes. An outlet of water on its south side, called Ramsey Creek, flowed eastwards. Ownership of the land was, by the late 18th century, in the hands of the Garland family who did little to improve it other than construct a dyke system around this area of 'Le Rey' or 'The Ray' in the early 19th century. This was undertaken by the Squire Garland in order to protect both the land and the main Harwich to London road against flooding.

Surveys had shown that the 'island' extended far enough into a deep water channel that would provide a sufficient depth of water on its northern side at all states of the tide - the requirement of the GER being that this be at least 14 feet at low water. Accordingly plans were put before Parliament in November 1873 along with a list of those landowners from whom land would need to be purchased either by consent or compulsion.

There were four main items in the GER's proposals. In summary these were that there be 1) - a quay or wharf in or near the River Stour at a point 1000 yards north of the dwelling house of Ray Island Farm extending eastward to a point 350 yards north of Ramsey Ray Point. 2) - a railway (turning north into the new quay area) from the GER Harwich branch at a point roughly 600 yards west of the level crossing at the west end of Ray Island over which the road ran from East New Hall to Ray Island Farm. This point is roughly 3 miles east of Wrabness station and this portion of new line would terminate 180 yards to the north of Ramsey Ray Point. 3) - a railway leading out from within the new quay area terminating on the Harwich branch line at a point 600 yards west of the locomotive sheds at Dovercourt station. And 4) - a host of reclamation works between the intended quay face and the existing river bank of Ray Island and between the end points of the two new lines of railway and the river bank noting that any further lands required may be taken into use. Also to be incorporated in the works were the even less developed areas of Sunk Island and Ray Creek located immediately west of Ray Island.

There exists the suggestion that the GER were disposed to leaving Harwich over a dispute involving the supply of water or the levying of a toll on coal supplies entering the town. A rate of 2s. per cauldron, this being roughly two and a half tons, was imposed by the Council in 1874 and the money raised was used to repave the local streets. The GER objected to paying the toll on coal arriving by rail and appealed against it. The Company lost, despite an appeal to the House of Lords, and they settled the outstanding balance of £1,300 on 1st January 1881. However there had been earlier tolls on coal such as one in 1819, when no railway existed, but whatever the reason the reality was that Harwich could not physically absorb the proposed plans of the GER and by the time of this latest toll the Company had already made plans to move out.

The proposed plans were approved in the Act of 16th July 1874 whereby the GER was authorised to construct a quay on the River Stour and connections therewith to the Harwich Branch. 'The above works called the Stour River Quay and connecting railways will be made and the lands and houses to be taken are situated in the parishes of Ramsey and Dovercourt or one of them in the County of Essex, and are within or will be defined by the Bill to be within the Port of Harwich'. Although still within the Port of Harwich it was however outside the jurisdiction of the Harwich Town Council, the boundary being the course taken by the Dovercourt Dock River which flowed out from Ramsey Creek and into the Stour at Ramsey Ray Point. This was an important consideration to the GER in that they could now develop their own quay without regard to any Harwich Council interference though any Council would surely have 'interfered' if they thought that their town was to be effectively flattened.

Once decided upon the issue was self evidently the way forward. Since 1876 the piers at Harwich had begun to get overcrowded and thus a new facility was most obviously needed. A related Act of 12th July 1877 authorised the GER to then allot separate capital to its new river quay project.

By the start of the 1880s traffic levels at Harwich were still managing to grow despite the out dated facilities and the ongoing problems at the Dutch end of its services. In February 1880 dredging in the New Waterway had ceased due to a lack of financial and physical resources caused by the continued decline in the overall fortunes of Rotterdam. Work on the channel resumed in 1881 only after agreement was reached in raising the cost of construction to 20 million Guilders. The work was greatly aided by the successful introduction of steam powered dredgers though it would not be until 1885 that the original transit requirements were met nor would it be until 1895 that the entire works were completed as per the original 1863 plans. By then the total cost would have risen to 36 million Guilders.

Since August 1879 the Great Eastern Railway Engineering Department had been responsible for constructing a 'fine commodious dock', ie the Stour River Quay, with the engineers in charge being J.S. Macintyre and John Wilson. Within the requirement of providing a new quay area some 600 acres of low lying land were being reclaimed and bounded by a two and a half mile long sea wall. Much of a nearby hill had been removed to provide material used in the stabilisation of marshlands and for building wide causeways across the island of Ray. The vast majority of this land, some 587 acres, had been bought from Squire Garland on 2nd December 1878 at a cost of £30,093.15s.0d..

The geology of the site chosen consisted of an uppermost layer of around 10 feet of soft silt beneath which lay a band of fairly tough green or brown clay mixed in with grit and broken sea shells which extended down to about -25 feet O.D.. Beneath lay a bed of shingle of variable depths up to 20 feet thick and then a band of stiff blue clay extending to about -100 feet O.D. until reaching a bedrock of chalk.

The quay itself would be built at the eastern end of the acquired lands and a contract for erecting this had been placed with the Horseley Foundry Company on 14th January 1879, the sum being £67,971.9s. and one penny!. This cost was for the construction of the quay only and work on building the required straight frontage, running east to west, was started in 1881.

At the quay face, between rows of cast iron screw piles, were sunk a double row of 9 feet diameter cast iron segmental cylinders each consisting of seven rings. As a consequence of the ground structure the piles were anything between 40 and 50 feet long with the shingle proving an excellent ballast foundation upon which to build. These cylinders were set upon the ballast and filled with concrete. A concrete surface was then overlaid on top. Behind, up to a distance of 60 feet from the quay face, lay further rows of cast iron screw piles whilst an additional 40 feet to the rear consisted of timber piles. In total over 1,000 piles were sunk with those near the front being 2 feet in diameter and those at the back being 1 feet 6 inches in diameter. The piles were connected by either steel or wrought iron bracing and joists over which lay timber bearers and a fully covering timber deck. A number of railway tracks were carried on special timber weigh beams supported by the main timber framing. A substantial brick culvert was built on top that would, in later years, house hydraulic power mains and cables and also carry the tracks for travelling cranes.

When completed the quay extended for 1,800 feet and was 100 feet wide. With ships then being around 260 feet in length there was sufficient frontage for six ships to lay alongside at any one time. In addition to these working berths, numbered 1 to 6 from east to west, there was a repair berth on the far east end where a seventh ship would partly overhang the quay and moor one end upon a dolphin. From the very start it was intended that all the berths would be strung with electric lights. When finished the quay had a minimum depth of 16 feet of water at low tide and 28 feet at high tide. A dredger for the purpose of maintaining these depths was bought for £1,000 in July 1882 from the Regents Canal in London. Beyond the extreme eastern and western ends of the quay was placed timber campsheeting, this being a facing of planks and piles placed along the bank of the river to prevent erosion, and the land behind was built up to the level of the quay. Off the quay, in mid river, were a further seven screw pile moorings for ships to lay up in line.

At roughly the centre point of the quay was constructed a 350 feet long three storey building, red bricked and ashlar dressed, which at ground level housed the railway station, offices and customs hall. Above this was a luxurious Great Eastern Railway Hotel. The building was part of a £47,846 contract awarded to Bennett Bros. in February 1882 which in itself was part of the £55,000 allocated by the GER for its construction and furnishings over a two year period. It was built next to a long platform that had a slight curve in it, this being on the down side, ie on the north side or river side of the railway lines. This through platform might be imagined as two platforms joined end on with a recessed bay platform at each extremity, the one at the eastern end being used for a shuttle service to the town of Harwich. A main line ran through the station as the middle line of three and joined the down line towards its eastern end. This hotel side platform was known as No. 1 platform. On the up side, ie the south or land side, was a single and much shorter No. 2 platform with an open fronted timber shelter at the London end. Connecting the two timber decked platforms was an iron footbridge close by the eastern side of the station building where an opening led onto the quay.

To the east of this opening was a two storey brick building that housed the Continental Offices, also known as the Dock or Marine Offices. About a quarter of a mile beyond the Harwich end of the station a locomotive depot was established alongside the seaward side of the track. Here there was a four road locomotive shed together with a 50 feet diameter turntable and between it and the sea wall fronting Bathside Bay were built extensive cattle pens.

On the western side of the station building, again in line, was a large brick built warehouse completed by July 1882. It was used as a bonded store and inside it was sub-divided to provide three smaller sections measuring 150 feet by 40 feet for the storing of wines and spirits, 81 feet by 40 feet for tobacco and 54 feet by 42 feet for dry goods. Large rooms were also made available for Customs officers and for those merchants and shippers who carried on their business there. Coaling facilities for the ships were provided close by the vicinity of this store as were stables for up to 96 horses which were used on hauling duties around the quay.

Out on the quay itself were built two large warehouses with one at either end. These were of steel and timber construction measuring 528 feet long by 60 feet wide. They were placed roughly 30 feet in from the quay face and fitted with steel framed trusses to support roofs that spanned wide side entrances through which railway lines ran. The east warehouse came to be known as the East Shed, later on as No. 1 Shed whilst the other was the West Shed or No. 2 Shed.

To access the 'mainland' a new road led away south from the station, over a causeway, and thence

A postcard of an early view looking east along the main or 'down' platform at Parkeston Quay.

through a cutting in the higher ground of the old Ray Island to join the rising ground towards Dovercourt and the main Harwich to London road. The causeway cut across an area of marshy ground behind the up platform and was intersected by a deep ditch. South of the ditch were numerous allotments and a footpath led out across them in line from the station footbridge. To the west of the causeway, between the mainline and the sea wall, was a formative goods yard consisting of 12 railway sidings.

In October 1881 the GER Board decided that this new quay would be named 'Parkeston Quay' in honour of its Chairman, Mr Charles Henry Parkes, though it would be a while before the name was officially adopted. However it soon came to be in public use as a foreign newspaper correspondent (NYT) wrote in August 1882 that *'the growth of Antwerp has created Parkeston, the new port of the Great Eastern Railroad, in addition to Harwich, where the accommodation was inadequate..'*.

This early reference to Parkeston was in connection with highlighting the growing importance of Antwerp which was then undergoing a massive change. In 1865 the inward tonnage of the port was 750,000; in 1880, it was over 3,000,000 and the Belgian Government were then building a new rail connected quay estimated to cost $10 US million, roughly £2m. *'...the old quay along the Scheldt, with its cafes and shady trees, is gone, ...the commercial advance of late has been unrivalled in Europe, ...the Germans have taken to travel by the line from Antwerp to Harwich to such an extent that the Great Eastern Railroad of England have started a daily service which now carries an immense amount of Italian produce to England via the St. Gothard Tunnel, Antwerp being nearer to Italy than any other port of Western Europe'*.

The GER ships were berthed at the Quai d'Herbouville in Antwerp's new Quai de Sud or South Quay at Hangar No. 9, or Shed No. 9, to where a railway line would soon be running alongside. As for the above mentioned daily service to Antwerp this had started on 1st July 1882 and was now daily except Sunday. In August 1882, via the Continental boat train, passengers now left London Liverpool Street at 7.10 pm., arrived at Harwich at 9.00 pm and were in Antwerp at 9.00 am the following morning. The return sailing left Antwerp at 4.30 pm and arrived at Harwich at 4.30 am. The boat train then left for London at 5.00 am to arrive at 6.50 am. The ships on the route were usually the *Pacific*, the *Claud Hamilton* and the *Adelaide*.

Further developments related to the works at Stour River Quay were the doubling of track along the Harwich branch throughout 1882 and the construction of a short length of embanked railway line, roughly a quarter of a mile long, known as the Manningtree North curve. Authorised by an Act of 4th July 1878 'to construct a new line from Lawford to the company's Harwich branch of 2 furlongs, 3 chains and 11 links' this line into the London to Norwich main line heading north created the third side of a now triangular junction. It opened on 29th August 1882 and would later prove to be of huge benefit to the new port.

The first commercial sailings from 'Ray Island Wharf' left on 3rd September 1882 when two unidentified vessels sailed to Rotterdam with surplus cargo stored on site as a result of an overflowing Continental Pier at Harwich. The new railway line into the quay opened on 6th September at a time when official plans still referred to it as 'Stour Quay' or 'Stour River Quay' and the first import of cargo arrived on 22nd September 1882 when the DFDS vessel *Riberhuus* unloaded cattle from Denmark.

The name 'Parkeston Quay' was first recorded as such on 7th October 1882 with confirmation occurring on 15th February 1883 when it was officially opened by Mr. Parkes. On 15th March 1883.the GER moved their Continental Ticket Office up from Harwich and this was accompanied by the movement upstream of their Rotterdam and Antwerp steamer services. The formal opening for business occurred on 17th March 1883. The original through railway line between Wrabness and Dovercourt was closed on the day of the move, 15th March, and shortly afterwards the railway station at Harwich itself was renamed as 'Harwich Town'.

The difference between the space available at Parkeston Quay and the cramped conditions experienced back at Harwich was enormous. The facilities offered were at that time the most magnificent anywhere in the country and it was not long after the Rotterdam and Antwerp services had transferred upstream, together with the Danish mail service, that

An early view looking west along the main or 'down' platform at Parkeston Quay. (Robert Clow collection)

interests were expressed in running services elsewhere. As early as October 1882 DFDS had applied for permission to run a service to the Swedish port of Gothenburg though such an idea was never to materialise for quite some time. However they were quick to introduce five cargo ships to the port, these being the *Thy* and the *Kursk* plus three recently acquired sister ships, *Charkow*, *Tula* and *Minsk*.

With the new quay at Parkeston now open for business all railway passenger boats ceased sailing to the Continent from Harwich. The town once again fell very quiet. '*What a contrast with the now deserted Continental Pier at Harwich, where all was bustle and life, now nothing but quietness reigns supreme*'. In time the old Continental Pier was reduced to being a fish jetty.

The provision of a station Hotel was seen by the GER as an integral part of the Parkeston Quay development and hugely important in offering visitors from abroad a decent establishment with full facilities. Prestige and pride was everything at their major new port of entry even though it was to be the smallest hotel the Company ever operated. '*..their splendid quay at Parkeston, Harwich, with its spacious hotel and waiting and refreshment rooms, all fitted up in the most luxurious style and electrically lighted throughout, is a striking proof of what untiring energy can accomplish, for it is quite unequalled at any point in England for embarkation to the Continent*'.

It featured twenty six bedrooms, these all being situated on the first floor, plus it offered both First and Second class restaurants, waiting rooms and lavatories and was connected to the landing stage by a covered way. This last feature was a huge improvement over having had to struggle with luggage through the backstreets of Harwich at all hours in all weathers. The existing hotel at Harwich was retained under GER management with a point of note being its silverware. Within the GER's group of hotels items such as knives, forks and spoons would often bear a company symbol together with a local mark. Those with H or HH on them signified the Harwich Hotel whilst those with a P were from the Parkeston Quay Hotel.

In association with the construction of their new quay the GER thought to provide accommodation for its new workforce by renting out houses that the Company itself would build. Conditions and wages were expected to be much better than many of the locals had hitherto enjoyed especially those attracted to move there from outlying villages and farms. Thus a new village and buildings close by the quay was considered an essential development and in December 1881 Directors of the Company came to visit the prospective site.

However by the time the quay was opened there existed no railway built housing whatsoever and the earliest reference to Company expenditure on any such accommodation for staff does not appear until the latter half of 1883. The first to be built were a Marine Superintendent's House, one pair of semi-detached Captains houses and one pair of semi-detached Clerks houses itemised as costing £880, £915 and £576.11s.5d. respectively. They were built on railway property, either side of what became Makins Road, close by the junction of Station Road and Coller Road.

Meanwhile an area of housing was being developed privately to the south and outside the confines of the GER's land. Garland Road, named after the local squire and landowner, was built to run due east off Station Road though initially houses were only built on its northern side. Leading off from between various groups of these houses, at right angles to Garland Road and heading north, were five parallel roads. From west to east these were named as Adelaide Street, Tyler Street, Hamilton Street, Princess Street and Parkeston Road. These consisted of narrow fronted terraced housing with the northernmost edge of each street laying up against the Company's boundary line. They were all built between 1883 and 1885 and the names given were in some way associated with either the quay or the Company. Adelaide Street, Tyler Street, Hamilton Street and Princess Street are all thought to have been named after the paddle steamers *Adelaide*, *Lady Tyler*, *Claud Hamilton* and *Princess of Wales* though Tyler Street and Hamilton Street could well have been named after Company Directors during the time of their construction. Parkeston Road takes its name from the quay as it was amongst the first to be built during the period 1883 to 1884. This area of housing formed the core of a Parkeston village and although they were privately built the houses were still only rented to GER quay employees.

The GER first started to build dwellings on their own land in 1884 when they spent £2,921.7s.11d. on twelve cottages at the north end of Hamilton Street. Close by was built a new school, opened on 4th October 1888, and which, although run by the Ramsey School Board in whose parish Parkeston was situated, was managed by the GER Board of Directors. Fees were payable of 2d. each for infants and juniors and 4d. for the older children prior to the introduction of free schools in 1891. Also built was a Wesleyan Chapel in Garland Road in 1887, a Garland Hotel, a village hall and St. Gabriels Church.

The population of Parkeston in 1886 was 600. In 1890 a further twenty cottages were built by the GER at a cost of £5,501.12s.0d., along an extended Tyler Street that ran into Coller Road. By 1891 the village population had risen to 1,050.

In later years, and to complete what essentially remains the present day residential layout of Parkeston village, the south side of Garland Road was lined with houses during 1897 and 1898. This marked the outermost limit of construction there due to the marshy nature of land further south. Between March 1899 and 1901 another twenty dwellings, together with an Enginemen's Barracks, were built on the south side of Foster Road, this being a new road on GER land to the west of Station Road. The Barracks were intended to be a place of overnight lodgings for up to fifty train crew who brought trains down one day and left the next. It was opened in February 1901 and, together with the cottages, cost a total of £10,248.15s.7d.. Foster was another Company Director and in 1913 work started on yet a further twenty cottages on the road's north side though these were built privately. The last phase of development took place on the west side of the village starting with Una Road, built privately prior to 1922, off which was built Edward Street during the 1930s. Una Road was named after Una Wood, the daughter of the Vicar of Ramsey who had earlier hoped to build a church on this land whilst Edward Street was named after Edward Saunder, the owner of a brickworks in Una Road.

Throughout the entire period that the future Parkeston Quay was under construction its funding had come wholly from resources within the GER and by the end of 1886 the Company had spent around

£475,000. The GER's original intention was to have previously raised additional funds to meet the cost but it was not until the half yearly General Meeting of the GER on 28th January 1887 that the issue of how to do that was finally resolved.

In his address to shareholders the Chairman, Mr. Parkes, said *'We spent not quite £500,000 but nearly. We had power to raise that by a separate capital charged upon this Parkeston Quay; but we deferred doing so, because there were no funds at the time, the progress of the works was going on, and we were allowed by Parliament and by you to defer the creation of that separate capital and to pay the money out of our usual expenditure. We have done so; and the time has now arrived, the Parkeston Quay having been opened several years and developed, when we ask you to create again a sufficient amount to cover that expenditure, as well as the £75,000 which we expended in the purchase of the East and West India Dock, with a further sum to make up the £750,000 which we were authorised to raise by the Act of 1875'.*

Two sets of figures were created in relation to the construction of Parkeston Quay. One was the overall capital expenditure, or gross costs, associated with developing and building the entire site including all the necessary railway infrastructure, this being the 'not quite £500,000 but nearly' figure referred to above. The other was the proportion of those costs allocated to the port via the Parkeston Quay Capital Account. This lower figure included only those elements more associated with the business of 'docks, harbours and wharves' rather than the business of running a railway. At the time of the Chairman's address to shareholders it is estimated that just under £320,000 had been allocated to the Parkeston Quay Capital Account.

In preparation for the anticipated increase in traffic, especially for that via Antwerp, the GER had been placing orders for new ships. These went to Earle's Shipbuilding and Engineering Company of Hull and resulted in the *Norwich*, launched in March 1883, followed by the *Ipswich*, launched in May 1883. These were the GER's last iron hulled vessels and their first twin screwed steamers. Their arrival ended the Company's ordering of any more paddle ships. Construction of both these 1,037 grt, 260 feet by 31 feet iron hulled vessels was overseen by the Company's Marine Superintendent, Captain Howard, and they supplemented the ten vessels the GER already had - these being the *Zealous, Harwich, Rotterdam, Avalon (II), Pacific, Richard Young*, *Claud Hamilton, Princess of Wales, Lady Tyler* and *Adelaide* - an amazing number even by the standards of the day and which between them had carried around 80,000 passengers in 1882.

Both the new ships made maiden voyages to Antwerp, the *Norwich* on 24th July 1883 and the *Ipswich* three months later on 23rd October. Each was very comfortably furnished. On the Main deck was a main saloon amidships, fitted out in panels made of rosewood, satinwood and oak, aft of which was a smoking room. Also on this deck was a Ladies saloon and a galley equipped with a hoist system that allowed stewards to convey meals directly to the First class cabins on the Bridge deck above without the need to go outside. There were berths for 84 travelling First class whilst for those in Second class there were 42 berths aft under the poop. The crew were berthed in the foc'sle. Overall accommodation was for a total of 440 passengers plus, due to their design, space for more cargo than the existing paddle steamers could carry. Each had three hatchways to the holds, three steam winches, several derricks plus space for carrying horses fore and aft of the main saloon.

The ships were heated by steam and lit with Swan's incandescent electric lights of which one was kept in action all night in every cabin. These were powered by Siemen's dynamos with the electrical gear supplied by Raworth of Liverpool. The saloons and cabins were so efficiently ventilated with fresh air that passengers 'often plug the ventilators to keep it out'. As both ships were mainly deployed on the overnight service to Antwerp there was no need for a high service speed. Little was gained by arriving at the port too early or much before the timetabled departure of the connecting trains and so a service speed of 14 knots was quite sufficient. When first built it was thought that the screw steamers might have had a tendency to roll more than the paddle steamers. To counteract this possibility they were fitted with water balance tanks capable of holding 200 tons of water for use in trimming the ship when the cargo was light. Over time they were deemed to be quite unnecessary. The arrival of the *Norwich* and *Ipswich* marked the start from when all future GER vessels bore the names of places served by the Company, both in England and on the Continent, and the beginning of a 25 year association with the Earle's shipyard.

Screw ships had a distinct advantage over paddle ships in being able to berth close up against the quay and this enabled cranes to transfer cargo directly between the quayside and the hold. With paddle ships the extra width of the paddle boxes meant that their holds were anything up to 20 feet off the quay and thus cargo had first to be winched out onto the deck before it could be craned ashore. Such improvements together with the new facilities available helped show an increase of 16% in the level of continental goods being handled.

On 20th May 1884 Parkeston Quay became a licensed slaughtering and quarantine point complete with the building of a new fodder store and in July 1884 two new two-ton steam cranes were erected in connection with a new service to Hamburg. This had been proposed by the Hamburg agency of H.J. Perlbach & Co., and whose service started with the arrival of the *Astronom* on 19th August 1884. What began as a weekly service, primarily for cargo, soon became twice a week with the arrival later that year of the *Roland*, a vessel more usually seen sailing between Hamburg and Rotterdam. Departures from Parkeston Quay were on Wednesday and Saturday and over the next few years other ships were variously seen on the route such as the *Germania, Minerva* and *Uranus*. All were British built iron hulled schooners originally from yards along the Humber, Tyne or Tees rivers and measured in the region of 200 feet long and between 600 and 700 grt although the *Uranus* was somewhat larger at 926 grt. The *Roland* was to become a frequent visitor to Parkeston Quay and she made 20 trips from Hamburg in 1884, and a further 30 in 1885, before moving onto a combined Hamburg to Parkeston Quay and Antwerp service in 1886. In 1885 the service had increased to three sailings a week with departures from Hamburg being each Tuesday, Wednesday and Saturday night at 10.00 pm.

Since the beginning of 1883 the DFDS ship *Esbjerg* was no longer in service at Parkeston Quay as a new ship had arrived to take over her role. This was the paddle steamer *Koldinghuus,* built by Lobnitz and Co. in Renfrew at a cost of £37,200. She was another cattle ship but with accommodation for 118 passengers, 48 in First class plus 70 in Deck, and made her maiden voyage from Esbjerg to Parkeston Quay on 19th July 1883. At 1,057 grt she had a much increased freight capacity and with a speed of 12½ knots this 269 feet long paddler was much faster on what was still a weekly service. The *Riberhuus* was then sent away in September 1883 to Lobnitz and Co. for conversion to a screw steamer and returned to work the Parkeston Quay to Esbjerg route in April 1884.

In June 1885 the service, as offered by the *Koldinghuus*, or another of DFDS's fine steamers, was advertised as leaving Parkeston Quay every Saturday 'on the arrival of the train which leaves Liverpool Street station, London at 5.30 pm'. The return sailing from Esbjerg was every Wednesday evening with the sea passage taking about 30 hours. Trains between Esbjerg and Copenhagen ran twice daily on a journey that required the use of two train ferries the first of which, when travelling from Esbjerg, was for crossing the Lillebaelt or Little Belt between Fredericia and Strib which opened in 1872 and the second for crossing the Storebaelt or Great Belt between Nyborg and Korsor which opened in 1883. The Little Belt crossing was a matter of only a few hundred yards but the Great Belt crossing was much longer at 13¾ n. miles.

The fare between London and Esbjerg by First class rail and saloon was £2.0s.0d. single or £3.0s.0d return for a ticket that was valid for one month. By Second class rail and saloon the fare was £1.17s.0d single or £2.15s.0d. return. For a saloon passage only, between Parkeston Quay and Esbjerg, the fare was £1.10s.0d. single or £2.5s.0d. return. For particulars one should apply to: Tegner, Price & Co., Billiter House, Billiter St., London. E.C.. With an evening departure and a 30 hour sea passage the arrival time at each port would have been in the very early hours of the morning.

By 1885 work on the New Waterway in Holland had successfully reached the stage whereby the depth of water within its channel was no longer an issue for concern. However there did remain the ever present natural hazard of fog that could still cause considerable delays to traffic and with its ever increasing use by relatively slow moving cargo ships there re-emerged the idea of a railway line to the Hook of Holland to speed up the transit times via Rotterdam.

Concern about the levels of traffic then going between Britain and Germany via the Scheldt estuary grew to such an extent that in September 1885 the GER's agents in Rotterdam, Hudig & Pieters, wrote to the Dutch Government stating that it was now ten years since the Act of 1875 had authorised such a railway and they feared that the GER would retire from Holland altogether if such a line was not built. Without specifically saying as much it was thought that the Dutch port of Terneuzen on the north bank of the Scheldt or a new port at Zeebrugge in Belgium were being considered as alternative destinations for the Harwich steamers. It was argued that the Hook of Holland was better placed geographically to serve the main centres of Holland with shorter distances and up to two and a half hours less travelling time to and from England if going via Parkeston Quay rather than via Flushing. The transport of fish from industries based in Scheveningen, Vlaardingen and Maassluis and fruit and vegetables from the Westland would benefit greatly as would the postal service. The GER service was said to have grown from being a local service between Harwich and Rotterdam into an international rail and boat connection between England and the Continent. Furthermore an essay at the time contained the point that the *'G.E.R. recognised that permanent success is only to be found by the support of the masses'* and as their service was by no means poor or inferior on account of the provision of luxurious ships, *'there is no outing so cheap and no change so entire as that offered by the G.E.R. route via Harwich'*. For full details passengers were recommended to consult the Continental Time Table, price 1d. The counter argument favouring the SMZ was that their route out of Flushing had managed a great expansion of business despite a fire at its Queenborough Pier in 1882 that saw services temporarily diverted to Dover and its cargo traffic being conveyed to and from London using chartered steamers. Also its business had now warranted a fourth paddle ship, the *Willem, Prins van Orange*, which joined the fleet in July 1883.

Despite the public endorsements and the very persuasive arguments made by the GER and Hudig & Pieters, the Dutch Government remained in favour of the Flushing service run by its State Railways, the SMZ and the LC&DR in England. The pier at Queenborough was fully restored in 1885 and at the instigation of the Continental postal authorities, especially in Germany where the mails were often late due to intolerable delays via the Dover to Ostend route, it was agreed that the SMZ should now run a day service in addition to its night boats. The pier at Queenborough was lengthened by 125 feet and with fresh capital having been raised on behalf of the SMZ the company built three new paddle ships. These were similar to those on the night service but specifically fitted out as day boats. They were named *Duitschland, Engeland* and *Nederland* and this new service commenced on 1st June 1887.

The route was to prove popular for those travelling from the Continent. London's Victoria railway station was closer to the sights than Liverpool Street but going back meant a morning departure from the station at 7.15 am and this was a little too early to endure on a regular basis. The train arrived at Queenborough at 8.35 am with the ship reaching Flushing at 5.00 pm. Onward connections then arrived at Cologne at 11.30 pm that night and Berlin at 7.39 am the next morning after. The sea crossing times were similar each way so that the boat from Flushing docked at Queenborough around 5.00 pm.

A timetable of the improved 1887 GER service to Antwerp. (Stephen Brown collection)

In anticipation of these developments the GER had earlier improved their own service between Parkeston Quay and Antwerp despite the Chairman of the LC&DR, Mr James Staats Forbes, himself a Dutchman, having said that *'Queenborough and Flushing is, in some sense, in competition with Dover and Calais, but it is much more in competition with the old tubs that used to go down the river from the Thames to Antwerp'*.

As from 1st March 1887 the twin screw steamers, *Norwich*, *Ipswich* and *Cambridge* were all used on the overnight service to Antwerp which ran daily, except Sundays. The *Cambridge* was another new ship almost identical to the *Norwich* and *Ipswich* except that she was 20 feet longer and the Company's first screw steamer to be built of steel. She was launched on 11th October 1886, underwent trials on 25th January 1887 and had only been in service since 12th February. Her overall layout was very similar to the *Norwich* and *Ipswich* though her extra length allowed for a more substantial superstructure within which were housed an additional 50 First class cabin berths, two luxury Deck cabins and a raised capacity for 737 passengers. The fares (from Belgium) were:

Brussels to London
    First class Single £1.10s.3d.   Return £2.6s.8d.
    Second class Single 18s.3d.   Return £1.9s.0d.
Antwerp to London
    First class Single £1.6s.0d.   Return £2.0s.0d.
    Second class Single 15s.0d.   Return £1.4s.0d.

On the evening sailing from Antwerp a dinner costing 3s.6d. consisting of Soup, Fish, Joint and Pastry was served at 6.30 pm whilst Second class passengers could travel in the steamer's First class Saloon upon payment of an extra fare of 6s. single and 9s. return.

Both ports were linked to their respective capitals and major cities by special boat trains with some exceptionally fast transfer times at the Belgian port. For example the morning train to Brussels left just 10 minutes after the arrival of the ship though passengers had only to walk a short distance in between. Luggage would have been dealt with by having had it through registered. The timings were:

Dep. London (L St)	8.00 pm	Dep. Brussels	4.43 pm
Dep. P. Quay	9.50 pm	Arr. Antwerp	5.46 pm
Arr. Antwerp	9.30 am	Dep. Antwerp	6.00 pm
Dep. Antwerp	9.40 am	Dep. P. Quay	5.00 am
Arr. Brussels	10.42 am	Arr. London (L St)	6.50 am

The London to Parkeston Quay boat train also conveyed passengers travelling to and from Holland and whose overnight steamer arrived in Rotterdam at 9.00 am and departed back at 6.30 pm.

From Parkeston Quay a second boat train headed north towards the major centres of Yorkshire and Lancashire. This had developed from a service first started on 1st September 1882 between Harwich and Doncaster and was one of Britain's earliest long distance cross country trains. In later years it would become known as the 'North Country Continental' and went via the new north curve at Manningtree and then by way of Ipswich, Bury St Edmunds, Ely, March, Spalding, Lincoln and Doncaster. Connections were available at March for Peterborough and Birmingham whilst from Lincoln connections ran through to Manchester and Liverpool. In 1885 destinations in Scotland had been added to those then reachable via connecting trains and in 1887 the following destinations, amongst others and via connections, were advertised as being possible from Parkeston Quay.

Dep. P. Quay	7.43 am	Dep. Glasgow	8.45 am
Arr. Doncaster	12.34 pm	Dep. Edinburgh	10.00 am
Arr. York	1.40 pm	Dep. Liverpool	2.00 pm
Arr. Manchester	3.00 pm	Dep. Manchester	3.00 pm
Arr. Liverpool	4.06 pm	Dep. York	3.25 pm
Arr. Edinburgh	7.00 pm	Dep. Doncaster	4.44 pm
Arr. Glasgow	8.20 pm	Arr. P. Quay	9.29 pm

Overall the services had vastly improved since Gilbert and Sullivan's 1882 opera 'Iolanthe' in which the Lord Chancellor sang his nightmare song: *'For you dream you are crossing, The Channel and tossing, About in a steamer from Harwich, Which is something between, A large bathing machine, And a very small second-class carriage.'*

Unfortunately the profits had not improved. Between 1884 and 1886 the GER had been the only railway company out of the five in Britain then operating short sea steamer services to the Continent, (the others being the London, Chatham & Dover, the South Eastern, the London, Brighton & South Coast and the London & South Western), not to have increased its overall steamboat receipts and it had the worst performance of them all between 1885 and 1886.

	1884	1885	1886
Receipts	£189,000	£188,000	£186,000
Expenses	£157,000	£159,000	£163,000
Net profit	£32,000	£29,000	£23,000

Extenuating circumstances were partly responsible such as in 1884-85 the Continent had been plagued with outbreaks of cholera, in 1885 the Antwerp Exhibition caused a reduction in travel and in 1886 there had been long periods of severe gales, bad weather and continual fog in the North Sea that had reduced the attractions of travelling at all. Fortunately the GER services were still profitable as were those of all the others companies.

Throughout the mid to late 1880s the GER had become embroiled in a Parliamentary debate over a proposal by the Felixstowe Railway and Dock Company (FRD) that they be allowed to run their own steamer services to foreign ports, mainly in Germany, and to form a 'Felixstowe, Ipswich and Midland Railway'. Felixstowe had only opened as a dock in 1886 and the debate raised suggestions that it was actually the GER who were behind the proposal for their own ends.

The origins of a dock at Felixstowe dated back to an Act of 19th July 1875 which incorporated the Felixstowe Railway and Pier Company (FRP). Work then started on building a 13½ mile long railway line from Westerfield, north of Ipswich, down to Felixstowe and this was opened on 1st May 1877. The idea of such a venture had come from a wealthy local landowner, Colonel George Tomline, who foresaw the development of a port on the Suffolk side of the estuary and opposite Harwich. The line cost £130,000 to build but despite a reasonable return on its passenger side the freight business was practically non existent. As such Tomline was unable to make it sufficiently profitable and in 1879 he had asked the GER to take over the running of it in exchange for buying stock and receiving 65% of the gross receipts. The FRP then became known as the FRD on 21st July 1879 and work on building a dock proper was begun in 1882. The arrival of its first ship, the collier *Crathie* with 471 tons of coal, was on 7th April 1886 just as the parliamentary debate was getting underway.

The problem for the GER was that the Felixstowe line had been vested to them since 17th November 1885 and thus any advantages to a new Bill being passed were assumed to be largely for their benefit. The Company was also being scrutinised for effectively poaching the Continental traffic of northern manufacturers and businesses by offering the same rate for goods going by rail all the way via Parkeston Quay as that charged by local companies for going via much nearer ports such as Hull. They were further accused of supporting the running of steamer services from Felixstowe to 'Amsterdam, Dunkerque, Bremerhaven, Hamburgh, Altona and Cuxhaven or any other port on the River Elbe'. as not only were they currently operating the railway into which these steamers would connect but the Elbe ports were amongst those previously denied them when the GER applied for parliamentary approval in 1869.

The accusations were strongly refuted in the House by, among others, the GER Director, Lord Claud Hamilton, who stated that his company had nothing whatsoever to do with the matter. Fellow Director, Sir Henry Tyler, added that the GER considered Felixstowe to be on the wrong side of the river for the type of trade envisaged. Eventually the proposals were rejected and having failed to attract the anticipated foreign trade an agreement was reached in November 1886 whereby Colonel Tomline would sell the railway element of the FRD to the GER. Approval was granted by an Act of 5th July 1887 with the sum involved being £221,000 made up of £57,000 in debentures and £164,000 in ordinary stock. Left with no railway of its own except for a few sidings the FRD was then re-titled the Felixstowe Dock and Railway Company (FDR). In the years to come the GER appeared to do the dock few favours as regards rates and the general carriage of goods but it did develop the town into a sizeable tourist resort.

The idea that steamers from Felixstowe should concentrate on sailing into northern waters and to Germany was because of the GER at Parkeston Quay having a local monopoly into Holland and Belgium. However there were various other competing services to both these countries from several ports along the east coast, these being mainly out of London St Catherine's Dock, Tilbury and the Humber ports of Goole, Hull and Grimsby with the latter ports serving Antwerp twice a week. In general most of this short sea trade was now going via the Scheldt estuary and in December 1887, from amongst the GER fleet of cargo ships, only the *Harwich*, rebuilt in 1884 as a twin screwed passenger and cargo ship, was left sailing to Rotterdam.

In 1887 the ageing paddle steamers *Zealous* and *Pacific* were sold for scrap and the *Rotterdam* was sent to Earle's in Hull for a similar conversion to that of her sister ship, *Harwich*. She was returned to passenger and cargo service after having been renamed *Peterborough*. The GER then chartered two smaller cargo ships, the 338 ton *Corsican* between 18th December 1887 and 1st December 1888 followed by the 388 ton *John o'Groat* from 8th December 1888 until 9th August 1889. The *John o'Groat* was built in 1877 by Gourlay Bros. of Dundee and was used whilst the *Richard Young* was sent away for conversion by Earle's into a twin screw steamer and cattle carrier. When she returned to service in February 1890 she had been renamed as the *Brandon*.

In 1887 H.J. Perlbach ceased sailings between Parkeston Quay and Hamburg and in 1888 transferred operations to Tilbury Docks where a new and commodious goods station closer to London was far better suited to their cargo trade. The Hamburg route from Parkeston Quay was then taken up by the General Steam Navigation Company in conjunction with their services from London. Starting on the 29th March 1888, with the arrival of the *Hawk*, the route then became one for both cargo and passengers. The GER, having once proposed a service of their own to Hamburg in 1869, might well have been able to do so in 1887 via their 'non involvement in the Felixstowe issue' but instead they decided to continue with leasing out the appropriate facilities on the quay.

The GER's *Avalon* was sold in 1888. Another new ship, the *Colchester*, arrived in February 1889 as a sister ship to the *Cambridge* and she too was put on the Antwerp route. As a sign of improving technology the GER decided that as from February 1889 all of its ships should be fitted with electric lamps.

The decade ended with news that in order to develop trade further the Danish government had given the Esbjerg to Parkeston Quay route a subsidy of Dkr 150,000 a year, the only subsidy ever paid to a Danish ship owner. Though it was seen as being more of a subsidy to Danish farmers it did have the effect of increasing sailings in 1889 from weekly to three times a week.

The principal DFDS passenger vessels were still the *Riberhuus* and *Koldinghuus* but in the previous two or three years there had been an increased assortment of cargo ships sailing in support. At varied or infrequent occasions these now included the *Expres*, *Kronen*, *Romny*, *Union*, *Christian IX* and *Lolland*.

GER Parkeston Quay Capital Expenditure to 31st December 1886

Particulars	to 1886	to 1886 Proportion applicable to Quay &c
Sea Walls and Works	69,026. 3. 9.	
Pile Foundations &c. for Buildings	49,184. 0. 0.	44,418. 11. 0.
Stables	2,226. 4. 4.	2,226. 4. 4.
Pile Foundations &c. for Engine Shed	6,608. 8.11.	
Marine Superintendent's House	880. 0. 0.	
Clerks' Houses, 1 Pair semi detached	576. 11. 5.	
Captains' Houses, 1 Pair semi detached	915. 0. 0.	
Cattle Lairs and Shoot	11,996. 0. 0.	11,996. 0. 0.
Electric Lighting Engine House	7,368. 18. 0.	
Works	4,158. 15.10.	2,466. 0. 0.
Ironworks, Stour Quay and Warehouses	97,732. 8. 0.	97,732. 8. 0.
Cylinder and work done Stour Quay	69,638. 15. 4.	69,638. 15. 4.
Mooring Buoys	1,298. 15. 0.	1,298. 15. 0.
Hydraulics and Crane	500. 0. 0.	500. 0. 0.
Parkeston Station Buildings	54,564. 11. 7.	14,621. 18. 7.
Meat Larder	250. 0. 0.	
Signalling Points and Coverings	3,548. 19. 6.	
Cooking Apparatus &c. Parkeston Hotel	1,566. 13. 5.	
Office Furniture	859. 12. 6.	
Steel Rails	2,235. 5. 6.	
Sundries and Departmental	34,201. 7.10.	25,470. 0. 0.
Land	34,970. 9. 6.	34,970. 9. 6.
Law Costs	524. 11. 0.	524. 11. 0.
Engineering Staff	10,743. 14. 7.	6,370. 14. 7.
Dredging	5,799. 5. 4.	5,799. 5. 4.
Electric Telegraph	452. 8.11.	
Furniture	1,915. 5. 5.	
	£ 473,742. 5. 8.	£ 318,033. 12. 8.

(Expenditure by the GER as detailed in accounts later compiled by the LNER)

THE 1890s

The 1890s saw a continued expansion in trade that moving to Parkeston Quay had brought about during the previous decade and the extra work had required the GER to provide a more efficient system of maintenance for its ships. In 1890 a new marine shops and repair facility was built at Parkeston Quay to the east of, and in line with, the Continental offices. Previously the Company had run a workshop facility in George Street in Harwich and made use of the western side of Halfpenny Pier to lay up its vessels and those requiring minor repairs. Their new workshop cost in the order of £550 and the repair facilities a further £2,500.

For the summer of 1892 the General Steam Navigation Co. introduced their newly built *Peregrine,* a slightly larger version of her namesake launched only the year before and which was sold after just one round trip. This second *Peregrine* measured just under 280 feet long, was of 1,681 grt and could travel at 16 knots with 250 passengers on board in two classes.

Her arrival followed an agreement made in 1890 between the GSN Co. and the GER regarding their continued use of berths and facilities at Parkeston Quay over the next twenty years. Since opening their new route to Hamburg in 1888 the GSN Co. had continued in maintaining their existing sailings from London, these being a daily cargo service and a once a week passenger service. In 1891 that passenger service closed and with fast new ships like the *Peregrine*, ably partnered by the well equipped *Seamew*, the journey time to Hamburg was reduced from the 30 hours it took from London down to just 24 hours from Parkeston Quay. Departures from the Quay remained as being on a Wednesday and Saturday with passengers making use of the boat trains from London Liverpool Street that connected with the GER's own steamer services.

The *Peregrine* arrived at a time of concern over an influx of aliens arriving in Britain. In 1892 the only ports compiling a list of those considered to be *'the residium, the worthless and the unfit'* were Dover, Folkestone and Harwich, ie Parkeston Quay, and even then those lists were only concerned with those *'deck passengers and persons who on landing proceed by train as third class passengers'*. At the time Hamburg was referred to as *'the great port from which the destitute aliens take ship to England'* and whose own law determined that *'no person without means is to land at that port'*. However most of this destitute class were heading for London on ships provided with basic or emigrant class accommodation. One, H.J. Perlbach's *Minerva,* was a former visitor to Parkeston Quay and was the subject of quite horrifying accounts of conditions on board.

That same year, 1892, saw DFDS maintaining their service of three passenger sailings a week to Esbjerg. Departures from Parkeston Quay were each Monday, Thursday and Saturday evening after the arrival of the train from London that departed Liverpool Street at 2.35 pm. The return sailings from Esbjerg were less regularly timed in that they departed on Tuesday afternoons, Thursday mornings and Saturday afternoons. A further two cargo vessels, the *Fano* and *Botnia*, had visited since 1890.

The GER services to Rotterdam and Antwerp were still sailing daily, except Sunday, as follows:

Dep. London (L St)	8.00 pm	Dep. Antwerp	6.00 pm
Dep. P. Quay	9.50 pm	Dep. Rotterdam	6.30 pm
Arr. Rotterdam	9.00 am	Dep. P. Quay	5.00 am
Arr. Antwerp	9.30 am	Arr. London (L St)	6.50 am

However in 1893 an event occurred that would forever link the name of Harwich with Holland, namely the opening of a new terminal at the Hook of Holland (HvH).

Its long overdue appearance came after an inquiry had looked into the poor financial situation of the Dutch national railways. This had led to a decision that in 1889 the Dutch Government would buy up the Dutch Rhine Railway Company (NRS) and distribute its assets between the Dutch Iron Railway Company (HIJSM) and the Dutch State Railways (SS). Unfortunately for Rotterdam this meant that their favoured railway company, the NRS, no longer existed and they were left with two unappealing candidates from which to choose who should build the line to the Hook of Holland.

In 1890 the HIJSM linked the former NRS Maas Station into their own system around Rotterdam with ambitions of running the new Hook line themselves. The State Railways also had ambitions but their presence was unwelcome because of having helped start the rail and sea routes out of Flushing. Eventually in 1890 the City of Rotterdam, somewhat reluctantly, gave preference to the HIJSM. The new line was completed and opened in stages, first from Schiedam to Maassluis in 1891 and then onto the Hook in 1893. The first train arrived there on 28th May and the station and the new steamer terminal built alongside was then officially opened on 1st June 1893.

Coincident with the terminal's opening the GER had built a new ship, the *Chelmsford*. She was launched at Earle's of Hull on 21st February 1893 as a development of the *Cambridge* and *Colchester.* Partly financed by the sale of the *Lady Tyler,* which was taken in part exchange after a short and uneventful career, the *Chelmsford* was 20 feet longer again and also 3 feet wider. This made her a fraction over 300 feet long and together with the extra beam allowed for more space on board and more cabins of which some were now set aside for Third class passengers.

On 27th May she was presented at Parkeston Quay to members of the London, German and Dutch press. Many had travelled down by train from London Liverpool Street, departing at 10.00 am, with various other guests and GER officials. One and a half hours later they were shown aboard the *Chelmsford* and then treated to a six hour cruise which went via the Cork and the Shipwash. This gave ample opportunity for admiring her accommodation which included a large dining room, a Ladies saloon and a Gentlemen's smoking room much of which was fitted out with a maple and satinwood finish. An especial feature was the large number of First class cabins able to berth two people and all cabins being fitted with a fresh air ventilator. She was equipped with two sets of self contained triple expansion engines, a Company first, that drove twin screws at a service speed of 17½ knots.

Also on board was a dynamo that powered 246 16-candle power lights. On her return to Parkeston Quay the GER's Continental Traffic Manager, Mr Gooday, invited all the crew to join him in a celebration dinner.

On the night of 31st May 1893 the *Chelmsford* made her maiden voyage to the Hook of Holland. Next morning, 1st June, after the disembarkation of its passengers and the unloading of any urgent cargo, two trains decorated with both the British and Dutch flags ceremoniously left the Hook, one for Amsterdam at 7.08 am, the other for Rotterdam at 7.16 am. Two international trains, the 'Noord Express' and the 'Zuid Express', then left for Berlin and Basle respectively. The *Chelmsford* later sailed on to Rotterdam Westerkade with the 'ordinary cargo' and any remaining passengers.

This new terminal saw the GER introduce a new Sunday sailing such that their services to the Hook of Holland and then onto Rotterdam now ran seven days a week.

Dep. London (L St) 8.00 pm   Dep. Rotterdam   6.00 pm
Dep. P. Quay   10.00 pm   Dep. HvH   10.30 pm
Arr. HvH   5.50 am   Arr. P. Quay   7.05 am
Arr. Rotterdam   8.00 am   Arr. London (L St) 8.45 am

The express boat train that ran between Parkeston Quay and the North now left York at 3.40 pm and consisted of a First class restaurant car and First and Third class corridor carriages complete with lavatories. Connections were made at York with Scotch and Northern expresses, at Lincoln for Manchester and at Peterborough for Birmingham. The Dining Car on this train had been in service since 1st July 1891, between Harwich and Doncaster, as one of the first provided by a railway company anywhere in the country.

The new terminal in Holland opened up what was advertised as the 'new short route' and meant that many European cities could now be reached much quicker than before. Amsterdam was now possible at 8.26 am whilst Berlin was reachable at 10.36 pm the day after having set out from London.

From now on travelling via the Hook of Holland was destined to become the GER's premier Continental service at the expense of the one to Antwerp though it would be many years yet before that process was complete. For the route's initial opening the *Cambridge* and the *Colchester* were moved off the Antwerp service, where the evening departures from Belgium were now at 5.45 pm., in order to run in conjunction with the new *Chelmsford* and when the new Hook of Holland terminal was fully opened on 3rd June it was the *Cambridge* that became its first commercial arrival from Parkeston Quay.

The GER now had on the route to Holland their three largest passenger steamers and it is interesting to note that some observers thought the new Hook route 'would prove a powerful rival to Ostend' when in fact it was more the SMZ who were engaged in that particular challenge. However the opening of the Hook route did have implications for the GSN Co. who earlier would appear to have requested of the GER that they ease off their enthusiasm for the new route's future possibilities. On 9th May 1893 the GSN Co. decided that their Hamburg service would now become 'summer only', the reason presumably being that the improved timings of the rail connections deep into northern Germany were thought more preferable to passengers than a long sea voyage. Despite this decision those passengers travelling via the Hamburg service were still welcome on board the GER's boat trains. In June 1896 they could travel by the 'express route from Liverpool Street Station, Wednesdays and Saturdays at 8.30 pm.' The single fare in First class and saloon was £1.17s.6d.

By 1893 the only GER paddle steamers still in service were the *Princess of Wales*, *Adelaide* and *Claud Hamilton*. These were soon to be replaced by three new ships that were similar to the *Chelmsford* in overall design but around 18 inches wider in the beam and able to carry an extra fifty passengers.

To enhance the significance of having opened up the service to the Hook of Holland and from there on new rail links into Europe the GER now started giving their new passenger ships names that better reflected its Continental connections. Thus when three new sister ships arrived at Parkeston Quay during 1894 they were named as the *Berlin* on 28th March, the *Amsterdam* on 28th April and the *Vienna* on 11th October. Their arrival coincided with the opening of the East train shed extension at London Liverpool Street station on 2nd April 1894 and which housed platforms eleven to eighteen. In the following month there opened its associated Great Eastern Hotel designed by Mr C.E. Barry and which later held the Abercorn Rooms and Masonic Hall.

The new GER ships each cost £75,000 to build, were 302 feet long with a 36 feet beam and fitted with the same machinery and basic layout of the public spaces as seen on the *Chelmsford*. They were rigged

A Dutch poster advertising the opening of the new 'short route' between Harwich (Parkeston Quay) and the Hook of Holland on 1st June 1893.

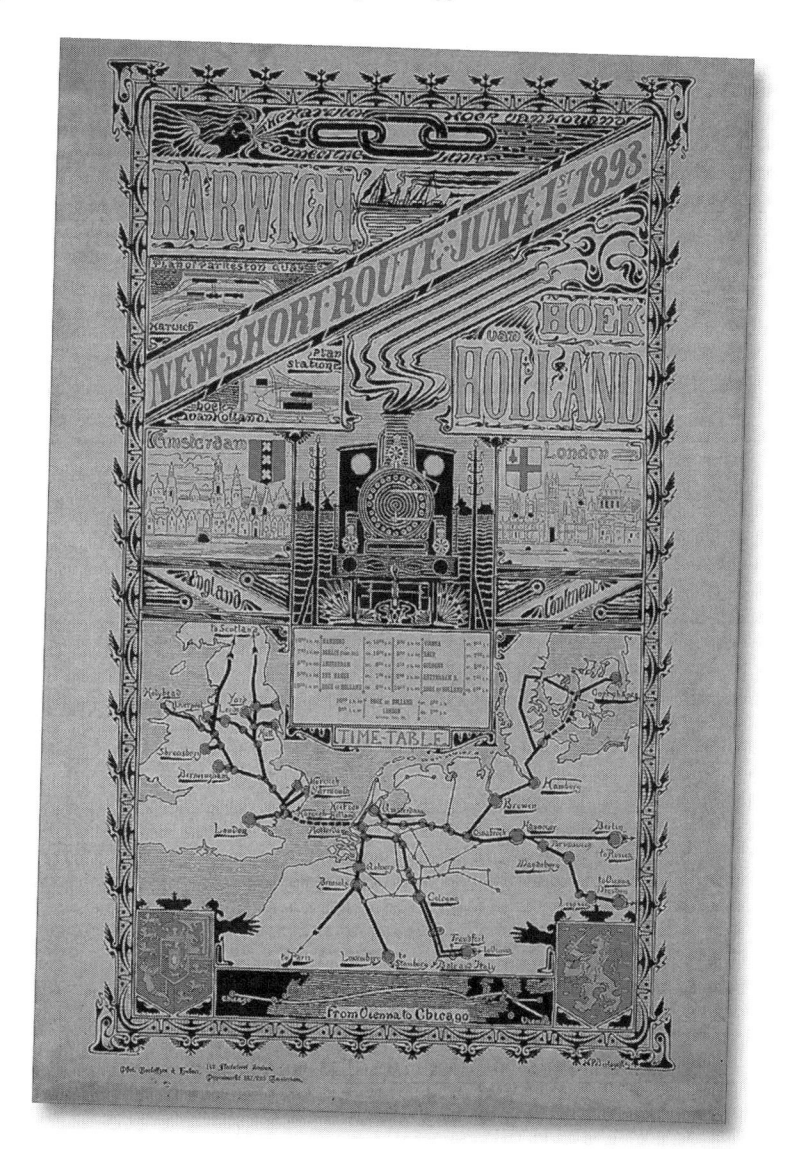

as fore and aft schooners with two masts and had hulls divided into eight watertight compartments. The passenger accommodation was located throughout three decks. An entrance hall, luxury cabins, the Ladies cabin and the dining room were all located on the Main Deck while extra cabins were fitted one deck below. The First class accommodation, again furnished and fitted in maple and satinwood, berthed 218 passengers while space for 120 in Second class was situated at the stern and the after 'tween deck.

Each vessel had a total passenger capacity of 780 and a crew of 49 that consisted of the Captain, 2 Navigating Officers, 3 Petty Officers, 3 Engineers, 10 Firemen, 8 Greasers, 1 Steward, 20 A.B.s, and 1 Pilot. On board were eight boats, of which six were lifeboats, and nearly 1,000 lifebelts which was a number 'in excess of those required by the Board of Trade'. Bunker capacity was roughly 150 tons of coal that was consumed at a rate of about 4 tons per hour as the ship made up to 18 knots. A feature retained on all these ships was that of providing luxury Deck cabins, at a supplementary charge, plus two large twin berth State Rooms on the Main deck, one of which was always reserved for use by Royalty. Following their respective maiden voyages throughout 1894 the *Berlin*, *Amsterdam* (9th May) and *Vienna* (25th October) eventually displaced the *Colchester*, *Cambridge* and *Chelmsford* back onto the Antwerp route and thus the ultimate demise of the *Princess of Wales*, *Adelaide* and *Claud Hamilton*, these then being the last GER paddle steamers left in service.

The introduction of these three new ships greatly increased the numbers travelling by the GER from 82,000 in 1892 to 95,000 in 1893 and 134,000 in 1894. They also severely affected the SMZ route at Flushing. To regain its traffic the Zeeland Company reduced its fares and for 1895 had Fairfield's yard at Govan build them three new ships of their own. These were yet again paddle steamers for their night service with each being larger and more powerful than the ones they replaced. They were named *Koningin Wilhelmina*, *Koningin Regentes* and *Prins Hendrik* and were launched on 23rd May, 9th July and 22nd August 1895 respectively. Fitted with triple expansion engines these 320 feet long 1,950 grt vessels had a service speed of 21 knots. They were put on the Queenborough route in the autumn of 1895 with the added benefit that their higher speed enabled a later departure time from London.

A large part of the goods imported through Parkeston Quay had consisted of live cattle and the quay's lairage, fodder store and quarantine facilities were kept in a state of constant readiness. In fact some of the advertisements for travelling on the GER boats not only said that the steamers were fitted with dining saloons, separate sleeping cabins, ladies saloons, etc but also that 'Cattle are carried on these boats'. It is presumed that this was by way of a warning to passengers rather than an appeal for any bovine travellers!. There was also, at the time, a significant number of horses being brought in by DFDS of which many had originated in Poland. However the livestock traffic was often interrupted by outbreaks of foot and mouth disease on the Continent, outbreaks that led to times such that imports of Dutch cattle were temporarily restricted on 8th October 1890 and soon afterwards banned altogether whilst imports from Denmark were likewise banned on 16th February 1892.

The response from farmers in Denmark to a total ban was to move away from being exporters of 'meat on the hoof' and move more towards being farmers of pigs and the exporters of bacon and finished farm products. To keep such products fresh they needed to be refrigerated and for the sea voyage they needed a new type of ship. In 1887 DFDS had already created probably the world's first refrigerated cargo vessel by installing a primitive cooling plant on board the 1883 built vessel *Kasan*. This had proved capable in maintaining a hold temperature at below freezing point and by the mid 1890s, when the technology had become much more efficient, DFDS had ordered three new refrigerated ships.

These were all built by Lobnitz and Co, Renfrew and all were launched during 1896, these being the *N.J. Fjord* on 14th May, the *Ficaria* on 7th September and the *Primula* on 5th November. All were in the region of 1,400 to 1,500 grt and overall were between 270 to 280 feet long. The *N.J. Fjord* was very slightly the smallest of the three and she entered regular service on the Esbjerg to Parkeston Quay run after her maiden voyage on 15th July 1896. The other two ships were placed on North Sea routes between Copenhagen, Newcastle and Grimsby although the *Primula's* first voyage was one round trip to Parkeston Quay in December 1896.

They were noticeable for not only being longer and faster, at 14 knots, than the existing DFDS ships at Parkeston Quay but also the first DFDS ships to have their hulls painted a light grey, this being done to indicate the installation of a cooling plant. Additionally each was fitted with comfortable passenger accommodation with space for 257 on board the *Primula* though only for a mere 59 on board the *Ficaria*. The *N.J. Fjord* was the most spacious by catering for up to 347 passengers.

The mid to late 1890s saw further arrivals from within the DFDS fleet, namely the *Nidaros*, *Olga*, *Storebelt*, *Tyr* and *Georg* whilst for the GSNCo. there was the *Gannet* and *Lapwing*. For the GER another new ship arrived in 1897 and again this was built by Earle's of Hull. She was named *Dresden* and was to be the only example of her class. With a similar length to the 1894 trio of 302 feet her beam had widened out another 2 feet to 38 feet and the gross tonnage raised to 1,805. Her layout was again similar to previous ships in that she was twin funnelled and twin masted and she represented a further modification to the established three island design that Earle's had supplied the GER with over the past 14 years. On the *Dresden* the GER were among the first to adopt Brown's new patent 'Telemotor' which was 'quite the most compact and effective steam steering gear in existence, by which all the chains and rods etc. leading to the steering engine are dispensed with'. The *Dresden* cost £63,750 and after entering service on the Antwerp route on 29th June 1897 she became renowned for her luxurious appointments that included a number of extra deck cabins. She would also become known for being the last passenger vessel that Earle's supplied the GER.

In 1896 the boat express to and from London was split into two separate trains with one carrying passengers for the Hook of Holland now departing Liverpool Street at 8.30 pm and the other with passengers for Antwerp departing at 8.40 pm. The journey time of the original boat express had been progressively reduced over the years from 1¾ hours to 1½ hours. The new trains were each allowed just 85 minutes.

Whilst the steamer services were becoming ever more fashionable it was unfortunate that Parkeston

Quay's GER hotel was proving impossible to make a profit. In part this was due to it being a relatively small establishment but it was still seen by the GER as being part of a 'package' with which to advertise the port and the Company to a wider audience. Fortunately their Continental services were enormously profitable and the Board considered that the money taken in baggage charges alone more than made up for any losses the hotel incurred. Consequently the establishment was still maintained to a high order and standard.

The conveyance of baggage was handled most efficiently and the service highly praised as a traveller in 1897 remarked to the NYT when travelling to Antwerp - *'At Liverpool Street.....on the Harwich route they weigh the trunks and charge so much a pound for carrying them, and give a receipt for a certain number of "pieces". Each trunk is then labeled with a big, foreign-looking yellow tab, reading "London to Antwerp", and the traveler need trouble himself no further about them till he lands in Belgium. In the two hours between London and Harwich the train ran at express speed, with no stops, and drew up at 10 o'clock on the pier close beside the steamer. The platform was brighter with electric lights than any part of London I have seen. The Amsterdam, the steamer that lay ready to carry us away from Merrie England, was so spic and span and bright and tight looking, so brilliant with electric lights, that it was easy to imagine ourselves in America instead of on the east coast of England... The steward opened the door for me of one of the best staterooms I ever saw - a big family room on deck, with beds for five or six persons, to be divided at will with thick curtains. .. For an hour we sat on deck under the awning, eating a luncheon from the restaurant below, which was still open and sending its emissaries out to take orders and deliver goods'*.

On the route to Holland those in a hurry were now disembarking at the Hook but those who sailed onto Rotterdam saw that *'From the Hook the boat continues its journey up the Maas to Rotterdam, one of the most interesting parts of the journey, the Maas running between meadows full of grazing cattle and fields of corn, intermixed with groves and orchards. The shipping is particularly interesting, especially when nearing Rotterdam. The landing place of the steamers at the West Quay, Rotterdam, is quite charming, with its avenue of trees and wooded park close by, and gives a very good idea of picturesque old-world Holland, now so famous as a tourist country. This year the brilliant season, with everything en fete owing to the coming coronation of the young Queen,* (the 18 year old Queen Wilhelmina in 1898), *will more than ever attract pleasure-seekers towards its shores. Here again, everything to do with the service is managed to perfection under the admirable direction of Messrs. Hudig and Pieters, the Rotterdam agents of the Company, whose large offices are just opposite the landing stage'*.

Whilst having some of the most luxurious ships afloat on one of the most important routes between England and all parts of Germany the services of the GER were, in 1898, also *' the cheapest of the first-class express routes to Copenhagen, Stockholm, Christiania, and all the beautiful parts of Norway, to romantic Switzerland and the picturesque Bernese Oberland, whilst naturally it was by far the quickest way to all the principal places in Holland. At present the route is not only the most direct and shortest by mileage than any other, but when the new line now in construction from the Hook to Capelle round Rotterdam is completed the distance will be further reduced by twenty-five miles, and a very great improvement in the services to and from North and South Germany, Russia, Denmark, Norway, and Sweden will be again made'*. That new railway line around Rotterdam was opened in June 1899 and did away with having to use the existing circuitous route via Amsterdam.

With the boat fare being the same to either the Hook of Holland or to Antwerp passengers were almost spoilt for choice as to where to enjoy their crossings. By now there were no GER paddle steamers still in service and the only major consideration on the Antwerp route was that apart from the *Dresden* it mainly ran slightly older vessels like the *Colchester, Cambridge* and *Chelmsford.* The paddle steamers *Princess of Wales* and *Adelaide* had been sold for scrap in 1895 and 1896 respectively whilst the very last survivor, the *Claud Hamilton,* once the pride of the GER fleet, was sold in 1897 to the City of London for the ignominious task of transporting cattle from Greenwich to Deptford until being dismantled in 1914.

In 1899 work began on constructing the Parkeston Power House. This was a sizeable brick built structure located along Station Road just north of the barracks building and connected to the railway station by a siding. A contract was awarded in May 1899 for Davey, Paxman and Co. of Colchester to supply three 100 hp steam driven generators, five Economic boilers each 14 feet long by 8 feet diameter and two condensers. The engines and boilers were delivered in May 1900 when the works were officially opened. When the condensers arrived in June 1901 the building was then fully completed and additionally housed three hydraulic pumps that supplied hydraulic power to the quay's cranes and capstans and the generators that supplied electric power for lighting the quay's 16 arc lamps, each of 2,000 candle power. The overall cost of the Power Station buildings, plant and machinery was around £26,000. Of this £6,333 went on the Paxman contract and £5,832 was spent on the provision and installation of electric lighting around the quay.

In June 1899 Signor Guglielmo Marconi, the famous inventor of wireless telegraphy, visited Harwich in order that he could further develop his new apparatus. A 200 feet high pole mast was erected above the seafront in nearby Dovercourt within the Cliff Gardens adjoining the Cliff Hotel A smaller version was fitted to a vessel within the GER fleet and each had a similar example of Marconi's invention attached to their mastheads.

Experiments into some form of a shore to ship communication system had earlier taken place locally back in 1885 when underwater telephone cables linked the shore at the Naze near Walton, a few miles south of Harwich, with the Sunk light vessel moored some 10 miles offshore. Experimental messaging, mainly enquiring about weather conditions, were conducted between staff from the Telegraphic Construction and Maintenance Company and the light vessel. It was soon envisaged that using the system to advise distant ports of the expected arrival of passing ships would be commercially advantageous as at the time an average of 90 ships per day were passing within the light vessel's vicinity. The range by telephone cable was thought to be viable in excess of 20 miles. The testing in 1899 of Marconi's 'cable-less' or wireless invention was to try and transmit a signal a distance of 30 miles out to sea.

Since 1876 the SMZ route out of Flushing had carried all the mail between Britain and Holland but in 1898 the GER became responsible for the daily conveyance of outward mails from Harwich, ie Parkeston Quay, to the Hook of Holland. The following year Parliament resolved *'That the contract, dated the 3rd day of April 1899, between the Postmaster-General and the Great Eastern Railway Company, for the daily conveyance of mails from Harwich to the Hook of Holland, be approved'* and the route duly became known as the Royal British Mail Route to Holland although the carriage of inbound mail from Holland remained the responsibility of SMZ. A further change affecting SMZ was that their affiliated railway company in England, the London, Chatham & Dover Railway Company (LC&DR), had since formed a working arrangement with its rival, the South Eastern Railway Company (SER) and together, on 1st January 1899, they created the South Eastern & Chatham Railway (SE&CR) who then became their new partners.

At the close of 19th century Parkeston Quay was operating a busy schedule of North Sea sailings. The GER were sailing to the Hook of Holland and Rotterdam every day and to Antwerp every day except Sunday. DFDS had three sailings a week to Esbjerg and the GSN Co. sailed twice a week to Hamburg during the summer months. All in all *'Everything, in fact, speaks of prosperity at Parkeston; and close to the quay a new colony has sprung up where many of the servants of the Company reside, over 1,000 of whom are employed at the quay alone'*.

This map of 1898 shows the original extent of Parkeston Quay, as built in 1883, and the subsequent development of a new community in Parkeston village. The original railway line to Harwich is now shown as disused. In later years the quay was twice extended westward whilst Parkeston village expanded a little further to the south and west.

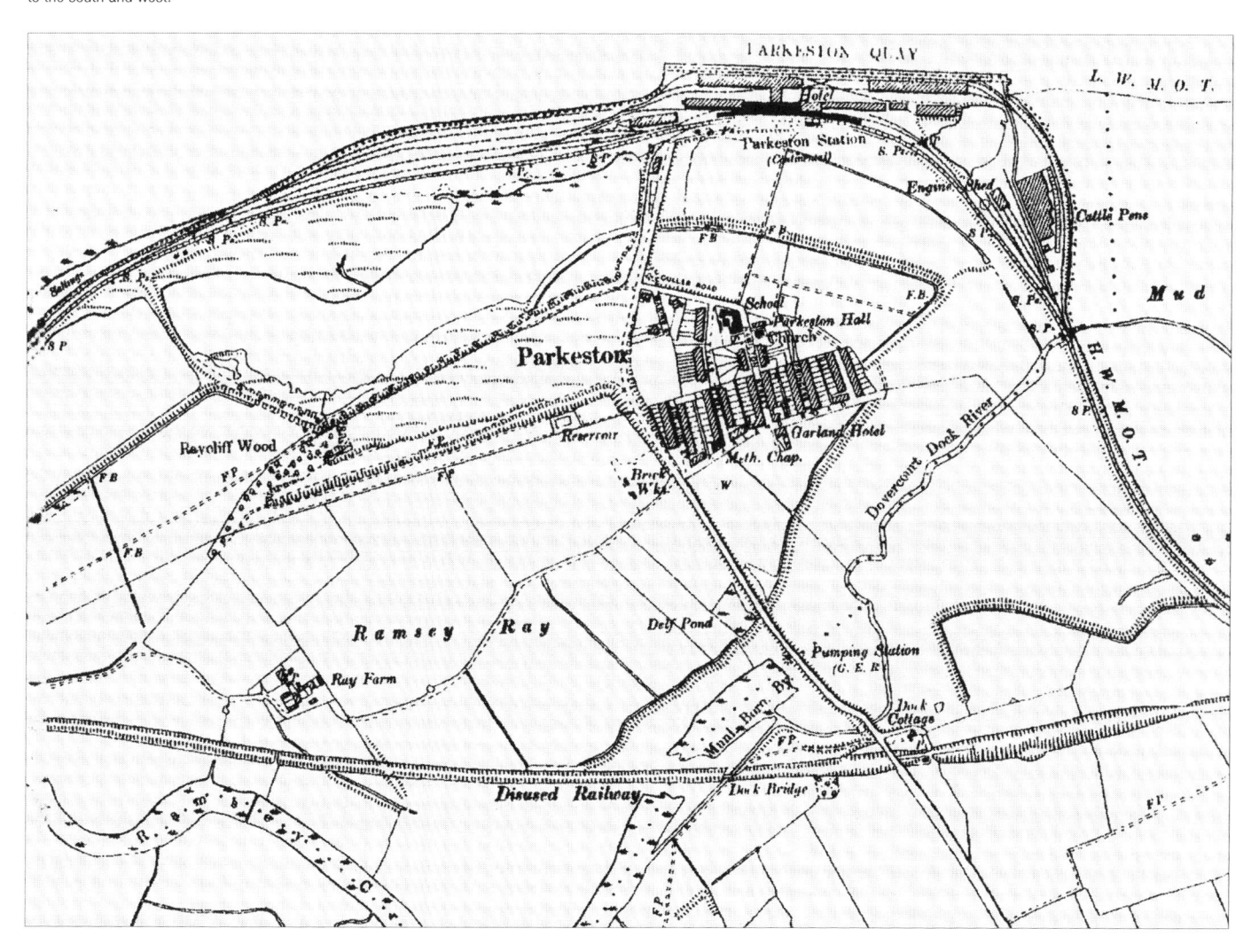

THE 1900s

Upon entering the new century everything at Parkeston Quay was indeed 'speaking of prosperity'.

In 1900 the GER's total wages bill for working the quay was £83,696.10s.2d. The Steam Boats Goods Traffic Received figures for the year up until 30th June were £78,650 plus a further £90,130 for the year's second half up until 31st December. Out of this total of £168,780 the Great Eastern Railway took a one third share for themselves of £56,260. The remaining £112,520 was set against the Parkeston Quay Account and this alone more than paid the quay's wage bill.

The revenues were earned by ships crews working a seven day week and with the exception of officers and stewards were required to supply their own food. Each man received just 14 days leave a year. An able seaman was paid £1.12s.5d. per week on the Hook of Holland route or £1.8s.0d. if on the Antwerp route. The rate for a fireman was an extra 2s. a week. Although there was no overtime paid these rates were above the then national average of around £1.6s.0d. a week. Amongst the lowest paid were the Deck boys who earned either 13s.2d. on the Hook boats or 11s.8d. on those to Antwerp.

Parkeston Quay Wages bill for 1900 per department:

	£.s.d.
Parkeston	6,237.10.2
Marine Engineer	9,702. 7.7
Crews	31,837.15.6
Coaling - Bargemen	196. 1.6
Coaling - Labourers	3,505. 5.7
Labourers	27,360.10.2
Hamburg	4,773.10.4
Harwich Quay	83. 9.4
Total	£ 83,696.10.2

Investment expenses were also incurred such as when, on 6th November 1900, the GER agreed to spend a contributory £10,000 towards the harbour authority deepening the harbour at Harwich which, when completed, would also improve access to its facilities at Parkeston Quay. The Company was already the beneficiary of an Act passed on 30th May 1895 giving them authority to dredge the River Stour themselves but with the overall costs being greatly in excess of £10,000 a suggestion was made that Harwich petition the Government for some financial assistance, this being on account of Harwich being 'an important coal station'.

The prosperous state of affairs at Parkeston Quay was in stark contrast to a run of bad luck that the SMZ were experiencing. Heavy storms in 1897 had so damaged the railway to their north Kent port that services were once again diverted to Dover. This was followed in 1900 by a second fire which destroyed the Queenborough pier and services this time being diverted to Port Victoria on the opposite bank of the River Medway.

As if to capitalise on this misfortune the GER launched a highly effective advertising campaign which would ultimately lead to the phrase 'Harwich to the Hook' becoming one of the most famous and well known throughout England. Starting from around 1900 a poster was seen at hundreds of railway stations that showed the coastlines of England and Holland with the ports of Harwich and the Hook of Holland being joined by a chain across the North Sea. It was designed by the Dutch artist, H.W. Mesdag at a time when more of the middle classes were taking holidays abroad and a modern version of the Grand Tour of Europe was being advertised to American visitors who would first arrive in Britain via the Transatlantic liners of the day and then in 'stepping stone' fashion use Harwich as their transit port to the Continent.

It was a time when anything Dutch had become all the rage. The recent accession of Queen Wilhelmina had helped further that interest even though some had thought that Dutch involvement in the recent South African Boer War had led to fewer English visitors travelling in protest. However there remained many visitors to Holland who were either German or American, one of whom was most unimpressed with travelling via Harwich in early 1901 - *how many of them who have once come that way and experienced the discomfort, scant courtesy, and downright extortion practiced on the steamers of the Great Eastern Railway Company ever care to repeat the journey. ...on the night boat from Harwich, unless he has secured one of the few habitable staterooms on deck, the American traveller is bound to suffer. First-class fare, which is not small, entitles one only to a berth, and in some cases there are six of these in a small closet. The ventilation is abominable and the servants of the ship do not even pretend to politeness. The two head stewards I know something of from personal observation are ill-bred fellows, who have the air of making a poor pretense at civility go a long way. These fellows assume that the passenger's sole duty is to pay his money uncomplainingly and hold his tongue. Some of them do that, rather than dispute with the stewards. Those who complain get no redress.'* (NYT)

By now the overall capital expenditure by the GER on their marine activities via the Parkeston Quay Account had breached the one million pound level at £1,083,218. Figures up until 29th January 1901 indicate that expenditure on the quay, its buildings and equipment had been £453,682 with that on steamboats having been £625,276 plus £4,260 on barges.

In 1901 there were two express trains leaving London Liverpool Street on a weekday. The one with passengers for Holland was now known as 'The Continental Express' which left from Platform 9 at 8.30 pm and arrived at Parkeston Quay at 9.57 pm. The other with passengers for Belgium was known as 'The Antwerp

Parkeston Quay wages bill for 1900. (Stephen Brown collection)

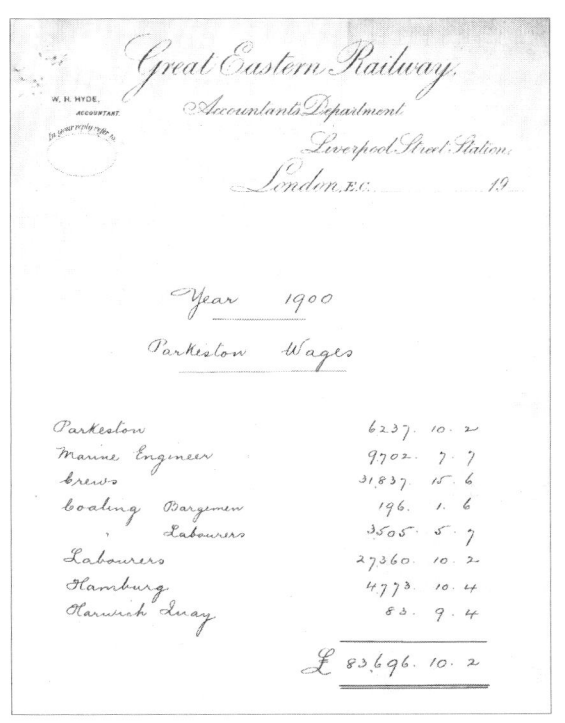

Continental' and left Platform 7 at 8.40 pm. This train arrived at Parkeston Quay at 10.07 pm and then carried on to arrive at Dovercourt at 10.19 pm and Harwich Town at 10.22 pm. On Sundays there was only the one express service from Liverpool Street and this left at 8.30 pm to arrive at Parkeston Quay at 9.57 pm, Dovercourt at 10.09 pm and Harwich Town at 10.22 pm. The three local stations were all listed in the timetable under Harwich and were suffixed as Parkeston Quay, Dovercourt and Town.

The 'North Country Continental' left York at 3.50 pm, via Doncaster at 4.38 pm and arrived at Parkeston Quay at 9.27 pm, Dovercourt at 9.37 pm and Harwich Town at 9.40 pm. The return timings were to depart Harwich Town at 6.35 am, Dovercourt at 6.38 am and Parkeston Quay at 7.00 am and then via Doncaster at 11.59 am the train would reach York at 12.56 pm.

Example fares for 1901, Doncaster to:

	Parkeston Quay	Rotterdam	Antwerp
Single 1st Class	£1.2s.8d.	£2.2s.9d.	£1.19.9d
Return 1st Class	£2.5s.4d.	£3.12s.6d.	£3.7s.6d.
Single 3rd/2nd	15s.0½d.	£1.5s.10d.	£1.2s.10d.
Return 3rd/2nd	£1.10s.1d.	£2.4s.7d.	£1.19s.7d.

The fares for 3rd/2nd are 3rd class rail to Parkeston Quay then 2nd class beyond. These result from the GER having abolished 2nd class on their rail services on 1st January 1893 though it was retained on their suburban services and on Continental express trains out of London. The single fares were valid for 7 days and returns were valid for 60 days. The normal train fares from Parkeston Quay to London Liverpool Street were 12s.10d single and 19s.6d. return, (or £1.0s.0d. from Harwich Town), in First class and 5s.10d. and 11s.8d. respectively in Third class. Even allowing for a certain degree of discounting and through bookings the above fares suggest a First class ticket for a boat to the Hook of Holland of around £1.0s.0d. single and to Antwerp of around 17s.0d. Second class was around half that of First and both classes had substantial reductions on return tickets especially on the Antwerp service. In general the GER considered that First class rail passengers were more the Saloon class of passenger on the boat with those travelling Second class by rail being more the Cabin class.

On a more local level there was a shuttle service of trains between Parkeston Quay and Harwich Town, mainly for the workers, where the fares were 3d. single and 4d. return in First class and 1d. single and 2d. return in Third class. With Parkeston village itself having a population of 1,060 in 1901 the provision of workers trains from Harwich suggests the port was indeed a hive of activity.

On 13th August 1901 the first purpose built passenger ship for the North Sea services of DFDS joined the Esbjerg to Parkeston Quay route on her maiden voyage. Built by the Elsinore Shipyard the 1,615 grt *J.C. la Cour* could carry 112 passengers in some luxury of which 76 were in First class. The route was still operating three passenger sailings a week with the advertised departures from Parkeston Quay being on Mondays, Thursdays and Saturdays. A further period of the Company's vessels then new to the quay saw the *M.G. Melchior, Christianssund, Frejr* and *Hengest* arriving in less than a year. The arrival of the *J.C. la Cour* was to relegate the *Koldinghuus* to the status of relief ship as the number of passengers carried on the Esbjerg to Parkeston Quay route in 1902 rose to 16,700.

At the GER's Annual General Meeting in January 1902 it was announced that the Company was to take delivery of two ships being built at the yard of Gourlay Brothers of Dundee. This broke the sequence of new builds from Earle's of Hull, the reason being that at the time Earle's had a full order book and could not deliver within the time specified. Such an enviable situation at Earle's was quite a turn round from just two years earlier when the yard was under threat of liquidation. It was only saved in June 1900 when it was bought by Thomas Wilson & Co. and the yard was now fully employed in building ships for its new owner when the GER had come calling for more.

The first ship to appear from Gourlay's was the *Cromer*, a twin screw steamer built as the GER's first cargo and cattle ship purposely constructed for the Rotterdam route. She was ordered in response to an ever increasing need for more freight capacity as that being carried by the passenger vessels was breaking all records. Accordingly she could carry 450 tons of cargo and 86 head of cattle. She was fitted with triple expansion engines that gave her a service speed of 13½ knots and she first entered service on 22nd April 1902. Crewing levels were much lower on the cargo boats than they were on the more luxurious passenger ships and those on board the *Cromer* numbered just twenty seven. This consisted of the Captain, 2 Navigating Officers, 2 Petty Officers, 8 A.B.'s 3 Stewards, 2 Engineers and 9 Firemen.

The next ship from Gourlay's made her maiden voyage on 19th June 1902. This was the *Brussels*, a ship which had been specifically built for the Antwerp route. Her external appearance was very similar to the three ships the GER had built for the Hook of Holland service in 1894 though she was slightly smaller in size by measuring 285 feet by 34 feet and of only 1,380 grt.. She had the usual array of saloons, cabins and Ladies rooms together with the Deck cabins and State Room that had become such popular features amongst the Company's other steamers. The *Brussels* was said perhaps to be 'one of the most sumptuously fitted steamers afloat'. She was to be the GER's last reciprocating steamer but the first to be fitted with a new wonder of the age, a 'sea to shore radio'. This was installed in order to further assist Signor Marconi with his ongoing experiments. The *Brussels* had cost £63,700 whilst the cargo ship *Cromer* had cost £37,498. So successful was the *Cromer* to prove that a sister ship, the *Yarmouth,* followed in June 1903.

At the Hook of Holland a new 'America Wharf' was opened in 1903. This was somewhat similar in construction to the one at Parkeston Quay inasmuch as it was built upon iron screw piles with a wooden decking and was used by the trans-Atlantic liners of the Holland America Line. In those days the depth of water at

Total capital expenditure on Parkeston Quay up to 1901. (Stephen Brown collection)

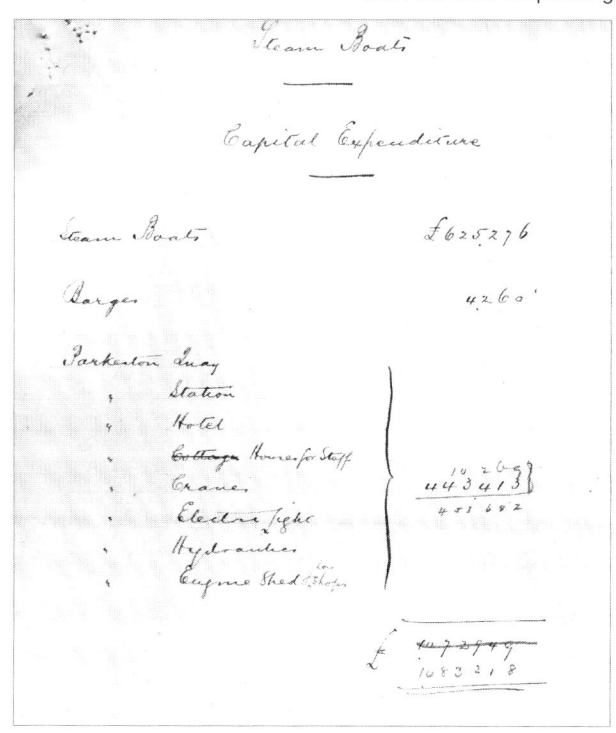

Rotterdam was not yet sufficient for these much larger liners to berth at all states of the tide and so passengers would be disembarked at the Hook of Holland and the ships would then sail up the river to Rotterdam on a high tide in order to discharge their cargoes.

In 1904 there came into effect a similar arrangement for passengers travelling to Holland from Parkeston Quay such that as from 1st June 1904 all passengers using the GER route could travel only as far as the Hook of Holland. Rotterdam was no longer to handle any passenger traffic but would still be used for the Company's cargo only ships. As a consequence and also because of the increased capacity per ship of recent additions to the fleet the frequency of GER sailings between Parkeston Quay and Rotterdam was reduced that year from six per week to just three.

Around this time the other users of Parkeston Quay were making changes to their own fleets though one was due to misfortune. On 5th January 1903 the DFDS vessel *Koldinghuus*, on passage from Parkeston Quay to Esbjerg, stranded off the Danish coast at a point south west of the island of Fano. Her passengers and crew were all saved by lifeboat but the ship was never to see active service again. In April 1903 she was re-floated and after having been towed into Esbjerg she was used as a storage ship before being sold for scrap in August 1906.

The *Koldinghuus* was quickly replaced by the *Primula* which was a sister ship to the *N.J. Fjord* though with slightly less passenger accommodation. She did however have 48,500 cubic feet of cargo space of which 36,150 was refrigerated. The route's main stay passenger ships were now, at various times, the *Riberhuus*, *N.J. Fjord*, *J.C. la Cour* and *Primula* although the *Riberhuus* was increasingly being used elsewhere. From 1904 onwards the cargo ships *Esbern Snare*, *Ceres*, *Eos* and *Valdemar* would, at some time or other, be seen assisting on the route along with the *Constantin* a few years later.

During 1905 the General Steam Navigation Co. put the *Hirondelle* onto their Hamburg route, alongside the *Peregrine,* and later used the *Woodcock* which was built in 1906. The *Hirondelle* had previously been a visitor to Parkeston Quay shortly after having been built when, on 14th June 1890, she made a trip from the quay to Gravesend. On board were a party of officials and invited guests there to witness her trials during which she attained a speed of 15 knots. At the time she was en route to London from where she would later be used on a fast service to Bordeaux.

Following on from the GER having ceased passenger sailings to Rotterdam the Company underwent a fleet reorganisation that saw the *Brandon,* (formerly the paddle steamer *Richard Young*) scrapped in 1905, their last iron built vessels, the *Norwich* and *Ipswich*, being sold in 1905 and the respective scrapping of the *Harwich* and *Peterborough* (formerly the paddle steamer *Rotterdam),* in 1907 and 1908.

During this time two new cargo ships were delivered as a second pair of sister ships to the *Cromer* and *Yarmouth*. These were the *Clacton* and the *Newmarket* and both were products from the yard of Earle's in Hull. They in turn entered service in February 1905 and August 1907 and were practically identical in both layout and machinery to the earlier pair delivered by Gourlay's.

By 1907 it is presumed that passengers were being much better treated on board the GER ships than that of the earlier referred to experience of 1901 as travelling for both business and pleasure was on the increase.

'Miss Hook of Holland' was a popular operetta in 1907 even though 'Miss Hook' herself was in fact a character of, as in from, Holland rather than an attraction at the Hook itself and music halls rang out to the strains of "By the side of the Zyder Zee" and its variety of versions of which not all were especially genteel.

Train passengers were further tempted by improvements to the Continental express services out of London when the GER introduced specially built trains with corridor coaches and restaurant cars. Dining on such trains had become justly famous when these first appeared for Hook of Holland passengers in May 1904 and Antwerp passengers in 1905. Departures from Liverpool Street remained at 8.30 pm and 8.40 pm respectively.

The 'North Country Continental' was similarly equipped as from 1st July 1906. This left Parkeston Quay at 7.02 am and was made up in sections that would split off for various northern destinations along the way. At March the two rear most carriages left for Birmingham to arrive at 12.11 pm. At Lincoln four more were detached made up of two each for Manchester to arrive at 1.38 pm and for Liverpool to arrive at 2.45 pm. The remaining six carriages then went on to York and arrived there at 12.32 pm. The return times departed Liverpool at 2.30 pm, Manchester at 3.20 pm, York at 4.00 pm and Birmingham at 4.00 pm. All sections joined up at the stations where they were earlier detached and the whole set arrived back at Parkeston Quay at 9.35 pm, just ahead of the boat trains from London. Apart from the carriages that went on to Manchester and Liverpool only one set of stock was needed for the return trip.

Two Acts were passed in 1904 relating to the GER. One, of 24th June, authorised the Company to additionally operate steam ships to Zeebrugge as an alternative destination for whenever Antwerp became ice bound. Previously the alternative destination had been Ostend which was said to have been last used for such an eventuality in 1895. The port of Zeebrugge was still in the process of being completed and although it had received its first ship in 1902 it would not be officially opened until 23rd July 1907 by King Leopold II.

The other Act, of 22nd July 1904, gave the GER powers to execute certain works in connection with Parkeston Quay. This was in relation to the fact that within the space of just twenty years since being built Parkeston Quay had started to suffer the same consequences as befell the workings of the original piers at Harwich, namely that success had led to its facilities becoming overloaded and that further expansion was again required. In fact congestion had become so great at Parkeston Quay that since 1901 the GER had been back down at Harwich and were using the Continental Pier to operate a limited cargo service. The original cattle pens had long been replaced by a large warehouse which was being leased out to private firms for the storage of timber and grain and the pier itself was also being used by the General Steam Navigation Co. for the export of fish to Hamburg and by Trinity House for berthing and storage purposes.

The July 1904 Act allowed the GER to lengthen Parkeston Quay by a further 900 feet in a westerly direction and a contract was awarded to Messrs A. Jackaman and Sons of Slough to build an extension sufficiently long for three extra berths. The proposed method of construction was different from the original quay in that it was one of the first examples of reinforced ferro-concrete being used for such a structural purpose. The work essentially comprised the building of a concrete pier, in line with the original quay face, that went out across the saltings bounding the river and behind which, ie to the south, would lie a 129 feet expanse of new quay area. On this would be built a large two bay concrete transit shed measuring 440 feet by 62 feet equipped with two overhead electric cranes running along its entire length. Being situated further west this became the 'new' West Shed or No. 3 Shed with the 'old' No. 2 West Shed being designated the Middle Shed. Although some preliminary work had started in 1903 it was not until 7th November 1906 that the first permanent concrete piles were being driven in.

Meanwhile changes in marine technology were undergoing another revolution. In June 1903 the South Eastern & Chatham Railway had introduced the world's first turbine driven cross Channel steamer onto the Dover to Calais route, this being 'The Queen' with a service speed of 21 knots. This was followed in September 1905 when the Belgian Government's 'Princesse Elizabeth' amazed the shipping world with a trials speed of 24¾ knots and a service speed of 22¼ knots.

The GER was not slow to see the advantages of this superior form of propulsion and soon set about acquiring similar vessels of their own. Unfortunately for their existing and well established supplier of vessels, Earle's of Hull, this change of technology meant a change of yard and the one the Company turned to for its orders, both now and in the future, was John Brown's of Clydebank in Scotland. In due course the GER's first turbine steamer, the *Copenhagen*, entered the water in October 1906 as one of a series of three sister ships all destined for the Hook of Holland route. She made her maiden voyage on 27th January 1907.

At a glance she had the appearance of being similar to the 1894 trio but with an extra 30 feet in length and 7 feet in the beam she was more than just an enlarged development. Within the *Copenhagen*'s 331 feet by 43 feet lay three spacious passenger decks with most of the accommodation amidships. The dining room and lounges were fitted out in maple and mahogany wood and draped with crimson curtains. In addition to the usual smoking room and Ladies room there was a full width dining room and cabin accommodation for 320 passengers in First class and 130 in Second class with the latter being situated aft. All passenger and crew accommodation was supplied with telephonic communication.

The turbine machinery was manufactured by Parsons which for the first time on the route drove a ship with triple screws. The centre screw was driven by a single high pressure turbine whilst the two outer screws were each driven by lower pressure wing turbines which were also equipped to provide power for going astern. Also a first was a boiler room designed with the closed stoke hold system of forced draught with steam supplied by five single ended Scotch boilers. Service speed was a somewhat modest 20 knots. When the Company was asked at the time why their ships were not quicker, their reply was the route offered comfort not speed and that passengers had to have sufficient time to sleep!

Amongst the numerous trans-Atlantic liner companies of the day was the American Line whose brochure for 1907 gave details of how it was possible to travel from Britain to the Continent by steamer. It listed a number of options aimed principally for those who had first visited London and included the routes out of Harwich, ie Parkeston Quay, as well as four alternative ways of reaching Paris. The steamer to Antwerp departed at 10.20 pm, daily except Sunday, whilst the one to Holland departed daily at 10.00 pm and arrived at the Hook of Holland at 5.05 am and Rotterdam at 6.07 am after having taken the train from the Hook. Interestingly the brochure included the option of reaching Rotterdam 'via Harwich and direct steamer' even though such a facility for passengers had supposedly been withdrawn in 1904. The price quoted was the same as for going to Antwerp.

Fares - London to:

	Rotterdam (via HvH)	Rotterdam (direct steamer)	Antwerp
Single 1st Class	$7.70	$6.40	$6.40
Single 2nd Class	$4.92	$3.75	$3.75
Journey Time	9½ hours	12 hours	11 hours

Based on an approximate exchange rate of $US5 to £1 it would appear that the cost of travel had changed very little in almost 20 years other than that of going via the Hook of Holland which now attracted a higher fare. However when compared to other routes crossing the English Channel the fares out of Parkeston Quay were noticeably cheaper than all the other options available even though the sea crossings were longer.

This 1907 brochure further noted that DFDS operated three sailings a week to Esbjerg that departed Parkeston Quay every Monday, Thursday and Saturday at 9.30 pm. Travelling the 500 miles between London and Copenhagen was possible in thirty three hours with the crossing by steamer to Esbjerg taking around twenty five hours.

Despite having previously made mention to ships of the GER as being luxuriously appointed for their day, with crew of the highest order, comfortable berths and with modern amenities of light and ventilation there were also some that were shown to be inadequate or having poor speed and others still liable to ground themselves or become lost in fog. Apart from such incidents and the likelihood that crossings could well be wild and storm tossed there has been nothing said as to the ships being unsafe. The worst that happened, not withstanding the stranding and sinking of the *Ravensbury* in March 1870 and without any loss of life, was that they arrived late and by 1907 over 1,200,000 passengers had been carried by the Company without a single fatality. However 1907 was to see the worst ever peacetime disaster to befall a service out of Harwich or Parkeston Quay - the loss of the GER's *Berlin*.

On Wednesday 20th February 1907 the *Berlin* set sail from Parkeston Quay at 10.00 pm for the Hook of Holland. On board were 91 passengers and 52 crew under the command of Captain Precious. The weather that night was bad. A strong north westerly gale was blowing as the ship left the quay and the subsequent crossing was terrible. However the *Berlin* was regarded as being in first class shape, having been overhauled just a few months before, and after riding out a night of gales and blizzards she arrived off the Dutch coast on the morning of Thursday 21st on time. Anticipating that disembarkation would also follow on time the passengers were awakened at 5.00 am as the ship came in sight of land. On the bridge were Captain Precious, the Mate Mr Morsley and a Dutch Pilot Mr Brondes.

As the ship was approaching the entrance to the New Waterway with barely half an hour to go before docking she was struck at about 5.15 am by a heavy sea on the port quarter. The force was such that the bow swung round to the north and with a strong northerly current running the *Berlin* moved dangerously close to the North Pier. In response to this Captain Precious succeeded in turning the ship to starboard only to be hit by a tremendous sea on her starboard side which uplifted the vessel and literally dropped her across the breakwater. Stranded on granite rocks at the end of a pier in one of the most exposed places along the Dutch coast the *Berlin* lay helpless. In an attempt to get the ship off Captain Precious rung double full astern on the telegraphs but the engines stopped, the vessel 'blacked out' and Chief Engineer Dennant ran to the bridge saying 'The stoke hold is flooded, the fires are out. 1 can do no more'. After the sighting of distress rockets fired from the ship a lifeboat and tugs were immediately sent to the mouth of the river. Huge breakers were now battering the *Berlin* and within 30 minutes of stranding all eight of her lifeboats had been smashed and the flying bridge swept into the sea together with its occupants.

The lifeboat *President van Heel* arrived on the scene around 6.30 am but owing to the force of the wind, still around gale force 8, and with high running seas it was unable to approach the *Berlin* safely as she was reachable only on her starboard side, ie the side of the worst conditions. Initially the sight of the lifeboat may well explain a lack of panic on board the *Berlin* but hopes of a major rescue were soon dashed as the lifeboat was forced to return to the Berghaven. A message sent by the GER's Dutch agents to Captain Howard, Marine Superintendent at Parkeston Quay read : 6.35am - '*Berlin* stranded at North Pier. Very dangerous. Heavy gale. Tugs and lifeboat going out to assist.'

With the *Berlin* perched upon the breakwater and continually lashed by the full force of the sea it was not long before she eventually broke her back. At about 7.30 am she split in two just aft of the funnels. The forepart separated and quickly sank into the icy water some seventy yards away whilst the other half remained jammed on the breakwater. Most of the passengers were on this forepart and from here about seventy or so were swept away. Only one person survived having been picked up by the lifeboat which, due to mechanical problems, then returned to the harbour.

The GER cargo vessel *Clacton*, which left Parkeston Quay for Rotterdam shortly after the *Berlin* had sailed, arrived on the scene at 8.00 am and had seen the forepart sink. She stood by for about an hour but the *Clacton*'s Captain Dale, thinking that it was impossible for anyone to have survived and being concerned for the safety of his own ship in that it might also be swept onto the breakwater, decided to proceed onto Rotterdam. On board the *Clacton* was able seaman Precious, son of Captain Precious.

A further message was received at Parkeston Quay stating - 'Position very dangerous. Heavy gale still blowing. Have tried to get passengers off with tug and lifeboat, but have not succeeded at present.' Then at

Querying the extension to Parkeston Quay in 1907. (Stephen Brown collection)

10.26 am came the fateful news - '*Berlin*, a total loss, with crew and passengers; no-one saved'. A similar statement was later made to the press by the GER Secretary, Mr. Peppercorne. The news was met with a stunned helplessness not only for the loss of passengers but also because the ship's crew were local personnel. By 11.00 am twenty five bodies had been washed ashore. Two men had been saved, one described as a seaman who had been carried unconscious to the 'Hoek van Holland Hotel'.

Only by late Thursday afternoon was it possible to get any definite news of the disaster. It was apparent that the forepart with the greater number of passengers and crew had sunk immediately but there were still some survivors on board with twenty five passengers and crew having taken refuge in the smoking room in the vessel's stricken aft section. This had settled on the shoals of a sand bank and several unsuccessful attempts had already been made to reach them by lifeboat and pilot tug. Gale force conditions continued throughout the day and by nightfall thirty three bodies had been recovered from the sea. These were placed within the Holland America Lines warehouse at the Hook which had been turned into a makeshift mortuary.

By noon of Friday the 22nd the sea had eased off though the gale still raged. Normal sailings from Parkeston Quay continued and when the *Amsterdam* arrived it was said that her passengers heard cries from the wreck as she passed by. In between snow squalls survivors could be seen clinging to the deck though their numbers were now down to just fifteen. Ten rescue volunteers managed to land themselves on the breakwater and crawl along the pier on their hands and knees as far as the lattice light. A rope was thrown to the wreck but the survivors were unable to catch it. Then one of the rescuers noticed a lifeboat on the *Berlin* left hanging from the ship's side and at great risk he waded through the treacherous seas to recover its rope end. This was eventually made secure by tying it some 20 feet up the light tower and by climbing along this rope ten exhausted survivors made their way down onto the pier. An eleventh person fell from the rope into the water but was rescued unconscious and later recovered in hospital. A rising tide then forced attempts at saving any others to be abandoned and the return of the lifeboat inside the harbour. The survivors were stretchered to a makeshift hospital in the 'Hotel America'. Those involved in the rescue attempt had been much encouraged in their efforts by the sight and actions of Prince Henry, Consort to Queen Wilhelmina, and who had earlier driven from the Hague and at the time was on board the pilot tug *Hellevoetsluis*.

By now forty four bodies had been recovered but there still remained three semi conscious women on the wreck whose rescue had been delayed by the rising tide. At midnight on Friday, when the tide was low, Captain Sperling, skipper of the salvage tug *Van der Tak*, set out with the tug *Wotan* and two of his nephews, the intention being to rescue the three women. When close by the *Berlin* they rowed the last few yards, landed on the pier, and by using the same rope to the fallen lifeboat Captain Sperling clambered on board the wreck. Close to a heap of bodies the women were in a poor condition, one of them still clutching her dead daughter in her arms. With great difficulty and bravery he managed to pass the women down to his fellow rescuers and safety. They were finally landed at 4.00 am on the morning of Saturday 23rd, almost 48 hours after the ship was swept to disaster.

Throughout Saturday the remaining bodies were recovered from the wreck and placed with those in the warehouse which the Dutch had reverently converted into a chapel. The walls had been draped with black and white and over each body was laid a trailing sash of crepe. On the 24th, Sunday, the British dead were loaded onto the *Clacton*, each coffin being draped with the Union flag. The GER had previously made arrangements to bear the costs of conveying the bodies of recovered victims to England and issued free passes to relatives who wished to travel to Holland for identification purposes. The GER had also provided staff to assist in the recovery of bodies at the Hook. Following her return as the *Clacton* slowly entered Harwich harbour at nightfall the guns of Landguard, Beacon Hill and several warships boomed out a sombre salute. In total 128 people lost their lives. Only fifteen survived including four crew.

As much as the loss of the *Berlin* was a local disaster for many of the families within Harwich it was also viewed as a national loss. When news reached the London Stock Exchange, the shares of the GER fell sharply though they soon recovered when it was learnt that, to a certain extent, the Company was protected against claims for compensation because the disaster happened at sea and also because the Company was well provided for as regards reserves of capital. But the human side of the incident also attracted great interest for it illustrated the nature of those travelling and the poignant tragedies played out at sea. Amongst the survivors was Captain Parkinson of Holt Line Shipping but amongst those who died were many members of the Berlin Operatic Company returning home after a concert tour of England. Also lost was Mr. Arthur Herbert, a King's Messenger, who was heading for Constantinople with documents for the British Embassies in Berlin, Vienna, Belgrade and Sofia. He was one of nine official couriers one of whom would travel on the Parkeston Quay to Hook of Holland route every week alternating between going to Constantinople one week and St. Petersburg the other. To accommodate a King's Messenger on his travels the GER was required to make special arrangements for him on board their ships.

Amongst the most touching of losses was that of five year old August Hirsch who was leaving his ill mother in London to join his father in Hanover. The GER had made arrangements for his travel and placed him in the personal charge of Chief Steward Moore. Both died and when the bodies were recovered the young boy was found still tightly clutched in the arms of the steward who had desperately tried to save his life.

The *Berlin* was replaced on the Hook of Holland route by the *Colchester* and a Board of Trade enquiry into the loss was held at Caxton Hall. The verdict was given in April 1907 with the blame laid upon the late Captain Precious as an 'Error of judgement of captain, error in attempting to enter New Waterway in prevailing weather and underestimating 'send' of the sea and force of tide and vessel was not navigated at all material times with a proper and seamanlike care.' The GER was to pay £25,541 to the Admiralty Court, the limited liability of £15 per ton, less crew space for claims.

Inevitably there were theories as to how the event happened, or might even have been allowed to happen, ranging from a huge underwater swell that rendered the ship unmanageable to criticism of the GER in pressuring their Captains to arrive on time, no matter what the weather, in order to connect with the waiting trains. It was known that around the time of the

Brussels approach to the channel other ships had managed to safely navigate past the pier though on the basis of reputation alone the GER could never have attracted such high levels of custom had it been operating their steamers recklessly in pursuit of financial considerations. It was thus that Captain Precious was blamed for having suffered 'an error of judgement'.

Money came in for the relief of the dependants and a special fund was opened to provide a memorial in All Saints' churchyard to Chief Steward Moore. Part of the insurance money was donated by the GER to St. Gabriel's Church in Parkeston to move, rebuild and renovate the organ at the new church of St. Paul's in memory of those who lost their lives. For their heroic efforts the British Government made awards to the Dutch lifeboat crews and separately awarded Prince Henry, whose esteem was now greatly enhanced with the Dutch public, the Grand Cross of the Bath. At the end of 1990 two steam boilers from the *Berlin* were salvaged during dredging works near the North Pier. One of the fire doors and some pieces of coal which were found in the furnace were later put on display in the local Lifeboat Museum in the Hook of Holland.

The first new berth in Parkeston Quay's extension came into use on 14th August 1907 with the arrival of DFDS's *Esbjern Snare*. This was only nine months after the first piles had gone in but a somewhat cautionary note as regards any further expansion was sent on 25th September 1907 from Mr. Gooday, General Manager of the GER to Mr. Hyde, Assistant General Manager stating - *'The question is how far we are justified in extending Parkeston Quay having regard to the remuneration we get from the Continental Traffic. I shall be glad if you will read attached memo from Mr. Busk* (Continental Traffic Manager) *and speak to me before getting out any figures on the matter'*.

The exact reason for the memo is unclear but it might well have been influenced by the matter of the Harwich Docks Bill of 1908 that yet again agitated for the development of a dock system on land adjoining Harwich. Dated 15th November 1907 the Bill was essentially an updated version of the various mid 19th century plans for infilling Bathside Bay between Harwich and Parkeston Quay. It was proposed by what might best be termed a consortium of interests marshalled by the Harwich Corporation.

The Bill sought powers for the incorporation of a company to make and maintain docks and to establish and carry on a dock undertaking at Harwich. The area of the site was to be 310 acres with sea walls or embankments sufficient to enclose a 30 acre dock, two miles of berths and two graving docks. The Bill also provided for the diversion of various waterways running across the mud flats plus powers for the company to dredge the bed and foreshore of the river to provide deep water channels with a depth at low water of 35 feet. Authorised capital was set to be £1,150,000 though it was said that the scheme would cost £2 million to construct. Work would be provided for 2,000 men engaged in building works that would last three years. Net revenue was estimated at around £80.000 per year.

There were also to be powers to control vessels and the piloting of them, the provision of buoys and beacons, together with the right to manage and regulate warehouses, to sell perishable goods, to own and let steamers, tug-boats, dredgers and lighters. The company sought powers to rent out their property, to make rules and by-laws for the control of the docks, and to make and recover tolls and rates. They were also to be empowered to enter into agreements with the railway company and the Bill also empowered the corporation of Harwich to hold shares or stock in the dock company, to lend money to the company and appoint directors to its board.

In 1906 imports and exports through Harwich, though this predominantly meant Parkeston Quay, totalled almost £25 million making it one of the largest ports in England. The proposal was apparently welcomed by the GER even though its Directors refused to take a financial stake in the new docks. That decision became one of the points used by counsel appearing for the Ipswich Dock Commission who argued against the project and for the retention of its own existence as an important port that was quite sufficient for all foreign going vessels. Furthermore Felixstowe Dock maintained that the new dock could not possibly pay nor was there any chance of the money required being raised.

Amongst the various petitioners for the Bill was Mr. Free of Mistley, who had paid into the Bank of England on behalf of the harbour syndicate, the reported sum of £57,924, this being the amount of the Parliamentary deposit. The petitioners included the Earl of Warwick, Sir Walter Gilbey, Sir Ernest Clarke and Mr R. A. Cave-Brown-Cave, RN. Yet despite such strong support the opposition from the Ipswich Dock Commission won through and .the scheme was thrown out by the Select Committee sitting in March 1908 on the grounds that the preamble of the Bill was not proved

Another factor possibly influencing Mr. Gooday's earlier caution was that the loss of the *Berlin* was affecting the number of people travelling and though it wasn't known at the time it would not be until 1910 that the figures were back up to those achieved in 1906. What was known was the increasing size of ships now using the quay. In the 1880s the average ship length was in the region of 260 feet but the latest GER turbine steamers were much longer at over 340 feet. Consequently they, and those that followed from other companies, required a longer length of quay to accommodate merely the same number of ships alongside and so the need for an extension really was a necessity.

In 1905 the Cullinan mine in South Africa produced the world's largest ever rough diamond. Known simply as the 'Cullinan diamond' it weighed 3,106 carats and was given to Britain as a reconciliatory gift following the Boer Wars. The job of cutting it was awarded to the firm of Asscher's of Amsterdam with the largest cut diamond it produced being used in Britain's Crown Jewels. Amidst reports of high security and a navy destroyer being deployed to safely transport the diamond to Holland it found its way to Amsterdam inside the hand luggage of Mr. Asscher senior when travelling home on board a GER steamer in January 1908.

Less fortunate that year was the loss of another GER ship in circumstances that created one of the mysteries of the North Sea. It concerned the cargo steamer *Yarmouth*. At 5.00 am on 27th October 1908 the vessel, under the command of Captain Avis, left Rotterdam part loaded with cargo and proceeded to the Hook of Holland to load on some more. She then left the Hook for Parkeston Quay at 10.30 am with 354 tons of cargo, 89 tons of meat, 3 three-ton furniture vans, one passenger and a crew of twenty one. She was next seen by the men on the Outer Gabbard lightship at around 5.00 pm, this being the time she was due to arrive at Parkeston Quay. She was rolling heavily and with a marked list to starboard of about forty degrees. The Captain of the *Yarmouth* made no request for any assistance and the vessel sailed on until she was soon lost in fog. She was never seen again.

At noon the next day the *Vienna* was sent out to assist in the search for any sign of her whilst *H.M.S. Blake* was already searching close by her last known position. Some wreckage and lifebelts were eventually found near the Outer Gabbard lightship together with just a single body which was recovered by *H.M.S. Blake*. After a search lasting some 30 hours the *Vienna* returned to Harwich with her flag at half mast - the *Yarmouth* was lost with all hands.

At the enquiry held on 1st January 1909 it was found that the ship, although seaworthy and not overladen as regards her deadweight, was deemed to be unstable due to the inappropriate stowing of the furniture vans. These had been unsatisfactorily secured on the poop and forecastle and her loss was presumed to be the result of heavy seas having shifted her cargo to the extent that she turned over and sank. The GER's liability was £6,024 though the Company received £5,949 in insurance compensation. As a result of the enquiry the GER discontinued loading any of its ships with goods on either the poop or forecastle.

In 1908 all GER ships on the Hook of Holland route were fitted with wireless telegraphy apparatus and this was followed by all ships on the Antwerp route being similarly equipped in 1909. The cost for fitting out the ships was £4,015.16s.11d. plus a further £844.5s.5d. for installing land based apparatus at the quay's Power House. Such developments were the end result of experimental work carried out within the Power House by the British wireless pioneer, Sir Oliver Lodge. A wireless transmitting station was set up with the call sign of GPU which was later changed to GUQ.

Despite the advances in technology the steamers were still unable to eradicate the dangers of fog. Thick fog had caused the *Amsterdam* to run onto the North Pier at the Hook of Holland on 22nd August 1906, this being the same pier that would later wreck the *Berlin*. The *Amsterdam* was re-floated the next day with the aid of local tugs and assistance from the cargo ship *Clacton* which then ran aground herself.

The *Vienna* ran aground during fog on the Massvlakte on 18th January 1908 whilst only a few days later on the morning of 23rd January a more serious incident again involved the *Amsterdam*. With 70 passengers and 50 crew on board she collided with the anchored American cargo ship *Axminster* in thick fog near the Maas lightship. As the *Amsterdam* started taking in water her passengers were transferred by lifeboats to the relatively undamaged *Axminster* which later landed them ashore in Rotterdam. The *Amsterdam* managed to discharge her cargo at the Hook of Holland and was eventually dry docked in Rotterdam. The *Vienna* crossed light from Parkeston Quay to take over the night service in her absence.

The two vessels ordered by the GER as sister ships to the highly successful *Copenhagen* were the *Munich*, launched in August 1908, and the *St. Petersburg*, launched in April 1910. The *Munich* entered service on 16th November 1908 and the *St. Petersburg* on 7th July 1910.

Each was similarly built with a large number of cabins on the Awning Deck and special State Rooms on the Main Deck. In addition there were numerous twin berthed cabins for which there was no extra charge if reserved by two First Class tickets holders. The *St. Petersburg* was additionally given a 'Cabine de Luxe', use of which was an extra £2.0s.0d., along with a major visual difference in that she was fitted with a raised foc'sle, experience having shown that this might better protect the forward part of the ship from heavy seas and spray.

Another newcomer to the port was the DFDS ship *Ficaria,* one of the three refrigerated ships the Company had built in 1896, and which entered a joint Esbjerg to Parkeston Quay and Grimsby service in 1909. Although a sister ship to the *N.J. Fjord* and *Primula* she had very limited passenger accommodation.

Work on the Parkeston Quay extension which had started in 1907 was finally completed in August 1910 at a cost of around £140,000 under the supervision of GER's Chief Civil Engineer Mr. Wilson. New electric cranes consisting of three with a 5-ton lifting capacity and six with a 1½ ton capacity had been installed to serve the new berths with electricity being considered a major improvement upon the hydraulic cranes in use on the old quay. Such was the improvement that during 1908 some 41 feet of the old quay was strengthened to allow the provision there of another 5-ton electric crane. To provide for the increased electrical power demand two Parsons steam turbo-generators were installed in the Power House.

The quay extension's second new berth was opened in September 1910 with the berthing of the troopships *Alnwick Castle* and *Neapolitan Prince*. These were there to pick up troops who had marched overnight from Colchester and rested in the new transit shed before embarkation. Events were marred somewhat when the departing *Neapolitan Prince* managed to hit and considerably damage the moored cruiser *H.M.S. Andromache*. The troopship sustained only minor damage and continued her voyage.

With no fixed installations jutting out from either the original or extended quay face the number of working berths was eventually re-adjusted to six. Still named and numbered from east to west, Berths 1 and 2 were adjacent to the East Shed, Berths 3 and 4 to the West Shed (later re-named Middle Shed) and Berths 5 and 6 to the new Transit or Tranship Shed (later re-named West Shed). The Repair berth remained on the extreme east end and the total quay frontage was now 2,700 feet.

THE 1910s

In 1910 came the start of a long awaited service to Sweden when, on the morning of 7th May, the *Balder* berthed at Parkeston Quay having sailed light from London and bound for Gothenburg. Such a service was first envisaged by DFDS as far back as 1882 but it was Angfartygs Aktiebolaget Thule or Thule Line of Gothenburg, established in 1870, that finally got one under way. It was created to cover the five months of an extended summer season that saw sailings once a week from each port departing at 10.30 pm on a Saturday night. Arrival time was at 6.30 am on Monday.

The *Balder* was built in 1898, of 1,486 grt, and had accommodation for 109 passengers. However she only made this one initial sailing as the route's regular ships were to be the *Thule* and the *Saga*. The *Thule*, of 1,969 grt, left Gothenburg on 7th May and arrived at Parkeston Quay late in the afternoon of 9th May, at 3.30 pm, when the first passengers from Sweden were landed together with around twenty tons of perishable cargo. Any passengers bound for London left by special train having cleared Customs in just twenty minutes. The ship then sailed on to London later that evening to unload the bulk of its cargoes. There she was later loaded in readiness to return to Parkeston Quay on the following Saturday and pick up any passengers and goods for the sailing back to Sweden. The *Saga* left Gothenburg a week later on 14th May thus relegating the *Balder* to the role of relief ship. The *Thule* was built in 1892 with accommodation for just 75 passengers but the much larger *Saga*, at 2,809 grt, was only a year old and carried up to 170 passengers. This Thule Line service was a change to the Company's normal schedule of a direct Gothenburg to London Tilbury service and it reappeared on a yearly basis.

At Harwich the old timber built Continental Pier which opened in 1866 suffered a disastrous fire on 18th June 1910. The seaward end of the warehouse was completely destroyed though the landward end was returned to use after temporary repairs were made. 1910 also saw the completion of work in deepening Harwich harbour towards which the GER had earlier contributed £10,000. The total cost had been £40,810 to which the Admiralty, concerned for the harbour's strategic importance, had made an additional contribution of £2,000.

By 1912 the Danish Government had ceased its subsidy on the Esbjerg route. Having started in the late 1880s the terms were amended in 1889 so that DFDS could reduce its freight rates and then be compensated for doing so out of State funds. In the twelve months up to 31st March 1911 the Esbjerg to Parkeston Quay route received 120,000 Danish kroner (Dkr) plus Dkr 180,000 for harbour dues. This total of Dkr 300,000 was equivalent to £16.666. By comparison a subsidy payment totalling Dkr 125.000 had been made for the Esbjerg to Grimsby service but with both routes now being sufficiently successful there was no longer a need for any such assistance. Also successful were the new GER turbine steamers and these had caused the withdrawal of two passenger ships, the *Chelmsford* being sold in June 1910 to the Great Western Railway and the *Cambridge* being disposed of in November 1912.

Since 19th September 1893 all railway ships had been coaled at Parkeston Quay as the coal in both Antwerp and Rotterdam was deemed to be of an inferior and unsuited quality and since 19th November 1907 the DFDS ships were also being coaled there as well.

The process itself was both arduous and dirty and was entirely carried out by hand. It consisted of drawing loaded railway wagons of coal out from the sidings and along to the east end of the quay where it was tipped into lighters or barges. These were then towed round to the steamers and the coal transferred on board by men carrying it up in baskets using ladders on the ship's side. The annual cost of doing so, in wages alone, had risen from roughly £3,700 in 1901 to around £4,200 in 1910 when it was now proposed to install a much less manually intensive system.

The use of cranes was considered impractical because bunkering took place at the same time as the handling of cargo and cargoes such as butter and

GER map of Parkeston Quay - 1912.
(Stephen Brown collection)

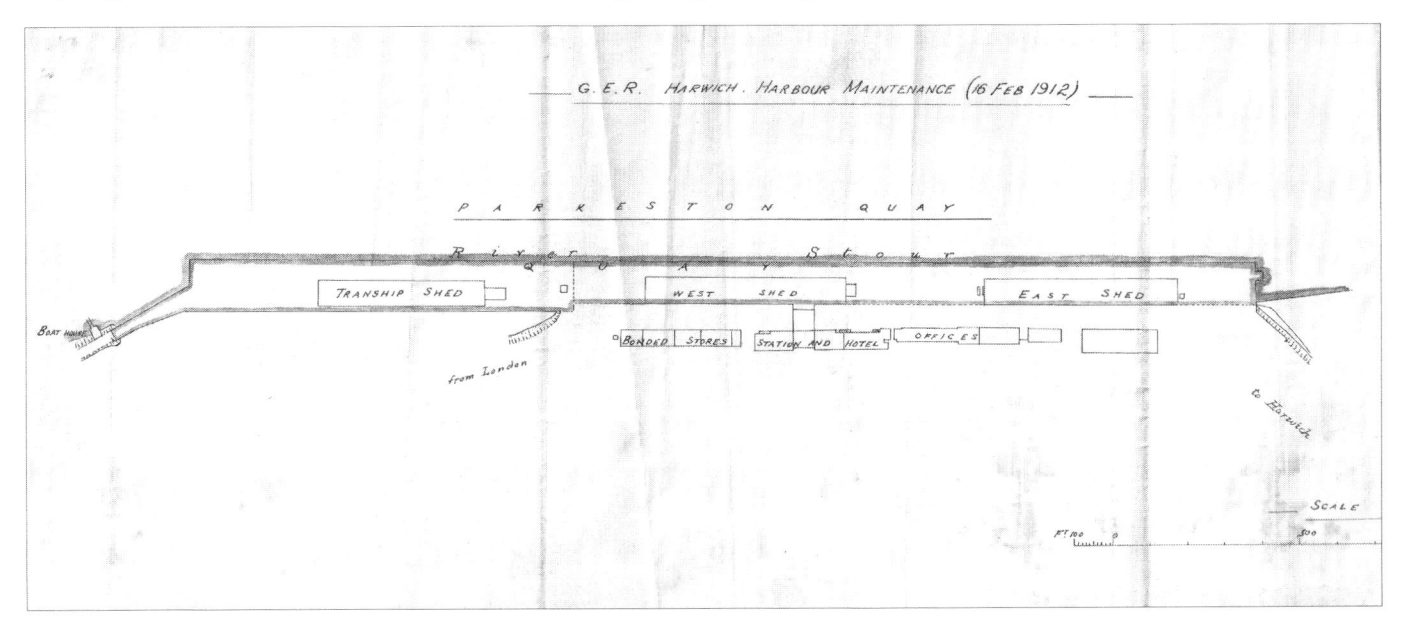

bacon risked being spoiled if covered in a sprinkling of coal dust. Instead a system involving the use of electrically driven conveyors and loading shoots was agreed in July 1911 and a suitable installation was later built in the space between the rear of the Bonded Warehouse, adjacent to the Hotel building and the back of Middle or No. 2 Shed.

To support the new coal shipping plant a series of timber and cast iron screw foundation piles were first driven in through the quay. The installation was designed by the GER's electrical engineer, Mr. Firth, and supplied by Messrs. Spencer and Co. of Melksham. When in use the loaded trucks of coal were brought round to this plant and then lifted up and emptied into a central hopper. The hopper then fed two conveyor belts, each 2 feet 6 inches wide, that ran out in opposite directions parallel to the back of No. 2 Shed. At either end was another elevated belt, running at right angles and along the side of the shed, onto which the coal was dropped and conveyed to ships moored in the Middle Quay Berth nos. 3 and 4. Swivelling arms that were adjustable to the position of the ship directed the coal to onboard shoots that were only 2 feet in diameter. In total around 1,000 feet of belt was installed and each had a maximum loading capacity of 100 tons per hour. The weight of coal on the belts was automatically weighed and for purposes such as on board trimming there were further automated controls that adjusted the delivery rate to as low as 30 tons per hour. The new apparatus was completed towards the end of 1912 at a cost of £11,786.11s.11d. Tests were carried out in December and the first ship to be coaled by this method was the GER vessel *Amsterdam* on 28th February 1913. The cost of installing the new equipment was partially offset by later selling the coal barges for £2,315 in 1913. A further development occurred at the east end of the quay where the 50 feet diameter turntable at the loco depot was replaced in 1912 by a larger one of 65 feet diameter in response to the use of larger locomotives. These were Class 1500 Sandringham's, the use of which had reduced the running times of 'The Continental Express' and 'The Antwerp Continental' from London Liverpool Street down to 82 minutes.

On the evening of 29th September 1913 the inventor of the diesel oil engine, Dr. Rudolf Diesel, left Antwerp on board the GER vessel *Dresden* in order to attend the annual meeting of the Consolidated Diesel Engine Manufacturers in London. When the ship arrived at Parkeston Quay at 6.00 am the next morning there was no sign of Dr. Diesel on board. His landing ticket had not been given up and it was therefore assumed that he had not yet gone ashore. A search of his cabin, which he had had to himself, showed his bed had not been slept in though his night attire had been laid out. Everything about the cabin seemed in perfect order. The previous evening he had dined with his two travelling companions and was said to have been in good spirits. He had last been seen at around 10.00 pm. Given that Dr. Diesel was prone to bouts of insomnia it was thought he might well have gone for a stroll on deck before retiring and had somehow managed to fall overboard. Though not a proven explanation nothing else was deemed plausible as suggestions of suicide were dismissed by his friends. The exact circumstances of his disappearance remain fully unresolved to this day though his body was found on the Flushing coast.

The introduction of the *Copenhagen*, *Munich* and *St. Petersburg* onto the Hook of Holland route had spurred the SMZ into building a further series of three fast twin screw steamers in order to improve their night

GER map of the piers at Harwich - 1912. (Stephen Brown collection)

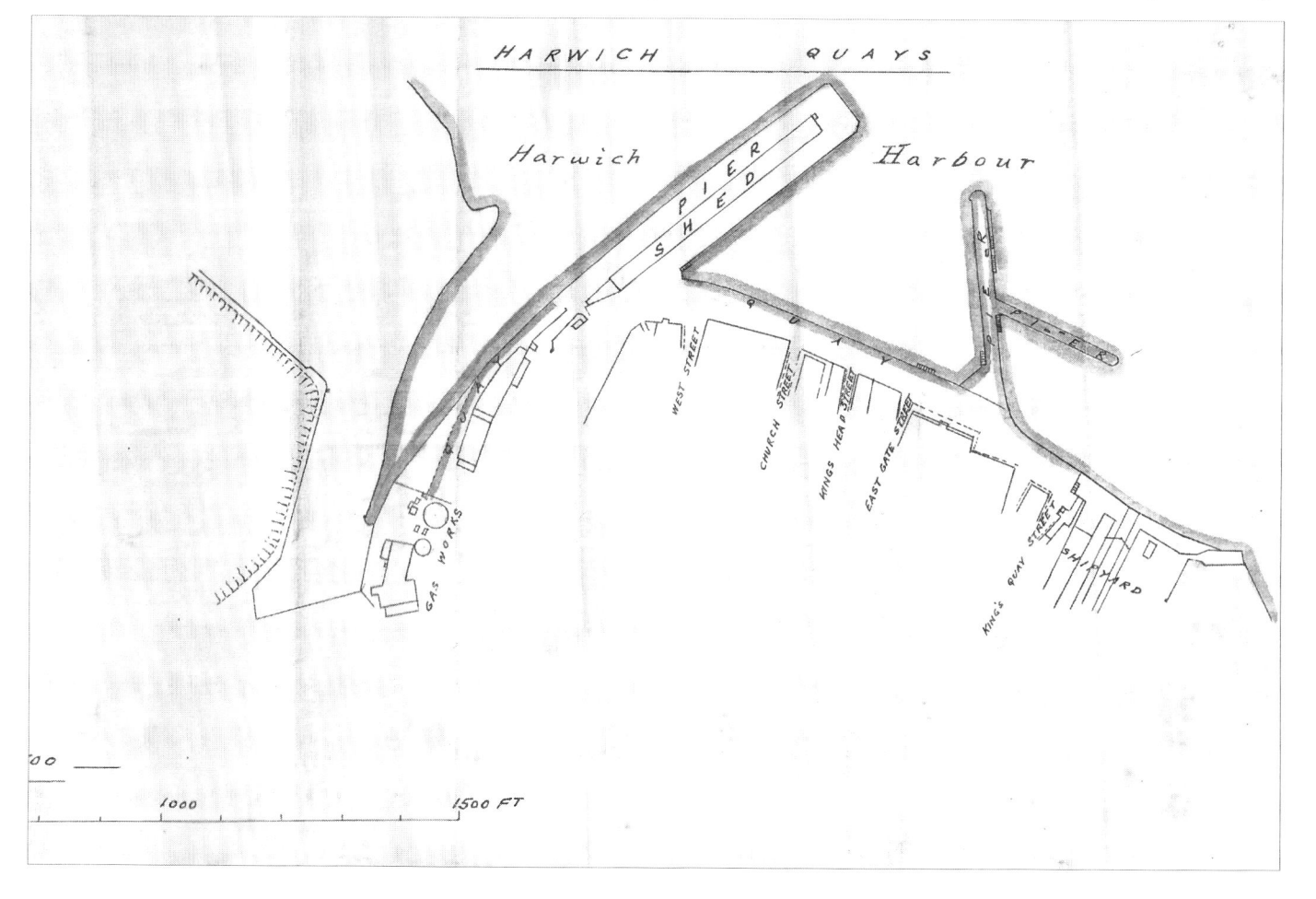

service out of Flushing. All three were built by Fairfield's of Govan and were over 1,200 tons heavier, at 2,885 grt, and over 60 feet longer, at 350 feet, than the three paddle steamers they replaced. Each had a service speed of 22 knots and were named *Princes Juliana*, *Oranje Nassau*, (after the Dutch Royal association with the German house of Nassau) and *Mecklenburg* (a province in north Germany). Of the 1886 trio of paddlers two were scrapped leaving only the *Duitschland* as a reserve ship.

The new ships variously entered service in April 1910. However the approach to Queenborough proved too shallow for them and so in May 1911 the night service was switched to Folkestone, a port much quicker to reach by sea as it was only 92 miles distant from Flushing as opposed to the 111 miles to Queenborough. Dover would have been nearer still, by 7 miles, but Dover's harbour and piers were not under the control of the SE&CR like those at Folkestone were.

The three remaining paddle steamers, dating from 1895, were refurbished and used to maintain the day service to Queenborough. The move to Folkestone and the new screw propelled ships brought about a big increase in traffic for SMZ such that the number of passengers carried rose from 128,000 in 1909 to 148,000 in 1910 and 159,000 in 1912. To achieve such figures the SMZ were running both a day and night boat service from Holland. By comparison the GER ran only a night boat from Parkeston Quay to the Hook of Holland and in 1910 that route alone carried 105,000 passengers. In 1912 a total of over 4,000 passengers a week were travelling through the port with those for Antwerp numbering only a little less than those for Holland.

Upon the opening of the GER hotel at Parkeston Quay in 1883 the original Great Eastern Hotel on Harwich quayside had become somewhat sidelined and after having consistently run up years of unsustainable losses it had been put up for sale by auction in February 1907. With the highest bid of £8,300 failing to reach the reserve price the GER closed the hotel on 27th April 1908. It re-opened on 30th March 1912 after a successful lobbying campaign by local interests and with the support of the GER's own Continental Steamship Committee who regarded its closure as having had an affect on its services.

The hotel's re-opening had a beneficial knock on effect upon the Parkeston Power House where the electrical generating plant was supplemented with new high voltage equipment which was described so: *'New motor generators, 60 kilovolt-amperes, of British Thomson-Houston Company's design, have been installed to transform current from 220 volts direct current to 3000 volts three-phase 50 periods. The transformer plant has been supplied by the British Electrical Transformer Company. There are some features of interest in the overhead transmission line which has been erected between the Parkeston power-house and Harwich station, cables being laid from thence to the Harwich Hotel. The high-tension switch gear has been supplied by Messrs. Ferranti.'*

As the 1910s progressed so too did tensions within Europe and the prospect of a war involving Britain began to loom ever more likely. As early as 28th June 1913 the Admiralty had issued a notice stating that in the event of hostilities arising they would require the use of Parkeston Quay. In the meantime another new DFDS passenger ship, the *A.P. Bernstorff*, arrived at Parkeston Quay on 30th July 1913 after her maiden voyage from Esbjerg. Substantially larger than the other DFDS ships, at 304 feet long overall and able to carry 407 passengers, she replaced the *N.J. Fjord* and was envisaged as the fore runner of a suitably modern and upgraded fleet of passenger liners for the Company's North Sea routes. Cargo ships were also being upgraded as only recently had there been the appearance of two new sister vessels, the *Diana* and *Hebe*. As events unfolded the whole process would not occur for quite some years but the *A.P. Bernstorff* was to sail alongside the *J.C. la Cour, Primula* and *Ficaria* on the Esbjerg route until war finally intervened. Of future interest *A.P. Bernstorff* could carry up to 15 cars in her hold.

The weekly pattern of sailings from Parkeston Quay in 1913 was a once every Saturday night sailing (May to September) by Thule Line to Gothenburg, a twice weekly General Steam Navigation Co. service to Hamburg every Wednesday and Saturday, four DFDS sailings to Esbjerg departing on a Monday, Wednesday, Friday and Saturday, a daily except Sunday GER service to both Antwerp and Rotterdam and a daily GER service to the Hook of Holland.

The times of the Antwerp service were:

Dep. London (L St)	8.40 pm	Dep. Brussels	5.22 pm
Dep. P. Quay	10.10 pm	Dep. Antwerp	7.00 pm
Arr. Antwerp	8.00 am	Arr. P. Quay	6.00 am
Arr. Brussels	9.11 am	Arr. London (L St)	7.35 am

whilst those of the Hook of Holland service were:

Dep. London (L St)	8.30 pm	Dep. HvH	11.30 pm
Dep. P. Quay	10.00 pm	Arr. P. Quay	6.35 am
Arr. HvH	5.10 am	Arr. London (L St)	8.00 am

All times are local with those at HvH being referred to as 'Amsterdam Time'

By the end of 1912 the GER Capital Account for Parkeston Quay showed a total Company expenditure of £714,652.8s.8d. of which £401,092.18s.8d. had been apportioned to the Parkeston Quay Capital Account. In addition the Quay's Capital Account had been wholly allocated costs of £54,529.10s.11d. towards the coaling scheme, barges and additional electrical plant and machinery that brought the total up to £455,622.9s.7d. Prior to the outbreak of war any further investment was somewhat limited such that by the end of 1915 the respective totals were £721,960.2s.5d. and £471,872.18s.4d. As regards the GER's total expenditure on the piers and works at Harwich that figure was now £65,918.14s.8d. none of which was apportioned to the Parkeston Quay Capital Account.

In February 1914 the GER appointed an American, Mr Henry W. Thornton, General Superintendent of the Long Island Railroad, as their new General Manager. The appointment of a foreigner created a storm of protest to which the GER Chairman, Lord Hamilton, responded by saying it was due to *'a dearth of proficient men in the British railway world'* and that *''there was something paltry about the British system which tended to interfere with the mental activity of employees, reducing them to automata as merit was sacrificed to seniority. Perhaps there are able men in the British railway system, the trouble is that under our present system, I never get to hear of them.'*

Mr. Thornton had earlier sailed over to England on board the *Campania* and upon his arrival back in America in late February, having sailed on the *Carmania* from Liverpool, he had this to say about his four weeks away. *'There are 32,000 employees of the Great Eastern Railway and I am sure there are several competent men among that number. I shall make it my business to get personally in touch with the staff and help along those who have merit. I went down to Parkeston Quay, where the company's steamers start for the Hook of Holland and Antwerp. The vessels are amongst the best in the English Channel, and the service is one of the big assets of the line. One thing is certain - I shall use my utmost endeavours to give the English travelling public a first-class service, and if I fail - well, I can pack up again and come back to New York.* He was scheduled to return to England on 31st March on board the *Lusitania* and take over at the GER in the first week of April 1914. Events soon overtook his good intentions.

On the 4th of August 1914 Britain declared war on Germany. As a harbour Harwich was requisitioned by the Admiralty for use as a major front line naval base. Here was stationed the Harwich Force made up of a Destroyer Fleet under the command of Commodore Reginald Tyrwhitt and a Submarine Fleet under the command of Commodore Roger Keyes. Both fleets were to play a full and engaging role in combating the enemy and also to keep the North Sea free of enemy shipping south of a line that roughly extended from Flamborough Head to a point on the German coast near to the mouth of the River Elbe. In addition they were also required to link up with the Patrol Force at Dover as and when events required. The defence of the harbour approach was strengthened by the installation of a gun battery at Beacon Hill, close by the 1850's stone pier at Harwich, whilst a similar defensive position was provided on the Landguard side. The GER's hotel in Harwich was taken over as a military hospital on 6th August and their hotel at Parkeston Quay was to become an accommodation centre for Naval officers. As a port Parkeston Quay was also taken over by the Admiralty with all passenger and cargo sailings either being suspended or ceasing altogether.

The 3rd August had already seen the closure of Thule Lines service to Gothenburg as well as the GSN Co. sailings to Hamburg. At the time the GSN Co. were currently advertising their twice a week service as being in the hands of the *Peregrine* and the 1,727 grt *Ortolan* though earlier the 1,171 grt *Corncrake*, built in 1910, had also been seen on the route. On a regular basis passengers from London who made use of this service into Germany travelled down on the 8.40 pm boat train out of Liverpool Street. The issue over the evacuation of British subjects from the Continent had also been addressed on 3rd August by H.M. Government having contacted their embassies abroad. On 4th August a GER vessel left Antwerp having ascertained that there were no further British subjects still waiting to leave whilst the next day saw Belgium 'clear' as there were none reported waiting at Ostend either.

The GER's *St. Petersburg* then crossed to the Hook of Holland on 6th August with the German Ambassador Prince Lichnowski on board together with 120 German Embassy staff, the Ambassador later telegraphing his appreciation of the courtesy shown to him throughout. The ship then brought back the British Ambassador, Sir Edward Goschen, who arrived at Parkeston Quay on the 8th on board a ship that was 'not nearly full'. The route to the Hook of Holland was then suspended.

The Antwerp service remained open with six sailings a week until 12th August when the British port of arrival was changed to Tilbury. The 12th of August was also the day that the DFDS service from Esbjerg was suspended with the Danish port now closed due to mines having been laid along its North Sea coast. All the DFDS ships returned home and sailings from Denmark were moved to Copenhagen although Aarhus and Odense were also used. The pre-war sailings to Parkeston Quay were initially transferred to Leith in Scotland and were mainly undertaken by the *N.J. Fjord* out of Copenhagen.

All sailings from Parkeston Quay were thus suspended from mid August onwards though they briefly resumed to Antwerp on 3rd September. However the port saw its 'normal' GER sailings again diverted to Tilbury as Parkeston Quay, by now a naval port, was barred to all aliens. None were allowed to pass through as it was thought that German spies might pose as Belgian civilians. Very soon several thousand Belgian refugees were being landed at Tilbury the first of which arrived at London Liverpool Street station on 11th September.

The route from Antwerp remained open until the 7th October, averaging three sailings per week, with the last British ships to safely leave being the *Brussels* followed by the *Amsterdam,* the latter bringing back the British Consul-General, Sir Cecil Hertslet and party. Also on board were a great many refugees fleeing the fall of Belgium and the subsequent German occupation of Antwerp that occurred on 9th October.

Throughout this short period the ships had moved back and forth a great many stranded holiday makers, refugees and a number of Germans returning to their own country. On one occasion some 300 English children, who had been boarding in Belgian schools, came home on one ship whilst on others a great deal of warehoused goods were also brought back. The British Government later conveyed their thanks to the GER's Agent at Antwerp, Mr. A.C. Pain, for services rendered.

GER traffic between Britain and Antwerp -
4th August to 7th October 1914.

Number of:	Voyages	Passengers	Goods in Tons
To Antwerp via P. Quay	8	367	653
To Antwerp via Tilbury	16	772	657
From Antwerp via P. Quay	7	1594	750
From Antwerp via Tilbury	20	2402	Nil

In addition 8007 Belgian Refugees travelled via Antwerp to Tilbury.

Prior to the outbreak of war the GER had 11 ships in commercial service, these being the three turbine steamers, *St. Petersburg*, *Munich* and *Copenhagen* to the Hook of Holland, four cargo vessels *Clacton*, *Colchester*, *Cromer* and *Newmarket* to Rotterdam and the four twin screw steamers *Amsterdam*, *Dresden*, *Vienna* and *Brussels* to Antwerp. Some of these would continue in commercial service though not always from Parkeston Quay whilst others were requisitioned for a fate more hazardous and which often ended in tragedy.

Their call up came at a time when the modern version of a passport and visa was being introduced with photos being required from 1915 onwards. It was also a time when anything vaguely Germanic in title, such as a ship's name, was subject to change with one of the early alterations being to adopt a more widespread use of the term 'North Sea' in favour of what had long been known as the 'German Ocean'.

In order of being taken up for military service the first was the *Vienna*. She was commandeered by the Admiralty on 28th August 1914 and used as an accommodation ship prior to being fully requisitioned in January 1915. She was renamed *Antwerp* and initially used as one of the very first Q-ships or decoy ships - innocent looking merchantmen armed with hidden guns that would open fire on any unsuspecting surfaced U-boat. Her time spent on anti-submarine duties was brief and largely uneventful and she later became an armed boarding steamer in April 1915. She survived the war and was returned to commercial service.

A total of seven GER ships were requisitioned during October 1914. The *Clacton* was taken up on 7th October for use as a mine sweeper. She was torpedoed by the German submarine U73 and lost at Levant on 3rd August 1916 whilst protecting *HMS Grafton*. The *Newmarket*, taken up on 8th October, was also used as a mine sweeper. She was lost off Kalymos in the Aegean on 16th July 1917 after being hit by a torpedo from U38.

All three turbine passenger steamers were requisitioned on 12th October. The *St. Petersburg* became a hospital and transport ship to and from various French ports. She was renamed *Archangel* on 7th May 1915 and survived the war. She was then used in repatriating both British and German prisoners of war between Rotterdam and Hull. The *Munich* was employed as a transport ship until September 1915. She was renamed *St. Denis*, after the first Archbishop of Paris, on 7th October 1915 and thereafter became a hospital ship though at the time this merely meant a 'floating ambulance' as such ships were not fully equipped with operating theatres or extensive surgical facilities. She also survived the war and both she and the *St. Petersburg* were returned to service.

The *Copenhagen* was not so fortunate. In September 1914 she had brought home a large number of British refugees recently released from detention in Berlin but after being requisitioned she also sailed as a transport ship to and from Holland up until November 1915. During this time she carried a great many Belgian refugees who the Germans accused of later joining the Belgian army. As a consequence the German High Command ordered that the ship be destroyed and Dutch authorities once arrested a young German caught trying to plant a bomb on board ship whilst alongside in Rotterdam. The *Copenhagen* was converted to a hospital ship in 1916 and from December 1916 ran a special mail service between Parkeston Quay and Holland when all ordinary merchant traffic was excluded from the North Sea. The Germans finally caught up with her off the Belgian coast on 5th March 1917 and she was sunk by a torpedo from U61 with the loss of six lives.

Of the three remaining twin screw steamers two were requisitioned on 31st October. The *Dresden* became an armed boarding steamer and was renamed in 1915 as *HMS Louvain* after a town in Belgium. She was lost by being torpedoed and sunk in the Eastern Mediterranean by U22 on 20th January 1918 at a cost of 7 officers and 217 men. The other was the *Amsterdam* which joined the *Vienna* in the role of armed boarding steamer and decoy ship on anti-submarine duties. As with the *Vienna* the *Amsterdam* also went on to survive the war and thereafter resume commercial service.

A limited merchant service to the Hook of Holland was resumed, via Tilbury, as from 2nd December 1914. following Germany's guarantee on the neutrality of Holland. The Rotterdam cargo service, suspended since 5th October, also resumed from Tilbury with sailings once a week. In addition the GER also resumed commercial services to Holland from Parkeston Quay and these were maintained throughout the entire period of the war except when they were banned from doing so upon instruction of the Admiralty. However with much of their fleet requisitioned the Company was left with just three ships, the *Brussels*, *Colchester* and *Cromer*, and these were initially used to transport large volumes of foodstuffs from Holland. Later on, when a passenger service developed, these ships were often the only means of communication with Holland. Alongside the need for war materials and foodstuffs the war produced a heavy demand for horses and by the end of 1914 the existing stable block at Parkeston Quay had been extended by an additional thirty six stalls and the number of horses having been sent abroad had reached over a thousand.

The service to Rotterdam was assisted from the start by the cargo passenger steamer, *Wrexham*, which the GER had chartered from the Great Central Railway (GCR) and whose own ships were, in many respects, now surplus to requirements as they were no longer able to work their usual routes into Germany. The *Wrexham* was a 240 feet long, 1,432 grt three island type cargo and passenger steamer. She was originally built for the Finnish Nord Co. of Helsinki as the *Nord II*, one of three sister ships for a service between Finland and Newcastle and for which her forward hull was specially ice strengthened. She could carry 189 passengers and had three holds that could carry 1,250 tons of cargo including dairy products kept cool by an onboard refrigeration plant.

Throughout the war the North Sea remained an obvious place of danger made all the more hazardous by the channels no longer being marked following the extinguishing of lightships and lighted buoys in December 1914. Also there was the ever present threat of running upon a mine. In the early days it was thought that enemy destroyers would pose the greatest threat to shipping but that was quickly changed to it being the German submarine. Although a certain degree of chivalry was still evident on both sides it was perhaps more noticeable on the part of a U-boat Commander given the more stealthily destructive nature of his craft. If coming across a civilian vessel they would first challenge it to stop, offer the crew the chance to escape by lifeboat and then sink it when all were clear. However not all the intercepted Captains were willing to do so.

On 11th December 1914, the *Colchester* was ordered to stop some 20 miles off the Dutch coast by a submarine which had surfaced close by. The *Colchester*'s Captain Lawrence had the fires double banked, ordered 'Full Ahead' and proceeded to outrun the submarine in a chase lasting twenty minutes. Captain Lawrence was later presented with a gold watch by the Chairman and Directors of the GER 'as a mark of their appreciation of his courage and skilful seamanship' amidst his comments of having previously been involved in six similar escapes.

In early 1915 the 'rules' relating to encounters at sea were redrawn. On 10th February the British Admiralty issued instructions that 'No British merchant vessel should ever tamely surrender to a submarine but should do her utmost to escape'. Further orders were that they should try and force a submarine to dive by aiming straight at it. An announcement then came from Germany stating that as from 18th February their U-boats were to attack, without warning, any vessel sighted in British waters. Their decision was in part brought about by having been caught out by the Q-ships, the use of which had led the Germans to suspect that all civilian ships were a threat and as such they would now just sink whatever they saw.

On 2nd March 1915 the *Wrexham* was ordered to stop by a German submarine whilst en route from Tilbury to Rotterdam. Instead of stopping she increased her speed and outran the submarine over a chase that lasted over 30 miles. A great deal of credit for this was awarded to the engineers and firemen as the *Wrexham* was not the fastest of ships. A gold watch was awarded by the Directors of the GER to her captain, Captain Fryatt.

Higher recognition of the heroics of both the ships and their crews came on 25th March 1915 when H.M. King George V visited Parkeston Quay and this was followed by a letter sent to the GER from the Admiralty dated 8th April 1915 which read:-

Sir;- I am commanded by My Lords Commissioners of the Admiralty to inform you that H.M. Consul-General at Rotterdam has called the attention of the Secretary of State for Foreign Affairs to the highly courageous and meritorious conduct of the masters of the s.s. Cromer, Brussels, Colchester, and Wrexham, which have run during the whole period of hostilities between Rotterdam and Harwich. The fact of these British boats running regularly is reported to have a great moral effect locally at a time when Dutch and other steamships had ceased running and showed nervousness. Mr. Maxsc states further that the Masters of these vessels have rendered him ready assistance on many occasions during the war. In forwarding this report, the Secretary of State for Foreign Affairs has expressed his appreciation of the services rendered by these officers. My Lords endorse Sir E. Grey's approbation, and desire that you will be good enough to convey his thanks and theirs to the officers concerned for their conduct which has reflected credit on British seamanship. I am. Sir. Your obedient Servant. (Signed) W. Graham Greene

The attacks continued as did the commendations. Just three days after the Royal visit, on 28th March, the *Brussels,* with Captain Fryatt in command, was sailing from Parkeston Quay to Rotterdam when she was sighted near the Maas light by U33 and ordered to stop. In accordance with Admiralty instructions Captain Fryatt again decided upon trying to evade capture. This time, as advised to do so, he set about causing the submarine to dive. In the event it was claimed that the ship either rammed it or clipped the conning tower as it submerged. Captain Fryatt did not report having felt his ship strike anything but one of the firemen did report a bumping sensation under the ship's hull. On this occasion his successful and heroic escape was recognised by the Harwich Town Council whose Mayor awarded him an inscribed watch. However the Germans saw this in a totally different light and put him down as a marked man. With the likelihood of the German Navy searching out the *Brussels* Captain Fryatt was offered, and refused, the command of another ship.

On 17th August 1915 the *Cromer* was the target of a torpedo fired from a submarine whose periscope was seen around four hundred yards away. Fortunately for the *Cromer* it missed and the ship escaped by skilfully outrunning the submarine after a chase lasting twenty minutes. Again the captain received a gold watch from the Chairman and Directors of the GER.

The use of German submarines in attacking on sight was widely condemned both by the shipping companies and countries who had remained neutral and after increasing protests Germany relented on such activities on 20th September 1915. In 1916 the Royal Navy introduced a convoy system between the Shipwash light vessel and the Maas light vessel off Rotterdam. The intention was to help protect merchant shipping from the dangers of a U-boat attack but it never managed to eradicate the problem.

The *Cromer* was again attacked on 2nd April 1916 when returning from the Hook of Holland. This time she escaped through the skilful manoeuvring of Captain Beeching who also managed to ram the submarine. This action earned him the Distinguished Service Cross for gallantry, this noticeably being a military award given to a civilian. Chief Engineer Smith and Chief Officer Stiff received honourable Mentions in Despatches from the Admiralty. The GER further awarded the officers and crew with inscribed watches. Similar watches were also presented to Captain Barren

GER poster from November 1918 headed with services suspended due to the European war. Similar posters first appeared in 1915. (Stephen Brown collection)

and Captain Stiff for dealing with other attacks from submarines. The *Cromer* was later used by the Royal Navy as a 'survivor collector' of ships sunk in convoys and survived the war.

The *Colchester* was moved to sailing from Tilbury on 8th March 1916 and was later captured by a German cruiser on 21st September 1916 when crossing back from Rotterdam. Captain Bennet and the crew of 27 were interned and the ship was put under the German flag for use as a minelayer. She was sunk in the Baltic by the Royal Navy on 2nd March 1918.

After having been chartered for almost two years the *Wrexham* was returned to the GCR and in November 1916 she was requisitioned for use as a naval armaments carrier. Her return was partly due to having become too slow, at 12 knots, at outrunning German submarines which, whilst only able to do 8 or 9 knots submerged, were increasingly capable of doing 15 to 17 knots when on the surface. Her replacement was the *Staveley*. This was another GCR vessel and one that had earlier been requisitioned in October 1914. When released from Admiralty duties on 8th July 1916 she was taken over by the GER even though she was barely any faster at escaping from enemy submarines. She was the same length at the *Wrexham* but otherwise smaller in capacity and size. When in civilian service she could carry 30 passengers in First class aft, the location being a feature at the time of GCR vessels, and 330 in Emigrant class forward.

Amongst all the wartime casualties of the GER the most notorious was not of a ship but that of the aforementioned Captain Fryatt. On the 23rd June 1916, whilst in command of the *Brussels*, his good fortune of escaping capture ran out. The ship had left the Hook of Holland around 11.00 pm on the 22nd bound for Tilbury. Just after midnight the ship was surrounded by five German destroyers. In accordance with instructions Captain Fryatt had managed to burn a number of confidential papers before seeing his ship boarded by an enemy crew. The *Brussels* was escorted to Zeebrugge where Fryatt and his crew were questioned about the incident involving U33. The crew were initially interned in Ruhleben camp and Captain Fryatt was later put up for trial before a German Navy court martial in Bruges on 27th July 1916. He was charged with being a 'franc-tireurs' which variously translates as a freebooter of the sea, a sharpshooter or a maverick.

His trial ended at 4.30 pm throughout which Captain Fryatt maintained that 'he had done no wrong'. Despite the best efforts of Major Naumann, a German acting on his behalf, and the intervention of the American Ambassador in Berlin acting on behalf of the British Government, (America still being a neutral country), a verdict was given at 6.30 pm that Captain Fryatt would be shot that evening. At 7.00 pm the sentence was carried out. A public notice in German, Flemish and French was posted up in Bruges: *'The English Captain of the Mercantile Marine, Charles Fryatt, of Southampton, though he did not belong to the armed forces of the enemy, attempted on March 28th 1915 to destroy a German submarine by running it down. This is the reason why he has been condemned to death by judgement of this day of the War Council of the Marine Corp, and has been executed. A perverse action has thus received its punishment, tardy but just.'*

The sentence was widely condemned even by legal minds in Germany. Had Captain Fryatt admitted acting in accordance with Admiralty instructions or had been armed with even so much as a revolver his capture would have resulted in him being treated as a prisoner of war, under the Germans own code of conduct, but being designated as a non combatant he had apparently acted outside the code of engagement even though he was entitled to save his ship at any cost. The situation was indeed perverse. The captured *Brussels* was re-named by the Germans as the *Brugge* and used as a submarine depot ship. The Germans then scuttled her at the entrance to Zeebrugge harbour on 14th October 1917 in order to protect their base.

For the loss of the *Brussels* the GER received £51,000 in insurance compensation. The ship was later raised in October 1919 and donated by the Belgian Government to the British Government who then sold her for £3,100. The proceeds went to charity and eventually towards the building of the Fryatt Memorial Hospital at Dovercourt, near Harwich. The ship itself was towed to Leith, rebuilt as a cattle carrier, renamed *Lady Brussels* and put in service between Liverpool and Dublin until being scrapped in 1929. Captain Fryatt's body was returned for burial in Dovercourt on 8th July 1919. He was posthumously awarded the Belgian Naval War Cross on 6th May 1920 and a memorial gravestone, presented by the GER, was unveiled by Lord Hamilton on 20th June 1920.

Sailings throughout the war to neutral Holland, as and when circumstances permitted, were not the sole responsibility of the GER. The General Steam Navigation Co. were also involved and they lost two ships that had previously been seen at Parkeston Quay. The first was the *Gannet* which was mined and sunk on 7th July 1916 close by the Shipwash light vessel. The other was the *Peregrine*. This ship had been requisitioned in 1914 as a supply ship and following her release from such duties in November 1915 was then used on services to Holland. She also was intercepted by a German U-boat, on 8th February 1917, but managed to safely outrun her attacker. However she was lost on 29th December 1917 after grounding on the Longsand near the Sunk light vessel and later washed onto the wreck of the *Isis* which had similarly grounded there just two days earlier. The *Peregrine* broke her back and of the 59 passengers on board, mainly French, and a crew of 33 all were saved by the Walton lifeboat.

Elsewhere the SMZ had seen all its normal services suspended and sailings transferred to Tilbury. These ran until June 1915 when all sailings were cancelled as a result of Germany's U-boat policy of attack on sight even though Holland and the SMZ were neutral. After Germany had relented this action the SMZ resumed services until struck by a tragic six month period in 1916 that saw their pre-war fleet of seven ships reduced by the loss of three. Each became victims of sea mines between Tilbury and Flushing and those lost were the *Princes Juliana* on 1st February, the *Mecklenburg* on 27th February and the *Koningin Wilhelmina* on 31st July. Thereafter the service was severely reduced and was later closed on 1st February 1917, this being the date when Germany resumed its earlier policy of attacking all ships in British waters, neutral or otherwise. A fourth ship was later lost in 1918 when the *Koningin Regentes* was torpedoed on 6th June whilst en route from Rotterdam to Boston, Lincolnshire exchanging prisoners of war. Thus only the *Prins Hendrik*, *Oranje Nassau* and *Duitschland* were left, the last ship having been re-named *Zeeland* in 1916 as Duitschland meant Germany in Dutch.

Throughout the period of hostilities the GER

timetables were regularly headed: 'Owing to the European War the services to and from the Continent via Harwich are Suspended.' but by the time of the Armistice on 11th November 1918 ships on what might be termed GER service had made 1,428 crossings to and from Holland, an altogether remarkable achievement given the circumstances. The main threat to shipping had throughout remained that from German submarines but the area around Harwich itself was not immune to being bombed, first by German planes and later by Zeppelins. When the war was over Harwich harbour became the main receiving port for the surrendering of German U-boats.

Through Parkeston Quay and Tilbury and with the help of the GCR vessels a total of 7,782 passengers had travelled 'via the GER' to Holland whilst 34,015, mainly Belgian refugees, were brought back. As regards cargo 59,663 tons were sent to Holland and 232,166 tons of foodstuffs returned. The ships transported around three quarters of all the parcels for prisoners of war that went via Holland totalling 1,962,420 bags or 15,700,000 parcels. Postal mail was also carried, this amounting to 129,657 ordinary parcel mail and 68,174 letter mails into Holland and 382,206 ordinary parcel mail and 154,359 letter mails to England. Many of the latter were 'war cards' sent from British prisoners of war via the International Red Cross.

Whilst the sight of such vessels arriving in Holland was greatly appreciated and Dutch morale suitably uplifted the war took a heavy toll on the GER's pre-war Parkeston Quay based ships. Six were lost, these being the *Brussels, Copenhagen, Clacton, Newmarket, Dresden* and *Colchester* leaving just five that eventually returned to service, these being the *Cromer, Vienna, Amsterdam, St. Denis* (formerly the *Munich*) and *Archangel* (formerly the *St Petersburg*)

In order to supplement such a depleted fleet the GER sought to build, purchase or charter in replacement tonnage although one of their early attempts at doing so was thwarted by the Royal Navy. Still under construction in 1917 at John Brown's yard was a sister ship to the original trio of *Copenhagen, Munich* and *St. Petersburg*. She differed in having turbines that were geared rather than directly driven and at one time was referred to as a future *Antwerp*. However she was commandeered that year by the Admiralty on 27th February, launched as the *Stockholm* on 9th June and re-named as the aircraft carrier *Pegasus* on 28th August 1917.

In August 1917 the GER then managed to purchase the passenger cargo ship *Kilkenny* from the City of Dublin Steam Packet Company, a company which at that time was being absorbed into a formative Coast Lines. She was used on sailings to and from Holland until November 1918 when she was then taken over by the Government for services across the Irish Sea.

Following the Armistice a limited cargo service had begun running out of Tilbury using the cargo passenger steamers *Notts* and *Staveley* to and from Rotterdam and the *Marylebone* to and from Antwerp. Throughout this time their passenger capacity was reduced to twelve and all three of these GCR vessels did occasional trips to the Hook of Holland. The GER's *Cromer* also sailed on the Rotterdam service out of Tilbury along with the occasional trip out of London's East India Dock. All services and sailings were somewhat irregular and often consisted of each ship making just one or two trips per fortnight.

The *Notts* was a sister ship to the *Staveley* and was originally launched into GCR service as the *Nottingham*. She had been requisitioned on 12th October 1914 for use as a store carrier and throughout the war had been known simply as the *Notts* so as not to be confused with HMS *Nottingham*.

The *Marylebone* was one of a pair of triple screw twin funnelled turbine steamers that the GCR introduced to their Grimsby to Rotterdam service in 1906. Each was fitted out in a more conventional arrangement inasmuch as the GCR now placed First class amidships, Second class aft with Emigrant class still within the tween decks. Despite improvements in the route's timings, a faster voyage and better accommodation they were expensive to run and were eclipsed in popularity by the GER services out of Parkeston Quay. The *Marylebone*, together with sister ship *Immingham*, were re-engined in 1911 with triple expansion machinery driving a single screw and the profile was altered to a single funnel by removing the forward one. The *Marylebone* had the distinction of making the first post war sailing to Antwerp of a vessel bearing the flag of a returning Great Eastern Railway and its arrival there on 17th December 1918 was furthermore the first British steamer to do so since the city had fallen in October 1914. On board was the returning British Consul-General, Sir Cecil Hertslet.

It was not until January 1919 that continental services were resumed at Parkeston Quay with the first commercial arrival being that of the *Marylebone*, from Antwerp, on 21st January. A few days later, on 26th January, she re-opened a once a week service to the Belgian port. The service became twice weekly with the brief introduction of the *Woodcock*, formerly used pre-war on the GSN Co. route to Hamburg. In February the *Notts* arrived from Rotterdam on the 19th followed by the *Staveley* on the 22nd. Each ship then did one trip to the Hook of Holland. The *Notts* re-opened the Parkeston Quay to Rotterdam route on 1st March followed by the *Staveley* on the 5th, each ship sailing once a week. The *Cromer* returned to Parkeston Quay on 1st March and from the 9th sailed mainly to Antwerp with the occasional trip to Rotterdam. Her schedules were both varied and relaxed often sailing just once a fortnight.

These four ships, *Notts*, *Staveley*, *Marylebone* and *Cromer*, were later joined by the cargo vessel *Felixstowe* which arrived at Parkeston Quay on 13th April 1919 straight from her builders, Hawthorn's of Leith. She underwent trials on the measured mile off Maplin Sands and made her maiden voyage by sailing to Rotterdam on 23rd April. She was then utilised with the *Cromer* on relief sailings to both Antwerp and Rotterdam.

By mid 1919 the first of the surviving passenger steamers were returning to the port. The *Archangel* was discharged from war duties on 19th April and sent to John Brown's yard on Clydebank from where she subsequently arrived at Parkeston Quay on 18th July 1919. A week later, on 25th July, the *Vienna* was returned having first visited the yard of Fletcher's in London. The *Vienna* had been discharged on 31st December 1918 and she arrived back at Parkeston Quay having since been re-named the *Roulers,* after a city in Belgium. Following local refit work the *Archangel* re-opened passenger sailings to the Hook of Holland on 3rd August whilst the *Roulers* returned to the Antwerp service on 3rd September. The Hook of Holland route then received its second passenger steamer with the return of the *Amsterdam*. She arrived back at Parkeston Quay on 13th September from a refit at Green & Silley Weir in London's East India Dock and resumed sailings to the Hook on 11th October 1919.

As the GER was slowly re-introducing its own ships into service it was also returning those it had chartered. Accordingly the GCR's *Notts* left on 1st August to resume her original name of *Nottingham*, followed by the *Staveley* on 1st September and the *Marylebone* on 2nd October with all three sailing back to Grimsby.

Earlier the *Kilkenny* had arrived at Parkeston Quay, on 26th July 1919 from Cork, following her spell on the Irish Sea. Some two months earlier, on 15th May, she had badly grounded in Knockadoon Bay, 25 miles east of Cork, during a voyage there from Liverpool and after her July appearance at Parkeston Quay she too was sent for a refit at Green & Silley Weir's on 12th August. She returned on 6th November and took up sailings to Antwerp on 13th November. Very soon afterwards she was re-named *Frinton* and made the first sailing to Antwerp under her new name on 18th December 1919. Although she was originally built with passenger accommodation for a mix of 154 in First and Third class her role now as a cargo ship meant that such facilities were not required.

Since November 1918 there had been a troop ship service running between Parkeston Quay and Rotterdam repatriating prisoners of war from both sides. This ceased on 7th November 1919 during which time some 10,000 British and 15,000 German troops were returned home. This service was operated by a further group of ships chartered from the GCR namely the *Dewsbury, Stockport, Accrington* and *Lutterworth*. Upon completion of their duties they left Parkeston Quay on the 11th, 12th, 12th and 14th November 1919 respectively in order to resume their own Company's services from Grimsby to Rotterdam and Hamburg.

Out of the pre-war services run by Thule Line, GSN Co. and DFDS the Danish company was the first to return to Parkeston Quay. Their service out of Esbjerg, diverted to Leith at the outbreak of war, had seen one of its pre-war vessels, the *N.J. Fjord,* captured by the Germans on 5th April 1917 whilst carrying coal from Blyth to Odense. She was sunk by the exploding of bombs that the Germans had placed on the hull though only after the crew were safely allowed to take to the lifeboats.

The other DFDS 'Parkeston regulars' all survived the war years and had principally been operating cargo sailings from Copenhagen. The *Ficaria* was used mainly on sailings to Hull and the *Primula* to both Hull and Newcastle with both ships having been utilised throughout the duration. The *A.P. Bernstorff* and the *J.C. la Cour* were also employed on the route to Hull before being laid up respectively from October 1915 to August 1917 and from January 1917 to November 1918. Three of these were chartered post-war by the British Government in order to repatriate British prisoners of war, principally from the German ports of Warnemunde, Lubeck and Stettin, with the *Primula* making 6 trips to the U.K. between 25 November 1918 and 17 March 1919 whilst the *A.P. Bernstorff* made 5 trips between 27 November 1918 and 9 January 1919. In addition the *J.C. la Cour* made 5 trips from Germany to Copenhagen between 27 November 1918 and 10 January 1919 and together they transferred around 20,000 personnel.

Upon the resumption of peace time services the one from Esbjerg initially ran to Grimsby and it was not until 26th October 1919 that it returned to Parkeston Quay. That day saw the arrival of the passenger steamer *A.P. Bernstorff* which was shortly joined by the *J.C. la Cour* which arrived on 29th October. Between them they ran a twice weekly service departing Parkeston Quay on Tuesday and Saturday and from Esbjerg on Wednesday and Saturday.

The war had placed an increased demand upon the Parkeston Power House with power lines from there being run out to a number of mine depots located upstream the River Stour at Wrabness and then lines being further extended as far as the railway premises at

HRH King George V reviewing sailors and marines on the quay behind the station hotel. On the left is the original location of the quay's own fire service whilst top right shows part of the housing for the conveyor belts of the coaling plant - 26th February 1918. (Essex Archives Online)

Manningtree. In 1918 five Paxman super heaters were ordered and these were delivered in February 1919 to improve the existing Economic boilers. The GER then took on 'commercial customers' such as malting companies in Mistley and Trinity House in Harwich.

In addition to the obvious dangers associated with the war Britain had also undergone a period of severe inflation. The assassination of the Archduke Ferdinand back in 1914 had caused a financial paralysis and the consequent drop in economic activity was only alleviated by central banks injecting more money into circulation. This resulted in years of high inflation with rates of 12.5pc in 1915, 18.1pc in 1916 and 22.5pc in 1917. It remained above 20pc until 1919 and thus by the time the war ended costs had roughly doubled and yet at Parkeston Quay the wages of GER staff had risen only upon promotion or in line with their normal incremental entitlement.

The quay's lowest rates were paid to messengers at 1s.6d. per day. Above them were labourers employed at 5d. per hour which, if they worked a full 8 hours for six days a week, was equal to a £1 a week. Further up the scales were those on daily rates with wide variations that saw firemen receiving 4s.3d. per day, blacksmiths 5s., drivers 5s.3d. and fitters 6s. These rates of between £1.5s.6d. and £1.16s.0d a week were at a time when the national average weekly wage in 1914 was £1.10s.6d. rising to £1.11s.6d. in 1915. In March 1916, when the GER boats temporarily ceased running, a number of staff previously employed within the Continental Department on board ship were re-deployed as labourers within the Electrical Department until being sent back in January 1917.

Throughout the war's early years pay rises were often modest at best but as from 17th February 1917 there came the introduction of a war bonus or war wage payment and rates began to show a reasonable increase. The rates for labourers were improved by the addition of a half-penny payment per hour, equal to a 10% rise, plus time and a quarter rate for working overtime or time and a half for working Sundays. For a few select key personnel the war bonus was worth up to 5s. a week but in general it gave most workers an extra 2s.6d. a week. It was even paid to six newly employed female labourers who were taken on in March 1917 at 3s. per day. Wages nationally rose from a weekly average of £1.14s.0d. in 1916 to £1.19s.0d in 1917.

Most staff still worked a six day week but some, such as the Parkeston Hotel Boiler Attendants, worked Sundays as part of their normal week. They were employed by the Hotel Department initially working a 12 hour shift from 6 am to 6 pm and 6 pm to 6 am, six days a week for 5s.6d. a day. Their relief came from within the Marine Superintendent's Engineering Department. In September 1916 they came under the Electrical Department and the hours were later changed to 8 hour shifts of 5 am to 1 pm and 1 pm to 9 pm, seven days a week. One attendant retired onto the pension fund in March 1917 and was next day re-engaged as temporary staff doing the same job at 3s.10d. per day.

By May 1917 the rate for a foreman was 8s. a day and his position was not only amongst the highest paid on the quay but one of the select few who were entitled to 14 days annual holiday, the others being the storekeeper on £1.10s.0d. a week, the chief telegraph clerk on £2.0s.0d. and the chief wireless operator at £2.6s.0d. Most others within the permanent staff were lucky to get just four days a year though drivers were entitled to a week off. Of all the jobs ashore the telegraph and wireless department undoubtedly offered the best paying jobs in line with its importance and the level of training required but even they were falling behind the national average which in 1918 had risen to £2.11s.0d. per week. For those lower down the pay scales the war had caused them to suffer a relative decline in their incomes due probably to the fact that the ships had for so long been out of revenue earning service.

By the end of 1919 the GER were sailing six ships out of Parkeston Quay, the *Archangel* to the Hook of Holland, the *Amsterdam* mainly to the Hook of Holland though with occasional trips to Rotterdam, the *Felixstowe* to Rotterdam, the *Roulers* and *Frinton* to Antwerp and the *Cromer* to both Antwerp and Rotterdam. However despite these and the anticipated return of many of the pre-war services it would be a few years more before the port resumed full operations.

London & North Eastern Railway Parkeston Quay Capital Expenditure to 31st December 1912

Particulars	to 1912	to 1912 Proportion applicable to Quay &c
Sea Walls and Works	69,026. 3. 9.	
Pile Foundations &c. for Buildings	49,418. 11. 0.	44,418. 11. 0.
Stables	2,835. 11. 9.	2,835. 11. 9.
Pile Foundations &c. for Engine Shed	6,608. 8.11.	
Marine Superintendent's House	1,008. 0. 2.	
Clerks' Houses, 1 Pair semi detached	576. 11. 5.	
Captains' Houses, 1 Pair semi detached	915. 0. 0.	
Cattle Lairs and Shoot	1,663. 16. 0.	1,663. 16. 0.
Work Shop	554. 16. 5.	554. 16. 5.
Electric Lighting Engine House	32,841. 14. 7.	
Works	4,158. 15.10.	2,466. 0. 0.
Ironworks, Stour Quay and Warehouses	97,732. 8. 0.	97,732. 8. 0.
Cylinder and work done Stour Quay	69,638. 15. 4.	69,638. 15. 4.
Mooring Buoys	1,298. 15. 0.	1,298. 15. 0.
Locomotive Shops for Boat Repairs	5,748. 0. 7.	
Hydraulics and Crane	29,032. 16. 6.	29,032. 16. 6.
Parkeston Station Buildings	54,621. 18. 7.	14,621. 18. 7.
Meat Larder	250. 0. 0.	
Signalling Points and Coverings	3,651. 3. 5.	
Cooking Apparatus &c. Parkeston Hotel	1,902. 7. 5.	
Office Furniture	859. 12. 6.	
Steel Rails	2,235. 5. 6.	
Sundries and Departmental	42,951. 14. 0.	25,470. 0. 0.
Cottages and Barracks	17,176. 18.11.	
Quay, Additional Sidings &c.	150,013. 12. 4.	97,507. 12.11.
Coaling Plant Scheme	11,786. 11.11	
Dredger	1,190. 19. 1.	1,190. 19. 1.
Land	35,495. 9. 6.	
Law Costs	547. 16. 0.	
Engineering Staff	10,743. 14. 7.	6,370. 14. 7.
Dredging	5,799. 5. 4.	5,799. 5. 4.
Electric Telegraph	452. 8.11.	
Furniture	1,915. 5. 5.	
Steam Cranes		430. 0. 0.
Venetian Blinds, Parkeston		60. 18. 2.
	£ 714,652. 8. 8.	401,092. 18. 8.
Coaling Scheme		11,786. 11.11.
Coal Barges		2,315. 0. 0.
Electrical Plant & Machinery on Quay		40,427. 19. 0.
		455,622. 9. 7.
Additional Summary Expenditure		
1913 Works	2,785. 1. 1.	2,785. 1. 1.
1913 Land		8,942. 15. 0.
1914 Works	4,524. 3.11.	4,524. 3.11.
1915 Works (credit)	(–1. 11. 3.)	(–1. 11. 3.)
	£ 721,960. 2. 5.	£ 471,872. 18. 4.

(Expenditure by the GER as detailed in accounts later compiled by the LNER)

THE 1920s

The early 1920s showed few signs that Britain was becoming a 'land fit for heroes' or for those who had otherwise survived the Great War. The economy was severely disrupted by a coal strike in 1921 that lasted from 1st April until the end of June and this led to thousands throughout the country being thrown on the dole. Whole swathes of industry either shut down or went onto reduced working at a time when it was often cheaper to import a wide variety of goods, especially those produced in Germany, than it was to manufacturer them in Britain.

Socially the hub attraction of London was considered to be a dull place for visitors with even the well to do country set staying away throughout 'The Season'. As a result it was being suggested that European bound Americans on board the trans-Atlantic liners were in receipt of telegrams en route pointing out the greater fun and gaiety to be had in Paris and were changing their plans accordingly. As a result Parkeston Quay became less and less a part of the 'Grand Tour'. Once significant rather than lucrative this feature of the port's activity would become increasingly replaced by those still able to afford the cost of travelling abroad. For many the lure of the Continent remained as strong as ever and the GER were keen to accommodate the demand.

Following the end of its use by the military authorities around £4,000 had been spent on the Company's hotel at Harwich and it re-opened for business on 21st April 1920. At Parkeston Quay the former attractions and frequency of the Hook of Holland service were soon to be resumed following the GER's purchase in June 1919 of the turbine steamer *St. George*. She had been built in 1906 for the Great Western Railway's Fishguard to Rosslare route and was later sold to the Canadian Pacific Railway in May 1913. After being requisitioned for war service in 1915 she subsequently returned to Britain where from 1917 onwards she was in use as a hospital ship. The GER paid £130,000 for her, this being an inflationary premium on the £110,000 she had originally cost to build, and on 2nd July 1919 the Company sent a crew from Parkeston Quay to join her in Southampton.

With a maximum speed of 22½ knots the *St George* became the fastest of the GER's ships though generally her service speed was a more normal 20 knots. Her external features were left unaltered from how she looked when new but internally her original accommodation was halved to now carrying just 498 passengers. She retained her original layout of First class amidships and Second class aft and her role was to replace the lost *Copenhagen*. By April 1920 the *St. George*, the *Archangel* (ex St Petersburg) and a recently returned *St. Denis* (ex Munich) were then providing a daily service to the Hook of Holland, except on Sunday. The *Amsterdam* was moved onto the Antwerp service in order to release the *Frinton* to join the service to Rotterdam and raise that route's sailings to three times a week.

The introduction of the *St. George* created several problems for regular passengers on account of the *Archangel* and *St. Denis* having almost identical levels of double and single berth cabin accommodation and the *St. George* having a very high number of cabins that were four berth. It thus became difficult for the booking clerks to arrange everyone's requirements satisfactorily with some passengers avoiding the ship altogether if they could not get their regular cabin.

A feature at the time of the *St. Denis* was her entitlement to fly the Blue Ensign. She was the only home trade vessel in Britain to do so as her captain, Captain Stiff, was a Lieutenant-Commander in the Royal Navy Reserve (RNR). A special Admiralty warrant had allowed him to fly the flag whenever he was in command of a ship's crew that included a number of RNR ratings.

In August 1920 the pre-war service between Gothenburg and London Tilbury via Parkeston Quay was re-instated by Fornyade Angfartygsakt Svenska Lloyd or Swedish Lloyd who, in 1916, had taken over the route's previous operator Thule Line. The two earlier ships, *Thule* and *Balder*, returned to the run with the *Thule* having been extensively refitted and modernised just prior to the service re-opening. The *Thule* left in 1921 followed by the *Balder* in 1923 with both ships being moved up to Newcastle. Their replacement was the *Patricia*, a vessel built in Italy in 1901 and which had seen extensive service in Russia, China and Australia before being acquired by Swedish Lloyd in 1919. She was altogether a much larger ship, at 2,981 grt, than those she replaced and after a refit in 1920 she could carry 572 passengers. She remained on the route until 1929 when Swedish Lloyd placed two new turbine vessels, the *Suecia* and *Britannia*, on the route which then ran three times a week in summer, once in winter, but which no longer called at Parkeston Quay.

For the summer of 1920 DFDS supplemented their Esbjerg to Parkeston Quay service between 4th July and 28th September with the addition of the *Dronning Maud*. Built in 1906 this 1,761grt passenger and cargo ship was used mainly for the Company's Copenhagen to Stettin and Oslo service as well as on domestic Danish routes. Now, in conjunction with the *A.P. Bernstorff* and the *J.C. la Cour*, she was part of a three times a week passenger service between Denmark and Parkeston Quay that was backed up with additional sailings by cargo vessels as and when required. From London Liverpool Street a connecting boat train departed at 3.15 pm though passengers had a long wait at the quay until their late evening sailing.

But it was Belgium that became the greater focal point for travellers due to it being the cheapest amongst the European countries for both living costs and travel. This gave rise to a vast number of short excursions and day trips which were further encouraged by the Belgians having abolished passport visas and the associated time and

Front side of a 1923 handbill advertising the LNER Harwich (P. Quay) service to Zeebrugge. (Robert Clow collection)

LONDON AND NORTH EASTERN RAILWAY

ROYAL MAIL AND DAYLIGHT SAVING ROUTE

Inexpensive Holidays in Belgium

via

HARWICH — ZEEBRUGGE

2nd JULY to 16th SEPTEMBER, 1923

TO ZEEBRUGGE:—MONDAYS, WEDNESDAYS AND FRIDAYS
FROM ZEEBRUGGE:—TUESDAYS, THURSDAYS AND SUNDAYS

LONDON ... dep. 8.40 p.m.	BRUSSELS (NORD) ... dep. 8.15 p.m.
(Liverpool St. Station)	GHENT ... „ 9.44 „
PARKESTON QUAY ... „ 10.30 „	BRUGES ... „ 10.31 „
ZEEBRUGGE ... arr. 6.30 a.m.	ZEEBRUGGE ... „ 11.15 „
BRUGES ... „ 7.33 „	PARKESTON QUAY ... „ 6.0 a.m.
GHENT ... „ 8.22 „	LONDON ... arr. 8.9 „
BRUSSELS (NORD) ... „ 9.27 „	(Liverpool St. Station)

Restaurant and Pullman Cars between London and Harwich. Restaurant Car Express between Liverpool, Manchester, Sheffield and Harwich. Through Carriage between Edinburgh, Glasgow, York, Birmingham, Coventry and Harwich.

FINE STEAMERS, SPECIALLY EQUIPPED FOR NIGHT TRAVEL.

Connection by Railway and Electric Trams (conveying luggage), between Zeebrugge, Heyst, Knocke, Blankenberghe, Ostend, Mariakerke, Middelkerke, Westende, Lombartzyde, Nieuport.

FARES : Single.

LONDON TO ZEEBRUGGE

1st Class.   2nd Class and Saloon.   2nd Class.
£2 : 5 : 0   £1 : 17 : 0   £1 : 10 : 0

HARWICH TO ZEEBRUGGE

1st Class.   2nd Class.
£1 : 10 : 6   £1 : 3 : 6

For further particulars see other side.

Details from any of the Company's Agents; the Continental Department, Liverpool Street Station, London, E.C.2; or the West End Ticket and Information Bureau, 71, Regent St., W.1.

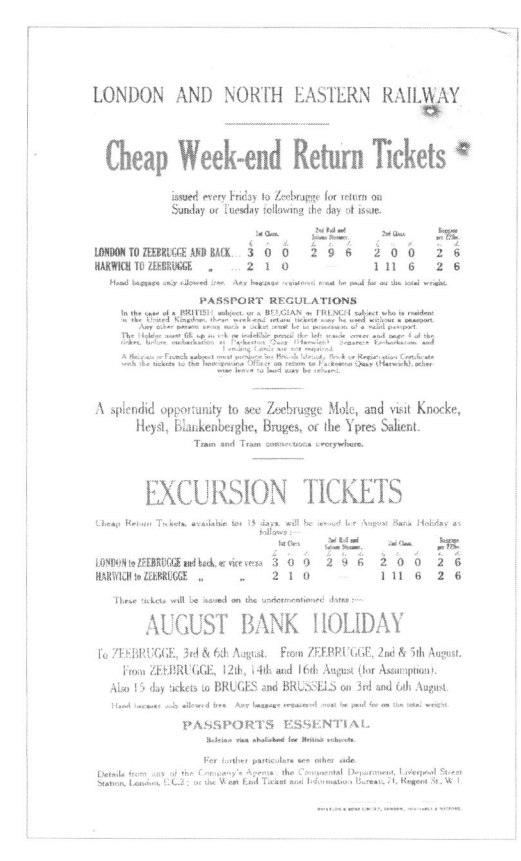

Reverse side of a 1923 handbill advertising the LNER Harwich (P. Quay) service to Zeebrugge. (Robert Clow collection)

Plan layout of the Harwich Train Ferry Terminal. (Railway Gazette, April 1924)

expense of acquiring one. Thus with quick and efficient formalities for both entering and leaving Belgium it soon became normal for the overnight steamers to Antwerp to sail full every trip. It was obvious though with ships on the route now over 25 years old that replacements were desperately needed and so in turn the GER ordered three much larger ships.

The first of these almost 3,000 grt vessels to arrive was the *Antwerp* which entered service in June 1920 followed by the *Bruges* some three months later on 30th September. With the benefit of a quarter of a century's advance in technology these ships were a major improvement over what was in service at the time. Both had been built by John Brown and each had the distinction of having had their forward upper part painted out in white. Although certificated to carry up to 1,680 passengers and very well appointed throughout there was only enough cabin accommodation for 350 of which 263 were in First class. The frequency of sailings to Antwerp was increased to four per week in June 1920 and then six per week from August 1920 onwards.

The third ship did not arrive until almost two years later. She was named the *Malines* and came not from the yard of John Brown's but instead from the High Walker yard of Armstrong Whitworth and Co. at Wallsend. When launched on 6th January 1921 she was said to be 'an accomplishment of which even that famous firm can be proud'. However her construction was so delayed that she did not undergo sea trials, off the mouth of the Tyne, until 9th March the following year and only entered service on 21st March 1922. She took her name from the first railway line to open in Belgium, on 5th May 1835, and which ran for 13½ miles between Brussels and Malines.

Her description at the time was equally suited to both the *Antwerp* and the *Bruges*. All had hulls with cruise sterns measuring 337 feet overall by 43 feet which were divided into nine compartments by steel bulkheads that extended up to the shelter deck. These were made completely watertight by closing doors controlled from the bridge. In the engine room were five main boilers, each over 16 feet in diameter and nearly 12 feet long that provided steam to four John Brown Curtis turbines. These spun at 2,710 rpm and were geared to drive bronze twin screws at 271 rpm. Total output was 10,500 shp giving a service speed of around 21 knots.

Passenger accommodation was of the highest standard. On the Boat Deck, between the line of boats and Welin davits, was the wireless telegraph office and officers quarters, a First class lounge and the Cabin-de-Luxe. From the lounge there descended a handsome staircase to the Shelter Deck which contained the ticket office and a First class dining saloon. The furniture, doors and columns were all made of a dark oak with the upholstery and carpets set out in green. All around were electric lights with rose coloured petal shades and large square windows in between. An electric fire was set beneath an Adams style mantle-piece and the tables were designed in a style described as 'intime' with moveable chairs. A separate First class Ladies saloon was decorated with silk panels, deep sofas, lounge chairs and another Adams electric fireplace. Off this saloon were found the Ladies cabins and lavatories. For those travelling Second class there was another dining saloon on the Main Deck, a further Ladies saloon and a Gentleman's smoking room. A fully equipped electric kitchen complete with a range, ovens and hot plates, grills and toasters was connected to the principal dining saloon by lifts and the pantry was fitted with a hot cupboard.

A high percentage of the cabin berths were in First class single berth cabins fitted with 'homely wood cot beds' and specially fitted spring mattresses of the largest size. Although the tendency had remained for single berth cabins there were increasing numbers of First class cabins that had twin berths. Being much larger ships each now had a crew of 60. The *Malines* was to be the last ship ordered by the GER.

The ongoing trend for wanting to visit Belgium, as well as to holiday abroad, saw the GER start a new experimental service between Parkeston Quay and Zeebrugge. This opened on 2nd July 1921 and was 'summer season only'. It was inaugurated by the *Bruges* but from the 4th July onwards the *Roulers* took over and she sailed three times a week until September. Departures from Parkeston Quay were on Monday, Wednesday and Saturday. Timings were such that passengers could leave London Liverpool Street at 8.40 pm on the Antwerp boat train and next morning arrive in Zeebrugge in time to catch the 6.10 am connecting train for Bruges and Brussels. The return sailings departed Zeebrugge at 11.30 pm on Tuesday, Thursday and Sunday with passengers arriving in London at 8.00 am the next morning.

The route was attractive to holiday makers and day-trippers keen to visit the resorts of Blankenberge, Ostend, Heyst or Knokke via the coastal electric tramway. As with the route to Antwerp it was possible for either businessmen to spend a full day in Brussels or for others to visit the Belgian battlefields. One particular advantage of this service was the Sunday night sailing from Belgium which compensated for the lack of one from Antwerp.

A further development for the summer of 1921 was

the resumption of the pre-war 'North Country Continental' complete with restaurant cars. This service had been discontinued throughout the war but was eventually restarted on 25th July 1921. The train would leave Parkeston Quay at 7.02 am and having travelled via March, Lincoln and Sheffield, would arrive at Manchester Central at 2.32 pm and Liverpool Central at 3.25 pm. The return journey left Liverpool at 2.30 pm, Manchester at 3.25 pm and Sheffield Victoria at 4.42 pm. A week later, starting on 1st August, the connection to Birmingham New Street was similarly restored with an arrival time there of 3.00 pm and departure at 3.55 pm. The various portions rejoined at March and the arrival time at Parkeston Quay was now 9.42 pm.

At Harwich the old Continental Pier that was damaged by fire in 1910 soon outgrew the temporary repairs that had kept it in service and its condition deteriorated to such an extent that it was decided to completely demolish it and build a new one. A contract worth £7,300 was awarded to Jackaman & Sons in April 1915 but due to the labour requirements of the War Office work on its construction was delayed and it was not until 1917 that any demolition work began. The process of building the new pier did not start until April 1919 by which time the cost had increased to £11,300. It was officially completed on 7th April 1921 and measured 310 feet long by 95 feet wide. As the main user was Trinity House it was now known as Trinity Pier.

At around the same time there was formed the Parkeston Social Club which took over the local premises of a former Sailors Rest Hostel in Parkeston village. This had been built in 1915, just north of the Power Station in Parkeston Road, as a place of recreation for off duty service personnel. It was purchased for £1,000 following a recommendation to do so at a meeting on 30th September 1920 and supported by the Company's General Manager, Mr. Thornton. By April 1921 the contents of the hostel had been purchased for £700 as had mowers and rollers for a further £220 for use on an adjacent recreation field. These costs were borne by the GER who then rented both premises to the Social Club for £260 a year. The field became known as Hamilton Park and was later equipped with a bowling green and tennis courts as well as being used as a venue for sports events and local flower shows.

In 1921 it was proposed that the SMZ should introduce sailings to Parkeston Quay though the reasoning behind the idea was not altogether one of their own. After the war the *Prins Hendrik* had re-opened their night service to Flushing on 31st January 1919 via a short lived association with the port of Gravesend. Normal services via the pre-war route to Folkestone were later resumed by the *Oranje Nassau* on the night of 23rd June 1919 followed by the return there of the *Prins Hendrik* and *Zeeland*.

In Holland the war had caused such a massive drop in transit trade and rail revenues that by 1918 the only way that both the Dutch Iron Railway Company and the Dutch State Railway could finance any necessary improvements was through their closer co-operation and for the Dutch Government to effectively underwrite both companies. Doing so would first require the Government to gain control of nearly all of Holland's railways and this they achieved in 1920. The 1921 proposal that SMZ should reinstate a day service was considered to be more advantageous if it ran from the Hook of Holland to Parkeston Quay instead of from Flushing to Folkestone. The main advantage lay with

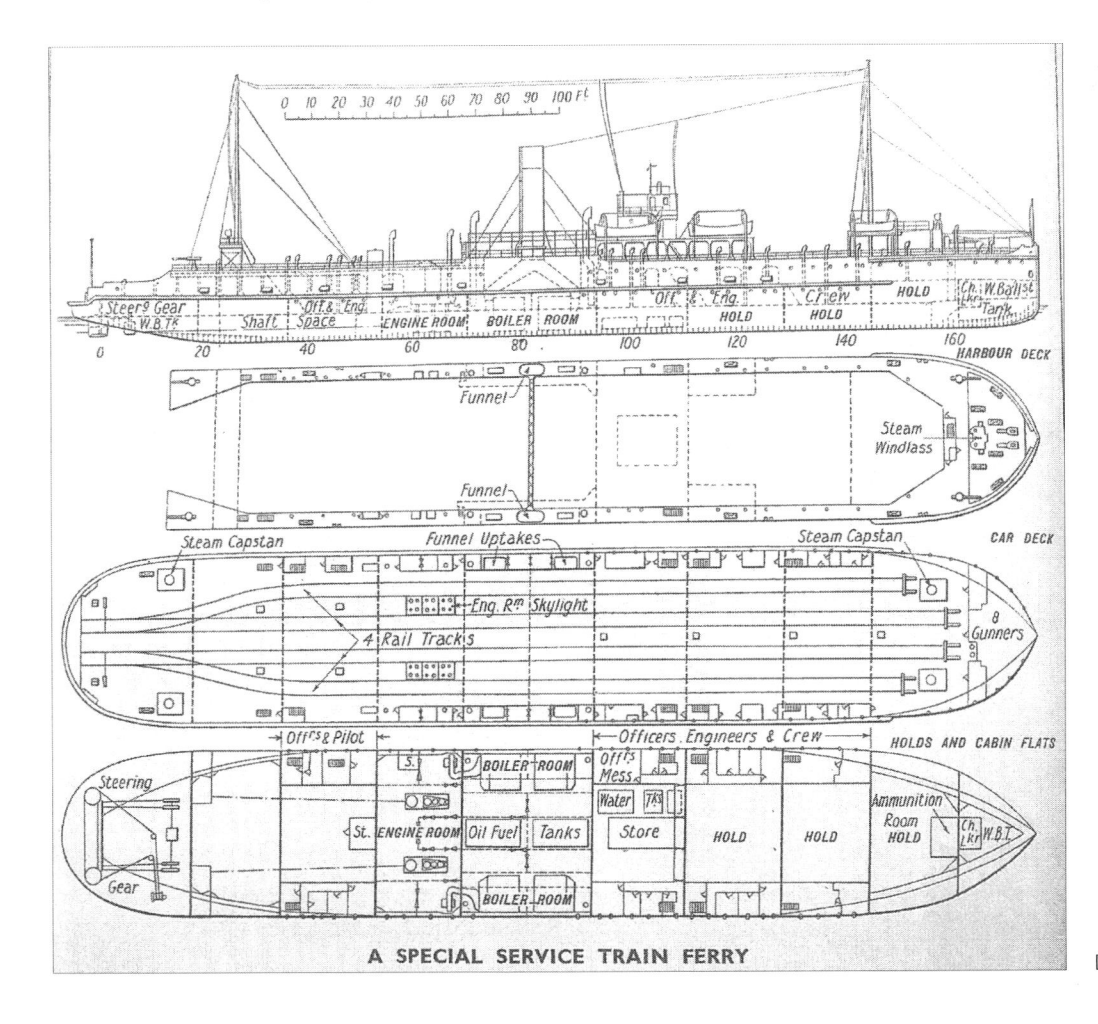

Deck plan of a train ferry. (Railway Gazette)

THE CROSS CHANNEL TRAIN FERRY STEAMER T.F.1
SIR W. G. ARMSTRONG, WHITWORTH AND CO., LIMITED, NEWCASTLE-ON-TYNE, BUILDERS

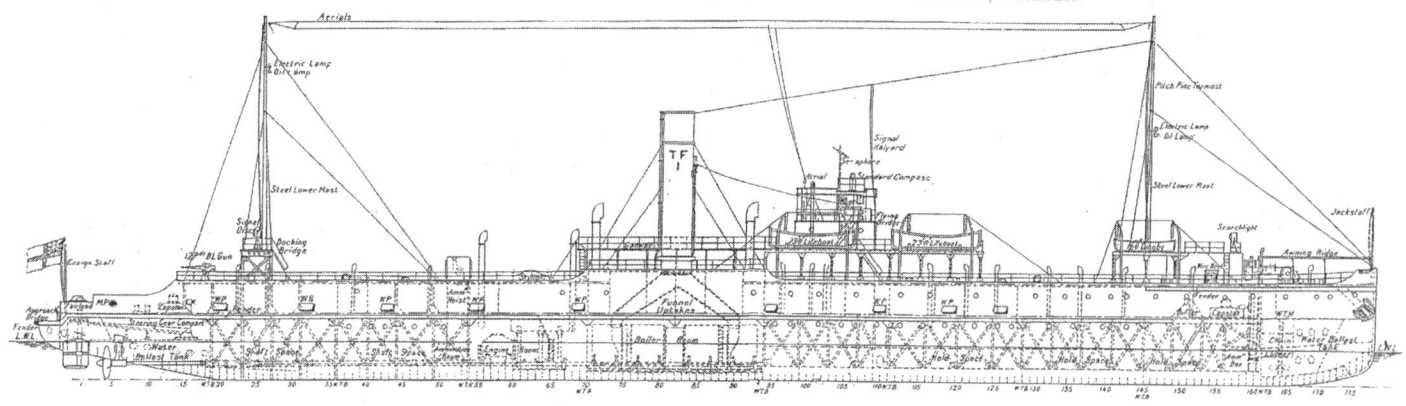

Side view plan of a train ferry.

View of the newly completed train ferry terminal at Harwich. (Robert Clow collection)

the Dutch railways who could then run both the GER and SMZ connected boat trains from just the one port thus making it the Government who effectively came up with the idea.

However after various negotiations with the SE&CR it was decided that any day service should remain as running between the existing ports of Flushing and Folkestone with a crossing time of 5½ hours. It was further decided that SMZ discontinue its night service altogether and that alternative arrangements be made by the SE&CR to run a replacement service in conjunction with suitable overnight steamers operated by the Batavier Line. This led to the inauguration of a new terminal, the Batavier Pier, at the SE&CR's West Street station at Gravesend on 15th June 1922. The SMZ day service to Folkestone had already started on 1st June, this having been the earlier proposed date for the change of route to Parkeston Quay. The owners of the Batavier Line were Wm.H. Muller & Co., a company which, in 1919, had been invited to take over as Managing Directors of SMZ. The SMZ Board then also included a Government representative on account of the Dutch Government having acquired a holding in the steamboat company worth 1 million Guilders via links dating back to when its State Railways helped create SMZ in 1875.

These re-arrangements coincided with SMZ rebuilding their fleet and from the same Fairfield plans as used in 1909 they had produced a *Prinses Juliana (II)* in 1920 and were then to follow this with a second *Mecklenburg* in 1922 to which Wm.H. Muller & Co. provided some financial assistance. Both were built at the Kon Maats de Schelde yard in Vlissingen and were distinguished from their predecessors by having their waste steam pipes hidden inside the funnels instead of being exposed as before. These new ships in turn had displaced the *Zeeland* and *Prins Hendrik* for scrapping.

Despite a depressed level of goods traffic and adverse European exchange rates the GER had, by the end of 1921, regained around 70 per cent of its pre-war passenger levels and were hopeful of soon reaching the full pre-war figures for both passengers and cargo. Various service improvements and attractions were introduced such as in October 1921 the Dutch railways added a restaurant car to their connecting train to Amsterdam Central that departed the Hook of Holland at 7.01 am to arrive in Amsterdam at 9.19 am and later, during the 1921 Christmas period, special cheap rate 15 day return tickets were available to Antwerp that left London Liverpool Street between 21st and 24th of December.

The return fares were:
London to	Antwerp	Brussels
1st Class throughout	£4.0s.0d.	£4.8s.6d.
2nd Rail/1st Steamer	£3.7s.0d.	£3.12s.0d.
2nd Class throughout	£2.13s.6d.	£2.18s.6d.

At the time the national average wage was £3.8s.0d per week which was roughly a quarter down on the highly inflated £4.11s.0d per week in 1920. The reduction was due mainly to a claw back of various war bonus payments, strikes and a depressed level of working.

For the summer of 1922, the year that 'GB' plates first came into use on motor vehicles, the Zeebrugge seasonal service started a month earlier, on 1st June, and was increased to six sailings a week with passengers still using the connecting Antwerp boat train to and from London Liverpool Street.

On 6th February 1922, just before the *Malines* entered service, the GER opened new offices at the Quai d'Herbouville in Antwerp's Quai Sud alongside which their steamers docked at 8.30 am. New warehousing space, a booking office, waiting rooms and a refreshment room were built to replace those former offices wrecked during the war by German troops. The works completed the Company's post war programme of investment in restoring the Antwerp service to its former glory which to some extent was now in preference to their Hook of Holland service. As a gesture of gratitude the Antwerp City Municipality presented the GER with a painting of the city and this was placed in the saloon on board the *Antwerp*. The arrival of these three new ships relegated the *Amsterdam* and *Frinton* to the role of reserve or relief ships.

On 1st January 1923 the London & North Eastern Railway (LNER) came into being through the merger of several railway companies operating throughout the eastern side of Britain. These were the North Eastern, the Great Northern, the Great Central, the Hull and Barnsley, the North British, the Great North of Scotland together with the Great Eastern Railway. This new organisation thus ended over 60 years of the GER's existence and Parkeston Quay now became part of a new Eastern Region division of the LNER. The new organisation inherited a local cross channel fleet consisting of eleven ships mainly deployed as follows. The two passenger routes had the *St Denis, Archangel* and *St. George* sailing to the Hook of Holland with the *Antwerp, Bruges* and *Malines* sailing to Antwerp. The Rotterdam cargo service was maintained by the *Cromer* and the *Felixstowe* whilst the *Roulers* sailed on the seasonal Zeebrugge route. The *Amsterdam* and *Frinton* were the relief ships.

As if the fates had conspired to mourn the passing of the Great Eastern Railway a fire broke out at Harwich's Halfpenny Pier, this being the pier from where the Company had originally sailed its vessels. The fire severely damaged the pier's northern end which was already in a poor state of repair following extensive wartime use by the Royal Navy. The date of the fire was July 1923 - Friday the 13th. This burnt out part of the pier remained derelict until being demolished in 1943. Some two months later the Harwich hotel was closed after having proved to be financially unviable since its recent re-opening. Whilst its closure at the end of September 1923 marked the direct ending of what the GER had started in 1863, ie the continental steamship services, the Great Eastern name was to survive at Harwich for a few years more.

Ever since the opening of their seasonal Parkeston Quay to Zeebrugge route the GER had become interested in an idea being proposed in Belgium that a cargo service might be developed utilising the concept of train ferries, a tried and tested form of transport that was already quite widespread in places such as Scandinavia.

The origins of a commercial train-ferry, literally a ferry that conveys a train or wagons upon its decks, began in Scotland. A purpose built vessel, the *Leviathan,* was completed in 1849 and was first used to cross the Firth of Forth between Granton Harbour and Burntisland on 3rd February 1850. The *Leviathan* was also used in the later opening, on 28th February 1851, of a similar service across the Firth of Tay linking Ferryport-on-Craig (Tayport) with Broughty Ferry. Thereafter this route was operated by another train ferry, the *Robert Napier*, and throughout the 30 years or so that these services ran a further four train ferries were built, these being the *Carrier* (1858), *Balbirnie* (1861), *Kinloch* (1865) and *Midlothian* (1881). All were paddle steamers. Their use across the Firth of Tay ended with the opening of the Tay railway bridge in May 1878. However following its disastrous collapse on 28th December 1878 the train ferries were reinstated across the Firth until the opening of a second Tay Bridge in June 1887. The service across the Firth of Forth ended with the opening of the Forth railway bridge in March 1890.

Another train ferry service to operate within Britain was a very short lived enterprise that the Isle of Wight Marine Transit Company started in 1885. This linked Langstone Harbour on the mainland with Brading Harbour on the island and used the *Carrier* until the route closed in 1888. It was not until the First World War that train ferries were again seen in Britain.

Their re-appearance was in response to the British Military Authorities (BMA) requiring an efficient means of moving heavy equipment and supplies abroad that would improve upon the existing methods of using cargo ships and towing barges that was both wasteful of resources and endlessly time consuming. With the merits of a train ferry system of transport having been studied and approved an order worth £560,000 was placed by the British Government on 17th February 1917 for three new purpose built vessels. Somewhat plainly named as *Train Ferry No. 1, Train Ferry No. 2* and *Train Ferry No. 3* they were delivered in camouflage paint and manned by the Inland Water Transport Division of the Royal Engineers. Each was armed with 4 twelve pounder guns and anti-submarine measures.

Two routes were chosen for their use. One was between Southampton and Dieppe, a distance of 113 nautical miles (n.miles), which opened in December 1917 using just the one ship, *Train Ferry No. 3,* with sailings every other day. The other route was a much shorter one of 31½ n.miles between Richborough and Calais. The French terminal was constructed at the town end of the Bassin Carnot which was accessed through a lock. This route opened on 10th February 1918 using two ships, *Train Ferry No. 1* and *Train Ferry No. 2,* each making a round trip sailing every day. Towards the end of the war a limited service ran from Richborough on the 47 n.miles route into Dunkirk and at the war's very end a fourth ship, the *Leonard*, was acquired from Canada and put on an additional route between Southampton and Cherbourg. She entered service on 6th November 1918, re-named *T.F.4.*, just days before the Armistice and remained there until the Southampton services ceased in March 1919.

By the middle of December 1918 the military had exported from Richborough goods and stores equal to 185,000 tons in 6,200 wagons plus 150 railway locomotives, 685 tanks and 4 railway mounted guns, the latter of which weighed an average of 300 tons apiece. The movement of such a large quantity of materials and the diversity of cargoes carried proved beyond doubt the advantages that using a train ferry offered.

The direct involvement of the War Department at Richborough ceased in December 1919 though train ferry services continued until 21st January 1921 to allow for the repatriation of military equipment to Britain. Thereafter the facilities there, as well as at Southampton, were left intact for use by any commercially interested parties and although some were attracted services at Richborough gradually declined throughout 1921 with the last ambulance train being landed there on 5th September 1921. The port closed in 1922. Thereafter the official receiver approved a shipbroker's offer of £125,000 for all three vessels and the steelwork from all the five terminals. The ships were then laid up in Immingham with their future undecided though one of them, *Train Ferry No. 2*, was used on several sailings between Dublin and Liverpool during 1922 in connection with the evacuation of British troops and military material from Ireland. Her last sailing was from Dublin on 19th December loaded with motor vehicles.

Back in 1918 the 'Syndicat Belgo-Anglais' had been formed with the object of organizing a regular commercial train ferry service between Britain and Belgium. Many issues were raised such as which ports, ships and even which railway gauge to use along with the matter of how the project would be funded. As time went by a more ambitious suggestion was made in January 1921 by a Swedish Naval Architect, Mr Hock, who proposed that they be used on a route between Immingham and Gothenburg.

In 1922 the GER first became interested in the Belgian syndicate's scheme and eventually it was decided that Zeebrugge and Harwich were the most suitable ports for such a venture. Richborough was deemed as being the most unsuitable as it was liable to silting up and this was the reason why the local railway company, the SE&CR, never took over the running of the service. In the first week of January 1923 it was announced that Belgian financiers and the firm of Wolfe, Barry and Company had signed an agreement to run a train ferry service between Harwich and Zeebrugge. However Harwich meant Harwich itself, not Parkeston Quay, and so after an absence of 40 years a railway operated shipping service would be returning to the town in the form of an international train ferry route out of Britain.

To run the service two new companies were formed. Although the region's railway company was, since 1st January 1923 the LNER, the British operator of the new service was named The Great Eastern Train Ferries Ltd (GETFL), of 17 Eldon Street, London EC2, and was set up on 14th March to operate the ships and the port terminal at Harwich. The Company was funded via the issue of 400,000 £1 shares. The Chairman was Lord Daryngton and the LNER were represented on the Board by Lord Ailwyn, a former Director of the GER. The other Directors were Sir George Stapylton Barnes, Sir Cyril K. Butler, Mr. Gerald T.J. Bevan and Mr. Hubert Robyn. Messrs Rowe and Pitman acted as the Company's brokers.

The GETFL's Capital Account of £400,000 was divided up in order that £200,000 be spent on the purchase of the three train ferries and the rail connecting bridges or linkspans at both Richborough and Southampton, £60,000 for transporting the landing stage from Southampton and re-building it at Harwich, £17,000 to set up an agency for the Company in Belgium and £33,000 for a range of legal expenses. This left £90,000 for use as working capital.

In Belgium the Societe Belgo-Anglaise des Ferry Boats S.A. (SBA) was founded on 16th April with a capital of 3 million Belgian Francs (Bfr) of which half was subscribed to by the GETFL. The first Managing Director of the SBA was the aforementioned Mr. Hubert Robyn who had been the most active within the original Syndicat Belgo-Anglais.

Though control of the service was entirely vested with the LNER each of the two founding companies were to contribute something towards the project. In simple terms this meant that the GETFL provided the ships, by acquiring them from Messrs. Bevan Churchill and Co., and the SBA provided the rolling stock by acquiring hundreds of specially adapted 12-ton wagons originally owned by the BMA and which formed part of a fleet of 15,000 wagons subsequently purchased by the Belgian Government.

Construction of the train ferry terminals began immediately. At Zeebrugge the 100 feet long linkspan from Richborough was re-installed behind the gates of the Visart Lock at the entrance to the Bruges Canal. Offices and customs examination facilities were located close by and the whole works cost around 1 million Bfr. At Harwich the site of its new terminal was west of the Continental Pier and linked to the Harwich branch line by a set of railway lines leading off sidings from alongside the station. Both the site and the tracks were provided by the LNER without charge. The marshalling and storage of wagons would be undertaken in the sidings at Parkeston Quay.

The terminal at Harwich was to be transported from Southampton by sea on board two barges towed side by side, the *Seathwaite* and the *Grisedale*. The various linkspans had been built of differing lengths due to the tidal variations encountered at each port and the one at Southampton was 120 feet long. When fitted at Harwich this would allow for the shunting of rail wagons to be carried out on a rising or falling gradient of up to 1 in 20. The linkspan was placed on board the *Seathwaite* lengthways and rested on timber baulks supported by scaffolding. Its side members were left overhanging the edge of the barge whilst part of its 200 tons weight was supported by being placed upon the *Grisedale*. The *Grisedale* also carried the lifting towers or gantry, its machinery and counter weights. These weighed in at a further 130 tons.

The barges left Southampton on 2nd September 1923 in the tow of the tug *Plumgarth*. Two days later, on the 4th, the cargo on both barges moved when they were about two and a half miles off the Cork Lightship. After attempts at retrieving the situation failed the barges sank. Early in October the linkspan was recovered and beached at Harwich. Unfortunately it was now 200 tons of an upside down structure that could not be righted. The only solution was to have it dismantled and to reassemble it on the required site and this was carried out by the company of Christian and Neilsen. As for the gantry and other machinery these were deemed to be unsalvageable and were later blown up. The one from Richborough was then brought round in replacement making the completed terminal at Harwich a combination of a Richborough gantry and a Southampton linkspan. In addition the berth was equipped with two reinforced arms or jetties. These were set upon steel piles and were of unequal length. The longer arm, on the western side, was 450 feet long whilst a shorter eastern arm was 110 feet long. Between them they enclosed a narrow basin just wide enough for the ships to dock stern first.

All shore structures were practically identical with the required machinery installed at the top of a gantry that consisted of two steel towers, measuring 42 feet high and 5 feet 6 inches square, and placed 36 feet 6 inches apart between centres that acted as supports to a bridge. Here was housed a 20 hp electric motor that powered a winding drum connected to four steel wire ropes that worked over pulleys to adjust the position of the linkspan relative to the ferry. If the power supply failed it was possible for two men to work the double tracked linkspan by hand. Whenever a ship was in its berth the linkspan would be lowered so as to sit upon a conical bollard, known as the pin, situated between the rail tracks on the ship's stern. Once in place the correct alignment of the railway tracks was secured and any sideways movement restricted to a list of about 5 degrees in either direction. Docking was normally to take only twenty to thirty minutes.

As regards the three ships purchased by the GETFL, *Train Ferry No.1*, *Train Ferry No. 2* and *Train Ferry No. 3* were all identical and built to a design by Sir W. G. Armstrong-Whitworth. *Train Ferry No. 1* and *Train Ferry No. 2* were built at the Low Walker yard of Armstrong, Whitworth & Co. Ltd. at Wallsend whilst *Train Ferry No. 3* was built on the Clyde by Fairfield Shipbuilding & Engineering Co. Ltd. in Govan. All three were registered in London.

Overall each were 363 feet 6 inches long with a beam of 61 feet 6 inches and with a full load on board had a draught of 9 feet forward and 10 feet aft. Their gross tonnage was a little under 2,700 tons and the total cargo capacity was 850 tons. Four single ended oil fired boilers, placed in pairs either side of the ship between which were two fuel tanks with a capacity of 80 tons, fed two sets of triple expansion engines of around 400 nhp. Steel hulled, twin screwed with twin rudders the ships could manage a maximum speed of 14 knots and a service speed of 12 knots. Each ship was to be converted from oil fired to coal fired before entering service at Harwich.

Two thin elliptical funnels were placed amidships at the extreme sides of the vessel and linked together by a steel lattice girder. Below and slightly forward of this was the Captain's bridge which spanned four rail tracks located on the one main deck. Here were 2 centre tracks each 310 feet long and 2 side tracks each 230 feet long that provided space for carrying 54 loaded 12-ton wagons or their equivalent in other forms of rolling stock. The four tracks converged to just two at the stern over which the wagons were hauled on and off by steam locomotives. If not carrying wagons and the rails were packed flush with wooden boards the deck space was sufficient for loading between 50 and 60 motor lorries.

The hull had nine watertight compartments and below the main deck was found all the officer and crew accommodation. During wartime conditions these would have housed up to 46 military personnel. Also under deck were a number of water ballast tanks used for trimming the ship during loading and unloading. Those at the extreme forward end were of 160 tons, at the aft end 210 tons, plus two side tanks of 40 tons each. Four steam capstans, two forward and two aft, each capable of exerting a pull of 20 tons, helped moor the ship and if required could also be utilised for transferring wagons on and off the ferry.

The opening ceremony of the Harwich to Zeebrugge Train Ferry service took place on 24th April 1924 and was conducted by H.R.H. Prince George, later to become the Duke of Kent. The Prince, his party and guests travelled by special train that left London Liverpool Street at 9.50 am and arrived at Harwich Town Station at 11.23 am. There the Prince was met by the Mayor, Clr. Lucy Hill, members of the Council and various officials of the Great Eastern Train Ferries Ltd.. His Royal Highness, in full naval dress, was then accompanied by the High Sheriff of Essex, Sir Carne-Rasch; and inspected a Guard of Honour formed by the Harwich Battery of the Royal Garrison Artillery, the Suffolk Coast Defence, Girl Guides and Boy Scouts.

After a tour of the terminal the Prince went aboard *Train Ferry No. 2* and from the Captain's bridge watched a number of wagons being shunted on. Having returned to the long arm jetty he then turned a little brass wheel that set the machinery in motion to raise the linkspan. To the sound of the British and Belgian national anthems *Train Ferry No. 2* then sailed out of its berth to Zeebrugge. On board were the wagons carrying general goods, agricultural implements and Royal Mail parcels and post.

Once the ferry had left Prince George and a host of invited guests departed Harwich on board the LNER paddle steamer *Norfolk* at 12.15 pm for a 10 minute trip over to Felixstowe. From there they were taken by car to the Felix Hotel for a celebration luncheon that commenced at 1.00 pm. The GER had earlier purchased this hotel in July 1920 for £3,227. Unfortunately Lord Daryngton, Chairman of the GETFL was unable to attend due to illness but amongst the guests was Colonel A. J. Barry who had long enthused the idea of a Harwich train ferry and was now the Company's Consulting Engineer.

In his speech proposing a toast to the 'The Train Ferry Service', Prince George talked about the expectations of success and that Harwich, which had served the Navy so well throughout the war, should be further connected to a country for which we bear such warm and friendly feelings. In reply, and on behalf of the LNER, Sir Hugh Bell spoke of the importance of continental trade and hoped the new service might be regarded '*as the beginning of a long career of satisfactory usefulness to the world*', this being a wonderful phrase that the Victorian promoters of Parkeston Quay would surely have been proud to have thought of themselves. At the conclusion of events the Royal party returned to London via a special train that was to leave Felixstowe Town station at 3.50 pm and arrive back at Liverpool Street station at 5.55 pm. That night a large number of GETFL officials sailed from Parkeston Quay to Zeebrugge on board the *Roulers* in order to attend a similar opening ceremony in Belgium the following day. This was officiated over by Prince Leopold, Duke of Brabant, and the occasion was later celebrated in the Palace Hotel on Zeebrugge seafront.

The second sailing from Harwich was undertaken by *Train Ferry No. 3* on 25th April, the day after the service opened, and sailings became daily except on Sundays. When *Train Ferry No. 1* entered service on 17th July the schedules allowed for any two ships to be in use with one in reserve or off on maintenance.

The distance between Harwich and Zeebrugge was 84 n.miles. The time scheduled for the overnight sea passage was about eight hours with a berth to berth time of between nine and ten hours. Arrival time at Harwich was 7.30 am and at Zeebrugge it was 9.00 am. The initial expectation was that each ship would carry around 480 tons of cargo per trip and that the service in total would carry roughly 160,000 tons in its first year of operation. In the event of severe or prolonged disruption it was noted that an additional facility existed in the form of a temporary train ferry berth at Immingham which had already been used for the conveyance of rolling stock to the Continent. The LNER undertook to operate the train ferries for a period of 30 years on the basis of cost price plus a share of the profits. The first £24,000 of net profit would go to the GETFL, the next £24,000 to the LNER and any balance was to be divided equally between the two Companies.

The service was only ever designed to carry goods and cargo and a major attraction was to be the reduced level of any loading and unloading and the subsequent reduction in damage, breakages and losses as compared to the man handling of such

Programme of events for the opening of the Harwich to Zeebrugge Train Ferry Service by HRH Prince George - 24th April 1924. (Robert Clow collection)

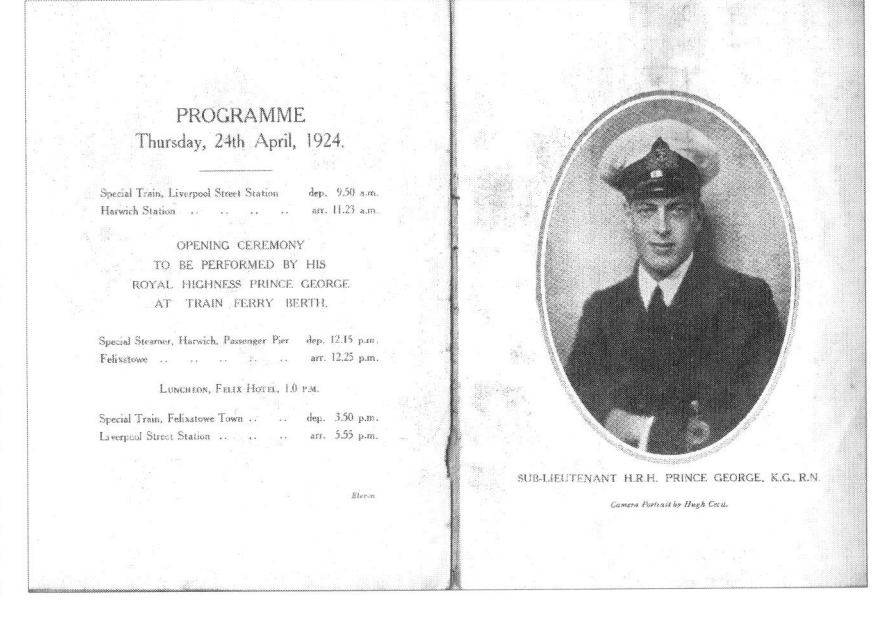

items. It was estimated that 40% of the cost of shipping goods across the English Channel was being spent, or wasted, on transhipping them first from wagons to steamer and then back again to wagons. Such a saving in the amount of handling required together with an increase in the speed of transit would bring about delivery times now measured in days rather than weeks. This was to be a great benefit to the Continental growers of fruit and vegetables as well as to manufacturers of delicate items such as pottery and glassware. Also all sorts of oversized goods such as heavy machinery could now be carried in ways not possible by conventional cargo ships.

One country that was highly supportive of the service was Italy and its representatives Societe del Ferry Boats Per l'Inghilterra located in Milan. They agitated for, as did others, for a system of through tariff charges to and from England which had long been delayed due to 'a stumbling block being the aloofness of the French Railway Companies'. With a through rail route going via new tunnels recently built in Switzerland, that bypassed much of France, trade over such a long distance was now a more practical proposition. Arrangements were made for the local examination of wagons by H.M. Customs at Parkeston Quay though a special dispensation was granted for suitably sealed imported wagons to be examined inland at London's Bishopsgate depot. For this the LNER were first required to put up a bond to cover any lost payment of duties through theft or other irregularities. This new method of transport did however provide customers with some relief on duty payments in general as with less packing involved in protecting the goods there was less duty to pay on items charged by weight.

Despite all the advantages the initial carryings fell way short of that predicted and only 26,148 tons of goods were conveyed by the end of 1924. It soon became apparent though that imports from abroad were going to outweigh exports from Britain. Also apparent was the wide variety of cargoes being carried. In June 1925, when motor vehicles were a rarity on board ships, the train ferries brought over a trial consignment of 500 Fiat cars imported all the way from Milan. On 9th January 1926 some 40 officers and men of the 70th Medium Battery Royal Artillery brought back around 100 horses in German rail wagons which were then let out and exercised before being put into British horse boxes and moved to Bournemouth. Later that month, on 24th January, a crowd gathered at 8.00 am to watch the feeding of 70 lions which were on their way from London Olympia to Brussels. In time the train ferry service was to gain an enviable reputation for reliability, even through the worst kind of weather conditions, and this led to a steady increase in traffic levels.

Elsewhere other changes in ships and technology were soon to be introduced by DFDS whose Esbjerg to Parkeston Quay service in 1923 had carried 23,000 passengers and 16,300 tons of cargo on board ships that were in need of replacing. The *Dronning Maud* had been modified from domestic to North Sea service the previous year and had since re-joined the Esbjerg to Parkeston Quay route on 13th May 1922. Her sister ship, the *Kong Haakon*, had likewise been modified slightly earlier, in September 1921, and from then on had been regularly sailing on the Esbjerg route. In 1923 the *Ficaria* had resumed her pre-war schedule of sailings between Esbjerg and either Parkeston Quay or Grimsby and these were being supplemented by those of the *Flora*, *Frigga*, *Tjaldur*, *Vidar*, *Rhone* and *Margrethe*. Now more modern tonnage was on its way via an order placed at the Elsinore Yard of Helsingors.

This saw a new 2,762 grt passenger ship launched as the appropriately named *Parkeston*. She departed Esbjerg on her maiden voyage to Parkeston Quay on 8th August 1925 as the 'm.v' *Parkeston* being as she was DFDS's first diesel engined motor vessel and the world's first diesel driven short sea passenger ship. She was powered by two Burmeister and Wain 6 cylinder 4 stroke single acting engines able to provide a service speed of 15 knots and was a major step forward for the company of 'Forende Line of Copenhagen Royal Danish Mail Steamers'.

The *Parkeston* was the first of four sister ships that would eventually arrive on the Esbjerg to Parkeston Quay route over the next seven years. Except for slight differences on board between the number of First and Third class passengers each ship was basically made up of four holds, two foreward and two aft, above which were two decks of passenger accommodation located amidships. They had straight stems and counter sterns, a raked funnel and were fitted with 2 pole masts around which were 2-ton and 6-ton derricks forward and 3-ton derricks aft. Up to 20 crane loaded cars could be carried in the holds where the total cargo space was 88,000 cubic feet of which 50,000 was refrigerated.

On the *Parkeston* there was First class accommodation for 124, either in single or double cabins, plus a further 88 in Third class cabins that were situated further aft. Each class had its own dining saloon. Accommodation for the crew was on the Awning Deck with lower ranks in the forecastle and officers amidships. The Promenade Deck contained a lounge, a smoking-room and a comfortable music room complete with grand piano.

The service became daily except Sundays with departures from Parkeston Quay being at 10.00 pm and arrival at Esbjerg not before 8.00 pm the next day. For many of those travelling to Copenhagen they might well have spent the night in Esbjerg and caught a train the next morning. For those travelling deeper into Scandinavia there was the option of a departing sleeper car train to Copenhagen with connections

HRH Prince George on the bridge of *Train Ferry No.2*. (Railway Gazette, May 1924)

through to Stockholm and Oslo. Most people took the train as those travelling by car were still few and far between. Normally only a handful of cars travelled each trip and these would have been loaded on board by crane. If stowed in the hold they avoided either being covered by tarpaulins that would chafe the paintwork in rough weather or left out uncovered and exposed to the corrosive salt air. Cars had to arrive at least two hours before sailing time and any petrol in them was drained off into canisters and placed in a special store to be collected upon arrival.

The *Parkeston,* which replaced the *Dronning Maud,* was followed into service by the *Jylland* which arrived at Parkeston Quay on 27th June 1926 following her own maiden voyage from Esbjerg. Although the *Dronning Maud* was returned to again sailing out of Copenhagen she was not entirely displaced from sailing out of Parkeston Quay and she remained an irregular visitor on the Esbjerg route up to and throughout the 1930s.

The 1920s saw the first beginnings of cruising out of Harwich harbour with the arrival of Bergen Lines *Meteor*. At 346 feet long in the style of a clipper ship she was originally built in 1904 by Blohm & Voss of Hamburg for the Hamburg America Line. She was acquired by Britain as part of war reparations in 1919 and used on repatriation work worldwide before being sold to Det Bergenske Dampskibsselskab or Bergen Line in 1921. She then became a cruise ship for up to 250 passengers who enjoyed summer season trips from Parkeston Quay to the fjords of Norway.

Such was her success that Bergen Line ordered a new and larger ship that when delivered in 1927 looked somewhat similar to the *Meteor* in overall style and design. The new ship was named *Stella Polaris* and was built by A.B. Gotaverken of Gothenburg. At over 5,200 grt and 360 feet long she was diesel powered by two sets of eight cylinder B&W engines that had her cruising at around 16 knots. She took over the fortnightly summer visits to Parkeston Quay in 1927 and luxuriously combined the traditional amenities of an ocean liner with the intimate charm of a private yacht. She had a crew of 130 to look after just 200 passengers. Gourmet meals were served at one leisurely sitting and the entertainment included nightly dancing, motion pictures and swimming in the outdoor pool. All cabins were equipped with a bath tub and overhead shower unit.

The first new passenger vessel that the LNER had built was the *Brightlingsea*, a small wooden hulled motor ship used on the harbour ferry service, but their first 'full-size' ship for use out of Parkeston Quay was the cargo vessel *Sheringham*. She was built by Earle's of Hull and would turn out to be the last that the yard would supply the port. Her first day in service was on the Rotterdam route on 15th September 1926 when sailings were increased to five days a week. She replaced the *Frinton*.

The aforementioned SMZ day service between Flushing and Folkestone lasted only until 31st December 1926. The next day they were sailing from Parkeston Quay after having earlier agreed terms with the LNER on a change of port and a pooling of revenues. The agreement provided SMZ with a share of the overall revenue yielded by passenger traffic on both the day and night services to Holland with a separate agreement covering freight traffic. The move severed links going back over 50 years between SMZ and the LC&DR, the SE&CR and its successor the Southern Railway and was the result of a financially disastrous decision for SMZ when, in June 1926, the British Board of Agriculture banned the import of Dutch meat of which SMZ were carrying around 35,000 tons a year

The arrangement at Parkeston Quay was that the LNER would continue to run its night service to the Hook of Holland and the SMZ would run its new day service to Flushing, the distance from Parkeston Quay being roughly the same as it was from Folkestone. Doing so meant that in addition to the LNER's usual timetable of night departures and morning arrivals there would now be the SMZ's timetable of day departures and evening arrivals. The train departure time from London to catch the SMZ daytime sailing remained at 10.00 am though now it left from Liverpool Street instead of from London Victoria. Travellers using either route to Holland continued to benefit from excellent railway connections into Germany and beyond.

The SMZ's first day boat sailing from Parkeston Quay was undertaken by the veteran steamer *Oranje Nassau* on 1st January 1927 at 11.30 am. She had earlier sailed light the previous day from Flushing and arrived around 3.00 pm complete with a celebratory group of Dutch Folk Dancers. The first SMZ ship to commercially arrive from Flushing was the *Mecklenburg (II)* at 6.30 pm that new year's day.

The original intention was for SMZ to depart Flushing at 11.30 am on a daily basis and arrive at Parkeston Quay at 5.30 pm from where any passengers travelling to London could do so via a luxury train complete with restaurant car facilities that left the port at 6.10 pm to arrive in London Liverpool Street at 7.45 pm. As events developed these times were amended slightly along with other changes that affected the existing boat trains.

The new luxury express that connected with the SMZ service was titled the 'Flushing Continental' whilst the existing express that connected with the overnight LNER sailings to Holland, and which had hitherto been known as the 'Continental Express' up until 1914 and the 'Hook of Holland Express' since 1919, was again re-named as the 'Hook Continental'. The express that served sailings to Belgium was revived as the 'Antwerp Continental' in 1928 and during the summer season this train continued to be used by passengers travelling via the route to Zeebrugge.

Although the names had changed the two LNER connecting boat trains had retained their traditional departure times from London Liverpool Street of 8.30 pm for Holland and 8.40 pm for Belgium. In 1927 both were allowed just 82 minutes to reach Parkeston Quay and thus at 9.52 pm and 10.02 pm the port was a veritable hive of activity as passengers transferred to their respective ships whilst the rear baggage vans of each train were being detached and shunted round to the ship's side. The times of these two trains back to London were 6.55 am and 7.00 am respectively.

By the winter of 1927 the advertised times of the 'Hook Continental' were showing a journey time of 87 minutes from London and services to and from Holland as being:

View of a train ferry wagon deck looking aft. Although the carriage of motor cars generally was still in its infancy this deck was already being referred to as the 'car deck'. (Robert Clow collection)

Impression of *Train Ferry No. 3* departing the Harwich train ferry terminal. (The Book of the Railway, J.R. Hind)

Early poster advertising the Harwich to Zeebrugge train ferry service.

Further examples of early posters advertising the Harwich to Zeebrugge train ferry service.

LNER (Hook Continental)		SMZ (Day Continental)	
Dep. London (L St)	8.30 pm	Dep. London (L.St)	10.00 am
Arr. P. Quay	9.57 pm	Arr. P. Quay	11.25 am
Dep. P. Quay	10.15 pm	Dep. P. Quay	11.30 am
Arr. HvH	6.00 am	Arr. Flushing	5.30 pm
Dep. HvH	11.00 pm	Dep. Flushing	12.35 pm
Arr. P. Quay	6.15 am	Arr. P. Quay	6.05 am
Dep. P. Quay	6.55 am	Dep. P. Quay	6.35 pm
Arr. London (L.St)	8.38 am	Arr. London (L St)	8.20 pm

The fares to Holland were the same by either route with cabins subject to an additional charge as were a number of 'exceedingly interesting tours' that were offered by arrangement at Flushing.

Fares from P. Quay to:	Single		Return	
	1st Class	2nd Class	1st Class	2nd Class
HvH or Flushing	£2.4s.0d.	£1.14s.0d.	£4.8s.0d.	£3.8s.0d.
Rotterdam	£2.6s.4d.	£1.15s.10d.	£4.12s.2d.	£3.11s.2d.
(From London add)	14s.6d.	6s.6d.	£1.9s.0d	13s.0d.

In addition to the boat trains from London was the 'North Country Continental' which continued its role as a luxury long distance express service. Over the years the journey times to major stations such as Manchester and Liverpool were reduced by about 25 minutes each way and the arrival time at Parkeston Quay brought forward from 9.42 pm to 9.12 pm. Being ahead of the London boat trains this was a less hectic time to arrive at the port as was the morning departure north when it was retimed from 7.02 am to 7.25 am. A direct service still ran through to Edinburgh and Glasgow at times little different from 40 years earlier though both cities could be reached far quicker if changing at York. A through coach that left Glasgow at 8.35 am and Edinburgh at 10.15 am had to wait at York for over an hour before joining the train that made up the 'North Country Continental' heading south. From the late 1920s onwards the following times were fairly standard.

Dep. P. Quay	7.25 am	Dep. Liverpool	2.20 pm
Arr. York	1.06 pm	Dep. Manchester	3.10 pm
Arr. Manchester	1.55 pm	Dep. York	3.30 pm
Arr. Liverpool	2.43 pm	Arr. P. Quay	9.12 pm

The SMZ dayboat service was strengthened by the arrival of the *Prinses Juliana (II)*. As both she and the *Mecklenburg (II)* had come from the same plans as used on the sister ships lost in the war these 3,000 grt vessels were equally stylish and elegant with their counter sterns, twin raked funnels and pole masts. For their time they were rather unique inasmuch as although they were high speed cross channel steamers they were still fitted with piston engines. They arrived at Parkeston Quay as ships built, or rather advertised, as the finest, safest and most up to date vessels that could be constructed with spacious sheltered promenade decks offering a day crossing that was cheerful, enjoyable and very restful. On board were five decks of accommodation with roomy saloons, ladies rooms, smoking rooms, vestibules and an excellent dining saloon service. Cabins, or rather state-rooms, were provided that varied from those with either one or two berths located on the Saloon Deck with larger ones on the upper deck. More upmarket were the beautiful Suites-de-Luxe which had a roomy drawing room, bedroom and lavatory whilst the most exclusive cabin was the Grand Cabin-de-Luxe that had its own lobby, a large sitting room, a bedroom, lavatory and bath. Charges for cabins varied hugely. In 1924 these had ranged between 5s. and £4.0s.0d.

Passengers travelling with SMZ were reassured that 'the safety appliances are in excess of Lloyds requirements', 'bulkheads divide the ship into eleven watertight compartments which make the steamers practically unsinkable' and 'Moreover the steamers are so fitted as to permit the lifeboats being lowered on the lee side, if desired, even though heavy lists occur. This unique invention is only workable on board steamers with clear decks, such as those of the Zeeland Steamship Company'.

In 1927 times were hard and Harwich was not immune from an era of industrial depression and unemployment. The Council opened up a soup kitchen in the town as merchant ships lay rusting in the River Stour beyond Parkeston. Though the port suffered a reduction in trade, and men were laid off, the arrival of SMZ had led to a new round of capital expenditure on a quay where apparently nothing new had been seen since 1915. For a grand total of £877.12s.10d. the LNER provided a new mooring dolphin, an electric

Right: A 1920s view of disembarking passengers walking along a wooden decked Parkeston Quay towards the Customs Hall. They are seen here passing underneath one of the coaling shutes. (Robert Clow collection)

Far right: An ornate staircase onboard the SMZ vessel *Mecklenburg (II)*. (Robert Clow collection)

trolley with three trailers and additional accommodation set aside for Customs. Meanwhile the train ferry service from Harwich had become a hugely successful operation, despite the recession in overall trade, and in 1927 it carried a total of 156,320 tons of goods.

There had been some other investments such as that which followed an agreement signed on 10th July 1924 whereby the LNER would supply electricity to the Harwich Corporation from its power house at Parkeston. New equipment and turbo-alternators were installed as a result but in 1926 came the founding of a national grid for the supply of electricity which would ultimately see the end of numerous local suppliers throughout the country. It was not until 1933 that power generation at Parkeston would finally cease yet such was the array of local equipment then in place that the station remained in use as a control and distribution centre for many years thereafter.

On the ships a token level of investment came after an announcement was made on 28th June 1928 that the *Antwerp*, *Bruges* and *Malines* were all to be supplied with gramophones. Such apparatus might well have helped pass the time especially during the following winter when the river at Harwich froze over and between 11th and 15th February the LNER service to Antwerp was suspended due to severe icing in the River Scheldt. Even a week later when sailings had resumed at their usual time of departing Parkeston Quay at 10.10 pm the ships were still not arriving in Antwerp until 10.00 am as sailing safely on past Flushing was only possible in daylight.

The tail end of the 1920s was to see the start of a fleet modernisation period with the first to arrive being a further addition for DFDS. On 26th April 1929 the *Esbjerg* arrived at Parkeston Quay following her maiden voyage from Esbjerg. She was the third in the series of sister ships that already included the *Parkeston* and the *Jylland*. Likewise the LNER were also acquiring new ships of their own to replace those on the Hook of Holland service which were now over 20 years old. An order had been placed with John Brown for three new ships which, although not as elegant perhaps as those of the SMZ, would nonetheless become most impressive additions to the fleet.

The first to arrive was the *Vienna* which appeared in early July 1929. On her way round from the Clyde she made courtesy calls in Amsterdam on 12th and 13th and then Rotterdam on 13th and 14th before making her maiden voyage, overnight from Parkeston Quay to the Hook of Holland, on 15th July 1929. Her sailing was duplicated by the *St. George* which then returned light. The *St. George* later left Parkeston Quay on 16th October 1929 bound for the breakers yard at Blyth. In doing so she was following the fate of the *Amsterdam* which had been sent there in December 1928 having ended her days on the Rotterdam cargo service.

Two views of the Grand Cabin-de-luxe onboard the SMZ vessels *Mecklenburg (II)* and *Prinses Juliana (II)*. (SMZ)

The arrival of DFDS's new motor ship *Esbjerg* upon the completion of her maiden voyage from Esbjerg - 26th April 1929. (NRM collection)

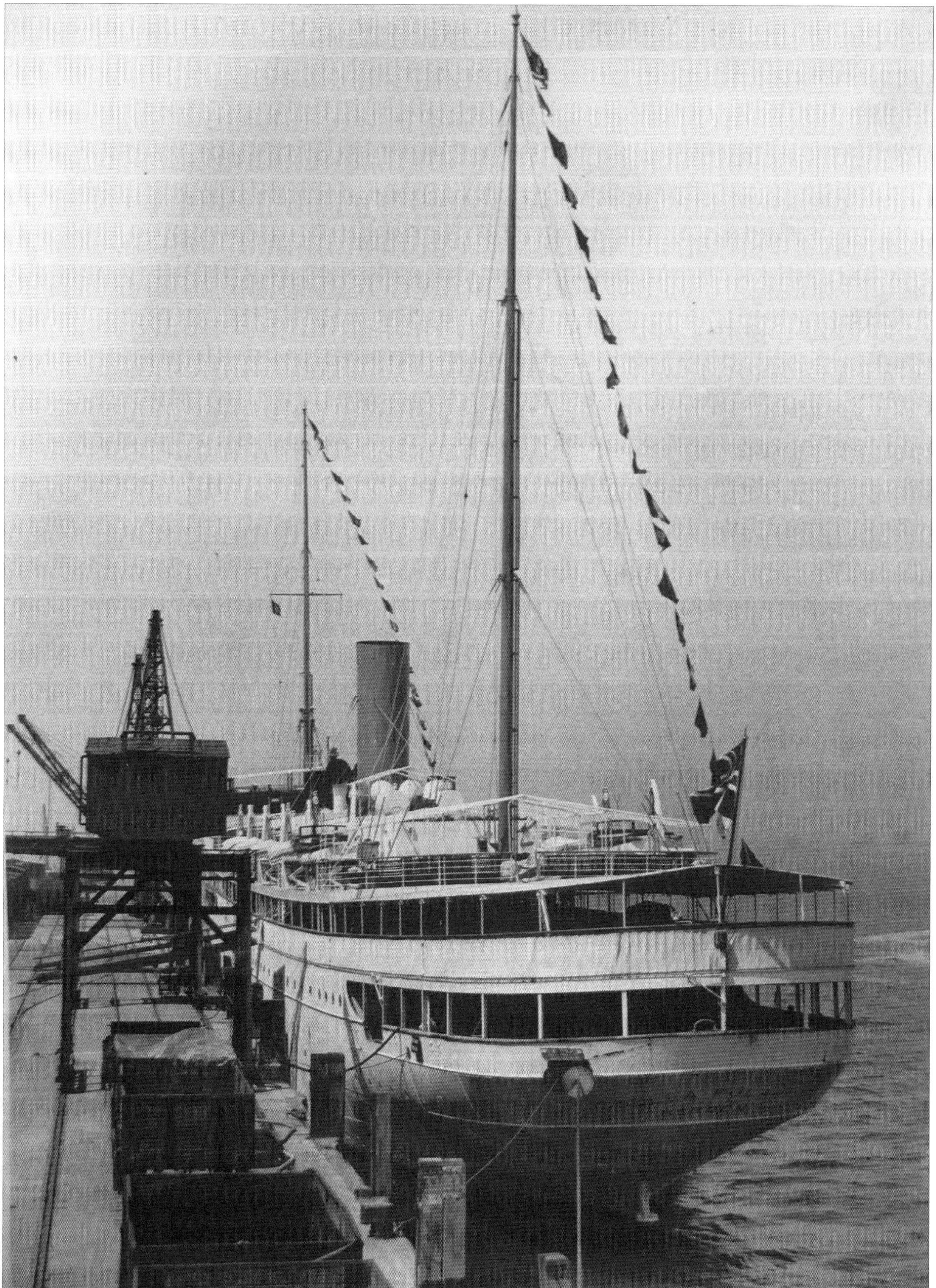

THE 1930s

The introduction of the LNER's *Vienna* was followed by that of the *Prague* which first arrived at Parkeston Quay on 22nd February 1930. Her maiden voyage was to the Hook of Holland on 1st March and in doing so she took over the sailings of the *St. Denis* whose last trip was on 28th February. The third sister ship, the *Amsterdam*, arrived on 13th March and she made her maiden voyage on 26th April 1930. The *Amsterdam* in turn released the *Archangel* whose last trip had been on 21st April.

The *St. Denis* and *Archangel* were later placed on the summer season service to Zeebrugge and together they operated the usual six sailings per week. They took the place of the *Roulers* which had earlier left Parkeston Quay on 23rd March for breaking up in Blyth. Both *St. Denis* and *Archangel* would also be used as off season relief ships making the occasional trip to the Hook of Holland.

The *Vienna*, *Prague* and *Amsterdam* were the largest and most luxurious cross channel ships of their type and time with each being capable of carrying 708 passengers. They were built substantially larger than their predecessors, at over 4,200 grt, and overall they measured 366 feet by 50 feet with a service speed of 21 knots. Each had spacious entrance lounges and were panelled throughout in polished wood to enhance the elegant nature of their interiors. Likewise the cabins, laid out over four decks, were equally enhanced with all having washbasins, hot and cold water, electric reading lamps and were ventilated by currents of fresh and warm air which could be controlled as required by the occupants.

First class cabin accommodation was provided for 427 passengers in a mixture of single berth cabins, some of which had inter-connecting doors, and cabins fitted with double berths. Those in Second class had a choice between two and four berthed cabins located aft comprising a total of 126 berths. Forward on the Promenade Deck were four Cabin-de-Luxe that emulated those of the SMZ with each being fitted with two cot beds, a private toilet and shared bathroom. There was also a 76 seat First class smoking room and two restaurants that catered for 48 in First class, 42 in Second class and whose meals were prepared in all electric galleys. Additionally the *Prague* arrived in service as the first ship to be fitted with a duty free shop.

Following on from the success of the Harwich to Zeebrugge train ferry service there had been a suggestion in 1928 of running a similar service from Harwich to Esbjerg. This would utilise three train ferries, each making two round trips per week, with facilities on board for 250 passengers or 800 tons of cargo. The crossing time was to be around 18 hours. The earlier suggestion that a service should run between Immingham and Gothenburg was again raised in 1929 with the idea that two train ferries might make three round trips a week. Here the proposed vessels were to cost £330,000 each, be 445 feet long and accommodate 300 passengers and up to 60 rail wagons. With turbines providing 7,200 hp and a service speed of 16½ knots it was estimated that the distance of 504 n.miles could be covered in 30½ hours incorporating two nights at sea. A further idea emerged in 1931 for a service between Immingham and the Swedish port of Varberg.

None of these suggestions were developed any further than the initial idea but in 1931 a new train ferry route did open from Harwich though only as far as Calais. This was a partnership between GETFL and the Compagnie Francaise des Ferry-boats of Paris and started on 8th November with a morning departure from the berth in Calais's Bassin Carnot. In a twist to the circumstances of 1923 when the Italians were in favour of the new Zeebrugge to Harwich service because it would bypass France so now were the French in favour of the Calais to Harwich service because it would bypass Belgium. In doing so it would save certain goods such as perishables, machinery, textiles and pottery from incurring additional customs duties. Ironically on board the first sailing were nine wagons of Italian merchandise. Sailings on this new route were three times a week using *Train Ferry No. 3* whose departures from Harwich were at 11.00 am.

Despite the ideas for opening up new train ferry routes the years of depression since the late 1920s were still affecting overall trade. Up until 1931 the GETFL had somehow managed to make a small profit but in 1932 this turned into a loss of £3,485 and no dividends were paid to its shareholders. Later that year the GETFL went into liquidation. In July 1933 the Company's assets, including the Harwich terminal and the three train ferries, were bought by the LNER for £150,000 who in turn disposed of part of their acquired holdings in SBA by selling them on to the Belgian State Railway (SNCB).

By the early 1930s there had been a rise in the number of passengers wishing to travel as motorists even though the sight of one's pride and joy being precariously lifted on and off ship by a crane and sling was not always a worry free experience. The rules and regulations on taking a car abroad were gradually being relaxed and motorists no longer had to drain their petrol tanks prior to shipment. Nor did they need to deposit customs duties on their car at each border point of entry only to have them refunded when the car then left the country. Motoring organisations were increasingly offering their services in the booking of tickets and generally streamlining the mountain of paperwork. In the 1930s the Automobile Association opened a port office at Parkeston Quay in order to assist the growing number of its members using the port. For those who preferred instead merely to drive to Parkeston Quay, leave the car there and then travel on board ship as a foot passenger, a new storage garage was built in 1930 close by the quay and which was capable of holding up to 30 cars.

In 1931 the passport regulations for passengers travelling into Holland were also relaxed and the steamer companies of the LNER, SMZ, Batavier Line and the Hull and Netherlands Steamship Co. were each allowed to issue special 'No Passport' tickets for stays in Holland of

Opposite: The cruise ship *Stella Polaris* alongside the Middle Quay prior to leaving for San Sebastian and Biarritz - 3rd June 1933. (NRM collection)

1931 handbill advertising a day in Antwerp via the LNER Harwich (P. Quay) service. (Robert Clow collection).

up to 15 days. This dispensation coincided with a general reduction in the cost of taking one's car abroad such that in the summer of 1931 a return ticket for a car from Parkeston Quay to either Holland or Belgium was: Up to 15 cwt - £4.5s.0d., up to 25 cwt - £5.0s.0d., up to 30 cwt - £6.10s.0d. and over 30 cwt - £7.10s.0d. Bearing in mind that the average wage was around £3 a week it was still an expensive exercise.

One particular attraction for motorists was that they could travel out on the Flushing, Antwerp or Zeebrugge services and return to Parkeston Quay from any of these ports on the same ticket. Any competition came mainly from services out of Dover where both the Southern Railway (SR) and Townsend Bros, (Ferries) Ltd. were each operating one round trip per day to Calais. Their prices were based on the length of a vehicle rather than on its weight with single fares ranging from £1.15s.6d. by SR or £2.0s.0d. by Townsend for a wheelbase of up to 8ft.6in. up to £5.0s.0d. or £6.0s.0d.. respectively for a wheelbase of over 10ft.6in. The passenger fare was an additional 10s.. Batavier Line were offering an alternative route to Holland between Gravesend and Rotterdam but their fares were higher than from Parkeston Quay.

On the DFDS route to Esbjerg the service had been greatly improved by the new class of motor ships and patronage was further improved by the availability of through connections between London and the various Scandinavian capitals. The service was still daily, except Sunday, and the boat train from London, which had earlier been known as the 'Esbjerg Continental', was re-named the 'Scandinavian' on 7th July 1930.

In 1931 a passenger could depart London Liverpool Street at 7.42 pm, Parkeston Quay at 10.00 pm and arrive in Esbjerg at 9.40 pm the following evening. From there, at just after midnight, the sleeping car service left for Copenhagen and arrived at 7.43 am. Alternatively passengers could join another sleeper service that would directly arrive in Gothenburg during the early afternoon on the next day or Stockholm and Oslo in the evening. The return journey departed from Oslo at 6.45 pm, or from Stockholm during the early afternoon, and via Gothenburg at 1.31 am and the Helsingborg ferry at 6.49 am, would arrive in Copenhagen at 9.05 am. The train to Esbjerg then arrived at the North Sea port at 4.23 pm with the opportunity to have taken lunch on board the 1½ hour train ferry crossing between Korsor and Nyborg. With the DFDS vessel sailing from Esbjerg at 5.15 pm the time of arrival back at Parkeston Quay was around 5.00 pm the next evening.

In 1932 the fourth, and last, in the series of sister motor vessels built for DFDS arrived at Parkeston Quay on 24th April. This was the *England* which in turn displaced the *A.P. Bernstorff*. The *J.C. la Cour* had earlier finished on the Esbjerg service in 1931 and like several other ships from Parkeston Quay in recent years had ended her days at the breakers yard at Blyth. The six days a week Parkeston Quay to Esbjerg service was now in the hands of the *Parkeston, Jylland, Esbjerg* and *England* with the *England* being perhaps the least seen of the quartet.

At around 5.30 am on 9th July 1932 the *Malines* was anchoring in the River Scheldt due to thick fog. There she was struck amidship by the oil tanker *Hanseat* which left her badly holed. The *Malines's* Captain Bennett managed to restart his engines in time to safely beach her on a sandbank and raise the SOS. All the passengers were safely rescued by climbing down ladders amidst what one described as *'the mildest bit of excitement I have ever had'*. Apparently everyone was calm and collected apart from *'one man who was not an Englishman got rather panicky and talked about taking his clothes off and jumping into the water'*. Assistance was given by a number of tugs and by the *Vienna* which was following behind on a cruise to Antwerp. The *Vienna* embarked the *Malines's* passengers and mails and landed them all in Antwerp around noon. The *Malines* was later towed to Antwerp for dry-docking and repair.

On 16th November 1931 work began on a second extension to Parkeston Quay. As with the first extension this was to be a further development at the western end and when completed would add a further 1,120 feet of quay, 146 feet deep, behind which would be built a new railway station and warehouse. The extension would have three new berths numbered east to west as 7, 8 and 8a and be known as Parkeston Quay West. The principal user was to be the SMZ whose vessels were currently sharing berths along a congested Middle quay. The contractors were The Yorkshire Hennebique Contracting Co. Ltd. of Leeds and London and each new berth would be equipped with one 5-ton and three 1½ ton electric cranes supplied by Stothert & Pitt Ltd. of Bath.

In some respects the works were a form of job creation scheme inasmuch as the overall cost, which exceeded £400,000, was subsidised by the Government as part of a wider scheme to alleviate unemployment during the depression. Construction would take three years to complete and was expected to absorb nearly all of the locally unemployed. The Harwich shipyard of Messrs. Cann was to be hired out and up to 200 men taken on with some being brought in from outside the area.

The extension started from the western end of the existing quay where there was then a Customs Boathouse and slipway. However the quay face would not join in a straight line, as was the case with the 1907 works, but angle back at just over 9 degrees towards the shore. Before such work could begin the site was dredged out to a depth of 20 feet at low

Deck plan of the DFDS motor ship *England* built in 1932. (Railway Gazette)

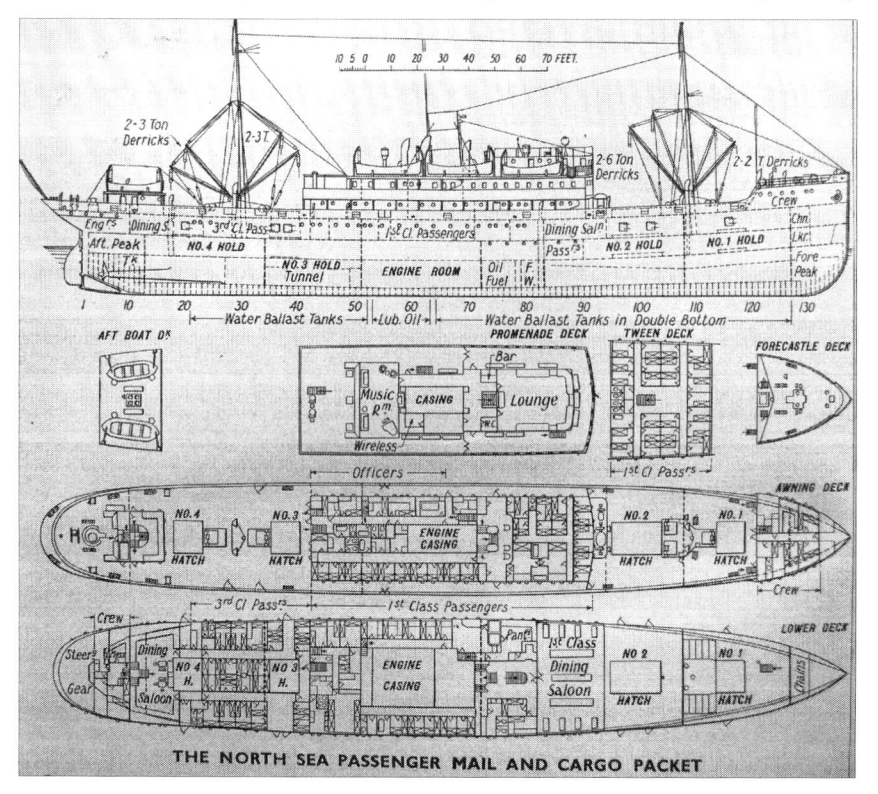

An early 1930s aerial view of Parkeston Quay looking west. (Robert Clow collection)

water. This resulted in the removal of 282,000 tons of material which was pumped a distance of half a mile in order to fill in a shallow lake just inland of the railway embankment.

Work on the main extension began via a series of stagings. A steam derrick crane, some barges to float out pile and decking material and a pile barge gradually built up an island of permanent structural works. This island was then connected to both the stagings and the existing quay by a gantry along which a standard gauge rail track ran that enabled the use of hand propelled wagons.

Behind the quay face were placed four front rows of 16 inch diameter reinforced piles and behind them were further rows of piles 14 inches in diameter. All piles were either 38 feet 6 inches or 40 feet in length of which 1,124 were used in the main quay and a further 310 elsewhere. In the front row of each main trestle were placed a pair of 16 inch piles pitched 16 inches apart. Around each pair of piles was placed a concrete cylinder, 24 feet long by 6 feet diameter, fitted with a steel cutting edge. When securely bedded into the underlying clay, or ballast, reinforcing bars were then fitted and the cylinder filled with concrete. Upon these foundations were placed the numerous series of trestles, transversely placed at 12 feet 6 inches apart at centre, and joined at their tops by decking and deck beams and lower down by bracings. An alternating series of main type and intermediate type trestle sizes ran throughout its length with the pattern type being modified throughout the 'joining curve' with the existing quay.

Upon this strengthened decking was built a two storeyed transit shed measuring 900 feet long by 63 feet wide which, on its lower level, housed the new railway station of Parkeston Quay West. This was connected to the existing railway lines by means of two reinforced concrete and trestle viaducts leading in from the west. The north viaduct, or the seaward side, carried two rail tracks serving the goods roads at the front of the quay. It measured 537 feet long by 27 feet wide and was built on a curve of 10 chains radius. The south viaduct, or the landward side, carried a single rail track leading to the passenger station. Again built on a curve it measured slightly shorter at 498 feet long by 16 feet wide with a radius of 11½ chains. The trestles were, as in the quay extension itself, placed 12 feet 6 inches apart at centre with those on the north viaduct resting on 14 inch piles and those in the south viaduct resting upon 16 inch piles.

The two storey station and main shed covered 56,800 square feet. The middle part of the lower storey was given over to being a fully equipped railway station for passengers complete with booking office, refreshment room and offices for Customs and Immigration complete with baggage examination facilities. The interiors were panelled in wood and pressed fibre boards with a decorative scheme consisting of maroon, cream and white.

The remainder of the building at platform level was given over to warehouse space accessed by sliding doors placed at frequent intervals. The floor level was at quay level and this lower storey had a ceiling height

Looking east towards No. 3 Shed in August 1931. The area to the left became the site for the new west end extension. (Robert Clow collection)

Work in progress on the west end extension looking west, January 1933. (Robert Clow collection)

View of the newly completed No. 4 Shed and the two connecting rail viaducts. (Robert Clow collection)

of 15 feet. The upper storey was entirely given over to warehouse space except for a small number of offices on the south side and had a headroom clearance of 12 feet 6 inches. Six lifts, plus stairways, connected the two levels. On the north side, facing the quay, were a number of cantilevered platforms onto which could be placed cargo craned directly from a ship's hold and then moved inside the building through sliding doors. The cranes could lift cargo from a hold 30 feet below quay level to a height of 52 feet above. This new shed became another 'new' West Shed with the existing and earlier renamed 'new' West Shed itself becoming another 'old' West Shed. It proved far better, and less confusing, to stick with No.3 Shed and to call this new one No.4 Shed.

Additional works included the building of a fully equipped single storey mess room for 200 men along with a new electricity sub-station that powered the entire extension premises. Also about 450 feet at the rear of the existing No.3 Shed, dating from 1907, was widened by 14 feet 6 inches so that room could be made for a roofed in platform whereby train ferry wagons could be examined by Customs. A new office and bonded store were also built here in what became nicknamed the 'SingSing' shed.

The entire extension and works consumed over 13,000 cubic yards of concrete, most of which was mixed in half cubic yard mixers and distributed by hand barrow. The cement used was 'Steelcrete' mixed in with sand and gravel that was sourced from the tidal beaches of the river Stour and brought in by barge. Any extra sand came from pits near Colchester whilst all the concrete piles and blocks required were made locally in Harwich.

Alongside these works the LNER enlarged the goods yard by giving it seven additional sidings creating standage for an extra 387 wagons. About 3 miles of new track was laid with two new signal boxes being needed to handle the new layout and signalling arrangements. One replaced the existing 34 lever signal box, located at the extreme western end of the yard since 1882, with a new 56 lever Parkeston Goods box that controlled access to both the sidings and the new extension. The other was a 50 lever box built adjacent to the road crossing onto the quay, close by the main station, and was named Parkeston West. This meant there were now three signal boxes at Parkeston, the third being the 1882 built 36 lever box at Parkeston East.

From the eastern end of Parkeston Quay West station a branch ran through the quay area and into the existing Parkeston Quay station which itself was partly re-built. Works here included the creation of a 'central hall'. behind the old booking hall, for the purpose of Customs examination of passengers luggage.

The first ship to open the Parkeston Quay West extension was the SMZ vessel *Mecklenburg* on 13th August 1934 which sailed just sixteen minutes after the arrival of the 10.00 am 'Flushing Continental' from London Liverpool Street. This was the first passenger train to arrive at the new extension and it brought down from London some 260 passengers and 300 bags of mail. On hand to meet the train were Mr. Gibson, LNER's Continental Traffic Manager, and Mr. Keep, Assistant Marine Superintendent at Parkeston Quay.

The terminal was officially opened on 1st October 1934 by Admiral of the Fleet, Sir Reginald Tyrwhitt. A special train had left Liverpool Street at 10.20 am conveying various guests and officials, including Sir Murrough Wilson, Deputy Chairman of the LNER, in order to arrive at the new station at noon. Initiating the proceedings Sir Reginald opened the gates to the new station premises using a special silver gilt key embellished with an enamelled LNER crest. Following a tour of inspection a luncheon was taken on board the *Vienna* with the ship later providing a short cruise around Harwich Harbour. Those guests who had travelled from London by train were back in the capital by 6.00 pm.

The new extension now gave the SMZ day boats their own terminal away from the area they had previously been sharing with the LNER night boats. The year 1934 also saw the name of Harwich being officially added to the station name of Parkeston Quay whose length of quay now measured 3,947 feet.

During the period that the extension was being built changes had been occurring in Holland. A long abandoned wharf and warehouse at the Hook of Holland had been taken over in August 1932 by the stevedore 'New Fruit Wharf'. It had fallen out of use since the New Waterway had been further deepened after the war and doing so had relieved liner traffic of the need to call in at the Hook first on their way up to Rotterdam. By 1933 the Hook of Holland had become Europe's largest importing port for fruit. A further change in 1933 was that the LNER cargo ships moved away from Rotterdam's Parkkade quay to a new terminal at Merwehaven in nearby Schiedam with the service remaining at three times a week.

Boat train connections at the Continental ports were improving all the time as were their reliability, comfort and an ever increasing choice of easily reached destinations throughout Europe. That choice was further increased in 1932 when the LNER started luxury cruising out of Parkeston Quay.

The use of a steamer for such cruises had already been seen during 1929 when the SMZ was sending their *Oranje Nassau* on weekend trips via the Hook of Holland on voyages as far afield as Cowes, the Isle of Wight and Torquay but when the LNER placed their *Vienna* in a similar role the number of destinations and the range of on board experiences was raised to a much higher level.

Starting in the summer of 1932 the *Vienna* offered a series of weekend cruises which variously combined visits to the Dutch ports of Amsterdam and Rotterdam, the Belgian ports of Antwerp and Zeebrugge or even a trip up the River Seine in France to visit Rouen. Occasionally a 'Mystery Cruise' would be offered though passengers usually awoke to find themselves in the Channel Islands. The season lasted from the end of June to early September and for all cruises no passports were required.

The cruises normally left Parkeston Quay at 11.00 pm on Friday and arrived back at around 6.00 am the following Monday. They became hugely popular and appealed to those unable to afford either the time or the cost of a longer ocean cruise. In fact the *Vienna* was advertised as being comparable in miniature to the large ocean liners of the time and the attractions on board were described in such a way that passengers would not feel as though they were missing out on much by choosing to cruise on a steamer. Their ship had a spacious entrance hall, dining rooms, a tastefully decorated lounge and a separate Ladies' saloon. There was also a cocktail bar and lounge, ample promenade decks and hundreds of well appointed cabins up to the level of Cabine de-luxe. In reality all this was little different to when the *Vienna* was normally sailing to the Hook of Holland but when cruising the numbers on board were limited to avoid overcrowding. Furthermore every endeavour was made to provide each passenger with the exclusive use of a cabin 'unless otherwise requested'.

What was different was the gaiety on board and the amusement to be had from dancing and the various deck games on offer such as quoits, shuffle-board, putting and wooden horse racing. In later years Ladies' cricket matches became highly popular events along with on deck shower bathing for those hot sunny days. The most popular of all the special attractions was undoubtedly the coronation of 'Queen Cruisiana', a novelty event that was basically an upmarket beauty pageant. For each cruise there was the modern day equivalent of an Entertainments Manager and on the *Vienna* this role was performed by Mr Simon Vernon-Harcourt whose 'day-job' was that of a statistician working for the LNER at Liverpool Street!.

Cruises that covered the August Bank Holiday weekend were extended by an extra day, at extra cost, and so arrived back at Parkeston Quay on the Tuesday. So successful did the cruising season become that in early 1936 the Marine Department at Parkeston Quay extended the *Vienna*'s boat deck aft in order to increase facilities.

Fares were attractively priced from the outset and by 1937 the fare, from London by 3rd class rail, was £3.12s.6d. per person and included a cabin berth and all meals. The Bank Holiday cruise cost £5.0s.0d. which that year went to Hamburg. To and from the port the travel times were:

Dep. London (L.St)	(Friday)	8.15 pm
Dep. P. Quay	(Friday)	11.00 pm
Arr. P. Quay	(Monday)	6.00 am
Arr. London (L.St)	(Monday)	7.53 am

In 1938 the respective fares were slightly higher at £3.16s.6d. and £5.5s.0d. The supplement for travelling by 1st class rail was 3s.6d. per adult or 1s.9d. per child each way. These prices were repeated in 1939 though the train times had since been amended to:

Dep. London (L.St)	(Friday)	8.30 pm
Dep. P. Quay	(Friday)	11.00 pm
Arr. P. Quay	(Monday)	6.20 am
Arr. London (L.St)	(Monday)	8.38 am

Passengers from the north and the midlands could travel via the 'North Country' train which arrived at Parkeston Quay at 9.16 pm and departed at 7.25 am. If starting from Parkeston Quay the prices were £3.5s.6d. for all except the Bank Holiday cruise which was £4.14s.0d. A great many other starting points were inclusively priced, mostly from LNER stations, and all cruises offered the options of shore excursions and cabin upgrades.

Additional charge for cabins:		(Bank Holiday)
Deck B outside	7s.6d.	10s.0d.
Deck A inside	7s.6d.	10s.0d.
Deck A outside	15s.0d.	20s.0d.
Promenade Deck inside	10s.0d.	12s.6d.
Promenade Deck outside	25s.0d.	30s.0d.
Cabine-de-Luxe	75s.0d.	84s.0d.

A reduction of 5s.0d. was made if taking more than one cruise per season whilst groups of 10 or more received a discount of 3s.6d. per person. For children, ie those under the age of 14, the fare was reduced by 15s.0d. A full set of meals were provided on each Saturday and Sunday consisting of Early Morning Tea, English Breakfast, Lunch, Tea and Dinner. The wearing of dinner jackets was optional. No meals were provided on the Friday night whilst on the Monday morning there was only Early Morning Tea. Those on the Bank Holiday cruise received a full day's set of meals on the Monday and Early Morning Tea on Tuesday.

From the tone of the advertising it would appear that there was a high percentage of repeat bookings as the itinerary for 1939 included a new cruise to nowhere. It was called a Week-end at Sea and was arranged for 'those passengers who have in past years visited the regular ports of call'. Perhaps the LNER had run out of interesting ports or their regulars had become bored of seeing the same old sights but on this one occasion the *Vienna* would not be calling at any of them.

Cover of the official guide to the opening of Parkeston Quay West - 1st October 1934. (Robert Clow collection)

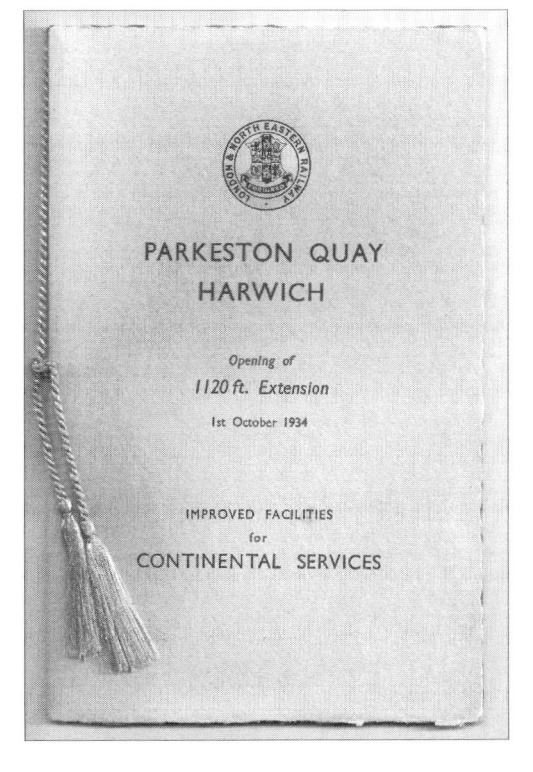

In June 1933 three ships of the LNER were engaged in experiments on enhancing ship to shore communication. In ways reminiscent of when the GER carried out work for Signor Marconi some 30 years earlier the *Vienna* and two other vessels were fitted with equipment to assist the Marconi International Marine Communication Co. Ltd. in trying to transmit wireless telephone messages over a range of up to 100 miles. The ultimate intention of the experiments was to provide businessmen with an affordable means of maintaining contact with their offices whilst at sea.

In 1934 the Danish State Railways and DFDS abolished Third class travel and in the following year Denmark's Little Belt Bridge across the 700 yard wide Aarosund was opened to traffic on 14th May 1935. Its construction was intended to reduce journey times from Copenhagen to a number of major towns on Jutland, including Esbjerg, by removing the need to use train ferries between Strib on the island of Funen and Fredericia on Jutland. The idea of a bridge had been mentioned as far back as 1922 when the cost of building a 1,000 yard bridge and the associated embankments was put at around Dkr45m. or £2,095,000. It was not until 1931 that work began on what eventually became a 1,095 yard long combined road and rail bridge.

New 'Lyntog' or Lightning express trains made up of three car diesel electric units were introduced and on the Copenhagen to Esbjerg service they had the effect of considerably reducing the 197 mile journey from around 7 hours to between 4½ and 5 hours. In conjunction with the opening of the Little Belt Bridge the sailing times of the Parkeston Quay to Esbjerg service were brought forward by 4 hours so that departures now left at 6.00 pm instead of 10.00 pm. This meant it was now possible to arrive in Copenhagen the night after leaving Parkeston Quay which was a vast improvement over what was formerly a breakfast time arrival on the third day.

During the summer seasons the 'Scandinavian' boat train, complete with restaurant car, was retimed to depart Liverpool Street at 4.10 pm and run non-stop to Parkeston Quay where it arrived at 5.45 pm before carrying on to arrive at Harwich Town at 6.06 pm. During the winter months passengers left Liverpool Street on the 3.10 pm to Great Yarmouth in carriages that were taken off at Manningtree. They were then separately hauled to Parkeston Quay where they arrived at 4.45 pm. In Denmark a special boat train known as the 'Vestjyden' or West Jutlander ran between Esbjerg and Copenhagen.

On 29th June 1935 a collision occurred at 6.40 pm in clear weather off the entrance to Harwich harbour between SMZ's inward bound *Prinses Juliana* and DFDS's outward bound *Esbjerg*. The *Esbjerg* and her 133 passengers returned to port for an inspection of damage which amounted to a broken stem and hose. Her passengers were later transferred to the *Jylland* which made a special midnight sailing for the journey to Denmark. The *Esbjerg* then sailed to London for repairs the next morning, 30th June, and was back in service on 8th July. By contrast the *Prinses Juliana* suffered far worse damage with a 87 feet gash along her starboard side. The ship, with 311 passengers on board, also made it back to port where medical teams were waiting to treat any injuries. Fortunately only three passengers were hurt, two of which were taken to the local hospital. Temporary repairs to the *Prinses Juliana* were carried out by the quay's boilermakers and shipwrights following which she sailed for permanent repairs in Rotterdam in the early hours on 4th July. She returned to service on 11th August.

By 1935 traffic levels on the Harwich to Zeebrugge train ferry service were on the increase due mainly to improved marketing by the LNER and who eventually restored a degree of profitability. The route to Calais only lasted until September 1936 when it was closed shortly before the opening of a new train ferry service between Dover and Dunkirk operated by the Southern Railways and which started on 12th October 1936. Despite this 'competition' carryings on the remaining Harwich to Zeebrugge route were still sufficient to keep two of the three train ferries in regular use. The importance of train ferries was such that in October 1937 the combined services from Harwich and Dover carried a total of 1,870 rail wagons, a figure that was practically the same as the number of motor vehicles imported by all the ferry routes then running into Britain.

At Harwich lay the long since closed and empty GER hotel. With the LNER having no need of it the building was transferred to the Harwich Borough Council on 27th February 1936 in exchange for the

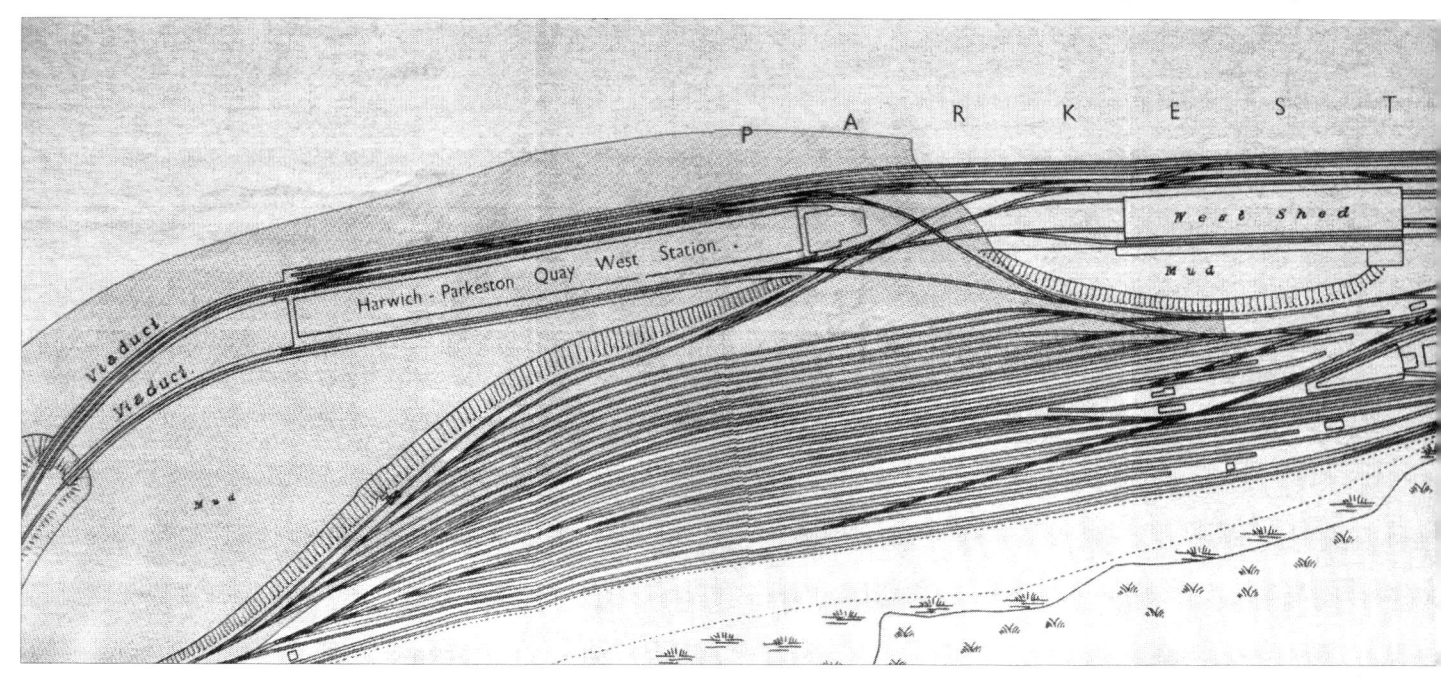

A plan of Parkeston Quay in 1934 showing the integrated west end extension. (Robert Clow collection)

Council taking over the LNER's ongoing responsibility for maintaining the road and quay face between the former naval shipyard and Halfpenny Pier. On 7th February 1938 the Council then purchased from the LNER that length of road from the shipyard along to Church Street. The last bit of railway owned road, from Church Street to George Street was sold to the Council by the British Railways Board on 7th February 1972. The hotel acted as the Council's Town Hall between October 1951 and December 1983 when it was sold off. In 1987 it was converted into residential flats.

The latter half of the 1930s saw a number of Royal personages pass through Parkeston Quay and ships from the LNER fleet taking part in a number of naval reviews. In 1935, on 15th July, the *Malines* attended the Spithead Jubilee Naval Review. On 6th August Princess Ingrid and her husband arrived from Denmark and the Queen of Holland and her daughters sailed in from Flushing. The King of Denmark arrived on board the *England* on 6th December to attend the funeral of Princess Victoria later departing on 9th December on board the *Parkeston*. In 1937 the *Amsterdam* and *Vienna* left on 19th May for the Spithead Coronation Review whilst the King of Denmark, with his Queen, was again seen at Parkeston Quay on 10th December having arrived on board the *Esbjerg*.

Other visitors to the port during July and August 1937 were the excursion steamers of the New Medway Steam Packet Company. Their *Queen of Thanet, Queen of Kent, Queen of the Channel* and *Royal Sovereign* were used in connection with the World Scout Jamboree in Holland as were the *Prinses Juliana* and *Oranje Nassau* which made some extra sailings.

The latter half of the 1930s was also a time of further improvements to boat trains and timings. In 1938 the LNER introduced a new and luxurious set for the Hook of Holland service that consisted of thirteen carriages including two restaurant cars and two Pullman cars. When loaded with passengers and luggage it weighed up to 500 tons which was more than the 455 tons of the set it replaced. After a brief period of when the old set had been timed to make the journey from Liverpool Street to Parkeston Quay in just 82 minutes this new improved 'Hook Continental' was slowed to a pre-existing time of 87 minutes with the departure time from London being brought forward to 8.15 pm. Arrival time at Parkeston Quay was now 9.42 pm whilst the return departure of 6.20 am was timed to reach London at 7.53 am.

The 'Antwerp Continental' was also brought forward and now departed Liverpool Street at 8.30 pm. It continued to run through to Harwich Town and arrive at 10.14 pm but its return working started from Parkeston Quay where it normally left at around 7.00 am to arrive in London at 8.38 am. However this varied between summer and winter and whenever the seasonal June to September service to Zeebrugge was running then passengers off that route would continue in using the Antwerp train. In 1937 however only a combined 'Hook and Antwerp Continental' express was running due to a depressed level of traffic.

Summer timetable from Holland

By LNER		By SMZ	
Dep. HvH	11.45 pm	Dep. Flushing	1.50 pm
Arr. P. Quay	6.15 am	Arr. P. Quay West	7.10 am
Dep. P. Quay	6.55 am	Dep. P. Quay West	7.55 pm
Arr. London (L.St)	8.38 am	Arr. London (L St)	9.30 pm

On 31st December 1937 Britain's railways saw the abolition of Second Class travel, except on Boat trains and Continental services, leaving just First and Third class. The next day, 1st January 1938, saw the emergence of Netherlands Railways Ltd, (NS), as the sole operator of railways in Holland after the Dutch Government had earlier dissolved the historic Dutch Iron and State railways.

In 1937 DFDS were still running six passenger departures per week between Esbjerg and Parkeston Quay. Their principal ships were the *Parkeston, Jylland* and *Esbjerg* with the only additions to the 'DFDS visitor list' having been the *Bellona, Vistula* and *J.C. Jacobsen*. In 1938 the Esbjerg route carried 48,250 passengers. To cope with the increasing numbers the Danish 'Vestjyden' train became a four car unit and was re-named the 'Englaenderen'. In 1938 and 1939 a Sunday sailing was introduced for the summer months of July and August whilst in the spring of 1939 DFDS had ordered another new ship from Helsingor's Yard.

By now the 'Flushing Continental' had become very similar to the 'Hook Continental' in having First class Pullman and restaurant cars. It also made an

The new quay front looking east along No. 4 Shed, 1934. (Robert Clow collection)

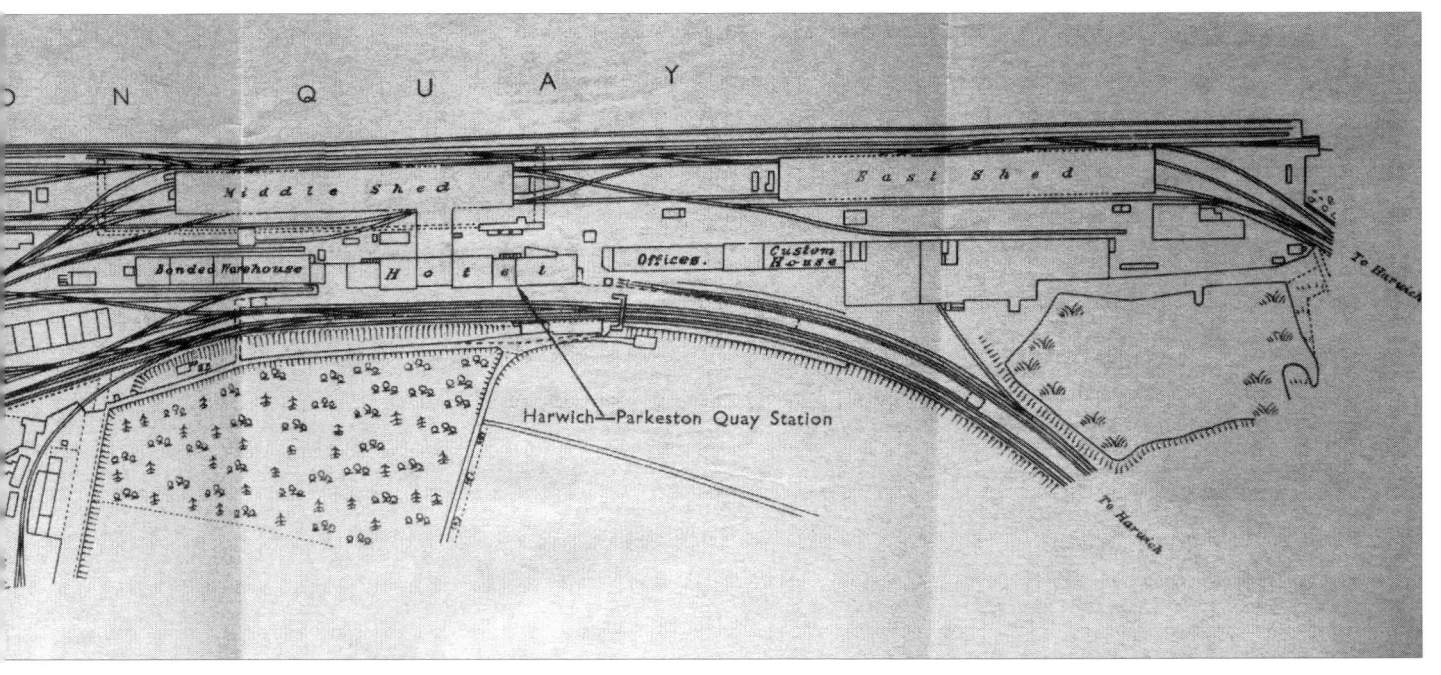

interesting short run along the quay between the two stations at Parkeston.

1938-39 winter		1939 summer	
Dep. London (L.St)	9.30 am	Dep. London(L.St)	10.00 am
Arr. P. Quay West	10.55 am	Arr. P. Quay West	11.30 am
Then to Arr. P. Quay		Arr. P. Quay	11.38 am
Dep. P. Quay	6.30 pm	Dep. P. Quay	7.45 pm
Dep. P. Quay West	6.45 pm	Dep. P. Quay West	7.55 pm
Arr. London (L.St)	8.13 pm	Arr. London (L.St)	9.30 pm

In 1939 SMZ introduced two new ships when the *Koningin Emma* and the *Prinses Beatrix* made their respective maiden voyages from Flushing to Parkeston Quay on 4th June and 3rd July. Both were products of De Schelde at Flushing with vastly different profiles from that of the rest of the fleet. Not only did they have grey hulls but of much greater significance was the fact that they were SMZ's first motor vessels. Each was powered by two ten-cylinder Sulzer diesel engines and thus the Company had gone from steam reciprocating engines to diesel power without ever having had a turbine steamer. The service speed of the new ships was around 21 knots but when on trials the *Koningin Emma* achieved fractionally under 24 knots she became the fastest ship on the North Sea.

The *Koningin Emma* was also the first ship on the North Sea which enabled cars to be directly driven on and off though this was subject to a suitably amenable tide. Opening on both sides of her hull led into a hold on D Deck where cars were then manhandled into position. However most of the 25 cars for which space was available were still craned on and off through hatches either in the Promenade Deck aft or B Deck forward.

Accommodation was for up to 1,800 passengers plus 58 crew but as these ships were designed to be day boats there was very little in the way of cabin accommodation. Just 90 berths in two classes were available in 52 cabins that each had either one, two and three berths. All had a wash basin and fresh air ventilation. Two Cabin-de-Luxe on C Deck, complete with toilet facilities, could by way of interconnecting doors be converted into one de-Luxe Suite.

The change to diesel propulsion did away with the need for an array of boilers and their associated uptakes and this allowed the accommodation a greater sense of space that was both well proportioned and tastefully appointed. Most of the public areas were aft of the funnel with First class being forward of Second class. The top deck or A Deck held a First class Sun deck and veranda whilst below on B Deck there was a large First class smoking room and lounge together with a separate Second class lounge that was capable of being extended by the use of folding side-screens consisting of heavy steel doors.

Both class of dining room were on C Deck aft which was also the main promenade deck whilst on D Deck were not only the garage spaces but also the passenger entrance halls which were panelled in light oak. Off these entrances were four retiring rooms which were rooms set out with comfortable settees and for use mainly by Ladies. Most of the cabins were on E Deck.

The provision of sheltered promenading areas and also heated outdoor spaces was in part associated with the idea that the new ships might undertake some form of future cruising. The differences between the two classes of accommodation on board was not that great and should the ships be put into cruising mode then the company was to install a number of shower baths.

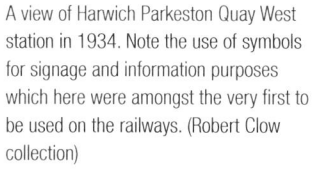

A view of Harwich Parkeston Quay West station in 1934. Note the use of symbols for signage and information purposes which here were amongst the very first to be used on the railways. (Robert Clow collection)

Unfortunately both ships were destined to enjoy only the briefest of time in civilian service before war broke out.

There had already been evidence of a worsening international situation since December 1938 when Parkeston Quay became a reception point for Jewish children fleeing from Germany. At 5.30 am on 2nd December the *Prague* had arrived with the first group and during that month both the *Prague* and *Vienna* between them brought in over 1,200 children. During the next 9 months a further 10,000 more would arrive in Britain, mostly through Parkeston Quay, giving rise to the term 'Kinder Transport'. There was also the 'Winton Train', a means of escape organised by Nicholas Winton who, between March and September 1939, succeeded in rescuing 669 children by train from Prague and who arrived in London having travelled via the Hook of Holland and Parkeston Quay.

Despite the international situation the 1939 seasonal services resumed as normal. The cruise ship *Stella Polaris* returned on 13th May whilst the *Vienna* started out on her own first cruise of the year on 23rd June. But during the summer the situation escalated. The Admiralty Trade Division took over control of the country's commercial shipping activities on 26th August and at Harwich and Parkeston Quay, as elsewhere, this quickly led to cutbacks and cancellations.

The *Vienna*'s weekend cruise scheduled for the 25th August had already been cancelled and all around the quay sandbags were being filled in order to protect the office windows and the all important telegraph room. On 31st August the Rotterdam service was suspended with the *Sheringham* making the last trip back. Then on 1st September, when Germany invaded Poland, both the Hook of Holland and Antwerp routes were closed with the last sailings being those of the *Prague* and the *Antwerp* departing for Parkeston Quay that same night. On 2nd September the whole of Parkeston Quay was closed on orders from the Admiralty and the eastern 1,200 feet part of the quay requisitioned for the Royal Navy.

With Holland and Denmark, along with Belgium, all being neutral their respective ships gradually returned to their home ports. Those of the SMZ fleet were all laid up in Flushing immediately following their last day sailings from Parkeston Quay. These in turn were the *Koningin Emma, Prinses Beatrix, Mecklenburg* and *Prinses Juliana* which sailed back to Vlissingen on 1st, 2nd, 3rd and 4th September respectively. The *Oranje Nassau* was retained to operate a three times a week service between Flushing and Tilbury which began on 14th September. This closed on 25th November following which the *Oranje Nassau* was also laid up in Flushing with the rest of the SMZ fleet.

The four DFDS vessels were also returned home for lay up. The *England* made her last sailing back to Esbjerg on 1st September followed by the *Jylland* on the 2nd with both ships being laid up there. The *Esbjerg* had arrived at Parkeston Quay on the 2nd September and was joined by the *Parkeston* on the 3rd. Both ships then left light on the 5th for an eventual lay up in Frederikshaven where they arrived on 8th September.

On 3rd September 1939 Britain declared war on Germany and events at Parkeston Quay very quickly followed a pattern of military and civil activity similar to those of 25 years before. The Royal Navy took over the quay and converted the marine workshops into an Admiralty repair station. Apart from a restricted number of railway employees only service personnel were allowed on the quay.

In summary the last sailings before war was declared were as follows:

Date	Ship	Arrived from	Sailed to
30 August	*Bruges*	Antwerp	Antwerp
30 August	*Amsterdam*	Hook	Hook
30 August	*Sheringham*		Rotterdam
31 August	*Antwerp*	Antwerp	Antwerp
31 August	*Prague*	Hook	Hook
31 August	*Koningin Emma*	Vlissingen	
31 August	*England*	Esbjerg	
1 September	*Bruges*		Antwerp
1 September	*Amsterdam*		Hook
1 September	*Sheringham*		Rotterdam
1 September	*Koningin Emma*		Vlissingen
1 September	*England*		Esbjerg
1 September	*Prinses Beatrix*	Vlissingen	
1 September	*Jylland*	Esbjerg	
2 September	*Antwerp*		Antwerp
2 September	*Prague*		Hook
2 September	*Prinses Beatrix*		Vlissingen
2 September	*Jylland*		Esbjerg
2 September	*Mecklenburg*	Vlissingen	
2 September	*Esbjerg*	Esbjerg	
2 September	*Train Ferry No 2*		Zeebrugge
3 September	*Mecklenburg*		Vlissingen
3 September	*Prinses Juliana*	Vlissingen	
3 September	*Parkeston*	Esbjerg	
3 September	*Train Ferry No.2*	Zeebrugge	
4 September	*Prinses Juliana*		Vlissingen
5 September	*Esbjerg*		Esbjerg (light)
5 September	*Parkeston*		Esbjerg (light)

During the last full year of peacetime services, in 1938, a total of 387,000 passengers had travelled through Parkeston Quay in what was described as having been a very good year. In that same year the Harwich to Zeebrugge train ferry service carried 70,780 tons of cargo. When the train ferries ceased civilian sailings on 1st September 1939 the Harwich to Zeebrugge route had, since opening in 1924, carried a total of 197,730 wagons and 1,281,670 tons of goods.

As in the First World War when ships of the GER were pressed into military service so too were those from the Harwich and Parkeston Quay fleet of the LNER. This even included the 22 ton harbour launch *Epping* which was renamed H.M.S. Badger on 13th September. This was the new name given to the naval establishment at Parkeston Quay and this tiny vessel was then assigned as the port's depot ship.

At the time the LNER had a local fleet of thirteen ships. The *Malines* and *Antwerp* were sailing a six days a week service to Antwerp with the *Bruges* as relief ship, the *Prague* and *Amsterdam* ran a nightly service to the Hook of Holland, the *Vienna* was on cruising duties and the *St. Denis* and *Archangel* were on the seasonal service to Zeebrugge. The two cargo ships, *Felixstowe* and *Sheringham* were mainly sailing just once a week to Rotterdam whilst the three train ferries, *Train Ferry No.1*,

Advert for the 1939 season of LNER cruises onboard the *Vienna* of which the final trip was cancelled on the outbreak of WW2. (Stephen Brown collection)

Inside the Customs Hall at Parkeston Quay West, 1934. (Robert Clow collection)

The joys of the Belgian coast, courtesy of the LNER service from P. Quay in 1934. (Stephen Brown collection)

Right: The crowning of 'Queen Cruisiana' by the captain of the *Vienna*, Captain Booth, with the 'Prime Minister', Mr. Vernon-Harcourt, officiating. Taken onboard one of the *Vienna*'s cruises in the 1930s. (Stephen Brown collection)

Below: The new 'Hook Continental' boat train, introduced by the LNER in 1938, is seen here on a trials trip at Parkeston Quay West. (The Railway Gazette October 1938)

Train Ferry No.2, and *Train Ferry No.3*, were fully engaged on the Harwich to Zeebrugge link.

On 5th September the *Bruges* and *Amsterdam* became the first ships to be requisitioned. They were ordered to Southampton, arriving there on the 8th and 12th respectively, to become troop ships primarily sailing to Le Havre and Cherbourg in France. Over the coming months several more of the LNER fleet were deployed in some form or other serving the needs of the British Expeditionary Force (BEF).

All three train ferries were requisitioned and transferred to running a nightly service to Calais. *Train Ferry No.1* and *Train Ferry No.2* were called up on 24th September and *Train Ferry No.3* on 11th October 1939. Their initial role was to transport ambulance trains to France for use by the BEF and the first four of these were shipped out via *Train Ferry No.1* and *Train Ferry No.2* on 26th and 27th September respectively. The train ferry terminal bridges were then strengthened to carry heavy road vehicles and the three train ferries had their rail lines packed out with wood to form a level deck suitable for the transport of guns, tanks and road vehicles. The work was carried out by the marine workshops at Parkeston Quay and on 21st October all three ships were put back onto the Harwich to Calais service. They were sailing on War Office service but still managed by the LNER.

In October 1939 the procurement of ships was done through a re-established Ministry of Shipping. The ships' crew were still classed as being merchant seamen though they were now subject to naval discipline. The Masters and Chief Engineers were offered commissions in the Royal Naval Reserve.

Three more ships departed Parkeston Quay, again for Southampton, when the *Archangel* was requisitioned on 30th November followed by the *Prague* and then the *Vienna* on 10th December. All were similarly used as troop ships to Le Havre and Cherbourg with occasional trips to Brest.

In December 1939 the *Felixstowe* and *Sheringham* were re-deployed to Ipswich with the intention of sailing out of the port's Cliff Quay on cargo services to Rotterdam, Antwerp and Zeebrugge. Sailings to Rotterdam were envisaged as being twice a week should circumstances permit and would supplement the existing once a week service then operated by the *Import*, a Dutch vessel chartered by the LNER since 9th November. Services from Ipswich to Antwerp and Zeebrugge were planned to open on 1st January 1940.

Just three ships were spared initial 'active service', the *Malines, St. Denis* and *Antwerp*, in case they were needed at short notice to evacuate British nationals from Holland. The *Antwerp* was temporarily used as a navy personnel accommodation ship before leaving on 12th January 1940 for trooping duties at Southampton.

By the end of 1939 the ineffectively small *H.M.S. Badger* was replaced by a much larger vessel requisitioned by the Royal Navy on 18th December. This was a former schooner, *Westward*, which became the new *H.M.S. Badger* on 12th January 1940. She was built in 1920 as a four masted schooner of 1,680 gross tons. On board was accommodation for up to 80 people complete with 12 bathrooms, a lounge, dining room and bars. Throughout the war the establishment at H.M.S. Badger was to oversee operations between Lowestoft and Shoeburyness and control an array of Harwich Destroyers, minesweepers, motor torpedo boats, submarines and anti-submarine vessels. Defences were strengthened with the placing of anti aircraft guns, barrage balloons and coastal artillery guns on both sides of the entrance to the Stour estuary plus a boom laid across its mouth from Harwich to Landguard.

Since September 1939 Parkeston Quay's station hotel had been occupied by the Naval Officer in Charge and various other senior personnel. In 1940 those offices and the work of an array of operations staff were then accommodated in Hamilton House, this being the former Railway Enginemen's Barracks that opened in 1901 and thereafter from 1913 having been the site of a corset factory. It later became the port's Custom House in 1935 as a result of the Import Duties Act of 1932. This Act created a huge increase in the workload of H.M. Customs and rendered the pre-existing Custom House, located in West Street, Harwich since the 1890s, becoming far too small to cope.

THE 1940s

With the first half of the 1940s being dominated by the Second World War, and both Harwich and Parkeston Quay having disappeared from the map as regards being commercial ports, ships of the LNER fleet were soon to be deployed in a wide and often disastrous array of situations.

During the first 3 months of 1940, in addition to the movement of equipment and supplies, the Harwich to Calais train ferry service conveyed a further eight ambulance trains each consisting of sixteen coaches made up of suitable rolling stock contributed by the various British railway companies. The coaches were initially sent to Cambridge where they were fitted out with bunks, hammocks, tables and other materials and from there moved down to Harwich.

For a while it remained possible to continue running limited cargo only services, under the control of the Ministry of Shipping, on routes initially suspended from using Parkeston Quay since September 1939. Thus the *Sheringham* and *Felixstowe* finally began weekly sailings from Ipswich to both Antwerp and Zeebrugge on 6th January 1940. The *Sheringham* made occasional trips to Rotterdam until replaced on 9th February by a chartered vessel, the *Brem,* which sailed once a week together with the still chartered *Import*. The Ministry of Shipping was later merged with the Ministry of Transport in May 1941 to create the Ministry of War Transport (MOWT).

Eventually the relative safety of national neutrality was lost. Denmark was invaded by Germany on 9th April 1940, being taken in as a Protectorate, following which many Danish ships were taken by their crews to Allied or other neutral ports. As regards those DFDS vessels last seen at Parkeston Quay, both the *Esbjerg* and the *Parkeston* were moved from Frederikshaven on 23rd April 1940 for a further lay up in Copenhagen. Later the *Jylland* left Esbjerg on 23rd June 1940 for Hamburg from where she left on the 29th to arrive in Copenhagen on 1st July. She was followed by the *England* making the same journey, leaving Esbjerg on 26th June and Hamburg on the 30th, to arrive in Copenhagen on 2nd July where both ships were again laid up.

Germany's advance towards Holland had earlier led to the ending of the cargo service between Rotterdam and Ipswich with the *Import* finishing on 6th May and the *Brem* making her final sailing from Rotterdam on 8th May as the last cargo ship to leave the Dutch port before the fall of Holland. This came on 10th May when Holland was invaded under the pretext that Germany 'was safeguarding its neutrality'. The SMZ vessels *Koningin Emma* and *Prinses Beatrix* escaped to England that same day followed by the *Mecklenburg* on the 11th and *Oranje Nassau* on 13th May. All arrived safely in the Thames despite Vlissingen having been bombed in an air raid on the 11th May which resulted in offices and buildings being destroyed. One major casualty was to be the *Prinses Juliana*. She had been given the task of carrying Dutch troops from Flushing to Ijmuiden and whilst on passage she was attacked by German aircraft on 12th May at the entrance to the River Maas. Having sustained damage to her hull and steering gear to the extent that she was both listing and unmanageable she was abandoned and towed to ground on the Terheide sandbanks north of the Hook of Holland. All those on board survived except one member of the crew. The ship eventually broke in two and was later

Bomb damage to the ARP Building adjacent to No. 3 Shed. (Robert Clow collection)

used as target practise by the Germans.

As a result of the deteriorating situation in Holland the two 'stand-by' ships at Parkeston Quay, the *Malines* and *St. Denis,* had already been chartered by H.M. Foreign Office and ordered to sail to Rotterdam in order to repatriate any trapped British civilians. The *Malines* arrived at the Dutch port on 26th April followed by the *St. Denis* on the 28th. On 10th May they were to leave Rotterdam at a moments notice. The *Malines*, in the command of Captain Mallory, escaped that evening under cover of darkness and after braving an onslaught of enemy fire she safely arrived at Tilbury the next day. There she disembarked 178 evacuees. The *St. Denis* was not so fortunate. On the 11th it was learned that her way out to sea was blocked by a sunken ship that had earlier hit a mine. On 12th May, after receiving instructions that the ship be scuttled, the crew opened the flooding valves, set her on fire and abandoned her. The crew then left Holland on board the last British destroyer to leave from the Hook of Holland and arrived back at Parkeston Quay at 11.30 am on 15th May. Their stricken ship was eventually raised by the Germans in November 1940 but was fit for nothing more than use as an accommodation ship which they re-named *Barbara*.

On the evening of 12th May the Dutch Crown Princess Juliana, Prince Bernhard and their children left Ijmuiden on board *H.M.S. Codrington* for the safety of Harwich. On the 13th May the Royal Navy landed a force of British Marines at the Hook of Holland to oversee the final evacuation of any remaining troops. During the morning Queen Wilhelmina of Holland arrived and was met by the senior naval officer with an offer of assistance. The Queen said *'I want to go to Flushing, please. Do you know where it is?'* adding *'Do you know the minefields?'*. The officer said yes to the whereabouts of British and German mines but no to where the Dutch were laying theirs. With it being decided that going to Flushing was too dangerous the Queen boarded *H.M.S. Hereward* and left the Hook at 12.00 noon and sailed for Harwich. Members of the Dutch Government later left the Hook at 5.20 pm that evening on board *H.M.S. Windsor* bound for London. Next day the Hook of Holland was in German hands and the final evacuation was from further up the coast at Scheveningen. From then on the Headquarters of the Dutch Navy was based at Parkeston Quay.

In Belgium the port of Antwerp fell into German hands on 18th May with the cargo ship *Felixstowe* just managing to escape in time. The *Felixstowe* was then transferred to the Great Western Railway's route between Weymouth and the Channel Islands before being requisitioned on 10th June 1940. Her replacement there was the *Sheringham* which had moved to Weymouth on 9th June.

Meanwhile the train ferry service between Harwich and Calais had been suspended since 10th May as a result of enemy bombing having damaged the locks at the entrance to Calais's Bassin Carnot and trapping *Train Ferry No.1* inside for a week. Upon her release and subsequent return to Harwich she then left for Southampton on 30th May followed by *Train Ferry No.2* and *Train Ferry No.3* on 2nd June. With no traffic then going via the Harwich train ferry terminal the railway's locomotives were moved back along the branch line to Manningtree as a safety precaution against enemy air attacks. Rolling stock was left where it was on the basis that an engine was a much more valuable asset.

Between 26th May and 4th June 1940 'Operation Dynamo' undertook the evacuation of an encircled British Expeditionary Force from the beaches of France and most notably those at Dunkirk. On 28th May the Germans had overrun Belgium. The *Malines*, recently requisitioned that month, made two trips to Dunkirk. On 29th May she went alongside the torpedoed *H.M.S. Grafton* and safely embarked over 800 men to Dover. This was the successor *H.M.S. Grafton* to that which had witnessed the loss of the GER vessel *Clacton* in August 1916. The *Malines* returned to bring back a further 700 troops to Folkestone on the 31st from where she left, apparently without permission, on 2nd June for Southampton.

The *Prague* made three successive Dunkirk trips between 29th May and 1st June. On the first two trips she safely landed almost 3,000 troops at Folkestone after coming under intense fire throughout though such was the load and equipment on board her second trip home, early on 31st May, that she needed the assistance of tugs to get her afloat and underway. On her third trip, on 1st June, she endured further air attacks whilst embarking 3,000 French troops at the western jetty. The narrow channel precluded attempts at zig-zagging out of danger and three bombs fell so close to her that she was lifted out of the water and suffered severe damage to her stern. She also sprang a leak and this led to her starboard engine having to be stopped. Her captain, Captain Baxter, then made his way out with the remaining engine running at full speed. Those on board were transferred to other vessels with *H.M.S. Scimitar* and another naval vessel each taking off around 500 men and the paddle mine-sweeper *Queen of Thanet* taking off a further 2,000. The *Prague* was then towed by the Dover tug *Lady Brassey* to safely beach near Deal. After receiving temporary repairs the *Prague* went on to London's West India Dock for more permanent repairs that would include the fitting of a new stern section. In recognition of their actions the Distinguished Service Cross was awarded to Captain Baxter and Chief Engineer Oxenham.

The *Archangel*, under Captain Greenham, had earlier been sent out from Dover on 27th May with several hundred troops on board in order to defend Calais and delay the German advance. However heavy shelling from the Gravelines batteries forced her return. She was then moved further west and on 31st May she arrived at Weymouth with troops from Cherbourg in company with the *Amsterdam*.

Whilst most of the evacuated troops were returned to places around England's southern coast some ships arrived back at Harwich. On 30th May the paddle steamer *Oriole* arrived around mid-day and set off back to Dunkirk that evening. On the 31st two further vessels arrived in the afternoon. Eight special trains were run at short notice to move the troops to the Midlands.

After Dunkirk attention turned to evacuating troops from around Le Havre in 'Operation Cycle'. The *Bruges,* which had been working as a troopship out of Southampton, was now engaged in moving retreating British troops from Le Havre to Cherbourg. On 11th June whilst anchored off Le Havre she was hit by a German dive bomber, beached and subsequently abandoned. All 72 of her crew were safely picked up by the *Vienna*.

On the next day, 12th June, the *Archangel* was at St. Valery-en-Caux, east of Le Havre, where her lifeboats ferried troops from the beach to the ship. Heavy air attacks forced a return with fewer than 100 French troops on board and the lifeboats left behind.

Meanwhile *Train Ferry No. 2* sailed that day from Southampton for St. Valery-en-Caux in order to evacuate the 51st Highland Division. Unfortunately, due to bunkering delays, she sailed late and alone and her voyage was further delayed by fog. In the meantime she failed to receive the message that St. Valery had fallen and that the evacuation convoy had been recalled. Whilst waiting offshore, on 13th June, she was shelled by the Germans and sunk. Some of the crew escaped by lifeboat and after rowing for several hours were picked up by a French minesweeper. Out of a crew of thirty seven, fourteen were lost.

The rendezvous vessel at St. Valery was the *Amsterdam* which saw the *Train Ferry No. 2* hit when about two miles distant. The *Amsterdam*'s Captain Sutton was then ordered to move the remaining troops from Le Havre to Cherbourg and Southampton. She was the last merchant ship to leave the port, doing so at night, with the town well ablaze. In July the *Amsterdam* was sent away for lay up in Swansea. There she remained until taking up service as a troop carrier between Aberdeen, Orkney and Shetland in February 1941.

The next area to be evacuated was the Channel Islands and during June 1940 no less than seven Harwich railway boats were seen assisting in various activities to and from Guernsey, Jersey and Alderney. The first to be involved were the surviving train ferries, *Train Ferry No.1* (between 17th - 19th June) and *Train Ferry No.3* (17th - 20th). These were joined by the cargo ships *Sheringham* (18th - 23rd June) and *Felixstowe* (18th - 20th), and then the passenger vessels *Archangel* (20th), *Malines* (20th - 23rd) and *Antwerp* (20th - 23rd). Those civilians and servicemen evacuated were mostly taken to Weymouth or Southampton with the whole operation essentially being completed on 23rd June. On 21st June the Harwich based Trinity House vessel *Vestal* collected the islands lighthouse keepers.

Following their evacuation work both the *Felixstowe* and the *Sheringham* reverted to commercial duties out of Weymouth. When the Germans first attacked the Channel Islands a week later, on 28th June, the *Felixstowe* was en route to Jersey and was turned back whilst the *Sheringham* was in the process of returning from Guernsey that night. German occupation started on 1st July 1940 and both ships were thus re-deployed. Between July 1940 and September 1941 the *Sheringham* was to variously sail as a military stores and cargo ship throughout the Irish Sea linking the ports of Preston, Belfast, Glasgow, Bristol and South Wales. Thereafter she carried commercial cargoes up until sailing for Coast Lines between Liverpool and Belfast in 1945. The *Felixstowe* also undertook commercial work elsewhere until once again being requisitioned whilst in London on 3rd August 1941. She was then used as the wreck dispersal vessel *H.M.S. Colchester* and retained both the role and name throughout the war.

In July 1940 the *Archangel* was laid up at Gareloch in Scotland and only resumed service in April 1941

The *Sheringham* resumed a railway boat presence on the post war Rotterdam route on 23rd March 1946. (Robert Clow collection)

when transferred for use on troopship duties between Aberdeen, Orkney and Shetland in conjunction with the *Amsterdam.* However her role as such was brief. Whilst heading for Aberdeen on the evening of 16th May 1941 the *Archangel,* with 400 troops on board, was bombed and severely damaged. She was beached the next morning some seven miles north of Aberdeen and broke up in pieces a fortnight later. Fifty troops and seventeen crew were lost, mostly from the engine room, whilst the Captain and a further sixteen were injured.

Since leaving Harwich in December 1939 the *Vienna* had taken part in trooping out of Southampton and rescue work at Le Havre and at Brest. On 5th July 1940 she was sent for lay up at Swansea and then to Portsmouth on 1st November for conversion to a fuel carrier. Work on the project ceased in April 1941 and she was instead converted in London to a depot ship for motor torpedo boats. She was purchased by the MOWT on 21st August for £257,500 and emerged on 15th June 1942 as *H.M.S. Vienna.* She was then based in Algiers in November 1942 before moving to Sicily in July 1943 and then on to Bari.

Back at Parkeston Quay events were such that by July 1940 the Royal Navy were in complete command and none of the railway ships had any commercial duties. The two remaining train ferries, *Train Ferry No.1* and *Train Ferry No.3,* were both taken over by the Royal Navy on 24th June 1940. They were respectively renamed *Iris* and *Daffodil* on 4th October 1940 with the chosen names being in memory and recognition of two Mersey ferries that bravely served in the First World War raid on Zeebrugge on 23rd April 1918. *Iris* become *H.M.S. Iris* when commissioned on 16th April 1941 though *Daffodil* was unchanged when she was commissioned on 12th June 1941.

The ships were converted at Southampton into Landing Ships with Stern-chute (LSS) via the installation of an inclined ramp at the stern down which the on board landing craft could be discharged directly into the water. Up to 14 such craft could be carried on the main train deck plus a further four launched by crane from the upper deck. An alternative configuration was to carry 13 craft along with 105 troops. Each landing craft weighed around 15 tons. Both ships had their twin funnels and connecting lattice work removed and replaced by one larger and centrally placed funnel. They were further equipped with four 2-pounder guns, five .303 Lewis guns and five 20mm cannon. They then spent much of their time shuttling landing craft around the U.K.. On 20th January 1942 both ships were purchased by the Government and on 17th September 1942 *H.M.S. Iris* was renamed *H.M.S. Princess Iris.* They each continued to be employed in moving landing craft mainly between the River Thames and ports along the south coast.

The sister ships *Malines* and *Antwerp* were requisitioned into the Royal Navy and converted to Convoy Escort vessels. They were renamed *H.M.S. Malines* on 15th November and *H.M.S. Antwerp* on 22nd November 1940. On 10th September 1941 *H.M.S. Malines* left from a refit on the Tyne bound for the Mediterranean via Londonderry in Northern Ireland on the 13th September and then via the Cape in South Africa. Acting in the role of troopship she reached Cape Town on 24th November and Port Said on Boxing Day. On 22nd July 1942 *H.M.S. Malines* was sailing off Port Said where she was hit by an aerial torpedo and beached. She was salvaged in December 1942 and towed to Alexandria in March 1943 where she was dry-docked. She returned to Port Said in November 1943 and was used as a training ship at Kabret under the management of the GSN Co. on behalf of the MOWT. She remained as such until 16th April 1944 when she was paid off as a constructive loss. In May 1945 she embarked on a tow to England that lasted six months. When she arrived at Wallsend on 7th November she was fit only for lay up and was later scrapped at Dunston on the Tyne in April 1948.

The *H.M.S. Antwerp* travelled the same route to the Mediterranean as did *H.M.S. Malines* leaving

The post war LNER service to Antwerp was reinstated by the GCR vessel *Accrington* on 29th July 1946. (Robert Clow collection)

Londonderry on 15th October and arriving in Alexandria on 23rd December 1941. Her duties during 1942 were as troop carrier and escort mainly along the North Africa coast and to Cyprus. She developed into a forward operations vessel culminating in becoming the Headquarters ship of the Eastern Naval Task Force that invaded Sicily on 10th July 1943. On board were Admiral Mountbatten and General Montgomery.

In December 1943 the *Amsterdam* was returned from Scotland to North Shields for conversion to an infantry assault landing ship (LSI-H). She left on 2nd March and sailed south in preparation for assisting in 'Operation Overlord', the D-Day invasion of Normandy on 6th June 1944. She was very quickly then sent to Glasgow for yet another conversion after which she emerged, on 13th July, as the hospital ship, *Hospital Carrier No. 64*. Upon returning to the Normandy beaches she only made two round trips before being mined when leaving Juno Beach on 7th August 1944. On board were 258 patients and 161 staff and crew. She sank in just eleven minutes during which time casualties were literally thrown overboard and then rescued from the sea. Due to heroic efforts and those of the Matron, who stayed on board to organise events, only 60 of the casualties were lost though in addition 36 of the crew were also lost. These included all of those in the engine room and Matron.

The *Amsterdam*'s sister ship, the *Prague*, was more fortunate. When she returned to service, fitted with a new stern, on 22nd December 1941 she was used as another troop ship sailing between Aberdeen and the Orkney and Shetland Islands. Despite the routes being bombed in air attacks she maintained this role until 23rd March 1944 after which she was sent to North Shields and converted into *Hospital Carrier No. 61*. Most of the cabins were removed to create spacious airy wards necessary for the relief of American casualties following D-Day. These were staffed by American medical staff though the ship remained crewed by the existing LNER personnel. The *Prague* made her first run from Southampton to the Normandy coast on 7th June 1944 and she successfully continued in doing so until her last arrival in Southampton on 11th June 1945.

Following D-Day the Army were given several berths at Parkeston Quay for the purpose of loading supplies onto various coasters and invasion craft required in the Normandy landings. To assist in the movement of heavy railway equipment both *H.M.S. Daffodil* and *H.M.S. Princess Iris* were subjected to another refit. On 15th May and 28th August 1944 respectively work began at Chatham Dockyard on fitting each of them with an additional stern gantry, the purpose of which was to land locomotives and rolling stock at ports that were not equipped with a suitable railway linkspan or shore ramp. Such loads were initially carried between Southampton and Cherbourg starting with *H.M.S. Daffodil* on 2nd August followed by *H.M.S. Princess Iris* in early September. By the end of September 1944 services were also running from Southampton to Dieppe, a route which later saw the loss of *H.M.S. Daffodil* when she hit a mine on 17th March 1945. She sank off Dieppe the next day taking with her a consignment of railway locomotives. *H.M.S. Princess Iris* had earlier reverted to handling just landing craft after having had her stern gantry removed in December 1944.

The war in Europe ended on 8th May 1945 with Victory in Europe (VE) Day and on 14th June the Royal Navy's Operations Room in Hamilton House was closed. This was followed on 18th June by the Flag Officer In Charge (FOIC) Rear Admiral F. Burgess-Watson hauling down his flag and the departure of his staff. The port then assumed its original name though the vessel *H.M.S. Badger* was not paid off until 21st October 1946 when it reverted to its former name of *Westward*.

Throughout the war the quay's workshop staff had carried out £1million's worth of maintenance work for the Army and the Royal Navy. The port had survived as the chief mine sweeping and destroyer escort base on the east coast and played host to a variety of mainly naval ships but also a number of paddle steamers. Five railway paddlers, the *Kylemore, Waverley, Marmion, Duchess of Fife* and *Oriole (ex Eagle III)*, were members of the Harwich 12th Flotilla of Minesweepers of which the last four had seen service at Dunkirk. Only three returned as the *Waverley* was lost on 29th May 1940. The *Kylemore* was then lost to a Luftwaffe attack off Harwich on 21st August 1940 and the *Marmion*, operating as an anti-aircraft ship, was bombed and sunk off Parkeston Quay on 9th April 1941 whilst actively engaging the enemy. Such raids were however comparatively rare as it was rumoured that the Germans were keen on keeping the port intact for their own eventual use.

The end of the war brought with it a disastrous tally of local ships lost. Out of eight pre-war passenger ships the LNER had lost five, the *St. Denis, Bruges, Archangel, Malines* and *Amsterdam* leaving just three survivors, the *Antwerp, Vienna* and *Prague*. However the *Vienna* was effectively 'lost' to the Company as she remained in the ownership of the MOWT and the *Antwerp*, though still owned by the LNER, was retained as a troopship. Of the three train ferries two were lost, *Train Ferry No. 1* and *H.M.S. Daffodil (ex-Train Ferry No. 2)* leaving just *H.M.S. Princess Iris (ex-Train Ferry No. 1)*. The only other survivors were the two cargo ships *Felixstowe* and *Sheringham*.

Those in the SMZ fleet fared relatively better as four of their five ships survived despite all having had equally eventful wartime careers. Following their escape to England the *Koningin Emma* and *Princess Beatrix* were used in the evacuation of troops and civilians from France and the movement of British troops to Iceland. They were requisitioned for Admiralty use in August 1940, converted at Belfast into attack landing craft (LSI-M) and renamed *H.M.S. Queen Emma* and *H.M.S. Princess Beatrix*. Their voyages were extremely varied and between them ranged from the Lofoten raid in March 1941, the Dieppe raid in August 1942, North Africa, Sicilian and Italian landings in 1943, D-Day and the Normandy coast in 1944 before both going on to the Far East in 1945 where the Japanese surrendered Malaya on board the *H.M.S. Queen Emma*. Victory in Japan (VJ) Day was not until 15th August 1945. In 1946 both ships assisted in the evacuation of Dutch civilians from Java.

The *Oranje Nassau* and *Mecklenburg* served out the war much closer to home, this the result of having much smaller bunker capacities than their newer fleet mates. The *Mecklenburg* was converted to an assault landing ship (LSI-H) and was the largest troopship to take part in the D-Day landings whilst the *Oranje Nassau* was used between August 1941 and August 1945 as a Royal Dutch Navy depot and accommodation ship based at Holyhead.

The four DFDS passenger ships had all remained in lay up until 1944 but their fates unfolded when eventually taken up by the Germans. The *England* and the *Jylland* were both seized on 19th January 1944. The *England* left Copenhagen on 22nd March under tow for Stettin. There she was renamed *Grenadier* and used as an accommodation vessel for U-boat personnel. In May 1944 she was moved to Kiel for repairs during which time she was bombed by the Royal Air Force on 27th August 1944 to such an extent that she was not worth repairing. She was scrapped in 1950. The *Jylland* also left Copenhagen under tow, on 5th April 1944, this time to Danzig where she was renamed *Musketier* and used as a barrack ship. In April 1945 she was towed to Kiel and shortly afterwards, on 3rd May, she was bombed and sunk off Travemunde whilst carrying 800 refugees from East Prussia.

The remaining pair, *Esbjerg* and *Parkeston,* were taken over on 20th January 1944. The *Esbjerg* left Copenhagen on 30th March for Pillau, renamed *Kurassier,* and later used in the evacuation of German refugees from East Prussia in December 1944. She was abandoned in Lubeck in June 1945 from where a Danish crew attempted to sail her to Copenhagen. Having left Lubeck on 23rd July she hit a mine off Stevns on 25th July 1945 and sank. She was salvaged in 1947and sold to Spanish interests who renamed her the *Cuidad de Ibiza*. She was scrapped in 1978.

The *Parkeston* left Copenhagen on 15th March 1944 for Gotenhafen and was re-named *Pioneer*. Whilst in use as a U-boat depot ship she was air attacked on 3rd May 1945 but suffered no damage. She was however beached and the crew abandoned ship. She left Lubeck on 23rd July, together with the *Esbjerg*, and safely arrived in Copenhagen on the 26th. On 27th July 1945 she was returned to DFDS, renamed *Parkeston* and became the only one of the four sister ships to be returned to service.

With all three of the principal pre-war users of the port having seen their fleets depleted it was obvious that the restoration of commercial services out of Parkeston Quay and Harwich would take quite a while to implement and start at a very low level of frequency. The Hook of Holland and Esbjerg services did not reopen until November and December 1945 whilst those to Rotterdam, Antwerp and the train ferry service to Zeebrugge had to wait until 1946. The pre-war passenger service to Zeebrugge was never resumed. It would not be until 1947 that the LNER received any replacement tonnage yet the end of the war did at least bring an immediate and welcome improvement to the local economy as a great many port related jobs could now be reinstated.

The first return to 'passengers' using the port, after an absence of nearly six years, began with the movement of thousands of troops, displaced persons and returning prisoners of war. Ever since D-Day, on 6th June 1944, preparations were in hand so that troops who had completed six months service abroad became entitled to ten days leave in the U.K. This led to the first official 'leave boat' sailing from Calais to Folkestone on 1st January 1945 though a limited service had earlier run between Antwerp and Tilbury.

The facilities at Tilbury had since become overcrowded and so an additional route was opened up between Calais and Parkeston Quay after the Royal Navy had agreed to release a berth. Sailings began on 4th January 1945 but the service only lasted a few weeks during which time a number of vessels, still under military command, made occasional trips which between them averaged a crossing only every other day.

The first such sailing was from Parkeston Quay by the *Lairds Isle* of Burns & Laird Lines. The other ships used were the Belgian ferries *Princess Josephine Charlotte* and *Princess Astrid,* both sailing with the prefix *H.M.S.* and transferred from an Ostend to Tilbury service, the Isle of Man Steam Packet Co's *Lady of Mann,* which made the most sailings, and the Southern Railway's *Biarritz* which closed the route on 27th February 1945 when sailing as the last ship to leave from Parkeston Quay. Carryings on board this highly infrequent service to Calais were restricted to 500 persons per crossing.

First and last dates of sailings:

Lairds Isle	4th January to 13th January
Princess Josephine Charlotte	5th January to 26th February
Biarritz	5th January to 27th February
Lady of Mann	13th January to mid February
Princess Astrid	17th January to 12th February

When these sailings to Parkeston Quay ended the trooping service returned to the Calais to Folkestone and Dover routes. After VE Day the numbers increased enormously and reaching Calais became beset with problems of logistics and the availability of sufficient trains of adequate quality. Journey times in from Germany and through Belgium for troops of the British Liberation Army (BLA) became longer and more uncomfortable and with the arrival of a new flow of troops returning from Italy, known as Medloc or the Mediterranean Line of Communication, Calais soon reached its limits when handling 7,500 a day in July 1945.

A new outlet was urgently needed and a Harwich, ie Parkeston Quay, to the Hook of Holland service was deemed the most suitable. It would be run by the MOWT who took over Berths 5 and 6 at Parkeston Quay together with No. 3 Shed and the use of Parkeston Quay West railway station. At the Hook they used the quay alongside the old 'Fruit Wharf' where the shed there later became a NAAFI.

The service got under way when the *Royal Ulsterman,* from the Burns & Laird Line's Glasgow to Belfast service, and the *Duke of York,* from the LMS's Heysham to Belfast service, left Parkeston Quay on the night of 31st July 1945. The route to the Hook of Holland had only recently become possible again following the location of enemy minefields and the Dutch railway authorities having undertaken to repair and reopen a number of badly damaged railway lines into Germany. Sailings were overnight in each direction.

The first trainload of troops to arrive at the Hook and then depart by ship did so on 1st August 1945 having travelled in from Hamburg on a far from direct route. The service improved as more and more railway lines were repaired and extra ships laid on for a movement of troops that was rising to a rate of 2,000 per day. Of the two Parkeston railway ships the *Vienna,* owned by the MOWT, had already been trooping since 1st April between Ostend and Tilbury. She joined the Parkeston Quay service on 1st August and was followed by the *Antwerp,* on charter to the MOWT, on 19th September.

By now these trooping movements were officially those of the British Army of the Rhine (BAOR) having been re-designated as such on 25th August 1945 from the BLA. Another service was opened from Dieppe to Folkestone to handle the Medloc traffic with duty travel, as opposed to leave, being maintained via Ostend and Dover. On 15th October 1945 a further service was opened up between Cuxhaven and Hull.

The transit arrangements at Parkeston Quay were

such that the inbound troops were met and taken away by four trains, two for London plus one each for Edinburgh and Manchester. A few hours later would arrive a similar number of trains loaded with troops coming off leave. These outward personnel were then moved by lorry to a specially constructed 'transit camp' a few miles from the port where they were housed and fed before returning to the port for embarkation on the night crossing. This newly constructed 20 acre camp site, capable of housing up to 4,000 troops at a time, was built during the summer of 1945 and on into 1946 in part using German prisoners of war as labourers. It had the look of a holiday camp and was fully equipped with a staff of three hundred. In the very early days an existing Warners holiday camp in Dovercourt had been used for up to 650 troops at times of delays or bad weather. Prior to a similar facility being built at the Hook of Holland troops there were temporarily housed near the Schiehaven and moved to and from the terminal by train.

The only pre-war LNER passenger ship available for commercial use was the *Prague* and on 14th November 1945 she resumed her former role on the Hook of Holland route. She made three sailings a week leaving Parkeston Quay on Monday, Wednesday and Friday evenings at 10.00 pm and returning from the Hook on Tuesday, Thursday and Saturday at 10.15 pm. Arrival times were 8.00 am at the Hook and 6.00 am at Parkeston Quay. As there were no Sunday sailings the lay-over time was used for maintenance work.

The *Prague* had re-entered civilian service following an austerity refit at the yard of John Thornycroft and Co. in Southampton though her upper decks remained much the same as when she was built. The Promenade Deck retained its 29 First class cabins plus the 4 double bedded Cabin-de-Luxe. There was no cabin number thirteen. Lower down on A Deck or Shelter Deck, forward, were a further 68 First class cabins whilst aft there remained the original 48 seat First class Dining Saloon and First class Lounge. The shop was adjacent to the First class Bar whilst at the extreme aft end was a separate Second class Lounge.

It was down below on her lower decks where austerity prevailed as the *Prague* retained the configuration of a wartime hospital ship. New passenger accommodation was installed in those areas previously laid out as long ambulance wards but due to the urgency of getting the ship back into service this merely consisted of double tiered bunks some of which were free standing. The only consideration given to privacy was that they were separated by curtains. Practically the whole of B Deck or Main Deck was fitted in this way. At the forward end were two large dormitory style open spaces that extended the full width of the ship and housed a total of 101 such berths. Moving aft were two side areas with a further 38 berths, a Ladies First class Saloon that included one double cabin and three designated Ladies Compartments containing a further 49 berths. At the aft end were 2 Second class double cabins, another bunk area with 30 berths and a Second class Dining Saloon with 28 seats. On C Deck or Lower Deck a further 104 bunk berths were installed forward along with 44 aft next to 9 existing Second class double cabins.

Thus the *Prague*'s cabin accommodation now comprised of 4 Cabin-de-Luxe, 72 First class singles, 26 First class doubles and 11 Second class doubles. Together with the 366 bunk berths this gave her a total of 520 sleeping places which, although little different from when she was first built, now had a much more utilitarian layout than her once luxurious days pre-war.

The following month saw DFDS resume their own service from Denmark. The sole survivor from the pre-war quartet of motor ships, the *Parkeston,* arrived from Copenhagen on 7th December 1945 on a once a week

A view of a twin funnelled *Duke of York* in LNER service at the Hook of Holland. She was later refitted and converted to a single funnel profile in early 1951. (Robert Clow collection)

service that was to leave Parkeston Quay on Saturday and Esbjerg on Wednesday.

December 1945 also saw the arrival of a ship specifically for the Hook of Holland trooping service. This was the *Empire Wansbeck,* a vessel originally built in 1939 as a fruit ship for North German Lloyd but served out the war as the German minelayer *Linz* following her completion in 1943. The MOWT had acquired her on 1st December 1945 as part of the war reparations scheme and sent her for an overhaul in Hull. There she was fitted with somewhat basic accommodation for 700 troops in tiered bunk bed dormitories plus cabin berths for 150 officers and those travelling with families. She was placed under the management of Ellerman Wilson Line and with Captain Johnson in command she first arrived at Parkeston Quay on 17th December 1945 sporting a black hull and EWL funnel colours. Her capacity was later raised to 1,050 but as she was less well appointed internally she found herself mainly in the role of spare or relief vessel and sailing at weekends when her higher capacity was used in moving those troops that the regular ships could not handle. Otherwise she just lay alongside together with all of her 50 crew on board.

When the LNER restarted their passenger service to the Hook of Holland it was hoped that this single ship service might be strengthened by using one of the returning SMZ vessels but these were still pre-occupied with their ongoing military or government duties. Since July 1945 the Dutch Government had been running a somewhat irregular trooping service of their own between Rotterdam and Tilbury for the benefit of Dutch military and government personnel, some repatriation work and a very limited cargo service. The agents at Rotterdam's Jobshaven were Wm.H. Muller & Co., owners of Batavier Line and managers of SMZ.

This Dutch run service commenced on 6th July 1945 using the *Batavier II* which was built in 1921. She was joined by the *Oranje Nassau* on 27th August and by the *Mecklenburg* on 21st November following their respective release from the Dutch and Royal Navies. Sailings to Tilbury ceased in March 1946 but since January that year a more regular service was running between Rotterdam and Parkeston Quay. The *Mecklenburg* was the first alongside at Parkeston Quay on 9th January followed by the *Batavier II* on the 10th. This service was usually twice a week with sailings from Rotterdam on a Wednesday and Friday and those from Parkeston Quay on Thursday and Saturday. The service could often be very busy with up to three ships being used on the same crossing.

By now the SMZ were facing major problems at Flushing. The port had been severely damaged during the war with much of the infrastructure in ruins, the harbour blocked, its offices and workshops destroyed and rail connections into Europe practically non existent. Whilst the situation was under review the Company relocated, on 1st April 1946, to temporary offices in the Jobshaven provided by Wm.H. Muller & Co..

During April 1946 three SMZ ships were released from military duties and preparations were made for their return to commercial services. The *Mecklenburg* was released on 16th April and was due an extensive overhaul. The *Prinses Beatrix* had already arrived at Flushing on 13th April and the *Koningin Emma* arrived there on the 29th April. A contract was awarded to the De Schelde yard to convert the *Prinses Beatrix* as the first one back into civilian use. However when the time came to start converting it was decided it would be quicker instead to convert the *Oranje Nassau* first. Whilst waiting the *Oranje Nassau* rejoined the Dutch Government service from Rotterdam on 24th April before leaving at the end of June.

Upon her return she was transferred to the Hook of Holland passenger service to run opposite the still lone running *Prague*. The route became every night, except on Sundays, when the *Oranje Nassau* made her first sailing from the Hook on 29th July 1946. With the service now running six days a week so too did the 'Hook Continental' boat train. Since November 1945 this had previously been running three days a week in conjunction with the sailings of the *Prague* and which departed London Liverpool Street at 8.00 pm and arrived at Parkeston Quay at 9.40 pm. The 'North Country Continental' did not resume running until 1949.

Replacing the *Oranje Nassau* on the Dutch Government service was the *Prinses Beatrix* which arrived on 3rd July 1946 and stayed on this route until she and the *Batavier II* closed it on 28th September 1946. Throughout their time together the *Batavier II* and *Prinses Beatrix* operated four sailings a week. When the service closed the *Koningin Emma* and *Prinses Beatrix* then received their major overhauls.

The four ships used between Tilbury/Parkeston Quay and Rotterdam sailed as follows:
Batavier II
    6th July 1945 to 28th September 1946
    (P. Quay from 10th January 1946)
Oranje Nassau
    27th August 1945 to 29th June 1946
    (P. Quay from 25th April 1946)
Mecklenburg
    21st November 1945 to 4th April 1946
    (P. Quay from 9th January 1946)
Prinses Beatrix
    (P. Quay from 3rd July 1946 to 28th September 1946)

Improvements to the DFDS route in March 1946 saw the *Parkeston* joined by the *A. P. Bernstorff* and the service becoming twice a week. She was on the route for just three months prior to the introduction of a brand new ship, the *Kronprins Frederik*. The appearance of a new ship so soon after the war had finished was due to it having been part built before the war and subsequently 'hidden'. Her story became almost one of folklore.

She was ordered in 1939 as one of three proposed sister ships. In the presence of Company directors she was launched at Elsinore on 20th June 1940 and named by H.R.H. Kronprins Frederik. At the time she was close to completion apart from being fitted out and would have been a valuable prize to the invading Germans had they taken her over. On the pretext that she could not be completed in Elsinore the ship was towed round to Copenhagen and placed in a part of the harbour where she could only be moved at exceptionally high tide and out past lifting bridges that were prone to mysteriously breaking down. The whole move had been a ruse to thwart the Germans who themselves, as a consequence of having sunk the *Algiers* in March 1940, had already disrupted her completion as the ship they sank was carrying her new propellers.

Whilst in Copenhagen parts of the new ship's machinery were dismantled and variously hidden in scrap yards and farmyards whilst the wooden fittings were stored in barges moored close by. She remained in Copenhagen throughout the war, was liberated in May 1945 and then towed back to Elsinore in

November. There she was completed after the removed parts had been retrieved and new machinery and propellers had been sent over from the United States. She was also fitted with radar, initially provided by the RAF, and electrical wiring taken from the German ship *Bremen*. After trials in the spring of 1946 she made her first crossing to Parkeston Quay on 26th May where she arrived next day for berthing trials. She entered commercial service when sailing from Esbjerg on 5th June, the occasion being marked by the presence on board of H.R.H. Kronprins Frederik.

At 3,895 grt and around 375 feet long she could carry 358 passengers with berth accommodation for 143 in First class and 159 in Second class comprising a mixture of one, two and four-berth cabins. Space was also available for 33 cars. With a service speed of 20¼ knots the crossing time was around 19 hours and the service increased to three times a week.

Meanwhile the LNER had set about sorting out their other pre-war services. A cargo service to Rotterdam had been resumed in February 1946 by using the chartered vessel *Lynn Trader* but after the *Sheringham* was demobilised on 8th March the service reverted to being run by a railway ship. The *Sheringham* made her first trip to Rotterdam on the 23rd March and from 1st April a twice weekly service operated with departures from Rotterdam on Monday and Wednesday. During the war Rotterdam's Merwehaven terminal had been destroyed and so a temporary berth in the Lekhaven was being used instead. The service went on to become three times a week with the return of the *Felixstowe* on 20th September 1946. The *Felixstowe* had been released on 19th January 1946 and given a refit following which she resumed her original name after having served as *H.M.S. Colchester*.

The service to Antwerp resumed a once a week service on 29th July 1946 though this would no longer be the prestigious passenger route it was in the days pre-war. With no local vessels available the LNER were forced to bring in tonnage from other routes and initially they acquired the use of the rather elderly passenger cargo ship *Accrington*. This vessel came off the Grimsby services and dated back to the days of the old Great Central Railway. Built in 1910 she was however no stranger to Parkeston Quay on account of having been used as a troopship to Rotterdam in 1919.

When launched she was fitted out to a luxury standard, at least for those 100 passengers travelling in First class. Their stateroom accommodation was located along the Bridge Deck amidships and supplemented by several four berth cabins and one luxury stateroom on the Main Deck. Those termed Cabin de-Luxe had armchairs, porcelain washstands and brass bedsteads. On the Main Deck was a full width saloon whilst on the Bridge Deck were two further lounges, one a Gentlemen's smoking lounge and bar, the other a Ladies lounge complete with easy chairs, bookcase and writing table. Second class accommodation consisted only of 10 berths under the poop. Further accommodation for up to 300 in Third class was located in fore and aft tween-decks though when first built these were classified as Emigrant class. Following her recent wartime activities as a convoy rescue ship the *Accrington* was returned to civilian use with her accommodation vastly altered. When she arrived for the Antwerp route she could carry 116 First class and 68 Third class passengers though slept just 77 in First class berths.

The service was quickly increased to twice a week on 30th August 1946 with the addition of the *Dewsbury*, also from the old GCR fleet, with accommodation for 197 passengers and 100 First class berths. Sailings now left from both Parkeston Quay and Antwerp on a Tuesday and Friday night. Connecting boat trains of just four coaches would leave London Liverpool Street at 3.00 pm, the ship sailing at 6.00 pm to arrive in Antwerp at 9.00 am next morning. In the return direction the sailing from Antwerp left at 5.00 pm and arrived back at Parkeston Quay at 6.00 am. It was noticeable that both ships were running to a slower crossing time of 14 hours compared with the 12 hours taken before the war.

The last LNER route to re-open was the Harwich to Zeebrugge train ferry service when operations resumed on 16th August 1946 utilising the sole surviving *H.M.S. Princess Iris*, formerly *Train Ferry No.1*. She had arrived on the Clyde on 6th May 1946 and was paid off on 20th May. The LNER then bought her back from the Government for £33,334 and gave her a £3,510 overhaul at John Brown & Co's yard on Clydeside. She was re-named *Essex Ferry* and resumed service making three round trips a week. The length of rail track on board was slightly amended from her original specifications to two inner lengths of 298 feet and two outer lengths of 211 feet. This gave a total length of 1,018 feet and sufficient room for 32 wagons, this lower number being due to the emergence of larger sized continental wagons since the days of when the original train ferries were able to carry 54 of the old style 12-ton trucks. However her old route was not an easy one to work. Zeebrugge and the train ferry linkspan behind the Visart Lock were so severely war damaged that it was thought the route might not re-open at all. The port was dangerously littered with wrecks and even after clearing a way through she could only manoeuvre safely in and out of port an hour either side of high tide.

Since 1st January 1946 there had been 20 troop trains a day arriving at the various Continental ports of which two went to Dieppe, ten to Calais, four to Ostend, one to Cuxhaven and three to the Hook of Holland. Arrival times at the Hook were at 1.09 pm from Hamburg, 1.45 pm from Kiel and 4.15 pm from Hannover whilst departures from the Hook were at 10.30 am for Hannover, 11.20 am for Hamburg and 12.20 pm for Kiel.

By the late summer of 1946 the number of troops having passed through Parkeston Quay was said to have reached the incredible figure of one and a half million. Ten different ships, mainly from Irish Sea routes, had been utilised during the past nine months alone, a figure that later rose to a total of twelve in all.

Royal Ulsterman
    31st July 1945 to 16th November 1945
Duke of York
    31st July 1945 to 14th November 1946
Ulster Monarch
    1st August 1945 to 16th August 1945
Vienna
    1st August 1945 to 1st July 1960
Duke of Rothesay
    7th August 1945 to 14th September 1946
St. Andrew
    18th August 1945 to 24th July 1946
Antwerp
    19th September 1945 to 1st May 1950
St. Helier
    18th November 1945 to 15th March 1946

Empire Wansbeck
   17th December 1945 to 26th September 1961
Manxman
   16th March 1946 to 24th February 1949
Empire Parkeston
   4th April 1947 to 25th September 1961
Biarritz
   6th September 1947 to 8th August 1948

Up until 6th April 1947 only troops on leave were being moved through Parkeston Quay. Thereafter the port additionally handled duty personnel diverted from Calais and this further work led to the introduction of a much larger vessel, the *Empire Parkeston*. Built in 1930 as the *Prince Henry* she was initially a passenger ship of some luxury sailing for the Canadian National Steamship Company. She was one of three sister ships constructed by Cammell Laird at Birkenhead via an order placed by the then President of the Canadian National Railway, Sir Henry Thornton, formerly the General Manager of the GER between 1914 and 1922.

In 1940 the *Prince Henry* became the Canadian Government's armed merchant cruiser *H.M.C.S. Prince Henry* having undergone a major structural conversion that saw the removal of most of her two upper decks and the forward two of her three original funnels being made into one much larger one. In 1943 she was further converted to an infantry landing ship with accommodation for 550 troops and eight landing craft and later loaned to the Royal Navy as *H.M.S. Prince Henry* in May 1945. She was then bought by the MOWT for £125,000 in late 1946 and converted to a troopship at Harland & Wolff's yard in Southampton. From there she emerged with a black hull, a light grey superstructure and black funnels. She was given the name *Empire Parkeston* on 17th March 1947 and arrived at Parkeston Quay on 4th April 1947 under the management of the General Steam Navigation Company.

At 5,576 grt she was the largest ship then regularly using the port. On board were forward saloons for the troops, aft saloons for the officers and 182 cabins that varied in size from 2 to 11 persons used by officers, women, civilian staff and families. Three tiered bunk accommodation was provided for up to 813 troops. Additionally she had a crew of 87 of which 27 were catering crew. As with the *Empire Wansbeck* no meals were served on board but a NAAFI was provided.

The *Vienna* was also refitted in 1947 and she emerged with 1,048 berths. Her wartime grey was likewise changed to a black hull and light grey superstructure though she resumed her LNER funnel colours. Conditions on board were similarly austere for the troops but the higher ranks enjoyed the luxury of an Officers Club. A refit of the *Antwerp* saw her accommodation amended to carrying up to 822 troops plus 86 cabin berths of which 36 were for officers and 50 for civilians travelling on duty. There were also a further 22 berths reserved for women only.

In early 1947 SMZ decided that as the port at Flushing was in such bad shape the Company's future would lay instead at the Hook of Holland. In July that year they left their temporary offices in Rotterdam provoking a difference of opinion that would last between themselves and the Dutch Government until 1953. Meanwhile SMZ set about re-commencing a day boat service to Parkeston Quay.

A three times a week service began using the *Mecklenburg* which had since been refitted at Wilton Fijenoord's yard in Schiedam. During that time she was converted to being oil fired and her accommodation was restructured to cater for 67 passengers in First class and 450 in Deck class. She left the yard on 13th June carrying invited guests for Parkeston Quay and made her inaugural voyage in passenger service from Parkeston Quay to the Hook of Holland on 14th June 1947. Sailings from Parkeston Quay were on Tuesday, Thursday and Saturday and from the Hook of Holland on Wednesday, Friday and Sunday. SMZ moved into their new offices at the Hook of Holland in July 1947 though they retained and rebuilt their workshops at Flushing and continued to use those facilities for laying up their ships.

The LNER's first post war new build passenger ship for Parkeston Quay was the *Arnhem*. She was built at John Brown's on the Clyde at a cost of £684,364 and launched by Her Excellency Madame H. Michiels van Verduynen on 7th November 1946. She was named in commemoration of the 1944 Battle of Arnhem and made her first appearance at Parkeston Quay on 12th May 1947. This was followed by a courtesy call to Rotterdam on 23rd May where she was inspected by H.R.H. Princess Juliana.

The *Arnhem*'s appearance was very different to her predecessors by having a much more enclosed superstructure and an extended upper deck. Her plans were originally based on a pre-war design that would have seen her looking as yet another twin funnelled coal fired vessel but these were changed to her being oil fired. This alteration resulted in just one overlarge funnel appearing where two smaller ones would have fitted. Her hull design was later used as the basis for the Royal Yacht *Britannia*.

At 377 feet long and 4,891 grt the *Arnhem* was built as a one class ship for 600 passengers with a layout designed to cater for a potential re-instatement of the Company's highly popular pre-war cruises. As such her cabin accommodation consisted of 4 'Specials' these being twin bedded Cabins-de-Luxe complete with private bathrooms plus 319 single cabins of which 95 were fitted with a second adjustable berth. However the total allocation of berths was categorised as being equal to 272 in First class and 150 in Second class though there remained just the one Lounge and one Dining Saloon both of which were on the Promenade Deck. Two sets of Parsons turbines produced an output of 12,480 shp that gave her a service speed of 21 knots. Her maiden voyage was from Parkeston Quay on 26th May 1947 and she was to be the last passenger ship built for the LNER. Her arrival displaced the *Oranje Nassau* which went off service on 23rd May 1947.

The train ferry service to Zeebrugge also received a new ship in 1947 when the 3,134 grt *Suffolk Ferry* entered service on 3rd September. Another product from John Brown's yard she was launched on 7th May 1947 as an unattractive floating box that was open at one end. Any attempt at elegance would have been wasted as the train ferry service was never to have any of the glamour associated with the passenger routes. Therefore the ships need only be built for the function they performed. However despite its plainness the *Suffolk Ferry* still cost £380,772.

Compared to the ageing *Essex Ferry* (ex *Train Ferry No. 1*) the *Suffolk Ferry* was about 40 feet longer overall at 404 feet 6 inches though her beam was the same as this was restricted to being able to fit through the locks at Zeebrugge. The train deck layout was broadly similar in having two rail tracks over the stern that branched into four on board and the total track length of 1,126 feet, made up of 2 x 340 feet inner rails and 2 x 223 feet outer rails, was ten percent more than that of the *Essex Ferry*. This allowed for a carrying capacity of between 32 and 38 of the larger sized continental wagons.

Much of the train deck was covered in and the officer and crew accommodation for 29 personnel was now located on a strengthened upper deck. In later years she would carry a number of trade cars aft on this upper deck though it would take the use of a forklift vehicle to place them there. In addition the *Suffolk Ferry* had limited passenger and sleeping accommodation for twelve people in 6 twin berth cabins, this being a throwback to the days of the GER's pre-war Zeebrugge passenger service. Power was provided by two 6-cylinder John Brown Sulzer diesel engines that gave her a service speed of just over 13 knots.

The arrival of the *Suffolk Ferry* saw the return of daily sailings but unfortunately she was a somewhat unstable vessel. Although she was fitted with twin screws she only had one central rudder and this made her almost unmanageable under certain conditions. After several precarious incidents involving heavy side on seas and twice heeling over with a list severe enough to sound the alarm bells she was quickly withdrawn from service and modified at the Tyneside yard of Palmer's at Hebburn. When she returned to service in December 1947 with twin rudders her handling was much improved.

In December 1947 it finally became possible to release the *Prague* for her first refit since the war. Her last trip was from the Hook of Holland on 24th December though this was delayed until 2.15 am on Christmas Day. She was then sent to John Brown's yard at Clydebank for refurbishing and a comprehensive overhaul. In her absence her sailings were taken up by a return of the *Oranje Nassau*.

One further development in 1947 had been the re-appearance of the *Stella Polaris* and the return to Parkeston Quay of luxury cruising. During the war she was seized by the Germans whilst in Norway and was afterwards recovered in Trondheim though in a somewhat dilapidated condition. After a thorough refit in Gothenburg she was returned to service for Clipper Line.

On 1st January 1948 a newly created British Transport Commission (BTC) took control of much of the nation's transport system and with it came the ending of the private railway companies. The LNER became part of the Eastern Region (ER) of a nationalised British Railways (BR) which included its quay and shipping services at Parkeston Quay and the Harwich train ferry service to Zeebrugge. At the time there were seven railway ships in service locally - the *Prague* and *Arnhem* to the Hook of Holland, *Accrington* and *Dewsbury* to Antwerp, *Sheringham* and *Felixstowe* to Rotterdam and the *Essex Ferry* and *Suffolk Ferry* to Zeebrugge.

The first ship to arrive at Parkeston Quay on that New Year's Day was the *Oranje Nassau* at 6.35 am from the Hook of Holland. The *Arnhem*, on her New Year's Eve overnight sailing to Holland, had left Parkeston Quay as part of the LNER and arrived at the Hook of Holland having been nationalised during the voyage.

The *Koningin Emma* finally emerged from her overhaul at Flushing in early 1948 and was chartered to BR as cover for the *Prague* in place of the *Oranje Nassau*. Her extensive conversion back to civilian use had changed her outward appearance by giving her a higher bridge and forward superstructure along with a lower profile funnel. Also her hull was now painted a more traditional black. Her passenger capacity was such that she could now carry up to 1,423 when running a day service and was fitted with berth accommodation for 203 passengers in First class and 94 in Second when on the night service. The *Koningin Emma*'s first trip back on the route was the night sailing from the Hook of Holland on 5th March 1948.

Just a few days later there occurred a major disaster with the loss of the *Prague* whilst being overhauled at John Brown's. On 14th March a fire broke out in the engine room. This led to an explosion that caused the vessel to heel over and end up resting against the dock wall. Despite firemen tackling the blaze for over twelve hours, during which time two were slightly hurt, the *Prague* could not be saved and the stricken ship was eventually sent away for scrap. As a consequence of having lost a ship that sailed to Holland the number of sailings from Parkeston Quay to Antwerp were increased that month from two to three times a week with services now leaving each port at 6.00 pm on a Monday, Wednesday and Friday.

As before, when replacement tonnage was sought, the now BR-ER again turned to ships from the Irish Sea and acquired those of what were once the LMS's during wartime and whose losses had not been so great. The *St. Andrew* from the Fishguard - Rosslare route was in use from mid April until replaced by the *Duke of York* from the Heysham - Belfast route. The *Duke of York* had recently been at Parkeston Quay on trooping duties but when she entered service as the Hook of Holland night service on 31st May 1948 she was to sail opposite the *Arnhem*. In doing so she displaced the *Koningin Emma*.

The *Duke of York* was built by Harland and Wolff in Belfast and launched in March 1935 for the LMS Railway. She originally sailed between Heysham and Belfast as a twin funnelled coal fired passenger and cargo ship with a large observation lounge or 'solarium' at the forward end of the boat deck. She was fitted with a raised foc'sle and roller hatches over the holds to which access was gained via four electric cranes. When first put into service on the Irish Sea she catered for a 'tourist' class of passenger which was likened to travelling in Third class though it was said that this felt little different to being in First Class. Cabin berths for 240 'tourists' were provided on the Main and Lower decks and aft whilst 139 First Class berths were located amidships. She served out the war as *H.M.S. Duke of Wellington* and when she arrived to join the Hook of

The first of the post WW2 new build train ferries, the *Suffolk Ferry*, entered service on 3rd September 1947. She is seen here alongside the Harwich train ferry berth in June 1972 little changed from new apart from her funnel markings. (NRM collection)

Holland service she then had berths for 129 in First Class and 206 in Second Class. She was re-registered at Harwich and in accordance with local tradition was fitted with the five pointed star on her bows.

That last day of May coincided with the SMZ day boat between Parkeston Quay and the Hook of Holland becoming a daily service when the *Prinses Beatrix,* back from her own overhaul, started sailings opposite the *Mecklenburg.* The *Koningin Emma* was then chartered out to Batavier Line for service between Rotterdam and Tilbury. There she joined the *Batavier II* and sailed on this route between 15th June and 30th September 1948.

During the summer of 1948 the *Felixstowe* was transferred to BR's Weymouth to Channel Islands service. This left the cargo service to Rotterdam solely in the hands of the *Sheringham* with sailings reduced to just twice a week. Cutbacks in sailings were similarly planned for the Antwerp service despite having recently been increased as a result of the *Prague* incident. For BR the service was not seen as being an ongoing concern even though it was said to have been profitable for the LNER in 1947. During September and October 1948 the *Duke of Argyll,* from the Heysham to Belfast route, covered the Hook of Holland route whilst the *Arnhem* and *Duke of York* went off for overhaul. In 1949 she and her sister ship *Duke of Rothesay* were both seen at Parkeston Quay on various occasions.

In response to increasing numbers on the Esbjerg route, which in 1947 had seen 51,100 passengers, a new ship was launched for DFDS in January 1948 and arrived at Parkeston Quay on 14th June 1949 following her maiden voyage. She was named *Kronprinsesse Ingrid* as a sister ship to the *Kronprins Frederik*. Although of the same design the *Kronprinsesse Ingrid* had an all welded hull as opposed to the riveted one of the *Kronprins Frederik* and her build price of around £600,000 was nearly twice that of the older ship. With two large passenger ships on the route the number of sailings were increased to six per week during the summer and the year ended with 69,763 passengers having been carried. The arrival of the *Kronprinsesse Ingrid* displaced the *Parkeston* to sailing between Newcastle and Copenhagen. In addition there had been several 'first arrivals' of DFDS cargo ships many of which were now over 25 years old. These were the *Thyra, Rota, Trondhjem* and *Tunis* to which later would be added the *Marocco* and *Bergenhus*.

During the summer season of 1949 two of the SMZ vessels were deployed on other routes. The *Oranje Nassau* was chartered to Batavier Line and the *Mecklenburg* was used in an attempt to revive a Flushing to Folkestone service as from 7th July. The *Mecklenburg* would sail two round trips at weekends but was not a great success due to the lack of a direct rail connection to Folkestone Harbour. However both ships repeated these respective summer season rosters until 1952.

In 1949 the Parkeston Quay to Hook of Holland trooping service was the only one left in use. Calais had since closed as a military port on 4th October 1947 with all its traffic diverted to the Hook. From the 5th October 1947 the times of the troop trains at the Hook of Holland were: Arrivals at 3.02 pm from Villach (Medloc), 5.03 pm from Hannover, 6.03 pm from Hamburg/Bielefeld and 8.05 pm from Hamburg with departures at 7.50 am for Hamburg, 8.56 am for Bielefeld/Hamburg, 10.13 am for Hannover and 11.30 am for Villach (Medloc).

The Cuxhaven to Hull service had ceased on 3rd June 1948 and with all troop movements now focused on the Hook of Holland there remained sufficient demand for daily troopship sailings to Parkeston Quay. Also there remained the three trains a day to and from the Dutch port and four a day when the Medloc service arrived. The three daily trains served the Northern, Central and Southern areas of the British Zone of Germany and were respectively colour coded Blue, Red and Green. They departed the Hook of Holland in time order as above with personnel being given a colour coded token to identify their correct train. The Medloc train was the White Train.

However by 1949 the number of BAOR troops being moved was in decline and by March 1949 only four ships remained in service, these being the *Antwerp, Vienna, Empire Wansbeck* and *Empire Parkeston*. Each were still under the control of their respective ship management company who had the responsibility of providing the crew, fuel and stores as well as undertaking any required maintenance and repairs. However all continued to be overseen and worked to the requirements of the Sea Transport Service acting on behalf of the Government. From April 1949 the number of weekly sailings was reduced to six by withdrawing those on Saturdays.

Ships of the LNER were ranked for the purpose of determining a Captain's rate of pay which the Company then scaled against the number of years served as a Captain. In 1949 those categories were as follows: Passenger Vessel over 15 Knots - Captain Sutton on *Vienna*, Captain Adams on *Antwerp*, Captain Pickering on *Arnhem* and Captain Baxter on *Duke of York*. Passenger Vessel under 15 Knots - Captain Bonser on *Accrington* and Captain Holland on *Dewsbury*. Train Ferry - Captain Nugent on *Essex Ferry* and Captain Good on *Suffolk Ferry*. Cargo Vessel over 1,000grt - Captain Greenham on *Sheringham*. Without a regular ship was Captain Stephenson. The various pay scales were:

	Passenger Vessel (+15 Knots)	Passenger Vessel (-15 Knots)	Train Ferry	Cargo Vessel (+1,000grt)
1st Year	815	775	730	710
4th Year	830	790	745	725
7th Year	850	810	760	740
10th Year	875	835	780	760

All except Captains' Bonser and Stephenson were on their 10th year rate of pay.

The end of the 1940s saw services in and out of Parkeston Quay and Harwich finally becoming settled again after a decade scarred by war. Figures for 1949 showed the number of passengers having passed through Parkeston Quay as being 176,000 departures and 180,000 arrivals. Cars totalled 9,149. At Harwich the amount of cargo carried by the train ferry service was 82,728 tons. Overall the quantity of freight was resuming the levels seen pre-war but passenger traffic was still slow in returning. Partly as a consequence BR announced in 1949 the impending end of the passenger service to Antwerp.

Although the war was over its legacy was ongoing. On her way to dry-dock at Elsinore on 2nd May 1947 the *Parkeston* hit a mine which severely damaged her stern and steering gear. Fortunately there were no casualties but in 1950 the *Frigga*, the first DFDS cargo ship to have arrived at Parkeston Quay just after the war had ended, also hit a mine and subsequently sank.

THE 1950s

British Railways decision to close the Antwerp passenger service came into effect in early 1950. The service had remained at three times a week up until the *Accrington* and *Dewsbury* made their last passenger sailings from the Belgian port on 1st and 3rd of February respectively.

It was hardly an unexpected scenario. The ships were now 40 years old and the attractions of earlier years no longer existed. The *Dewsbury* was withdrawn from service but the *Accrington* continued on the route as a cargo only vessel. However the situation quickly changed following a string of complaints and the *Accrington* resumed passenger sailings on 17th April 1950 albeit with a restricted capacity of just twelve travellers.

The Hook of Holland trooping service was reduced to five sailings a week as from 26th February 1950 with the cancellation of those on a Sunday. This was followed by the withdrawal of the *Antwerp* on 1st May, leaving just three ships in service, and this led to a further reduction in sailings to every other day as from 15th May 1950. The *Antwerp* was laid up on the buoys pending a sale but was eventually sold for scrap the following year.

On a more positive note the war damaged Hook of Holland railway station had since been rebuilt and the Hook service was in receipt of a brand new night boat. Built at a cost of £904,514 the *Amsterdam* was launched at John Brown's Clydebank yard on 19th January 1950 and arrived at Parkeston Quay under the command of Captain Baxter on 29th May.

Beforehand the early months of 1950 had seen the Hook service covered by two more Irish Sea vessels acting as relief ships. The *St. David* came round from Fishguard and relieved between late January and mid February followed by the *Duke of Lancaster* from Heysham from mid April until 20th May.

The *Amsterdam* was a modified sister ship to the *Arnhem* and undertook her maiden voyage on 10th June 1950. She was the third ship to bear the name *Amsterdam* and her naming was a further symbolic gesture towards the people of Holland. She could carry 675 passengers though unlike the *Arnhem* she was built as a two class ship from the outset. On board was cabin accommodation for 321 in First class single and double berth cabins with 236 in Second class made up of doubles and four berths. In addition there were four Cabin-de-Luxe. Her layout was similar to the *Arnhem* in that she had two main cargo holds and First Class accommodation forward with Second Class and holds for motor cars aft. In common with the *Arnhem* she could carry up to 18 cars but the *Amsterdam* had a clear difference visually in that her lifeboats were raised higher up in gravity davits.

The BR Hook of Holland night service was still operating a 'daily except Sunday' schedule but for the summer of 1950 this was increased to a sailing every day thus matching, temporarily, that of the SMZ day service. The timings of the respective services were:

BR 'Hook Continental'		SMZ 'Day Continental'	
Dep. London (L.St)	20.00	Dep. London (L.St)	09.25
Arr. P. Quay	21.40	Arr. P. Quay West	10.58
Dep. P. Quay	22.00	Dep. P. Quay West	11.30
Arr. HvH	05.45	Arr. HvH	18.40
Dep. HvH	22.50	Dep. HvH	11.30
Arr. P. Quay	06.00	Arr. P. Quay West	18.40
Dep. P. Quay	06.45	Dep. P. Quay West	19.45
Arr. London (L.St)	08.23	Arr. London (L.St)	21.20

From 25th September onwards the 'Hook Continental' from Parkeston Quay reverted to its regular out of season timing of 07.15 and the 'Day Continental' was brought forward to depart at 19.35. For those travelling out of season with DFDS the 'Scandinavian' boat train left London Liverpool Street at 10.05 and by means of a mid-day sailing from Parkeston Quay reached Esbjerg at about 08.00 the next morning. The 'Scandinavian' ran through to Harwich Town and from there it formed a return working that left at 13.45.

The recently resumed 'North Country Continental' left Parkeston Quay at 08.00 daily, except Sunday, and throughout the early 1950s would often run as follows:

Dep. Parkeston Quay	08.00	Dep. Liverpool (Central)	12.50
Arr. Sheffield (Victoria)	13.11	Dep. Manchester (Cent.)	13.50
Arr. Manchester (Cent.)	14.37	Dep. Sheffield (Victoria)	15.12
Arr. Liverpool (Central)	15.30	Arr. Parkeston Quay	20.43

After Parkeston Quay the train would run on to arrive at Dovercourt Bay at 20.53 and Harwich Town at 20.55 though when heading north it only ever started out from Parkeston Quay. A restaurant car was conveyed to and from Sheffield.

Passengers arriving at Parkeston Quay station in 1950 were greeted by a series of multi lingual announcements in order to speed up their progress through Customs and Immigration and to further assist foreign travellers in passing through the port. A system designed by the General Electric Co. Ltd. and equipped with pre-recorded tapes now informed Continental passengers in English, Dutch and German what to do and where to go whilst Scandinavian passengers were informed in English and Danish. This

Launch of the BR train ferry *Norfolk Ferry* at John Brown's yard at Clydebank - 8th March 1951. (NRM collection)

The DFDS passenger vessel *Kronprinsesse Ingrid* alongside No. 2 Berth - 13th May 1952. (Robert Clow collection)

facility proved so successful that in the summer of 1952 a similar system was installed on the 'Hook Continental' boat train, this being the first of its kind to be fitted on a British main line train.

With the *Amsterdam* and *Arnhem* now in charge of the Hook of Holland night service the *Duke of York* became the relief or spare ship and for the summer of 1950 she was sent to join BR's Southern Region services out of Southampton. From early July until late September she operated a twice weekly service to St. Malo plus a Friday night sailing to Guernsey. On completion of this she went back to her builders at Harland & Wolff in Belfast for an extensive refit.

By the end of 1950 the Hook of Holland night service had carried 220,569 passengers, 2,934 vehicles and 19,994 tons of cargo. A revenue of £1,152,052 more than covered an expenditure of £529,901 giving rise to a profit of £622,151. During that year the twice weekly cargo service to Rotterdam had resumed the use of its terminal at Merwehaven, tying up at the Hudig & Pieters Wharf, whilst the Antwerp service was still running three times a week. However both the latter services were running at a loss with the year end figures looking hugely disappointing.

P. Quay to:	Cargo (t)	Vehicles	Receipts	Expenditure	Balance profit (loss)
Rotterdam	16,289	1,350	£84,149	£87,803	(£3,654)
Antwerp	16,774	1,086	£94,772	£107,898	(£13,126)

As a result the sole survivor on the Antwerp route, the *Accrington*, was to make her last sailing from Antwerp on 6th January 1951. She was soon sold for scrap, realising £19,000, and left on 30th April for the breakers yard at Dunston on the Tyne. This was only a few days after the *Antwerp* had similarly left on the 26th for breaking up at T.W. Ward's of Milford Haven.

Yet despite losing money the Antwerp service was again saved 'by popular demand' and the ageing *Dewsbury* returned to the route on 10th February 1951. Sailings became twice a week with departures from Parkeston Quay on Monday and Thursday and from Antwerp on Tuesday and Friday. As had been the case with the *Accrington* the accommodation on board the *Dewsbury* was also reduced to carrying just 12 passengers in what must have been the most unusual of First class surroundings that were both comfortable and decidedly old fashioned.

The *Duke of York* re-entered service in May 1951 with both her crew and passenger accommodation having been thoroughly reconfigured and modernised. Her passenger certificate had been reduced from 1,500 down to 675 in keeping with her role as a night boat and this made for a much more comfortable ship to be on. Improvements were made to upgrade her First class accommodation and she now had 198 First class cabins containing 360 berths though only 54

Fire onboard the *Kronprins Frederik* in No. 2 Berth - 19th April 1953. (Robert Clow collection)

Second class cabins with 160 berths. Much of the extra accommodation was placed in the tween decks formerly used for cargo or, in her early days, for cattle. In addition she had been converted to oil burning and her two funnels replaced by a single elliptical one. Her aft docking bridge was also now removed.

Throughout her time in Belfast the Hook of Holland relief ships had been the *Duke of Argyll* for the first three weeks of February 1951 and the *St. David* from mid-April until mid-May. On 20th May 1951 the Hook of Holland night boat resumed its year round seven days a week service. However the newly refitted *Duke of York* was still the spare vessel and during the 1951 summer season she was again sent away, this time to the Holyhead to Dun Laoghaire service.

The Hook of Holland night service was now carrying upwards of a quarter of a million passengers per year, mainly businessmen throughout the year supplemented by large numbers of holiday makers during the summer. According to BR *'This is a service which has long been accepted as the natural route to Holland and Germany and which is able to hold it's own with air competition. Considerable quantities of perishable cargo are also carried by this service'.*

At the time the development of competition from air transport was referred to as 'a more disquieting element' against which cross-channel shipping services could not possibly hope to compete with in terms of speed. The boat's advantage was in terms of comfort with a need to better improve the facilities. *'The average passenger likes to feel that his well being and comfort on any journey is very much the consideration of the transport officials and staff. The boat train is the passenger's first introduction to the cross-channel service, and care should be taken to see that the stock is kept quite clean, an ample supply of hot water is available for washing together with towels and soap. Restaurant facilities should be ample and the food tastefully prepared and well served. It is of course desirable that the ships and associated shore facilities should be up to date. Consideration might also be given to the inclusion of meals and tips in the fares, the introduction of special tourist rates and an extensive publicity campaign'.*

In contrast to the loss making general cargo routes to Rotterdam and Antwerp the train ferry service from Harwich to Zeebrugge was highly profitable and in July 1951 there arrived another new vessel from John Brown's yard. Launched on 8th March and built at a cost of £459,796 the *Norfolk Ferry* was a sister ship to the *Suffolk Ferry* and these two modern vessels then relegated the *Essex Ferry* to the status of relief. The overall design of the *Norfolk Ferry* was essentially the same as the *Suffolk Ferry* except for some modifications made to her forward superstructure and her being 5 feet shorter overall. These were the result of earlier issues that affected the *Suffolk Ferry* in bad weather though in general all the train ferries would forever 'roll about a bit'.

Demand for using the train ferries was now growing by up to 30% a year and at times during the summer months the service required two sailings a day.

Harwich - Zeebrugge figures

	Tons Cargo	in Wagons	Receipts	Expenditure	Balance profit (loss)
1950	102,242	13,689	£372,707	£309,165	£63,542
1951	139,322	16,851	£490,602	£391,872	£98,730
1952	131,881	15,683	£505,660	£407,644	£98,016

The DFDS service to Esbjerg ran six days a week in summer and twice a week in winter. In between seasons there was an interim service of four sailings a week. For both this and the summer season the 'Scandinavian' boat train left London Liverpool Street at 15.10, the ship from Parkeston Quay sailed at 18.00 and Esbjerg was reached at 13.00 the next day. From there the connecting 'Englaenderen' boat train for Copenhagen left at 14.22 and reached the Danish capital at around 19.40. In the return direction the 'Englaenderen' left Copenhagen at 12.15 and arrived in Esbjerg at 17.30. There the ship departed at 18.00 and arrived at Parkeston Quay by 13.00 the next day. Passengers for London then boarded the 'Scandinavian' that left at 13.30 and arrived in Liverpool Street at 14.58 or, on Sundays, at 15.28.

During the interim timetable the *Kronprinsesse Ingrid* left Esbjerg on Monday and Thursday and the *Kronprins Frederik* on Wednesday and Saturday. Their combined schedules involved a regular pattern of layovers at each port with the *Ingrid* departing Parkeston Quay on Wednesday and Saturday and the *Frederik* on Friday and Monday.

(Mon, Wed, Fri, Sat)		(Mon, Wed, Thurs, Sat)	
Dep. London (L.St)	15.10	Dep. Esbjerg	18.00
Arr. P. Quay	16.40	Arr. P. Quay	13.00
Dep. P. Quay	18.00	Dep. P. Quay	13.30
Arr. Esbjerg	13.00	Arr. London (L.St)	14.58

For the winter service the twice weekly departures saw either the *Kronprinsesse Ingrid* or the *Kronprins Frederik* leave Parkeston Quay on Tuesday and Friday. The departure time was brought forward to 12.30 with arrivals in Esbjerg being at 09.00. Sailings from Esbjerg departed on Wednesday and Saturday at 18.00.

(Tues, Fri)		(Wed, Sat)	
Dep. London (L.St)	10.05	Dep. Esbjerg	18.00
Arr. P. Quay	11.42	Arr. P. Quay	13.00
Dep. P. Quay	12.30	Dep. P. Quay	13.30
Arr. Esbjerg	09.00	Arr. London (L.St)	14.58

1951 fares from London to: Esbjerg   Copenhagen
First class throughout - Single £11.11s.3d. £13.18s.7d.
                      - Return £22.3s.8d. £26.9s.9d.
Third class throughout - Single £7.10s.3d. £9.1s.8d.
                      - Return £14.11s.1d. £17.8s.3d.
Cabins and meals were extra.

A stricken *Kronprins Frederik* seen half submerged in No. 2 Berth. (Robert Clow collection)

On 11th February 1952, as the troopship *Vienna* was being readied for her 23.30 sailing to the Hook of Holland, an explosion occurred in her engine room at 21.45 causing the deaths of two of her crew. At the inquiry held in November that year the cause of the explosion was determined as being the result of the failure, through corrosion and fatigue, of a series of wrought iron combustion chamber stays within No. 3 boiler that had caused a plate to bulge loose and break open thus filling the stokehold with steam, scalding water and furnace contents. It was not an event that could have been predicted through normal inspections or periodic surveys that, to date, had been fully carried out. A point noting the current role of the *Vienna* was that ever since 1945 she was to have operated on the basis of two weeks on and two weeks off but the trooping service had been so demanding that this had not been possible.

In 1952 work began on reconstructing the eastern end of Parkeston Quay, this being the original 1881 structure along which the Hook of Holland night boat and the DFDS passenger boats were berthed. Upon inspection both the concrete cylinders and the cast iron piles were found to be in a satisfactory condition and the timber piles were generally sound. However a few on the seaward side were in need of replacement and so new steel box piles were installed. The original timber deck and supporting wrought iron joists were removed and replaced by a new reinforced concrete deck that covered the northern most 60 feet of quay to the quay face. The remaining 40 feet to the rear, or to the south of this, was repaired as built using recovered timber.

A new system of fendering was installed to cope with ships of up to 5,000 tons in size. This consisted of hanging timbers, mounted through rubber springs, onto reinforced concrete buttresses and the quay wall. On the quay itself new sections of sleepered rail were laid upon ballast and the ground level raised flush to rail height by a macadam roadway. The old dolphin at the extreme east end beyond the repair berth was replaced by a new structure made from steel box piles and capped in concrete. The work was designed to cause the minimum of disruption to day to day operations and was spread out over two years. Considering that this area was over 70 years old its condition at the time was remarkable.

Equally remarkable was a series of events that occurred in 1953 that centred on celebrations for the nation and dramas for Harwich and Parkeston Quay. It was a year for conquering Everest and the Coronation of Queen Elizabeth II but locally it was a year that saw a disastrous flood, a fire that sank a ship and a collision that sliced another in two.

On the night of 31st January 1953 an exceptional high tide and gale came down the east coast of Britain causing extensive flooding, damage and loss of life. At 00.30 on 1st February the surging tide reached Harwich and caused eight people to be drowned. This wave of destruction flowed further south and severe damage was caused on both sides of a narrowing North Sea. Coastal Holland was especially devastated.

All sailings from both Harwich and Parkeston Quay were suspended. The Hook night boat, the *Arnhem*, was cancelled and ships were moved off the quay face for fear of being damaged. The *Amsterdam* broke loose from its mooring on the river buoys though she managed to remain unscathed. Others were less

The *Duke of York* passing the capsized *Kronprins Frederik*. (Robert Clow collection)

fortunate. The *Koningin Emma* suffering damage to 76 feet of her belting and the harbour ferry *Pin Mill* was sunk though this little boat was successfully salvaged four days later. At Harwich the train ferry terminal's linkspan was severely damaged as was the *Suffolk Ferry* which was left hanging on its berth end after having been lifted up on the flooding tide.

Once the conditions had abated sailings from Parkeston Quay were soon back to normal except for the Hook day boat which, for a month, was re-routed to the Jobshaven in Rotterdam such was the damage at the Hook of Holland. It was also the only occasion that the MOWT trooping service was cancelled, on 2nd February, this being due to the earlier flooding in Holland.

The local railway stations also suffered badly by either being cut off or submerged. The Parkeston marshalling yard and motive power depot were inundated. As a result through trains to Harwich Town were impossible to run with the nearest usable railway station being Wrabness. Here the main line services ended and a connecting bus service went on as far as Dovercourt. It was not until 5th February before trains again reached Parkeston Quay whilst trains through to Harwich itself were delayed until 23rd February. The resumption of the train ferry service was further delayed until 5th March.

On 19th April 1953 at around 19.00 a small fire was discovered in a third class cabin on board the *Kronprins Frederik*. At the time the ship was alongside the quay discharging cargo and the fire was not thought to be all that serious. However it soon spread to engulf the whole ship and over 100 firemen were engaged in fighting a raging inferno. Some of their hoses were positioned high up on the quayside cranes and assistance was received from the Royal Naval Reserve Fleet based at Harwich and a fire float from the RAF depot at Felixstowe. At around 02.30 next morning the blazing ship capsized after having had so much water directed on board that she had become disastrously unstable. She keeled over to rest on the mud on her starboard side.

The cause of the fire was thought to have been an electrical short circuit and the resultant blaze eventually burnt out a third of the ship's interior. Fortunately there were no casualties. Messages of sympathy were sent to her Captain Lauridsen including one from H.M. King Frederik. The ship was so badly damaged that the underwriters condemned her but DFDS were to buy her back as a wreck.

The *Kronprins Frederik*'s place on the Esbjerg service was taken by the return of the *Parkeston* between 23rd June and 15th September with sailings on the route being amended to five times a week. It was most opportune that the *Parkeston* had had her passenger certificate increased during 1952 to 274 by the addition of further accommodation aft. A further development that year was that DFDS first started passenger sailings between Esbjerg and Newcastle using the elderly *A.P. Bernstorff* to operate a summer only timetable between 17th June and 17th September.

Just three weeks after the fire on board the *Kronprins Frederik* a third disaster struck the port when in the early hours of 6th May the *Duke of York*, inbound from the Hook of Holland, was hit by the 7,607 ton American freight ship *Haiti Victory*. The incident occurred at 04.17 in thick fog roughly 40 miles out from Harwich close by the Outer Gabbard light. The *Duke of York*, with 437 passengers and 72 crew on board, was struck on the port side and sliced almost in two just forward of the bridge. Thinking that the ship would sink the *Duke of York*'s Captain Adams and First Mate leapt to board the American vessel and from there gave the order to abandon ship. An SOS was sent out at 04.45 and was answered by several ships including the *Norfolk Ferry* and the *Dewsbury*.

Despite the impact the *Duke of York*'s bulkheads held out and a rescue operation was mounted by the crew who smashed down cabin doors in order to free any trapped passengers. The severed bow section fell away when the *Haiti Victory* went astern and it quickly flooded and sank. Fortunately most of the passengers inside had already been saved. Survivors and crew were transferred by lifeboat to the *Haiti Victory* and another American ship, the *American,* which was sailing from Dover to Germany. Some had been in boats for up to two hours. The *Haiti Victory* landed 351 passengers and 45 crew at Parkeston Quay at 15.00 that afternoon whilst the *American* landed 78 passengers and 12 crew at Dover.

Captain Adams and 14 members of the *Duke of York*'s crew returned on board their stricken vessel as a salvage operation was got underway. The ship was eventually towed back to Parkeston Quay, stern first, by the tug *Empire Race* and arrived at one of the river buoys at 23.00 that night. Staff from the Marine Workshops then boarded the ship in search of any further survivors. The next morning she was towed alongside No. 5 berth to discharge her cargo and then onto No.1 berth, aft of the sunken *Kronprins Frederik*, for temporary repairs.

With the *Duke of York* out of service and the regular vessel *Arnhem* then in dry-dock, BR were forced into chartering a replacement. This was the *Koningin Emma* which was then at the Hook of Holland

BR leaflet introducing the *Amsterdam*. (Robert Clow collection)

Two views of an extensively damaged *Duke of York* following her collision at sea on 6th May 1953. Having first discharged her cargo she is seen here being moved to lay up in No. 1 Berth behind the sunken DFDS vessel *Kronprins Frederik*. (bottom left, Stephen Brown collection; below, Stephen Gooch collection)

Loading the *Amsterdam* with wooden containers whilst alongside No. 2 Shed - 12th April 1954. (Robert Clow collection)

Offloading wagons at the Harwich train ferry terminal in November 1953. (Robert Clow collection)

preparing for a cruise. She sailed over to Parkeston Quay and took up the night service the same day of the collision. She continued doing so until the *Arnhem* returned on 18th May. The *Duke of York* left Parkeston Quay on 28th May and was towed to Jarrow on the Tyne for repairs.

From the damage sustained it was remarkable that the casualties were not higher than the six lives lost, eight injured and one unaccounted for. No doubt this was due to the strength and design of the ship's construction though lives were also saved through acts of bravery, one of which was that of Bosun Warner who rescued a deck boy stranded on the sinking bow section. It was the deck boy's first trip. The body of one passenger was not found until 22nd June when discovered in one of the ship's holds. At an inquest at Harwich in January 1954 the Coroner said there was no evidence with which to apportion blame and the jury returned verdicts of accidental death.

A more favourable event occurred on 27th June 1953 when a new train ferry terminal was officially opened in the outer harbour at Zeebrugge. A 160 feet long linkspan, able to cope with a tidal range of 16 feet, had been designed and installed for use by both rail and road vehicles. The position of this new terminal did away with the need to transit the old lock system and this resulted in the train ferries reaching their berth some ninety minutes earlier than before. The turn round time was thus reduced by three hours and the crossing time could now be as little as 7 hours each way.

During the summer months of 1953 the elderly *Oranje Nassau* was chartered by BR to operate extra sailings. She left lay up at Schiedam on 17th July for a very leisurely roster that saw her make just seven round trips. These departed from Parkeston Quay on Fridays and from the Hook of Holland on Saturdays and during the week she would lay up at Parkeston Quay. Her final arrival at Parkeston Quay was on the morning of 30th August, as a duplicate for the *Arnhem,* following which she returned directly to Schiedam. August 1953 was also the time when the Dutch Minister of Public Works conceded that SMZ were better served by operating from the Hook of Holland rather than Flushing. This followed the Company having negotiated a route pooling arrangement with British Railways in 1952 and despite SMZ having earlier rebuilt its base at Vlissingen where newly installed workshops for in-house repair and ship maintenance had been officially re-opened in March 1951.

All throughout had lain the still partly submerged *Kronprins Frederik*. On 8th May a salvage contract was awarded to the Liverpool and Glasgow Salvage Association with work starting on 10th May. After several months of preparation a start was made at 02.00 on 26th August on pumping the ship out. By

10.00 she was afloat and by 22.00 she was listing at a 'mere' 21 degrees. Eventually she became upright enough to be moved and on 13th September she left Parkeston Quay in the tow of the tugs *Seaman* and *Superman*. Her destination was her builder's shipyard in Elsinore where she arrived on 18th September. On board were Captain Lauridsen, who had been in attendance nearly all the time since the fire, and he and a skeleton crew acknowledged the well wishers watching her leave by raising a large new Danebrog, the Danish flag. On the funnel was painted a black cat, the traditional mark of a salvaged vessel.

During September and October 1953 BR Southern Region's *Normannia*, normally the overnight ship on the Southampton to Le Havre route, made ten round trips as a relief vessel on the Hook of Holland service. By the end of 1953 total traffic levels at Parkeston Quay were such that 243,000 passengers had departed, 240,000 had arrived and 12,535 cars had driven through.

After eight months away the *Duke of York* returned to service on 25th January 1954. During her time at Palmer's yard on the Tyne she had been fitted with a wholly new 90 feet long forepart. This gave her a raked stem and increased her length by about 7 feet to 359 feet overall. The opportunity had also been taken to fill in the fore well and when she returned to service she looked somewhat similar to the *Arnhem* having had the black paintwork on her hull raised by a deck. Her gross tonnage was now 4,325 and her passenger accommodation higher by just one First class berth. She remained configured as First class forward and Second class aft though with a number of Cabins de-Luxe now located along the starboard side of her Promenade Deck.

The *Kronprins Frederik* also returned to service that year. She returned from the shipyard on 23rd April and later left Copenhagen for Parkeston Quay on 3rd May. She resumed her passenger sailings on 7th May 1954 when she left Parkeston Quay for Esbjerg. Throughout the remainder of the 1950s the *Kronprins Frederik* and *Kronprinsesse Ingrid* would operate the Esbjerg service with six sailings a week during the summer peak and two a week during the winter.

During the spring of 1954 the *Arnhem* underwent a refit. Her certificate was raised to 675 and her passenger accommodation formally converted to a two class layout. Following work that cost £20,000 she emerged with 375 First class berths and 201 in Second class. The changes brought the berth allocation more in line with the *Amsterdam* though with a slight emphasis still towards First Class.

In 1954 the Parkeston Quay to Hook of Holland troopships received a livery change. The *Empire Parkeston* was dry-docked in May and repainted with a grey hull, white superstructure and grey funnels though later on these were repainted yellow with black tops. A narrow band of blue was painted along her new hull colour to represent her status as one of Her Majesty's Troop Ships (HMTS). It was around this time that the *Vienna* and *Empire Wansbeck* were similarly repainted.

The *Empire Parkeston* and the *Vienna* would normally undertake alternate sailings and from when the *Amsterdam* had joined the Hook of Holland service each trooping ship would usually sail the same nights as her. The troopship would leave Parkeston Quay shortly before midnight and arrive at the Hook of Holland by 07.00. This was after the arrival of the railway ship whose passengers had been given time to clear the terminal before the troops disembarked.

Troopship departures from the Hook were at 22.00 with an arrival time at Parkeston Quay of 06.00. The *Amsterdam* was scheduled to leave an hour later, at 23.00, and overtake the troopship by the Sunk Light Vessel as she had to berth at Parkeston Quay on time in order to connect with the waiting trains. If she was late the *Empire Parkeston* would circle around so that

A view of reconstruction work that began in 1952 along part of the original quay face that dated back to the 1880s. (Railway Gazette October 1954)

A view of the new Car Examination Hall adjacent to the level crossing - June 1954. (Robert Clow collection)

Opposite: A single berth cabin on the Promenade Deck of the *Duke of York* - January 1956. (NRM collection)

the 21 knot *Amsterdam* could catch up and pass. The reason for circling rather than just slowing down was said to be 'something to do with boiler pressures' to which she would normally use just two of her four boilers at any one time. If it was the *Empire Wansbeck* in service she could more easily be passed as she was much the slower ship.

By the end of 1954 the number of passengers travelling on the SMZ day boat service had passed the 100,000 a year mark for the first time but the Company's fleet was now minus the veteran *Oranje Nassau*. Her propellers and propeller shafts had already been removed in April prior to being her sold for scrap on 10th July 1954. She arrived at Hendrik-Ido-Ambacht in Holland two days later after having completed a remarkable 44 years of service.

By now the train ferry service to Zeebrugge had developed a regular pattern of sailings of 19.45 each evening from Harwich. However the ship only sailed as far as an anchorage point a few miles out and where she would lie until midnight. This was because docking at Zeebrugge could only occur at 07.00, usually with a tug in attendance, and unloading would not start before 08.00. Turn round time was 4 hours and departure from Zeebrugge was 12.00 noon. The ferry would then berth at Harwich at 20.00 that night having waited for the other ship in service to sail and move out of the way at its own time of 19.45. There the arriving ship lay until she again sailed the next day. At busy times with three ships in service there was ample scope to slot in another sailing.

In 1954 the amount of cargo handled by the train ferries had risen dramatically to 176,001 tons. However the aging *Essex Ferry* was too slow to work the required return trip every 24 hours and so an order was placed for a further vessel estimated at costing in excess of £600,000. It was not expected to arrive for another three years but once in service would save over £20,000 a year in operating costs when compared to the *Essex Ferry*. As for speed of crossing, in January 1956 the *Suffolk Ferry* set a new record for a round trip to Zeebrugge of 13 hours and 43 minutes! Both trips were with a full load and beat the previous record of 14 hours and 22 minutes.

Year on year growth in the number of loaded train ferry wagons and tonnage carried.

	Harwich-Zeebrugge		Zeebrugge-Harwich		Total	
Year	Wagons	Tonnage	Wagons	Tonnage	Wagons	Tonnage
1948	3,019	26,432	7,087	56,485	10,106	82,917
1949	3,403	30,367	7,375	52,361	10,778	82,728
1950	3,947	34,481	9,742	67,761	13,689	102,242
1951	3,824	31,940	13,027	107,382	16,851	139,322
1952	4,932	41,306	10,751	90,575	15,683	131,881
1953	5,691	48,719	11,111	83,363	16,802	132,082
1954	7,134	62,735	15,876	113,266	23,010	176,001

The number of motorist cars now passing though Parkeston Quay was such that a new Customs examination shed was needed and construction on one was completed during 1954. Located on the west side of the approach road adjacent to the level crossing this modern structure was 120 feet long by 47 feet wide. Inside was space for examining up to 6 vehicles at a time, an inspection pit and offices for quay officials and representatives of the two motoring organisations, the AA and the RAC. A new garage measuring 125 feet by 40 feet was also built just south of here.

During a House of Lords debate in July 1955 Lord Gifford described Parkeston Quay as being 'about the worst of the blackspots in our ports'. Blackspot or not it was becoming ever more popular. Duplicated sailings were now a feature throughout the summer months to Holland such that extra boat trains and LNER steamers were departing Parkeston Quay on a Wednesday and

View of the Harwich train ferry terminal - August 1955. (Stephen Brown collection)

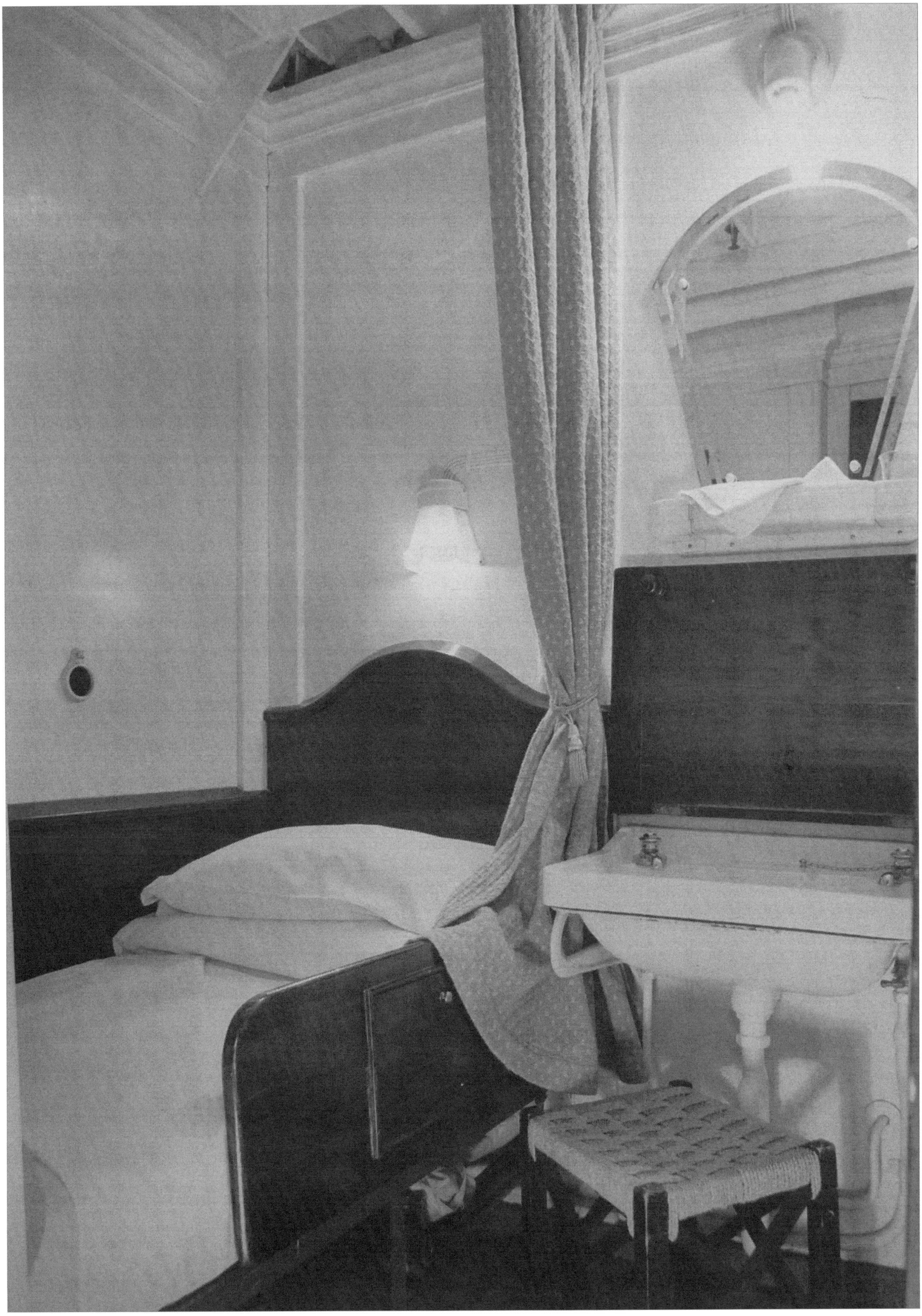

Above: The DFDS cargo vessel *Rota* alongside No. 1 Shed - 18th July 1958. (Derek Genzel collection)

Below: In this view of the pedestrian approach to Parkeston Quay the scene is still recognisable as the original Station Approach from the 1880s - January 1959. (Douglas Brown)

The *Duke of York* on the river buoys - February 1959. (Douglas Brown)

The *Norfolk Ferry* on the river buoys - February 1959. (Douglas Brown)

PARKESTON QUAY UNDER RAILWAY OWNERSHIP

Left: A view of all three troopships alongside No. 3 Shed. Nearest is the *Empire Parkeston*, ahead of which lies the *Vienna* with the smaller *Empire Wansbeck* alongside - February 1959. (Douglas Brown)

Below left: An impressive bow view of the *Amsterdam* as she lies in No. 3 Berth - February 1959. (Douglas Brown)

Below: The SMZ vessel *Mecklenburg* seen departing the Hook of Holland at the start of her dayboat run to P. Quay - March 1959. (Douglas Brown)

Bottom: Loading the *Colchester* at No. 1 Berth - 10th April 1959. (NRM collection)

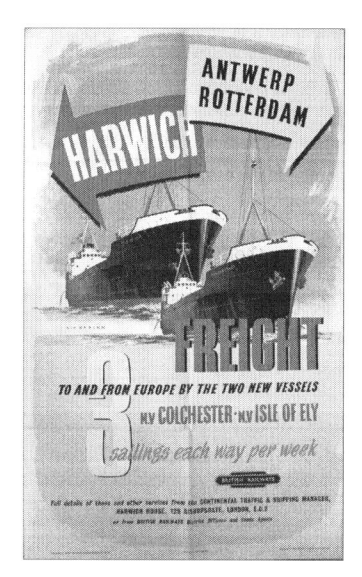

Poster advertising the introduction of the new BR cargo ships, *Isle of Ely* and *Colchester*.

A 2nd Class 4-berth cabin onboard the *Duke of York* - January 1956. (NRM collection)

Friday night and from the Hook on a Thursday and Saturday night. Also the SMZ service was being duplicated at weekends. At the Hook there were five continental trains waiting to connect with the night boat and three similar trains waiting upon the day boat.

Lord Gifford's comments led to further attention being brought before Parliament in December 1955 regarding the generally poor passenger facilities encountered at Parkeston Quay. Issues were raised about passport and immigration controls, paperwork and the arrangements for baggage which were giving a bad first impression to travellers and in particular to foreigners. Such comments were equally applicable to other cross-channel ports but Parkeston Quay was especially criticised for its arrangements as regards the stabling of trains in the platforms, the almost simultaneous arrival of relief boats that led to double loads of endless queuing by passengers and that much of this queuing was out in the open exposed to the elements.

Following a tour of the port Lord Gifford reported to the House that, as well as noting that *the paintwork and general appearance of our British boats did not compare in smartness with that of either the Danish or the Dutch boats*' he stated *'There is no doubt that Parkeston Quay is quite out of date and not suited to modern conditions'*. Overall nothing much had improved since BR's earlier aspirations that *'It is of course desirable that the ships and associated shore facilities should be up to date'*. It was to be quite a while before Parkeston Quay, with its 1,500 staff, had its issues over being 'suited to modern conditions' adequately addressed.

On 3rd June 1956 British Railways reclassified Third Class as Second Class. Later that year Harwich saw a temporary return to 'cattle class' when consignments of up to 30 animals a time were being handled and shipped out on the train ferries. The reason was due to a high demand in Holland for live beef and the normal cattle boats then sailing between Britain and Holland being fully loaded. Three or four consignments a week were exported to Rotterdam via the Harwich to Zeebrugge route with the cattle having first arrived at Parkeston Quay by rail from Reading. There they underwent a veterinary examination before being transferred into train ferry wagons.

The long anticipated new train ferry, having cost £695,652, was a new *Essex Ferry* which was launched at John Brown's on 24th October 1956. She underwent trials on the Clyde in the following January before first arriving at Harwich on 12th January. She entered service on 15th January 1957 when she sailed for Zeebrugge carrying 29 loaded wagons and 4 empties. The *Essex Ferry* was a third sister ship to the *Suffolk Ferry* and *Norfolk Ferry* and was almost identical in design except for being fitted with an overhead travelling crane that was fixed to the deck head and ran the length of the rail tracks. Capable of handling 10 ton containers the crane was installed in order that the ship might relieve on the Antwerp route. The old *Essex Ferry*, (ex HMS Princess Iris, ex Train Ferry No.1), had since been re-named *Essex Ferry II* before being sold for scrapping at Grays later that year. She was forty years old.

In late 1957 work commenced on a new examination shed at the west end of the quay designed to handle train ferry wagons. The shed provided a covered area measuring 600 feet long by 47 feet wide. Inside were two rail tracks capable of holding either 38 train ferry wagons or 54 standard wagons which, in total, was equal to a complete train ferry load. Each track ran alongside the outer walls and were separated by a 20 feet wide central platform onto which cargoes could be unloaded. The platform was built on piled foundations over which a single span pitched roof was built that was fitted with windows and glazing for natural light.

The gable ends were 15 feet high and both ends of the shed were open. The rail tracks came in from the sidings at the western end whilst the platform at the eastern end, behind the buffer stops, ran level to a separate examination block. Alongside were single storey offices and mess rooms for both BR staff and H.M. Customs, the latter designating this new location as their 'Western Station' in order to differentiate it from offices they already had within the old Continental Building and which became known as their 'Eastern Station'. In addition there was a separate circular oil fired boiler house complete with toilets for the dock staff. Although the buildings were constructed of a light yellow brick the whole complex became known as the 'White City'.

Throughout 1957 the train ferry service from Harwich to Zeebrugge had carried 225,000 tons of cargo which was very similar to the 240,000 tons being carried on those sailing between Dover and Dunkirk. The number of passengers travelling on the Hook of Holland services was 478,000 whilst a further 56,000 travelled with DFDS on the Esbjerg route.

The inclusion of a travelling crane on board the new *Essex Ferry* and the idea that she might relieve on the Antwerp route was related to major changes being planned not only for services to Antwerp but also the Rotterdam route as well. An order had been placed in 1956 for a pair of general cargo ships, one for each route, that would carry 42 standard type wooden box containers though with no provision for any passengers. The ships would be quite modest in size, at only 866 tons, and with a service speed of 13½ knots. Each would cost around £280,000.

As one was to be a replacement for the *Dewsbury* the lack of passenger accommodation was criticised by the local MP, Mr. Julian Ridsdale, who suggested in Parliament that more should be done to boost the attractions of the route to Antwerp. He said bookings were being discouraged as *'for two years the clerks at Liverpool Street's Continental booking service were instructed to deny the existence of the route to casual inquirers'* and that he was merely asking *'that there should be some passenger accommodation in the new packet'*. His reference to the term 'packet' was an interesting one yet out of keeping with the current situation as the carrying of 'small parcels' had long since vanished as had practically all of the passenger traffic. It was a situation deemed unlikely to change due to competition from ferries elsewhere and the increase in air travel. Also any accommodation on board the new ships would reduce space for the more important purpose of carrying cargo.

For those who still wished to visit Antwerp there were alternative routes available via the Hook of Holland or Dover to Ostend plus a new London to Brussels sleeper service, via Dover and connecting train, planned for the summer of 1957. The cost by sleeper would be £19 which was quite a lot more than the £8 it cost on the twice a week service from Parkeston Quay. In 1956 the Antwerp service ceased carrying passengers.

The first of these new ships into service was the *Isle of Ely* when she sailed to Rotterdam. This route had seen a twice weekly service maintained solely by the *Sheringham* except when away on overhaul or dry dock. Her reliefs had usually been found from amongst BR's Southern Region fleet of cargo vessels such as the *Hythe* but she was now being replaced by the route's first new ship in 32 years. The *Sheringham* made her final arrival at Parkeston Quay on 25th October 1958 and the *Isle of Ely* made her maiden voyage to Rotterdam on 27th October. Sailings were increased to three times a week that left Parkeston Quay on Monday, Wednesday and Friday.

Meanwhile the *Dewsbury* had survived on the Antwerp route in many ways similar to the *Sheringham* had been to Rotterdam and her times away in dock had likewise been covered by the *Hythe* and other BR-SR vessels such as the *Haslemere* and *Ringwood* that dated back to 1925. The *Dewsbury* made her last arrival at Parkeston Quay on 30th January 1959. Her replacement was the *Colchester,* sister ship to the *Isle of Ely,* which commenced her own three times a week schedule to Antwerp on 2nd February 1959. The *Sheringham* was sent for scrapping in December 1958 and the *Dewsbury* in March 1959.

Both the *Isle of Ely* and the *Colchester* were open hold general cargo ships designed to take an assortment of wooden box style containers and other goods that were loaded on and off by the use of shore side cranes. Built at a cost of £279,740 and £281,317 respectively each had a crew of 22 with all the accommodation, engine spaces and navigation housing located at the extreme aft end. Their carrying capacities of 89,171 cubic feet were arranged within No. 1 Hold forward - 7,093 cu.ft., No. 1 Tween Decks - 16,852 cu.ft., No. 2 Hold aft - 25,635 cu.ft. and No. 2

Two views of the 'White City', the new examination shed for train ferry wagons that was built at the west end of P. Quay in 1957. (Railway Gazette November 1957)

106　HARWICH FERRIES

The *Amsterdam* on the river buoys - 8th May 1959. (Douglas Brown)

The *Norfolk Ferry* laid up at the East End of P. Quay - 2nd June 1959. (NRM collection)

From the deck of the *Amsterdam* the DFDS vessel *Kronprinsesse Ingrid* is seen departing for Esbjerg - 16th June 1959. (Douglas Brown)

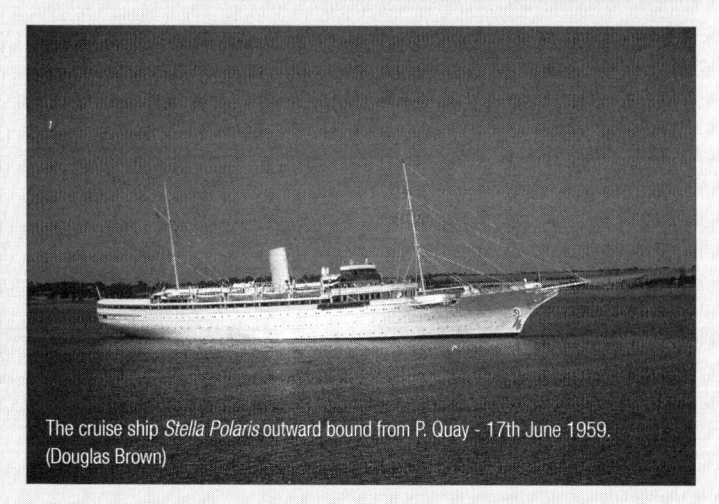

The cruise ship *Stella Polaris* outward bound from P. Quay - 17th June 1959. (Douglas Brown)

Postcards from the 1950s. Above shows the *Vienna* alongside No. 3 Shed. Right is a view of Parkeston Quay station looking east from Parkeston West signal box.

The SMZ day boat *Koningin Emma* outward bound from P. Quay - 17th June 1959. (Douglas Brown)

PARKESTON QUAY UNDER RAILWAY OWNERSHIP 107

A view of the troopship *Vienna* at the Hook of Holland in the new livery she adopted in 1954. (Philip Williams collection)

Cutaway drawing of the *Kronprinsesse Ingrid*. (Stephen Gooch collection)

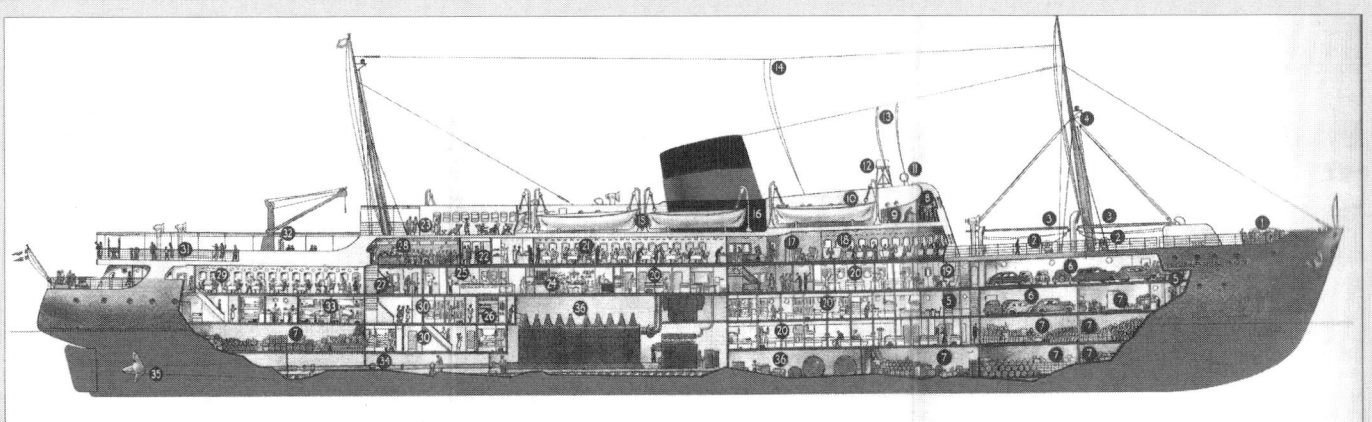

1 Windlass	8 Wheel House	16 The Funnel housing the Ventilation Units	21 1st Class Restaurant	29 2nd Class Restaurant
2 Cargo Winch	9 Chart Room	17 1st Class Hall and on the deck below the Enquiry Bureau and Purser's Office	22 1st Class Promenade Deck	30 2nd Class Cabins
3 Derricks	10 Officers' Accommodation		23 1st Class Sun Deck	31 2nd Class Sun Deck
4 Siren	11 Direction Finder		24 Galley	32 Crane
5 Crew's Accommodation	12 Radar	18 1st Class Lounge	25 Pantry	33 Tweendeck Accommodation
6 Car Deck	13 Signal Halliard	19 Cabins de Luxe	26 Stores and Provisions	34 Propeller Shaft
7 Refrigerated Hold	14 Aerial	20 1st Class Cabins	27 2nd Class Hall	35 One of the Twin Propellers
	15 Lifeboats		28 2nd Class Lounge	36 Engine Room

Tween Decks - 39,591 cu.ft.. These figures were usefully more than the 64,560 cu.ft. available on the *Sheringham* and the 65,012 cu.ft. on the *Dewsbury*. On top of the hold spaces were a series of MacGregor steel hatch covers. Power was provided by a single Ruston & Hornsby turbo charged diesel engine driving a single screw. As well as by their appearance they brought a modern and dramatic change to the manner in which general cargo would be handled.

Despite the port's out of date conditions the number of passengers travelling through it continued to rise. In 1958 there were 313,838 arrivals and 327,668 departures of which 'aliens' amounted to 124,572 and 137,668 respectively. The figures included all those travelling on the troopships though by now the numbers doing so were still in decline due to a reduction in the strength of the BAOR. Since 1st March 1958 the number of troopship sailings had been reduced to just three times a week.

The boat trains had continued running much as before though the 'North Country Continental' had seen the journey to Liverpool reduced by 30 minutes. Timings in 1957/1958 were then:

Dep. P. Quay	08.00	Dep. Liverpool (Cent.)	13.15
Arr. Sheffield (Victoria)	12.52	Dep. Manchester (Cent.)	14.15
Arr. Manchester (Cent.)	14.04	Dep. Sheffield (Victoria)	15.30
Arr. Liverpool (Central)	15.00	Arr. P. Quay	20.40
		Arr. Dovercourt Bay	20.51
		Arr. Harwich Town	20.53

As ships on BR's cargo routes were being replaced by those with a wholly new modern design it was noticeable that those that had arrived throughout the 1950s for DFDS were often more advanced and also refrigerated. The *Ficaria*, *Primula*, *Bellona* and *Blenda* were all such newly built examples whilst of the more traditional vessels ie. the *Alexandra*, *Diana*, *Lemnos*, *Melos* and *Klintholm*, only the *Alexandra* was then approaching 25 years old.

An aesthetic design stage further came from SMZ when they launched a thoroughly futuristic looking *Koningin Wilhelmina* as a replacement for their *Mecklenburg*. Supplied by the 'De Merwede' yard in Hardinxveld-Giessendam she was launched on 30th May 1959 by H.M. Queen Juliana. She was built as a traditional passenger vessel but was the first ship on the Hook of Holland route specifically designed with stabilizers and was further equipped with a 400 hp bow thrust propeller.

The *Mecklenburg* was withdrawn from service on 25th October 1959 and three days later she sailed to Schiedam for lay-up pending a sale. She survived only until 15th May 1960 when she was broken up in Ghent in Belgium. She was the port's last example of a passenger ship propelled by steam reciprocating machinery.

The scrapping of the old general cargo ships, the launch of container or unitised load vessels and the soon to be introduced *Koningin Wilhelmina* were as if slowly marking the end of an era. Hopes were raised that the 1960s would not only celebrate the centenary of the formation of the Great Eastern Railway but that Parkeston Quay would move on from being 'quite out of date and not suited to modern conditions'.

Postcard view below shows the *Kronprinsesse Ingrid* alongside No. 1 Shed.

PKN.20F   The Kronprinsesse Ingrid at Parkeston Quay.

THE 1960s

On Manningtree railway station the platform signs read 'Manningtree - For Harwich Branch and the Continent'. It was as if Harwich and the attractions of the Continent were of equal importance yet the facilities at Parkeston Quay remained woefully unappealing. However the 1960s were to be Parkeston Quay's transformation years as out would go the old and in would come the modern. It was to be a decade during which boring old British Railways, perhaps left behind by their competitors at other ports, would somehow get their act together and bestow the port with initiatives that were bold and exciting and much in keeping with the visionary nature of their Victorian predecessors.

The *Koningin Wilhelmina* made her maiden voyage from the Hook of Holland on 7th February 1960. Her low profile superstructure, manufactured by the De Schelde shipyard in Flushing, was topped by a distinctively squat and elongate funnel designed by the engineering firm of Vlieger in Amsterdam. Manufactured from a light metal alloy it helped reduce both the ship's weight and roll. Such was her resemblance to one the *Koningin Wilhelmina* soon became affectionately known as the 'clog'.

Overall the *Koningin Wilhelmina* was almost 395 feet long and was built as a two class day boat with a passenger certificate for 1,600. Those travelling First class were treated to their own forward Observation lounge located beneath the Bridge on B Deck. Access was via a staircase from a First Class lounge and bar that was directly underneath on C Deck and where most of the public areas were located. Aft of the First class lounge was a 12 seater Conference room amidship with a First class cocktail lounge to port and a First class restaurant to starboard. Second class accommodation was at the stern with a lounge and self service restaurant on C Deck and a cafeteria on D Deck both of which extended the full width of the ship. An additional seating lounge was located forward on E Deck. Being primarily a day boat there was relatively little in the way of cabin accommodation. First class cabins, including ten De-luxe, on B Deck and a number of Second class cabins on E and F Decks provided a total of only 217 sleeping berths though couchettes were available on the lowest deck. Hold space was sufficient for 200 tons of cargo plus up to 50 cars that were hoisted on and off by crane.

On 1st April 1960, following a proposal first made by Captain Louter on the *Koningin Emma,* an arrangement commenced whereby the incoming SMZ day boat would relay a weather forecast to Parkeston Quay for evening transmission by Anglia Television. The forecast was initially sent to the port's office and from there it was phoned through to Anglia TV's weather desk.

The arrival of the *Koningin Wilhelmina* helped SMZ see passenger carryings in 1960 exceed 200,000 for the first time, these figures having doubled in just six years. In addition the port was handling well in excess of 300,000 travelling with BR and around 60,000 with DFDS.

In 1960 it was decided that the BAOR trooping service between Parkeston Quay and the Hook of Holland would in future be replaced by the use of air transport. The service by sea was still handling 115,000 personnel a year but at a cost of £2m. A move to air transport would initially save an estimated £90,000 then needed to overhaul one of the ships and further save almost £1m in annual running costs. Ultimately it would save the huge cost of having to replace three old and out of date ships if trooping by sea was to continue at all.

Of the trooping trains still leaving the Hook of Holland the Red Train was revised and renamed 'Crossed Swords' on 29th May 1960 and left at 09.12 on a new and more direct daytime route to Hannover with a connection to Berlin that arrived at 21.40. The timings compared well with the best of the international trains of the time though it is interesting to note that when the Hook of Holland first opened in 1893 the Great Eastern Railway were advertising arrivals in Berlin only slightly later at 22.36. The 'Crossed Swords' ran just three times a week in connection with the existing troop ship sailings.

As part of the anticipated winding down of sailings the *Vienna* was withdrawn after making her last arrival at Parkeston Quay on 2nd July 1960. Two months later she was scrapped. From 1st October 1960 the sailings were reduced to just twice a week with the air service expected to account for roughly one third of the traffic. Sailings were from the Hook of Holland on Monday and Thursday and from Parkeston Quay on Tuesday and Friday.

Trooping by air began on 3rd October 1960 using Silver City Airways flying between Manston in Kent and Germany. The journey time between London Victoria station and places like Dusseldorf was just 4¼ hours, a considerable reduction in that by rail and sea, and this gradually brought about the demise of the Green Train from the Hook of Holland. The sea service eventually closed in 1961 when the *Empire Parkeston* made her final sailing from the Hook of Holland on the evening of 25th September. She arrived at Parkeston Quay the next morning and was later joined the same day by the *Empire Wansbeck* which arrived at 16.00

Quayside loading of a rail wagon with palletised goods - 4th May 1960. (Robert Clow collection)

having sailed back light from the Hook. The 26th September also saw the last departures of both the Blue Train and the 'Crossed Swords', the latter leaving the Hook of Holland at 09.12.

The trooping service had lasted 16 years and its closure saw the end of the *Empire Parkeston*. Following a short lay up she was sold for scrapping in La Spezia where she arrived on 20th February 1962. The *Empire Wansbeck* survived to become a passenger ferry when sold in 1962 to Kavounides Shipping Co Ltd of Piraeus in Greece. She was renamed *Esperos* in 1964 and extensively refitted for service between Venice and Greece. She too would eventually be sold for scrap but not until 1980 when she left Piraeus on 14th March for Gandia in Spain.

The closure of the troopship service had freed up Berth Nos. 5 and 6 for alternative uses though there were doubts as to how such uses might be brought about. Nothing much had occurred as regards investment in the port since the matter was raised in 1955 and there were allegations that traffic, especially the car traffic, was being lost to more modern ports as the process of craning on and off was becoming old fashioned, laborious and unappealing. At the time conditions locally were undergoing a series of changes to a labour market that could ill afford the loss of a shipping service. The Royal Navy had only recently vacated its Harwich base and Parkeston's BR motive power depot had since finished with steam locomotives on 2nd January 1961. Across the estuary it was thought that the port at Felixstowe was expanding faster than Parkeston Quay at a time when there was much discussion over the merits of private versus state labour.

The urgent case for more investment in the railway owned ports of Harwich and Parkeston Quay had already been resumed in July 1960 when Mr. Ridsdale M.P. asserted that the Hook boats were being worked too hard and as a consequence were insufficiently maintained. Also that the new Antwerp and Rotterdam boats, the *Isle of Ely* and the *Colchester*, were unsuitable vessels in all weathers and often needed assistance by the train ferries merely to maintain a service and that this

Unloading containers from the *Isle of Ely* at No. 7 Berth - 4th May 1960. (Stephen Brown collection)

was causing the train ferries own services to suffer accordingly. A point was made that during the first 18 months in service the *Suffolk Ferry* had already earned more than enough to have paid for the cost of her construction and yet despite this example of investment having been adequately rewarded, and other points raised in favour of doing so, the wait for any substantial investment at Parkeston Quay continued.

On the evening of 9th September 1962 London Liverpool Street station saw its last steam train workings. The up 'Day Continental', having left Parkeston Quay West at 19.30, arrived at 21.00 whilst Liverpool Street's last ever steam hauled departure had been the down 'Hook Continental' at 20.00 that was scheduled to arrive at Parkeston Quay at 21.25. Both trains were headed by a B1 class of locomotive and were the last cross channel boat trains still being hauled by steam. Steam had been used since the port's first commercial sailing some 80 years and six days previous.

Equally long ago had been the existence of the clock tower on top of Parkeston Quay station's former Great Eastern Hotel. By now this had fallen into a state of disrepair and the zinc tiles covering its four sided pyramid shaped roof were corroding away. With the cost of replacement being considered as much too expensive the tower's top was removed during the weekend of 16th-17th February 1963.

Back in September 1961, just as the troop ship service was ending, BR had placed an order with Alexander Stephen & Sons of Linthouse in Glasgow for a replacement for the *Duke of York*. Launched on 7th May 1963 this new ship was given the name *Avalon* which revived the memory of the pioneering GER steamer of the same name. Unfortunately when she was officially named at Parkeston Quay by Mrs Beeching, wife of Dr. Richard Beeching, Chairman of the BRB, on 25th July 1963 some wondered if that pioneering spirit had been lost as she was, from the outset, a ship that should never have been built as she was.

Working the *Colchester* at No.7 Berth with the troopship *Vienna* on the river buoys and the *Empire Wansbeck* in No. 5 Berth - 11th July 1960. (NRM collection)

The troopship *Empire Parkeston* on the river buoys in 1961 from onboard the *Duke of York*. (Douglas Brown)

The problem was that the *Avalon*, which broke the £2m cost barrier at £2,023,708, was a traditional passenger ship like the *Koningin Wilhelmina* and as such had no car deck. She was designed with facilities that could offer short 'out of season' excursions in ways that emulated the pre-war days of cruising which the LNER had made so popular and as the product of a British Railway mindset that persisted in thinking that its business in passenger shipping was for the carriage of those on foot, commonly referred to as 'classic passengers', and who would continue to arrive at the Company's various ports by train. Unfortunately for BR more and more passengers were now wanting to travel with their cars.

The basic idea of what would become known as roll-on roll-off car ferries had already been successfully demonstrated elsewhere and several routes had been offering such a service for years. Although they were not yet 'drive through' there were enough ferries equipped with side doors or stern doors giving access to holds or full length car decks to show what could be done even if with limited terminal equipment. As far back as 1939 the SMZ had developed a system at Flushing for the side loading of cars by driving them over a floating pontoon that was moored between the ship and the quay face whilst services across the English Channel had seen car ferries at Dover since 1948. At Tilbury there was a drive on service for commercial vehicles as far back as 1946 and earlier than all of these initiatives there had been ramps and duck boards slung across the gaps between quay and ship.

The *Duke of York* made her last arrival at Parkeston Quay on the morning of 20th July 1963. She was later sold to Chandris Lines, re-named *Fantasia* and became a cruise ship in the eastern Mediterranean. The *Avalon* then made her maiden voyage to the Hook of Holland on 25th July 1963 from a port still without any ro-ro facilities whatsoever and whose basic layout was much the same as it had been for years.

There remained the 8 working berths plus, at the

View of a busy Parkeston goods yard looking towards the east. On the left is Parkeston Quay West and No. 4 Shed whilst in the middle distance centre is the 'White City' examination shed beyond which can be seen the *Empire Parkeston* alongside. To the right is No. 3 Shed and the main station - 28th August 1961. (Robert Clow collection)

The cargo ship *Jacaranda* was chartered to sail on the service to Rotterdam throughout 1962 and 1963 and is seen here being worked on in No. 7 Berth. (Robert Clow collection)

extreme eastern end, a lay-up and Repair Berth. Moving west, alongside No. 1 (East) Shed, lay No. 1 Berth which was used for the Antwerp service with the *Colchester* or *Isle of Ely* providing two or three sailings a week, and No. 2 Berth used for a three times a week service to Esbjerg which, in summer, became daily except on a Monday. Alongside No. 2 (Middle) Shed was No. 3 Berth used by the BR Hook of Holland Night Boat vessels, *Amsterdam*, *Arnhem* and the brand new *Avalon,* which sailed every night except Christmas Day and were carrying 350,000 passengers per year, and No. 4 Berth which was either used by the Hook Night Relief Boat or, on Mondays and Tuesdays, by the Danish cargo vessels. During the summer season it was also used by the long serving cruise ship *Stella Polaris*.

Further upstream lay No. 5 and No. 6 Berths and the adjacent No. 3 (Old West) Shed. Since the closure of the BAOR Military Transport service this area remained largely unused though No. 3 Shed was later to become the Provender Stores supplying all the local railway boats. At the far west end lay Parkeston Quay West station complete with No. 4 (New West) Shed and No. 7 Berth which was used by the Rotterdam service with sailings provided by the *Colchester*, *Isle of Ely* or, at the time, the *Jacaranda,* a ship then on charter from Hudig & Pieters. Sailings to Rotterdam were every day except Sunday and Wednesday. Further up was No. 8 Berth used by the SMZ Hook of Holland Day Boat vessels *Prinses Beatrix*, *Koningin Emma* or *Koningin Wilhelmina* which sailed every day except Christmas Day.

Despite the criticism surrounding her functional design the *Avalon* was nevertheless well appointed throughout. Two lounges were fitted on her Promenade deck whilst below on the Shelter deck forward was a First class restaurant and lounge and at the aft end a Second class cafeteria and a smoking room. Cabin accommodation was provided for 331 in First class and 287 in Second class from amongst a certificate to carry up to 750 passengers. The Cabine-de-luxe each had their own private bathroom and each Special cabin its own private shower. Her three holds could carry 1,000 tons of cargo including the inevitable crane loaded cars. She was the first BR ship at Parkeston Quay to be fitted with stabilizers and full air conditioning and at the time she was the largest ship in the entire BR fleet.

The ability of the *Avalon* to 'go cruising' saw her running a Dr Barnardo's London Centenary Charity Cruise to Amsterdam on 27th September 1963 though this was not the first time that a British Railway's ship had cruised out of Parkeston Quay. The *Duke of Lancaster,* which had run seasonal cruises from north west England to the Western Isles of Scotland, had earlier visited Parkeston Quay during 1962 and 1963 en route to various destinations within Holland and France.

In 1964 there appeared the prospect of competition from a newly constructed port in Harwich. This took the local name of Harwich Navyard Dock on account of having been built on reclaimed land beyond the eastern boundaries of that formerly worked by the old Great Eastern Railway and on the site of the former naval shipyard. It extended over 11 acres, cost £500,000 to construct and was owned by the Harwich Dock Company Ltd. which in turn was a part of the Mann & Son International Ltd group of companies. It officially opened for business on 3rd January 1964 primarily as a car import and export terminal with just one berth.

General goods and palletised cargo stored on the upper floor of No. 4 Shed. (Robert Clow collection)

The first vessel to unload cars was the *Traviata* on 4th January when sailing for Wallenius Lines of Sweden.

Soon afterwards the Navyard was handling a wider variety of cargoes such as general goods, manufactured items, ro-ro and trailers. A measure of its success was that in 1961 Parkeston Quay handled 196,000 tons of general goods and 229,000 tons in 1965. In 1965 the Navyard Dock was already handling 201,000 tons. The site was, and still is, somewhat restricted due to its location within Harwich and thus for the storing of trade cars and trailers the Company made use of land then available at the former Transit Camp which had lain dormant following the end of the troop ship services.

At the far western end of Parkeston Quay, beyond No. 4 Shed, some 25 acres of land were being leased from British Railways by Carless Capel & Leonard, nowadays known as Petrochem Carless, for the purpose of building and operating an oil refinery. Terms had initially been agreed in December 1962 and work began on constructing a new tanker berth, just beyond Berth No. 8a, along with 2 eight inch diameter carbon steel pipelines to feed the new refinery. The new berth was first used on 27th February 1964 when the 807 grt tanker *Tillerman* discharged 1,000 tons of petroleum spirit. Refining commenced shortly afterwards and the complex was officially opened on 23rd June 1964. The 203 feet long *Tillerman* was built in 1963 and at the time was operated by Rowbotham & Sons of London. Over the ensuing years Rowbotham tankers were to become a regular sight at the oil berth as production of refined products increased.

The *Avalon's* first official British Railway cruise was a weekend trip to Amsterdam on 24th April 1964 when she left Parkeston Quay at 22.15 on the Friday night and arrived back at 07.00 on the Monday morning, these timings being very similat to those of the *Vienna* during the 1930s. In cruise mode she was configured to accommodate a maximum of just 350 passengers with a full programme of entertainment, deck games and other traditional cruising activities. The Amsterdam trips were repeated twice more in May with prices that ranged from £15 to £28 per person depending on the chosen grade of cabin. These were to be followed by an 8-day cruise to Amsterdam, Hamburg and Copenhagen in late May and an 8-day cruise to Amsterdam, Kiel and Copenhagen in early June with prices of between £40 and £80. These cruises would also leave Parkeston Quay at 22.15 but arrive back at 10.00.

The *Avalon* was scheduled to arrive back from her Kiel cruise on 10th June. Just two days later came evidence of the out datedness of her design when a new flagship for DFDS arrived as the North Sea's first drive-on drive-off passenger car ferry. This was the 8,117 grt *England* making her maiden voyage from Esbjerg and whilst she first arrived commercially at Parkeston Quay on 12th June 1964 she had earlier made a trials and presentation visit on 3rd June.

The almost 460 feet long *England* arrived at a time when changes on ship and shore generally were such that ships no longer had their public rooms, cabins and storage spaces subdivided vertically within a series of bulkheads rising the full height of the hull but instead

Passengers boarding the SMZ dayboat at Parkeston Quay West - 19th December 1962. (NRM collection)

had their facilities arranged horizontally layer upon layer. Increasingly cars and cargoes would no longer be hoisted and lowered deep into holds only to come out again the same way but would either be driven or self propelled on board at one end of the ship and emerge onshore at the other.

The reduction in time spent handling a ship in this way meant there was now an increasingly limited future for the old ways of crane loading and man handling cargoes with new ro-ro styled freight ships already being designed and put into service. At the forefront of these changes was DFDS who were also developing a large fleet of purpose built refrigerated trailers in order to better transport the ever important Danish farm products.

Although the *England* was provided with a full length car deck she was not a bow and stern loader for vehicles. Instead access was via side doors at the bow and stern quarter, on the starboard side, with the stern quarter door normally being the one through which cars drove onboard. A shore crane was used for adjusting the ramp. Height restrictions meant she could only carry around 100 cars and small caravans with no space at all for any lorries. This lack of height was due to the car deck being a deck higher than desired as the ships diesel engines were so high themselves that they intruded into where the required lower deck space would have fitted. As such she was not the most advanced ship as regards the overall carrying of freight but with facilities for 467 passengers she fully catered for what motorists might expect on board a luxurious ship designed for the longer sea routes.

Cabin accommodation for 155 passengers in First class and 244 in Second ranged from those with four berths on the lower decks and up through the various grades of those with either wash basins or en-suites. The highest grade cabins were on A Deck and these included two luxury First class suites complete with their own sitting room and bathroom. Those in Deck Class endured basic group accommodation at the aft end of D Deck.

Overall the *England* introduced a much improved range of cabin options with the supplementary price for a berth in 1964 varying between 10s.6d. in a basic 2nd class cabin up to £3.2s.6d. for a 1st class single en-suite. A Cabin-de-Luxe cost £10.7s.6d. which was almost the same as the fare.

Boat fare only:	Single (from 1st May)	
P. Quay to Esbjerg	1st Class	2nd Class
Adult	£12.5s.0d.	£9.2s.6d.
Child (4-12 years)	£6.2s.6d	£4.11s.3d.

The overall layout was First class forward and Second class aft with many of the public spaces being decorated with paintings and various works of art that emphasised a distinctive Danish atmosphere. Each class had its own shop. Most of the public rooms were on the Saloon Deck where forward was a First class lounge and bar, a writing room and a separate dining room. Further aft was the Second class dining room which led on to a lounge. All these areas extended the full width of the ship in an attempt to provide a light and airy atmosphere. A combined bar and night club was located below on A Deck.

The *Kronprins Frederik* had ended her sailings at Parkeston Quay in April and the arrival of the *England* displaced her onto DFDS's routes out of Newcastle. Locally a change of ship did little to alter the service throughout 1964 as schedules remained much the same as before - Dep. P. Quay 17.15, arr. Esbjerg 12.15, dep. Esbjerg 17.30 and arr. P. Quay at 11.30 (or 12.30 from 22nd March until 24th October). It was still a daily service during the summer season, from 12th June to 12th September, except for no sailing on a Sunday from Esbjerg or on a Monday from Parkeston Quay. During the off-peak periods, between 11th April and 11th June and from 13th to 25th September, sailings were three times a week with sailings from Esbjerg on a Tuesday, Thursday and Saturday and from Parkeston Quay on Wednesday, Friday and Sunday. Prior to April the winter service was only twice a week with sailings on Monday and Friday from Parkeston Quay and from Esbjerg on Tuesday and Saturday. During this time the departures from Parkeston Quay were at 12.30 and arrivals in Esbjerg at 08.30. Sailing times from Esbjerg remained at the normal time.

In reality sailing times varied little from year to year and those to the Hook of Holland were equally similar in 1964 as they had been before. These were:

by BR Night Boat		by SMZ Day Boat		
Dep. P. Quay	22.00	Dep. P. Quay West		11.20
Arr. HvH	06.15	Arr. HvH		18.45
Dep. HvH	23.40	Dep. HvH	12.00	17.45
Arr. P. Quay	06.45	Arr. P. Quay West	17.30	05.45

These times remained throughout the year except from 22nd March to 24th October when the day boat left Parkeston Quay West at 12.20 and arrived back at 18.20. Boat fares between Parkeston Quay and the Hook of Holland were the same by either company though cabins were charged extra.

	Single		Return	
	1st Class	2nd Class	1st Class	2nd Class
Adult	£5.3s.6d.	£4.7s.0d.	£10.7s.0d.	£8.14s.0d.
Child (3-14 years)	£2.11s.9d.	£2.3s.6d.	£5.3s.6d.	£4.7s.0d.

The SMZ day boat service was principally undertaken by the *Prinses Beatrix* and *Koningin Emma* whilst an additional afternoon departure from the Hook at 17.45, which sailed each Monday and Thursday from 13th July to 27th August, was operated by the *Koningin Wilhelmina*. She would arrive off Parkeston Quay around midnight and berth at 05.45 with passengers holding First class tickets being accommodated overnight in cabins at the following rates:

Impression of the new BR vessel Avalon. *(Stephen Brown collection)*

Opposite top: Passenger Lounge onboard the *Cambridge Ferry* - December 1963. (NRM collection)

Opposite bottom: One of six two-berth passenger cabins onboard the *Cambridge Ferry* - December 1963. (NRM collection)

View of the new *Cambridge Ferry*'s rail deck showing the overhead gantries fitted for the handling of containers - December 1963. (NRM collection)

	Berth in a 2-berth cabin	Cabin for sole use
Cabine-de-Luxe	£1.5s.0d.	£2.10s.0d.
Boat Deck	15s.0d.	£1.10s.0d.
B Deck	10s.0d.	£1.0s.0d.

Breakfast was an extra 6s.0d. Those with Second class tickets were able to book a couchette for 4s.0d and a breakfast for 5s.0d.

In the reverse direction, throughout July and August, a limited number of motorists could be accommodated overnight on the Dutch boats on a bed and breakfast basis upon payment of 16s.0d. on either the *Prinses Beatrix* or the *Koningin Emma* and £1.1s.0d. for the *Koningin Wilhelmna*. De-luxe and Special cabins were available for an extra 10s.0d. Motorists had to have booked in advance and be at Parkeston Quay by 22.00.

It is interesting to note the emphasis placed on accommodating motorists as none of the ships then in service were drive-on drive-off car ferries and the idea of accommodating them overnight on board the SMZ day boats appears a little strange when they might easily have been able to sail with BR. However an aspiration of SMZ back in 1939 was that the *Prinses Beatrix* and *Koningin Emma* might one day undertake some form of cruising activity and this overnight bed and breakfast arrangement offered on board the *Koningin Wilhelmina* gave some the opportunity of taking a North Sea mini-cruise.

The number of passengers passing through Parkeston Quay rose steadily from 624,919 in 1962, through 630,000 in 1963 to 640,413 in 1964 but it was still the train ferries where growth was all the more impressive. Figures of just under 200,000 tons of cargo carried in 1955 had become 271,000 in 1960 and the year on year rises were showing no signs of slowing down. Such growth levels inevitably led to yet another new train ferry being ordered though this came not from John Brown's yard on the Clyde but from Hawthorn Leslie Shipbuilders Ltd of Hebburn.

This new addition was named the *Cambridge Ferry* which entered service on 2nd January 1964. She was similar in design to the three existing train ferries yet perhaps slightly less severe looking in her overall appearance. She was the first to be fitted with a flume stabilisation system whereby the roll of the ship was dampened by moving sea water between port and starboard tanks within the hull, the primary purpose of which was to help prevent wagons derailing in bad weather. She was fitted with recessed rails, variable pitch propellers and further equipped with an overhead gantry system to handle box containers similar to that on the *Essex Ferry*. Consequently she was able to cover the Rotterdam and Antwerp services if required and was the first Harwich train ferry purposely able to carry road vehicles.

By the end of 1965 carryings on the Harwich to Zeebrugge route had jumped to 345,000 tons and since September 1965 the train ferries had formally been accepting bookings for ro-ro traffic with space being made available for up to 6 vehicles per sailing. The rates were somewhat unusually charged on a 'per square foot' basis with loaded vehicles being charged 4s.3d. per sq. ft. whilst outward bound empty vehicles

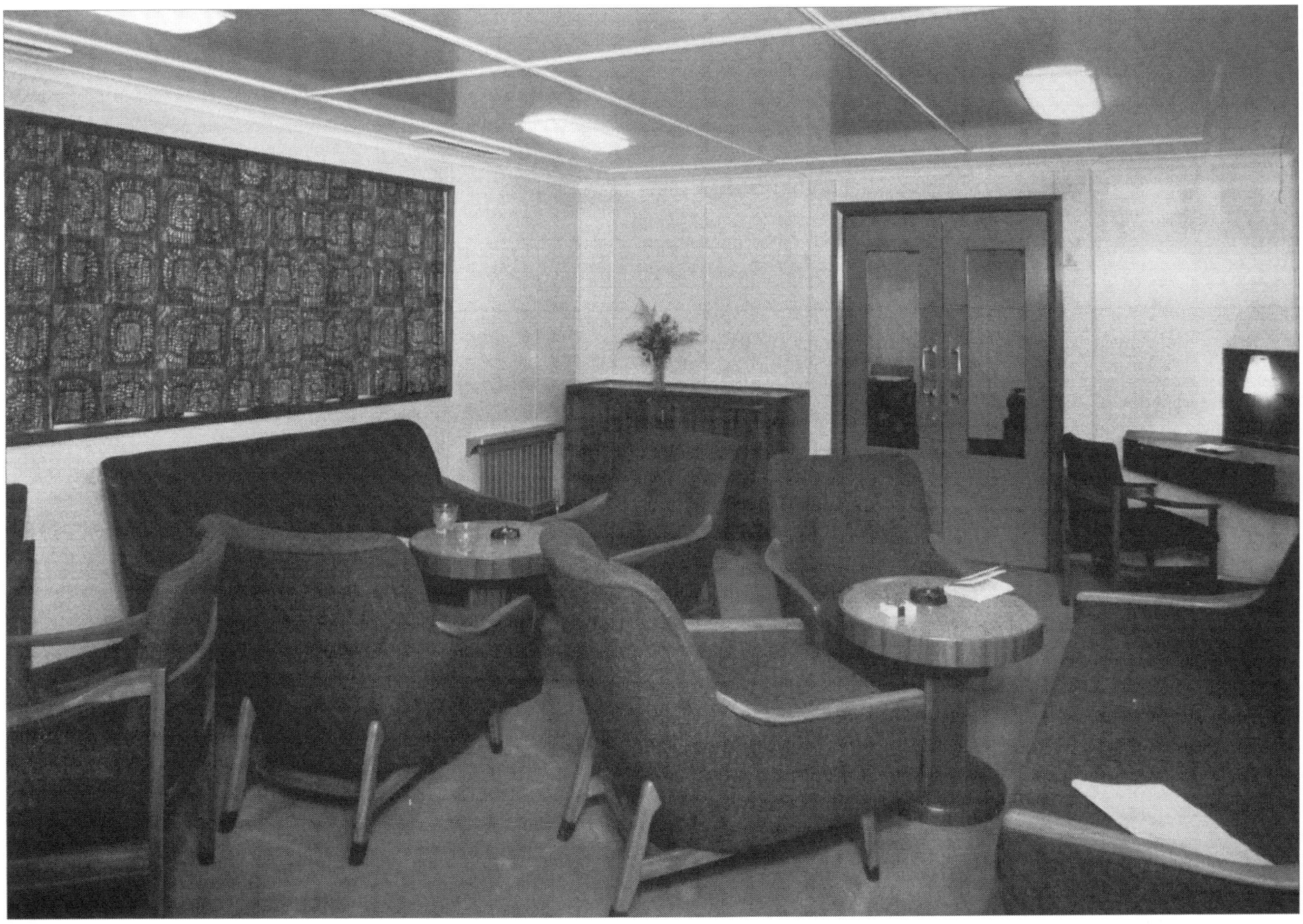

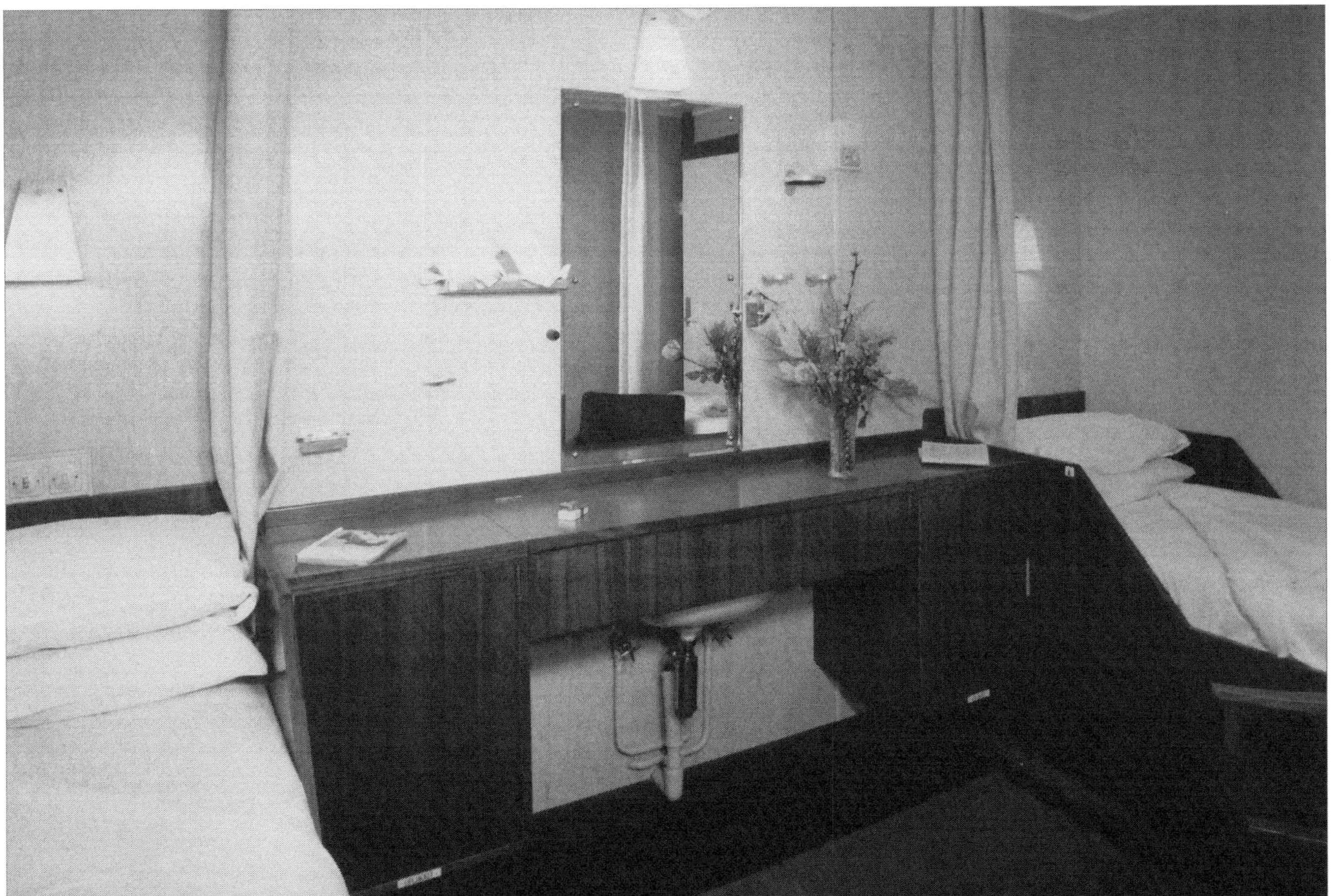

were charged 3s.3d. per sq. ft. and returning empty vehicles 2s.9d per sq. ft.

A short lived cargo service between Parkeston Quay and Hamburg was started in the spring of 1964 under the name of the Harwich Hamburg Line. The operator was the Zim Israel Navigation Co. who chartered a small Dutch coaster, the 398 grt *Deo Gratias*. Arrivals at Parkeston Quay were on Monday mornings with departures on Tuesday. Traffic levels were low to non existent and remained so even after combining services with the Star Shipping Agency and their vessel, *Flavius*, to create a twice weekly service. After 10 months the route closed.

In April 1964 British Railways commissioned a design agency, the Design Research Unit, to create an entirely new look that would incorporate within the railway industry a modern and recognisable house style. The new image was rolled out in January 1965 and featured the now iconic white painted double arrow logo on a red background. The company name was shortened to British Rail and the extensive re-branding process was also to include the BRB's fleet of ships. For them the new corporate colour scheme came to consist of a deep monastral blue hull, white superstructure and a red funnel topped out in black. On either side of the funnel would be placed the new double arrow logo, the top arrow of which pointed to the right. For use on the ships it was decided that on the port side of the funnel the top arrow could be reversed so that it was always seen to be facing forwards. The first to be given the new colour scheme was the Parkeston Quay based cargo vessel *Colchester*. Originally it was intended that all superstructures be painted a light blue grey but this was changed to white due to problems with reduced sighting and visibility in bad weather. On shore the house flag of the shipping business was a white double arrow logo on a blue background.

Since the ending of the BAOR troopship service in 1961 the quay area it vacated was still being underutilised at a time of growing interest in the creation of a direct ferry service between Germany and the UK. The various German companies involved had so far met with little success on finding a suitable route and the idea was also being taken up by the Swedish car transporting company of Wallenius Lines.

In 1965 negotiations took place between Wallenius and another Swedish company, Lion Ferry A.B. of Halmstad, which resulted in the formation of a joint operating company called Wallbon Ship A.B., the 'bon' part being in recognition of the Swedish company, Bonnier Group of Halmstad, which had founded Lion Ferry in 1959. Together they would start a ro-ro service from the German port of Bremerhaven to their chosen UK port of Parkeston Quay. Wallenius Lines were already familiar with the location of Parkeston Quay on account of their ongoing car carrying activities that linked Harwich Navyard Dock with Gothenburg, Amsterdam and Ghent and via their local agents of Mann and Son (London) Ltd. This new passenger route was to start the following year and be marketed as a Lion Ferry service.

Loading Sprite caravans onto the *Essex Ferry* at P. Quay - 15th April 1964. (NRM collection)

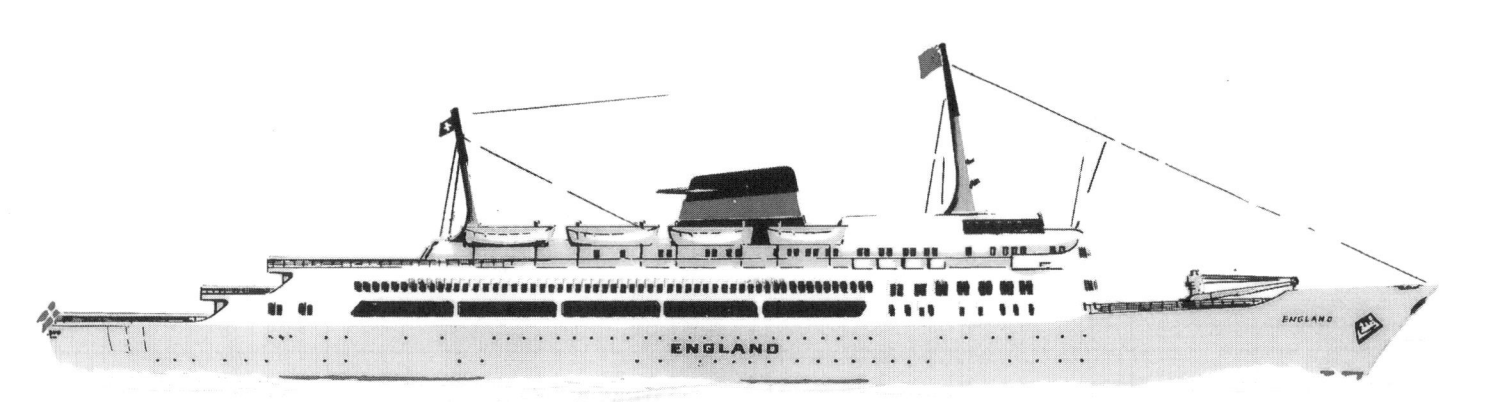

At Parkeston Quay this now meant the provision of a suitable ro-ro berth. Planning regulations meant that any fixed installation that projected out into the river required Parliamentary permission but non fixed structures did not. Therefore a decision was made that the best solution would be to build a floating pontoon structure with work on its construction beginning in the autumn of 1965. Upon this pontoon would rest a linkspan comprising a single lane roadway that angled into the quay. This came ashore at the western end of the Middle Quay at No. 6 Berth with the linkspan facing down river and the ship tying up alongside No. 3 Shed. The new berth was linked to the port's exit at the level crossing by a new road that later became known as the M1.

The level crossing and exit had been updated in early 1965 by the installation of new boom gates, an electrically driven pair of motorised gates that spanned the 18 feet 6 inch wide roadway though extending only part way across the width of the railway tracks. The new gates greatly speeded up the opening and closing of access to and from the quay which hitherto had been done by a crossing keeper whose services were then no longer required.

The new pontoon berth came into commercial use on 24th May 1966 when the new £3m Lion Ferry vessel, *Prins Hamlet,* arrived after completing her maiden 303 n.mile voyage from Bremerhaven. She was the first ro-ro passenger ship equipped with both a stern door and a bow ramp to berth at Parkeston Quay although she was not fitted with a bow visor. This was because of cabin accommodation that extended into the foremost part of the peak. Instead she had bow doors that hinged open to the side and through them disembarked the port's first roll-off traffic. She arrived with a blue hull, white upper decks and a pair of smallish yellow funnels set aft within which was a red 'B' to denote the Bonnier company. She was Swedish flagged and Swedish crewed.

The 7,658 grt *Prins Hamlet* had been launched on 17th December 1965 as the third in a class of ships built at Turku in Finland, the previous two having gone to Finnlines as *Finnhansa* and *Finnpartner,* though she differed from her sister ships by having fully enclosed bridge wings. On board the *Prins Hamlet* was space for over 800 passengers with the main facilities being located on the Restaurant Deck. Measuring around 440 feet long she was the longest passenger ferry to have berthed at Parkeston Quay and was the first alongside with some of the public rooms having been given names rather than simply designating them according to class. This was a feature that would take many years before appearing on board the railway oriented services to the Hook of Holland. Thus there was a full

Impression of the new DFDS vessel *England*. (Stephen Gooch collection)

The DFDS approach to attracting passengers onboard their new *England* was a more modern and inviting affair. (Stephen Gooch collection)

width a-la carte restaurant facing forward and a full width Ophelia Lounge that faced aft, this being a modern Scandinavian feature combining a night club, bar and casino area. The Restaurant Deck also housed a shop and a hairdressers. Below was a deck given over entirely to cabins and these, together with 10 Deluxe twin berth cabins on the Boat Deck above, provided a total of 444 berths in 116 cabins. The Boat Deck also housed a forward facing Neptune Bar and a cinema at the aft end. Below the cabin deck were two car decks with space for 268 cars or 26 lorries.

With only the one ship in service sailings were every other day with crossing times being around sixteen hours. The *Prins Hamlet* would leave Bremerhaven at 17.30 and arrive at Parkeston Quay at 10.15 the next day from where a connecting boat train left at 11.45 for London Liverpool Street. The return sailing left at 17.00.

When she finished the summer sailings at the end of August 1966 the *Prins Hamlet* closed a highly successful first season by carrying 42,651 passengers and 6,134 cars with very often a fully booked car deck. Afterwards, starting on 1st September, the *Prins Hamlet* was sent away on cruising voyages from Malmo and Copenhagen to the Canary Islands. She was replaced by Thoresen Line's *Viking III* which normally sailed throughout the summer season on Thoresen's Southampton to Le Havre and Cherbourg routes. She was a much smaller ship than the *Prins Hamlet* at 3,824 grt and only had 284 berths, 70 reclining seats and a car deck that held 180 cars or 17 lorries. When on the Bremerhaven service the crossing times of this chartered vessel, which first arrived on 19th September, were slower by about 2 hours each way and her arrivals at Parkeston Quay were either 12.15 or 12.45 with sailings back at 16.00 or 16.30.

The day of the first arrival of the *Prins Hamlet* came barely a week after a long overdue announcement concerning plans for the modernisation of Parkeston Quay. On 18th May 1966 Mr. Stanley Raymond, Chairman of the BRB, visited the port and opened a new car examination hall built on the west side of the approach road to the quay and behind where the garage stood. Mr Raymond then gave a Press Conference on board the *Arnhem* where he outlined decisive plans that would eventually lead to the wholesale clear out of old sheds, buildings and working practises. Practically everything on the East Quay and much of the Middle Quay would go. It was to be the biggest ever redevelopment of Parkeston Quay since the port was first built.

The Hook of Holland route was to be a fully integrated operation and become a proper roll-on roll-off service with both BR and SMZ supplying their own purpose built car ferries that would each make one round trip per day. The British vessel would sail day boat from Parkeston Quay and night boat from the Hook of Holland whilst the Dutch vessel would sail day boat from the Hook and night boat from Parkeston Quay. They would be the largest vessels ever built for the route each with space for around 200 cars on decks accessed via both bow and stern doors. New terminals with linkspan berths would be constructed at both the Hook of Holland and Parkeston Quay with those at Parkeston Quay being built within the area of the Middle Quay focusing on where Berth Nos. 3 and 4 currently were. A new passenger terminal complete with Customs and Immigration halls was envisaged as leading off from the railway station together with quay staff housed in a six storey round tower office block.

The area of the East Quay would be entirely flattened ready for the construction of Britain's first short sea container terminal from where British Rail would operate their own container services to Zeebrugge and Rotterdam using brand new purpose built container ships. This new terminal development was to be overseen by Mr Posner who was appointed Manager of BR International Container Services in 1966 whilst responsibilities in Zeebrugge were placed in the hands of the Societe Belgo-Anglaise des Ferry Boats S.A. or SBA.

These developments coincided with the appearance of new container terminals elsewhere such as Tilbury, Southampton and, more importantly, one which opened at nearby Felixstowe on 1st July 1967. By March 1968 Felixstowe's initial 500 feet long

An impression of cars driving onboard the new passenger vessel England. *She was introduced by DFDS in June 1964 as the North Sea's first drive on-drive off car ferry. (Stephen Gooch collection)*

Landguard terminal had been extended by a further 800 feet and the port also opened a second ro-ro berth to add to the one it opened in 1965. However such container terminals throughout the UK were primarily designed to attract trans-ocean or deep sea traffic thus ensuring that the one at Parkeston Quay would be Britain's very first purpose built short sea terminal.

Such terminals ushered in a new size of metal container, one that was constructed to standards established by an International Standards Organisation (ISO), and at Parkeston Quay these replaced the existing wooden box container services that had been sailing to Antwerp from No.1 Berth and Rotterdam from No. 7 Berth since the late 1950's.

In those intervening years the container and general cargo service to Rotterdam had since become five days a week after the *Jacaranda* was chartered in early 1962. She joined the *Isle of Ely* and in 1962 the route carried 15,000 containers via Rotterdam's Merwehaven terminal. The two ships sailed together until 31st December 1963 with departures from Parkeston Quay being on Monday, Tuesday, Thursday, Friday and Saturday. From 1st January 1964 the *Isle of Ely* and the *Colchester* were made interchangeable between the Rotterdam and Antwerp routes and the frequency of sailings was amended to reflect changing demand. With the *Jacaranda* having gone off charter on 31st December 1963 the Rotterdam service went down to four days a week with departures from Parkeston Quay being on Sunday, Tuesday, Wednesday and Friday. The service to Antwerp was reduced to just two days a week with departures on Sunday and Thursday.

The decision to replace the movement of old wooden box containers with shiny new metal ones produced an impressive list of requirements for the new container terminal. These included two 30 ton capacity Stothert and Pitt designed 'Transporter' cranes for working containers on and off the ships, a stacking ground beneath the cranes, a twin track Freightliner rail terminal complete with two 'Goliath' cranes and track capable of accommodating a standard 15 wagon train, three sidings with a stacking ground for 250 containers, a control office, workshops and an electrical sub-station. With all this equipment in place it was planned for each ship to make one round trip every 24 hours with a turn round time of 5 hours.

It was all a complete revelation to those who regarded British Rail as staid and old fashioned. As regards ro-ro it was not the case that BR had suddenly woken up to the concept at Parkeston Quay, as they were already in the process of introducing it with the Lion Ferry development, but there was certainly an element of playing catch up through having earlier underestimated its potential and the apparent misjudgement of having introduced the *Avalon*. On the other hand the idea of a container service was a truly pioneering development. By December 1966 BR had been authorised to spend £2.5m on the quayside redevelopment works and when the cost of the new ships was included the total spend at Parkeston Quay would be around £8m.. During the three years following Mr. Raymond's initial presentation the pace of activity around the port would often border on the frenetic.

In 1966 the old GER Hotel on Parkeston Quay Station was finally closed to fare paying guests and much of the interior was later converted into offices for the Port Management and its staff. At ground level there remained platform access to a public bar and restaurant whilst at the rear a back room with access from the quay became a refreshment room for the dock workers.

Throughout 1966 the *Avalon* remained the reserve vessel and in May she was sent away cruising to Oporto and Lisbon. On 22nd August she was chartered to Ellerman Wilson Line and sent to Hull in

The reality of loading of cars onboard the *England* at P. Quay. (Stephen Gooch collection)

The cargo ship *Colchester* was the first British Rail vessel to be given the new corporate colour scheme. She is seen here on 1st October 1964. (NRM collection)

order to operate the inaugural sailing of their new service to Gothenburg on 28th August. This was due to the late delivery of Ellerman's new vessel *Spero*. The *Avalon* returned to Parkeston Quay directly from Gothenburg with Ellerman's *Salerno* handling the car traffic. In the autumn the *Avalon* was again off cruising, this time to Tangier.

Unlike the Pontoon Berth, the proposed new ro-ro linkspans were structures that did require the necessary Parliamentary approval and this, with that also required to construct the Container Terminal, was granted in August 1966. However work had already begun prior to approval being granted and by August that year No. 2 Shed was already demolished. From then on the Quay literally became a massive building site as work commenced on constructing the two new linkspans which would be known as the East and West Portal Berths.

These works involved the building of a central apron of concrete that extended the face of the Middle Quay out into the river. This structure rested on piles and provided a common surface leading out to two longitudinal ramps running parallel to the quay, one facing east and the other facing west. The shore end of each 160 feet long ramp was hinged to the quay. The far end, ie the ship end, was suspended by a series of wire ropes that came down from a steel framed gantry supported on two concrete foundation blocks. These blocks rested on the river's gravel bed and were contained within a sheet piled coffer dam. The linkspans were 9 feet wide and could be raised or lowered within a working lift of 30 feet. On the ship side of the concrete foundation blocks was a 'crash barrier' of protective timbers. This consisted of 20 lengths of greenheart timbers, each 55 feet long and 14 x 14 inches square, packed four high and five deep and placed widthways across the berth. The barrier was faced with timber planking, weighed 70 tons and could be separately hoisted up and down.

During such time as these building works were in progress the normal day to day working of the quay was severely disrupted with shipping services being moved along to the far west end. Berth No. 8a became a temporary repair berth whilst Berth No. 8 was used by the Hook Night service and Berth No. 7 by the Hook Day service. DFDS were likewise moved up to using the Quay's west end with Lion Ferry continuing to use the Pontoon Berth.

The new West Portal was the first to take shape and its skeleton framework was already up by mid January 1967. This was closely followed by that of the East Portal a month later. The ramps were then lifted into place and by early May the ramp's winching gear and crash barriers were all fitted and weight load testings were underway.

Meanwhile work on the new Container Terminal was also underway. As late as February 1967 the East Quay was still being worked as normal with cargo ships such as DFDS's *Blenda* unloading their cargoes either into rail wagons that were shunted alongside or into store inside No. 1 Shed. By the middle of April 1967 much of this area was demolished. Gone was No.1 Shed along with an assorted collection of old sheds and buildings, some brick, some clad with corrugated iron and some made entirely of timber. These included the former locomotive depot whose

The loading of Ford motor cars for export onboard the DFDS cargo ship *Blenda* at the West Quay - 1967. (Derek Genzel collection)

site was needed for a new rail terminal and preparations were in hand to pile the quay and quay face in order to provide the strengthened support for the new cranes.

The first of the new portal berths to come into service was the West Portal when, on 19th May 1967, the *Viking III* arrived from Bremerhaven. This was a change from her usual berth at the Pontoon Berth which, on that day, was being occupied by Fred Olsen Line's *Black Prince* which had arrived to inaugurate a new service to and from Kristiansand in Norway.

Built in Lubeck the *Black Prince* was launched in May 1966 as a ship with a dual personality. She was designed to be a tourist and car ferry during the summer but in winter could operate as a refrigerated fruit carrier and since October 1966 she had adopted this latter role between London and the Canary Islands from where she would mainly bring back tomatoes. Her lower holds and car deck were designed to be temporarily subdivided and were equipped with a pallet and conveyor system for loading and unloading the cargo. Forklift trucks gained access to the refrigerated compartments through doors in the ship's side. On the decks above she retained accommodation for up to 350 passengers who could enjoy a bit of winter sunshine whilst the ship cruised south throughout the 5 day trip.

A sister ship, the *Black Watch,* was owned jointly by Fred Olsen Lines and Norway's Det Bergenske Dampskips-Selskap or Bergen Lines. She too sailed on Fred Olsen's winter route south but was also built to sail a summer season service between Newcastle and Bergen in Norway for Bergen Line. This she had done throughout the summer of 1966 when she was known as the *Jupiter*. Her entry into service had earlier brought about the building of Newcastle's first ro-ro berth which opened earlier that year.

When the *Black Prince* arrived at Parkeston Quay at the start of her tourist season sailings to Norway she was then the largest ship to use the port at 9,499 grt and was just under 465 feet long. Her layout had been re-configured from a one class ship in winter to a two class ship in summer and for the first time she now sailed with her full compliment of up to 587 passengers. Those in First class could choose between 11 single and 64 double berth cabins on the Boat Deck plus a double and five De-luxe cabins on the Sun Deck. Those in Tourist class were provided with 134 double or triple berth cabins located throughout the Upper, Main or A decks. All 215 cabins were en-suite. Most of the public spaces were located on the Lounge Deck with the forward most area being a First class lounge. Moving aft was a 120 seat First class restaurant that operated on a smorgasbord basis, a Tourist class cafeteria with seating for over 200 and a combined lounge and bar complete with the requisite night club and dance floor. Her car deck held space for 185 cars, once a hanging or mezzanine level was in place, with access being via stern doors only. Her appearance was notable for having a funnel said to resemble that of a fireman's helmet.

The service to Norway remained seasonal and was three times per fortnight with arrivals at Parkeston Quay on Monday, Saturday and Wednesday at 13.00 and departures the same day at 16.00. The crossing time was 22 hours and in between her trips to

The Lion Ferry vessel *Prins Hamlet (I)* is seen here arriving at the new pontoon berth following her maiden voyage from Bremerhaven - 24th May 1966. (Derek Genzel collection)

Another view of the Lion Ferry vessel *Prins Hamlet (I)* is seen here arriving at the new pontoon berth following her maiden voyage from Bremerhaven - 24th May 1966. (Derek Genzel collection)

Parkeston Quay the *Black Prince* also sailed between Kristiansand and Amsterdam. In subsequent years she returned to Parkeston Quay each May to September whilst her winters were spent away on the Canary Islands run.

The *Black Prince* was the first ship to use the new East Portal berth on 26th June 1967 with special arrangements being made for doing so as the berth was not ready for completion until the beginning of July. A short while earlier DFDS had introduced a new vessel of their own, the 8,658 grt *Winston Churchill*, and on 2nd June 1967 from the recently opened West Portal she had embarked on her maiden voyage to Esbjerg.

The *Winston Churchill* was built at the yard of Cantieri Navali del Tirreno e Riuniti near Genoa in Italy. She was named after Britain's wartime Prime Minister in a purely emotional gesture by DFDS to mark a sense of gratitude towards him by the Danish nation. Launched in April 1967 the vessel first arrived at Parkeston Quay for berthing trials on 29th May and this was following by an official naming ceremony at Greenwich on 30th May conducted by Lady Churchill.

Internally the *Winston Churchill's* layout was similar to that of the *England* as was the number of passengers she could carry at 462. The Saloon Deck contained a forward facing First class lounge, a bar and a 135 seat Dining Room whilst aft was a Second class Dining room with 220 seats and a separate lounge. Each class had their own entrance hall and the facilities on the Saloon Deck were fully class segregated as on the *England*. Featured throughout were wood panelling, glass bulkheads and screening which, together with all spaces again extending the full width of the ship, helped to create the all important light and airy feeling. Below on A Deck was a night club aft, Second class cabins amidships and First class cabins forward that included two side cabins designated as De-luxe Suites A and B that had their own sitting room, bedroom and bathroom. The rest of the cabins were on Decks B, C, and D. All First class cabins were en-suite and either single or double berthed whilst those for Second class passengers were either 2 or 4 berthed and fitted with washbasins only. In total there were 124 First class berths and 274 in Second class.

One advantage the *Winston Churchill* had over the *England* was that she could carry almost twice the number of cars at 180, or 40 x 20ft trailers, plus 55,656 cubic feet of hold space of which 33,000 was refrigerated. She had displaced the *Kronprinsesse Ingrid,* which had left Parkeston Quay on 15 December 1966, onto seasonal sailings between Esbjerg and Newcastle that began on 23rd June 1967 and by the end of the year had helped raise the number of passengers travelling on the Parkeston Quay to Esbjerg route into exceeding 100,000 for the first time ever, this being up from the 90,000 carried in 1965.

The crossing time had been reduced to 18 hours with arrivals at both ports being 12.00 and departures at 18.00. During the summer the service was daily and DFDS had now introduced a new car and motorist tariff with only two rates - for cars under 14 feet long with one driver/passenger the rate was £6.6s.0d. whilst for those over 14 feet long it was £7.18s.0d. If a car under 14 feet long was accompanied by two passengers the car's fare was reduced to £4.4s.0d., by three passengers it became £2.2s.0d. and with four passengers the car went for free. Separately there was a passenger fare to pay that started at £6.10s.0d single for a berth in four, six or eight berth group accommodation that included 'a proper berth with full

The *Prins Hamlet (I)* maintained the summer season service to Bremerhaven from 1966 to 1968. (Stephen Gooch collection)

bedding'. Alternatively the cheapest single fares berthed in Second class were £10.3s.0d or £13.11s.0d. in First class. DFDS considered such rates as being 'ideal for the holiday motorist on a tight budget or the man with a big family'. At a time when the average wage was then £16 a week the lowest all-in family fare for a car, two adults and two children was £39 return.

Perhaps more important than carrying passengers and tourists was the Winston Churchill's ability to carry freight. Though she was only a few inches longer than the England she was 4 feet wider in the beam at just over 67 feet and was widely regarded as being a much improved version of the earlier ship in regards to having a much greater headroom on her car deck. She arrived as the route's first drive through ship fitted with bow and stern doors which not only allowed for the carrying of road vehicles but also, with particular reference to Danish traffic, the all important future ability to transport bacon and butter in refrigerated trailers and containers. Her arrival was co-incident with DFDS implementing a fleet modernisation programme whereby their traditional cargo vessels were being replaced with larger and more modern roll-on roll-off freight ships that were able to carry both accompanied and unaccompanied units as well as the aforementioned refrigerated trailers. Danish farmers and meat producers were being encouraged into switching consignments away from loose loaded to trailer loaded and at Esbjerg a new bacon terminal was completed at the end of 1966 to handle the changing means of shipment.

The first DFDS cargo ships equipped with a bow visor were respectively launched in 1965 and 1966 as the 999 grt Suffolk and Sussex with each being capable of carrying up to 50 x 20ft trailers. An alternative method of defining carrying capacity was to quote the number of teu's or twenty foot equivalent units though this was a measure more often used in the carrying of metal boxed containers. DFDS made a wide use of such terminology even when transporting road based trailer units and thus the Suffolk and Sussex had a capacity for 50 teu's. Their main routes were out of Copenhagen, usually loaded with Carlsberg lager, with the Suffolk entering service in May 1966 when sailing to Felixstowe followed by the Sussex first sailing to Antwerp in September.

Visually, apart from the addition of a bow visor, they were not too dissimilar from BR's Isle of Ely and Colchester and were just 19 feet longer at 260.8 feet overall. However with an open plan deck space the DFDS ships boasted almost 40% more cargo capacity than the railway ships at 126,751 cu.ft. Both were somewhat infrequently seen at Parkeston Quay. The Suffolk first appeared in January 1968 whilst the Sussex first appeared in December 1969 only after both ships had recently been lengthened by 48.2 feet and now accommodated up to 85 teu's. Each made use of the new West Portal berth. However their time at Parkeston Quay was after the first fully drive through cargo vessel equipped with both a bow visor and a stern loading door had already arrived at the port. This was DFDS's Stafford.

Launched in January 1967 the 2,245 grt Stafford

Unloading boxes of tomatoes from the Avalon - September 1964. (NRM collection)

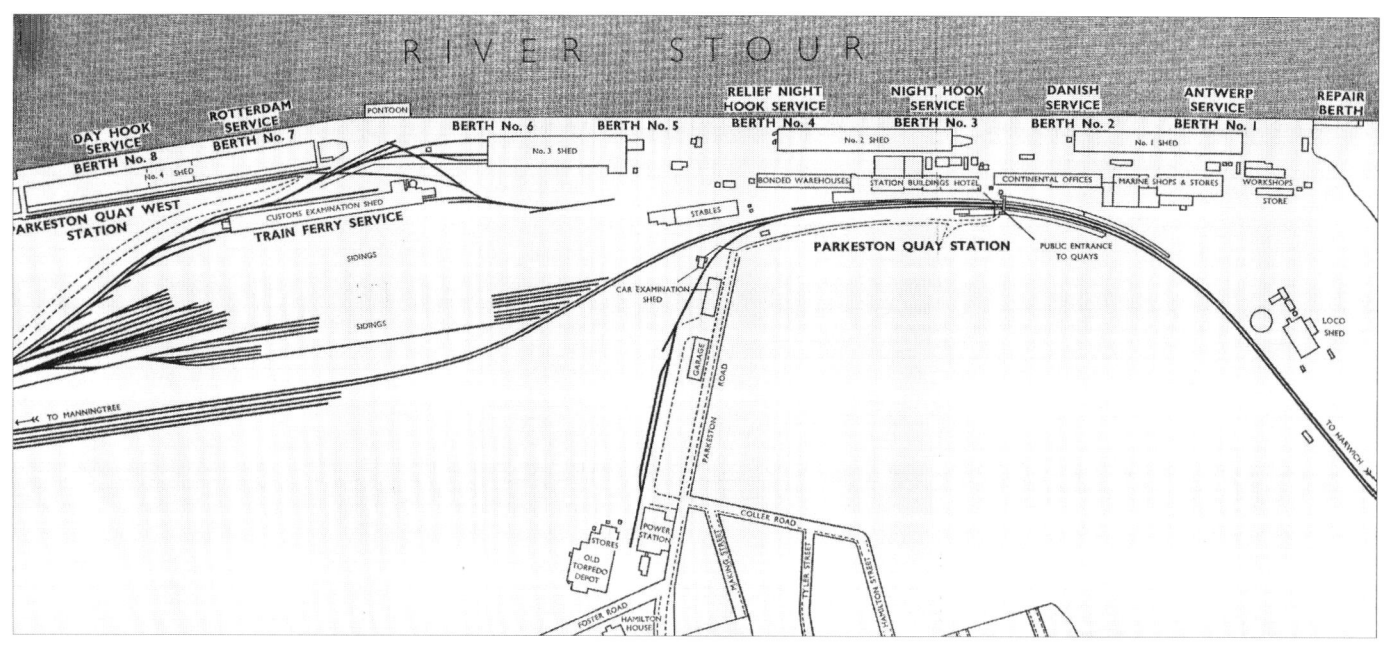

A plan layout of P. Quay in 1963. (Stephen Brown collection)

berthed at the West Portal on 9th June 1967 on her maiden voyage from Esbjerg, this being just a week after the *Winston Churchill* had entered service. The *Stafford* was a sister ship to the *Somerset* which, when sailing to Grimsby in January 1967, had been the first ship to handle the new method of shipping Danish agricultural products. Each ship could carry the equivalent of 100 teu's with passenger accommodation for 12 drivers.

The summer season sailings of the Lion Ferries service from Bremerhaven resumed on 1st June 1967 and were again undertaken by the *Prins Hamlet*. Her off season role as a cruise ship had been highly successful though during that time she had been restricted to carrying only around 350 passengers, mainly Swedes and Danes, who enjoyed the experience at a much cheaper price than on the established liners of the time. Every effort was made in creating the atmosphere of being on board a cruise ship rather than being on just a car ferry.

However it was her initial success at being merely a ferry and the consequent need for more passenger accommodation on the Bremerhaven route that a sister ship was proposed in joining her for the 1967 summer season. This was to be named *Prins Albert* and operated by a German subsidiary of Wallenius Lines. Instead in November 1966 the *Prins Hamlet* had earlier been sent to Gothenburg for a refit and an extra 60 cabins were installed equally throughout the starboard side of both the car decks. When the work was completed in fitting these four berth economy cabins she then had a total of 684 berths though her car decks had space for only 165 cars or 16 lorries. A swimming pool was placed on the aft deck and her tonnage raised to 8,688 grt..

The alterations were such that the *Prins Hamlet* was now equipped to handle all of the summer season passenger traffic on her own and thus there was no need for the second ship that Wallenius had on order. Wallenius later withdrew from their joint agreement and their planned *Prins Albert* was eventually built as the cruse ship *Boheme*.

An aerial view of P. Quay in the mid 1960s looking east. (Robert Clow collection)

The schedule for 1967 was therefore similar to the previous year with the *Prinz Hamlet* leaving Bremerhaven at 18.00 to arrive at Parkeston Quay at 10.15 from where a connecting boat train now left at 11.20 to arrive in London Liverpool Street at 12.45. The return journey left London at 14.10 and arrived at Parkeston Quay at 15.36 for a 17.00 sailing that arrived in Bremerhaven at 09.15 next day.

By the time the *Viking III* returned to take over the winter service on 25th September the *Prins Hamlet* had carried 46,033 passengers, 5,770 cars and 2,000 freight units. The passenger fare in 1967 was £6.11s.0d. single or £10.16s.0d. return with cabin accommodation starting at £1.7s.6d. per berth. Rates for a car up to 14 feet long were £8.11s.0d. single and £13.10s.0d. return.

As a result of provisions within the 1967 Transport Act BR were authorised to open up new sea routes if they were deemed to be financially viable and on 27th September 1967 an inauguration ceremony was held on board the *Norfolk Ferry* to mark the opening of a new train ferry service between Harwich and Dunkirk. This was to be run in conjunction with the French Railways (SNCF) and started on 2nd October with the *Norfolk Ferry* having been suitably modified in order to fit the berth in France. The schedule was daily except Sunday: Dep Harwich 06.00, arr Dunkirk 14.15, dep Dunkirk 16.15 and arr Harwich at 02.00. Although rates were the same as on the existing service to Zeebrugge the route got off to a slow start and by the end of the year it had carried just 5,000 tons of cargo.

At Parkeston Quay the redevelopment of the East Quay had created a problem of where to site the existing marine workshops. As a result of the planned integration of the Hook of Holland services the SMZ would no longer be berthing their ships at the West Quay and it was thought that that area would become almost redundant. Accordingly it was planned to relocate the workshops there and create a repair berth out of No.7 Berth. However a proposal that No. 4 Shed might one day be used to accommodate a general cargo service meant that the workshops had to go elsewhere and a new site was chosen to the west of the new car examination shed. Work on the new workshops began towards the end of 1966 and by June 1967 they were sufficiently operational to allow the final demolition of the old ones. When fully completed and opened in 1968 the port was then capable of undertaking all manner of marine based repair and maintenance work up to and including a complete vessel survey thanks to a staff of between 150 and 180 fitters, electricians, boilermakers, scalers and shipwrights. The only thing it could not do was dry dock a ship.

By January 1968 the container terminal was beginning to take shape. To take traffic from Station Road to the new terminal area a new roadway had been built, named East Dock Road, together with a new East Gates level crossing. The down side railway station platform was shortened to make way for this new crossing and the railway line to Harwich Town was made into single line working with the old down line being used as a long siding for the storage of container trains. The Goliath and Transporter cranes were nearing completion as were most of the other works. An examination shed for containers, known as 2 Block, was built alongside East Dock Road almost in a line due south of the old No. 2 Shed.

Contrary to the existing method when shipping the

Presentation by the Chairman of the BRB, Mr. Stanley Raymond, onboard the *Arnhem* outlining plans for the redevelopment of P. Quay - 18th May 1966. (Derek Genzel collection)

An artist impression of BR's plan for a new quay layout. (Stephen Brown collection)

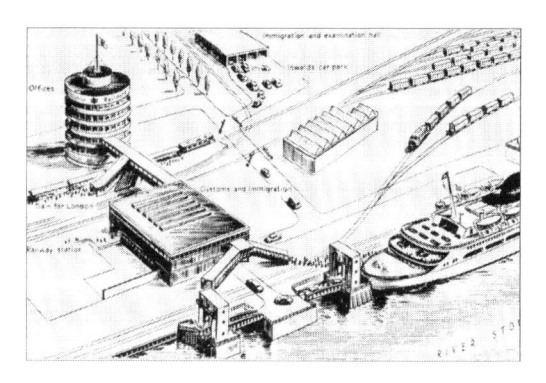

An alternative impression with a more 'continental' design theme. Both impressions include the 'Railport Tower' which was never built.

An artist impression of the working arrangements for the new container ships. (Stephen Brown collection)

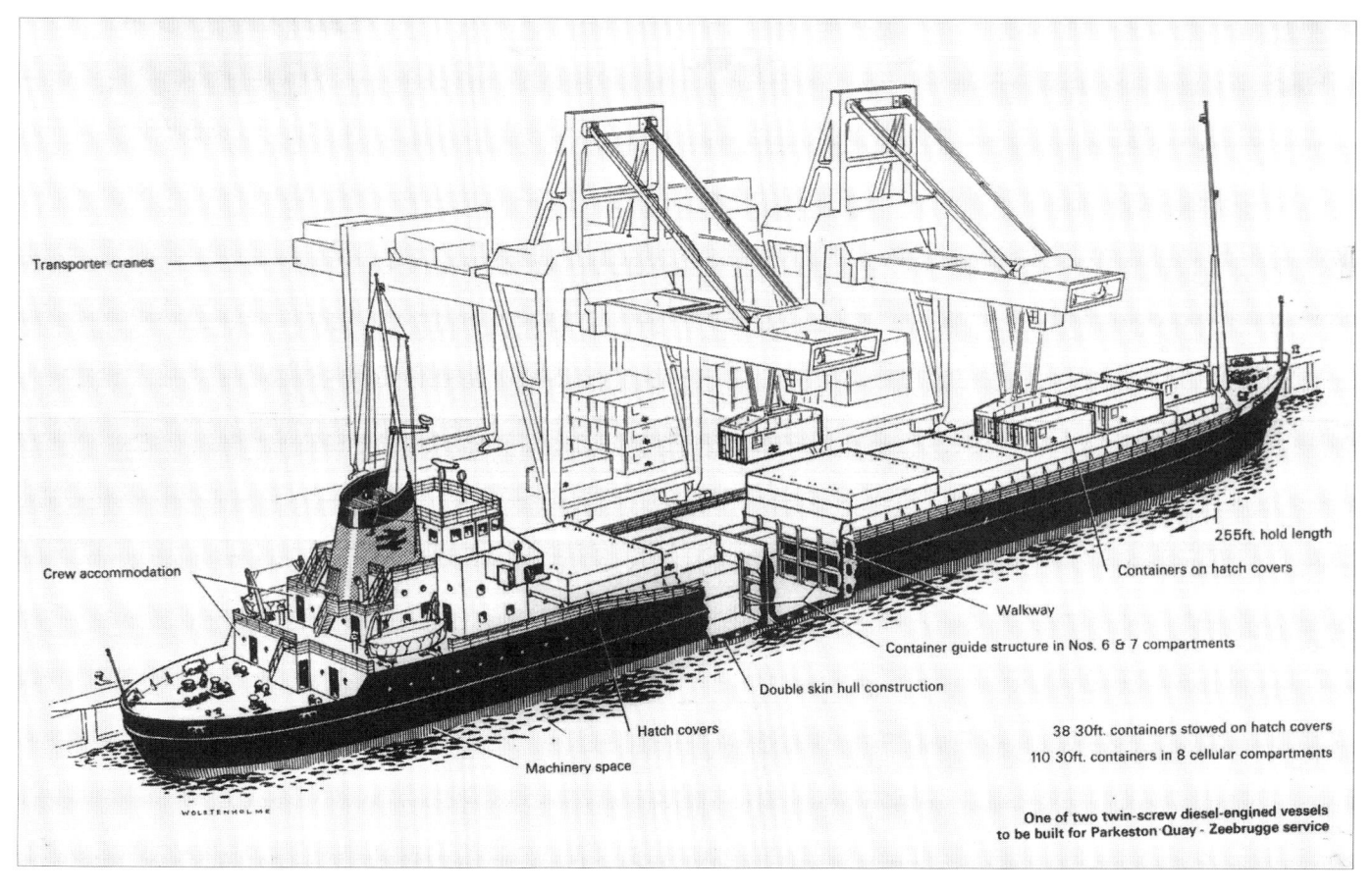

wooden box containers there was to be no provision for taking the new containers directly to the ship's side by rail. All movement of containers between the ship and the rail terminal would be by road using flat bed trailers hauled by a fleet of Bedford TK tractive units known locally as 'tug units'.

By now construction of the two new container ships was also nearing completion at the yard of John Readhead & Sons Ltd in South Shields. They were developed from a basic design of Mr. Rogan, BR's manager of ship construction, and were launched as Sea Freightliner I on 2nd December 1967 and Sea Freightliner II on 15th March 1968. Both ships were registered at Harwich and as such their bows were adorned with the traditional five pointed gold stars.

Measuring 388.5 feet overall with a beam of 53 feet these 4,034 grt sister ships were built as Britain's very first cellular container ships at a total cost of £1.75 million. They were powered by two Mirrlees National diesels providing a service speed of 13½ knots and were equipped with a bow thrust unit, a bow rudder and twinned spade rudders aft. The machinery spaces, stores and accommodation for the 18 crew were all situated in the aft section, this taking up a quarter the length of the vessel, whilst the cargo spaces, built as sectionalised holds containing cellular compartments, extended 255 feet almost to the bow. Containers were stowed 3 deep and 5 across within 4 longitudinal sections each 60 feet long. Three such sections each held 30 x 30 foot containers, or boxes, whilst the foremost section held a further 20 x 30 foot containers.

The cargo space was capped by a series of sliding hatch covers which when slid into place formed a secure base upon which another single layer of containers could be loaded. In total each ship could carry 148 x 30 foot containers arranged as 110 below the hatch covers plus 38 above. This was equal to 218 teu's in any assortment of 20 foot, 30 foot or 40 foot containers including those that were temperature controlled. Bridge controlled wing trimming tanks ran along both sides of the vessel at deck level in order to keep the ship literally on an even keel, this being so that containers could be accurately guided into place.

In the 1960s the end-on height and width of a standard ISO container was 8 feet by 8 feet and the capacity of a container ship was measured in terms of the number of teu's that could be slotted inside. However for commercial purposes the number quoted would often refer instead to 30 foot containers, the reason being that a container 35 foot long was then the maximum size allowed onto British roads. Under such criteria the two Sea Freightliners were classified as carrying 45 x 20 foot and 80 x 30 foot containers in cells plus a further 56 x 20 foot containers on top of the hatch covers. When the Road Construction and Use Regulations later permitted the movement of longer 40 foot containers the ship's cell guides could simply be moved further along in order to fit in the new size. The introduction of ISO containers led to the removal of the overhead gantry system on board the Cambridge Ferry.

The first of these pioneering vessels to arrive at Parkeston Quay was Sea Freightliner I which left South Shields at 12.22 on 11th March 1968. After a leisurely 246 mile delivery voyage she arrived at the quay in early afternoon the next day. She then made her first berthing trials trip to Zeebrugge during the 15th March, the times being: Dep. P. Quay 06.13, arr. Zeebrugge 12.55, dep. Zeebrugge 15.07 and arr. P. Quay at 21.13. A further trip was made on the 17th though she was forced to turn back when off Zeebrugge due to bad

One of two twin-screw diesel-engined vessels to be built for Parkeston Quay - Zeebrugge service

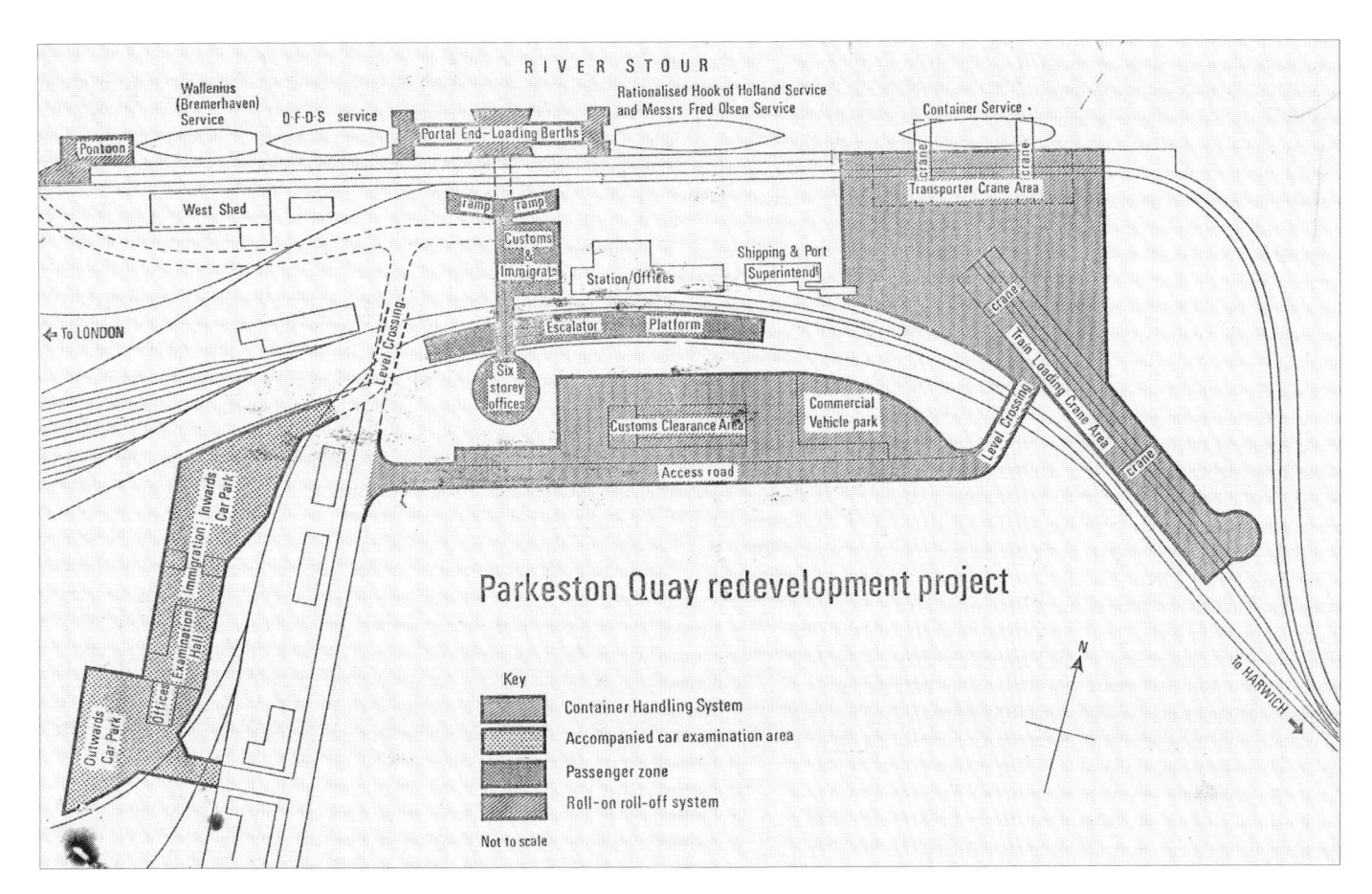

Parkeston Quay redevelopment project

The 1966 plans for a redeveloped Parkeston Quay. (Stephen Brown collection)

weather and gale force winds. On the 18th March she underwent the first test loading of a container from one of the quay's Transporter cranes and later that night she sailed on her first loaded voyage to Zeebrugge where the first to be landed there were taken off on the 19th March. The voyage times of her inaugurating run were: Dep. P. Quay 23.37, arr. Zeebrugge 07.20, dep. Zeebrugge 13.22 and arr. P. Quay at 21.12.

The *Sea Freightliner I*'s early days in service were marred by spells of exceptionally bad weather which often added an hour or two onto the 7 hours that were scheduled for the 84 n. mile crossing. As the service was new and containers relatively few on the ground this lost time could partly be made up by shorter turn round times at each port. The initial cost of transporting a 20 foot container, quay to quay, was £25 and to Zeebrugge from a container terminal at London Stratford the cost was £34.

The Container Terminal was officially opened on 21st May by H.R.H. Princess Alexandra. The occasion included a tour of the new terminal and a visit on board *Sea Freightliner I*, the arrangements being highly reminiscent of when her father, H.R.H. Prince George, opened the Train Ferry terminal in 1924. In Belgium a similar ceremony took place on 28th June in the presence of H.R.H. Prince Albert.

This new modern steel box container service brought about the end of the 'old fashioned' wooden box service to Antwerp. The route itself was closed on 31st May 1968 thus terminating a link between the two ports that had lasted for 85 years. The last sailing was by a chartered vessel, the *Derwent Fisher*, which was acting as cover for the *Isle of Ely* which, on 5th May, had been sent away to Readheads for conversion into a cellular ship similarly able to carry the new design of containers.

Sea Freightliner II arrived at Parkeston Quay on 3rd June. At 04.45 on 18th June she left to open the new container service to Rotterdam's Princesmargrithaven. She made only three round trips before being replaced on 24th June by the newly converted *Isle of Ely*. The wooden box service to Rotterdam later closed on 29th August 1968. This displaced the *Colchester* for a brief period of lay up before she was moved to sail between Weymouth and the Channel Islands on 18th October 1968.

The return of the *Isle of Ely* had released *Sea Freightliner II* to finally join *Sea Freightliner I* in running the planned twice daily each way service to Zeebrugge. Sailings from Parkeston Quay were at 23.00 Sunday to Friday and 17.00 Monday to Friday. In the first year of operation the new Container Terminal handled 23,177 containers. However

The Essex Ferry arriving at the Harwich train ferry berth - 4th July 1966. (NRM collection)

throughout its lifetime it suffered from having a quay frontage that was insufficient to fully accommodate two Sea Freightliners being alongside together. The length of quay available for mooring up was around 625 feet through which the ship to shore Transporter cranes could only move along around 580 feet. This meant that on the extreme east end one ship would 'overhang' by about 150 feet and necessitate being moored up alongside the dolphin. The reason was that enough space had to be left for ships to moor up at the new East Portal Berth and the required land to the east into which the quay would have needed to extend was not owned by British Rail.

At the same time as the new Container Terminal was coming into use arrangements were being made for the new Hook of Holland car ferry and ro-ro service to start as planned in July 1968. Of the two new ships on order it was the *Koningin Juliana* for SMZ that entered the water first. She was launched on 2nd February 1968 at Cammell Laird's yard at Birkenhead by Madame A. van Roijen, wife of the Dutch Ambassador. British Rail's vessel, the *St. George*, was built at Swan Hunter's on Tyneside and was launched a short while later on 28th February by Mrs. Johnson, wife of the BR Chairman. The *St. George* would become the last railway ship to be registered at Harwich and the last to bear the five pointed stars on her bow.

Although each ship had their own individual design characteristics they matched each other on their required capabilities. Each could carry up to 1,200 passengers by day or 750 by night and their car decks had space for up to 220 cars or 80 cars and 32 lorries. As regards sleeping arrangements the 6,682 grt *Koningin Juliana* had a total of 537 berths in 243 cabins whilst the 7,356 grt *St George* had 565 berths in 239 cabins.

The arrangements on board the new car ferries were broadly similar though the reverse of tradition in that Second class was now situated forward and First class was aft. Thus the Boat Deck had a forward facing Second class lounge behind which was the cafeteria. Moving aft was the First class restaurant and a First class smoke room and bar. The Second class smoke room and bar was forward on A Deck which led off the Second class entrance hall. On either side of this hall were two sleeping lounges. First class passengers boarded further aft and off their entrance hall, located amidship, were 6 De-luxe and 2 semi De-luxe cabins, each with private bathrooms. The aft section of A Deck was given over to First class double berth cabins and a First class rest lounge. A shop was located between the two classes.

On B Deck were a variety of cabins, both insides and outsides, arranged along both sides of the upper Car Deck. These extended the full length of the deck with an assortment of doubles and singles for First class and doubles and four berth cabins for Second class. The deck below was the main Car Deck and further below, forward on C Deck, was an area of predominately 4-berth cabins amongst which, on the *Koningin Juliana,* were 22 such cabins classed as 4 berth couchette or economy cabins that converted into 6 seat day cabins.

The *St. George* was the railway's first diesel driven passenger ship on the Hook of Holland route and the first to have an enclosed bridge and a bulbous bow. She was also equipped with twin controllable pitch propellers, twin stern rudders and a bow-thrust unit. Unfortunately events would show that she was not equipped with particularly reliable engines. Those fitted were a new design of Ruston AO diesels and it was often said that the *St. George* would move off the berth on four engines, turn on three, sail on two and

The *Cambridge Ferry* departing the Harwich train ferry berth - 1st November 1966. (NRM collection)

PARKESTON QUAY UNDER RAILWAY OWNERSHIP   131

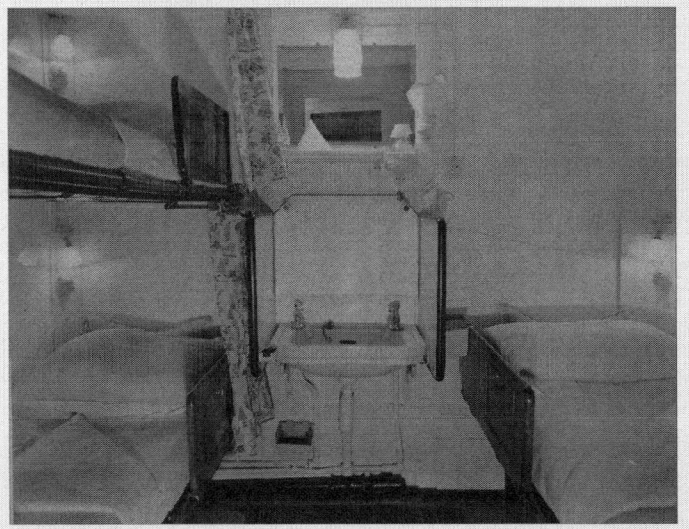

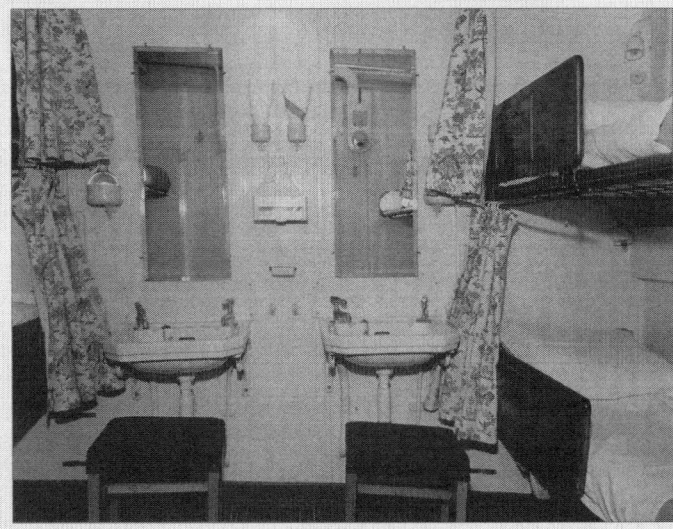

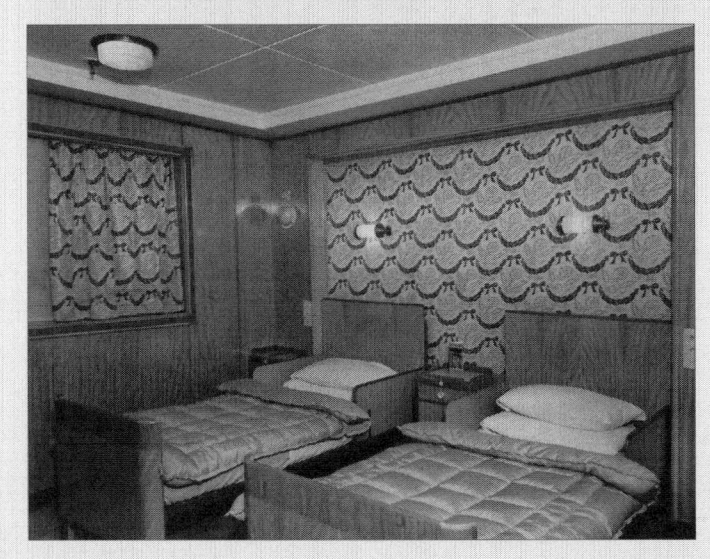

Top: A First class Cabin-de-luxe on A Deck onboard the *Arnhem* - 26th April 1967. (NRM collection)

Above left: A Second class 3-berth cabin onboard the *Arnhem* - 26th April 1967. (NRM collection)

Above right: A Second class 3-berth cabin on B Deck onboard the *Amsterdam* - 27th April 1967. (NRM collection)

Left: A Promenade Deck Cabin-de-luxe onboard the *Amsterdam* - 27th April 1967. (NRM collection)

These four pictures were taken towards the end of their careers and show the dated design of the BR ship's accommodation.

arrive with just one left working. Despite their poor reputation the *St. George* never lost a sailing due to a problem with her main engines.

Also unfortunate was a delay to the planned July start date as the *Koningin Juliana* suffered fire damage on 13th June whilst being fitted out at Cammell Laird's. It thus befell the *St. George* alone to open the ro-ro era between Parkeston Quay and the Hook of Holland when she made her maiden voyage with the night sailing of 17th July 1968. She sailed as the night ship in both directions whilst awaiting the arrival of the *Koningin Juliana* and sailed opposite the *Avalon* with the *Amsterdam* being used to duplicate sailings as required. The SMZ vessels *Koningin Emma* and *Koningin Wilhelmina* maintained the day service on an interim basis only.

Two older ships, one British and one Dutch, were withdrawn from service and quickly disposed off. The *Arnhem* had made her last trip from the Hook of Holland on the evening of 27th April 1968 and on 13th August she left Parkeston Quay for the yard of T.W. Ward Ltd in Inverkeithing where she was scrapped the following year. The *Prinses Beatrix* finished her services on 6th September and four days later was sent for lay up at Schiedam pending sale.

The delayed *Koningin Juliana* eventually left Birkenhead in early October and after calling in at Parkeston Quay for berthing trials on the 10th she finally arrived at the Hook of Holland on 11th October. She then sailed on up to the Parkkade in Rotterdam for inspection and two 'fly the flag' cruises. The first was from Rotterdam on the 13th for the benefit of SMZ personnel and the second was on the 14th from the Hook of Holland where H.M. Queen Juliana boarded the ship for her own special cruise into the North Sea. The ship returned to the Parkkade and was now ready to enter service.

On the morning of 17th October the *Amsterdam* arrived at the Hook and gave way to the *Koningin Juliana* which then made her maiden voyage to Parkeston Quay around midnight. The *Koningin Emma* had earlier arrived at the Hook of Holland around 18.00 on what was her final day boat sailing from Parkeston Quay. Next morning she sailed to Flushing for lay-up. Her place on the day boat service was taken up next day, 18th October, by the *Amsterdam* which now sailed opposite the other day boat, the *Koningin Wilhelmina*. The two laid up Dutch vessels both went to Jos de Smedt's yard in Antwerp for breaking up with the *Koningin Emma* leaving Flushing on 18th December and the *Prinses Beatrix* leaving Schiedam on 19th December 1968.

The *St. George* was to be plagued for some time with vibration problems caused by her controllable pitch propellers and on 25th October she was sent to Immingham where stiffeners were fitted between the frames around her stern. With the *Avalon* away on charter to Gulf Oil for the opening of the Bantry Bay oil terminal in Ireland the *Amsterdam* was switched back into covering the night service. The *Amsterdam* was herself covered for one trip by the BR Southern Region car ferry *Normannia,* which was on lay up at Parkeston Quay pending her annual survey there, and by the Holyhead to Dun Laoghaire passenger vessel *Hibernia,* which arrived on 25th October, for a further two trips.

The *St. George* returned to Parkeston Quay on 2nd

The West Portal under construction - 23rd January 1967. (NRM collection)

View of the East end of Parkeston Quay with the DFDS cargo ship *Blenda* being worked on alongside No. 1 Shed - 14th February 1967. (Derek Genzel collection)

November and finally the new integrated service was ready to commence. This occurred on 8th November 1968 when the *St. George* became the day boat from Parkeston Quay, dep 12.00, and night boat back from the Hook, dep 23.15 whilst the *Koningin Juliana* became the night boat from Parkeston Quay, dep 22.00 and day boat back from the Hook, dep 11.30. This regular pattern of sailings would then service the route for almost thirty years.

The *Amsterdam* had completed her final voyage on 7th November and was then laid up before being sold for around £200,000 in April 1969 to Chandris Line of Greece. This was the same company that had previously bought the *Duke of York*. The *Amsterdam* left Parkeston Quay on 1st May and was converted into a cruise ship and re-named *Fiorita*. The *Koningin Wilhelmina* sailed from the Hook of Holland on the morning of 8th November 1968 for a winter lay up in Flushing. To handle the new integrated service BR's agents at the Hook of Holland, Hudig & Pieters, had joined forces with those of SMZ's, ie Wm.H. Muller & Co., to form the Harwich Ferry Agency (HFA).

As if two new ro-ro berths, new British and Dutch ferries, a passenger service to Norway, a totally new container terminal with two innovative new ships, a new ro-ro passenger ship and freight ships to Denmark and a new train ferry route into France were not enough for Parkeston Quay and Harwich to contend with within the space of just 18 months there had been the added possibility of yet another new passenger service arriving when the Belgian ferry *Koningin Fabiola* underwent berthing trials on 19th September 1967 at the West Portal berth.

An announcement was later made on 6th December that the Belgian Marine Administration (BMA) would next year commence a year round car ferry service between Parkeston Quay and the Belgian port of Ostend. After berthing trials by their *Roi Baudouin* on 10th May 1968 the service opened with her arrival on 29th May 1968, this being just two days before the closure of BR's route into Antwerp. The *Roi Baudouin* was to operate just the one sailing a day and left Ostend at 14.30 and arrived at Parkeston Quay's No 6 pontoon berth at 19.30. She would then depart Parkeston Quay at 21.45 in summer and 22.30 in winter.

The *Roi Baudouin* was built in 1965 and had accommodation for 850 passengers and 160 cars. At 3,241 grt she was quite small in comparison to more recent arrivals at the port and suffered from a low clearance height on the car deck such that only cars, trade cars and caravans could be carried in any great numbers. Access was via a stern door only with the number of lorry spaces restricted to just five. Crossing times were 5 hours each way or 6½ hours during the winter.

The 82 n.miles from Ostend to Parkeston Quay was around twenty miles further than that of BMA's established 3¾ hours route between Ostend and

The *Viking III* is seen passing the West Portal berth having arrived on her overnight sailing from Bremerhaven - 13th April 1967. (NRM collection)

Dover but the hopes were that motorists would see that by using a port further up the east coast of England it was worth the extra time at sea in order to save the effort of having to crawl through the roads of London and the south east of England. However bookings were never very high due perhaps to the awkward timings involved. The *Roi Baudouin*'s sailings from Ostend to Parkeston Quay were in between those she was regularly making to and from Dover and although she had all the requisite amenities of a restaurant, a cafeteria and a bar there was only limited sleeping accommodation to alleviate a very early 03.45 arrival in Ostend. For those who preferred a berth the options available ranged from couchettes to a De-luxe grade cabin.

Yet the idea of such a route into Belgium had much to commend it. Ostend was served by a number of international train services that went deep into south and central Europe in ways similar to those that set out from the Hook of Holland and heading further to the north and east. Also there was a good motorway network close by. However the carriage of foot passengers, and thereby potential train passengers, was somewhat strangely discouraged by the BMA despite the Company's original intention to add a second ship to the route, this being the newly launched *Princesse Astrid*. Unfortunately as the initial service was to see a distinct lack of advance bookings the idea of a second ship was cancelled.

Several other ships were associated with this route including the *Koningin Fabiola* and *Prinses Josephine Charlotte* with the latter being used during the winter months when demand was lower until replaced on the list by the *Artevelde*. The passenger fare from Parkeston Quay to Ostend was £4.0s.0d single as opposed to £2.12s.0d from Dover whilst a car cost the same on both routes at £8.10s.0d each way.

It is noticeable that a car cost roughly the same no matter which route was used when leaving Parkeston Quay. The price to Ostend was mid-way between the £8.0s.0d it cost to Esbjerg with DFDS and the £9.0s.0d with Fred Olsen to Kristiansand. British Rail charged £18.5s.0d return to the Hook of Holland. The major differences were in the fares charged for passengers which then started at £4.11s.0d. single to the Hook of Holland, £12.0s.0d. to Esbjerg and £10.10s.0d. to Kristiansand.

In 1968 the Lion Ferry service to Bremerhaven again saw the *Viking III* replaced, on 13th June, by the return of the *Prins Hamlet* which then ran the summer service until 25th September. However because of the alterations that were made to provide more cabin accommodation the *Prins Hamlet* was increasingly unable to handle all of the freight on offer and so the freight ship *Don Juan* was put on the route to assist. From September onwards the *Viking III* again returned to take over the off season sailings though not before the *Prins Hamlet* had earlier that month grounded

The East end of P. Quay following the demolition of No. 1 Shed in preparation for the site of the new container terminal - 13th April 1967. (NRM collection)

herself off Harwich and required the services of the tugs *Ocean Cock* and *Ionia* to successfully re-float her.

These seasonal changes occurred just as in previous years but there were other changes occurring to both to the *Prins Hamlet* and Lion Ferry. The style of cruising that the *Prins Hamlet* offered had now become less popular and less profitable. She had spent the first months of 1968 and then her 1968-69 off season period chartered to an American travel firm who operated her from Lisbon to Recife in Brazil and ports along the South American coast. When she returned from Brazil in May 1969 she sailed straight for berthing trials at the St. Pauli Landungsbrucken pier in Hamburg arriving there on 22nd May.

This change of port was due to events in October 1968 whereby a consortium of interests in Hamburg had created the company 'Deutschland - England Fahrexpress GmbH' to run their own ferry service to England. The group consisted of F. Laeisz, Hamburgische Landesbank, Holsten Brauerei and the Hamburg shipping company of Hafen - Dampfschiffahrt AG (HADAG). Instead of trying to compete against this new company Lion Ferry A.B. entered into a 50-50 partnership agreement on the basis that Lion Ferry A.B. would maintain a majority interest in the service from Bremerhaven whilst Fahrexpress would be the majority interest at Hamburg. A new marketing brand was formed, called Prinzenlinien or Prins Line, which the public would come to know better as Prins Ferries.

As far as Parkeston Quay was concerned the relevance of these changes meant that Lion Ferry would be leaving. However they were not moving far as their new port of arrival was only a couple of miles down river at Harwich Navyard Dock. The first day of Prins Line at Harwich was on 2nd January 1969 when the still chartered *Viking III* arrived from Bremerhaven. This event marked the first arrival of a continental

Work in progress on the two Portal berths with the linkspan now in place at the West Portal - 25th April 1967. (NRM collection)

The West Portal first opened on 19th May 1967. It is seen here on 17th May with the *England* in the berth behind. (NRM collection)

Passengers disembarking from the *Avalon* upon completion of a 13 day cruise to the Baltic - 15th June 1967 (NRM collection)

Both linkspans in position - 20th July 1967. (NRM collection)

October. Able to carry just 40 lorries and 12 drivers she carried on doing so for a short while after the passenger service was resumed with the return of the *Viking III* in late September. The initial forecast for the Hamburg service was to carry 30,000 passengers but this was greatly exceeded at 68,676 and for both the Bremerhaven and Hamburg routes combined the year's total was 103,498 passengers plus 11,611 cars.

Dates in service between
Bremerhaven and Parkeston Quay: Ship
23 May 1966 to September 1966 *Prins Hamlet (I)*
19 September 1966 to 1 June 1967 *Viking III*
1 June 1967 to 25 September 1967 *Prins Hamlet (I)*
25 September 1967 to 13 June 1968 *Viking III*
13 June 1968 to 25 September 1968 *Prins Hamlet (I)*
25 September 1968 to 31 December 1968 *Viking III*

Bremerhaven and Harwich Navyard:
1 January 1969 to 31 May 1969 *Viking III*
1 July to 26 October 1969 *Celtic Ferry*
(freight only service)

Hamburg and Harwich Navyard:
31 May 1969 to November 1970 *Prinz Hamlet (I)*

passenger service at Harwich since they all moved up to Parkeston Quay in 1883.

In May 1969 the *Prins Hamlet* was overhauled at the German shipyard of Blohm & Voss. She was then sold to HADAG on 29th May, given a German flag and re-named in the Germanic form of *Prinz Hamlet*. To reflect the change in ownership her funnel colours were changed to those of HADAG which were silver with a central green band. She then opened the new 365 n.mile Prins Line Hamburg to Harwich Navyard service when leaving the new St. Pauli terminal at 12.00 on 31st May 1969. The crossing time was 21 hours and on board this inaugural sailing were 350 passengers and 50 cars.

With the *Viking III* off charter and the *Prinz Hamlet* now sailing from Hamburg there was no replacement passenger ship sailing from Bremerhaven during the summer of 1969. Instead a chartered freight ship, the 2,226 grt *Celtic Ferry*, ran between 1st July and 26th

At Parkeston Quay the loss of Lion Ferry was partly offset by attracting another new service, one that went to Dunkirk in France. This was a combined ro-ro and container service operated by a brand new vessel, the *Transcontainer I,* which had been ordered by SNCF at the time of BR having started the train ferry service to Dunkirk from Harwich. Delivered in February 1969 *Transcontainer I* arrived at Parkeston Quay's Container Terminal on 6th March for berthing trials and made her maiden commercial voyage from Dunkirk on 13th March 1969. An on board presentation took place on 7th May in the presence of various BR officials and Mr. Graff, Chief Shipping Manager of SNCF.

At 341 feet long and 2,760 grt this dual mode stern loading twin deck freight ship could carry up to 192 containers or lorries and had accommodation for 36 passengers. In service she would arrive at Parkeston Quay at 23.00, after the Sea Freightliner had sailed, and be worked on overnight until sailing back to Dunkirk at 05.00. Her schedules on the 6 hour 72 n.mile route were initially three sailings a week though these were later increased to five and her introduction in March 1969 brought in regularly Sunday night working on the quay for the first time since the war.

Since operating the three times a week service to Rotterdam the *Isle of Ely* had been struggling to cope with demand and so in December 1968 SMZ chartered in an additional ship, the *Domburgh*, a 1,117 grt 77 teu container ship. Her first sailing was on 2nd January 1969, and in partnership with the *Isle of Ely*, she helped raise the frequency of sailings to daily except Sunday with departures at 07.30 and arrivals back at 23.30 the following day.

A further boost to capacity saw the *Colchester* recalled from the south coast in June 1969 and sent to the Ailsa Shipbuilding Co. in Troon. There she was lengthened by an additional 54 feet and converted into being another cellular ship. When she returned to Parkeston Quay in September 1969 she now had three holds, No.1 hold being 41 feet long and No.'s 2 and 3 each being 62 feet 6 inches long. With a tier of containers able to be stowed upon new flush fitting

The Fred Olsen ferry *Black Prince* arriving at the East Portal - 7th August 1967. (NRM collection)

Below left: The *Koningin Fabiola* of the Belgian Marine Administration arriving for berthing trials at the West Portal berth - 19th September 1967. (NRM collection)

Below right: The car ferry service to Ostend was opened by the BMA vessel *Roi Baudouin* on 29th May 1968. She is seen here arriving for berthing trials on 10th May 1968. (NRM collection)

138 HARWICH FERRIES

Top left: Yard No. 621, the future *Sea Freightliner 1*, under construction at John Readhead & Sons Ltd., South Shields - 26th July 1967. (Stephen Brown collection)

Top right: Construction of the first of the ship to shore Transporter cranes at the new container terminal - 26th January 1968. (Derek Genzel collection)

Above left: Britain's first container ship, *Sea Freightliner 1*, arriving at P. Quay following her delivery voyage from South Shields - 12th March 1968. (Stephen Brown collection)

Above right: The first loading of containers onboard *Sea Freightliner 1* prior to the first loaded run to Zeebrugge - 18th March 1968. (Derek Genzel collection).

Right: The official opening of the new Container Terminal by Princess Alexandra - 21st May 1968. (Stephen Brown collection)

deck hatches she emerged from conversion with the capacity to carry 86 x 30 foot containers or 129 teu's. It was intended that she would provide cover for when the two *Sea Freightliner*'s were away in dry dock but a short while after replacing the *Isle of Ely* a collision put the *Colchester* back into dry dock herself.

The investment made in the new Container Terminal and the new ro-ro berths quickly led to a substantial growth in traffic. The total throughput of containers rose rapidly in 1969 to 83,721, (at Felixstowe it was 74,033), but it was the new ro-ro service to the Hook of Holland that was seeing even more dramatic increases.

During the mid 1960s the number of passengers travelling on the Hook of Holland route was in region of 500,000 with an extra 50,000 travelling as motorists in roughly 20,000 cars. Following the introduction of the new ro-ro ships those figures had soared with the route being supported during the summer months by duplicated night boat sailings undertaken by the *Avalon* and *Koningin Wilhelmina*.

P. Quay to Hook of Holland figures:
Year	Classics plus	Motorists	Cars
1964	514,767	45,995	18,398
1965	522,489	52,842	21,137
1966	497,773	50,812	20,325
1967	488,542	53,200	21,280
1968	526,948	70,568	28,227
1969	608,485	143,492	60,210

The 1960s had certainly proved to be the transformation years of Parkeston Quay. No longer was it an out of date port. New developments and building works were expanding the facilities available and the mainstay routes into Holland, Belgium and Denmark were being supplemented by new routes to Norway and France together with a short period of sailings to Germany. More exotic places were reached by the *Avalon* such as Helsinki and Leningrad when she was away cruising in 1967 and, two years later, the North Cape of Norway, the Baltic, Spain and North Africa. Sadly such opportunities would no longer be available by the *Stella Polaris* as she was sold in 1969.

Year end Totals for Parkeston Quay (all services combined):	1968	1969
Passengers	765,537	930,338
Acc. cars, caravans and coaches	57,495	92,330
Lorries and trailers	8,300	16,572
Containers	23,177	83,721
Rail wagons	59,824	52,985
Lorries by train ferry	775	678
Trade cars	20,898	15,502
Total tonnage of goods	854,182	1,530,249

On 1st January 1968 British Rail formed a Shipping & International Services Division (British Rail SISD) and later adopted the brand name, Sealink. Whilst the new

The new ro-ro route to Holland and artist's impression of how the British Rail vessel may have looked.

BR's *St. George* arriving at Parkeston Quay for the first time - 13th July 1968. (NRM collection)

The BR container vessel *Sea Freightliner II* at sea having departed P. Quay for Zeebrugge - 20th August 1968. (NRM collection)

Above: The first arrival of the new SMZ ro-ro vessel *Koningin Juliana* as she undergoes berthing trials at the East Portal - 10th October 1968. (NRM collection)

organisation, with its head office at 50 Liverpool Street, London EC2, took away the individual railway regions control over any BR shipping services within their area it created one of the most famous and well remembered of all consumer brands into which BR, SMZ, SNCF and the BMA all contributed their ships and operations.

Below: The SNCF vessel *Transcontainer I* seen here on her first arrival at the Container Terminal - 6th March 1969. (NRM collection)

The *Duke of York* sails past the *Isle of Ely* on her morning arrival as night boat from the Hook of Holland - June 1962. (Douglas Brown)

The troopship *Vienna* on the river buoys in August 1960. (Douglas Brown)

THE 1970s

In November 1970 DFDS (UK) Ltd started running their own agency service at Parkeston Quay. Previously such work had been undertaken by The United Shipping Co. Ltd., an associated company of Ellerman's Wilson Line Ltd., in offices located at the eastern end of the original Continental Offices. These were behind where No.1 Shed used to be and close by the former No.2 berth once used by the DFDS ships. By now both shed and berth were buried beneath the new container terminal. The link with Ellerman's Wilson Line Ltd originated in 1916 when Sir John Ellerman took over Thomas Wilson Sons & Co. of Hull, a company which itself had earlier taken over the North Sea shipping firm of Bailey & Leetham in 1903. Bailey & Leetham were agents for the United Steamship Company of Denmark, ie. DFDS, and the role was subsequently incorporated and maintained for over fifty years.

In 1970 DFDS abolished the practise of class distinction by making their passenger ships one class only and the year ended with the number of passengers travelling on their Parkeston Quay to Esbjerg route rising to 127,000. In 1971, the year when DFDS adopted the marketing name of DFDS Seaways, both the *England* and the *Winston Churchill* were sent away to be fitted with more cabin accommodation. Thus the *England* returned from Aalborg Werft with a total of 566 berths and the *Winston Churchill* from Elsinore with 757 berths via extra cabins having been built in former hold spaces. The following year saw the closure of DFDS's conventional freight services between Denmark and the U.K. with the last such sailing at Parkeston Quay being the departure of the *Skyross* on 23rd April 1972. By 1973 98% of all freight between Denmark and Britain would be carried in ro-ro ships.

Out on the quay developments that had begun in the mid 1960s were extended into the 1970s with attention now focused on the need for a new passenger terminal providing better access to and from the ships, an overhaul of the railway station and some remedial work on the new ro-ro berths.

Since 1968 the quay next to the two portal berths had suffered some structural problems and by now was starting to move. This was the result of severe scouring that was undermining the front supporting cylinders and was a problem that lay with the design of the new ships. In the 'old days' the ships had required only a relatively low use of power in conjunction with using a system of ropes, wires or anchors to manoeuvre themselves into position. Now the new breed of car ferries were using a damaging combination of bow thrusters and main engines to power their way on and off the quay. The solution was to replace the old cast iron pile and timber structure by re-piling the quay face, backing it with concrete and then strengthening the deck. Work on this had begun

Looking east from the Parkeston Goods yard towards the level crossing. On the left are the former stables beyond which lie the original bonded warehouse and station buildings - 29th April 1970. (Derek Genzel collection)

Structural work on the site of the former No. 2 Shed which was demolished in August 1966. In the West Portal berth is the DFDS vessel *Stafford* - November 1970. (Derek Genzel collection)

Below: A view from the East Portal berth showing the *Avalon* alongside with work in progress for new passenger walkways - 20th April 1971. (Derek Genzel collection)

Below right: A quayside view of installing one of the covered walkways leading off the new passenger terminal. Passengers are seen in the then traditional mode of leaving the station building and walking across the quay, here to board the *St. George* - 25th June 1971. (Derek Genzel collection)

in September 1969 and was completed in May 1971 after a lull for the 1970 summer season.

Meanwhile, over a two year period that started in 1970 a number of old buildings by the west level crossing were demolished. These included the old bonded warehouse and the Customs and Immigration Hall. The railway station itself was given a major overhaul involving platform extensions and the construction of new roof canopies. The railway line in from Harwich was slewed across to a fully lengthened upside platform and a new enclosed footbridge was built at its western end. This bridge connected into what became an ultra modern passenger terminal complete with escalators and baggage conveyors.

Passengers were now under cover from leaving the train to boarding the ships as glass sided covered walkways eliminated the long standing complaints of passengers having to walk out across a windswept quay. The terminal also had a baggage hall with spiral ramps at its extreme western end via which luggage would be driven to and from the ships in trolleys. The public address system of pre-recorded announcements first introduced in 1950 was updated by the installation of new speakers and other equipment supplied by the Millbank Electronic Group. The new terminal cost £750,000 and was officially opened on 12th September 1972 by Sir Alexander Glen, Chairman of the British Tourist Authority. The two storey building was designed to cope with up to 1,000 passengers and their baggage being cleared within 30 minutes with the lower level being used by outgoing passengers and the upper level for those arriving.

The upper works of the terminal were faced with a series of glass reinforced plastic panels bonded with a sandwiched core of polyurethane foam for both strength and lightness of construction. The use of these 20 feet by 10 feet sections, most of which were fitted with windows, was a first for Sealink. It was a bold contrast of the very new alongside the old Victorian station building. At the end of October 1972 work began on another Victorian building, namely the demolition of the old power house.

The opening of the new passenger terminal meant the closure of the station at Parkeston Quay West.

Notice had earlier been given in July 1970 that British Rail would cease using the station at some point in the future as, since the introduction of the integrated Hook of Holland ro-ro service in November 1968, it was only being used for when boat trains and the conventional ships *Avalon* and *Koningin Wilhelmina* were operating relief sailings.

In September 1972 work began on constructing a new accommodation building for dock staff and other railway personnel who hitherto had been housed in an assortment of mess rooms and old kitchen huts around the quay. A modern single storey structure was built on the site of the former stables by the West Gates crossing and when completed in April 1973 it not only had offices, mess rooms, toilets and locker rooms for the dock staff but also facilities for the port's ambulance crew and firemen as well as the railway's signal and telegraph staff.

Alongside and also completed in 1973 was a new single storey office block built for DFDS. This was conveniently close to the West Portal Berth and the Middle Quay pontoon berth where many of their ships would normally berth. The contractors were Spooners of Hull who supplied an open plan building designed in a Scandinavian style of dark woodwork with yellow and red Danish brickwork. Inside was a separate office provided for the Danish Vice Consulate.

In 1970 the overall traffic figures for Parkeston Quay were 1,029,065 passengers, 106,134 cars, 102,669 ISO containers and 27,104 road haulage vehicles. In 1972 those figures had jumped to 1,140,000, 123,000, 110,000 and 30,000 respectively. Of these the Hook of Holland service was by far the most important for both passengers and motorists, having been Sealink's fastest growing route, with summer seasons being supplemented by the *Avalon* and *Koningin Wilhelmina* sailing as relief night boats. P. Quay to Hook of Holland figures:

Year	Classics plus	Motorists	Cars
1970	684,606	170,973	73,123
1971	679,539	188,903	78,416
1972	667,384	198,037	82,478

In addition there was a growing market in ro-ro with 11,500 units being carried in 1972 together with 11,000 trade cars. Combined with the traffic going through BR's terminal at Harwich, which included a further 3,500 ro-ro units, the two ports overall tonnage of cargo handled in 1972 amounted to 2,350,000 tons of which 60% was being moved either by containers or in train ferry wagons. These cargo figures represented a four fold increase since 1967.

The seasonal Fred Olsen service to Kristiansand had seen regular rises in bookings and for 1970 they were markedly up on the previous year with 32,000 having already been made for the months of July and August alone. In response a new and much larger ship to replace the *Black Prince* was already under construction. Unfortunately it was late in being delivered and the *Black Prince* had already been committed to working Bergen Lines summer season

Artist's impression of the new Passenger Terminal. (Stephen Brown collection)

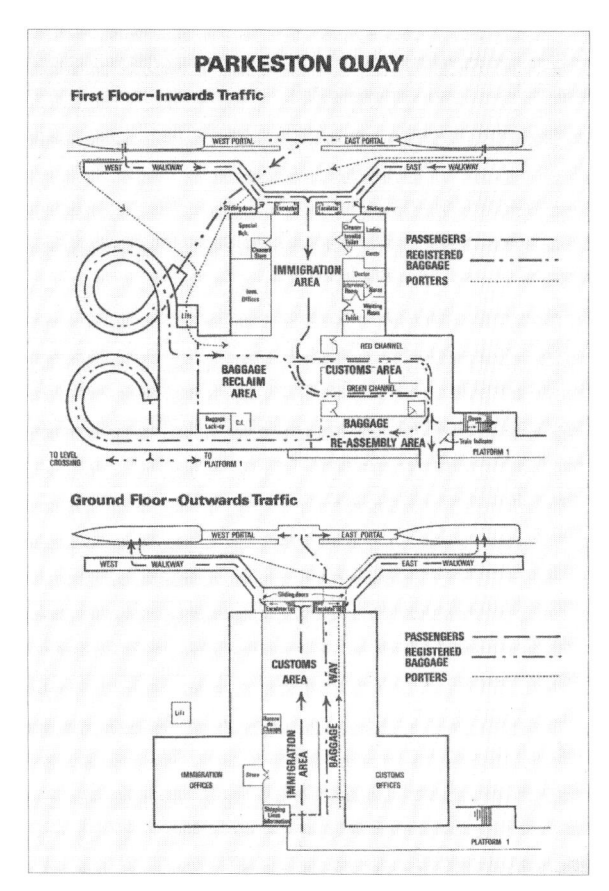

Layout of the Passenger Terminal showing the planned movements of passengers and baggage. (Stephen Brown collection)

sailings out of Newcastle, a service for which she was re-named *Venus*. As a result Fred Olsen chartered the 3,777 grt *Vikingfjord* between 1st July and 30th September to again run their regular roster of Parkeston Quay - Kristiansand - Amsterdam - Kristiansand - Parkeston Quay. Her first arrival at Parkeston Quay was on 4th July and thereafter the service remained at the usual three times per fortnight with arrivals on Wednesday, Monday and Saturday.

Although almost new herself, having been launched in May 1969, the *Vikingfjord* was much too small. She was originally ordered for the Hamburg based company of Partenreederei Nordlandfahre and since August 1969 this 650 passenger vessel had been sailing between Cuxhaven in Germany and Stavanger and Bergen in Norway. Her general size was more in keeping with that of the *Viking III*, still chartered during the off season by Prins Line, than with the size required by Fred Olsen during the peak season. With only 364 cabin berths plus 151 recliners and freight space for either 156 cars or 14 lorries she would often set sail for Kristiansand with insufficient accommodation to handle all of those who had booked. Instead of sailing to Norway many passengers found themselves being flown there, usually from Gatwick, or forced into cancelling altogether.

The new Fred Olsen ship eventually appeared in time for the 1971 season when, on 29th May, the *Blenheim* arrived at the East Portal as the port's largest passenger ship to date at 10,419 grt. The service remained at three trips per fortnight but with the Wednesday sailing now changed to Thursday.

The *Blenheim* was built as a near sister ship and larger version of the *Black Prince*. She emerged with a very similar layout on board and was able to carry up to 1,107 passengers. The Sun Deck had an increased number of ten De-luxe cabins located amongst the Officer grade cabins whilst the Boat Deck below consisted of First class single and double berth cabins. The Lounge Deck was arranged as First class forward and Tourist class aft with each class having their own lounge and restaurant facilities. The Upper Deck was entirely given over to Tourist class double and four berth cabins with additional cabins at the forward end of both Main and A Decks. In total the *Blenheim* had 580 berths plus space for 300 cars. As with the *Black Prince* she also had a swimming pool fitted aft on the Boat Deck for when she went cruising with just 400 passengers on board, her first such outing having been her maiden voyage to the Canary Islands on 10th September 1970. During the summer tourist season this area was covered over and used as a deck lounge.

The BMA route between Parkeston Quay and Ostend had, since 1970, been reduced to a summer season only service with just one daytime sailing that left Ostend at 09.25 and Parkeston Quay at 15.30. The crossing time was now 4¾ hours which gave an arrival time in Ostend of 21.15. On 1st November 1971 the BMA became the Belgische Regie Voor Maritiem Transport (RMT) and continued with running the service on a seasonal basis.

In contrast to all the other routes heading out of Parkeston Quay the service to Ostend proved not so attractive or popular and two years later the route closed with the *Roi Baudouin* making the last sailing on 10th September 1973. The route's demise was regarded by many as a shame as it certainly had potential if given the right ships and back up. Unfortunately it suffered problems in its overall

Right: The Passenger Terminal under construction following the demolition of a number of old buildings - 25th June 1971. (Derek Genzel collection)

Opposite top: The original footbridge joining the two station platforms was removed in the autumn of 1972. Removed somewhat earlier, in February 1963, was the clock tower above the station hotel building - 19th November 1970. (Derek Genzel collection)

Opposite bottom: A view from the original footbridge looking west towards the new passenger terminal and connecting footbridge - 25th June 1971. (Derek Genzel collection).

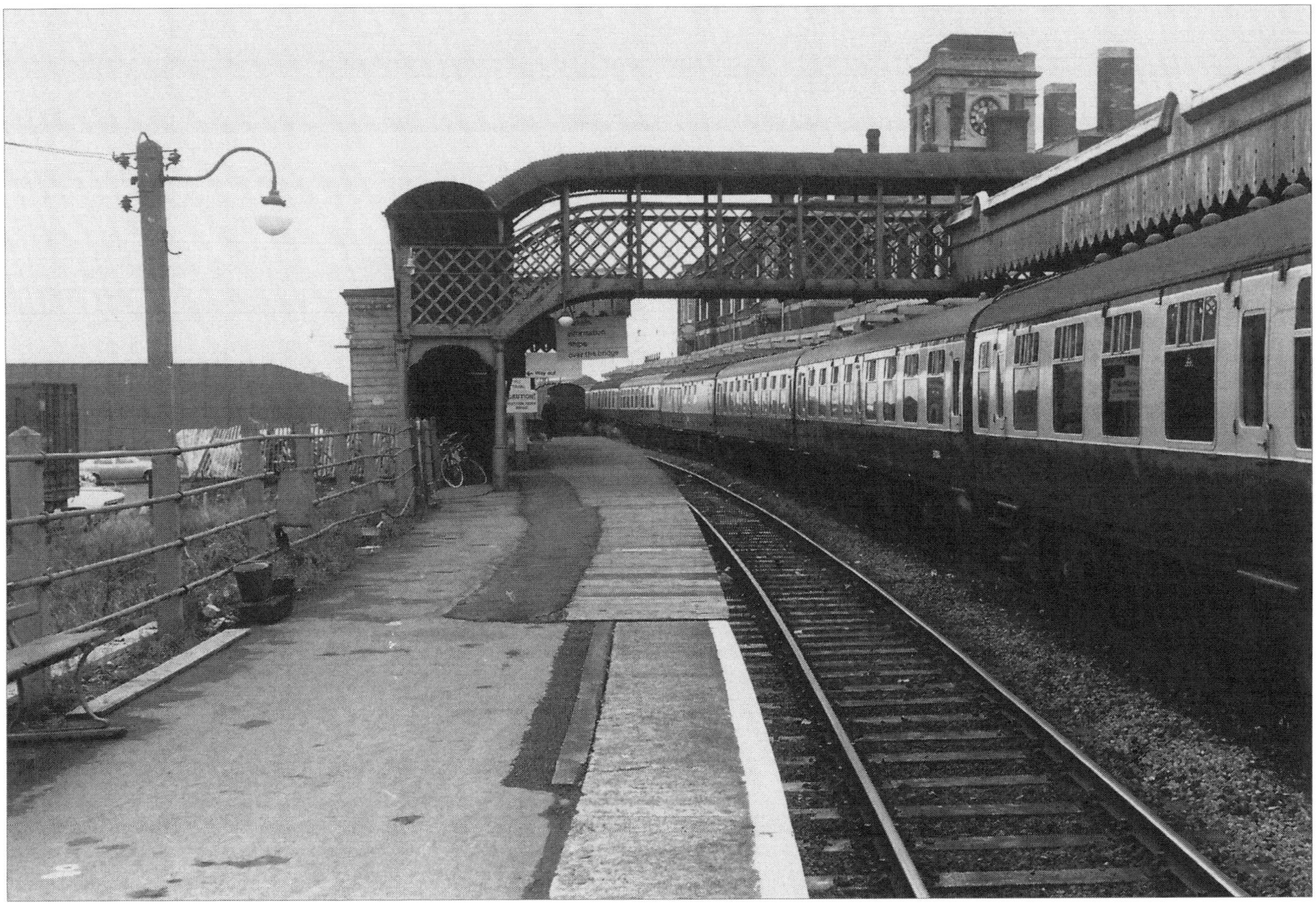

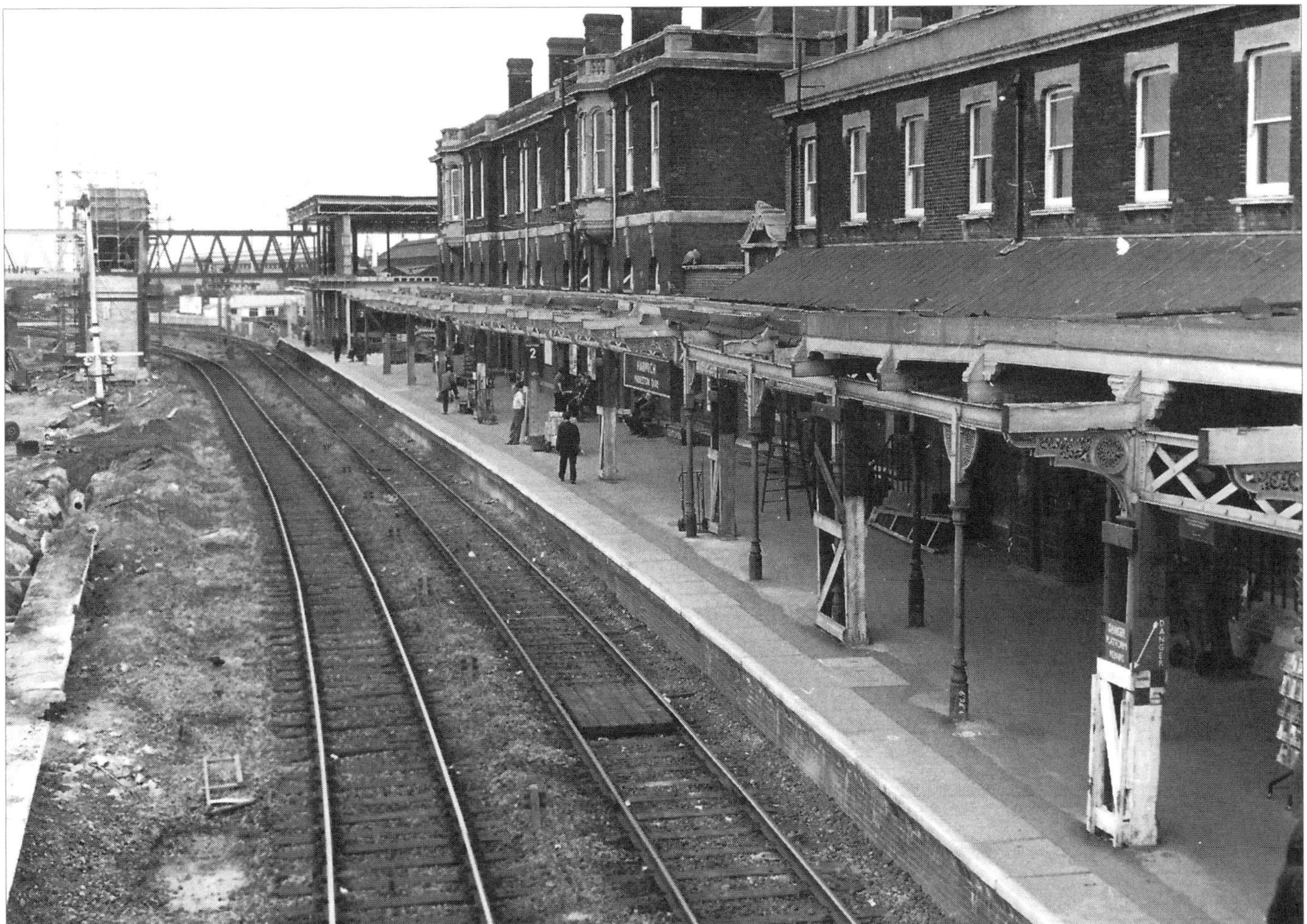

Above: Parkeston Quay station building stripped bare of its canopy and showing much of how it would have looked when first built - October 1971. (Derek Genzel collection)

Left: Looking east from the new footbridge showing work on a new 'up' side platform - 23rd July 1971. (Derek Genzel collection)

Below: Prefabricated cladding walls being lifted into position at the new passenger terminal - 25th June 1971. (Derek Genzel collection)

PARKESTON QUAY UNDER RAILWAY OWNERSHIP 147

A view of the new passenger terminal with much of the external work completed - 15th February 1972. (Derek Genzel collection)

Spiral ramps for use by the baggage trailers that would link the passenger terminal and the quayside berths - 15th February 1972. (Derek Genzel collection)

Arrival of the new Kone crane at the container terminal. This was hauled off the barge directly onto a specially constructed track and then moved into position - 18th February 1972. (Derek Genzel collection)

A composite photo of the new overbridge for cars that allowed them to bypass the congested crossing gates - 23rd July 1974 (based on Derek Genzel collection)

marketing though there had been belated attempts at encouraging a greater number of foot passengers. In its last year of operation the Ostend route carried some 37,000 passengers and 10,000 cars and had coincided with a time when Parkeston Quay was uniquely the only port ever to have handled ships from all of the constituent trading partners of Sealink, ie BR, SMZ, SNCF and RMT.

Despite the loss of the Belgian service the ever growing numbers of motorists wanting to travel via Parkeston Quay was highlighting its situation of being a port divided by a railway line and crossing that line via the West Gates crossing was creating a bottleneck in the movement of vehicles.

In order to improve matters it was decided to bridge these gates by means of a concrete flyover supported on piled foundations that would enable outward bound cars to run up and onto the upper deck of the new Passenger Terminal and then down one of the spiral ramps to quay level. Inward bound cars would use the flyover in the reverse direction on the basis of a one way system. By linking the quayside berths directly with the marshalling area and car hall, where Customs and Immigration continued to check both incoming and outgoing vehicles, it would help separate the cars from the heavy road vehicles which would continue to access the quay via the level crossing. Additional work had already seen the approach road to the port widened and resurfaced in preparation for accessing an extended car marshalling area that was capable of holding up to 335 cars. This area covered the ground once occupied by the old power house. Work on the £250,000 flyover scheme began in December 1973 and was officially opened in 1974 by the port's Shipping and Port Manager, Mr Taylor.

In 1974 a brand new leisure centre for the port's staff was opened in Hamilton Street, Parkeston to replace the one in Parkeston Road that had been in use since the 1920s. The £70,000 British Rail Staff Association (BRSA) building, fully equipped with a ballroom and bar, lounge, café and car park, was opened by Mr. Claydon, Deputy General Manager of SISD. Membership of the club numbered around 1,100 of whom 85% were shipping personnel.

At the Container Terminal the early 1970s was a period of adjustment and expansion amidst a host of different vessels appearing and disappearing. In 1970 the British Rail services handled nearly 70,000 containers via Zeebrugge plus a further 17,000 via Rotterdam. With such a rapid growth in traffic the terminal was already being stretched to capacity and thus an extension was built inland further to the east. This area was equipped with two more 30-ton cranes designed to handle containers arriving and departing by road. The first crane, built by Liebherr of Ireland, arrived in August 1971. The second, built by Kone, arrived in February 1972 from the Company's Hanko works in Finland fully erected on board a floating barge

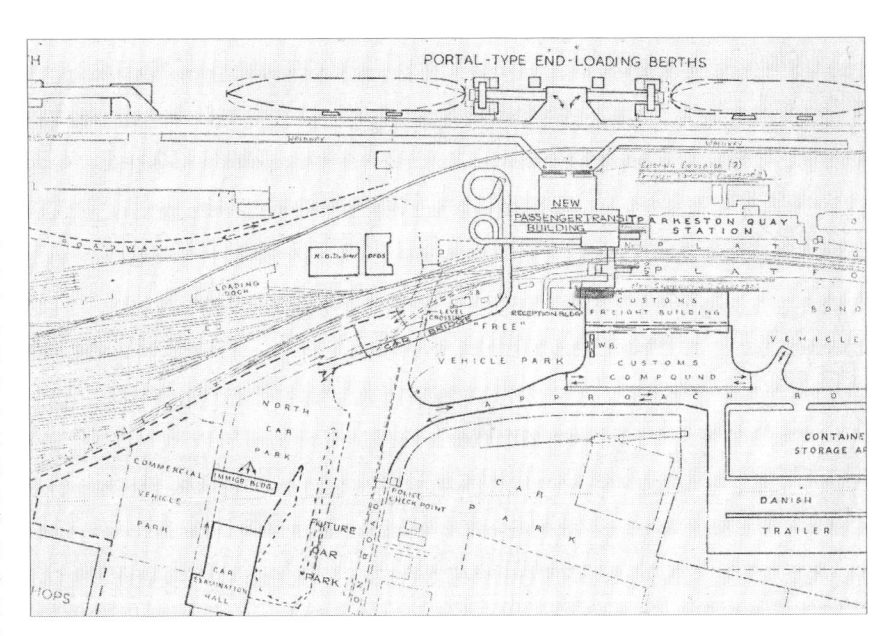

Plan location of the overbridge. (Stephen Brown collection)

Koningin Wilhelmina arriving at the East Portal - 24th July 1976. (Stephen Brown)

from which it was then moved ashore via a specially created temporary track. When this extension was completed the standage capacity had increased by a further 300 containers and around this time the terminal took delivery of its first mobile straddle carrier.

The total number of containers handled in 1971 was 103,859 of which 64,914 went via Zeebrugge, 17,932 via Dunkirk and 16,045 via Rotterdam. The remaining 4,968 were shipped on the DFDS Esbjerg route. By the end of 1972 Parkeston Quay was Britain's second largest container terminal, second only to Tilbury in terms of throughput, and the 110,000 containers handled that year had conveyed nearly 1.5m tons of cargo.

During their respective periods of dry docking in autumn 1970 the *Sea Freightliner I* and *Sea Freightliner II* were covered by the *Brian Boroime*. Similar in design to the Sea Freightliners the 184 teu *Brian Boroime* was one of a pair of container ships that had only recently been built for a new cellular container service from Holyhead to Dublin and Belfast. Unfortunately a fire on the Britannia Bridge on 23rd May 1970 had cut Holyhead off from the railway network and this had caused the introduction of the new sea services to be cancelled. A temporary arrangement was made, as from 15th June, for using a disused railway goods yard at Caernarfon and transhipping around 45 containers a day to and from Holyhead, and then onto Ireland. by road. After her time at Parkeston Quay the *Brian Boroime* was transferred in December 1970 to Heysham from where she would then operate her intended Holyhead services. It was not until January 1972 that Holyhead was again connected by rail and the planned new containerised services could finally begin.

The *Brian Boroime,* launched in March 1970, and her sister ship, the *Rhodri Mawr,* launched two months later, were shorter than the Sea Freightliners by the length of a 30 foot container having been built with only three cell guided holds but were wider in the beam by about 4 feet. The extra width was because of a problem that had arisen when loading the Sea Freightliners. Their cell guide clearances were rather tight which resulted in the guide tops often being damaged whenever a container was being aimed into its cell. Also moving the guides themselves had often become a difficult operation. The solution was to increase the guide clearances hence the extra width. With containers still being stowed five abreast both the *Brian Boroime* and *Rhodri Mawr* each had capacity for 136 containers below deck and 48 above on the hatch covers. A further ship, the *Brathay Fisher*, was built the following year to a slightly altered design and she covered for the Sea Freightliners absence in autumn 1971.

The *Isle of Ely* was finally displaced from the Rotterdam route in 1971 by the recently lengthened *Colchester* following which she initially went to Holyhead. The *Colchester* was herself withdrawn from the Rotterdam route on 1st September 1972 and also sent to Holyhead following BR's decision to no longer provide a ship for this service. Accordingly it was left to the *Domburgh* to carry on alone. Further changes occurred when the *Domburgh* was replaced by the SMZ chartering in the 658 grt *Nassau* and reducing the service to only three sailings a week. Such a limited service with a smaller ship eventually become totally uneconomic and the Dutch withdrew from the Rotterdam service by closing it on 27th November 1973.

Meanwhile a return to the handling of general cargo occurred when, in November 1973, Arrow Line began

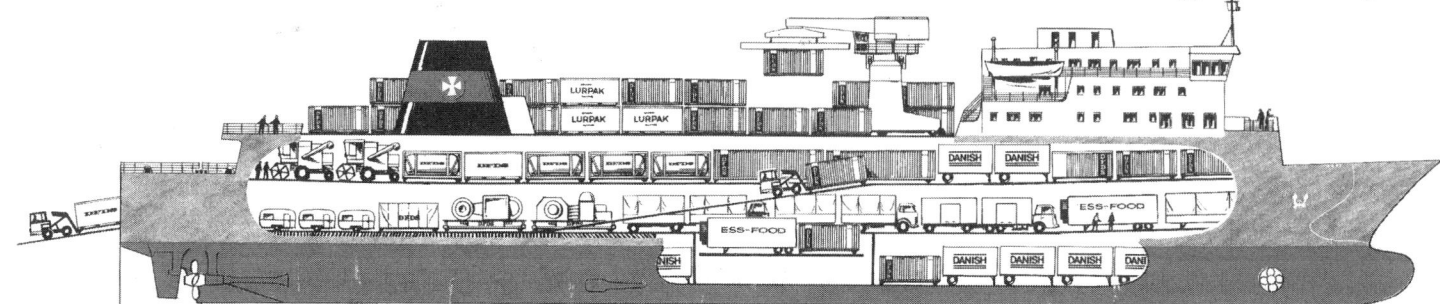

Impression of the new DFDS freight ship, *Dana Futura*, introduced in January 1976. (Stephen Gooch collection)

This is the new DFDS super roll-on/roll-off freight ferry

Dana Regina arriving from Esbjerg - 5th August 1976. (Stephen Brown)

running a fortnightly service to the Mediterranean ports of Piraeus, Famagusta and Beirut from a berth at what was formerly Parkeston Quay West. This was followed later that year by the formation of Parkeston Shipping Services Ltd., a joint venture between Sealink and James Fisher and Son Ltd., which took over the use of the Berths 7 and 8 and the adjacent No. 4 Shed. That part of the west quay became known simply as 'Fishers' and although it operated under the control of the Shipping and Port Manager it was run with its own manager and employed staff.

The first Arrow Line ship alongside had been the 4,000 ton Greek freighter *Tara* which discharged 38,000 cases of citrus fruit and other goods. Two other ships were employed on a fortnightly service between Parkeston Quay and the Mediterranean. Parkeston Shipping Services Ltd were to handle ships for other services including Reever Line who ran a three weekly service to Florida with their 4,271 ton general cargo ship *Northern Ice* bringing back both perishable and general goods. In addition Reever Line also brought in fruit from the Mediterranean. By May 1974 'Fishers' had handled 23 vessels from as far afield as the Canary Islands, Egypt and Israel.

The SNCF service to Dunkirk was still being maintained by the *Transcontainer 1*. There was additional weekend support from the *Colchester* between 27th November 1971 and 11th August 1972 plus, in late 1973, from one of the Sea Freightliner's which was also making two trips a week on this route. Thus in the five years since the opening of the container terminal no fewer than nine ships had already been utilised, *Sea Freightliner I, Sea Freightliner II, Isle of Ely, Colchester, Domburgh, Nassau, Brian Boroime, Brathay Fisher* and *Transcontainer 1*.

The *Transcontainer 1* left Parkeston Quay in August 1974 for conversion for use as a train ferry. After undergoing berthing trails at Dover on 24th October she then joined the service between Dover and Dunkirk. It was thought that she might also serve Harwich as well but the closest she was seen there again was when she ran a once a week service each

Winston Churchill alongside the East Portal - 24th August 1976. (Stephen Brown)

To distinguish between the two Sea Freightliner vessels, *Sea Freightliner I* had a small vertical white line painted uppermost aft on her funnel - 25th August 1976. (Stephen Brown)

St. Edmund departing from Parkeston Quay and passing the BR container ship *Rhodri Mawr* - 9th February 1977. (Stephen Brown)

Wednesday between Dunkirk and Felixstowe from 8th January 1975. The Parkeston Quay to Dunkirk service was initially taken over by one of the Sea Freightliner's whose absence on the Zeebrugge route was covered by the *Brathay Fisher* which, since August 1974, was on a two year charter. However the *Brathay Fisher* was soon to maintain the Dunkirk service herself by sailing three times a week until December 1975. Afterwards she was substituted by the *Rhodri Mawr* which became the tenth ship to have used the container terminal.

The movement of containers passing through Parkeston Quay was restricted in 1975 due to it having been noticed in late 1974 that the 1,080 feet long rails beneath the original Goliath cranes in the container terminal were failing as a result of metal fatigue. Rather than replace them, which would have meant digging up the foundations and effectively closing the terminal off for four months, a concrete beam into which new rails were embedded was superimposed upon the existing tracks. The work carried out provided the opportunity of raising the cranes operating level by 18 inches. This then allowed them to handle the larger size of 8 feet 6 inch high containers that were increasingly being used in preference to the original containers that were only 8 feet high.

On the Hook of Holland service the growth experienced since the introduction of the *St George* and *Koningin Juliana* had by now made it necessary to add a further new ship to cope with the ever increasing demand. Despite gales delaying her launch by 24 hours this new ship was named as planned on 13th November 1973 by Mrs Caroline Marsh, wife of the BRB Chairman, at Cammell Laird's yard at Birkenhead. Given the name *St. Edmund* she was viewed as a much improved version of the *St. George* and her extra size at 8,987grt made her the largest ship in the BR fleet. Compared to the *St. George*'s ability to carry up to 220 cars or 32 lorries the *St. Edmund* could handle roughly a third more at up to 296 cars or 148 cars and 40 lorries. She cost £7.5 million but was not the much more substantial ship, capable of carrying a far greater number of lorries, that some managers at the time were advocating for the route.

Another feature less substantial than perhaps expected was the menu provided on launch day. Consisting of 'Cream of Asparagus Soup, Cold Sirloin of Scotch Beef with salad and New Potatoes, Fresh Cream Gateaux, Petit Fours and coffee' it looked very much as though Cammell Laird had engaged the same caterers as for the launch of the *Koningin Juliana* over five years earlier when guests then celebrated to a menu of 'Melon Cocktail, Poached Turbot & Shrimp Sauce with New Potatoes and Green Peas, Pineapple Cream, Petit Fours and Coffee'!

The *St. Edmund* could handle 1,400 passengers by day or 1,000 by night and was originally envisaged as making three single crossings every 24 hours. However despite the potential to do so and thereby boost the route's capacity the idea never materialised as it would have meant an unbalanced timetable. Thus when she was ready for service she would take over from the *St George* on the existing round trip roster. However a series of strikes and other delays in her fitting out meant that she was delivered far too late for the 1974 summer season and her first arrival at Parkeston Quay was not until 24th December 1974. She then made her maiden voyage to the Hook of Holland on 19th January 1975.

As with the *St. George* and *Koningin Juliana* the two class layout on board the *St. Edmund* was Second class forward and First class aft. On A Deck was a First class restaurant for 88 persons, a Smoking room plus two port and starboard lounges. For Second class passengers there was a 104 seat cafeteria and a 236 seat tea-bar. Both passenger entrances were on B Deck and were linked by a series of circular seating areas noted for having centrally placed mushroom shaped fibreglass pillars. Here were found the Pursers office, Bureau-de-change, Passport office and first aid room. Forward was a 192 seat full width bar and disco with two port and starboard sleeping lounges amidship each with 72 Second class recliners. Aft was all

First class with a 33 seat sleeping lounge, a tv lounge, 10 twin berth De-Luxe cabins each with private bathroom plus 45 single and 13 twin berth cabins. In total the *St. Edmund* had 269 cabins with 671 berths many of which were located along both sides of car decks C and D. These consisted of First class twin berths aft and Second class four berth cabins forward whilst below the Car Decks, forward on E and F decks, were additional four berth cabins and Pullman berths for Second class only.

The arrival of the *St Edmund* very quickly saw the end of the *Avalon*, which left Parkeston Quay on 29th December 1974 for Swan Hunter's yard on Tyneside. There she had many of her cabins removed and was converted to being a stern loading car ferry for BR's Fishguard to Rosslare route. Also to see the end was the former No. 3 Shed which was demolished during 1974 to make way for a ro-ro storage area.

For the summer of 1975, the Centenary year of the founding of SMZ, the *St. George* and the *Koningin Wilhelmina* operated a new service of additional round trips throughout July and August. The *St. George* sailed as a day boat from the Hook of Holland at 14.00, arriving at Parkeston Quay at 20.15, whilst the *Koningin Wilhelmina* departing as day boat from Parkeston Quay at 09.30. Both sailed back as relief night boats. In Holland the centenary was suitably marked by members of the Dutch royal family. On 24th July Princess Beatrix and Prince Claus sailed on board the *Koningin Wilhelmina* from the Hook of Holland to Rotterdam there to receive a civic reception whilst two days later on 26th July, 100 years to the day that SMZ first sailed, Queen Juliana and Prince Bernard were on board the *Koningin Juliana* from Ijmuiden to Amsterdam, there to visit the National Maritime Museum and to receive a memorial book about the Company's history.

Unlike the late arriving *St. Edmund* one ship that did arrive in time for the 1974 summer season was the new 12,192 grt *Dana Regina*. She was constructed at the shipyards of Aalborg Vaerft A/S to further improve DFDS's service to Esbjerg and at 504 feet long was the largest passenger ship to have been built in Denmark. She was also the first DFDS passenger ship where the engines were directly controlled from the bridge. The *Dana Regina* was officially named in Copenhagen on 1st July 1974 by Queen Margrethe II of Denmark and later went on public display in London's Upper Pool on 4th July. Afterwards she was presented at Parkeston Quay from where she made her maiden voyage to Esbjerg on 8th July 1974.

On board were facilities for 1,006 passengers all of whom had sleeping accommodation either in one of 878 cabin berths or the 128 bunks in couchette class. Two four berth cabins were additionally set aside for disabled passengers. Almost half the cabins were located below the two Car Decks which were aft on Copenhagen Deck and both aft and forward on Britannia Deck. Above the Car Decks was the Anglia Deck which was given over entirely to cabins. One deck higher was the Restaurant Deck which, at the forward end, contained a full width 288 seat Codan Restaurant offering both a la carte meals and a smorgasbord buffet. On the port side was the Codan Lounge from where a promenade arcade led aft past a boutique, the Admiral Pub and a shopping centre. At the aft end was the 235 seat Scandia coffee shop and self service cafeteria, again full width, and this led on to the Compass Club disco and bar. One notably stylish feature was a spiral staircase that directly connected the Codan Restaurant with the Bellevue Lounge and Mermaid Bar up on the Boat Deck. This deck also housed two De-luxe cabins adjacent to the lounge, several other cabins and all of the couchettes which were at the aft end overlooking the Sun Deck. The two car decks held space for 250 cars or a combination of cars, lorries and trailers.

The *Dana Regina* sailed on the Esbjerg route on alternate days opposite the *Winston Churchill* and between them they provided a 6 days a week service that increased to daily during the summer. Her arrival displaced the *England* onto the Esbjerg to Newcastle and Torshavn Faroe routes.

In 1974 the number of passengers travelling between Parkeston Quay and Esbjerg was 189,000. This jumped to 266,000 in 1975 when the route was also carrying 1.6 million tons of freight. As well as introducing new passenger ships the route had also benefited from having had existing freight ships lengthened such as the *Somerset* in November 1972 and the *Stafford* in January 1973, each by an additional 41 feet that raised their capacity from 100 teu's to 148 teu's, or by the building of much larger vessels such as the 3,375 grt *Surrey*.

Built in 1969 primarily for the route between Esbjerg and Grimsby the *Surrey* had earlier been used on sailings to Parkeston Quay in November 1970 but it was only since 1972 that her arrivals had become more frequent. When first built the *Surrey* was 375 feet long and had a capacity equivalent to 226 teu's throughout four decks but she too was lengthened, in early 1975, by a further 59.7 feet and had her upper deck raised by 2.3 feet. When converted she had a capacity of 300 teu's but even this was to be superseded by the arrival of two even larger freighters with the capacity to carry up to 400 teu's in the usual mix of unaccompanied trailers and refrigerated units plus limited accommodation for 12 drivers.

These two sister ships, measuring 475 feet long and of 5,991 grt, were delivered in 1976 with their respective first arrivals at Parkeston Quay being the *Dana Futura* on 12th January and the *Dana Gloria* on 12th July. Their most notable features were their huge upper and main deck stern doors and a travelling gantry crane on the top deck that could lift up to 25 tons. Each was designed to make three round trips per week at 23 knots amidst plans for a new double deck linkspan to the east of the Container Terminal. Nothing came of such plans and the ships themselves only briefly served the port before spending much of their time on charter.

The *Dana Futura* left early in March 1976 and was re-named *Dammen Express* and was again re-named in April 1977 as *Drosselfels*. The *Dana Gloria* also managed just two months in service between Esbjerg and Parkeston Quay before likewise being moved and renamed, first as *Drachenfels* in September 1976 and then as *Dana Hafnia* in November 1977. Both ships were to spend most of the late 1970s variously chartered and sailing between North America and Europe, the Persian Gulf and Africa. The *Dana Hafnia* briefly reappeared at Parkeston Quay in September 1978 whilst the former and since re-named *Dana Futura* reappeared throughout 1978 and the latter part of 1979.

The build up of traffic at the Container Terminal had led to a reduction in the number of wagon movements at the Harwich Train Ferry Terminal. In 1968, when the Container Terminal opened, the train ferry service shipped 59,824 wagons. By 1975 that figure had almost halved to 32,622 at a time when there were nine container service sailings a week between Parkeston Quay and Zeebrugge.

The decline was thought largely due to a policy of British Rail who wanted goods to be transported in containers rather than in railway wagons. Amidst background accusations of a subsidised pricing policy the container did have the advantage of a direct door to door delivery service rather than a train ferry and goods depot system of delivery and collection. It appeared as though the advertising slogan of 'Save Packing, Time and Money', used by the LNER in the days of the original train ferry service, was now being given a modern containerised interpretation. Yet this notion of a price bias in favour of containers had long been disputed by BR as from the outset they claimed that the lower rates simply reflected the greater efficiency associated with that particular mode of transport. Whatever the truth was the figures for the different units carried were clearly setting a trend yet all was not what it seemed. Actual levels of goods transported continued to rise as new privately owned high capacity ferry wagons capable of carrying much heavier loads were being delivered into service and several specialised or large industrial users had built, or were building, railway sidings of their own such was their ongoing preference for using wagons. Somewhat inconveniently there had been reports from Zeebrugge of far more claims being made for damage to goods packed inside containers than there were for goods packed inside rail wagons with a suggestion that containers were not being very well built.

Meanwhile the train ferries at Harwich were still sailing a minimum of two round trips a day to Zeebrugge and during recent years were handling an increasingly wide range of goods that included caravans, combine harvesters and agricultural machinery. The service to Dunkirk was equally versatile as seen in the carrying of Portakabins. They also handled a variety of out of gauge industrial plant and machinery that could often weigh 50 to 60 tons or more and an increasing number of the heavier wagons such as specially designed Polybulk hopper wagons which, when loaded with grain from France, weighed a massive 80 tons each.

During 1972 the *Cambridge Ferry* and the *Essex Ferry* between them made 10 trips from Harwich to Dublin carrying new rolling stock for the Irish Railways (CIE). A total of 95 items were transported, all manufactured at British Rail's engineering works in Derby, and included passenger and restaurant coaches, steam heated vans and electric generator brake vans. Each ship berthed alongside the 100 ton crane at the Alexander Basin at Dublin's North Wall where the carriages were crane lifted off their standard gauge bogies and lowered onto wider 5 feet 3 inch Irish gauge bogies of which 190 had earlier been transported from Holyhead on board the *Slieve Donard*. In all some 3,250 tons of cargo were involved with a consignment value of £2.6m.

A nostalgic return to the days of steam occurred in January 1976 when the *Maid of Kent* arrived at Harwich fresh out of dry dock at Immingham. She was used for about a fortnight to help clear a backlog of trade cars on the Zeebrugge service and carried up to 200 cars per trip. Another unusual event in 1976 involved the *Cambridge Ferry* when she called in at Falmouth on her way back from one of her seasonal spells on the Stranraer to Larne service. There she was loaded with an assortment of over 100 wartime vehicles, tanks and guns which she then took to Zeebrugge. The vehicles were offloaded and later used in the production of the film 'A Bridge Too Far' which was being made around the Dutch town of Arnhem.

In July 1976 a new port was opened at Gravelines in France, otherwise known as Dunkirk West. This was roughly 12 miles nearer to Dover than was the existing port at Dunkirk and contained a new train ferry terminal which opened on 5th July. It was not only nearer but also much quicker to access as there were no locks to negotiate. British Rail then launched a new nationwide advertising campaign to encourage the movement of goods by train ferry under the slogan of 'Speed your Exports by Ferry Train - it's like the Channel wasn't there'. Although the campaign followed largely in response to the opening of Dunkirk West, where a shorter crossing time of 2 hours 20 minutes from Dover saw an increase from four to six in its number of daily train ferry departures, the campaign was also a general one that emphasised faster trains, faster crossings and extra trains on all services from October 1976 onwards. The two ports of Dover and Harwich were then carrying 677,000 tons of train ferry freight a year of which 45% was being sent via Harwich.

The opening of Dunkirk West had also shortened the distance for services from Harwich and the container service from Parkeston Quay was now a six hour crossing covering just 72 n.miles. *Sea Freightliner 1* or the *Rhodri Mawr* were still operating a 3 round trips a week service that departed Parkeston Quay at 23.00 on Monday, Wednesday and Friday and returned from Dunkirk West at either 17.00 or 18.00 on Tuesday, Thursday or Saturday.

These developments coincided with the U.K. Government having abandoned plans for a Channel Tunnel Project and Sealink then planning a major investment programme. A part of that investment included plans for three new train ferries at Harwich which were said to be in the preliminary planning stage though this somewhat confused the situation as to whether BR was decidedly pro-container at Parkeston Quay or pro-train ferry at Harwich. Whatever the thinking none of these three train ferry ships were ever built and the decline in the numbers of wagons, though not the tonnage of goods, being moved through Harwich had reached a point where the *Suffolk Ferry* was being earmarked for withdrawal. However she was saved for further service due to the movement of trade cars and caravans on the Hook of Holland route.

The traffic in trade cars was already playing a significant contribution to the overall viability of the train ferries and in 1974 some 15,000 vehicles had travelled via Zeebrugge. These mainly consisted of the importing of cars from Audi and Mercedes and the exporting of cars from British Leyland Austin and Morris. A nearby storage area had been created on the edge of Bathside Bay at Gas House Creek and although Audi left in August 1975 this was later expanded upon as trade increased. At the same time the numbers being shipped via Parkeston Quay was rising rapidly.

The origins of importing cars through Parkeston Quay date back at least as far as 1958 when Volvo started sending their cars over from Sweden and whilst traffic was low volume and infrequent it could often be varied. In February 1963 the Ford Motor Company once exported a consignment of cars from Dagenham to Denmark via DFDS's 1,481 grt vessel *Bellona* which left the quay for Copenhagen. However it was not until 1969 when Ford's brought in cars from Amsterdam on board the 500 grt *Rynstroom* of the Hollandsche Stoomboot Maatschappij (HSM) that numbers became significant. In subsequent years vessels such as the 1,597 grt *Carway* and the 1,159 grt *Clearway* of Elder Dempster & Co. Ltd. were also seen at Parkeston Quay, the latter being 300 feet long with a beam of 55 feet and fitted with five interconnected decks with access to the quay via twin hoistable ramps on either side of the ship. Capacity per ship was around 400 cars. In total the number of cars imported through Harwich train ferry and Parkeston Quay in 1969 was 15,000 and this grew to 47,000 in 1972.

In 1974 the movement of trade cars from Holland changed to using the regular ships on the Hook of Holland route and a specialist trade car operation was established at Parkeston Quay by the Toleman Delivery Group who, since 1st January 1972, had been running a national car delivery service from the old Transit Camp. Traffic solely through the Hook of Holland had risen rapidly from the 11,000 vehicles in 1972, to 22,000 in 1975 and then 54,000 in 1976. Such growth had made the passenger ferries increasingly unable to cope with their normal motorist traffic and with a forecast for 1977 of 95,000 units the *Suffolk Ferry* was retained in service as a train ferry in order that the *Essex Ferry* and *Cambridge Ferry* could be released to sail as car carriers on the Hook of Holland service.

The primary customer remained the Ford Motor Company who provided a balanced flow of traffic by exporting Escorts from their Halewood factory and importing Granadas from the Continent. The *Essex Ferry* also made several trips to the Hook of Holland full with mobile homes and caravans. The level of business was such that keeping the *Suffolk Ferry* on was worth £300,000 more to the port than if she had been withdrawn. During the early part of 1977 the *Cambridge Ferry* was modified at a cost of £90,000 on extending her boat deck aft by 68 feet in order to carry twenty five more cars per trip and was further modified so as to fit the new train ferry berth at Dunkirk West.

In March 1977 the Parkeston Quay to Dunkirk container service was temporarily suspended. Resources were then concentrated on the route to Zeebrugge utilising the *Sea Freightliner I*, *Sea Freightliner II* and the *Rhodri Mawr* and this was followed in late 1977 by the sales force of BR-SISD becoming more involved in the selling and marketing of the service.

Purely from Parkeston Quay to Zeebrugge the rates were now £113 for a 20 foot container, £135 for a 30 foot and £155 for a 40 foot. However the quoting of international through rates was the responsibility of an organisation called 'Intercontainer', a co-operative of railway administrations that had grown from an initial 12 in 1967 to now numbering 23 and of which both BR-SISD and Freightliner Ltd were members. Rates were quoted in 'Union Internationale des Chemins de Fer Francs or UIC Francs'. This was 'a unit of account based on the weighted average of 17 European currencies, which has been adopted by the UIC and is used as the tariff currency for many international tariffs in order to avoid excessive fluctuations which might occur if a national currency were to be used'. Through quotes in Sterling were to be avoided as the actual billing was made in Swiss Francs. The cost of transporting a single 20 foot container from Parkeston Quay through to eg, Cologne was quoted as being 913 UIC Francs, to Milan 1,421 and to Berlin 1,637.

Departure of the *St. George* from the East Portal - 16th November 1977. (Stephen Brown)

The *Dana Anglia* on the day of her first arrival at P. Quay - 6th May 1978. (Stephen Brown)

The first day of arrival for the *Prinses Beatrix* as she approaches the East Portal for berthing trials - 11th June 1978. (Stephen Brown)

The timetable of container ship sailings for 1978 provided for up to 11 round trips per week although the departures from Parkeston Quay on Monday at 08.00 and Friday at 10.00, and from Zeebrugge on Monday and Friday at 23.00, were subject to there being sufficient demand. On a full schedule of sailings the ships would each make 3 or 4 round trips per week

	P. Quay Dep.	Zeebrugge Arr.		Zeebrugge Dep.	P. Quay Arr.
Sunday	14.00	21.00			
Monday	08.00	15.00	Monday	11.00	18.00
Monday	23.59		Monday	23.00	
Tuesday		07.00	Tuesday		06.00
Tuesday	16.30	23.30	Tuesday	14.00	21.00
Wednesday	01.00	08.00	Wednesday	05.00	12.00
Wednesday	16.30	23.30	Wednesday	14.00	21.00
Thursday	01.00	08.00	Thursday	05.00	12.00
Thursday	16.30	23.30	Thursday	14.00	21.00
Friday	01.00	08.00	Friday	05.00	12.00
Friday	10.00	17.00	Friday	14.00	21.00
Friday	22.00		Friday	23.00	
Saturday		05.00	Saturday		06.00
			Saturday	14.00	21.00

The summer service to Kristiansand, which had been in the hands of the *Blenheim* since 1971, saw a change of ship for the 1976 season caused by developments at Newcastle whereby services from there to Norway had been re-organised, as from 1st October 1975, to operate under the joint title of Fred Olsen Bergen Line. The changes resulted in the *Blenheim* being more usefully employed at Newcastle with her replacement at Parkeston Quay being the *Borgen*, a recently built car ferry for use between Denmark and Norway that could also be used as an 18 wagon train ferry between Kristiansand and Hirtshals.

The service between Parkeston Quay and Kristiansand remained summer seasonal but was reduced to a once a week sailing that left Parkeston Quay on a Wednesday. At 5,330 grt. the *Borgen* was half the size of the *Blenheim* and was fitted with a panoramic bar, a restaurant and café, 87 double berth cabins, 20 four berth cabins, 246 reclining seats and 42 couchette bunks. Although able to carry 270 cars her limited passenger accommodation, much of which was below the car decks, meant she was ill suited for the long overnight crossings and so for 1977 the *Borgen* gave way to the *Jupiter*, sister ship to the *Black Prince*, and the service changed to departing Parkeston Quay on a Monday and the Kristiansand sailings being extended on to Oslo.

In 1976 the number of passengers travelling on the Parkeston Quay to Esbjerg route had further increased to 293,000. The figures had more than doubled in just three years and so an order was placed for a larger ship that would replace the *Winston Churchill*. It went to Aalborg Vaerft in Denmark who, in April 1978, delivered a ship costing £23m. The vessel left Aalborg for the Pool of London where on 4th May it was officially named *Dana Anglia* by the Danish born Duchess of Gloucester.

The *Dana Anglia* left London to arrive for berthing trials at Parkeston Quay on 6th May from where she then sailed back to Denmark for further trials and presentations before entering service on 13th May 1978. Although she was 3 feet shorter than the *Dana Regina* she was, at 14,399 grt, the largest ferry to have berthed at Parkeston Quay. She arrived with yet again another extensive array of typically Scandinavian facilities on board but her design was a little less generous when it came to cabins. Although there was now sleeping accommodation for 1,250 passengers, all in either two berth or four berth cabins with private facilities, they were now more compactly arranged with a greater number of them being inside cabins. The cabin arrangement remained similar to the *Dana Regina* in that there were still cabins located below the car decks on both the Copenhagen Deck and Britannia Deck though here they were now all forward. Above was an Anglia Deck which was similarly made up entirely of cabins.

The superstructure of the *Dana Anglia* extended for and aft to a greater extent than on most other ships of her time and this not only allowed for the carrying of more passengers and cargo but also provided a more spacious air to her Restaurant Deck. Here were located all of the public rooms. The Bellevue Lounge and bar areas remained at the forward end, having been lowered a deck from its location on the *Dana Regina*, and this led onto a similar port side promenade arcade that on the *Dana Anglia* extended to well over half her length. Along this arcade were gaming machines, a playroom, the Admiral Pub and the Shop whilst at the aft end was the Compass Club on the port side and the 236 seat Scandia Coffee shop on the starboard side. The main dining room was now divided into a smaller a la carte Codan Restaurant with

The Fred Olsen vessel *Jupiter* arriving from Kristiansand/Oslo - 7th August 1978.
(Stephen Brown)

134 seats and a new Tivoli Restaurant and smorgasbord with 203 seats. Both were now on the starboard side amidships. Five rooms were set aside for conferences or private parties although two were later converted into use as cinemas. The relocation of the Bellevue Lounge allowed more space for cabins on the Boat Deck and here, amongst a number of others, were 13 De-luxe cabins with varying configurations that offered a total of 36 berths. Down below her Car Decks could carry up to 470 cars or the equivalent to 135 teu's.

The *Dana Anglia* arrived at a time when oil prices were becoming increasingly unstable and so in the interests of fuel economy the crossing time to Esbjerg was now slowed into taking 19 hours. In the tradition of DFDS's new North Sea ships first going into service on the Esbjerg to Parkeston Quay route so too was tradition upheld whereby the older ship was displaced to the Tyne. As from June 1978 the *Winston Churchill* was transferred to services into Newcastle from either Esbjerg or Gothenburg though she continued to reappear at Parkeston Quay as a relief ship each May until 1983.

Only a few weeks after the appearance of the *Dana Anglia* came the arrival of a new ship for SMZ, this being in response to yet further growth on the Hook of Holland service. The *Prinses Beatrix* was launched on 14th January 1978 by H.R.H. Princess Beatrix at the yard of Verolme Scheepswerf in Heusden. She then arrived at Parkeston Quay for berthing trials on 11th June and undertook her maiden voyage from the Hook of Holland on 29th June 1978. She was powered by four Stork-Werkspoor diesel engines, the same as those on the *St Edmund*, and at 9,238 grt was then the route's largest ship.

In comparison to the *Dana Anglia*, the term 'largest ship' did not signify a particularly big one but the *Prinses Beatrix* could still carry up 1,500 passengers whilst still operating as a two class ship with strictly segregated accommodation. In addition her car decks could hold up to 320 cars or 44 trailers in various combinations thereof.

Second class sleeping accommodation was located on H Deck, below the car decks, and consisted of 13 two berth and 67 four berth cabins all with just a washbasin. First class cabins were located on E Deck with 9 two berth De-luxe cabins amidship, 54 singles which were nearly all outside cabins and 76 two berth inside cabins. All First class cabins had en-suite facilities and those advertised as singles were fitted with an additional bunk. The main public rooms were on D Deck with a full width Second class bar and lounge forward behind which lay a cafeteria on the port side. First class dining was further aft with a restaurant amidship on the starboard side and a full width lounge and bar at the aft end. On the overnight sailings the numbers of passengers was reduced to 1,024 and with only 572 being offered a berth.

Despite their being an additional 267 reclining seats in the observation lounge on B Deck for Second class passengers and a further 97 on D Deck for those travelling First class it was noticeable that nearly everyone travelling on board DFDS's new *Dana Anglia* was in berthed accommodation. Furthermore those on the Danish service had cabins equipped with their own private facilities whilst on board the *Prinses Beatrix* such luxury was only available to those travelling in First Class. Although both ships were of the same age and thus equally modern these differences in berthing facilities were due to the nature and length of the crossing with expectations of comfort being much higher on the longer routes.

Prior to the arrival of the new SMZ ship the Hook of Holland route had continued in running summer season relief sailings with the *St. George* backing up the *Koningin Juliana* and the *Koningin Wilhelmina* assisting the *St. Edmund*. Upon entering service the *Prinses Beatrix* took over the timings of the *Koningin Juliana* which in turn took over the *St. George*'s 14.00 departure from the Hook. The *St George* then sailed as relief day boat from Parkeston Quay by departing at 09.30. This left out the *Koningin Wilhelmina* which was withdrawn on 28th June 1978 as the last passenger only ship on the Hook of Holland route. She was laid up at Flushing and sold at the end of 1978 to the Ventouris Group in Greece who re-named her *Captain Constantinos*. The end of 1978 also saw the end of the laying up of SMZ ships at Flushing, the closure of the workshops there and thus the ending of SMZ's long association with the town of Vlissingen.

During the past few years it had become noticeable that whilst the Sealink service to Holland was carrying ever more passengers and accompanied cars it was falling behind in the carrying of ro-ro units. Overall the Anglo-Dutch traffic in ro-ro grew by around 10% between 1975 and 1978 but the Hook of Holland's market share had dipped from around 8% to just 6%. However it had maintained an overwhelming 70% share of the passenger market and around 45% of the motorist market. Local competition came from Townsend Ferries at Felixstowe who in 1974 had started a twice daily passenger service to Zeebrugge, and had supplemented this by upgrading a freight route to Rotterdam in 1978, and also from Sheerness where in 1975, one hundred years on from when SMZ first arrived there, a twice daily service to Flushing was started by Olau Line.

Comparison figures for ro-ro ferry services (000's):

Classic/walk-on	1975	1976	1977	1978
P. Quay - Hook of Holland	664	710	820	790
Felixstowe - Zeebrugge	48	55	49	50
Felixstowe - Rotterdam	-	-	-	30
Sheerness - Flushing	101	195	171	200

Motorists				
P. Quay - Hook of Holland	96	114	127	126
Felixstowe - Zeebrugge	54	79	103	114
Felixstowe - Rotterdam	5	5	5	25
Sheerness - Flushing	41	75	65	74

Ro-Ro units (acc. lorries and/or unacc. trailers)				
P. Quay - Hook of Holland	16	17	15	15
Felixstowe - Rotterdam	52	63	65	70
Felixstowe - Zeebrugge	18	27	29	30
Sheerness - Flushing	13	17	24	26

Despite the competition it remained the case that Parkeston Quay was comfortably the country's second busiest passenger port and, together with the Harwich train ferry services, was on a par with the busiest short sea port for the handling of trade cars which at that time was Harwich Navyard. In line with those at Dover the train ferries were also rapidly growing the volume of traffic carried in wagons due to better marketing by the BRB whilst the number of containers handled at the Quay's Container Terminal had remained steady at around 110,000 containers a year. By now Felixstowe had taken the lead in the movement of containers, handling 150,000 in 1977, and was well on its way to

The *Prinz Oberon* alongside P. Quay having arrived from Bremerhaven following Prins Line's return to the quay after a 10 year association with Harwich Navyard Dock - 1st May 1979. (Stephen Brown)

ultimately becoming Britain's premier container port.

One issue that had the potential to derail the prospects for continued growth concerned the train ferries. Both those at Harwich and at Dover were running at a loss. This had caused the BR-SISD to enter into a contractual agreement with the BRB 'which underwrites the Shipping Division on losses relative to the movement of empty and loaded railway wagons'. The agreement did not cover the carrying of any other type of traffic. In 1978 the Harwich to Dunkirk service was running 4 times a week with net receipts pooled and split 50-50 between BR and the SNCF whilst on the Harwich to Zeebrugge service, where sailings were up to three times a day throughout the week, all the receipts went to BR. BR also received all of the receipts from the Harwich to Zeebrugge container service whilst splitting those from the Hook of Holland service 50-50 with SMZ.

Figures for train ferry services (000's):

	1975	1976	1977	1978
Tons in wagons				
Harwich - Zeebrugge	218	245	325	331
Harwich - Dunkirk	63	55	42	57
Dover - Dunkirk	324	377	501	510
Ro-Ro units				
Harwich - Zeebrugge	4	3	3	2
Harwich - Dunkirk	1	-	-	-
Dover - Dunkirk	17	16	15	19
Trade cars				
Harwich - Zeebrugge	23	33	31	30
Harwich - Dunkirk	1	2	1	-
Dover - Dunkirk	26	35	20	20

Despite the losses 1979 saw Harwich and Dover train ferries handle a combined total of 1,093,000 tons of cargo, the first time that figures had exceeded 1 million tons. Out of this record total the Harwich to Zeebrugge and Harwich to Dunkirk services were responsible for around 470,000 tons. This was 80,000 tons up on 1978 and overall it meant that the Harwich train ferry services were consistently maintaining a mid 40% share of the market despite the huge increases at Dover brought about by the recent opening of Dunkirk West. It was also consistent with an earlier forecast of an extra 70,000 tons a year through Harwich when 200 new privately owned ferry wagons were introduced in mid 1977 rising to 350 by the autumn.

On 1st May 1979 Prins Line returned to Parkeston Quay after having spent 10 years downriver at Harwich Navyard Dock. The move back was prompted by a need for more space to further expand what had since become two routes into Germany and which had already seen considerable growth throughout the 1970s. Their return that day saw the arrival of the *Prins Oberon* from Bremerhaven. This was followed on 2nd May by the *Prins Hamlet* from Hamburg though this was not the same *Prins Hamlet* from 10 years before.

When Prins Line moved to the Navyard Dock in January 1969 they were running a chartered *Viking III* on their initial service from Bremerhaven. In May 1969 this had changed to running the *Prinz Hamlet* on a new route from Hamburg. At the time a new ship was being built for Lion Ferry at the yard of Werft-Nobiskrug of Rendsburg in Germany and on 21st February 1970 this was launched as the 7,993 grt *Prins Oberon*.

At 440 feet long this Swedish flagged vessel, with a white hull and superstructure and a yellow funnel containing a blue 'P' for Prinzenlinien, could carry up to 1,040 passengers and 238 cars of which 180 were housed on the main car deck and the remaining 58 on a separate hoistable deck. Alternatively there was space for up to 30 road vehicles or 47 x 40ft trailers. For passengers there was a Boat Deck with 100 Pullman berths below which was the Restaurant Deck that housed a 300 seat restaurant forward and a 205 seat cafeteria aft. In between, along the starboard side, was a pub, shop, casino and a bar. The Main Deck consisted entirely of cabins with 6 De-luxe three berth cabins located amidships, each with private baths, along with mainly four berth outside cabins that were all en-suite and four berth inside cabins that were not. A and B Decks were two car decks accessed only via a stern ramp below which were C and D Deck each of which contained a number of four berth economy cabins towards the forward end. In total there were

183 cabins with 702 berths made up of 165 four berth, 12 two berth and 6 De-luxe.

The off season sailings were still undertaken by the *Viking III* and when these finished on 31st May 1970 the *Prins Oberon* then made her maiden voyage from Bremerhaven to Harwich on 8th June. Together with the *Prinz Hamlet* arriving on alternate days there now commenced a daily passenger service between Harwich and Germany.

In connection with the Prins Line sailings boat trains had resumed running again between London and Harwich Town and an inaugurating train had earlier left Liverpool Street at 10.32 on 20th March 1970. In normal circumstances the departure from Harwich Town would be by a separate train leaving at 11.20, or 11.25 on Sundays, but on that first day the ship, the *Vikingfjord* which was covering for the *Prinz Hamlet*'s absence on overhaul, arrived late and so the same train from London was retained to form a return working from Harwich Town. The 10.32 from Liverpool Street ran in connection with the 13.00 sailing to Hamburg whilst for Bremerhaven the train left London at 13.52 to connect with the 16.30 sailing. The only timetabled stop en-route was at Dovercourt and on both ferry routes the arrival time in Germany was 09.00.

In November 1970 the *Prinz Hamlet* was sold to CGTM in Marseilles. Her successor on the Hamburg route was to be the *Vikingfjord,* recently seen at Parkeston Quay on charter to Fred Olsen, and which Prins Line now chartered and re-named *Prinz Hamlet* (II). Her first sailing from Hamburg to Harwich Navyard was on 15th November 1970. However just as she was when in service for Fred Olsen the new ship was to prove too small and was often worked to capacity. On 10th December 1971 she broke a crankshaft and was out of service until 19th February 1972. Her absence was covered by chartering the 499 grt *Landmark*, a 345 feet long German freight ship with capacity for 30 trailers and 12 passengers.

In early 1973 Fred Olsen's newly built *Bolero* covered the Bremerhaven route between 17th and 23rd February and then the Hamburg route from 24th February to 3rd March whilst the regular ships went away to dry dock.

To better serve the Hamburg route another new ship was on order from the yard at Rendsburg and this was launched in May 1973 as yet another *Prinz Hamlet* (2). At 5,830 grt she was much larger than the ship she replaced whilst in appearance she resembled that of a smaller version of the *Prins Oberon* being as she was around 50 feet shorter and had been given the same paintwork and funnel colours. She cost Dm40 million and as with the *Prins Oberon* economies were made in her construction by making her a stern loader only.

She could carry 1,034 passengers though only 570 had any cabin accommodation. She did however have a much improved cargo capability with space for 225 cars which was around 50% up on the existing *Prinz Hamlet* (II). Facilities on board were similarly laid out as those on the *Prins Oberon* though with certain facilities having been modernised or updated. All cabins on the Main Deck were now supplied with en-suite facilities but those on C and D Decks still remained without them. The Restaurant Deck had a bar and 198 seat restaurant at the forward end and a 221 seat cafeteria aft. The only major changes were that the one Suite and three De-luxe cabins, all en-suite but with a shower instead of a bath, were now on the Boat Deck aft of which was the conveniently, or otherwise, located disco. The Pullman berths had been moved down below to the aft end of C Deck.

The maiden voyage of this latest *Prinz Hamlet* (2) was from Hamburg on 12th November 1973 during which she encountered especially bad weather and a force 10 gale. Despite the conditions she was only three hours late in arriving at Harwich Navyard.

The *Prins Oberon* and *Prinz Hamlet* (2) became the long term regulars on their respective routes and although they had some appealing visual qualities the interiors and general standard of service on board was often considered to be less than impressive. Overall both appeared as if built down to their price. The public areas were largely of plastic and a large number of cabins were to remain equipped with only basic facilities. An air of cheap and often not quite so cheerful was perceived throughout ship as the years wore on.

On balance the *Prinz Hamlet* (2) was perhaps the better ship to sail on as she had the more interesting route. Her crossing time of 20 hours included almost 4 hours cruising along the River Elbe on her way up to Hamburg as opposed to a straight 16½ hours at sea on board the *Prins Oberon* to Bremerhaven. These two routes into northern Germany might not have appeared as all that far removed from the area into which DFDS was sailing from Parkeston Quay and with better facilities on board the Danish ferries there might well have been some serious competition issues. However Prins Line considered their main competition to come from routes further south and thus they offered a cheaper alternative to and from northern Europe without threatening the established Scandinavian routes. The figures bore out a successful strategy.

Since 1969 those on the Hamburg service had almost doubled in five years such that in 1974 the *Prins Oberon* was carrying 122,666 passengers plus 13,405 cars. That same year saw an additional 120,235 passengers and 13,289 cars travelling via Bremerhaven on the *Prinz Hamlet* (2). In 1975 the two routes combined had further grown to a total of 261,261 passengers and 31,419 cars.

Although the ever increasing figures were impressive the financial results were not. The company periodically encountered difficulties in the face of growing dissatisfaction with the service together with increasing costs associated in employing Swedish crews and the price of fuel. Eventually the experience of travelling on these cheaper services developed into travelling in a cheap fashion. On 30th September 1978 the Swedish flagged *Prins Oberon* was sold to Deutsche Leasing AG of Bremen and then chartered back as *Prinz Oberon* having been re-flagged under the cheaper German flag. The German investor consortium had also handed over to Lion Ferry their 50% interest in Prinzenlinien.

The sailing times throughout the 1970s had remained constant such that in 1978, the last full year of services from Harwich Navyard, those times were:

Hamburg service		Bremerhaven service	
Dep. St Pauli Pier	13.00	Dep. Columbus Pier	17.00
Arr. Harwich Navyard	09.30	Arr. Harwich Navyard	09.30
Dep. Harwich Navyard	13.00	Dep. Harwich Navyard	16.30
Arr. St Pauli Pier	09.00	Arr. Columbus Pier	09.00

In peak season the single fare for a passenger was £26 to Bremerhaven and £28 to Hamburg. For those travelling as motorists the fare for a car up to 14 feet long was also £26 to Bremerhaven and £28 to

Hamburg, if driven with either 1 or 2 fare paying passengers, or £10 on either route with 3 or more.

In comparison the same sized car on the Hook of Holland service cost £17.60 with each driver and passenger paying £14.30 First class and £11.50 Second class. The standard fare for a foot passenger was:

	Single		Return	
Fares from London	1st Class	2nd Class	1st Class	2nd Class
To Hook of Holland	£21.75	£16.55	£43.00	£32.80

Rest chairs were available at £2.00 each. Accommodation rates varied from £3.00 for a berth in a Second class four berth cabin up to £18.00 for a First class cabin de-luxe. Generally the cabin prices on the Hook route were around half those being charged by Prins Line.

Compared to years gone by the Hook of Holland route was still recognisably the same and much in keeping with the old railway philosophy of 'passengers having to have sufficient time to sleep'. What had changed over the years was the cost. The above fares for those travelling in 1978 were eight times higher than those in 1927 but wages had since risen twenty four fold from £3 a week to £72 a week thus making the price of a ticket that much cheaper in real terms. Service times were then by:

Night Boat		Day Boat	
Dep. London (L St)	19.40	Dep. London (L.St)	09.40
Arr. P. Quay	21.03	Arr. P. Quay	11.03
Dep. P. Quay	22.00	Dep. P. Quay	11.30
Arr. HvH	06.45	Arr. HvH	19.00
Dep. HvH	23.00	Dep. HvH	11.15
Arr. P. Quay	06.45	Arr. P. Quay	17.00
Dep. P. Quay	07.50	Dep. P. Quay	17.35
Arr. London (L.St)	09.14	Arr. London (L St)	19.05

At the Hook of Holland three continental trains waited upon the arrival of the night boat. These were the 'Rheingold', a luxurious Trans-Europ-Express that went down to Switzerland and Italy via Germany, the 'Rhine Express' that also headed south towards the cities of southern Germany but which then went on to Austria and the 'Holland-Scandinavian Express' which headed north through northern Germany and then on to Copenhagen. Awaiting the day boat was the 'Britannia Express' that followed the route of the 'Rhine Express' and the 'Nord-West Express' that headed out in the same direction as the 'Holland-Scandinavian Express' as far as Berlin but afterwards continued on to Warsaw. For the truly adventurous the Nord-West still offered the opportunity of taking a sleeper coach all the way through from the Hook of Holland to Moscow, the 48 hour 1,800 mile journey first being introduced on 29th May 1960.

In England the 'North Country Continental' was still running north though only as far as Manchester and was now more commonly referred to as the North Country Boat Train. It no longer ran to Sheffield via March and Lincoln but instead via March, Peterborough, Grantham, Nottingham and Chesterfield.

Dep. P. Quay	07.17	Dep. Manchester	15.15
Arr. March	09.08	Dep. Sheffield	16.25
Arr. Peterborough	09.32	Dep. Nottingham	17.23
Arr. Grantham	10.01	Dep. Grantham	18.05
Arr. Nottingham	10.41	Dep. Peterborough	18.41
Arr. Sheffield	11.38	Dep. March	19.02
Arr. Manchester	12.49	Arr. P. Quay	21.10

A new service for motorists occurred in 1979 with the provision of a Motorail train from Parkeston Quay to Scotland. It was principally aimed at those motorists making use of the day boat to and from the Hook of Holland and was an extension of an existing Motorail service that ran overnight between Cambridge and Edinburgh. A single width concrete ramp was constructed at the end of the track on Platform 3 over which cars were driven on and off the train. Despite the destination in Scotland being extended on to Stirling the service only lasted for a couple of seasons, its demise being due mainly to the high cost of using it.

Parkeston Quay's operations at the Fishers terminal had, by the end of the 1970s, expanded to include deep sea services from both South America and the Arabian Gulf. Arrow Line remained its main customer with a monthly general cargo service to Buenos Aires, Montevideo, Santos and Rio de Janeiro using vessels of between 6,000 and 10,000 tons and a monthly service to the Eastern Mediterranean with vessels of around 5,000 tons. The Gulf region was served with sailings on a 3 to 4 week frequency by the Gulf Integrated Shipping & Supply Company as was the Black Sea by the Balkan Black Sea Line. The terminal was accommodating vessels up to 500 feet in length and it was also making use of the existing rail link running alongside No. 4 Shed to load wagons with fruit and other foodstuffs for national distribution.

Beyond Fishers, at the Petrochem Carless oil refinery, a third pipeline was laid in 1978 that connected the works with the tanker berth. Made from stainless steel it was named P099, the original two dating from 1964 having been named P100 and P101.

In 1979 a programme of over £4m worth of improvements was started at Parkeston Quay that either replaced existing equipment or provided for new storage areas. The greatest expense was for a new berth as the ever increasing size of DFDS's freight ships had outgrown the capabilities of the single width No.6 pontoon berth. Accordingly £2½m was allocated to provide a new double width linkspan berth plus an additional 3½ acre standage area.

The new 1,000 ton structure, comprising a berth and a ramp, was designed by MacGregors Naval Architects Ltd. and built by Cleveland Bridge & Engineering Co. Ltd. at Port Clarence on Teeside. It arrived in January 1980 as a complete unit on the deck of a floating barge that had undergone a 48 hours tow from the Tees in the care of the Alexandra tug *Wellington*. The constituent parts were off loaded by a pair of giant floating cranes which then manoeuvred them alongside the quay and sank them into position. The ramp had a lifting range of 30 feet and faced upstream, in the opposite direction to the old pontoon berth, and overlapped part of No. 7 berth. The new linkspan opened in February 1980 with the first ship to use it being the *Dana Futura*. The old berth was laid up at the far east end beyond the container terminal

The work of the Toleman Delivery Group's trade car operation had expanded enormously from when it first started in 1974 and on 14th November 1979 a new 12 acre site costing £1m was opened to the south of Parkeston Quay's west end. Built on reclaimed marsh land the new complex of engineering workshops, vehicle preparation facilities and storage for 2,000 vehicles replaced the former depot at the transit camp and employed a workforce of 170 staff. Imported vehicles left the quay either in one the Company's car transporters, of which they had around a hundred, or by rail in specially designed double deck car carriers or 'cartics'. An area in the south east of the port previously in use as a car park for Ford's was then converted into a 4½ acre standage area to store 240 x 40ft trailers.

At the Container Terminal the services of the *Rhodri Mawr* had ended in October 1978 and were replaced by a return of the *Brathay Fisher* in November 1978. Throughput in excess of 100,000 containers a year was still being maintained and now some £500,000 was being spent on providing three extra lanes of stacking ground adjacent to the Kone crane and a new third area of standage to increase capacity there from 300 to 450 containers. Also new was a mobile straddle carrier built by Ferranti Engineering in Manchester.

The number of containers handled by the Container Terminal each year were:

Year	1974	1975	1976	1977	1978	1979
Containers	112,329	103,644	116,856	108,800	108,490	109,301

At Harwich the number of wagons shipped via the train ferries had remained fairly consistent though the use of larger wagons meant an increase in the tonnage handled.

Year	1974	1975	1976	1977	1978	1979
Wagons	41,327	32,622	30,765	33,549	32,651	30,423

A new meat inspection facility complete with a freezer room and offices was built on the end of No. 2 Shed on East Dock Road at a cost of £160,000 whilst out on the quay a further £180,000 was being spent on jacking up the covered walkways. By September 1979 the one to the East portal berth had been raised to a height of 14 feet above quay level. The scheme would later see two mechanised gangways, designed by Power Lifts Ltd, installed that would link the walkway to any ship using the berth plus new conveyor belts fitted in order to relieve the load of passengers carrying their baggage. This work was completed in 1980. Elsewhere work costing £600,000 saw sheet piling take place at the rear of the Middle West quay in order to provide a new 60 vehicle standage area for Prinz Ferries and a new walkway extending westward from the West Portal berth to the new Pontoon Berth. Additional work due for completion by autumn 1981 went on a new electrical sub station and a general upgrade costing £330,000.

Despite the money being spent on the quay there were many complaints over why nothing was being spent on the poor state of the railway station. The reason why the port had apparently done little, if anything, to improve matters was that the station at Parkeston Quay was the responsibility of British Rail Eastern Region, not Sealink UK Ltd, this now being the new wholly owned subsidiary of the BRB into which, on 1st January 1979, all aspects of the business formerly in the hands of BR-SISD had been transferred. In the 1980s Sealink UK Ltd would also not be responsible for Parkeston Quay either.

A jeep emerges from the starboard side bow ramp of the *England* when the ship was chartered for NATO duties - Autumn 1979. (Stephen Gooch)

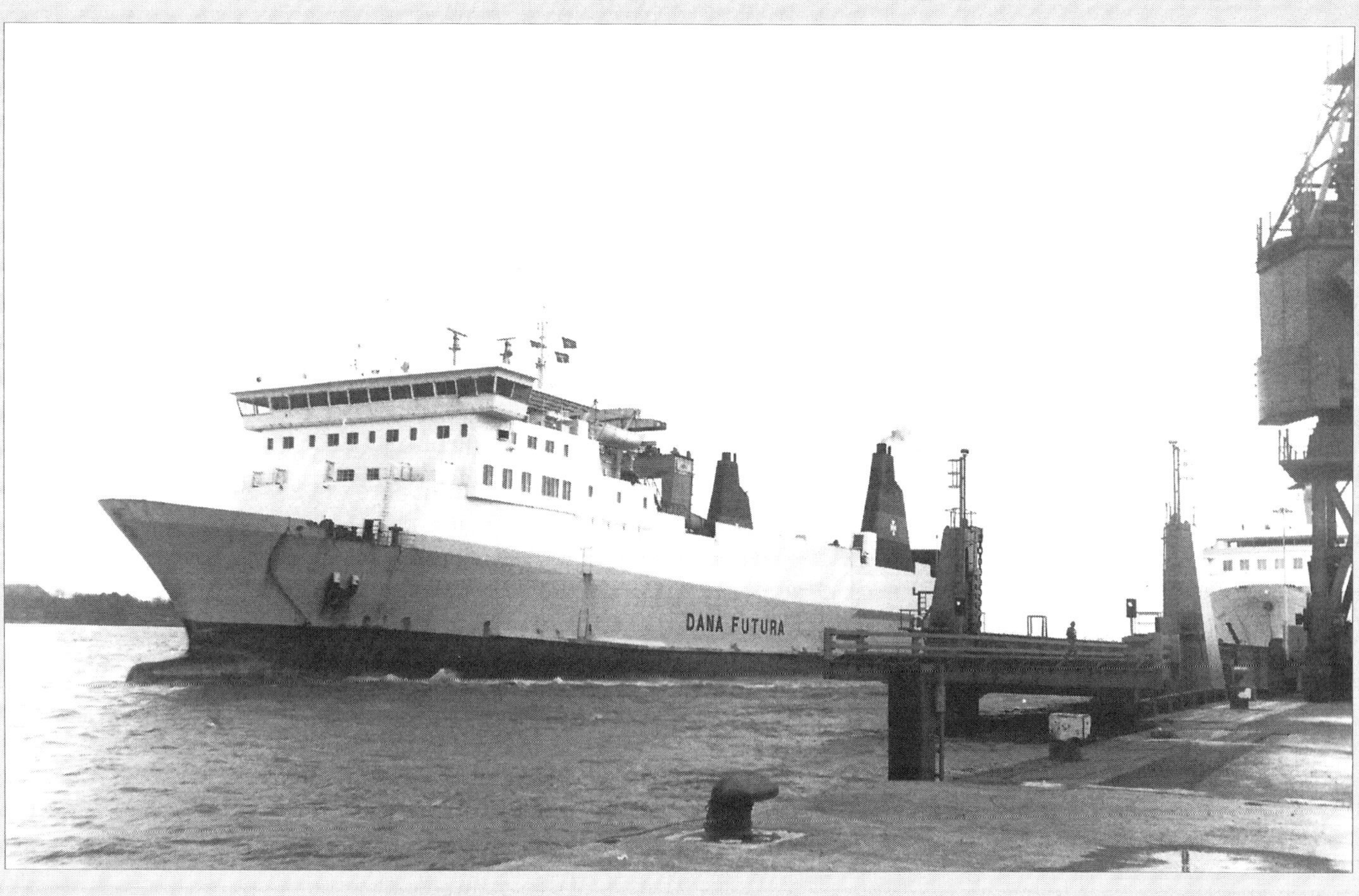
DANA FUTURA

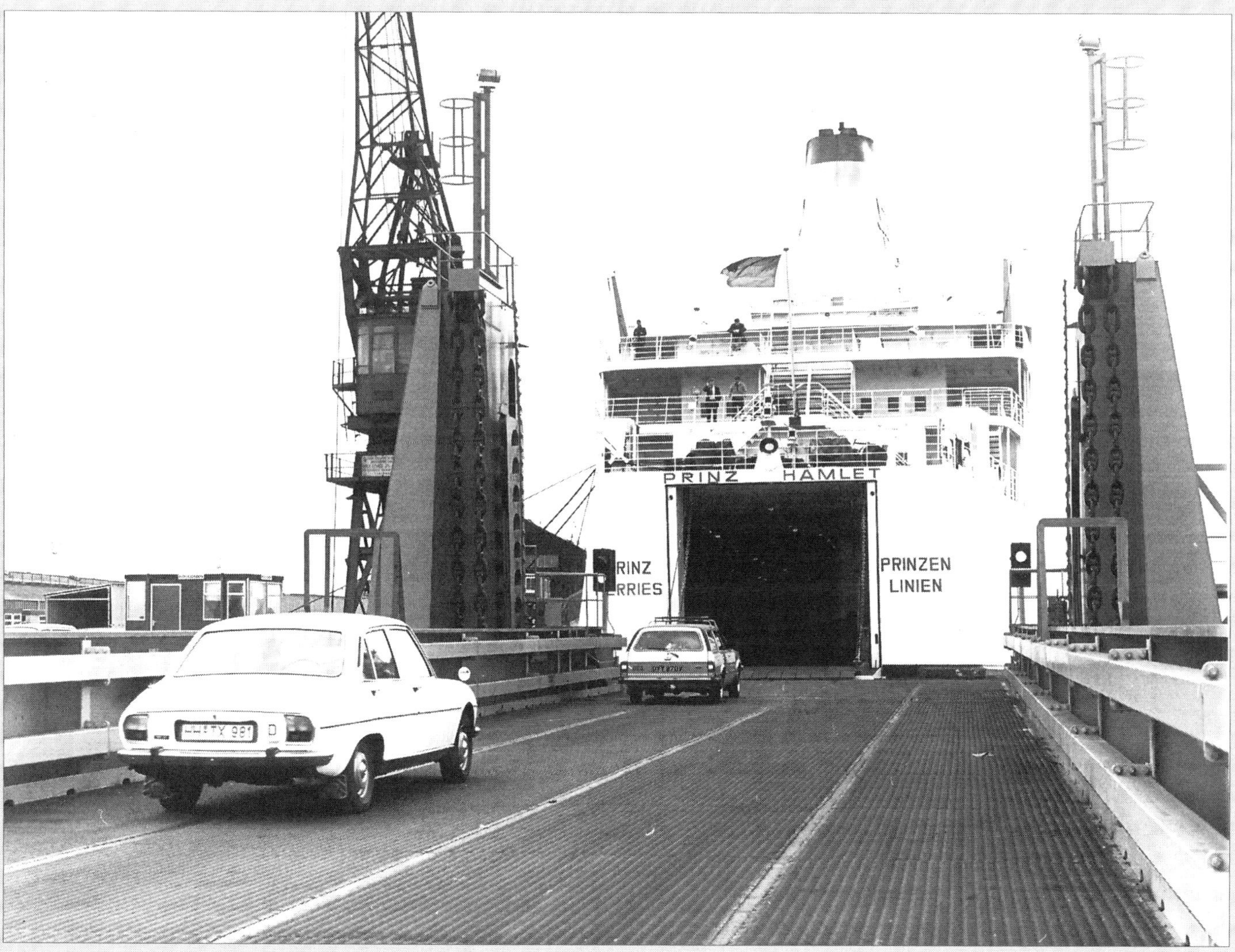
PRINZ HAMLET
RINZ
RRIES
PRINZEN
LINIEN

THE 1980s

Throughout the 1980s a multitude of ferry services could be seen criss-crossing all of the sea routes out of Britain building up to over 40 routes throughout the North Sea alone. Normal competition amongst the established operators was heightened by an array of new arrivals who sought to attract traffic mainly by chartering in tonnage and then undercutting rates. Although they often survived for only a short period of time these challengers caused a wider variety of ships to visit ports than would otherwise have been the case. As the decade progressed Parkeston Quay would welcome many such visitors as well as seeing many regulars leave.

On 4th June 1980 DFDS celebrated a centenary of sailings between Esbjerg and the ports of Harwich and Parkeston Quay. In their first month of operation back in 1880 the Company ran six sailings to Harwich bringing in 1,208 oxen, various other livestock and 110 tons of general cargo. In 1980 DFDS were importing 15,000 tons of cargo each week. Since May 1980 they had embarked on a new joint venture service between Parkeston Quay and Hamburg under the name of Prins Ferries/DFDS Hanse Ferries. The ro-ro freighter *Dana Futura* left Hamburg twice a week on Wednesday and Saturday and from Parkeston Quay on Thursday and Sunday. Combined with the normal Prins Ferries service there were now five or six sailings a week to and from Hamburg.

During the past century the ports of Harwich and Parkeston Quay had witnessed much to be proud of and during the 1980s Parkeston Quay would host its greatest ever variety of passenger services, Harwich would see its largest ever train ferry and, in 1982, the two together would then employ the greatest number of Sealink staff at 1,800. However both ports were to undergo a decade of change and uncertainty as a result of the preparation, implementation and consequential aftermath of the Government's privatisation of Sealink.

As far back as 1977 the BRB had been looking at ways to attract outside capital into its shipping division and an unsuccessful bid for Sealink from European Ferries in 1979 had since delayed that process. It was originally envisaged that BR would still maintain an ongoing and sizeable interest in any joint venture investments that were deemed suitable in developing the business further but that intention had, on 14th July 1980, been dropped in favour of British Rail Investments Ltd. being given the job of divesting the BRB of its entire interest in its shipping division. It would be a few years yet before the process was completed but in the early 1980s an optimistic British Rail was proposing a major investment locally in the train ferry service at Harwich. Or rather a major investment in its relocation to Parkeston Quay.

In December 1979 there appeared a BR Special Projects Report that detailed plans for a new train ferry terminal at Parkeston Quay West and for the replacement of the four existing ships with two jumbo train ferries. The cost was shown as being £36m. The report was set in the context of train ferry traffic being on the increase but the service being in the hands of an ageing infrastructure that needed replacing. In 1978 the Harwich to Zeebrugge service had made 1,750 vessel trips, was handling roughly 400,000 tons of cargo a year in 24,000 loaded wagons plus the return of 9,800 empties. It was noted that the traffic flows were unbalanced in that imports into the UK represented about two thirds of the total, a figure that had remained fairly constant from when the route first opened in 1924. The service was also losing £1.4m a year.

The report proposed replacing both the *Suffolk Ferry* and *Norfolk Ferry* with two new jumbo train ferries with an option of perhaps keeping on the *Essex Ferry* and the *Cambridge Ferry*. The new ships would each have three decks, the upper and lower decks being serviced via hoists from the main loading deck. Two size options were under consideration with each having two decks of rail wagons and the upper deck left open for the carriage of dangerous goods. One option was for a ship costing £13m that was five rail tracks wide per deck and had a capacity for 68 x 40ft units or rail wagons. The other was for a six track ship costing £16m and a capacity for 104 x 40ft units. The report did not detail the dimensions of these ships but each would have a speed of 19 knots. The crossing would take 5¼ hours which, with a turn round time of 2¾ hours, would allow each ship to make three single trips per day.

The new ships would have twin tracks over the ramp onto a new terminal at Parkeston Quay West and simulated research had shown that a six track train ferry could discharge and load 100 wagons off and 100 wagons on within the specified turn round time. The new terminal was said to cost £4m.. It would all require a major operational rethink as regards wagon movements, train marshalling and quayside procedures but the benefits were such that with a start date of 1983 the whole operation would show a substantial profit and that the route capacity would be able to cope with a potential quadrupling of traffic by 1990.

Whilst the plans were being developed a large capacity train ferry entered service at Harwich in the form of the *Speedlink Vanguard,* a re-named deep sea

Opposite top: The *Dana Futura* approaching the new No. 3 Berth - 2nd April 1980. (Derek Genzel collection)

Opposite bottom: Cars driving onboard the Prinz Ferries vessel *Prinz Hamlet* at No. 3 Berth - 24th April 1980. (Derek Genzel collection)

Lifting into position the new double width linkspan, later known as No. 3 Berth, which replaced the old pontoon berth - 14th February 1980. (Stephen Brown)

freight ship on a two year charter from Stena Line that had been specially converted at the South Bank ship repair yard at Smith's Dock in Middlesborough. Formerly the *Stena Shipper* she arrived at Smith's Dock on 4th May 1980 for a £4m refit and emerged in August as a double deck train ferry with wagons being stowed on an upper deck after having been hoisted from the main deck below. The loading arrangements were such that any wagons for the upper deck would be shunted onto the main deck as normal and moved towards two parallel lifts at the forward end. Once hoisted up to the upper deck they were then moved aft by mobile tractor units of the Trackmaster type. Unloading was achieved by reversing the process.

The *Speedlink Vanguard* was four tracks wide on both decks and fitted the berth the same as did the existing train ferries by having the all important matching breadth. She was however around 65 feet longer than the other train ferries and this gave her an increased overall carrying capacity of 56 wagons of which 32 were on the Main Deck and 24 on the Upper Deck. In keeping with the older train ferries she was provided with six twin berth cabins for passengers whilst the crew now benefited from all their cabins having private en-suite facilities.

The *Speedlink Vanguard*'s first day in service was to Zeebrugge on 21st August 1980 following berthing trials at Harwich the previous day. Speedlink was the brand name for BR's Railfreight services and the *Speedlink Vanguard* arrived with the purpose of initiating the planned replacement of the older and smaller ferries that were becoming ever more costly to operate. The first to leave service was the *Suffolk Ferry* which had already made her final trip the previous month and during her career had sailed just over one million miles. In August 1980 she was sold for scrapping in Belgium, towed to Antwerp in September and broken up at Tamise in April 1981. The *Norfolk Ferry* was then reduced to becoming the relief ship.

Meanwhile the 1979 proposals for two brand new train ferries had been modified and eventually agreed and in March 1981 the plans were with the Department for Transport for approval with Parliamentary powers being sought in the 1980/81 BR Bill. The chosen size of ferry was the six track 104 unit version and a new terminal at Parkeston Quay West was to have a 120 metre long dual level linkspan running out in a north easterly direction and capable of simultaneously serving both the main and top decks of the new ships.

A new secondary yard of sixteen sidings was to be built on reclaimed land and the whole yard layout and workings remodelled. The existing connections to No. 4 Shed would be removed, as probably would the shed itself, and nearby would be built a new staff accommodation block. Once Parliamentary powers had been granted work was expected to start in late 1981 and be completed by August 1983 in time for the arrival of the first new ship. The second ship would arrive in 1985 and of the existing train ferries only the *Cambridge Ferry* would be retained. Unfortunately the period of decision making coincided with a recession and a drop in foreign trade and the necessary financial backing by the Government never materialised. As a result none of these proposals were ever implemented.

A further significant factor was that the end of October 1980 had seen the demise of the famous 'Night Ferry' service via Dover, an overnight sleeper train that directly connected London with Paris and

The *Dana Anglia* returning to Parkeston Quay after a commemorative sailing marking the centenary of DFDS at Harwich - June 1980. (Stephen Gooch collection)

which first ran on 14th October 1936. Through sleeping carriages had ever since travelled on board one of the Dover to Dunkirk train ferries and in its last year of operation some 27,000 passengers were using it. However its ageing rolling stock had become too expensive to replace for so relatively few passengers per year and so closure had become an inevitable conclusion. Its ending created a net gain for Dover as amongst the six return train ferry sailings a day to Dunkirk the night sailing had only ever carried sleeping cars. Closing the 'Night Ferry' service meant all sailings could now carry rail wagons and thus from 1981 onwards Dover was operating with a 20% boost to route capacity.

To make matters worse for Harwich British Rail were later reported as having lost £15m on their international rail freight services throughout 1981 of which the Harwich train ferry service was said to have been responsible for having lost £7m. This was a five fold increase in losses in just three years and BR were no longer prepared to continue with such a disastrous situation. Their response led to the closure of the Harwich to Dunkirk service with the *Cambridge Ferry* making a final trip on 18th April 1982, the rationalisation of the service to Zeebrugge and the consequent scrapping of two more train ferries.

Thus the *Norfolk Ferry* made her last commercial voyage in October 1981 and was thereafter laid up in the River Blackwater. On 14th April 1983 she was towed from there to Ouderkerk in Holland where she arrived two days later at the breakers yard of Vianen bei Marel BV. The *Essex Ferry* hung on for another two months until she made her own final voyage in December 1981. She was first laid up on the river buoys before likewise being moved to the River Blackwater. On 27th April 1983 she was towed to Rainham on the River Medway where her accommodation was removed and her hull converted into a floating pontoon. She was re-named *Essex Ferry Pontoon* and towed to Haugesund in Norway for use

Below and overleaf: Plans for the new train ferry terminal at P. Quay's west end that would have seen a double deck linkspan installed for the loading and unloading of rail wagons and a re-modelling of Parkeston Yard - March 1981. (Stephen Brown collection)

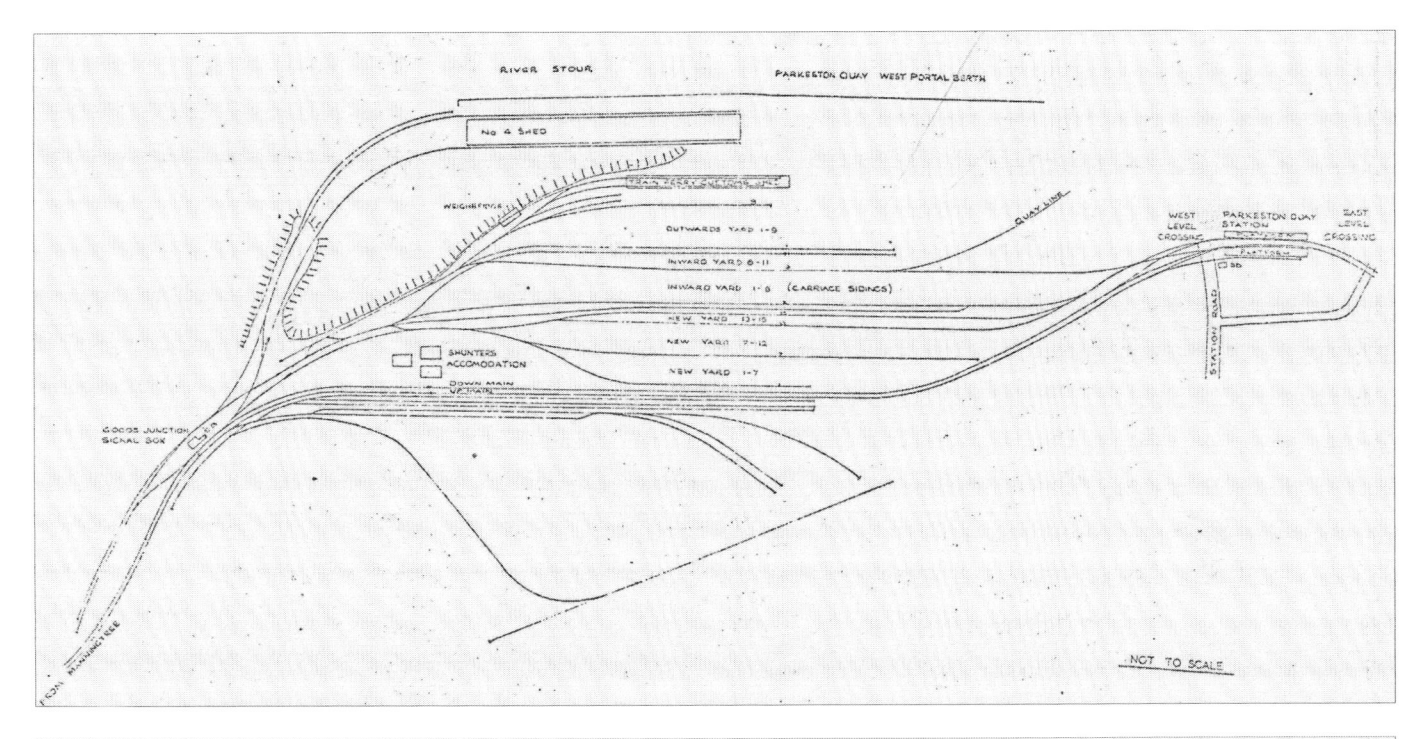

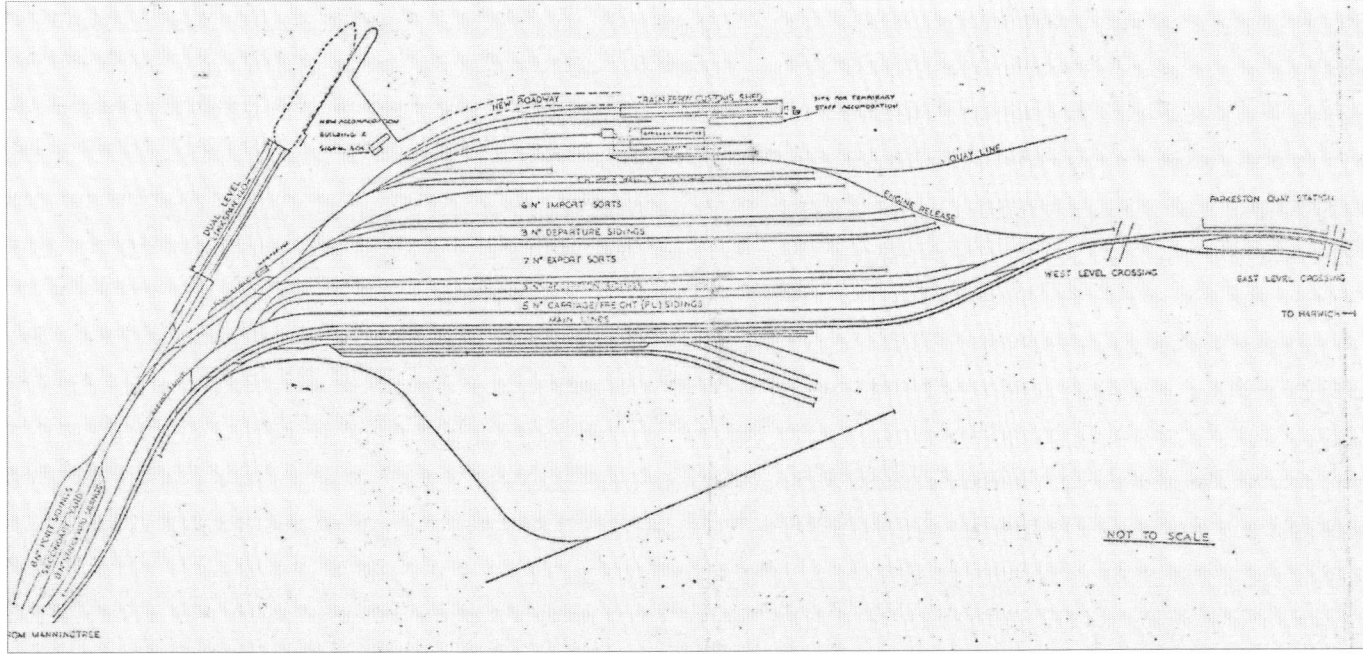

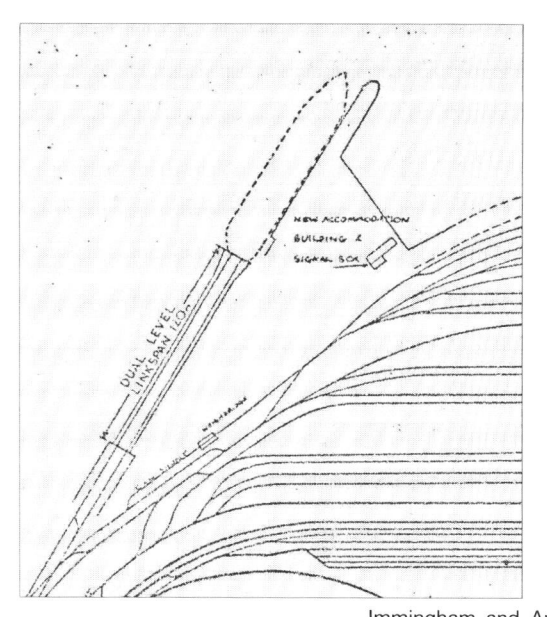

Below: The Royal Yacht *Britannia* lies in the East Portal berth awaiting to embark The Queen and the Duke of Edinburgh - 2nd May 1981. (Stephen Brown)

Bottom: Departure of the *St. Edmund* for the Hook of Holland - 19th November 1981. (Stephen Brown)

in the salvage of the capsized Norwegian oil platform *Alexander Kielland* before being broken up in late 1983.

On the passenger front there were increasing concerns about new tonnage and over capacity on services within southern Scandinavia that were affecting, amongst others, the operations of Lion Ferry. Also there were suggestions of a merger between Lion Ferry and either of two Swedish ferry companies, Tor Line and Sessan Line.

Tor Line AB was founded in 1965 by AB Trans-Oil and AB Rex with the purpose of running passenger ferries from Gothenburg to the UK.. These initially linked Gothenburg with Immingham and Amsterdam on a triangular circuit which lasted until 2nd June 1975 when Felixstowe took over from Immingham and the leg between the UK and Holland being dropped. The move to Felixstowe was accompanied by Tor Line introducing two new fast and super sleek sister ships, these being the *Tor Britannia* in 1975, a vessel which had barely been acquainted with Immingham before being moved. and the *Tor Scandinavia* in 1976. With a speed of 24½ knots these Tor twins could depart Gothenburg and be in Harwich harbour just 22 hours later.

Sessan Line was the trading name of R/A Goteborg - Frederikshavn Linjen (GFL) whose origins went back to 1936. In 1980 Sessan Line briefly went into partnership with Tor Line to form Sessan Tor Line as a way of avoiding being taken over by a predatory Stena Line, another Swedish company who were then undergoing a corporate overhaul and fleet renewal.

A merger between Lion Ferry and Tor Line, sailing into Felixstowe, would have rationalised Lion Ferry's interests at Parkeston Quay, viz. Prinz Line, but the whole situation changed dramatically upon the involvement of DFDS. The Danish company acquired Tor Line's passenger business from its then owners Salen Group in 1981 and this was followed in 1982 by the purchase of Tor Lloyd AB which then gave DFDS all of Tor Line's feight business. Both activities were wholly absorbed within DFDS with the passenger business being marketed at DFDS Tor Line and the freight business re-launched as a 'new' independently managed Tor Line.

In between times, on 1st May 1981, DFDS had also taken over the entire operation of Prinz Line after Lion Ferry had earlier sold them their original 50% interest and then the remaining 50% they had received back from the German investment consortium. This led to the creation of DFDS Prinz Line and a subsidiary company, DFDS (Germany) GmbH, that acted as agents for both its Bremerhaven and Hamburg routes. New funnel markings were adopted for the former Prinz Line vessels whereby the blue 'P' of Prinz Line was changed to red and placed within the white Maltese cross of DFDS. DFDS were no strangers to the Hamburg to Parkeston Quay route as, in addition to their *Dana Futura*, some occasional extra freight services had been provided by the *Stafford* and the *Surrey*.

On 2nd May 1981 Parkeston Quay played host to Queen Elizabeth II and the Duke of Edinburgh when they arrived to board the royal yacht *Britannia* before heading out on a state visit to Norway. Lesser personages travelling to Norway had to wait until 1st June when Fred Olsen then recommenced their service to Kristiansand and Oslo. Sailings were now twice a week with the Monday sailing being supplemented by another one on Thursday. The ship was again the *Jupiter* which arrived at the East Portal at 12.00 and sailed at 14.00. When the season ended on 17th August 1981 Fred Olsen then closed the route down. What had earlier been knocked down was a quayside crane when, on 14th August, the *Mercandian Transporter* collided with one as she was approaching no. 3 Berth. The ship, chartered for DFDS's service to Esbjerg, sustained only minor damage to her bow but the crane was totally wrecked.

Between January and June 1982 Sealink chartered the 2,353 grt *Stena Sailer* for service to the Hook of Holland. Able to carry up to 35 trailers on the main deck, 100 trade cars on the top deck and with passenger accommodation for 12 lorry drivers she became noted for having sailed to Antwerp in March 1982 with 400 trade cars on board and become the first 'railway boat' to do so in almost 14 years. On 4th July 1982 responsibility for the running of Parkeston Quay and the Harwich Train Ferry Terminal was transferred to Sealink Harbours Ltd., a wholly owned subsidiary of Sealink UK Ltd.

Meanwhile, on 19th March 1982, around 50 Argentinians, mainly scrap metal merchants, had landed on the South Atlantic island of South Georgia and were reported to have raised the Argentinian flag in order to begin 'an occupation of British territory'. On 2nd April Argentine armed forces invaded the Falkland Islands. On 3rd April Prime Minister Margaret Thatcher sanctioned 'Operation Corporate' in order to reclaim the islands. A task force was quickly assembled and the first Royal Navy ships left Portsmouth on 5th April. The Royal Navy was to be supported by a whole host of other ships supplied by the Merchant Navy ranging from tugs to cruise liners. These were known as STUFT's or 'Ships Taken Up From Trade' and ship number 40 on a list that would eventually became a total of 52 was the St. Edmund.

On 11th May staff from the Ministry of Defence had made a 2 hour inspection of her at Parkeston Quay. On 12th May after her normal 06.30 arrival from the Hook of Holland she was officially requisitioned at 08.00 and at 14.30 she left for the dockyards at Devonport under the command of Captain Wood. There she was converted into a floating garrison for the transport of army personnel and was fitted out with extra fuel and water tanks, loaded with stores and had two helicopter pads fitted aft, one large enough on which to land Chinooks. She had her bow visor welded shut, the car deck fitted with water purification plant and was further modified for refuelling at sea. She left Devonport on 20th May with Captain Stockman in command of a crew of 79, all Harwich volunteers, and 700 troops mainly from the 5th Infantry Brigade.

The St. Edmund officially entered the war zone on 7th June by which time British forces had secured some important advances. On 12th June, along with Europic Ferry, she was formally escorted closer towards the Falklands by H.M.S. Brilliant. From now on there were no more drills - all alarms meant action stations. On the night of 13th June reports were coming in that Port Stanley, the island's capital. had been successfully re-captured and this led to General Mario Menendez, Commander of the Argentine garrison in Port Stanley, signing the surrender document on 14th June. A little humour on board the St Edmund was that the Argentinians could withstand the effects of SeaDart, SeaSlug and SeaWolf missiles but not the imminent arrival of SeaLink ! The serious reality though was that the war had lasted 74 days and led to 255 British, 649 Argentine and 3 Falklanders being killed.

The St Edmund first arrived in Port Stanley harbour on 17th June and was used to ferry troops along the coast before becoming an accommodation ship for General Menendez and around 600 'specials', or suitably senior officers and technicians. These personnel were being held back as a guarantee that Argentina would not fight on because although a surrender document had been signed there was some 'difficulty' over the inclusion of the word 'unconditional'. It was not until 12th July that Argentina finally gave their official acceptance of its meaning. The next day saw the St Edmund repatriate what had become the last batch of prisoners by sailing for the Argentine port of Puerto Madryn. On board were 593 prisoners, including General Menendez, and when she arrived on 14th July she was escorted into port by an Argentine warship amid tight security. For the voyage she was granted cattle boat status by the Argentine authorities, ie a ship with no weapons on board or in any way constituting a threat. Whilst disembarking the prisoners many on board were drawn to the Company's advertising slogan back home - 'Let Sealink set you free'!

Upon her return to Port Stanley the St. Edmund then left on 17th July for Ascension, a voyage that

The 'Stanley Hilton'. A view of the St. Edmund anchored in Port Stanley harbour in the Falklands - 1982. (Stephen Brown collection)

Advertising logo in use by Sealink at the time of the Falklands War - 1983. (Stephen Brown collection)

Captain D.W. Jarvis, in the presence of Mr. L. Merryweather, M.D. of Sealink, being presented by Vice Admiral R.R. Squires with a plaque in recognition of the role played by the *St. Edmund* during the Falklands War - 28th February 1983. (Stephen Brown collection)

lasted 10 days. By 11th August she was back in Port Stanley and from mid August onwards she was used as a floating barracks for hundreds of soldiers. The comparative luxury of life on board ship earned her the nickname of the 'Stanley Hilton' - run by 'Forget-Me-Not Travel'. The ship's mailing address was *'H.M.S. St. Edmund, B.F.P.O. 666, H.M. Forces, South Atlantic. No stamp needed.'* By now she was one of around twenty civilian vessels still under requisition and for her services Sealink UK were reportedly being paid up to £50,000 per day.

At the time of the *St. Edmund*'s call up Sealink had previously made an announcement that they intended withdrawing both her and the *St George* from the Hook of Holland route, with the loss of 130 jobs, in favour of operating just one much larger vessel and when it came to sending out a change of crew for the *St. Edmund* in August a strike over the Company's proposals had only recently ended. The relief crew of 77 further volunteers, led by Captain Jarvis, finally flew out to Ascension on 2nd September. From there they sailed south on board the ferry *Norland* and took over on the *St Edmund* on 14th September.

The initial crew, having been away for just over 4 months, arrived home by sailing back on board the *Norland* as far as Ascension from where some flew into RAF Lyneham on 28th September and the rest into RAF Brize Norton the next day. On 5th October the British Rail Social Club at Parkeston hosted a welcome home party whilst on 12th October the City of London hosted a salute to the entire Task Force with Purser Stevens representing the *St. Edmund*'s crew.

From Mr Len Merryweather, Managing Director of Sealink, the crew received cards that read 'Nice to have you back'. Admiral Sir John Fieldhouse, Commander of the Falkland Islands Task Force, saw fit to further comment. 'Without the ships taken up from trade, the operation could not have been undertaken, and I hope this message is clearly understood by the British nation'.

Despite the patriotic feeling and local pride the Hook of Holland route was nevertheless still losing £1m a year and the prospect of losing ships saw the National Union of Seamen (NUS) again urging rejection of Sealink's plans in a December ballot. On 17th January 1983 Sealink met with SMZ management in Rotterdam with a view to handing the route over entirely to the Dutch with the possible loss of up to 440 jobs. A further meeting took place between Sealink and the NUS and this led to improved offers over leave and redundancy payments. A second ballot came out in favour of Sealink's revised offer and this enabled the Company to again meet with SMZ with a view to remaining on the route.

Such meetings had taken place amidst the aftermath of the first major tragedy for nearly 30 years. On the evening of 19th December 1982 at 22.50 an inward bound *Speedlink Vanguard* collided with an outward bound *European Gateway*, a 4,263 grt ro-ro freighter operated by Townsend Thoresen on their service between Felixstowe and Rotterdam. The collision occurred two miles off Harwich with the bow of the *Speedlink Vanguard* striking the *European Gateway* below the waterline on her starboard side and creating a 200 feet long gash.

The sea poured into her auxiliary engine room and then into the main engine room through an open watertight door which proved impossible to close against such a vast inflow of water. Within 90 seconds the *European Gateway* was listing to starboard by 15 degrees and within ten minutes she was touching bottom. Twenty minutes later she had rolled over to lie on her side half submerged on a sandbank with the loss of four crew and two passengers. A rescue operation co-ordinating a variety of local tugs and Trinity House craft was controlled by a local pilot on board the DFDS freight ship *Dana Futura* which was being used as shelter against both the current and a force six wind. On board the *European Gateway* many of her surviving 32 crew and 32 passengers were rescued after having clambered out onto the vessel's port side hull.

The ship had come to rest in 30 feet of water atop a relatively shallow ledge just beyond which was the deep water channel. Had she been struck further out it is most probable that casualties would have been far greater. The *Speedlink Vanguard* sustained severe damage to her bow but was able to safely reach Harwich at around 03.30 and without any casualties. She was returned to service on 29th December. The half submerged *European Gateway* was righted on 26th February 1983 by the salvage barge *Super Servant 3* and later removed to Holland. After being sold in May she was then towed to Perama in Greece for a reconstruction from which she emerged in August 1984 as the passenger ferry *Flavia* sailing between Greece and Italy. The ship was to see almost another thirty years in service either in the Mediterranean or the Baltic before being scrapped in Aliaga, Turkey in July 2013.

The inquiry began on 7th November 1983 at Riverwalk House, London amidst claims of fault on the part of both the Captains. The main accusation was in failing to notify each other of their intended course once it was realised that a course alteration on one or either vessel was necessary. Both had entered the Harwich channel in their correct positions but just east of the Cork Spit the *European Gateway* failed to alter course to starboard and instead headed northwards out of the channel. The *Speedlink Vanguard* crept to starboard in order to anticipate the *European Gateway* resuming her correct course when in fact a move to port would have prevented the fateful collision. However a move to port would have placed the *Speedlink Vanguard* in the direct path of the *European Gateway* had the *European Gateway* altered course as she was expected to and the inquiry heard of a message being sent from the *European Gateway* to

Harwich Harbour saying that she would in fact be staying north of the channel after the Cork Spit. Also under consideration were allegations of poor look out procedures, a poor use of direct vhf radio communication between the two ships and the role played by watertight doors.

The Inquiry's conclusion in August 1984 stated that the collision was caused by the wrongful act and default of both Captain McGibney, Master of the *European Gateway*, and Captain Bolton, Master of the *Speedlink Vanguard*, in the navigation of their respective vessels with Captain McGibney being censured for his actions and Captain Bolton being admonished.

Coinciding with the time of Sealink's financial difficulties DFDS had, by the middle of December 1982, also run into difficulties. Their take-over boom had since gone to bust as a result of having over extended themselves in acquiring both Prinz Line and Tor Line in so short a space of time. Also their plight was made all the worse throughout 1982 when their subsidiary company, Scandinavian World Cruises operating in America between the Bahamas and Florida and New York, suffered enormous losses of Dkr 200m. Cutbacks became inevitable and to help raise cash the *Dana Anglia* was sold to Dansk Investering Fond (Difko) for £22m and then leased back for a period of ten years with an option to re-purchase after five years.

DFDS's acquisition of Prinz Line had led to better marketing and some improvements on board the two ships with the result that carryings on the Hamburg service had markedly increased throughout 1982. However there had been no similar improvement on the Bremerhaven service and thus with insufficient traffic to fully support both routes into Germany it was decided that the Bremerhaven route would close. The last sailing left Parkeston Quay on 17th December 1982 with the departure of the *Prinz Oberon* though in keeping with the gloomy circumstances she was nine hours late in leaving due to bad weather and only got away around midnight. Thus far Prinz Line had lost DFDS close on Dm10m.

To compensate for the route's closure DFDS improved the freight service from Hamburg to twice a week principally using the *Stafford* and *Dana Futura* though both ships were not exclusive to this route. For a short while in 1983 the *Stafford* also sailed from Bremerhaven as had the *Dana Futura* in October 1982 but in common with many of the DFDS freight ships they operated on a multi port schedule between Denmark, Germany and the UK and thus their appearance on the route could be somewhat erratic. However the Hamburg freight run saw a core timetable for 1983 based around the *Stafford* departing Parkeston Quay on a Sunday and arriving back on a Wednesday with the *Dana Futura* departing on a Thursday and arriving back on a Saturday. Departures from Hamburg were at 18.00, crossing times were 24 hours and the ships were worked on at Parkeston Quay overnight in time for an early morning departure. In between these Hamburg sailings the two ships usually operated a freight service to and from Esbjerg or from there to other UK ports such as Newcastle.

	Stafford	*Dana Futura*
Dep. P. Quay	Sunday	Thursday
Arr. Hamburg	Tuesday	Friday
Dep. Hamburg	Tuesday	Friday
Arr. P. Quay	Wednesday	Saturday

In June 1983 the Sunday sailings were alternately operated by the *Tor Finlandia* and the *Fichtelberg* both of which were then on charter to Tor Line.

Following the closure of the Bremerhaven route the *Prinz Oberon* was laid up in Copenhagen but she returned to Parkeston Quay when SMZ chartered her between 11th February and 11th March 1983, as cover for when the *Prinses Beatrix* went away on overhaul, and then again between 12th March and 10th June when chartered by Sealink as cover for a mechanically ailing *St. George*.

March 15th 1983 marked the centenary of Parkeston Quay and the day was commemorated by a visit from Sir Peter Parker, Chairman of the British Railways Board and Mr. Len Merryweather, Managing Director of Sealink UK Ltd.. After a tour of the port conducted by Mr Colin Crawford, Shipping and Port Manager since 1979, a lunch was provided for over 200 guests on board the *Prinz Oberon*. A number of speeches were made that included those by Mr. Feke Hendrikse, General Manager of SMZ and Mr. Jim Davis, Chairman of DFDS (UK) Ltd. Also present were four former Shipping and Port Managers - Mr. Stanley Claydon (1955-57), Mr. Tom Tulloch (1957-70), Mr.

Five Shipping and Port Managers were present at the celebrations held to mark the centenary of Parkeston Quay - 15th March 1983. from left to right: Mr. J. Bernard Taylor, 1st July 1970 to 31st July 1978; Mr Stanley Claydon, 1st January 1955 to 30th November 1957; Mr Colin Crawford, February 1979 to 25th June 1989; Mr Tom Tulloch, 1st December 1957 to 30th June 1970; Mr Bill Henderson, 1st August 1978 to February 1979. (Stephen Brown collection)

Demolition of the old Continental Offices that dated back to the very origins of P. Quay - 15th March 1983. (Stephen Brown)

Bernard Taylor (1970-78) and Mr. Bill Henderson (1978). Sir Peter also opened a new Continental Travel centre on the station platform and unveiled a commemorative plaque supplied by the local Harwich Society.

When DFDS took over Tor Line's passenger business in 1981 they continued to operate the *Tor Britannia* and *Tor Scandinavia* from Gothenburg to Felixstowe and Amsterdam but in 1983 they changed from using Felixstowe as their passenger terminal in favour of the East Portal berth at Parkeston Quay. A few preparatory works were made to the berth in anticipation of the change that included dredging it out so that its depth of water was increased from 21 feet to 26 feet. One advantage to DFDS's move was that passengers requiring London would now have a direct 83 minute journey by rail instead of the existing and much longer journey by coach from Felixstowe. One disadvantage was that the extra length of the Tor vessels would compromise workings at the adjacent Container Terminal and require any ship being worked there to move eastwards by around 150 feet. Although this effectively reduced the terminal to working just one ship at a time the inconvenience was only for the few hours of the Tor ship's turn round time.

The first vessel to cross over the river was the *Tor Scandinavia* whose inaugural arrival at Parkeston Quay was on 1st April 1983. In contrast to the *Tor Britannia*, whose hull was adorned with DFDS Seaways, the *Tor Scandinavia*'s was showing DFDS Tor Line when she arrived from Gothenburg's Skandiahamnen with 1,330 passengers on board, the first of an anticipated 300,000 passengers a year. The day was a Good Friday and a record 13,000 passengers passed through what looked to be more of a port belonging to DFDS rather than one owned by Sealink as also alongside were DFDS's *Dana Regina* from Esbjerg, the *Prinz Hamlet* from Hamburg and the *Prinz Oberon* on charter to the Hook of Holland service.

The service to Sweden ran three times a week:

Dep. Gothenburg	11.00 (Thurs)	17.00 (Sat)	18.30 (Sun)
Arr. P. Quay	10.30 (Fri)	16.00 (Sun)	18.00 (Mon)
Dep. P. Quay	13.30 (Fri)	19.00 (Sun)	21.00 (Mon)
Arr. Gothenburg	14.00 (Sat)	19.30 (Mon)	22.00 (Tues)

At a fraction under 600 feet long the two Tor ships were significantly longer than most other ferries yet barely any wider as they were built to pass through the 86 feet wide locks at Immingham. Their distinctive long and sleek profiles and immensely powerful engines gave them a service speed of 24½ knots with sufficient in reserve, though at exorbitant cost, to attain up to 26 knots if called upon to make up for lost time. Neither ship had any access through the bow and so the loading and unloading of the freight decks was over the stern only via two large double width doors of which only one at any time could engage with the portal berths at Parkeston Quay.

Despite their extra length their carrying capacity of 1,357 passengers and 440 cars was on a par with that of the *Dana Anglia*. On Deck 7 there was the Mermaid Lounge and bar amidships along with two cinemas and three conference rooms. At the aft end was a night club and disco café. This deck also had a number of cabins made up of 29 three or four berth insides, 14 single or twin berth outsides plus 12 that were top class Commodore or De-luxe grade. Deck 6 contained a block of cabins forward consisting of 30 single or

The *Tor Scandinavia* inaugurating the transfer from Felixstowe to P. Quay of DFDS's passenger service to Gothenburg - 1st April 1983. (Stephen Brown)

twin berth outsides and 29 three or four berth insides, a cafeteria, two conference rooms amidships and the Tivoli a la carte restaurant aft. Deck 5 housed a full deck of three or four berth cabins, 113 outside and 55 inside, along with a shopping centre and information desk. Below were two freight decks whilst further down on Deck 2 were 176 couchettes or economy class berths with the lowest deck, Deck 1, containing a sauna. In total there were 845 berths in 282 cabins of which 169 were outsides, this being in contrast to the comparatively cramped *Dana Anglia* where the majority of cabins were inside.

The arrival of the *Tor Scandinavia* came only a few days after the demolition of the quay's original Continental Offices, the buildings having just managed to survive for a full century.

The charter of the *Prinz Oberon* ended with the arrival of Sealink's 'Big One', a ship the Company had been preparing for since the spring of 1982. The ship they had chosen was the *Princessan Birgitta*. She was one of two ships originally ordered by Sweden's Sessan Line in January 1979 at a time when routes within southern Scandinavia were under threat from the aforementioned overcapacity of new builds and intense competition not least of which being that between Sessan Line and Stena Line on the route between Gothenburg and Frederikshavn in Denmark.

Both these companies had ordered new sister ships but the French yard building for Stena Line were unable to deliver their ships before the expected arrival of those being built for Sessan Line. As a means to protecting their own operations Stena Line made a bid to buy out Sessan Line and a successful outcome was announced on 15th December 1980. By then the first Sessan Line ship, the *Kronprinsessan Victoria*, had already been launched, in October 1980, and following her completion in April 1981 she was put into service as planned by a newly merged Stena Sessan Line.

The second ship was launched as *GV 909*, ie without a name, on 22nd May 1981 and work on her was then halted to allow time for Stena's own new ships to arrive first. Stena Line then bought the vessel directly from her builders, the Gotaverken Arendal yard, for £30m in May 1982 just prior to her final completion on 19th May as the *Princessan Birgitta*. She too was put on the Gothenburg to Frederikshavn service as planned, her first sailing being on 3rd June 1982. She remained on the route until the first of the French built Stena Line ferries arrived in February 1983 following which she was chartered to Sealink on 28th February 1983. She then returned to her builders in Gothenburg for her cabin accommodation to be increased from 616 berths to 1,061 in readiness for her new role as a night ferry to the Hook of Holland.

Sealink's 'big-one' first arrived at Parkeston Quay's West Portal berth on 6th June 1983 still under the Swedish flag but now re-named the *St. Nicholas*. The name was chosen via a 'Name-a-Liner' competition run by the BBC children's programme 'Get Set' and was suitably appropriate in being both the name of the parish church in Harwich and the Dutch 'Santa Claus'.

Her maiden voyage was to the Hook of Holland on 10th June 1983. In view of the ongoing plans to privatise Sealink her external appearance was left little changed from that of her time with her owners, Stena Line, with only the Stena emblem having been removed from the funnel and a small 'Sealink' painted in blue on her hull. She remained under the Swedish flag until 15th June when she was officially named at Parkeston Quay by Mrs. Henderson, the wife of Sealink's Deputy Managing Director. The ceremony was followed by a short cruise along the coast and thereafter she was transferred to the ownership of Hill Samuel Trading and put under the British flag.

The savings sought by Sealink in order to make the Hook of Holland route viable had now risen to £1.3m. However hopes were high that the *St. Nicholas*, offering mini cruise liner standards of service, would put the route back into profit even when being chartered at a rate of £27,000 per day.

When originally built the *St. Nicholas* was a one class ship but she arrived at Parkeston Quay with her cabins re-assigned to either First or Second class. The only concession made towards any other kind of class demarcation was at the aft end where a First class Lounge on Deck 8 and a First Class cocktail bar on Deck 7 led off from her most impressive feature on board, that of a 500 seat tiered or terraced bar that overlooked a night club, stage and disco dance floor. A first on board a ship on this route was the novel attraction of a self service Smorgasbord buffer which was available in the 311 seat Compass a la carte restaurant on Deck 8 adjacent to the coffee shop where there were seats for 248. The more usual attractions of a duty free supermarket, boutique, gift

Above and below: 'Sealink's Big One'. The *St. Nicholas*, still registered in Gothenburg, lies alongside the quay prior to entering service on the Hook of Holland route - 7th June 1983. (Stephen Brown)

The morning of the first commercial arrival of the St. Nicholas from the Hook of Holland - 11th June 1983. (Stephen Brown)

shop and two bars were located below on Deck 7.

All the First class cabins had either one or two berths, were all en-suite, of which 166 were located forward on Decks 7 and 8. Each of these decks also had 2 four berth Staterooms and 6 two or four berth De-luxe cabins overlooking the bow. For those travelling Second class there were 220 two berth en-suite cabins located throughout Decks 5 and 6 with Deck 6 housing a further 34 cabins for First Class use. At the forward end on Deck 2, below the car deck, were 43 four berth and 22 two berth Second class economy cabins, all without private facilities. Two two berth Second class cabins were provided on Deck 7 for disabled passengers. In total the St. Nicholas could carry 2,100 passengers and her 503 cabins offered 401 berths in First class and 660 in Second class. In addition there were 635 reclining seats. Her car decks had space for 460 cars or 16 cars and 52 x 15 metre lorries. At 17,043 grt she was undoubtedly the port's 'big one'.

Meanwhile the St. Edmund had been employed as a troop carrier making round trip voyages between the Falklands and Ascension. On 9th February 1983 she left the Falklands for a refit back in Britain and when in Ascension on 16th February she was sold by Sealink to the Ministry of Defence for £7.75m. She arrived at Tyne Shiprepairers in Wallsend on 28th February and there Captain Jarvis was presented with a plaque from Vice

The mud dredger Landguard in action off the east end. Beyond the dolphin lies the old No. 6 pontoon berth - 8th June 1983. (Derek Genzel collection)

Admiral Squires which read *'Presented by the Admiralty Board in recognition of the role played by MV St Edmund in the Falkland Islands Operation 1982'*, VA Squires adding 'We couldn't have done the job without you'. This sentiment contrasted greatly with events at Harwich where she had failed to call in en route to Wallsend over fears that her crew might have gone on strike in response to their jobs not being needed there. Many of the other returning ships that made up the nation's Task Force were treated to joyous civic receptions but the *St. Edmund* was never to return to Harwich and as such she was denied any such welcome home celebration. Whilst still in dock she was boarded by the Royal Navy on 1 April and re-named *H.M.S. Keren* in a dispute with the NUS over crew rates. A few days later she reverted to *m.v. Keren* and put into service ferrying troops between Ascension and the Falkland Islands.

The arrival of the *St. Nicholas* also meant the end of the *St. George* which had been standing in for the long absent *St. Edmund* though with increasing degrees of difficulty due to a series of mechanical failures. The *St. George* made her final sailing from the Hook of Holland on 5th June 1983 and was then laid up on the buoys. From there she sailed on 20th September for repairs at Immingham before going on to Falmouth for a further lay up. She was later sold to Ventouris Line of Greece in 1984 and re-named *Patra Express*.

Throughout 1983 the Esbjerg service had remained in the hands of the *Dana Anglia* and *Dana Regina* operating a daily service whilst the one to Hamburg, utilising the *Prinz Hamlet*, was still operating a service on alternate days except during the off peak periods when, as with the other DFDS routes, the service was reduced to three times a week. Their respective sailing times were:

Dep. Esbjerg	17.30	Dep. Hamburg	15.30
Arr. P. Quay	11.30	Arr. P. Quay	11.00
Dep. P. Quay	16.30	Dep. P. Quay	15.00
Arr. Esbjerg	13.30	Arr. Hamburg	12.00

On 2nd October 1983 the *Dana Regina* made her final sailing from Parkeston Quay to Esbjerg. She was then transferred to DFDS's route between Copenhagen and Oslo as from 12th October thus breaking a 'tradition' whereby passenger vessels displaced from Parkeston Quay ended up in Newcastle. The timing of the *Dana Regina*'s departure from Parkeston Quay coincided with DFDS having closed their weekly Gothenburg to Amsterdam service on 1st October and this enabled the under utilised *Tor Scandinavia* and *Tor Britannia* to move onto the Esbjerg route in lieu of the *Dana Regina*. Each Tor ship undertook alternate sailings with a change of roster each Sunday, these being in addition to their normal Gothenburg duties. From Parkeston Quay the Esbjerg service was daily except Monday with the *Dana Anglia* departing on Tuesday, Thursday and Saturday and one of the Tor vessels on Sunday, Wednesday and Friday.

The changes were in part prompted by another disastrous performance from DFDS's Scandinavian Cruise Lines that lost a further Dkr321m in 1983. This led to the closure of the New York operation and the transfer of the lead vessel, the *Scandinavia*, onto the Copenhagen to Oslo route in December that year. DFDS then sold both the *Dana Futura* and *Tor Scandinavia* to Difko of Esbjerg on 19th December 1983 for £5.7m and £18.5m respectively with both being leased back on a 15 year bareboat charter with an option to purchase after five years.

At Parkeston Quay DFDS achieved some further savings via some inventive re-scheduling of services and by utilising the superior speed of the two Tor ships it was made possible throughout 1984 for the Company to fully operate both the Esbjerg and Gothenburg routes using just the *Dana Anglia*, *Tor Britannia* and *Tor Scandinavia*.

During the peak season months of early June to the middle of August, and wholly dependent upon the Tor ships being able to make the 342 n. mile crossing to Esbjerg in just 15 hours, it was possible for these three ships to provide a daily service to Esbjerg and an every second day service to Gothenburg. Thus one of the Tor ships would arrive at Parkeston Quay from Esbjerg at 08.30 one day, 4 hours earlier than the *Dana Anglia* could manage, and sail out at 11.30 for Gothenburg. In doing so she would pass her sister arriving from Gothenburg which would then sail out to Esbjerg that evening. In between times the *Dana Anglia* made her regular sailings to Esbjerg as did the *Prinz Hamlet* to Hamburg.

In order to handle Tor Line's freight traffic transferring across from Felixstowe a much larger scheme of works was required at Parkeston Quay than merely dredging out a berth. Consequently, Sealink

The *Landguard* in a piece of innovative advertising. (Stephen Brown collection)

Offloading rail wagons from the train ferry *Speedlink Vanguard* at Harwich - 20th August 1983. (Stephen Brown)

The container ship *Sea Freightliner I* being worked on at Parkeston Quay - 14th September 1983. (Stephen Brown)

Chartered by SMZ the *Zeeland* arrives at Parkeston Quay in the days when it was still possible to approach a berth with the bow visor raised - 13th April 1984. (Stephen Brown)

During the summer of 1984 the *Prinz Oberon* linked Parkeston Quay with Cuxhaven. She is seen here arriving past the Bremerhaven ferry, *Prinz Hamlet*, which is tied up alongside the West Portal. (Stephen Gooch)

Harbours Ltd., in agreement with Sealink UK Ltd. and British Rail Investments Ltd., submitted plans to the Secretary of State for authorisation under Section 9 of the Harbours Act 1964 to sheet pile and reclaim land for a new linkspan berth and standage area for primary use by Tor Line. Approval for a £5m scheme, which was upstream of the linkspan built in 1980, was granted by September 1983. The agreed timetable for Tor Line moving out of Felixstowe had been that their passenger service should vacate Felixstowe by the end of March 1983, which they had already done so, but the freight traffic could stay on until this new berth at Parkeston Quay was ready.

By February 1984 the required work was well under way at the quay's west end, alongside No. 8 Berth, and when fully completed the quay's frontage then consisted of a Container Terminal and four multi purpose ro-ro berths for both passenger and feight ships. The East Portal was now designated as No.1 Berth able to accommodate a ship up to 150 metres long and with a breadth of 22 metres, the West Portal became No. 2 Berth for ships up to 140m x 22m, the 1980 Linkspan was No. 3 Berth, for ships 180m x 25m whilst this latest linkspan became No. 4 Berth, 180m x 30m. No's.1, 2 and 3 Berths had a maximum depth of water of 8 metres whilst No.4 Berth's maximum depth was 5.5 metres.

In early 1984 British Rail spent £32,500 locating a new ticket and parcels office on the upper level of the passenger terminal. It was opened on 12th June by the local MP, Sir Julian Ridsdale, and replaced the old platform level office on Platform 1. This old office was refurbished and taken over by port staff who had previously been housed in a series of portakabins laid out to the south of the railway lines adjacent to the east gates crossing. These were originally built to house a number of shipping agents and were locally referred to as the 'rabbit hutches'.

On 8th March 1984 the *St. Nicholas* went to Dunkirk for her first overhaul from where she emerged in the new colours of Sealink UK Ltd prior to the Company's looming privatisation. On 27th March she went on show at Dover displaying a livery designed by H & P Associates who intended that the symbol of a double looping yellow band *'conveys authority and professionalism through its association with the badge of a naval officer'* and *'use of an italicised letter form for the Sealink name combined with a strong horizontal stripe gives the impression of power and purposeful direction'*. The *St. Nicholas* then sailed on to Parkeston Quay where she arrived later that evening.

Whilst the *St. Nicholas* was away she had been covered by the *Koningin Juliana* which was soon to leave the route in favour of a larger ship. As a temporary arrangement the Larvik - Frederikshavnferjen (Larvik Line) vessel, *Peter Wessel,* a ship with a greater capacity for freight, was taken over by SMZ at the end of March on a two year charter. Having re-named her *Zeeland* this 6,801 grt vessel, which had herself been displaced the previous month by a larger new build for Larvik Line's service between Norway and Denmark, entered service from the Hook of Holland on 2nd April 1984 initially in partnership with the *Koningin Juliana*. When the *Koningin Juliana* made her last trip from Parkeston Quay on 7th April the *Zeeland* then sailed nightly, except Sunday, alongside the *Prinses Beatrix* which had returned from having been away on her own refit.

Facility wise the 1,500 passenger capacity *Zeeland* was a poor partner for the *Prinses Beatrix*. All of her public rooms were on the one deck, the Salon Deck, and here there was a Second class café, bar and lounge forward, a First class restaurant amidship and a First class bar and lounge at the aft end. Below lay the Cabin Deck which housed 119 cabins, 54 couchettes and a duty free shop. On the Lower Deck aft, below the car decks, were a further 16 cabins whilst on the Boat Deck aft there were 24 economy cabins. Although the *Zeeland*'s total of 544 cabin berths was roughly the same as on the *Prinses Beatrix* she had a far larger proportion of multiple occupancy cabins with none that were originally built as singles. The one advantage of introducing the *Zeeland* to the Hook route was her ability to carry up to 300 cars. This was an increase of a third over the outgoing *Koningin Juliana* and more evenly matched that of the *Prinses Beatrix*.

The outgoing *Koningin Juliana* was laid up in Rotterdam's Waalhaven for several months before being sold in December 1984 for conversion to an exhibition ship and the promotion of Dutch goods abroad. Having been re-named *Holland Trade Ship* the venture collapsed due to financial problems and the ship was moved to Amsterdam in February 1985. She was then sold in October to the Italian company Navarma for service between Naples and Sardinia. Re-named *Moby Prince* she took up her new role in December 1985.

A surprise visitor during the summer of 1984 was a returning *Prins Oberon* running additional services for DFDS. Between 23rd June and 19th August she sailed twice a week to Cuxhaven, departing Parkeston Quay on Sunday and Tuesday as well as making a weekly sailing on a Thursday to Gothenburg.

Throughout 1984 the DFDS routes out of Parkeston Quay to Gothenburg, Esbjerg, Hamburg and Cuxhaven provided a common tariff of standard fares for motorists. Outside of high season, which ran from 13th July to 12th August, cars up to 6 metres long and accompanied by either 1, 2 or 3 adults were charged £31 or free if accompanied by 4 adults. Within high season the charge of £31 was levied even with 4 adults. The adult fare to Gothenburg started from £42, Esbjerg from £35, Hamburg from £26 and Cuxhaven from £34. All prices were for single journeys and included a couchette on all routes except to Gothenburg which included a berth in an economy cabin. Children under 16 were half price. The earlier mentioned cheapest fare of £39 back in 1967 for a high season family plus car return to Esbjerg was now £272 with comparable fares to Gothenburg being £314, Hamburg £218 and Cuxhaven £266. Sealink's Hook of Holland route was around £228 whilst Fred Olsen's seasonal service to Kristiansand was a much more expensive £330. The Norwegian service charged a relatively modest £23 for a car if accompanied by up to 3 adults or free if accompanied by 4 adults but the cheapest adult fare was £55 and only included a sleeper or reclining seat. However all fares were still rising at a slightly slower rate than wages, the average now being £124 a week, and this was helping to drive the growth in passenger ferry usage. Year round offers such as mini-trip deals and motorist packages brought prices down to ever more affordable levels and the figures for people travelling confirmed Parkeston Quay's popularity as Britain's second busiest passenger port.

In November 1984 DFDS sold the *Stafford* and increasingly utilised the *Dana Futura* on routes elsewhere. Their places on the freight run between Parkeston Quay and Hamburg were taken over by medium sized freight ships on charter such as the *Mercandian Governor* and the *Linnea* and now by the *Gabriele Wehr* and the *Romira*.

By 1984 the process of privatising Sealink had come down to two main contenders. One was 'The Sealink Consortium' made up of a Sealink UK Ltd management team partnered by the National Freight Consortium, James Fisher & Sons Ltd, Charterhouse J. Rothschild and Globe Investment Trust. It was headed by the Sealink Managing Director, Mr Len Merryweather.

The other was Sea Containers Ltd., a Bermuda based company with assets of £600 million, headed by Mr. James B. Sherwood. Its principal activity was in the leasing of ships and containers and in 1983 the company had made a profit of £30m.. Its associate company, Seaco Inc., had already bought a number of British Transport Hotels from British Rail in 1983.

Aerial view of Parkeston Quay looking east towards Bathside Bay and Harwich. In the lower left is the new No. 4 Berth located alongside the site of a recently demolished No. 4 Shed – 28th May 1985. (Stephen Brown)

Sea Freightliner I under the cranes at the container terminal - 28th May 1985. (Stephen Brown)

The *Speedlink Vanguard* lies in her berth at the Harwich train ferry terminal - 28th May 1985. (Stephen Brown)

Construction of the new Leibher ship to shore crane at the container terminal beneath which lies a strike bound *Sea Freightliner I* - 23rd January 1986. (Stephen Brown)

The spoils eventually went to Sea Containers Ltd. who acquired the Sealink business on 18th July 1984 for £66m. The deal was completed on 30th July and in future Sealink ships would trade as Sealink British Ferries owned within a wholly owned subsidiary of Sea Containers Ltd known as British Ferries Ltd. The price paid was viewed as somewhat low for the purchase of a business that included 37 ships and 10 harbours and it soon led to it being dubbed the sale, or steal, of the century. Even Mr. Sherwood admitted that the assets were worth two to three times more than the figure he paid but within the balance sheets all was not as generous as first appeared.

Although the asset value of the 37 ships alone was given to be £170m some £80m of that was leased and despite Sealink UK Ltd's Annual Report for the year ending 31st December 1983 having shown a gross income of £264.8m and a gross operating surplus, ie before interest and taxes, of £12.8m the Government had instead judged that during the previous five years Sealink's ships had been losing an average of £2.5m a year and that the £100m British Rail had spent on Sealink could arguably have been better spent instead on Britain's railways. Accordingly the Government viewed the £66m it received as having been a good price which, after expenses, all went back to British Rail. Two years later the Harwich M.P., Sir Julian Ridsdale, was to state that Sea Containers had paid far too high a price for Sealink and that the next offer had been as low as single figures.

The average number of employees employed by Sealink UK Ltd in 1983 was 9,633 and their total remuneration was £86.7m. Despite Sea Containers having to contend with what they regarded as being this highly unionised labour force 'lacking the flexibility to adapt quickly to a changing business climate' and a company 'performing a host of services for the railways at a loss because it has been ordered to do so', they considered themselves to have got their hands on some of the best ferry routes in the country. If they were restructured with the right ships then those loss making routes had the potential to make a good profit and if decision making was restructured and delegated down to port level then so much the better again. Although the Company was to be slimmed down the intention was for the same number of people to be on the payroll in five years time but generating three times the revenue.

Since 1983 the *Speedlink Vanguard* was sailing 6 days a week, departing Harwich at 02.00 Monday to Saturday, and was supplemented 4 days a week by the *Cambridge Ferry* sailing at 19.30 Tuesday to Friday. In May 1984 traffic levels were still increasing and there existed the possibility that one of the *Speedlink Vanguard*'s sister ships might be similarly converted for use at Harwich. In October 1984 when BR were in negotiations over renewing contracts with Dunkirk there were rumours that all train ferry traffic might be moving via Harwich but as the year ended with a downturn in the number of wagons handled at Harwich that idea soon went away.

By January 1985 the Sea Containers plan for Parkeston Quay had already been unveiled. At the time Harwich Harbour Board were spending £10m on deepening its 6 mile long main entrance channel and the resultant 1.5 million cubic metres of dredged sand and gravel were being pumped into an area east of Parkeston Quay in order to reclaim an initial 90 acres of ground. This was viewed as work having started on the long awaited infilling of Bathside Bay in the hope of converting it into the major deep sea container port that would rival Felixstowe. The project was estimated at costing £90m in order to provide 2,000 feet of quay for new deep sea berths, with a minimum depth of water of 37 feet, plus five ro-ro berths at its eastern end.

A second stage to reclaim and develop up to 520 acres of ground would provide for container standage, trailer parks, warehousing and offices as well as make possible the construction of a bypass for Dovercourt that would help take away the heavy road traffic then heading for the docks at Harwich Navyard. The expectation was that work on the initial acreage adjacent to Parkeston Quay would be completed by early 1988 and the bypass by 1990. Pending completion of the first container berth on this reclaimed land the existing No. 4 ro-ro berth would be converted into a deep sea container berth by further dredging it out, sheet piling the quay face and 'pulling down the big shed on the quay', ie No. 4 Shed. Two container gantries supplied by Sea Containers would be installed on the quay with the new facility up and running by the middle of the 1985.

On the Hook of Holland route losses were now much lower since the arrival of the *St. Nicholas* and a freight only ship would arrive on the route if suitable manning levels were agreed. Also new would be a Sealink British Ferries service from Parkeston Quay to Scandinavia using a British flagged vessel. The container service was to see only one ship sailing regularly to Zeebrugge whilst the other made two trips a week to Rotterdam plus one or two others to Zeebrugge. Space on the Rotterdam route would be chartered out in full with a longer term proposal that Freightliners would appoint an agent in Rotterdam to start a new service. Manning levels on the container ships were to be reduced with any crew displaced being transferred to the new Hook of Holland freight ship. The train ferry service at Harwich was safe until at least the end of 1986 though afterwards it was now presumed that the service would eventually transfer to Dover. Neither the container ships or the train ferries were to be re-branded in the new corporate colours of Sealink British Ferries as they each remained on contract to British Rail. An earlier idea of turning Parkeston Quay into the main UK container base for Sea Containers Ltd and using it for the repair and refurbishing of containers had been dropped but not before a huge container ship had already dumped hundreds of broken or damaged containers on the quayside that lay around for months.

Notwithstanding any of Sea Containers plans there had been a welcome return to Parkeston Quay of the service to Norway last seen in 1981. The Fred Olsen vessel *Bolero* re-opened the route from Kristiansand in the summer of 1984 from 19th June until 30th August. Departures from Parkeston Quay were at 16.00 each Wednesday, the first being on 20th June.

Although built for Fred Olsen in 1972 the first sailings of the 14,264 grt *Bolero* had actually been between Bremerhaven, Hamburg and Harwich Navyard whilst on charter to Prins Line in February 1973. Thereafter her early days were spent sailing between Maine and Nova Scotia at a time when she was thought too luxurious for the role of a ferry between the ports of Portland and Yarmouth. Such niceties as wall to wall carpeting, air conditioning and cabins 'with showers where the water temperature was individually thermostatically controlled' were considered the height of luxury along with interiors decorated with expensive pieces of artwork. The

Above: Parkeston West signal box - 23rd January 1986. (Stephen Brown)
Below: Parkeston West signal box partly demolished - 7th March 1986. (Stephen Brown)

public spaces consisted of a bar and lounge area on A Deck supplemented by a Lido bar and sun deck aft whilst on B Deck there was the main restaurant, a cafeteria and shopping centre. Following a short period with Stena Line as their *Scandinavica* she returned to Fred Olsen in 1981 as the *Bolero* and by now could carry 1,600 passengers and 410 cars with 620 cabin berths, 204 reclining seats and 48 couchette berths. The cabins had either two, three or four berths and most were en-suite. Her three lounges and two bars were supplemented by a restaurant that offered either a Norwegian buffet or a table d'hote service.

For 1985 the brochures suggested the reappearance of the *Bolero* after Fred Olsen had announced her as having been a remarkable success. However it was a ship new to the North Sea that resumed the service in June 1985 with the *Bolero* having been chartered out to the Baltic company of Vaasanlaivat for service between Sundsvall in Sweden and Vaasa in Finland.

The new ship was a level above the *Bolero* having originally been launched as the 13,879 grt *Viking Song* for Viking Line's prestigious Baltic capitals route between Stockholm and Helsinki. She was bought by Fred Olsen for £30m, given a £2.5m refit in Hamburg and re-named *Braemar* prior to entering service between Kristiansand and Hirtshals. In and amongst a regular pattern of sailings between these two ports she made a once a week 'detour' directly from Kristiansand's Europakaien to Parkeston Quay where she arrived each Wednesday at 13.30 and departed at 16.00. Her first arrival at Parkeston Quay was on 12th June 1985. On board were nearly 900 passengers and she left with roughly the same number.

In a break with tradition the *Braemar* was given an all over white hull rather than a grey hull and white superstructure and was adorned with buff funnels and a buff stripe on two levels along her upper hull. Internally she was designed with all her public rooms aft and all the cabins forward, the majority of which took up the forward half of Decks 6 and 7 and the middle section of Deck 1 which was below the Car Deck. All cabins throughout were either two or four berth en-suites and housed a total of 1,256 berths with the highest graded being in three forward facing De-luxe cabins on Deck 6 and five Comfort cabins on Deck 7.

The public rooms were built up vertically at the aft end throughout Decks 6 to 9. On Deck 6 was the Reception counter, a centrally located Tax Free shopping centre, a full width Brasserie, snack bar and the Black Watch and Black Prince Lounges. Above, on Deck 7, was an orchestra based music and dance floor, a bar and two restaurants these being the gourmet Bali a la-carte on the port side and the Restaurant Bandeirante on the starboard side which offered a traditional Norwegian self service buffet. Decks 8 and 9 contained a two deck atrium and conservatory styled Tropic Garden lounge which doubled up as a disco in the evening. Here were two further bars whilst outside on Deck 9, forward of the twin funnels, was an open air terraced seating area known as the Romantic Circle. A Friskotek was provided on Deck 1, this being a fitness centre complete with saunas, solarium, a whirlpool, swimming pool and gymnasium.

Decks 2, 3, 4 and 5 housed two full length freight decks apart from a few cabins at the forward end of Decks 4 and 5. In total the car decks could hold up to 486 cars or 56 trailers with such a huge facility for freight being unique on a service between the UK and Norway. Although an emphasis was placed on trying to fill the car decks foot passengers were connected with both Oslo and London by rail, the latter via special boat trains to and from Parkeston Quay. During the *Braemar*'s 1985 summer season the times were:

Dep. Oslo (S) (train)	08.00 (Tuesday)
Arr. Kristiansand	12.55 (Tuesday)
Dep. Kristiansand	15.00 (Tuesday)
Arr. P. Quay	13.30 (Wednesday)
Dep. P. Quay	14.25 (Wednesday)
Arr. London (L.St)	15.45 (Wednesday)
Dep. London (L.St)	13.35 (Wednesday)
Arr. P. Quay	14.55 (Wednesday)
Dep. P. Quay	16.00 (Wednesday)
Arr. Kristiansand	16.30 (Thursday)
Dep. Kristiansand	17.05 (Thursday)
Arr. Oslo (S) (train)	21.55 (Thursday)

At the end of her first season the Parkeston Quay to Kristiansand route was changed and the *Braemar* sailed instead to Hirtshals in Denmark and from there there was the opportunity of remaining on board and

A most unusual sight of smoke rings blowing up out of the *Zeeland* as she starts up her engines for a day boat trip to the Hook of Holland - 7th March 1986. (Stephen Brown)

sailing straight through to the Norwegian capital. This was the result of a timetable change on 5th September whereby the *Braemar* no longer sailed between Kristiansand and Hirtshals but instead sailed on a new route between Hirtshals and Oslo's Sorenga Quay. The 'detour' to Parkeston Quay would now be from Hirtshals with the Wednesday arrival at Parkeston Quay being changed to a Saturday, the first of which was on 7th September. A more significant change was that the service would now operate all year round rather than just seasonal. The arrival time was changed to 10.30 and the time of departure was now 17.00, or 16.00 in high summer. This new service to Norway was further accompanied by an extensive array of breaks, mini-cruises and winter holidays promoted by Fred Olsen had also opened a freight and agency office in Hamilton House on 1st July 1985. The new all year service as from September 1985 were:

Dep. Oslo	23.30 (Thursday)
Arr. Hirtshals	08.15 (Friday)
Dep. Hirtshals	10.30 (Friday)
Arr. P .Quay	10.30 (Saturday)
Dep. P. Quay	11.25 (Saturday)
Arr London (L.St)	12.45 (Saturday)
Dep. London (L.St)	14.32 (Saturday)
Arr. P. Quay	15.50 (Saturday)
Dep. P. Quay	17.00 (Saturday)
Arr. Hirtshals	20.00 (Sunday)
Dep. Hirtshals	22.30 (Sunday)
Arr. Oslo	07.30 (Monday)

This direct sea route to Oslo took a lot longer than via Kristiansand and from there taking the train and was probably the longest through ferry service of any route out of the UK. It was also an interesting experience not only for the novelty of two nights on board but also, at least to any British travellers, to note that amongst the first 'quayside personnel' to board the ship at Hirtshals on a Sunday evening were Danish butchers offering to sell meat products at prices far cheaper than they were in Norway. In the reverse direction the service offered Norwegians a 4 night mini-cruise experience which at times proved quite popular.

In future years, between 17th June and 21st August 1986 and 16th June and 20th August 1987, services to Norway were further boosted by the *Bolero* making an additional midweek sailing from Kristiansand to Parkeston Quay.

Dep. Kristiansand	14.45 (Tuesday)
Arr. P. Quay	13.30 (Wednesday)
Dep P. Quay	14.30 (Wednesday)
Arr London (L.St.)	15.43 (Wednesday)
Dep. London (L.St)	13.50 (Wednesday)
Arr. P. Quay	15.06 (Wednesday)
Dep P. Quay	16.00 (Wednesday)
Arr Kristiansand	16.30 (Thursday)

A continued growth in overall traffic was requiring ever more space for storage and concrete was fast taking over every spare piece of ground. By August 1985 a new trailer park was being built on the site of Parkeston Railway Football Club's ground in Hamilton Park, the work involving the digging up of the turf and then laying down a surface of hand laid block paving. This left the last remaining bit of greenery being that of the Parkeston BRSA Bowls Club who, in April 1986,

The *Tor Scandinavia* departing for Gothenburg - 7th March 1986. (Stephen Brown)

Testing the spreaders on the new Leibher crane - 7th March 1986. (Stephen Brown)

The *Tor Britannia* arriving from Gothenburg – 7th March 1986. (Stephen Brown)

The *Armorique* battling in blustery conditions to come alongside the East Portal berth after her day boat crossing from the Hook - 10th April 1986. (Stephen Brown)

A view of the upper deck of the *Speedlink Vanguard* as she lays up alongside the container terminal - 18th April 1986. (Stephen Brown)

The *Prinses Beatrix* is seen arriving at Parkeston Quay for the last time - 21st April 1986. (Stephen Brown)

were told to vacate their green after 60 years in existence. The site was likewise built over for a further extension to the new trailer park. The football club moved to a pitch in nearby Dovercourt whilst a new bowls ground was built close by BRSA club in Hamilton Street.

During the course of the first few months since having taken over Sealink James Sherwood had, in his own words, 'ruffled a few feathers' and was later to implement changes that more than ruffled feathers but rather killed the bird itself. In comparison to the latest breed of superferries arriving in northern Europe and the Baltic several of his newly acquired services were somewhat dowdy and his aim of upgrading them to a more luxurious state was most laudable. Unfortunately his early initiatives, such as on the Channel Island routes, resulted in fares to which the travelling public baulked at paying and this eventually led to the end of the islands' long established Sealink service. Although this and several other adverse consequences of 'feather ruffling' were largely self inflicted there were problems to come at Parkeston Quay and Harwich that were largely outside of his control and his earlier comments about the company slimming down were soon to become a local reality.

The main problem was that although Harwich, and in particular Parkeston Quay, had benefited greatly from the imaginative ideas and investments made by British Rail, i.e. the new container terminal, new linkspans and ro-ro facilities, that same almost over dependence on British Rail quickly led to a decline in fortunes once privatisation took place. The pressure was now on to reduce costs in all areas, especially regarding the container and train ferry services, as the existing financial arrangements were no longer acceptable. Costs that British Rail had borne whilst services were under their complete control were now considered far too expensive for them to pay to a private owner operating similar sailings and services under contract. The first casualty was the container terminal.

On 2nd December 1985 British Rail Freightliner announced that they would be terminating their contract with Sealink to run the Harwich to Zeebrugge service on 31st December 1985. The main reason given was that Freightliner wanted to consolidate their short sea services with their deep sea services at Felixstowe. Doing so would help reduce the number of trains they ran but operational costs were also a factor. The Sealink ships, once so pioneering at the time of their launch, were now, by international standards, over manned and uncompetitive. The two Sea Freightliner vessels employed a total of 92 staff consisting of 47 officers plus 45 seamen and sailed with a crew of 18 per ship. With competitors running newer ships with often just 10 crew per ship Freightliner were intent upon using two German flagged vessels from Comar Containerline and sailing six times a week to Zeebrugge from Felixstowe's new Trinity Terminal.

A protest sit-in on board *Sea Freightliner I* lasted from the date of BR's announcement until March 1986. After some 13 weeks it became the longest sit-in of its kind in British maritime history during which time the container terminal was entirely out of action. Proposals aimed mainly at retaining a single ship service to Rotterdam were thwarted by the way the shipping of containers had developed from when they were first started in 1968 by British Rail's Shipping & International Services (BR - SISD). Following the creation of Sealink UK Ltd the 'International Services' part of SISD was transferred to BR's European Rail Traffic Organisation (BR - ERTO). The Harwich to Zeebrugge container service was then transferred out of BR- ERTO into another BR subsidiary, Freightliners Ltd.. Upon notice of closure the idea of running an alternative service in competition was duly considered but ultimately deemed impossible because operators booked space through 'Intercontainer' to which BR's agent in the UK was now solely Freightliners Ltd.

Throughout the 1980s the BR contract had provided the Container Terminal with the bulk of its business that overall had remained at around the 100,000 level.

Year	1980	1981	1982	1983	1984	1985
Containers	102,761	115,828	92,514	103,547	93,096	96,000

Its ending saw the loss of a further 100 shore based jobs that reduced the total number of staff employed by Sealink at Harwich and Parkeston Quay from 1,400 to 1,200.

Both Sea Freightliners were laid up in the River Stour until 30th July 1986 when *Sea Freightliner I* was towed for a further lay up in the River Blackwater. The *Sea Freightliner II* followed likewise on 1st August and lay there until 26th September when she left the Blackwater for Tilbury. There she was loaded with empty containers and sailed three days later for Naples in Italy from where, on 8th October, she later left loaded with scrap pipe bound for Pakistan. Upon arrival at Karachi on 2nd January 1987 she was immediately beached in readiness for demolition. *Sea Freightliner I* left the River Blackwater on 9 February 1987 for Falmouth from where, loaded with stores, she also sailed to Naples. At the end of March, carrying electrical cables for China, she sailed first to Colombo and finally to Kaohsiung in Taiwan where she arrived on 4th May 1987 and was then scrapped.

The announcement by BR of their intention to terminate their contract coincided somewhat ironically with the arrival of a new container crane. With the *Sea Freightliner I* laid up alongside the quay the barge vessel *Hans Behren* arrived on 8th January 1986 to discharge the sections of a £1.7m Leibher ship to shore crane that had a lift capacity of 35 tons and could work faster than the two existing Transporter cranes on whose eastern side the new crane was constructed. On 7th March it was almost complete and was then undergoing testing. In addition a new 22,500 sq ft standage area made up of hand laid concrete blocks was located adjacent to the terminal on reclaimed land within Bathside Bay.

Meanwhile a new freight service had started in December 1985 between Parkeston Quay and Esbjerg operated by Stena Portlink Service, a collaboration within the southern North Sea between Stena Line and Tor Line AB. The service made use of the *Stena Gothica* but lasted only until early 1986.

The arrival of the *St. Nicholas* on the Hook of Holland route had led to a rapid growth in traffic and by the spring of 1984 SMZ had already proposed similar plans of their own in replacing two ships with just one. In late 1984 they placed an order with the yard of Van der Giessen-de-Noord for a £40 million super-ferry that was broadly based upon two ships recently delivered by Seebeck Werft (A.G. Weser) of Bremen for the German company TT-Line.

Prior to its expected delivery in April 1986 the *Prinses Beatrix* was sold to Brittany Ferries on 1st October 1985, re-registered in Caen and chartered

Above: The largest and the smallest! The *Koningin Beatrix*, having completed her 'flag day cruise', towers over the harbour workboat, the *Pinmill* - 21st April 1986. (Stephen Brown)

Below: The first commercial arrival of the *Koningin Beatrix* - 22nd April 1986. (Stephen Brown)

The Fred Olsen Lines vessel, *Braemar*, arriving at P. Quay from Oslo and Hirtshals - 26th April 1986. (Stephen Brown)

The two redundant container ships, *Sea Freightliner I* and *Sea Freightliner II*, were laid up in the River Stour - 27th May 1986. (Stephen Brown)

A very much under utilised container terminal. Tied up alongside is the mud dredger *Landguard* - 27th May 1986. (Stephen Brown)

back to sail across the North Sea under the French flag. The *Zeeland* made a final sailing from Parkeston Quay to the Hook of Holland on 25th March 1986 and was replaced by the 5,732 grt Brittany Ferries vessel *Armorique* which sailed day boat from the Hook of Holland on 26th May and night boat from Parkeston Quay up until 23rd April. The *Armorique* was quite a small ship by comparison and when in partnership with the *Prinses Beatrix* she only provided facilities for 700 passengers and 165 cars.

The new SMZ super-ferry required new facilities at the Hook of Holland and a £8.3m investment project saw the construction of a third ro-ro berth at the old Fruitwharf at the eastern end of the quay. The berth's ramp measured 42 metres long with a maximum width at the seaward end of 26 metres. It could cope with a tidal variation of 8.6 metres and was said to be the largest of its type in Europe. New gangways and a covered walkway, complete with a moving floor or travelator, connected the new 185 metre long berth with the customs hall and the railway station. Additional work went into creating new trailer parks on areas of reclaimed land with the fully completed project being finally opened on 1st April 1987.

In view of the scale of the works at the Hook of Holland it was no surprise that when the new ship arrived it was huge. She was launched on 9th November 1985 and named by Queen Beatrix of the Netherlands as the *Koningin Beatrix*. In terms of size she raised the level of 'big one' to a whole new level. At 31,189 grt and 530 feet long she was by far the largest ship anywhere on the North Sea and her all white hull only served to emphasis her bulk. Her design was perhaps the most angular of any passenger ship previously seen at Parkeston Quay with a very square forward superstructure that was likened by some to a floating block of flats. However her interior, able to carry 2,100 passengers, conveyed an air of luxury and comfort such that 'the competition is left behind for the next decade'.

Amidst advertising proclaiming 'from a Princess to a Queen' the *Koningin Beatrix* was to enter service displaying no reference to Sealink. Instead she had the words 'Hoek-Harwich' on her port side and 'Hook-Harwich' on her starboard side. Her buff coloured funnel was topped in black beneath which lay the Zeeland colours of blue, white and red arranged in narrow bands. With Royal approval she was to enter service with a large golden crown fitted on both sides of her funnel.

The *Koningin Beatrix* first arrived at Parkeston Quay for berthing trials on 13th March 1986 during which time her massive bow ran into the upper part of the West Portal berth causing extensive damage to its structure. The impact hardly broke the ship's paintwork but the berth was out of use to bow loading vessels for two weeks. She then re-appeared on 21st April for a 'flag day' visit and cruise along the coast which ended somewhat unceremoniously when she became stranded on the mud in mid river on her return to the quay and then having great difficulty in getting alongside due to strong winds. Next day, on 22nd April 1986, she successfully made her maiden voyage from the Hook of Holland and in so doing immediately displaced both the *Prinses Beatrix* and the *Armorique*.

The original plans for the *Koningin Beatrix* were for the single ended loading of cars and vehicles over three stern doors and then turning them round inside the ship so as to be ready for disembarking. Instead changes were made to the bow to incorporate butterfly type bow doors that opened and moved outwards through which a 14 metre long articulated bow ramp would emerge to engage the relevant linkspans. By such means the *Koningin Beatrix* had full ro-ro facilities and on her main freight deck, No 3 Deck, there were 1,000 lane metres of space that could hold either 265 cars or 76 trailers.

The ship was in some ways designed similar to Fred Olsen's *Braemar* inasmuch as the cabin accommodation was all located forward throughout Decks 4 to 9 and the public rooms located aft throughout Decks 6, 7 and 8. The after half of Decks 4 and 5 were given over to cars where a further 220 could be stowed whilst lower down on Deck 2 was the provision to stow trade cars. Passenger accommodation started on the lowest deck, Deck 1, with 108 couchettes and these were supplemented by the provision of 324 reclining seats throughout Decks 4 and 5. A total of 559 First and Second class cabins, all ensuite, contained 1,296 berths. These included 8 Luxury suites with tv, video and fridge, 61 De-luxe grade cabins and 2 cabins set aside for use by disabled passengers.

Deck 6 contained the information desk, a large duty free shopping centre, casino and a 350 seat Second class bar and lounge aft. From the lounge a staircase led up to the Coffee shop and a 261 seat self service Globetrotter restaurant on Deck 7. Here was featured a unique five metre diameter rotary carousel that was equipped with a variety of trays for dispensing both hot and cold food. By making one rotation per minute diners merely waited until the appearance of their required selection and then repeatedly helped themselves for a fixed price of £6.20. It was a novelty that in later years was removed. A more permanent feature was the 234 seat Rembrandt a la carte restaurant located amidship. The First class bar and lounge was located aft on Deck 8 with this deck also having 2 cinemas and 2 conference rooms. Deck 9 was the crew accommodation deck. At the extreme aft end the decks were tiered and the open spaces referred to as Sun Decks. Sailing times were:

by: *Kon. Beatrix*		*St. Nicholas*	
Dep. P. Quay	21.45	Dep. P. Quay	11.15
Arr. HvH	06.45	Arr. HvH	19.00
Dep. HvH	11.30	Dep. HvH	22.45
Arr. P. Quay	18.15	Arr. P. Quay	06.45

Foot passenger fares were:

	Single		Return	
Fares from Harwich	1st Class	2nd Class	1st Class	2nd Class
To Hook of Holland	£26.00	£20.00	£52.00	£40.00

Night boat accommodation started at £2.50 for a rest chair or £5.50 for a berth in a Second class economy cabin onboard the St. Nicholas up to £48.00 for a First class Stateroom onboard either ship. All cabins, except in economy grade, were en-suite and all were half price on the day boat with rest chairs being free. Cars cost between £20.00 and £48.00 depending on the season.

All cabins were en-suite, except economy grade, whilst on the day boat all were half price and rest chairs were free. Cars cost between £20.00 and £48.00 depending on the season.

The *Koningin Beatrix* was expected to boost carryings by around 50,000 passengers a year and coincident with preparations for her arrival had been the electrification of the Harwich branch railway line.

Fred Olsen Lines *Bolero* outward bound for Kristiansand - 6th August 1986. (Stephen Brown)

The new DFDS ferry *Hamburg* arriving at P. Quay for the first time - 5th April 1987. (Stephen Brown)

The 'prison ship' *Earl William* alongside the Harwich train ferry terminal - 12th May 1987. (Stephen Brown)

Above: Aerial view of P. Quay looking west with the initial attempts at infilling Bathside Bay seen adjacent to the container terminal. This reclaimed area was locally known as 'The Mud' - 3rd May 1988. (Stephen Brown)
Below left: The cruise ship *Argonaut* being brought alongside the container terminal in order to discharge her passengers - 9th July 1987. (Stephen Brown)
Below right: The *St. Nicholas,* in the East Portal berth, dwarfs over the original station buildings - 3rd May 1988. (Stephen Brown)
Bottom left: The *Tor Scandinavia* arriving at No. 3 Berth - 3rd May 1988. (Stephen Brown)
Bottom right: A versatile port. The *Autotransporter* car carrier departs past a Bell Line container ship whilst the passenger ferry *St. Nicholas* loads for her day boat trip to Holland - 3rd May 1988. (Stephen Brown)

PARKESTON QUAY UNDER RAILWAY OWNERSHIP

Top left: An outward bound *St. Nicholas* passing the paddle steamer *Waverley* which operated a one off passenger cruise from P. Quay to London. By way of a comparison the dimensions of the *Waverley* are broadly similar to those of the original paddle ships operated by the G.E.R. from Harwich - 28th September 1988. (Stephen Brown)
Top right: The *Earl Granville* seen covering for when the *St. Nicholas* went away for overhaul in 1989 - 10th January 1989. (Stephen Brown)
Above left: The *Bell Reliant* being worked on at the container terminal - 10th February 1989. (Stephen Brown)
Above right: An evening view of the container terminal with Railfreight's *Geranta* (ex - *Karen Oltmann*) and Bell Line's *Angela Jurgens* underneath the cranes - 30th March 1989. (Stephen Brown)
Below: The *Koningin Beatrix* inward bound from the Hook of Holland in Crown Line livery - 25th July 1989. (Stephen Brown)

HARWICH FERRIES

15th August 1989

15th August 1989

20th August 1989

24th August 1989

From a Queen to a Queen - The various stages of repainting the *Koningin Beatrix* following the acquisition of SMZ by Stena Line in June 1989. (Stephen Brown)

24th August 1989

The first electric hauled passenger train from London arrived at Parkeston Quay on 21st April, the day of the *Koningin Beatrix*'s 'flag day', having first had its locomotive named 'European Community' by the former Prime Minister, Edward Heath, in a ceremony held at Liverpool Street station. As from 12th May 1986 a fleet of 100 mph locos would then haul the boat trains from Parkeston Quay to London in just 68 minutes, a saving of 10 minutes on the previous time taken to cover the 70 mile journey.

The *Koningin Beatrix* entered service at a time when the Hook of Holland service was in need of yet more capacity during the summer, and especially during the week, than even she could provide. To help cope with moving around 1,000 freight units a week the *Stena Sailer* was chartered for an initial period of three months with forty seamen being temporarily taken on. After a refit in Glasgow she commenced Monday to Friday sailings from Parkeston Quay on 30th June 1986 on a schedule that saw her depart at 10.00 having earlier arrived from the Hook at 06.00. She served on the route until the end of August.

The appearance of the *Stena Sailer* came shortly after DFDS had opened up a new freight service between Parkeston Quay and Rotterdam. Since May 1986, mainly to relieve the pressure on their services out of Immingham, they were sailing three times a week form Parkeston Quay using a chartered vessel, the *Belinda*, which had earlier been seen at the port as the *Linnea*. Able to carry up to 120 trailers or 302 teus her sailings were increased to six a week in July when Townsend Thoresen's services out of Felixstowe were disrupted by strike action. However DFDS closed this service in 1987 when it fell victim to strike action in Rotterdam.

In common with most other traffic flows the movement of trade cars had also been on the increase with around 500 being imported each day, mainly by the Ford Motor Company. These arrived on ships run by Ugland Car Ships that docked at the Quay's west end berth and from where it had long been a circuitous drive round to the 18 acre Tolemans storage depot. On 8th July 1986 a new £300,000 bridge was officially opened by Sealink's chairman, Mr. Lenox-Conyngham, that provided a short cut over the railway lines and directly connected the ships with the 3,000 car capacity depot. The bridge had its concrete foundations and approaches built by Tilbury Construction of Ipswich and a 130 feet long steel bridge span built by Depledge & Co Ltd of Leeds.

Purpose built car boats had been sailing to and from Parkeston Quay since the mid 1970s and were originally from a fleet of vessels owned by Hoegh-Ugland Auto Liners (HUAL), a company jointly created in 1970 between the oil tanker operator, Leif Hoegh & Co., and ro-ro operator, Ugland Car Carriers. Such multi-deck car transporter ships had been appearing from yards throughout Europe since the early 1970s with a few being able to also handle ro-ro units and lorries. Most had either six or seven levels on which cars could be stored as if in a floating garage and were between 300 and 340 feet long. The two most recent arrivals, the *Autoline* and the *Autotransporter*, were sister ships built in Japan in 1983 and were now the more regular of the car boats that would sail up to six times a week to either Zeebrugge or Flushing. The Company was later reconstructed as United European Car Carriers (UECC) and bought by NYK in 1990 when the fleet then numbered nineteen ships in service. Amazingly all nineteen at some time or other had arrived at Parkeston Quay with several having come from as far afield as Spain when loaded with Ford Fiestas.

Whilst there was an air of optimism surrounding the Hook of Holland service following the introduction of the *Koningin Beatrix* this was entirely lost as regards the Harwich train ferries. On 15th September 1986 British Rail formally announced, after months of speculation, that they would be terminating their contract with Sealink to run the Harwich train ferry service on its behalf and that the route to Zeebrugge would close on 31st January 1987.

In order to try and maintain some sort of service Sealink proposed an alternative based upon running just the one ship but this was never going to be enough to outweigh BR's stated losses of £3m a year. The *Speedlink Vanguard* and the *Cambridge Ferry* were too small, too slow and too inefficient to be cost effective and were not even covering their operating costs. The Government backed BR's decision, saying

The final sailing of Fred Olsen Line at P. Quay was the *Braemar*'s departure for Kristiansand seen here passing the harbour ferry *Brightlingsea* - 29th August 1989. (Stephen Brown)

such losses were 'shattering', and accepted the need for a one route operation based at Dover where the potential for growth was greater. Suspicions arose that on a political level the transfer of all train ferry traffic to Dover and then finding it could no longer cope on its own might well be useful in strengthening the case for a Channel Tunnel. Figures throughout the 1980s show a steady decline in the number of wagons shipped via Harwich especially from when the proposed new terminal at Parkeston Quay West was shelved and an increase in capacity at Dover.

Year	1980	1981	1982	1983	1984	1985	1986	1987
Wagons	30,166	30,355	20,879	24,591	20,957	23,480	19,450	1,100

In reality the demise of the train ferry at Harwich was in part blamed on the *Speedlink Vanguard* which had proved to be both unreliable and wholly unsuited to the stop start operations of a short sea route. She often broke down and was slow to berth and discharge, this being a reputation she maintained to the very end when her final trip from Harwich, on 30th January 1987, was delayed by four hours. On her way across she was making such slow progress that a following ship radioed up to ask 'Speedlink Vanguard, have you stopped?'. She arrived at Zeebrugge so late that her return sailing to Harwich was cancelled and instead she sailed direct to the Tyne for handing back to Stena Line. The journey took 42 hours. It was an ignoble end to an enterprise that had given almost 63 years of service and which had indeed provided that '*long career of satisfactory usefulness*' envisaged way back in 1924.

The remaining vessel, the *Cambridge Ferry*, had made her own final crossing from Harwich to Zeebrugge on 24th December 1986 from where she left on 29th December for Immingham and a refit. She would then be transferred to Dover and join two equally small and ageing French train ferries, the *Saint Germain* built in 1951 and the *Saint Eloi* in 1975. The *Saint Germain* had once been a visitor to Harwich when, on 31st March 1985, she arrived for berthing trials and was never seen there again. The loss of the Harwich train ferries saw a total of 115 sea going jobs lost although 60 of them were 'saved' by crew working on board the *Cambridge Ferry* at Dover. A further 40 shore based jobs also vanished.

The closure of the Zeebrugge route was especially criticised by interests in Germany and over time there were suggestions that the *Cambridge Ferry* might run a daily service between Zeebrugge and Dover or that German operators might run one of their own out of Cuxhaven to either Harwich or Immingham. As with the many previous suggestions made for new train ferry routes nothing materialised and Sealink later considered investing £350,000 on converting the Harwich train ferry berth into a fifth ro-ro terminal which again came to nothing. The berth and its gantry eventually became totally redundant and today it languishes as a Grade II listed building.

Upon arriving at Dover the *Cambridge Ferry* started on the Dunkirk route on 16th March 1987, ten days after the tragic loss of the *Herald of Free Enterprise* off Zeebrugge on 6th March, and was soon off service herself after colliding with the *Saint Eloi* on 1st May. Damage to her bow was so severe that she was sent away to Smith's Dock in North Shields for repairs.

On 15th April 1987 a new 13,727 grt jumbo sized train ferry, the *Nord-pas-de-Calais*, was launched for SNCF. Built at a cost of £23m this 521 feet long multi-purpose vessel had two decks, the lower of which was a main rail deck fitted with four tracks and space for 33 wagons and an upper deck that housed a freight deck able to carry up to 45 road vehicles. Her forward superstructure contained a lounge and cafeteria area for 80 passengers plus individual en-suite cabins for 35 crew and similar facilities for up to 30 drivers.

The *Nord-pas-de-Calais* first entered service in January 1988 as a 90 trailer capacity ro-ro vessel sailing between Dover and Calais whilst she awaited the completion of a new £10m train ferry berth that was being built at Dover's Admiralty Pier. Designed as a double deck linkspan able to cope with a tidal range of 7.2m this new structure consisted of a 105 metre long lower bridge built in three jointed and hinged sections of 30m, 50m, and 25m lengths along which ran two rail tracks that branched out into four at the seaward end in line with the four tracks on board the ship's main deck. Above was an overhead road bridge that directly connected with the vessel's upper freight deck. A new berth was also built at Dunkirk a cost of Ffr55m.

Following berthing trials on 15th April 1988 the new ship first entered service as a fully fledged train ferry on 9th May 1988 operating 4 round trips a day. The old lock systems at Dover and Dunkirk were closed on 16th May though these were briefly re-activated in October and December 1988. The *Nord-pas-de-Calais* had been contracted by BR to handle rail wagons for an initial period of 10 years and her design and shore installations were quite possibly based on the ideas originally planned for Harwich only a few years before.

The *Saint Eloi* left the service in March 1988, the *Saint Germain* some three months later and finally the *Cambridge Ferry* on 13th October 1988. By the end of 1988 the Dover to Dunkirk service had handled 1,080,623 tons of cargo, the first time the route had exceeded 1 million tons by train ferry, plus 347,906 tons of road freight. Following the official opening of the Channel Tunnel on 6th May 1994 the days of maintaining any sort of train ferry service were numbered and the Dover to Dunkirk service closed on 22nd December 1995.

Back at Parkeston Quay the number of passengers travelling with DFDS in 1986 had reached 810,000. Route by route the figures were 363,000 via Esbjerg, 300,000 via Gothenburg and 147,000 via Hamburg. By way of comparison DFDS's services from Newcastle carried only 46,000 passengers to Esbjerg and 23,000 to Gothenburg whilst the Sealink BF /SMZ service to the Hook of Holland carried 926,000.

The *Surrey* had now become the main freight ship on the Hamburg route and operated most of the twice weekly sailings herself on the following schedule:

Dep P. Quay	05.00 (Sunday)
Arr Hamburg	07.00 (Monday)
Dep. Hamburg	18.00 (Tuesday)
Arr. P. Quay	18.00 (Wednesday)
Dep. P. Quay	05.00 (Thursday)
Arr. Hamburg	07.00 (Friday)
Dep. Hamburg	18.00 (Friday)
Arr. P. Quay	18.00 (Saturday)

In addition the *Dana Cimbria* had been assisting on the Esbjerg route in September and then on the Hamburg route in December. The figures for the Parkeston Quay to Hamburg service also included 21,400 cars and overall were little different from those in 1983 when 143,700 passengers and 22,200 cars were carried following the closure of the Bremerhaven service.

However in the intervening years the *Prinz Hamlet* had been upgraded with new Commodore class cabins, new carpets to replace old flooring and a generally improved standard of on board service. During March 1985 DFDS chartered the *St. Patrick (II)* from the Irish Continental Group as cover for the *Prinz Hamlet* and again in September 1985 when she re-appeared for a further month. By the end of 1985 the route's finances were in much better shape and with it being run close to maximum capacity it was announced in September 1986 that DFDS were to acquire a much larger vessel for this route.

This was the *Kronprins Harald* which had been sailing on Jahre Line's premier Oslo to Kiel route ever since being built in 1976. She was purchased by DFDS Seacruises (Bahamas) Ltd. for around $18m on 27th February 1987 and made her last sailing with Jahre Line on 1st March. She was then overhauled in Hamburg at a cost of Dkr21m and changed from her original two class status to being one class only. A number of cabins were fitted with extra bunks and a lounge at the forward end of her Restaurant Deck was replaced by a block of 21 three or four berth cabins.

She re-emerged on 3rd April as the 13,141 grt *Hamburg*. She was officially re-named in Hamburg on 4th April following which she then made her first sailing for DFDS and arrived at Parkeston Quay on 5th April 1987. Thereafter she maintained an alternate day service throughout the summer period before reverting to the standard three times a week service during the winter.

The *Hamburg* was over twice the tonnage of the now displaced *Prinz Hamlet* and could carry roughly twice the number of cars or freight at 400 cars or 45 trailers as opposed to 225 cars or 24 trailers and for her 1,035 passengers the *Hamburg* offered 862 berths in 281 mostly en-suite cabins plus a further 270 bunks in couchette class.

On Deck 9, formerly the upper Bridge Deck, there were 21 Commodore class cabins of which a further 10 were located on Deck 8. Each had one, two or three berths and in total could sleep 80 passengers. On Deck 7 were 57 outside and 8 inside three or four berth cabins plus a five room conference centre at the aft end. Deck 6 was the original Restaurant Deck and here, in addition to the newly installed block of 13 outside and 8 inside cabins, was the Navigator Bar and Four Seasons a la carte Restaurant forward and the Alster Restaurant and Mayfair Lounge aft. A promenade arcade that held a bar area, casino and video room was situated on the starboard side. Deck 5 was the main entrance deck complete with an Information Desk, a Tax free shop, 78 outside and 31 inside two berth cabins plus 55 two or four berth economy cabins of which the latter had only a washbasin facility. Below were the Car Decks 3 and 4 whilst further down were the couchette cabins of which there were 25 on Deck 2 and 52 on Deck 1.

The *Prinz Hamlet* had made her last arrival at Hamburg on 4th April 1987 and next day she was sold to DFDS for Dm18m., put under the Danish flag and later re-named as the *Prins Hamlet*. She then transferred to sail between Esbjerg and Newcastle as from 13th May 1987 before returning to Parkeston Quay between 21st November 1987 and 2nd March 1988 for occasional work as a freight ship on the Esbjerg route. There she sailed in conjunction with the *Dana Anglia* and with weekly assistance from the *Dana Cimbria*.

In May 1987 an unusual new service was announced that would directly link Parkeston Quay with North America. A joint Fednav - Camar operation between the USA company Fednav and Canada's Canada Maritime would see two Fednav vessels, the 15,005 grt *Federal Lakes* and the 15,036 grt *Federal Seaway* sailing a monthly schedule from Parkeston Quay to the Great Lakes port of Toledo and ports along the US east coast. They were to carry a variety of general goods, wheeled traffic and trade cars with the first sailing being that of the *Federal Seaway* from Parkeston Quay on 6th June 1987.

Ports do not normally become a focus of controversy, except perhaps when dealing with issues over expansion or the handling of livestock, but when the British Ferries vessel *Earl William* docked alongside the now disused train ferry terminal at Harwich on 11th May 1987 it sparked a storm of local protests. Its purpose in being there was to act as a floating reception centre for up to 120 Tamils suspected of being illegal immigrants.

In reality its arrival prompted an alternative description as being that of a prison ship run by the Home Office and this prompted concerns over 'nobody being safe in their beds' and that tourism would suffer as a result. Feelings ran high despite promises that 'there will be no searchlights and barbed wire' and that no-one was likely to jump overboard or try to escape. Jobs for up to twenty seamen were boycotted whilst a private firm, Securicor, was employed to maintain security on board the ship.

The 3,882 grt *Earl William* was originally built for Otto Thoresen A/S in 1964 as the *Viking II*, sister ship to the *Viking III* which Lion Ferry had used on their services from Bremerhaven to Parkeston Quay and Harwich Navyard back in the 1960s. In more recent times the *Earl William* had been employed in 1985 on Sealink British Ferries upgraded Weymouth to Channel Islands route in what became a ruinously expensive exercise in competition with the newly formed company of Channel Island Ferries. In 1986 she was re-branded as sailing for British Ferries and became surplus to requirements in September 1986 when Sealink gave up the island services altogether. The ship was then laid up in the river Fal before being chartered by the Home Office in Spring 1987 for an initial period of three months. Following her taking on stores at Weymouth the *Earl William* arrived at Harwich offering facilities on board which were reported as being quite luxurious especially the 'cells'. These in fact were outside cabins complete with their own en-suite and toilets with the 'in-mates' being served three meals a day in the ship's restaurant. Recreational pursuits such as football and table tennis were available on the car deck.

During the course of the summer it was argued that the ship needed planning permission to stay where she was. However all issues surrounding the ship were literally swept out to sea during the famous hurricane of 1987. On the morning of 16th October the ship broke away from its moorings at what one report called 'George Street Quay', a term not normally used in

Above and overleaf: Visions of an unrealised future - impressions of how an infilled Bathside Bay was intended to rival Felixstowe as a major deep sea container terminal. (Stephen Brown collection)

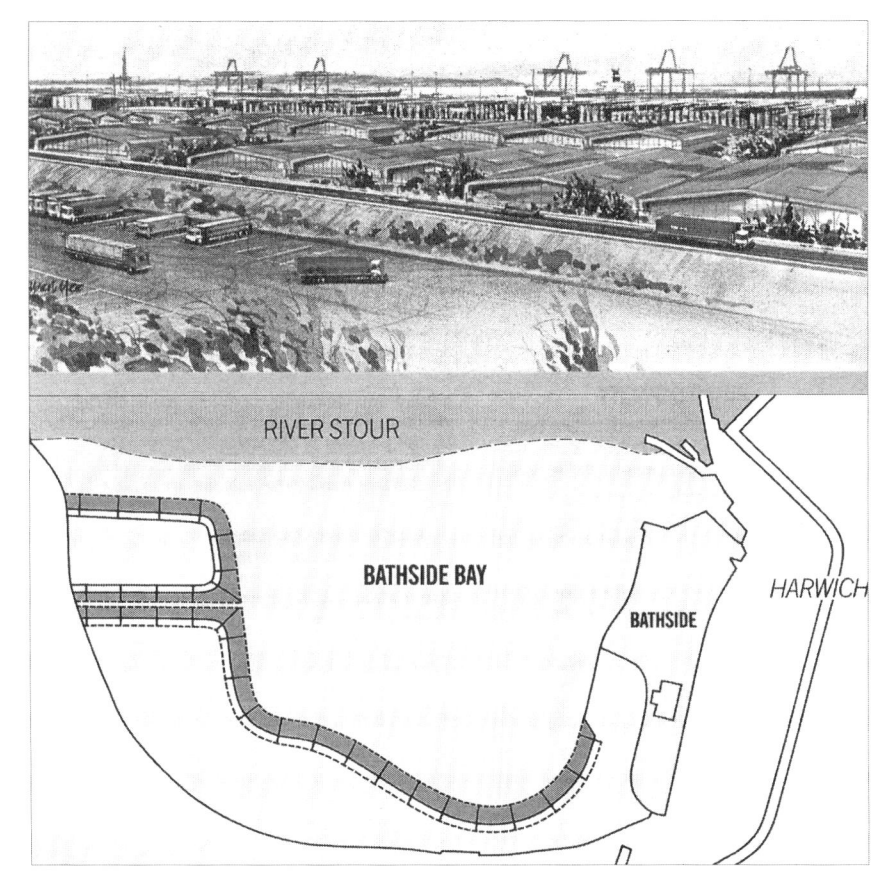

reference to the train ferry berth but whose street name most certainly would have been known to the many Victorian travellers who had earlier trudged down its path on the way to the continental steamer at Harwich's Corporation Pier.

The *Earl William* came to rest on a sandbank off Shotley Point on the opposite side of the river Stour. No-one amongst the crew and 65 detainees on board were injured whilst the ship drifted out of control but a hole was made in her side when she struck a small barge through which a quantity of water entered an engine room storeroom. The ship was re-floated that evening and moved to dock at Parkeston Quay where the detainees were disembarked and transferred to a reception centre in Wimbledon.

The contract for her use as a floating reception centre had earlier been extended by a further three months but was then terminated at the end of November with the *Earl William* leaving Harwich on 4th December 1987 for lay up at Falmouth. By the time of her breaking free in October her hulls had been painted over in white so as to remove any unwanted publicity as to what 'british ferries' were being used for. She went on to commence a new Sealink British Ferries service from Liverpool to Dun Laoghaire in April 1988. During her time at Harwich a few local traders were said to have benefited from retailing the ship with supplies and electrical goods whilst seamen engaged as watch-keepers were reported to have earned up to £170 a week.

During the summer of 1987 the number of weekly sailings from Parkeston Quay were: by Sealink BF/SMZ to Hook of Holland - 14, by DFDS to Esbjerg - 8, Gothenburg - 3½, Hamburg 3½ (plus 2 ro-ro by the *Surrey*), Helsingborg - 1 (by the *Dana Futura*) and by Fred Olsen to Hirtshals/Oslo - 1. In addition there were the car ship sailings and a container terminal that since early 1986 had been operating at only a quarter of its capacity handling independent operator vessels. On 9th July 1987 the terminal received one of its more unusual visitors in the form of the 4,007 grt cruise ship *Argonaut* whose arrival displayed a mixture of old fashioned style and design together with an engaging episode of Mediterranean style chaos and disorder as passengers and their baggage were being landed on the open quayside next to the cranes.

Better prospects for the terminal's future came in August 1987 when Bell Lines decided to transfer its operations from the Thames and instead sail to their Rozenburg terminal in Rotterdam from Parkeston Quay. Bell Lines had recently become a part of HES Beheer, a Dutch based shipping and transportation group and Europe's leading short sea container operator. From Rotterdam they also ran services to Teesport, Waterford and South Wales and from Waterford to France and Spain. Since 1976 their existing terminal on the Thames had been at the Victoria Deep Water Container Terminal at Greenwich and from where they were operating twice a week sailings to Rotterdam that took between 16 and 18 hours to complete. From Parkeston Quay they envisaged sailing five times a week with crossings taking only between 8 and 10 hours.

Bell Lines first set up their new operations on 1st November 1987 employing 23 staff. Their inaugural sailing was from Rotterdam on 11th November and was undertaken by the 262 teu vessel *Jan Becker* which made its maiden voyage in just eight hours. Their initial target was to handle 20,000 containers a year using the *Jan Becker* and her sister ship the *Amazone*. Both ships had a service speed of 14½ knots and were built by J.J. Sietas Schiffswerft of Hamburg at a cost of £4.5m each. J.J. Sietas was then the oldest shipyard in Germany, dating back to 1625, and specialised in building small container feeder ships. Most were in the order of 300 to 320 feet long and over the next few years several of them would be seen at Parkeston Quay. The *Jan Becker* and the *Amazone* were built to carry Bell Line's new '425 container', a container measuring 40 feet long by 2.5 metres high that was designed to better compete for trailer type traffic.

The arrival of DFDS's *Hamburg* had brought about a substantial increase in traffic on the Hamburg route with 178,000 passengers travelling in 1987 and 195,000 passengers and 30,200 cars in 1988. Previously the Hamburg route had been supplemented with twice weekly sailings by the *Surrey* and during April 1987 the route had been further assisted by the freight ship *Beaverdale*. Eventually however the greater capacity of the *Hamburg* reduced the need for an extra ship and the *Surrey* instead made just the one round trip a week to Germany with the other then going to Esbjerg instead.

By now the Landungsbrucken terminal in Hamburg was becoming much too small and thus the building of a new terminal at Fischereihafen, a mile and a half downriver on the Elbe's north bank, was agreed to in 1988. It opened in May 1991 having been built at a cost of Dm36m. to which DFDS had contributed Dm14m.for facilities that included a 190 metre long quayside and storage areas.

The overall growth in business to both Germany and Scandinavia was such that former services were either re-instated or enhanced. The former collaboration between Stena Line and Tor Line that had once created Stena Portlink was partially revived in 1987 through a joint venture involving Stena Line and DFDS. Togther they created Stena Tor Line AB and on 1st October began a six days a week service between Gothenburg and Parkeston Quay/Felixstowe using the vessels *Stena Gothica* and *Stena Britannica*.

Later on DFDS were to re-instate a service to Bremerhaven after an absence of almost six years. On 18th August 1988 they started twice a week freight sailings from Parkeston Quay, on Thursday and Saturday, and from Bremerhaven on Monday and Friday. The route was mainly operated by the *Surrey* with support from two chartered vessels, firstly the *Dana Cimbria* and then the *Saga Star*. However in February 1989 sailings were reduced to just once a weekend:

Dep Bremerhaven 18.00 (Friday)
Arr P. Quay   18.00 (Saturday)
Dep. P. Quay   06.00 (Sunday)
Arr. Bremerhaven 06.00 (Monday)

In September 1988 DFDS took out one month charters on the *Trapezitza*, to sail between Parkeston Quay/Immingham and Helsingborg/Copenhagen, and her sister ship, the *Tzarevetz*. The *Trapezitza* was to briefly take over from the *Dana Futura* which had been on the Helsingborg service since 1985 whilst the *Tzarevetz* covered for the *Surrey* on the Bremerhaven route. Both these chartered ships went on to become more widely known as the *Fantasia* and the *Fiesta* sailing out of Dover.

Summary of yearly traffic figures through Parkeston Quay (000's)

	1981	1982	1983	1984	1985	1986	1987	1988
Passengers	1,518	1,549	1,828	1,941	1,979	2,038	1,932	1,937
Accompanied veh.	172	191	227	243	252	272	267	270
Trade vehicles	219	186	195	164	177	170	175	220
Acc. ro-ro	36	32	33	54	45	60	58	78
Un-acc ro-ro	29	32	40	44	46	52	45	43
Bacon trailers	14	12	11	9	7	4	4	3
Containers	116	93	104	93	96	27	33	72

A further absence that was re-instated followed an announcement in September 1988 that Freightliner Ltd were to transfer back to Parkeston Quay its short sea container operations at Felixstowe. This reversal of their earlier decision to have left the Quay was so that Freightliner could better develop Felixstowe's booming deep sea potential and was expected to involve around 57,000 containers a year. As the move would substantially increase the annual throughput of Parkeston Quay's container terminal a £2.7m scheme of works was approved to include extra standage and marshalling areas, the creation of a new centralised port control office, an extension to the Kone crane track and ultimately installing a fourth container gantry.

This resurrected Parkeston Quay to Zeebrugge service started on 3 January 1989 with two container ships, the *Karen Oltmann* and the *Petuja*. Arrivals at Parkeston Quay were at 06.00, the same as for Bell Lines, but as each was shorter than an original Sea Freightliner both company's ships could be worked whilst alongside together. Unfortunately a series of breakdowns involving a new computerised documentation and tracking system saw the Freightliner service temporarily reverting to Felixstowe's Landguard Terminal after only a week in operation. Once the teething problems had been resolved the service resumed from Parkeston Quay as planned though with the *Karen Oltmann* having meanwhile been re-named as *Geranta*.

January 1989 also saw Bell Lines introduce two new 262 teu vessels, *Jan Kahrs* and *Angela Jurgens*, onto their service to Rozenburg. As with the two ships sailing for Freightliner so too were these sailing for Bell Line a product of the J.J. Sietas yard. However Bell Lines were to make future use of several older and smaller capacity vessels all of which were built by the Kagoshima Dock & Iron Works company in Japan. Chartered in and prefixed 'Bell' these were the 168 teu *Bell Racer*, *Bell Ruler* and *Bell Ranger* and the 132 teu *Bell Reliant*, *Bell Renown*, *Bell Resolve* and *Bell Rover*.

A third container service arrived later that year when DFDS began one from Bremerhaven using the feeder vessels *Concord* and *Clipper*. Both had originated at the yard of J.J. Sietas in Hamburg and together they offered an alternative mode of transport to the existing ro-ro service then running between Parkeston Quay and Germany.

The privatisation of Sealink in 1984 had curtailed the railway's involvement in its passenger ferries but the contracts for the carriage of containers and railway wagons on British Rail's behalf had since prolonged a residual interest. Thus the final sailing of the *Speedlink Vanguard* can be regarded as having brought those interests to an end, interests that had been carried on ever since 16th September 1854 when first they started at Harwich. Even the boat trains were not immune to change.

The 'Scandinavian' had long since finished in 1975 but the 'Hook Continental' and the 'Day Continental' carried on until making their final runs at the end of May 1987. An un-titled train still ran to and from London Liverpool Street in connection with the boats though now it was no longer an express service. As regards the North Country boat train that had become more of a regional cross country service than a prestigious boat train. In 1983 the Parkeston Quay to Manchester service was re-vamped as the 'European'. This ran daily except Sunday and left Parkeston Quay at 07.17 and via Manchester it arrived in Edinburgh at 17.11. This was replaced in 1987 by the 'Rhinelander' linking only Parkeston Quay and Manchester which in turn became the 'Lorelei' in 1988 which then ran on to include Blackpool. In 1989 the 'Lorelei' was used to link in Birmingham and Liverpool whilst another train, the 'Britannia', ran between Parkeston Quay and Manchester.

A further long standing enterprise that was soon to end was that of SMZ. At the time SMZ was 70% owned by the Dutch state with a further 25% of its shares being held by Internatio Muller in Rotterdam and the remaining 5% being traded on the stock market. In 1988 the Dutch Minister of Transport and Public Works announced that the Government was to sell its controlling interest in the company and this led to SMZ adopting Crown Line as an interim trading name. They then advertised the *Koningin Beatrix* with a cruise ferry concept and replaced the 'Hoek/Hook-Harwich' logos on her hull with one displaying Crown Line.

When the *St. Nicholas* went away to Schiedam for an annual overhaul on 8th January 1989 her schedules were taken over by the former Sealink Channel Islands ferry *Earl Granville* with ro-ro traffic being carried on board the chartered *Mercandian Universe*. The *St. Nicholas* returned to service on 19th January and four days later the *Koningin Beatrix* also sailed to Schiedam for her own overhaul. In her place on a two weeks charter was Brittany Ferries' newly purchased *Duchesse Anne*, fresh from a £2.4m refit in Germany. This 400 feet long vessel dated from 1979 when she was built as the *Connaught* for the Irish company of B&I Line. On board were facilities for 1,300 passengers including 388 reclining seats and 156 cabins offering 471 berths. Her car decks could carry around 270 cars or 30 lorries and she covered on the Hook route between 22nd January and 2nd February 1989.

By early 1989 four prospective buyers, Sealink British Ferries, Nedlloyd, Johnson Line and Stena Line had expressed an interest in purchasing SMZ. Despite a strong bid from Sealink BF it was the offer by Stena Line to pay 6,750 Guilders for each 250 Guilder share that was finally accepted.

The official transfer of the Dutch Government's holding in SMZ took place on board the *Koningin Beatrix* on 22nd June 1989, when the Minister of Transport, Mrs Smit-Kroes and the President of Stena Line, Mr. Lars-Erik Ottosson completed the necessary documentation. The cost of securing the *Koningin Beatrix* and the Crown Line business was reported as being £33 million or 110m Nlg. SMZ had been one of the oldest shipping companies in Holland and could proudly boast that throughout its 114 years it had never lost a ship during peace time.

Throughout August 1989 the funnel of the *Koningin Beatrix* had its crowns removed and was repainted in Stena Line red with the large white 'S' symbol. On the 31st August the ship's new Stena Line house-flag was officially presented to Captain Nagel and this was raised at 10.00 on the following day when the SMZ house-flag was lowered for the final time. Thus from 1st September 1989 'De Stoomvaart Maatschappij Zeeland Koninklijke Nederlandsche Postvaart N.V.' became known as Stena Line BV, a subsidiary of Stena Line AB which itself was 60% owned by the Sten A Olsson family via Stena Rederi AB. Crown Line became Stena Line with the *Koningin Beatrix* now owned by Stena Line AB and chartered back to Stena Line BV.

One further change that year was the closure of Fred Olsen's service to Norway. Since September 1985 the *Braemar* had regularly arrived from Oslo and Hirtshals at 10.30 on a Saturday morning and left at 16.00. This she continued to do up until 19th June 1989 whereupon the link with Norway was changed on 26th June to a once a week summer season sailing between Parkeston Quay and Kristiansand. This arrangement saw the day of arrival changed to a Tuesday and a timetable as follows:

Dep. Kristiansand	14.00 (Monday)
Arr. P .Quay	13.00 (Tuesday)
Dep P. Quay	14.00 (Tuesday)
Arr London (L.St.)	15.20 (Tuesday)
Dep. London (L.St)	13.25 (Tuesday)
Arr. P. Quay	14.38 (Tuesday)
Dep P. Quay	16.00 (Tuesday)
Arr Kristiansand	16.30 (Wednesday)

The route was then closed on 30th August 1989 and the *Braemar* moved to a new Oslo/Kristiansand service to Newcastle which not only offered Norwegians a shorter crossing of the North Sea but also far better shopping opportunities ashore.

In September 1989 Cobelfret, a Belgian operator more normally associated with Harwich Navyard, opened up a ro-ro service between Parkeston Quay and Zeebrugge. Sailings were 5 times a week, Monday to Friday, using the 61 trailer capacity feight ship *Seafowl* and followed a series of trial trips that took place during the previous June and July. The *Belvaux* later took over until the service closed at the end of November 1990 due to a lack of traffic.

On 8th November 1989 the *Hamburg* was struck on her starboard side by the ro-ro freightship *Nordic Stream* when 10 miles south of Helgoland en-route to Parkeston Quay. She was left with a huge gash in the vicinity of the Mayfair Lounge and with three passengers having been killed in the impact. The *Hamburg* was towed first into Bremerhaven and then to the yard of Blohm & Voss in Hamburg for repairs. She returned to service on 22nd December 1989.

In November 1989 Sea Containers somewhat surprisingly announced plans for a £200m property development in Bathside Bay consisting of a mix of residential, industrial and recreational facilities. Initial plans were for a new business park and 600 houses on existing land which would later be supplemented by a further 650 houses on reclaimed land. Additional features were to include a number of warehousing and manufacturing units, a 120 room hotel, a health and fitness centre, a primary school and a shopping centre. The scheme was said to 'allow for the natural expansion of the port and also provides alternative uses for an area of Harwich which is currently underutilised'. This 'new town', complete with a park and lakes, would cover up to 330 acres of tidal mudflats yet in keeping with most other plans for Bathside Bay nothing much came of this one either.

The 1980s closed with Parkeston Quay and Harwich having lost their railway ownership and the ships associated with that ownership all gone. Gone altogether were the Sea Freightliners and the Train Ferries whilst the historic link to the Hook of Holland was now in the hands of a private company. Also gone was the presence of the British Transport Police in January 1989 thus ending a period of 80 years of them patrolling the quay. As from 1st February the port's security was in the private hands of Capitol Security Services. However the 1980s were probably the best time to have been a passenger travelling out of Parkeston Quay with Norway, Sweden, Denmark, Germany and Holland all having been easily reached on a regular basis by ferries that were amongst the most comfortable of their era.

In future years Parkeston Quay was to see further changes both in ownership and operation that arguably never quite matched the supposed heydays of previous years. That process had already begun as in March 1989, on the New York stock exchange, Stena Line AB acquired a 9% holding in Sea Containers. What followed is another story.

The River and Harbour Services

When the Eastern Counties Railway (ECR) took over the Eastern Union Railway (EUR) in 1854, the company also took over the EUR's fleet of local paddle steamers then sailing between Ipswich and Harwich. Some of these had earlier been operated by the Ipswich Steam Navigation Company (ISNC) and whose *River Queen* was used on 15th June 1846 between Ipswich and Harwich in connection with the opening of the EUR's line from Ipswich to Colchester whilst the *Orwell (I)* was used on 17th June 1846 when the EUR and ECR jointly embarked on their demonstration voyage from Ipswich to Rotterdam.

As early as 1815 a service briefly operated between Ipswich and Harwich using the River Orwell's first steamer, also named the *Orwell*, but it was not until the mid 1820s that more established or longer distance routes ran out from the Suffolk town. A steamer service into London was started in April 1826 with paddlers of the ISNC taking around 11 hours to complete the journey up to London Bridge having made calls each way at Harwich. Early examples were their sister ships, the *Ipswich* and the *Suffolk*. When the *River Queen* arrived in 1839 the 110 mile journey from Ipswich became possible in a little over 8½ hours and passengers onboard were able to partake of both breakfast and dinner along the way.

The arrival in Ipswich of the railway in June 1846 saw the town increasingly become a centre for both river and coastal paddle steamer services with the attractions of the River Orwell gaining a wider recognition amongst travellers at leisure. In 1851 it was considered that many of those leaving London as tourists felt compelled to take their annual holidays in places such as Ramsgate or Margate such was their ease of accessibility but now '*One can vary the scene at less expense, by visiting the far-famed banks of the picturesque Orwell, or the enchanting country in the neighbourhood. Fast, and well appointed steamers, ply constantly between London and Ipswich, and many of the passengers, who land at, or otherwise visit, Harwich, will most probably proceed to Ipswich, allured by the beauty of the river scenery, the shortness of the distance, and the accommodation offered by the constant trips of steamers to and from Harwich*'. Even after the long awaited arrival of the railway at Harwich in August 1854 the steamer service remained a viable and often cheaper way of travelling to and from London.

The eight paddle steamers acquired by the ECR were at the time often the outright property, registered ownership or the subject of a co-operation arrangement between the EUR and its now chief engineer, Peter Bruff. Bruff, together with J.C. Cobbold, had earlier helped to create the EUR in 1844 and since 1850 had personally been acquiring a number of vessels.

Thus in 1854 when the ECR took over the *Pearl*, *Orwell (I)*, *River Queen*, *Orion*, *Atalanta*, *Prince Albert*, *Cardinal Wolsey* and *Prince* all were in some way associated with Bruff with the exception of the *Orwell* and the *River Queen*, these two vessels having been bought by Alfred Cobbold in May 1853 following the liquidation of the ISNC. Sailings from Harwich were from the new Corporation Pier which opened on 2nd July 1853 and one vessel, the *Orion*, was large enough to be used by the ECR on several of its sailings between Harwich and Antwerp during the summer of 1855.

The *Pearl*, *Orwell (I)*, *River Queen*, *Orion* and *Prince Albert* were later sold or disposed of by the ECR leaving the *Atalanta*, *Cardinal Wolsey* and *Prince to* become a part of the Great Eastern Railway (GER) when it was formed in 1862. The GER then sold the *Cardinal Wolsey* and *River Queen* and replaced them in 1864 by two new sister ships, the *Ipswich (I)* and the *Stour (I)*.

The *Ipswich (I)* was the first new build river steamer of the GER and like the *Stour (I)* was 120 feet long, of 87 tons and able to accommodate up to 150 *passengers*. By the end of the 1860s the last remaining ex-EUR/ECR vessels, the *Atalanta* and *Prince,* had been sold leaving the river service in the hands of just two regular paddle steamers.

In July 1871 Bruff, having since resigned from the GER in 1867, built a new pier at Clacton-on-Sea which attracted calls from vessels sailing between London and Ipswich though sailings to Ipswich from Harwich remained a river service only.

In 1873 the *Ipswich (I)* was transferred to Lowestoft and replaced by the arrival of another new ship, the *Orwell (II)* and she was joined by a sister ship, the *Stour (II)*, in 1878 as a replacement for the *Stour (I)*. In 1881 the Thames Ironworks Co. Ltd. built the *Suffolk (I)* and followed this a year later with the *Norfolk (I)*. Both these ships were 140 feet long and 114 tons. However the *Suffolk (I)* was only in service for a short while as she was sold in 1883.

Some fifteen years later came a further pair of new and much larger paddlers that were designed as 'double enders', ie they were built as looking the same from either end, in order to make it easier to arrive and depart within the narrow confines of the channel at Ipswich's river side quay. Twin funnelled and fore and aft masted the first to appear was the 165 feet long *Suffolk (II)* in 1895. The second ship, the *Essex (II)*, arrived in 1896 and although built as a sister ship she was 10 feet longer than the *Suffolk* and 52 tons heavier at 297 grt. Each could carry 450 passengers and not only did they sail between Harwich and Ipswich but

The harbour ferry *Brightlingsea* lies alongside her berth at Harwich's Halfpenny Pier - 11th December 1976. (Stephen Brown)

they also made excursion visits to Felixstowe and Great Yarmouth. Both were built by Earle's Shipbuilding & Eng. Co. Ltd. of Hull who at the time were also providing the GER with their cross channel ships out of Parkeston Quay.

By now the coastal services of other operators was greatly expanded. The railway had reached Clacton-on-Sea in 1882 and what was becoming a thriving seaside resort was now attracting tourist boats. These included those from the fleet of Belle Steamers Ltd whose vessels would visit Clacton and then Harwich en-route to and from Ipswich.

In 1898 the Coast Development Company was formed as a successor to Belle Steamers Ltd. and they took over a newly built pier at Walton-on-the-Naze and then built a new one at Felixstowe in 1905. Again Harwich benefited from the intensifying network of coastal services that successive pier constructions brought about.

The local GER fleet was augmented in 1900 by the arrival of the *Norfolk (II)* which was the largest and the last of the paddle steamers built for the river service. Designed as a single funnelled version of the *Essex (II)* her dimensions of 184 by 24.1 feet were broadly similar to those of the *Esbjerg* that DFDS had used for crossing the North Sea.

These latest river paddlers had well appointed accommodation for those in First class with polished woods, velvet cushioned seats and a separate ladies toilet all provided for their comfort and pleasure as they viewed the surrounding countryside. Second class was rather more austere with wooden seats and toilets outside on deck. Their arrival displaced the *Norfolk (I)* and *Stour (II)* for sale in 1896 and 1900 respectively.

In 1912 the GER acquired the rights to running a new service between Harwich and the inner harbour dock at Felixstowe. Sailings began on 22nd July 1912 and this was followed by another new service that linked Harwich with Shotley Gate that began in April 1914. Services were initially operated by using a small 40 feet long wooden harbour launch, the *Pinmill,* an 11 ton motor vessel that was built in Kent in 1910 but fitted out in Ipswich.

In May and June 1914 Vosper & Co. of Portsmouth delivered a pair of larger vessels, the *Epping* and the *Hainault*, and between them they maintained a three way service between Harwich and Shotley/Felixstowe. Though larger these vessels were only 50 feet long and were described as single screw wooden harbour ferries, diesel powered, and were built at a cost of £1,157 each.

In December 1913 the *Essex (II)* was sold off and put into service between Southend and Sheerness. At the outbreak of WW1 the two remaining river boats, the *Suffolk* and the *Norfolk*, and the three harbour boats were all requisitioned by the Royal Navy for various harbour duties and as supply launches. Services were resumed post war with the one to Ipswich being restarted by the *Suffolk* on 26th May 1919.

The last river or harbour vessel the railway had built for them was the *Brightlingsea*. She arrived in October 1925 as the very first ship newly built for the LNER and upon arriving at Harwich she relegated the *Pinmill* to the status of work boat. The wooden hulled and motor driven *Brightlingsea* was the largest of the harbour service vessels with accommodation for 231 passengers.

The *Suffolk* and *Norfolk* maintained the river service to Ipswich until it was closed on 4th October 1930 due to consistently having lost money throughout the late 1920s. Both ships were sold off in 1931.

For the duration of WW2 all four harbour vessels were requisitioned for harbour duties with the *Epping* having an unusual, though short lived, career change. Upstream at Parkeston Quay the Royal Navy had taken over the port and re-named it as *H.M.S. Badger*. The *Epping* was assigned the role of the port's depot ship and sailed as *H.M.S. Badger* until being replaced on 12th January 1940 by a much larger and more suitable ship, the *Westward*.

The B*rightlingsea* re-opened a post war service to Felixstowe on 1st February 1946 together with the *Hainault* resuming sailings to Shotley. Crossings times were 15 minutes to Felixstowe and 10 minutes to Shotley.

Timetable from 17th September 1956 to 16th June 1957. Monday to Saturday departures from:

Harwich to Shotley
07.40 09.00 11.00 13.45 16.00 17.00
Shotley to Harwich
07.50 09.15 11.15 14.00 16.15 17.15
Harwich to Felixstowe
08.00 09.55 11.55 14.10 14.55 17.25
Felixstowe to Harwich
08.25 10.30 12.30 14.35 15.30 17.45

Sunday departures from:
Harwich to Shotley
10.00 12.45 14.15 16.50
Shotley to Harwich
10.15 13.00 14.30x 17.15†
† via Felixstowe
Harwich to Felixstowe
10.55 14.15x 15.30 16.50†
† via Shotley
F'stowe to Harwich
11.30 15.00 16.00 17.30

The service continued in operation throughout the 1950s though always at a loss to its owners. British Rail Eastern Region reported deficits ranging between £3,800 and £6,000 a year and in 1959 were threatening to withdraw the service entirely. Figures showed that throughout 1958 some 103,573 passengers had used what was undoubtedly a highly seasonal service with the months of July and August alone accounting for around two thirds of that total. The fare was 1s.6d. single and 3s.0d return and it was estimated that BR's losses that year of £4,600 were equivalent to losing 10d, or roughly half the fare, for every passenger they carried. Furthermore the Felixstowe Dock and Railway Co. had raised their landing fees from a long since agreed £150 a year to £1,000 though this was still much lower than a Statute that allowed the FDR Co. to charge up to 1s.0d. per passenger, equivalent if based on 1958 carryings to around £5,000.

Based on a totally uneconomic situation BR later announced that they would cease what they referred to as the Harwich Motor Boat Service as from 31st December 1961. All vessels except the *Pinmill*, which was retained as a workboat, were laid up and put on the market. The *Epping* and *Hainault* were quickly sold to non-commercial private owners but the *Brightlingsea* was saved for future service by George Goodhew of Great Oakley and the establishment of the Orwell & Harwich Navigation Company. Having bought the vessel this privately owned company operated the *Brightlingsea* between Harwich and Felixstowe as from 1st May 1962. She was also employed on excursions around the harbour though a service to Shotley was not resumed. The owners partnered the *Brightlingsea* in the excursion trade with the *Orwell Haven* until April 1968 and then by the *Torbay Prince* until 1972.

1971 Summer season timetable. Daily departures from:

Harwich to Felixstowe
   09.00† 10.00 11.00† 12.00 14.00 15.00 16.00 17.00 18.00
Felixstowe to Harwich
   09.30† 10.30 11.30† 12.30 14.30 15.30 16.30 17.30 18.30
(†) not Saturday and Sunday

1971-1972 Winter season timetable. Monday to Friday only departures from:
Harwich to Felixstowe   08.15   17.15
Felixstowe to Harwich   08.30   17.30

The Orwell & Harwich Navigation Company was sold on 1 October 1979 to the Felixstowe Dock & Railway Company, then owned by European Ferries, though the Orwell & Harwich Navigation Company title was retained for trading purposes. The service again changed ownership in November 1985 when it was taken over by Alan Pridmore of Harwich. An enhanced schedule of regular sailings and excursions was introduced but eventually the service was to close in the autumn of 1993 after Felixstowe Dock withdrew permission for the *Brightlingsea* to continue to berth at its inner dock basin. Their decision was based upon concerns over the safety of passengers making use of a footpath that passed through an area of the dock that was earmarked for future development. Despite having sold 20,000 single tickets in 1993 the *Brightlingsea* was thus withdrawn from regular passenger service and put to use in offering harbour cruises instead. She was later laid up at a marina at Walton-on-the-Naze and then moved to Woodbridge in Suffolk where she was overhauled and refurbished for further use as a river cruiser. The *Brightlingsea* briefly re-appeared at Harwich during the summer of 2007.

Since 1998 a privately operated harbour service has linked Harwich with Felixstowe and Shotley utilising the *Explorer 12* on a seasonal basis. This twelve passenger landing craft type of vessel runs between Halfpenny Pier at Harwich, a floating pontoon at Shotley and the beach at Felixstowe where it runs up onto the shore.

Land and property purchases made by the GER.

Vendor	Date of Conveyance	A.	R.	P.	Yds.	Consideration	Solicitor's Costs
Narborough	21 March 1864	0	0	21	0	£1400. 0. 0	
Brice	14 January 1867	0	0	8	0	£500. 0. 0	
Commissioners of Woods & Forests (Harwich)	1871					£200.0.0	£34.13.0
Watts	1 August 1872	0	1	6	0	£5250.0.0	
Harwich Corp.	1872	4	0	32	0	£41365.0.0	£1002.14.11
Hesseltine	6 October 1875	0	0	16½	0	£2500.0.0	£52.10.0
Garland	2 December 1878	587	3	20	0	£30093.15.0	£312.0.0
Pattrick	1878					£1500.0.0	£75.0.0
Cobbold	31 October 1884	88	2	0	0	£11000.0.0	
Evans	5 March 1895	5	1	3	0	£1500.0.0	
Bruff	14 December 1896	0	0	27	0	£2250.0.0	
Vincent	25 January 1899	0	0	8½	0	£750.0.0	£4.0.6
Wilson	10 December 1913					£500. 0. 0	£27. 10. 0
Groom & Voots	22 April 1919	13	2	3	0	£8000. 0. 0	
Groom Trus.	22 April 1919	0	1	3	0	£4000. 0. 0	£120. 10. 0
Power & Ors	18 December 1919					£500. 0. 0	£2. 10. 0
Randall	31 December 1919					£0. 5. 0	

(Expenditure by the GER as detailed in accounts later compiled by the LNER in 1928)

Shipping & Port Managers

The overall responsibility for the working of both port and shipping at Parkeston Quay was initially that of the Marine Superintendent, a title which lasted until the 1950s when it become known as the Shipping & Port Superintendent and in the 1970s as the Shipping & Port Manager. Upon privatisation the role was split into two with responsibility for the port resting with a General Manager whilst a separate Ferryline Manager handled the residual interests of BR's passenger service.
Those past managers responsible for the port were:

Captain W. Rivers (1875-1877),
Captain Daniel Howard (1877-1910),
Captain W.H. Coysh (1910 to 31st December 1925),
Captain R. Davis (1st January 1926 to 31st December 1954).
Mr. Stanley Claydon (1st January 1955 to 30th November 1957),
Mr. Tom Tulloch (1st December 1957 to 30th June 1970),
Mr. Bernard Taylor (1st July 1970 to 31st July 1978),
Mr. Bill Henderson (1st August 1978 to February 1979),
Mr Colin Crawford (February 1979 to 25th June 1989)
Mr Ian McWilliams (26th June 1989 to October 1991)

Fleet List

This fleet list should be read in conjunction with the text so that a fuller history of each ship can be seen. The term 'First ref:' means the first reference of a ship being seen at Parkeston Quay.

NOTES
Each set of notes is pre-fixed as follows:
Pps - passenger paddle steamship
Cps - cargo paddle steamship
Pcps - passenger and cargo paddle steamship
Ps - passenger steamship
Cs - cargo steamship
Pcs - passenger and cargo steamship
Rcs - refrigerated cargo steamship
Pms - passenger motor ship
Cms - cargo motor ship
Pcms - passenger and cargo motor ship
Rcms - refrigerated cargo motor ship
Pcms ro-ro - passenger and cargo motor ship roll-on roll-off
Cms ro-ro - cargo motor ship roll-on roll-off
Cms tf - cargo motor ship train ferry
Cms lo-lo - cargo motor ship lift-on lift-off
Cms cc - cargo motor ship car carrier

Engines and Power Outputs are simplified down to:
s.o.- simple oscillating
c.o.- compound oscillating
Tr. exp. - Triple expansion
srg - single reduction geared turbines
diesel - showing engine type.
nhp - nominal horsepower
ihp - indicated horsepower
shp - shaft horsepower
bhp - brake horsepower
kw - kilowatt power

Accrington; GCR
Built: by Earle's Shipbuilding & Eng. Co. Ltd., Hull - yard no. 565
Launched: 7 June 1910
Dimensions: 276.0 / 265.0 x 36.0 x 17.4 ft
Tonnage: 1680 grt / 879 nt / 1098 dwt
Engines: Earle's Tr. exp. 22", 35" & 60" - 42"
Power Output: 309 nhp / 1912 ihp
Speed: 13 knots
Passengers: 450 (B:140 First, 10 Second and 300 Emigrant class)
First ref: November 1918 repatriation sailings between Parkeston Quay and Rotterdam. Returned to the GCR on 12 November 1919.

Pcs. (m/v) was from Grimsby to Antwerp in August 1910. Survived being requisitioned in WW2 as a convoy rescue ship and was again at P. Quay post war. The *Accrington* re-instated the Antwerp service on 29 July 1946 and sailed on the route until 6 January 1951. Passengers: 184 (B: 77 First class). She was then sold for scrapping by Clayton & Davie Ltd at Dunston-on-Tyne where she arrived on 2nd May 1951. For further details see *Dewsbury*.

Adelaide; GER
Built: by Barrow Shipbuilding Co. Ltd, Barrow in Furness.
Launched: 8 May 1880
Dimensions: 254.2 x 32.3 x 13.0 ft
Tonnage: 927 grt / 441 nt / 757 dwt
Engines: Barrow Shipbuilding c.o. 2 cyl 45" & 87" - 72"
Power Output: 300 nhp / 2000 ihp
Speed: 14½ knots
Passengers: 705 (B: 113 First & 58 Second class)
First ref: 23 July 1880 Harwich to Rotterdam (m/v)

Pcps. Launched by Mrs Simpson, wife of one of the Directors, as the first GER ship built from steel and the last ship they ordered driven by paddle wheels. Replaced by *Amsterdam (I)* and sold to T.W. Ward in 1896. Sold on to J. Bannatyne & Sons in 1897 for scrap.

Alexandra; DFDS
Built: by A/S Helsingors Jernskibs-og Maskinbyggeri, Elsinore - yard no. 200
Launched: 20 December 1930
Dimensions: 280.0 / 265.0 x 39.0 x 17.6 ft
Tonnage: 1463 grt / 766 nt / 1700 dwt
Engines: Helsingors J&M Tr. exp 4 cyl. (2) x 18.3" & (2) x 39.4" - 39.4"
Power Output: 1570 ihp
Speed: 12 knots
Passengers: 12
First ref: 1955

Cs. Cost: Dkr 1,172,658. Was the last steamer ordered by DFDS. Made 110 trips between Esbjerg and P. Quay, many of which were from 1961 to 1963. Sold on 3 December 1964 to Greek interests. Stranded off Tripoli on 21 February 1965 and thereafter scrapped in Split.

Amazone; Bell Line; IMO: 8703256
Built: 1987 by J.J. Sietas Schiffswerft, Hamburg, Germany - yard no. 985.
Dimensions: 94.50 / 87.81 x 15.90 x 5.05 m
Tonnage: 2749 grt / 1110 nt / 3178 dwt
Engines: 1 x Wartsila diesel type 6R32D
Power Output: 1353 hp / 995 kw
Speed: 14 knots

Cms lo-lo. Space for 262 teus. One of 5 Sietas Type 122 feeder ships. Re-named *Ilha da Madeira* in January 1997. Last owner: Vieira & Silveira Transportes Maritimos, Lisbon, Portugal. Sister ships: *Jan Becker, Angela Jurgens, Jan Kahrs* and *Otto Becker*.

Amsterdam (I); GER
Built: by Earle's Shipbuilding & Eng. Co. Ltd., Hull - yard no. 380
Launched: 24 January 1894
Dimensions: 302.4 x 36.0 x 16.2 ft
Tonnage: 1745 grt / 556 nt / 1131 dwt
Engines: Earle's Tr. exp. 6 cyl in 2 sets 26", 39½" & 61" - 36"
Power Output: 447 nhp / 5800 ihp
Speed: 18 knots
Passengers: 780 (B: 218 First & 120 Second class)
First ref: 9 May 1894 Parkeston Quay to Hook of Holland (m/v)

Pcs. Collided with *Axminster* on 23 January 1908 near the Maas lightship. First ship to use the new coal bunkering equipment at P. Quay on 28 February 1913. Requisitioned in October 1914. Sold for scrapping at Blyth in December 1928. Sister ships: *Berlin, Vienna (I)*.

Amsterdam (II); LNER
Built: by John Brown & Co. Ltd., Clydebank - yard no. 529
Launched: 13 January 1930
Dimensions: 377.0 / 350.7 x 50.1 x 15.3 ft
Tonnage: 4220 g2 / 1988 nt / 3028 dwt
Engines: 2 x 2 John Brown Curtis srg turbines
Power Output: 1520 nhp / 11500 shp
Speed: 21 knots
Passengers: 708 (B: 427 First & 126 Second class)
First ref: 26 April 1930 Parkeston Quay to Hook of Holland (m/v)

Pcs. Requisitioned in September 1939 as a troopship and later converted to a hospital ship in July 1944. Re-named *Hospital Carrier No. 64*. Mined and lost off Juno Beach, France, on 7 August 1944. Sister ships: *Vienna (II), Prague*.

Amsterdam (III); BR; IMO: 5015440
Built: by John Brown & Co. Ltd., Clydebank - yard no. 659
Launched: 19 January 1950
Dimensions: 377.0 / 360.8 x 52.0 x 15.2 ft
Tonnage: 5092 grt / 2633 nt / 1113 dwt
Engines: 2 x Parsons turbines - direct drive
Power Output: 12000 shp
Speed: 21½ knots
Passengers: 675 (B: 321 First & 236 Second class)
First ref: 10 June 1950 Parkeston Quay to Hook of Holland (m/v)

Pcs. Served on the Hook of Holland route until displaced by new ro-ro vessels. Space for 18 cars. Left P. Quay on 1 May 1969 having been sold to Chandris Line of Greece. Arrived in Piraeus 9 May for conversion to a cruise ship for cruises around the Mediterranean based in Venice. Re-named *Fiorita* on 13 May 1970. Laid up on 9 May 1979 until sold in early 1983 to Ef-Em Handels GmbH, Munich, then to Sommerland Handels GmbH and then in April to Oren Tur Turizm ve Isletmcilik Tatirim AS of Istanbul. Arrived in Kas, sw Turkey on 5 April 1983 for use as a hotelship. Sank following a storm in Fethiye Bay in 27 January 1987. Sister ship: *Arnhem*.

Angela Jurgens; Bell Line; IMO: 8815293
Built: 1988 by J.J. Sietas Schiffswerft, Hamburg, Germany - yard no. 967
Dimensions: 94.50 / 87.81 x 15.90 x 5.05 m
Tonnage: 2749 grt / 1110 nt / 3376 dwt
Engines: 1 x Wartsila diesel type 6R32D
Power Output: 1353 hp / 995 kw
Speed: 14 knots

Cms lo-lo. Space for 262 teus. One of 5 Sietas Type 122 feeder ships. Other names: *Inishowen* (1996), *Gera* (1998), *Arfel* (2001), *Gera* (2003), *Vera* (2003), *Marti Pride* (2006), *Princess Sira* (2008) and *Montaser M* (2001). Last owner: Nour Shipping, Marshall Islands. Sister ships: *Amazone, Jan Becker, Jan Kahrs* and *Otto Becker*.

Antwerp; GER
Built: by John Brown & Co. Ltd., Clydebank - yard no. 493
Launched: 26 October 1919
Tonnage: 2957 grt / 1286 nt/ 2373 dwt
Engines: 2 x 2 John Brown Curtis srg turbines
Power Output: 1476 nhp / 10500 shp
Speed: 21 knots
Passengers: 1680 (B: 263 First & 87 Second class)
First ref: June 1920 Parkeston Quay to Antwerp (m/v)

Pcs. Launched by Lady Blythwood. Able to accommodate 430 First class and 1250 Second class passengers though only had 350 berths. Requisitioned in January 1940, later becoming *H.M.S. Antwerp* in November 1940, and served mainly throughout the Mediterranean. Returned to P. Quay as a BAOR troopship to HvH from 19 September 1945 until 1 May 1950. Sold for scrap in April 1951 at T.W. Ward, Milford Haven where she arrived on 4 May 1951. Sister ships: *Bruges, Malines*.

A.P. Bernstorff; DFDS
Built: by A/S Helsingors Jernskibs-og Maskinbyggeri, Ellsinore - yard no. 140
Launched: 26 April 1913
Dimensions: 304.5 / 290.0 x 41.5 x 17.3 ft
Tonnage: 2316 grt / 1162 nt / 1352 dwt
Engines: Hels. J&M. Tr. exp. 27", 44" & (2) 52" - 42"
Power Output: 355 nhp / 3300 ihp
Speed: 16 knots
Passengers: 407 (138 First & 269 Third class)
First ref: 29 July 1913 Esbjerg to Parkeston Quay (m/v)

Pcs. Cost Dkr 1,217,024. Space for 15 cars. Initial service was interrupted on 12 August 1914 by WW1. Having been mainly laid up in Copenhagen she re-opened the Esbjerg to P. Quay route on 25 October 1919 and there remained until 5 May 1932. Thereafter sailed between Esbjerg and Antwerp / Dunkirk with very occasional calls at P. Quay. Refitted in 1935. Passengers: 210 (112 First & 98 Second class). Mostly laid up from 1940 onwards until seized by the Germans on 18 April 1944. Re-named *Renate* and used as a hospital ship in 1945. Post war she was refitted and returned as *A.P. Bernstorff* to the Esbjerg to P. Quay route from 5 March 1946 to 7 June 1946 and then again between 17 January 1947 and 11 October 1948. Rebuilt in late 1947 in Frederikshavn and converted to oil burning. Transferred to various other North Sea routes until finally laid up in July 1955. Sold for £50,500 on 27 March 1957 to Eisen und Metal K.G. & Co of Hamburg and scrapped by September 1957.

Aquila; ECR
Built: by James Henderson & Sons, Renfrew - yard no 7
Launched: 1854
Dimensions: 180.4 x 21.4 x 9.7 ft
Tonnage: 264 grt / 123 nt
Engines: McNab & Clark, Greenock s.o. 2 cyl 42 3/8 " - 42"
Power Output: 110 nhp
Speed: 13 knots
First ref: 16 September 1854 Harwich to Antwerp. Operated by the North of Europe Steam Navigation Co. on behalf of the ECR.

Pcps. Iron paddle steamer with a clipper bow, two masts and two tall funnels abaft the paddles. Launched for the North of Europe Steam Navigation Co. Made 12 trips from Harwich on behalf of ECR in 1854 and a further 47 in 1855 when chartered by the ECR from 23 April 1855 until 16 December 1855. The first sailing in ECR service was on 2 May 1855 from Harwich to Antwerp. Once more chartered for one trip to Rotterdam on 16 October 1856. Sister ship: *Cygnus*.

Armorique; Chartered; IMO: 7108203
Built: by Nouvelle des Ateliers et Chantiers du Havre, France - yard no. 205
Launched: 24 April 1971
Dimensions: 116.65 / 108.20 x 19.90 x 4.80 m
Tonnage: 5732 grt / 3036 nt / 1128 dwt
Engines: 2 x Semt-Pielstick 12 cyl diesels type 12PC2V400
Power Output: 12000 hp / 8825 kw
Speed: 19 knots
Passengers: 700 (B: 410))
First ref: March 1986 Hook of Holland to Parkeston Quay.

Pcms ro-ro. Launched as *Terje Vigen* for Da-No Line, Oslo, Norway for service between Oslo and Aarhus, Denmark. Space for 165 cars or 36 cars and 19 trailers. Sold in 1973 to Scan-Fahrt KG of Hamburg. Sold in 1975 to Brittany Ferries, Morlaix, France. Re-named *Armorique* and refitted for service between Plymouth and Roscoff or St. Malo. Also on sailings to Santander and Cork and sailings from Portsmouth. Chartered to SMZ from 25 March to 23 April 1986 between P. Quay and HvH. Sold on 18 December 1993 to Xiamen Ocean Shipping Co., Xiamen, China and re-named *Min Nan* for service between Xiamen and Hong Kong. Sold in 1998 to Wei Hai Ferry Co, China and re-named *Sheng Sheng*. Sold on 30 June 2003 to Dharma Lautan Utamea in Belize. Re-named *Tirta Kencana 1* in 2005 for service between Surabaya and Makasar. Re-named *Musthika Kencana II* on 2 April 2010. No details beyond July 2011.

Arnhem; LNER
Built: by John Brown & Co. Ltd., Clydebank - yard no. 636
Launched: 7 November 1946
Dimensions: 377.0 / 350.0 x 52.0 x 15.3 ft
Tonnage: 4891 grt / 2450 nt / 875 dwt
Engines: 2 x Parsons turbines - direct drive
Power Output: 12480 shp
Speed: 21½ knots
Passengers: 600 (B: 8 First & 414 Second class)
First ref: 26 May 1947 Parkeston Quay to Hook of Holland (m/v)

Pcs. Launched by Her Excellency Madame H. Michiels van Verduynen. Was the first Harwich based railway ship to be oil fired. Originally built with a one class cabin arrangement though berths were categorised as being equal to 272 First & 150 Second class. Space for 18 cars. Berth allocation was increased in 1948 to 296 First & 150 Second class. Refitted in spring 1954 and formally converted into a two class vessel for 675 passengers (B: 375 First & 201 Second class) and Tonnage: 5005 grt / 2538 nt / 1139 dwt. Withdrawn from service on 28 April 1968 prior to the introduction of ro-ro on the P. Quay to HvH route. Arrived at T.W. Ward Ltd of Inverkeithing on 16 August 1968 for resale or scrapping. Broken up in June 1969. Sister ship: *Amsterdam (III).*

Artevelde; RMT; IMO: 5025586
Built: by S.A. Cockerill-Ougree, Hoboken, Belgium - yard no.794
Launched: 1 February 1958
Dimensions: 383.1 x 50.7 x 12.4 ft
Tonnage: 2812 grt / 1417 nt / 775 dwt
Engines: 2 x Sulzer 12 cyl diesels type 12MD-510
Power Output: 9600 bhp / 7061 kw
Speed: 21 knots
Passengers: 985 (B:135)

Pcms ro-ro. (m/v) was on 2 June 1958 from Ostend to Dover. Capacity for 160 cars and 7 coaches. Served on this route until 1975, then laid up or chartered to Sealink at Dover. Sold to Vasilios Agapitos, Piraeus on 3 October 1976 and re-named *Aigaion* on 6 November. From 1977 until November 1993 was in service between Piraeus and various Greek islands after which she was laid up in Perama. Caught fire on 19 February 1996 during a refit at Drapetsona and sank whilst being towed to the island of Atalanti.

Astronom; H.J. Perlbach
Built: 1863 by M. Samuelson of Hull
Dimensions: 201.4 x 28.4 ft
Tonnage: 700 grt / 421 nt
Engines: Humphreys & Pearson of Hull c.o. 2 cyl 26" & 48" - 30"
Power Output: 90 hp
First ref: 19 August 1884 arrival at Parkeston Quay from Hamburg

Pcs. Formerly known as *Kestrell*

Atalanta; River Services
Built: 1841 in Deptford, Kent.
Dimensions: 100.4 x 14.8 x 6.8 ft
Tonnage: 72 grt.

Pps. Purchased by P. Bruff from owners in London in 1850. Powered by a 36 nhp engine. Owned by the EUR in 1851 and then by the ECR in July 1854 by which time she had been lengthened by 9 feet. Dimensions: 100.4 x 14.8 x 6.8 ft. Tonnage: 72 grt. Owned by the GER in 1862. Scrapped in 1868. Sister ship: *Cardinal Wolsey*

Autobahn; UECC; IMO: 7129207
Built: 1972 by Batservices Verft, Mandal, Norway
Dimensions: 92.45 x 14.50 x 3.87 m o.a.
Tonnage: 499 grt / 241 nt / 858 dwt
Speed: 13 knots
Stowage area: 4659 sq.m. on 6 levels
Trade car capacity: 420

Cms cc. Arrived at Aliaga on 17 April 1998 for scrapping

Autocarrier; UECC; IMO: 8100519
Built: 1982 by Flender Werft, Lubeck, Germany
Dimensions: 89.52 x 18.00 x 4.26 m o.a.
Tonnage: 1000 grt / 461 nt / 1472 dwt
Speed: 14½ knots
Stowage area: 6640 sq.m. on 7 levels
Trade car capacity: 683

Cms cc. Was known as *Castorp* until January 1990. Scrapped in 2009.

Autofreighter; UECC; IMO: 7533393
Built: 1977 by Vuijk & Zonens, Capelle Aan Den Ijssel, Holland
Dimensions: 89.56 x 18.02 x 4.23 m o.a.
Tonnage: 999 grt / 459 nt / 1303 dwt
Speed: 12½ knots
Stowage area: 5500 sq.m. on 7 levels
Trade car capacity:

Cms cc. Known as *Fredenhagen* until re-named *Autofreighter* in January 1990. Re-named *Freighter* in August 2005, *Kebbi* in October 2005 and *Elduga* in July 2010. Last owner: Natie Shipping, Vladivostok, Russia.

Autoline; UECC; IMO: 8200565
Built: 1983 by Tsuneishi Shipbuilding, Fukuyama, Japan
Dimensions: 99.99 x 17.00 x 4.82 m o.a.
Tonnage: 986 grt / 508 nt / 1550 dwt
Speed: 16 knots
Stowage area: 6114 sq.m. on 6 levels
Trade car capacity: 650

Cms cc. Re-named *Al Mahmoud Express* in November 2009 and *Express 1* in February 2013. Last owner: Sunlight Shipping of Panama and in service as a livestock carrier.

Autoroute; UECC; IMO: 7822079
Built: 1979 by Mitsui Tamano Eng. & Shipbuilding, Tamano, Japan
Dimensions: 99.99 x 17.40 x 4.20 m o.a.
Tonnage: 2462 grt / 721 nt / 1894 dwt
Speed: 15½ knots
Stowage area: 6767 sq.m. on 7 levels
Trade car capacity: 695

Cms cc. Scrapped

Autostrada; UECC; IMO: 7109219
Built: 1971 by Langvik Sarpsborg Mekaniske Verksted, Greaker, Norway
Dimensions: 92.45 x 14.50 x 3.87 m o.a.
Tonnage: 610 grt / 230 nt / 843 dwt
Speed: 13 knots
Stowage area: 4729 sq.m. on 6 levels
Trade car capacity: 420

Cms cc. Arrived at Aliaga on 13 August 1996 for scrapping

Autotrader; UECC; IMO: 7361166
Built: 1974 in Schulte & Bruns Schiffswerft, Emden, Germany
Dimensions: 89.86 x 16.60 x 4.59 m o.a.
Tonnage: 921 grt / 415 nt / 1307 dwt
Speed: 13 knots
Stowage area: 6020 sq.m. on 7 levels
Trade car capacity: 660

Cms cc. Known as *Warendorp* until 1990 and the *Autotrader* until September 1997. Scrapped.

Autotransporter; UECC; IMO: 8200577
Built: 1983 by Tsuneishi Shipbuilding, Fukuyama, Japan
Dimensions: 99.99 x 17.00 x 4.82 m o.a.
Tonnage: 997 grt / 516 nt / 1566 dwt
Speed: 16 knots
Stowage area: 6114 sq.m. on 6 levels
Trade car capacity: 650

Cms cc. Re-named *Al Mahmoud Orient* in November 2009. Last owner: Livestock Export of Panama and in service as a livestock carrier.

Autoweg; UECC; IMO: 7325576
Built: 1973 by Batservices Verft, Mandal, Norway
Dimensions: 91.30 x 15.00 x 3.84 m o.a.
Tonnage: 498 grt / 260 nt / 981 dwt
Speed: 14½ knots
Trade car capacity: 565
Stowage area: 5772 sq.m. on 7 levels

Cms cc. Scrapped

Avalon (I); GER
Built: by Messrs J. & W. Dudgeon, Cubitt Town, London
Launched: 26 March 1864
Dimensions: 245.0 / 230.0 x 27.1 x 11.8 ft
Tonnage: 613 grt / 455 nt / 499 dwt
Engines: J & W Dudgeon s.o. 2 cyl 54" - 30"
Power Output: 220 nhp / 950 hp
Speed: 12 knots
Passengers: 150
First ref: 13 June 1864 Harwich to Rotterdam (m/v)

Pcps. Built with a straight stem instead of a clipper bow that was more usual of the time. Twin funnelled, twin masted and schooner rigged with 16 feet diameter paddle wheels and a crew of 28. Sold back to J & W Dudgeon on 21 December 1864 for £23,500. Sister ship: *Zealous.*

Avalon (II); GER
Built: by Messrs J. & W. Dudgeon, Poplar, London
Launched: 3 June 1865
Dimensions: 239.8 x 27.1 x 14.0 ft
Tonnage: 670 grt / 478 nt / 571 dwt
Engines: J & W Dudgeon s.o. 2 cyl 54" - 54"
Power Output: 220 nhp / 1000 ihp
Speed: 14 knots
Passengers: 483
First ref: September 1865 Harwich to Rotterdam

Pcps. Built at a cost of £30,556, schooner rigged and with 18.8 ft diameter paddle wheels. In 1876 she was given new engines and boilers at The Victoria Graving Dock Co., London and a service speed of 12 knots. Sold to Earle's Co. Ltd. of Hull in 1888 as part payment for the *Colchester.* Converted to single screw vessel in 1890, saw service in Norway and Caribbean until wrecked in Bluff Bay, Jamaica in 1909. Sister ship: *Ravensbury.*

Avalon (III); BR; IMO: 5418915
Built: by Alexander Stephen & Sons of Linthouse, Glasgow - yard no. 680
Launched: 7 May 1963
Dimensions: 404.5 / 372.4 x 59.7 x 15.8 ft
Tonnage: 6584 grt / 3542 nt / 842 dwt
Engines: 2 x Pametrada turbines - direct drive
Power Output: 15000 shp / 10950 kw
Speed: 21 knots
Passengers: 750 (B: 331 First & 287 Second class)
First ref: 25 July 1963 Parkeston Quay to Hook of Holland (m/v)

Pcms. Cost £2m. Was the last traditional BR ship at P. Quay and well known for her off season cruises for up to 320 passengers organised by BR. Over a period of 8 years her destinations ranged from Scandinavia and the North Cape, the Baltic and Leningrad, Amsterdam and the Bulb fields, Portugal, Spain, Gibraltar and North Africa. Displaced in 1974 and sent to Swan Hunter Ship Repairs Ltd, North Shields on 29 December for a £1m rebuild as a stern loading car ferry. Emerged with two car decks in lieu of cabin decks and space for 210 cars and 1200 passengers. Tonnage: 5142 grt. Placed on the Fishguard to Rosslare route on 18 July 1975. Moved onto Holyhead to Dun Laoghaire route in January 1976. Hit breakwater on 17 March 1976 causing a 20 ft gash and three weeks off service. Returned to serve mainly as relief ship out of Holyhead until finishing on 8 September 1980. Laid up in Barrow and then sold in December 1980 to Seafaith Navigation Co, Limassol, Cyprus. Re-named *Valon.* On 22 January 1981 she arrived at HH Steel Ltd., Gadani Beach, Pakistan for scrapping.

Balder; Thule Line
Built: by Blackwood & Gordon, Port Glasgow - yard no. 239
Launched: 23 June 1898
Dimensions: 246.2 x 34.1 x 14.1 ft
Tonnage: 1486 grt / 829 nt / 1250 dwt
Engines: 3 cylinder Tr. exp.
Power Output: 212 nhp / 920 ihp
Speed: 12 knots
Passengers: 109 (58 First, 39 Second & 12 Third class)
First ref: 7 May 1910 Parkeston Quay to Gothenburg

Pcs. Entered service between Gothenburg and Granton, later to London Tilbury. Transferred to Rederi Ab Svenska Lloyd of Gothenburg (Swedish Lloyd) in January 1916. In August 1920 resumed Gothenburg to P. Quay / London calls until 1923 when transferred to Newcastle route. Passengers: 117 (25 First, 28 Second & 64 Third class). Rebuilt in 1930 with a refrigerated hold and re-named *Northumbria.* Tonnage: 1396 grt / 792 nt / 1250 dwt. Seized by Germans on 10 April 1940 at Stavanger and used as the U-boat trials escort vessel *Eupen.* Bombed by Allies on 9 October 1943 in Gdynia, raised in May 1944 and scrapped.

Batavier II; Dutch Trooping Service; IMO: 5605438
Built: by Wilton Machinefabriek & Shipyard Co., Rotterdam - yard no. 292
Launched: 1920
Dimensions: 260.0 x 35.0 x 15.5 ft
Tonnage: 1573 grt / 956 nt / 960 dwt
Engines: 3 cylinder Tr. exp. 24", 38" & 62" - 36"
Power Output: 231 nhp / 2250 ihp
Speed: 15 knots
First ref: 10 January 1946

Pcs. Built for Wm. Muller & Co. for Batavier Line service between Rotterdam and London. Passengers: 151 (98 First & 53 Second class). (m/v) was on 5 January 1921. Following cross channel evacuation duties in early 1940 she was requisitioned by the Royal Navy in Falmouth on 12 July 1940 for use as an accommodation ship. Returned to commercial service with Wm. Muller & Co. in 1942. Rebuilt in 1945 Tonnage: 1726 grt / 928 nt / 960 dwt. Passengers: 42 First class. Operated a service on behalf of the Dutch Government between Tilbury / P. Quay and Rotterdam from 6 July 1945 to 28 September 1946, (P. Quay from 10 January 1946). Resumed commercial service in June 1947 until withdrawn on 12 April 1958 and ending the Batavier Line passenger service between London and Rotterdam. Sold in September 1959 to NV Vereenigde Utrechtsche Ijzerhandel, Utrecht for scrapping in January 1960 at Hendrik Ido Ambacht.

Belinda; Chartered; IMO: 7389194
Built: by Ab Lodose Varv., Lodose - yard no. 180
Launched: 7 September 1978
Dimensions: 161.37 x 18.03 x 6.70 m
Tonnage: 11235 grt / 3338 nt / 8538 dwt
Engines: 2 x Zgoda Sulzer diesels type 8ZL40/48
Power Output: 7650 kw
Speed: 17¼ knots
Passengers: 12
First ref: May 1986

Cms. Capacity for 120 trailers or 302 teus. Sold to Belinda Shipping S.A., Panama in October 1985 and re-named *Belinda.* Chartered to DFDS in May 1986 for use on a new P. Quay to Rotterdam freight service. Route closed in 1987. Other names: Launched in 1978 as the 5236 grt *Linnea* which was seen on the P. Quay to Hamburg route in September 1984. Became the *Belinda* in 1985 then *Nordborg* (1988), *Dana Hafnia* (1994), *Kattegat Syd* (1999), *Dana Hafnia* (1999), *Tor Hafnia* (2001), *Strada Corsara* (2001) and *Indus* (2011). Scrapped at Alang, India in January 2012.

Bell Pioneer; Bell Line; IMO: 8907668
Built: 1990 by Teraoka Shipyard, Minamiawaji, Japan - yard no. 288
Dimensions: 114.00 x 17.00 x 4.0 m
Tonnage: 6111 grt / 5100 dwt

Cms lo-lo. Space for 301 teus. The first hatchless container ship. Other names: *Ultra Contship* (1997), *Ashdod Express* and *MF Ranger* (1998), *Ultra Container* (2000), *Zim Novorossiysk I* (2001), *Nile Express* (2002), *Med Power* (2003), *Alcione* (2004) and *Egy Group* (2009). Last owner: Mahoney Shipping & Marine Services, Alexandria, Egypt.

Bell Racer; Bell Line; IMO: 7613428
Built: 1977 by Kagoshima Dock & Iron Works, Kagoshima, Japan - yard no. 93
Dimensions: 92.00 x 13.61 x 6.8 m
Tonnage: 2213 grt / 3342 dwt
Speed: 13 knots

Cms lo-lo. Space for 168 teus. Launched as 1936 grt. Other names: *Blue Sky 1* (1997), *Zhen Yu,* and *Xin Chang* (2000). Scrapped.

Bell Ranger; Bell Line; IMO: 7613442
Built: 1976 by Kagoshima Dock & Iron Works, Kagoshima, Japan
Dimensions: 92.82 x 13.54 x 6.8 m
Tonnage: 2213 grt / 3342 dwt
Speed: 13 knots

Cms lo-lo. Space for 168 teus. Launched as 1948 grt. Other names: *Als* (1996), *Perma Glory* (1996), *Iran Glory* (2003) and *Mataf Star* in 2004. Last owner: Al Mataf Shipping, Dubai, United Arab Emirates.

Bell Reliant; Bell Line; IMO: 7709409
Built: 1978 by Kagoshima Dock & Iron Works, Kagoshima, Japan
Dimensions: 79.71 x 13.54 x 6.8 m
Tonnage: 1593 grt / 2159 dwt
Speed: 13 knots

Cms lo-lo. Space for 132 teus. Other names: *Erizo* (1991). Scrapped.

Bell Renown; Bell Line; IMO: 7709382
Built: 1978 by Kagoshima Dock & Iron Works, Kagoshima, Japan - yard no. 117
Dimensions: 79.71 x 13.54 x 6.8 m
Tonnage: 1593 grt / 2159 dwt
Speed: 13 knots

Cms lo-lo. Space for 132 teus. Launched: 25 February 1978. Other names: *Ola* in 1991. Scrapped.

Bell Resolve; Bell Line; IMO: 7709394
Built: 1978 by Kagoshima Dock & Iron Works, Kagoshima, Japan - yard no. 118
Dimensions: 79.58 x 13.54 x 6.8 m
Tonnage: 1592 grt / 2159 dwt
Speed: 13 knots

Cms lo-lo. Space for 132 teus. Other names: *Fareast Brilliant* (1993), *Hua Jie* (1995), *Hai You* (2008), *Mansengo Maru* (2010) and *Ocean Win* (2011). Last owner: Vision Shipping, Hong Kong.

Bell Rover; Bell Line; IMO: 7613430
Built: 1976 by Kagoshima Dock & Iron Works, Kagoshima, Japan
Dimensions: 79.58 x 13.54 x 6.8 m
Tonnage: 1593 grt / 2159 dwt
Speed: 13 knots

Cms lo-lo. Space for 132 teus. Other names: *Ling Feng* (1993) and *Hai De Li* (1998). Scrapped.

Bell Ruler; Bell Line; IMO: 7613454
Built: 1977 by Kagoshima Dock & Iron Works, Kagoshima, Japan - yard no. 96
Dimensions: 92.00 x 13.61 x 6.8 m
Tonnage: 2213 grt / 3342 dwt
Speed: 13 knots

Cms lo-lo. Space for 168 teus. Launched as 1936 grt. Other names: *Blue Sky 2* (1997) and *Hai Xiang Tong* (2001). Scrapped.

Bellona (I); DFDS
Built: by Deutsche Werke A.G. Kiel - yard no. 172
Launched: 3 November 1923
Dimensions: 241.0 / 230.0 x 33.9 x 14.6 ft
Tonnage: 840 grt / 418 nt / 1030 dwt
Engines: Deutsche Werke Tr. exp 19.75", 32.25" & 52.4" - 35"
Power Output: 1100 ihp
Speed: 12 knots
Passengers: 12
First ref: early 1930s.

Cs. Cost: Dkr 760,000. Infrequent visitor to P. Quay during the 1930s. Other names: *Bellona II* (1940). Lost by German air attack off Gourdon, Scotland on 9 October 1940.

Bellona (II); DFDS; IMO: 5040029
Built: by Frederikshavns Vaerft & Flydedok A/S, Frederikshavn - yard no. 222
Launched: 9 December 1955
Dimensions: 89.31 / 82.25 x 12.91 x 5.69 m
Tonnage: 1481 grt / 716 nt / 2022 dwt
Engines: 1 x B&W 5 cyl diesel type 550-VF-90
Power Output: 1680 bhp
Speed: 13 knots
Passengers: 8
First ref: 1958

Rcms. Occasional user of P. Quay until withdrawn from the North Sea in 1972. Sold on 12 April 1972 to William Lines Inc., Cebu. Other names: *Tagbilaran City* (1972), *Davao City* (1972) and *Wilcon IX* (1984). Stranded off Tulungin Point on 18 May 1986 and was later towed for scrapping in Manilla in October 1987. Sister ship: *Blenda*

Bergenhus; DFDS
Built: by A/S Helsingors Jernskibs-og Maskinbyggeri, Elsinore - yard no. 167
Launched: 23 September 1922
Dimensions: 242.2 / 230.0 x 35.0 x16.6 ft
Tonnage: 1399 grt / 798 nt / 1380 dwt
Engines: Helsingors J&M Tr. exp 18", 30" & 50" - 36"
Power Output: 900 ihp
Speed: 11 knots
Passengers: 8
First ref: late 1940s.

Pcs. Cost: Dkr 1,788,401. Infrequently seen at P. Quay. Sold on 30 September 1961 to Brugse Scheepssloperij N.V. Belgium for scrapping. Sister ship: *Trondhjem*

Berlin; GER
Built: by Earle's Shipbuilding & Eng. Co. Ltd., Hull - yard no. 379
Launched: 10 January 1894
Dimensions: 302.4 x 36.0 x 16.2 ft
Tonnage: 1745 grt / 556 nt / 1131 dwt
Engines: Earle's Tr. exp. 6 cyl in 2 sets 26", 39½" & 61" - 36"
Power Output: 447 nhp / 5800 ihp
Speed: 18 knots
Passengers: 780 (B: 218 First & 120 Second class)
First ref: April 1894 Parkeston Quay to Hook of Holland (m/v)

Pcs. Was wrecked on the Hook of Holland breakwater on 21 February 1907 with the loss of 128 lives. Sister ships: *Amsterdam (I), Vienna (I).*

Biarritz; Trooping Services
Built: by Wm. Denny & Bros., Dumbarton.
Launched: 7 December 1914
Dimensions: 352.0 / 341.2x 42.1 x 12.8 ft
Tonnage: 2388 grt / 936 nt / 461 dwt
Engines: 2 x Parson srg turbines
Power Output: 859 nhp / 10000 ihp
Speed: 22 knots
First ref: 5 January 1945

Pcs. Cost £90,545. Built for the South Eastern & Chatham Railway but first entered service for the Admiralty in March 1915 having been requisitioned as a minelayer. Was operated by the SE&CR / Southern Railway post war between Dover / Folkestone and Calais / Boulogne. Passengers: 1320 (120 First & 1200 Deck class). Requisitioned on 9 September 1939 as a troopship. Sent to Rotterdam on 11 April 1940 as a stand by ship to evacuate British civilians until replaced by the P. Quay based vessel, *Malines*, on 26 April 1940. Became a landing ship in 1942. Had two spells of trooping at P. Quay. Firstly, between P. Quay and Calais from 5 January 1945 to 27 February 1945 that included a period between Tilbury and Ostend in early February and secondly, between P. Quay and HvH from 6 September 1947 to 8 August 1948. Could carry up to 1104 service personnel. Did not resume commercial service and instead was scrapped in November 1949 by Dover Metal Industries.

Black Prince; Fred Olsen; IMO: 6613328
Built: by Lubecker Flender-Werke, Lubeck, Germany - yard no. 561
Launched: 14 May 1966
Dimensions: 464.7 x 65.7 x 20.0 ft
Tonnage: 9499 grt / 5272 nt / 3440 dwt
Engines: 2 x Crossley Pielstick 18 cyl diesels type 18PC2V
Power Output: 15500 bhp / 12310 kw
Speed: 22½ knots
Passengers: 587 (B: 151 First & 376 Tourist)
First ref: 19 May 1967 arrival at Parkeston Quay from Kristiansand

Pcms ro-ro. Built for Fred Olsen & Co of Kristiansand, Norway with a dual purpose role of a car ferry in summer (May to September) and a 350 passenger cruise ship to Canary Islands in winter. (m/v) was in October 1966 from London to Canaries. Space for 185 cars. Left the Kristiansand to P. Quay route in September 1969. When Fred Olsen integrated their ferry services with Bergen Lines in May 1970 she was re-named *Venus* when used as a ferry from Newcastle to Norway and as *Black Prince* when cruising from Rotterdam to Canary Islands. Re-fitted in 1986 in Turku, Finland as a cruise ferry sailing from Southampton to the Mediterranean with charter work in Scandinavia. Sold May 2009 to Servicios Acuaticos de Venezuela CA, re-named *Prince*, then *Ola Smeralda*. Chartered in 2010 to interests in Mexico. Sister ship: *Black Watch / Jupiter*

Blenda; DFDS; IMO: 5046310
Built: by Frederikshavns Vaerft & Flydedok A/S, Frederikshavn - yard no. 223
Launched: 1 August 1956
Dimensions: 89.31 / 82.25 x 12.91 x 5.69 m
Tonnage: 1481 grt / 717 nt / 2032 dwt
Engines: 1 x B&W 5 cyl diesel type 550-VF-90
Power Output: 1680 bhp
Speed: 13 knots
Passengers: 8
First ref: late 1950s.

Rcms. Seen at P. Quay throughout the 1960s. In 1971 she ended her North Sea services by sailing from P. Quay to Copenhagen, arriving there on 18 May. Sold on 17 March 1972 to William Lines Inc., Cebu. Other names: *General Santos City* (1972). Lost by sinking off San Nicolas Shoals, Manilla following an onboard fire on 24 December 1976. Sister ship: *Bellona (II)*

Blenheim; Chartered
Built: by William Denny & Bros., Dumbarton
Launched: 1854
Dimensions: 220 feet long
Tonnage: 514 grt / 412 nt
Power Output: 450 nhp
First ref: 3 October 1863 Rotterdam to Harwich

Pcps. Chartered by the ECR from Tod & McGregor of Glasgow from 24 September 1863 to 24 February 1864. Engines by Tulloch & Denny

Blenheim; Fred Olsen; IMO: 7008001
Built: by Upper Clyde Shipbuilders Ltd., Glasgow - yard no. 744
Launched: 10 January 1970
Dimensions: 488.7 x 65.6 x 22.0 ft
Tonnage: 10419 grt / 5540 nt / 3721 dwt
Engines: 2 x Crossley Pielstick 18 cyl diesels type 18PC2V-400
Power Output: 18000 bhp / 13428 kw
Speed: 23 knots
Passengers: 1107 (B: 580)
First ref: 29 May 1971 arrival at Parkeston Quay from Kristiansand

Pcms ro-ro. Delivered to Fred Olsen Ltd, London on 1 September 1970 six months late due to shipyard delays. (m/v) was on 10 September 1970 when in cruising mode for up to 400 passengers between London, Funchal, Tenerife and Las Palmas. In May 1971 she ran as a car ferry from Kristiansand to P. Quay / Amsterdam. Space for 300 cars. Alternated between cruise ship and car ferry until leaving the P. Quay route in September 1975 and transferring to Newcastle. Sold to DFDS Seacruises in 1982 and thereafter to various interests in Florida and Bahamas. Re-named *Discovery 1* and *Scandinavia Sea* in 1982 and *Venus Venturer* in 1984. Caught fire off Bahamas on 8 May 1996, towed to Freeport and laid up. She arrived in Alang, India on 29 August 1997 for breaking up by Goyal Traders Ltd.

Bolero; Fred Olsen; IMO: 7221433
Built: by Dubigeon-Normandie S.A., Nantes - yard no. 133
Launched: 13 June 1972
Dimensions: 464.1 x 71.8 x 18.7 ft
Tonnage: 11344 grt / 6350 nt / 1828 dwt
Engines: 2 x Pielstick 12 cyl diesels type 12PC3V
Power Output: 20400 bhp / 15000 kw
Speed: 21½ knots
Passengers: 975 (B: 620)
First ref: February 1973 at Harwich Navyard Dock from Bremerhaven and Hamburg

Pcms ro-ro. She first entered service in 1973 on charter to Prins Line between Bremerhaven and Harwich Navyard from 17 to 23 February and then between Hamburg and Harwich Navyard from 24 February to 3 March. Space for 270 cars. Chartered to Commodore Cruise Line between 1973 and 1976 to run between USA east coast and Bermuda, then Nova Scotia to Maine. In November 1976 she commenced year round sailings from Newcastle to Norway until May 1978 when chartered to Stena Line and re-named *Scandinavica* for use between Gothenburg and Kiel. Returned to Fred Olsen in 1981 as the *Bolero*. Re-fitted and given side door access to freight decks. Tonnage: 14264 grt / 6325 nt / 1829 dwt Passengers: 1600 (B:620) plus 410 cars. Sailed Hirtshals to Kristiansand in summer and to Stavanger / Bergen in winter. In summer 1984 she sailed between Kristiansand and P. Quay from 19 June to 30 August. Chartered to Vaasanlaivat's Sweden - Finland service between Sundsvall and Vaasa, June to 1 September 1985. Thereafter extensively used between Denmark and Norway with seasonal work on the Kristiansand to Hirtshals / P. Quay routes from 17 June to 21 August 1986 and 16 June to 20 August 1987. Transferred to Color Line A/S, Oslo on 15 December 1990 and re-named *Jupiter*. Passengers: 1400 (B:530) plus 342 recliners, 48 couchettes and 245 cars. Re-named *Crucero Express* in October 1994 and sold to B. Skaugen Holding A/S, Nassau. Served out the rest of her career under various owners cruising in the Mexican Gulf and Florida being re-named *Seminole Empress* in October 1996, *Magic 1* in February 1999, *Mirage* in March 2003 and *Mirage 1* in 2004. Broken up in Aliaga, Turkey in March 2012.

Borgen; Fred Olsen; IMO: 7358315
Built: by Aalborg Verft A/S, Aalborg - yard no. 206
Launched: 17 December 1974
Dimensions: 355.7 x 58.3 x 16.1 ft
Tonnage: 5330 grt / 2763 nt / 1180 dwt
Engines: 4 x Stork Werkspoor 6 cyl diesels type 6TM410
Power Output: 16000 bhp / 11770 kw
Speed: 21 knots
Passengers: 776 (B: 254)
First ref: June 1976 arrival at Parkeston Quay from Kristiansand

Pcms ro-ro. Built as an 18 wagon train ferry or 270 car ferry for service between Kristiansand and Hirtshals. (m/v) was on 26 June 1975. Covered the 1976 summer season between Kristiansand and P. Quay. Substantially rebuilt and lengthened at Aalborgs Vaerft in 1981. Dimensions: 427.1 x 64.9 x 16.4 ft. Tonnage: 7570 grt / 4285 nt / 1824 dwt. Passengers: 900 to 1574 depending on route and season (B:410), 392 recliners, 42 couchettes and 430 cars. Sailed as *Skagen* for Color Line, Oslo in 1991 and rebuilt in Gothenburg in 1992. Tonnage: 12333 grt / 5300 nt / 2520 dwt. Resumed sailings on various routes between Norway and Denmark until laid at Sandefjord in August 2004. Sold in 2005 to El Salam Shipping, Egypt and re-named *Fedra*, then to Arab Bridge Maritime Co., Jordan and re-named *Shehrazade*. Further re-named *Shehrazad* in 2011 and sold for breaking up at Alang, India.

Botnia; DFDS
Built: by Lobnitz & Co., Renfrew - yard no. 364
Launched: 7 October 1891
Dimensions: 209.5 / 199.5 x 31.0 x 15.1 ft
Tonnage: 1032 grt / 578 nt / 1056 dwt
Engines: Lobnitz Tr. exp 18", 30" & 48" - 36"
Power Output: 1050 ihp
Speed: 11 knots
Passengers: 243 (73 First, 40 second & 130 Third class)
First ref: 1892

Pcs. Cost: Dkr 658,557. Variously seen at P. Quay until 1904 and then again in 1909. Sold on 12 March 1935 to Hughes Bolckow Shipbreaking Co Ltd at Blyth for scrapping.

Braemar; Fred Olsen; IMO: 7827225
Built: by Oy Wartsila Ab., Turku - yard no. 1248
Launched: 23 March 1980
Dimensions: 476.2 x 83.6 x 18.1 ft
Tonnage: 14623 grt / 7236 nt / 2830 dwt
Engines: 4 x Wartsila Pielstick diesels type

12PC2SV
Power Output: 24000 bhp / 19480 kw
Speed: 21½ knots
Passengers: 1900 (B: 1256)
First ref: 12 June 1985 arrival at Parkeston Quay from Hirtshals

Pcms ro-ro. Built as the *Viking Song* for Viking Line. Tonnage: 13879 grt / 7236 nt / 2830 dwt. Passengers: 2000 (B:1238). (m/v) was on 30 August 1980 between Stockholm and Helsinki. Sold to Fred Olsen in May 1985, refitted at Blohm & Voss, Hamburg and entered summer service in June 1985 between Kristiansand and Hirtshals / P. Quay. Freight space: 486 cars or 56 x 18m trailers. Sailings were amended on 5 September 1985 to an all year service from Oslo to Hirtshals / P. Quay until June 1989. Reverted to Kristiansand only until the P. Quay link closed on 30 August 1989. Transferred to new Oslo - Hirtshals / Kristiansand / Newcastle service on 7 September 1989. Sold in December 1990 to Rigorus Shipping Co. Ltd, Limassol, Cyprus. Chartered in January 1991 to Baltic Shipping Co., St. Petersburg, re-named *Anna Karenina* and put on Baltic Line's St. Petersburg to Nynashamn and Kiel service. Laid up as *Anna K* in March 1996, sold to Empremare Shipping Co. Limassol, re-named *Regina Baltica* for Estline service between Stockholm and Talllinn. Thereafter variously chartered to Estonian and Latvian interests for services principally between Stockholm and Tallinn / Riga until 2009. Summer charters in 2010 and 2011 to Acciona Trasmediterranea, Spain between Almeria and Nador. Re-appeared at P. Quay during 2012 when chartered as a floating hotel ship servicing offshore wind farms. Since March 2013 in service for Sweoffshore. Sister ship: *Viking Saga*

Brathay Fisher; BR; IMO: 7103033
Built: by Van Der Werf Scheeps n.v., Deest, Holland. - yard no.
Launched: 26 March 1971
Dimensions: 347.5 x 55.1 x 18.0 ft o.a.
Tonnage: 3604 grt / 2015 nt / 5463 dwt
Engines: 1 x Kloeckner-Humboldt-Deutz, Cologne 12 cyl diesel
Power Output: 4800 bhp
Speed: 14½ knots
Passengers: Nil
First ref: Autumn 1971 Parkeston Quay to Zeebrugge / Rotterdam

Cms lo-lo. Built for James Fisher & Sons, Barrow. Used as cover at P. Quay for when the *Sea Freightliners* were away on overhaul in autumn 1971. Chartered for two years in August 1974 by BR at P. Quay. Was the main ship on the Dunkirk service from 11 August 1974 until 23 December 1975 when she was displaced by the *Rhodri Mawr*. Chartered to Mac Andrews & Sons in 1976 and re-named *Calderon*. Reverted to *Brathay Fisher* in 1978 and chartered to assist between P. Quay and Zeebrugge / Dunkirk from 12 November 1978 to 25 October 1980. Left Dunkirk route in November 1980 and in 1981 was sold to Salwa Marine Co. Ltd, Cyprus and re-named *Haje Naime*. In 1983 was re-named *Violette* for Amrid Shipping Co. Ltd, Syria before reverting to *Haje Naime* in 1984. Was further re-named *Newpoint* in 1985 whilst still with Salwa Marine and again in 1985 re-named as *Pel Carrier*. In November 1994 was re-named *Pancon3* and in August 2002 re-named *Progress3*. On 28 June 2003 she arrived at Chittagong for scrapping.

Brian Boroime; BR; IMO: 7015327
Built: by Verolme Cork Dockyard Ltd., Cobh - yard no. 809
Launched: 23 March 1970
Dimensions: 351.9 / 324.8 x 57.0 x 13.5 ft
Tonnage: 4098 grt / 1882 nt / 3150 dwt
Engines: 2 x Mirrlees Blackstone 6 cyl diesels type KLSSGMR
Power Output: 4200 bhp
Speed: 14½ knots
Passengers: Nil
First ref: October 1970 Parkeston Quay to Zeebrugge / Rotterdam

Cms lo-lo. Cost £1m. Built for new BR container services between Holyhead and Dublin and Holyhead to Belfast. Space for 184 teus. 18 crew. Services never started as planned due to a fire on the Britannia Bridge on 23 May 1970. Used as cover at P. Quay for when the *Sea Freightliners* were away on overhaul from 13 October to 5 December 1970. Then transferred to sail from Heysham on 10 December 1970 to Belfast / Dublin until the Britannia Bridge was repaired and her planned sailings from Holyhead were able to start on 30 January 1972. Her last sailing from Holyhead was to Belfast on 21 December 1989. Sold in 1990 to Satinwave Shipping Co, Cyprus. Re-named *Peltainer* for Sarlis Container Services around the eastern Mediterranean. Sold in 2004 to Arados Shipping and re-named *Abdul H*. Was scrapped at Aliaga, Turkey having arrived there on 17 April 2012. Sister ship: *Rhodri Mawr*.

Brightlingsea; River Services
Built: 1925 by Rowhedge Iron Works Co. Ltd., Colchester
Dimensions: 70.0 / 67.5 x 16.0 x 3.8 ft
Tonnage: 51.16 grt / 24.39 nt
Engines: 2 x Bergius Co. Ltd, Glasgow 6 cyl diesels
Power Output: 80 bhp
Speed: 9 knots
Passengers: 231
First ref: October 1925

Pms. Cost £4,656. Wooden hulled and the first ship built for the LNER. Requisitioned in 1939-45 for harbour duties. Re-opened Harwich to Felixstowe service on 1 February 1946. Re-engined in 1956. Engines: 1 x Kelvin 4 cyl diesel. Power Output: 88 bhp. Service closed on 31 December 1961. Sold to George Goodhew of Great Oakley. Service resumed on 1 May 1962 by the Orwell & Harwich Navigation Co. Ltd. Service sold on 1 October 1979 to Felixstowe Dock & Railway Co. Sold on 5 June 1985 to Harry Rodger of the O&HNC but withdrawn on 15 August with engine failure. Sold to Alan Pridmore in November 1985 who returned her to service in summer 1986. Following the route's closure in autumn 1993 she was used for harbour cruises. Laid up at Walton and then Woodbridge. Refurbished for current service as a river cruiser.

Bruges; GER
Built: by John Brown & Co. Ltd., Clydebank - yard no. 494
Launched: 20 March 1920
Dimensions: 337.0 / 321.5 x 43.1 x 17.8 ft
Tonnage: 2949 grt / 1286 nt / 2373 dwt
Engines: 2 x 2 John Brown Curtis srg turbines
Power Output: 1476 nhp / 10500 shp
Speed: 21 knots
Passengers: 1680 (B: 263 First & 87 Second class)
First ref: 30 September 1920 Parkeston Quay to Antwerp (m/v)

Pcs. Inaugurated the seasonal P. Quay to Zeebrugge service on 5 July 1921. Requisitioned on 5 September 1939 as a troopship. Was bombed off Le Havre on 11 June 1940 and lost. Sister ships: *Antwerp, Malines*.

Brussels; GER
Built: by Gourlay Bros. & Co., Dundee - yard no. 202
Launched: 2 September 1901
Dimensions: 285.3 x 34.0 x 15.5 ft
Tonnage: 1380 grt / 523 nt / 950 dwt
Engines: Gourlay's Tr. exp. 6 cyl in 2 sets 20", 33" & 54" - 36"
Power Output: 350 nhp / 3900 ihp
Speed: 16 knots
Passengers: (B: 164 First & 88 Second class)
First ref: 19 June 1902 Parkeston Quay to Antwerp (m/v)

Pcs. Launched by Miss Drury. Cost £63.700. Noted for the ship commanded by Captain Fryatt and captured by the Germans on 23 June 1916. Scuttled at Zeebrugge on 14 October 1917, raised 14 October 1919 and returned to the GER who sold her for £3,100 in August 1920 for use as a cattle carrier between Liverpool and Dublin. Re-named *Lady Brussels*. Sold for scrapping at Port Glasgow in May 1929.

Cambridge; GER
Built: by Earle's Shipbuilding & Eng. Co. Ltd., Hull - yard no. 299
Launched: 11 October 1886
Dimensions: 280.5 x 31.0 x 15.2 ft
Tonnage: 1196 grt / 519 nt / 906 dwt
Engines: Earle's 2 sets comp. 2 cyl 30" & 57" - 36"
Power Output: 275 nhp / 2200 ihp
Speed: 14½ knots
Passengers: 737 (B: 134 First & 56 Second class)
First ref: 12 February 1887 Parkeston Quay to Antwerp (m/v)

Pcs. Was the GER's first screw steamer built of steel. Similar to *Norwich* and *Ipswich* but 20 feet longer. Engines indicated 2350 hp on trials. Was in a collision with *H.M.S. Salmon* on 12 December 1911 with two of the destroyer's crew killed. Sold to the Anglo Ottoman Steamship Co. Ltd. of Greece on 25 November 1912. Sold in 1919 to Admin. de Navine a Vapeur Ottomane Galata, Constantinople and re-named *Gul Nehad*. Sold in 1922 to Admin. de Navine a Vapeur Turque Galata and re-named *Gulnihal*. Sold for scrap in 1937. Sister ship: *Colchester*.

Cambridge Ferry; BR; IMO: 6400044
Built: by Hawthorn, Leslie Shipbuilders Ltd., Hebburn - yard no. 754
Launched: 1 November 1963
Dimensions: 406.0 x 61.3 x 11.3 ft o.a.
Tonnage: 3294 grt / 1111 nt /1854 dwt
Engines: 2 x Mirrlees National Ltd., Stockport 7 cyl diesels
Power Output: 3720 bhp / 2736 kw
Speed: 13½ knots
Passengers: 12 (B: 12 First class)
First ref: 2 January 1964 Harwich to Zeebrugge (m/v) for BR.

Cms tf. Fitted with flume stabilisation system to counteract rolling. Freight capacity: 38 continental wagons. Also designed to carry ro-ro traffic and box containers. Modified in 1977 to fit the berth at Dunkirk. Made her last sailing at Harwich on 24 December 1986 and was then refitted at Immingham for service at Dover. Berthing trials at Dover on 2 February 1987, then in service to Dunkirk from 16 March 1987 until 13 October 1988. Sold to Stena Line Ab, Gothenburg in January 1990 and used on Irish Sea services until sold to Sincomar, Valetta, Malta on 21 April 1992 and re-named *Ita Uno*. Further re-named *Sirio* in 1993. Used intermittently as a freight ship in eastern Mediterranean, eg Italy to Albania. Sold in May 2003 for scrap at Huzur Gemi Sokum Ltd, Aliaga, Turkey where she arrived on 26 May 2003.

Canabal; UECC; IMO: 7409102
Built: 1976 by Astilleros Construcciones, Vigo, Spain
Dimensions: 88.55 x 15.96 x 5.18 m o.a.
Tonnage: 1323 grt / 697 nt / 2175 dwt
Speed: 13 knots
Stowage area: 4882 sq.m. on 6 levels
Trade car capacity: 540

Cms cc. Other names: *Tamara* (1993) and *Tamara 1* (1994). Scrapped.

Cardinal Wolsey; River Services
Built: 1845 by Bedlington Ironworks, Northumberland.
Dimensions: 104.0 x 14.3 x 6.7 ft
Tonnage: 57 tons

Pps. Built for the Eastern Union Railway. Fitted with a simple oscillating single cylinder engine and space for 150 passengers. Purchased by P. Bruff in 1850 and operated in arrangement with the EUR. Owned by the ECR in June 1854 though still registered to Bruff. Sold to the GER in August 1862 who re-sold her in 1863 to interests in Middlesborough. Scrapped in 1865. Sister ship: *Atalanta*.

Ceres; DFDS
Built: by Kochums Mekaniska Verkstads A/B. Malmo - yard no. 36
Launched: 30 September 1882
Dimensions: 237.4 / 228.7 x 30.0 x 17.1 ft
Tonnage: 1166 grt / 730 nt / 1022 dwt
Engines: Kochums c.o. 2 cyl 34.75" & 61.4" - 38"
Power Output: 1000 ihp
Speed: 11 knots
Passengers: 117 (54 First, 36 Second & 27 Deck class)
First ref: 1900

Pcs. First delivered to Sydsvenska Angfartygs A/B of Malmo on 21 February 1883. Purchased by DFDS on 14 April 1899 for Dkr 250,000. Occasional winter visitor to P. Quay until 1914. Sunk by the German submarine U88 in the North Atlantic on 13 July 1917.

Charkow; DFDS
Built: by Palmer Bros & Co. Jarrow - yard no. 66
Launched: 2 November 1857
Dimensions: 197.5 x 25.6 x 16.0 ft
Tonnage: 689 grt / 518 nt / 720 dwt
Engines: Day, Summers & Co. Southampton c.o. 2 cyl 26" & 52" - 36"
Power Output: 450 ihp
Speed: 8 knots
Passengers: 88 (42 First & 46 Second class)
First ref: early 1880s.

Cs. First delivered to Norddeutscher Lloyd, Bremen in 1857. Purchased by DFDS on 30 November 1881 for £6.000. Sold on 27 May 1898 to C.J. Lundvall & Co., Helsingborg. Other names: Delivered as *Mowe* in 1857 then *Charkow* (1881) and *Onsala* (1898). Sank off Ijmuiden 7/8 October 1905. Sister ships: *Romney, Minsk, Tula*.

Chelmsford; GER
Built: by Earle's Shipbuilding & Eng. Co. Ltd., Hull - yard no. 367
Launched: 21 February 1893
Dimensions: 300.3 x 34.5 x 16.2 ft
Tonnage: 1635 grt / 596 nt / 1076 dwt.
Engines: Earle's Tr. exp. 6 cyl in 2 sets 26", 39½" & 61" - 36"
Power Output: 5000 ihp
Speed: 17½ knots
Passengers: 730 (B: 200 First & 64 Second class)
First ref: 31 May 1893 Parkeston Quay to Hook of Holland (m/v)

Pcs. Launched: by the Mayoress of Chelmsford. Fitted with some Third class berths. Was the ship that opened the new Dutch terminal at the Hook of Holland on 1st June 1893. Sold in June 1910 to the GWR who re-named her *Bretonne*. Transferred in 1911 to sailing in Greek waters as the *Esperia* and then as the *Syros* in 1920 until she was sold for scrap in 1933.

Christian IX; DFDS
Built: by A/S Burmeister & Wain's Maskin-og Skibsbyggeri, Copenhagen - yard no. 84
Launched: 12 April 1874
Dimensions: 232.2 / 224.0 x 30.2 x 16.0 ft
Tonnage: 1236 grt / 890 nt / 1415 dwt
Engines: B&W c.o. 4 cyl (2) 21" & (2) 44" - 30"
Power Output: 500 ihp
Speed: 9 knots
Passengers: 16 (10 First & 6 Second class)
First ref: late 1880s.

Pcs. Sold on 6 April 1916 to Asgeir Pjetursson, Reykjavik. Other names: *Halvar* (1917) and *Hammarby* (1921). Lost by stranding off Biskopson, Sweden on 25 November 1925. Wreck sold for scrap in Stockholm.

Christianssund; DFDS
Built: by Lobnitz & Co., Renfrew - yard no. 190
Launched: 6 August 1881
Dimensions: 180.0 x 25.0 x 13.5 ft
Tonnage: 574 grt / 351 nt / 450 dwt
Engines: Lobnitz c.o. 2 cyl 24" & 44" - 30"
Power Output: 420 ihp
Speed: 9½ knots
Passengers: 300 (34 First, 14 Second & 252 Deck class)
First ref: early 1900s.

Pcs. First delivered to T.H Adolphs Enke, Copenhagen in September 1881. Purchased by DFDS on 23 January 1888. Sold on 28 April 1903 to A/S Sondmore D.S. of Aalesund. Other names: *Hjorungavaag* (1903) and *Havda* (1921). Sunk by allied air attack off Floro, Norway on 9 December 1944.

Clacton; GER
Built: by Earle's Shipbuilding & Eng. Co. Ltd., Hull - yard no. 488
Launched: 28 November 1904
Dimensions: 245.0 x 31.3 x 15.2 ft
Tonnage: 820 grt / 209 nt / 702 dwt
Engines: Earle's Tr. exp. 6 cyl in 2 sets 15½", 25¼" & 41" - 36"
Power Output: 202 nhp / 1970 ihp
Speed: 14 knots
Passengers: Nil
First ref: 7 February 1905 Parkeston Quay to Rotterdam (m/v)

Cs. Requisitioned in October 1914. Sunk by U73 near Kavalla Bay, Aegean Sea on 22 October 1917. Sister ship: *Newmarket*

Claud Hamilton; GER
Built: by John Elder & Co., Govan, Glasgow - yard no. 187
Launched: 3 June 1875
Dimensions: 251.6 x 30.2 x 13.7 ft
Tonnage: 962 grt / 565 nt / 677 dwt
Engines: J. Elder c.o. 2 cyl 54" & 95" - 63"
Power Output: 350 nhp / 1596 ihp
Speed: 14 knots
Passengers: 558
First ref: 14 August 1875 Harwich to Rotterdam (m/v)

Pcps. First GER ship built on the Clyde and the first GER ship fitted with compound oscillating machinery. Named after a Director of the GER and was the last GER paddle steamer still in service when sold in 1897 to the Corporation of the City of London for use as a cattle carrier between Gravesend and Deptford. Sold in July 1914 for scrapping in Holland and arrived at the yard of Hendrick-ido-Ambacht on 26 August 1914.

Clipper; Chartered; IMO: 7928756
Built: 1980 by J.J. Sietas Schiffswerft, Hamburg, Germany - yard no. 854
Dimensions: 92.3 / 86.7 x 15.5 x 6.3 m
Tonnage: 3228 grt / 5050 dwt
Engines: 1 x Klockner Humbold Deutz diesel
Power Output: 1470 kw
Speed: 14 knots

Cms lo-lo. 263 teus. Chartered by DFDS in 1989 for service between P. Quay and Bremerhaven. Other names: Launched in 1980 as *Clipper* then re-named *Manchester Clipper* (1980), *ECL Cadet* (1991), *Jupiter* (1992), *Iberian Bridge* (1992), *Jupiter* (1993), *Borstel* (1993), *Paaschburg* (1997), *Lady Marah* (2008), *FGM Istanbul* (2010), *Pendik* (2011) and *My Violet* (2013). Still in service. Last owner - Viramarine Denizcilik of Istanbul. Sister ship: *Concord*.

Cobres; UECC; IMO: 7409114
Built: 1977 by Astilleros Construcciones, Vigo, Spain
Dimensions: 88.55 x 15.96 x 5.18 m o.a.
Tonnage: 1323 grt / 697 nt / 2175 dwt
Speed: 13 knots
Stowage area: 4882 sq.m. on 6 levels
Trade car capacity: 540

Cms cc. Other names: *Eleonore* (1993) and *Elenore* (1993). Scrapped.

Colchester (I); GER
Built: by Earle's Shipbuilding & Eng. Co. Ltd., Hull - yard no. 312
Launched: 1889
Dimensions: 280.8 x 31.0 x 15.2 ft
Tonnage: 1160 grt / 517 nt / 907 dwt.
Engines: Earle's 2 sets comp. 2 cyl 30" & 57" - 36"
Power Output: 275 nhp / 2440 ihp
Speed: 14½ knots
Passengers: 730 (B: 160 First & 56 Second class)
First ref: 27 February 1889 Parkeston Quay to Antwerp (m/v)

Pcs. In 1900 she was re-boilered and her engine room rebuilt with triple expansion steam engines comprising 8 cyl in 2 sets, (2)14½", (2)23" & (4)27" - 33". Captured by the Germans on 21 September 1916, sunk by Royal Navy on 2 March 1918 off Kiel and in 1919 was towed back to England for scrapping. Sister ship: *Cambridge*.

Colchester (II); BR; IMO: 5076987
Built: by Goole Shipbuilding & Repairing Co. Ltd., Goole - yard no. 513
Launched: 14 October 1958
Dimensions: 241.8 / 226.0 x 37.0 x 13.2 ft
Tonnage: 866 grt / 278 nt / 935 dwt
Engines: 1 x Ruston & Hornsby Ltd 8 cyl diesel type VOXM
Power Output: 1806 bhp
Speed: 13½ knots
Passengers: Nil
First ref: 2 February 1959 Parkeston Quay to Antwerp (m/v)

Cms. General purpose cargo ship for unit load / box containers. Capacity of 42 'B' type box containers. Was the first ship to appear in 1965 with the new BR colours of blue hull, white superstructure, red funnel with black top and double arrow logo. Lengthened by 54 feet and converted to a cellular container ship in June 1969 at Ailsa Shipbuilding Co. in Troon. Emerged able to carry 86 x 30 foot containers or 129 teus. Also served on routes to Rotterdam and Dunkirk. Withdrawn from P. Quay in September 1972 and moved to Holyhead and Heysham in 1973. Chartered in November 1973 by MacAndrews & Co. for services between Liverpool, Spain and Portugal and in March 1974 by J. Fisher. Sold in 1975 to Corinthian Nav. Co., Cyprus and re-named *Taurus II*. Other names: *Gloriana* (1979), *Sea Wave* (1984), *Taurus* (1985) and *Diana* (1991). No further details after 1993. Sister ship: *Isle of Ely*

Concord; Chartered; IMO: 8024155
Built: 1981 by J.J. Sietas Schiffswerft, Hamburg, Germany - yard no. 884
Dimensions: 92.3 / 86.7 x 15.5 x 6.3 m
Tonnage: 3149 grt / 1698 nt / 4519 dwt
Engines: 1 x Klockner Humbold Deutz diesel
Power Output: 1470 kw
Speed: 14 knots

Cms lo-lo. 269 teus. Chartered by DFDS in 1989 for service between P. Quay and Bremerhaven. Other names: Launched in July 1981 as *Concord*, then re-named *Eastmed Queen* (1982), *Concord* (1983), *Australian Eagle* (1983), *ECL Concord* (1991), *Concord (1992)*, *Prime Venture II* (1993), *Phoenix* (2000), *Egypt Star* (2000), *Frey* (2004) and *Kaja* (2008). Still in service. Last owner - Hansa Shipping of Tallinn. Sister ship: *Clipper*.

Constantin; DFDS;
Built: by Kochums Mekaniska Verkstads A/B. Malmo - yard no. 24
Launched: 23 January 1880
Dimensions: 237.8 / 228.5 x 30.0 x 17.0 ft
Tonnage: 891 grt / 517 nt / 975 dwt
Engines: Kochums c.o. 2 cyl 34" & 60" - 38"
Power Output: 800 ihp
Speed: 11½ knots
Passengers: 18
First ref: late 1900s.

Cs. First delivered to C.K. Moller of Copenhagen in April 1880. Purchased by DFDS on 3 May 1880 for Dkr 470,000. Sold on 31 January 1923 to Carl Marius Engholm of Copenhagen and later scrapped in Kiel.

Copenhagen; GER
Built: by John Brown & Co. Ltd., Clydebank - yard no. 380
Launched: 22 October 1906
Dimensions: 343.0 / 331.2 x 43.2 x 17.8 ft
Tonnage: 2410 grt / 708 nt / 1498 dwt
Engines: 3 Parsons Turbines - direct drive
Power Output: 1325 nhp / 9208 ihp
Speed: 20 knots
Passengers: (B: 320 First & 130 Second class)
First ref: 27 January 1907 Parkeston Quay to Hook of Holland (m/v)

Pcs. Launched by Miss Ida Hamilton, daughter of Lord Claud Hamilton, as the P. Quay to HvH route's first turbine steamer. Also triple screwed. First arrived at P. Quay on 24 January 1907. Requisitioned in October 1914. Was sunk on 5 March 1917 by UC61, 8 miles off the North Hinder lightship whilst sailing from P. Quay to HvH. Sister ships: *Munich, St. Petersburg*.

Corncrake; GSNCo
Built: by Ailsa Shipbuilding & Co, Troon - yard no. 223
Launched: 12 May 1910
Dimensions: 240.0 x 35.1 ft
Tonnage: 1171 grt / 555 nt
Engines: Tr. exp.
Power Output: 251 nhp
Speed: 12 knots

Pcs. Seen on the GSNCo. P. Quay to Hamburg route. Sold in 1937 to Moss Hutchison Line and re-named *Chloris*. Sold in 1948 to SARGA and re-named *Sarga*. Sold in 1953 to P. Cossi and re-named *Gianandrea*. Scrapped at Savona in 1955.

Cromer; GER
Built: by Gourlay Bros. & Co., Dundee - yard no. 201
Launched: 22 February 1902
Dimensions: 245.3 x 31.3 x 15.3 ft
Tonnage: 812 grt / 253 nt / 706 dwt
Engines: Gourlay's Tr. exp. 6 cyl in 2 sets 15½", 25¼" & 41" - 36"
Power Output: 201 nhp / 1952 ihp
Speed: 13½ knots
Passengers: Nil
First ref: 22 April 1902 Parkeston Quay to Rotterdam (m/v)

Cs. Launched by Miss A Howard. Cost £37,498. Was the first GER ship to fully serve her time as cargo only. Able to carry 450 tons of cargo and 86 head of cattle. Manned by a Captain and 26 crew. Sold for scrapping at Hendrick-ido-Ambacht. Left for Rotterdam under tow on 30 August 1934. Sister ship: *Yarmouth*

Cygnus; Chartered
Built: by James Henderson & Sons, Renfrew - yard no 8
Launched: 1854
Dimensions: 182.0 x 21.4 x 9.7 ft
Tonnage: 250 grt / 133 nt
Engines: McNab & Clark, Greenock s.o. 2 cyl 423/8" - 42"
Power Output: 120 hp
Speed: 13 knots
First ref: May 1855 Harwich to Antwerp

Pcps. Completed in October 1854 for NESN Co.. Chartered by ECR from 23 April 1855 to October 1855 and made 32 trips. Sister ship: *Aquila*.

Dana Anglia; DFDS; IMO: 7615414
Built: by Aalborg Verft A/S, Aalborg - yard no.210
Launched: 24 June 1977
Dimensions: 501.0 / 448.0 x 79.0 x 18.7 ft
Tonnage: 14399 grt / 7758 nt / 3511 dwt
Engines: 2 x Lindholmen Pielstick 18 cyl diesels type 18PC2-5V
Power Output: 20800 bhp
Speed: 21 knots
Passengers: 1372 (B:1250)
First ref: 13 May 1978 Esbjerg to Parkeston Quay (m/v)

Pcms ro-ro. First arrival at P. Quay was on 6 May 1978 for berthing trials. Space for 470 cars. In service on the Esbjerg to P. Quay route until 28 September 2002. Was sold to K/S Difko, Esbjerg on 29 December 1982 for £22m and leased back for 10 years. Short term charter to Sealink for P. Quay to HvH service from 16 January to 31 January 1987. Re-sold to DFDS on 29 December 1989. For a few months from 15 January 1999 departures from P. Quay sailed to Esbjerg via Ijmuiden. On 2 October 2002 was re-named *Duke of Scandinavia* and opened new route linking Copenhagen, Trelleborg and Gdynia. Moved to sailing between Ijmuiden and Newcastle on 24 November 2003. Chartered to Brittany Ferries in January 2006. Re-named *Pont L'Abbe* on 28 February and put in service from Portsmouth to Cherbourg on 6 March 2006. Sold to Brittany Ferries on 19 December 2007. Sold to Moby Lines, Livorno in November 2009 and re-named *Moby Corse* for service between Toulon and Bastia as from 20 May 2010. Still in service.

Dana Cimbria; DFDS; IMO: 8413992
Built: by Frederikshavn Vaerft A/S. Frederikshavn, Denmark - yard no. 417
Launched: 12 December 1985
Dimensions: 145.01 / 135.01 x 20.40 x 6.62 m
Tonnage: 12189 grt / 3656 nt / 7057 dwt
Engines: 1 x MAK diesel type 6M601
Power Output: 9000 bhp / 6615 kw
Speed: 17½ knots
Passengers: 12
First ref: September 1986

Cms ro-ro. Space for 2080 lane metres of freight or 458 teus. Briefly in service between P. Quay and Esbjerg in September 1986, Hamburg in December 1986.and Bremerhaven from August to October 1988. Other names: Launched as *Mercandia Express II* (1985) then *Dana Cimbria* (1986), *Tor Cimbria* (2001), *Aquae* (2006) and *Cimbria Seaways* (2011).

Dana Futura; DFDS; IMO: 7358731
Built: by Helsingor Voerft A/S, Ellsinore - yard no.407
Launched: 11 July 1975
Dimensions: 144.56 / 130.99 x 22.99 x 7.09 m
Tonnage: 5991 grt / 1977 nt / 6900 dwt
Engines: 2 x B&W 18 cyl diesels type 18U50LU
Power Output: 27540 bhp / 20190 kw
Speed: 22½ knots
Passengers: 12
First ref: 12 January 1976 arrival at Parkeston Quay from Esbjerg

Cms ro-ro. Capacity of 402 teus. (m/v) was on 3 January 1976 from Esbjerg to Felixstowe. Chartered to Atlanta Shipping Corp, Houston on 4 March 1976 and re-named *Damman Express*. Chartered to DDG-Hansa, Bremen on 15 April 1977 and re-named *Drosselfels*. Re-named *Dana Futura* on 31 December 1977. Extensively chartered and / or variously used throughout the North Sea including Esbjerg to P. Quay from January 1978 through to 1985, Hamburg to P. Quay from 1980 and Bremerhaven to P. Quay in 1982. Sold to K/S Difko, Esbjerg on 19 December 1983. Lengthened by 32m at Frederikshavn Vaerft A/S in November 1985. Dimensions: 176.55 / 162.52 x 22.99 x 7.09 m. Tonnage: 18787 grt / 6097 nt / 10150 dwt. Capacity now 562 teus. Sold to Rederi ab Nordo-Link, Malmo on 29 November 1988, re-named *Skane Link*. Passengers:130 (B:130) for the Helsingborg to Travemunde service. Sold to Ventouris Ferries, Limassol in December 1991 and re-named *Polaris* for service between Bari and Patras. Chartered to Nordo-Link of Malmo in September 1998. Returned to Ventouris and Bari in 2000. Sold in 2011 for scrapping in India. Sister ship: *Dana Gloria*.

Dana Gloria; DFDS; IMO: 7358743
Built: by Helsingor Voerft A/S, Ellsinore - yard no.408
Launched: 9 February 1976
Dimensions: 144.56 / 131.02 x 22.99 x 6.88 m
Tonnage: 5991 grt / 1977 nt / 6604 dwt
Engines: 2 x B&W 18 cyl diesels type 18U50LU
Power Output: 27540 bhp / 20190 kw
Speed: 22½ knots
Passengers: 12
First ref: 12 July 1976 arrival at Parkeston Quay from Esbjerg

Cms ro-ro. Capacity of 402 teus. (m/v) was on 3 July 1976 from Esbjerg to Felixstowe. Chartered to DDG-Hansa, Bremen on 14 September 1976 and re-named *Drachenfels*. Re-named *Dana Hafnia* on 7 November 1977 and extensively chartered from 1978 onwards. Rarely seen at P. Quay, eg September 1978 and late 1985. Sold to Molslinien A/S, Esbjerg on 26 November 1985. In service Esbjerg / Hamburg to P. Quay from 4 January to 19 February 1986. Sold to GT Linien A/S on 21 March 1986, converted to car ferry, re-named *Gedser* for Gedser to Travemunde route. Tonnage: 14540 grt / 4362 nt / 2150 dwt. Passengers: 600 (B:200), 350 cars. Sold to GT-Link in 1986 and re-named *Gedser Link*. Sold to Ventouris Group, Limassol in December 1989 and re-named *Venus* for service between Patras and Bari and *Siren* in 2004. Sold for scrapping in India in March 2010. Sister Ship: *Dana Futura*.

Dana Maxima; DFDS; IMO:7708778
Built: by Hitachi Shipbuilding & Eng. Co Ltd., Ariake Shipyard, Nagasu, Japan - yard no. 4603
Launched: 20 April 1978
Dimensions: 141.51 / 132.47 x 20.60 x 6.56 m
Tonnage: 4928 grt / 2159 nt / 6552 dwt
Engines: 2 x Nigita Pielstick 14 cyl diesels type 14PC2-5V-400
Power Output: 15600 bhp / 11475 kw
Speed: 18 knots
Passengers: 12
First ref: 28 September 1978 arrival at Parkeston Quay from Esbjerg

Cms ro-ro. Space for 2160 lane metres of freight or 390 teus. Made one round trip from Esbjerg to P. Quay on 27 September 1978. Thereafter in service between Esbjerg and Grimsby / North Shields. In 1983 she also sailed from Hamburg to Grimsby / P. Quay and from Esbjerg to P. Quay. Other names: *Tor Maxima* (2000) and *European Trader* (2008). Scrapped in April 2012 in Turkey.

Dana Optima; DFDS; IMO: 7708649
Built: by Helsingor Vaerft A/S, Elsinore, Denmark - yard no. 417
Launched: 16 June 1978
Dimensions: 105.62 / 96.02 x 18.98 x 4.97 m
Tonnage: 1599 grt / 840 nt / 3450 dwt
Engines: 1 x MAK diesel type 12MU453AK
Power Output: 4500 bhp
Speed: 15¼ knots
Passengers: Nil
First ref: October 1983

Cms ro-ro. Space for 274 teus. Arrived at P. Quay on 19 October 1983 for a brief service to Hamburg until 1 November 1983. Sold on 14 February 1984 to the Ethiopian Shipping Lines s.l. in Assab. Other names: *Nopal Optima* (1979), *Optima* (1983), *Dana Optima* (1983), *Meskerem* (1984), *Marag III* (2000), *Noora* (2000), *Marine Star I* (2001) and *Noora* (2003). Last known as *Dubai Moon* in 2008.

Dana Regina; DFDS; IMO: 7329522
Built: by Aalborg Verft A/S, Aalborg - yard no.200
Launched: 31 August 1973
Dimensions: 504.6 / 456.0 x 73.1 x 16.4 ft
Tonnage: 12192 grt / 6311 nt / 2703 dwt
Engines: 4 x B&W 8 cyl diesels type 8S45HU
Power Output: 17600 bhp / 12945 kw
Speed: 21½ knots
Passengers: 1006 (B:878)
First ref: 8 July 1974 Parkeston Quay to Esbjerg (m/v)

Pcms ro-ro. Cost Dkr 101.5m. Space for 250 cars or 100 teus. Hoistable car deck enlarged in January 1977 increasing space to 370 cars. Served on the Esbjerg to P. Quay route until 3 October 1983. Transferred to the Copenhagen to Oslo route as from 12 October 1983 until 1 June 1990. Sold to Nordstrom & Thulin AB, Stockholm in 1989 who took the ship over on 2 June 1990. Re-named *Nord Estonia* on 5 June 1990. In service for Estline between Stockholm and Tallinn from 18 June 1990 to 1 February 1993. Chartered to Larvik Line and re-named *Thor Heyerdahl*. Sailed between Larvik and Frederikshavn from 7 March to 29 November 1993. Sold on 27 April 1994 to Mandalika Shipping Co Ltd, Nicosia and re-named *Vana Tallinn*. In service for Tallink between Tallinn and Helsinki from 13 May 1994 to 25 August 2002. Two starboard engines replaced in March 1996 with 2 x Sulzer diesel type 6ZAL40S. Two port engines replaced in June 2001 with 2 x Sulzer diesel type 8ZL40/48. Combined power now 12250 kw. From 11 October 2002 to 14 April 2009 sailed mainly between Paldiski and Kapellskar. Was in service instead between Riga and Stockholm from 26 April 2007 to 2 August 2008 plus other short term eastern Baltic charters. Chartered on 1 June 2011 to All Ferries SA., Majuro Marshall Island and re-named *Adriatica Queen*. Refitted in Montenegro for service since 15 June 2012 for Albanian Ferries between Durres and Bari. Sold to All Ferries SA on 11 December 2013. Sold for scrapping at Aliaga where she arrived on 22 April 2014.

Deo Gratias; IMO: 5088704
Built: by Scheeps & Masch., Holland-Nautic, Haarlem, Holland.
Launched: January 1954
Tonnage: 398 grt

Cms. First delivered to J & H Boll, Delfzijl, Holland. Briefly sailed between P. Quay and Hamburg in 1964 for Harwich-Hamburg Line when chartered by Zim Israel Navigation Co. Later sailed in co-operation with the Flavius (details unknown) until the service closed in early 1965. Other names: *Dinkelstroom* (1965), *Deo Gratias* (1967), *Leandros* (1973), *Zafiri* (1980) and *Greenland* (1982). No further details.

Derwent Fisher; Chartered; IMO: 6602018
Built: by Nieuwe Noord Nederlandse Scheepswerven, Groningen, Holland - yard no. 343
Launched: 1966
Dimensions: 216.9 x 34.1 ft o.a.
Tonnage: 1096 grt / 1467 dwt

Cms lo-lo. Launched for James Fisher & Sons Ltd of Barrow. Chartered by BR in spring 1968 for service between P. Quay and Antwerp. Made the route's last sailing on 31 May 1968. Other names: *Parham* (1979), *Sofia* (1984), *Saint Anthonys* (1989), *Golduen Bird* (1990), *Mariya* (1991), *Swene* (1991) and *Baris B* (1996). Scrapped in April 2002 at Aliaga, Turkey

Dewsbury; GCR
Built: by Earle's Shipbuilding & Eng. Co. Ltd., Hull - yard no. 564
Launched: 14 April 1910
Dimensions: 276.0 / 265.0 x 36.0 x 17.4 ft
Tonnage: 1631 grt / 878 nt / 1102 dwt
Engines: Earle's Tr. exp. 22", 35" & 60" - 42"
Power Output: 309 nhp / 1912 ihp
Speed: 13 knots
Passengers: 450 (B:140 First, 10 Second and 300 Emigrant class)
First ref: November 1918 repatriation sailings between Parkeston Quay and Rotterdam. Returned to the GCR on 11 November 1919.

Pcs. Built as one of four sister ships for the GCR service from Grimsby to Hamburg, (m/v) on 17 June 1910, the others being the *Accrington*, *Blackburn* and *Bury*. The *Blackburn* was lost on her maiden voyage on 8 December 1910 and so the *Stockport* was ordered in her place. The *Bury* was not seen at P. Quay. Each ship cost £41,500 and were single funnelled passenger and cargo vessels with First Class accommodation amidships. The Bridge deck had 100 berths in staterooms, a smoking room and ladies lounge. The Main deck had 40 berths in four-berth cabins plus one luxury state room and a full width saloon. Ten second class berths were under the poop with 300 in Emigrant class housed in fore and aft tween decks. With the exception of the *Bury*, which was seized in Hamburg on 4 August 1914, the remaining three ships were used during WW1 in various duties for the Admiralty. Post WW1 the *Dewsbury*, *Accrington* and *Stockport* were all engaged in repatriation work between P. Quay and Rotterdam until returning to the GCR in November 1919. Was requisitioned in July 1941 as a convoy rescue ship. Post WW2 was again at P. Quay sailing on the Antwerp service from 30 August 1946 until 3 February 1950. Dimensions: 276.2 / 265.0 x 35.9 x 18.0 ft. Tonnage: 1686 grt / 907 nt / 1464 dwt. Passengers: 197 (B:100 First class). Resumed P. Quay to Antwerp service again from 10 February 1951 until 30 January 1959, Passengers: 12 (B:12 First class). Sold on 7 March 1959 and arrived in Antwerp on 10 March for scrapping by Brussels Shipbreaking Co.

Diana (I); DFDS
Built: by A/S Kjobenhavns Flydedok og Skibsvaerft, Copenhagen - yard no. 90
Launched: 5 August 1911
Dimensions: 242.0 / 230.0 x 33.9 x 14.6 ft
Tonnage: 942 grt / 431 nt / 915 dwt
Engines: Kjobenhavns Flydedok Tr. exp 19.5", 32" & 53" - 36"
Power Output: 1100 ihp
Speed: 12 knots
Passengers: 38 (22 First & 16 Third class)
First ref: early 1910s.

Pcs. Cost: Dkr 495,000. Lost by sinking in a German air attack north west of the Faroes on 9 June 1941. Sister ship: *Hebe*

Diana (II); DFDS
Built: by A/S Svenborg Skibsvaerft, Svenborg - yard no. 49
Launched: 13 August 1944
Dimensions: 79.86 / 73.15 x 10.92 x 4.78 m
Tonnage: 1082 grt / 546 nt / 1320 dwt
Engines: Helsingors Skibsvaerft c.o 4 cyl (2) 16.5" & (2) 35.4" - 35.4"
Power Output: 1200 ihp
Speed: 11¼ knots
Passengers: 5
First ref: August 1958

Rcs. First delivered to C. Clausen d.s. A/S, Svendborg on 3 February 1945. Purchased by DFDS for Dkr 3.5m. on 23 February 1950 as the last steamer they ever purchased. Made 42 crossings from Esbjerg to P. Quay between August 1958 and April 1965. Sold on 23 November 1965 to Greek interests in Piraeus. Grounded off Reggio di Calabria on 14 May 1968 following an onboard fire. Condemned and later sank whilst in Messina on 10 February 1969. Other names: Delivered as *Linda* then *Clausen* (1945), *Diana* (1950) and *Twiga* (1967).

Domburgh; Chartered; IMO: 5091808
Built: by Werf De Noord, Alblasserdam - yard no. 616
Launched: 1949
Dimensions: 280.7 x 40.2 x 14.1 ft
Tonnage: 1117 grt / 500 nt
Engines: 1 x N.V. Werkspoor 8 cyl diesel
Power Output:
Speed: 16 knots
Passengers: Nil
First ref: December 1968 Rotterdam to Parkeston Quay

Cms. Cargo ship delivered in August 1949 to Wm. H. Muller & Co. for service between Rotterdam and London. Dimensions: 253.5 x 40.2 x 14.1 ft. In 1962 was lengthened to 280.7 feet and rebuilt as a 77 teu cellular container ship. Chartered by SMZ in December 1968 for service between Rotterdam and P. Quay in conjunction with BR's *Isle of Ely*. In September 1972 was sole ship on route sailing three times a week until displaced by *Nassau*. Sold in 1973 to Carib Shipping Co. London, then to Trincargo Shipping Services Ltd, Trinidad. Sold in 1975 to Magic City Corp., Panama and re-named *Forwarder*. 1983 sold to Pioneer Shipping Inc., Miami and re-named *Nuevo Rio*. Was sunk as an artificial reef near Key Largo on 6 February 1986.

Donington; UECC; IMO: 7424463
Built: 1976 by Ateliers & Chantiers du Havre, Le Havre, France
Dimensions: 105.50 x 15.90 x 4.15 m o.a.
Tonnage: 1591 grt / 801 nt / 1350 dwt
Speed: 14½ knots
Stowage area: 6053 sq.m. on 6 levels
Trade car capacity: 650

Cms cc. Previously known as *Tertre Rouge* then re-named *Donington* (1987) and *Goodwood* (May 2003). Scrapped in June 2003 at Aliaga.

Dresden (Louvain); GER
Built: by Earle's Shipbuilding & Eng. Co. Ltd., Hull - yard no. 410
Launched: 17 November 1896
Dimensions: 302.1 x 38.1 x 16.3 ft
Tonnage: 1805 grt / 496 nt / 1173 dwt
Engines: Earle's Tr. exp. 6 cyl in 2 sets 26", 39½" & 63" - 36"
Power Output: 476 nhp / 6000 ihp
Speed: 18 knots
Passengers: 780 (B: 216 First & 128 Second class)
First ref: 29 June 1897 Parkeston Quay to Antwerp (m/v)

Pcs. The last GER ship supplied by Earle's of Hull. Noted for the ship from which Dr Rudolph Diesel disappeared in October 1913. Requisitioned in October 1914 and re-named *HMS Louvain* in 1915. Sunk by U22 in Kelos Strait, Aegean Sea on 20 January 1918.

Dronning Maud; DFDS
Built: Built: by A/S Burmeister & Wain's Maskin-og Skibsbyggeri, Copenhagen - yard no. 252
Launched: 10 August 1906
Dimensions: 287.2 / 273.0 x 38.0 x16.9 ft
Tonnage: 1761 grt / 871 nt / 1131 dwt
Engines: B & W Tr. exp. 25½", 42½" & (2) 51" - 42"
Power Output: 337 nhp / 2450 ihp
Speed: 15 knots
Passengers: 422 (134 First, 68 Second & 220 Deck class)
First ref: 5 July 1920 arrival at Parkeston Quay from Esbjerg

Pcs. Cost Dkr 909,000. Built for the Copenhagen to Stettin and Oslo service. (m/v) was on 10 October 1906 from Copenhagen to Stettin. In service between Esbjerg and P. Quay from 4 July to 28 September 1920, then from 13 May 1922 to 19 June 1926 and at various times throughout the 1930s. Survived WW2 mainly laid up or chartered to the German Navy. Thereafter briefly used as a British Government troopship out of Tilbury, including to and from the Hook of Holland in February 1946. Sold 25 August 1947 to A/B Orient of Turku and re-named *Bore II*. Transferred to A/B Bore of Turku in December 1947 and refitted at A/B Crichton-Vulcan, Turku for service throughout the Baltic until 1966. Sold on 16 March 1966 to Finska Angfartygs A/B of Helsinki and re-named *Silja II*. Sold on 12 June 1967 for scrapping by Helsingin Romuliike of Finland. Sister ship: *Kong Haakon*.

Duchess Anne; Chartered; IMO: 7615048
Built: by Verolme Cork Dockyard Ltd., Cork, Ireland - yard no. 955
Launched: 20 June 1978
Dimensions: 122.0 x 18.83 x 4.83 m
Tonnage: 9796 grt / 3818 nt / 1373 dwt
Engines: 4 x MAK diesels type 8M551AK
Power Output: 13248 kw
Speed: 19 knots
Passengers: 1300 (B: 471))
First ref: 22 January 1989 Hook of Holland to Parkeston Quay.

Pcms ro-ro, Built for B&I Line of Dublin as the *Connaught*, originally with space for 332 cars. Variously in service between Cork and Swansea or Pembroke Dock and between Dublin and Liverpool or Holyhead. Sold in June 1988 to Societe Anonyme Economie Mixte d'Equipment Navale, (Brittany Ferries), Morlaix, France and taken over on 3 October 1988. Refitted by Jos. L. Meyer Werft in Papenburg and re-named *Duchess Anne* in December 1988. In January 1989 was chartered to Crown Line (SMZ) for service between HvH and P. Quay. In service with Brittany Ferries from 13 February 1989 until 30 September 1996 initially between St. Malo and Portsmouth, later on routes linking St. Malo, Cork, Roscoff and Plymouth. Sold in October 1996 to Jadrolinija p.o., Rijeka, Croatia and re-named *Dubrovnik* for service between Croatia and Italy. Still in service between Dubrovnik and Bari.

Duitschland (Zeeland); SMZ
Built: by Fairfield Shipbuilding & Eng. Co. Ltd., Govan, Scotland - yard no. 313
Launched: 25 November 1886
Dimensions: 286.5 x 35.3 x 16.6 ft
Tonnage: 1653 grt / 870 nt / 1530 dwt
Engines: Fairfield c.o 2 cyl 60" & 104" - 84"
Power Output: 826 nhp
Speed: 17 knots
Passengers: 700
First ref: June 1887 Flushing to Queenborough (m/v)

Pcps. Built by Fairfields - formerly known as J. Elder's - for a new dayboat service starting 1 June 1887. Laid up as reserve ship in 1910. Re-named *Zeeland* in 1916 and in 1918 was used as hospital ship between Rotterdam and Boston (Lincs.). Broken up in 1922 at Diedrichsen Shipbreakers in Bremen. Sister ships: *Engeland*, *Nederland*

Duke of Argyll (II); Relief ship
Built: by Wm. Denny & Bros. Ltd., Dumbarton - yard no. 1194
Launched: 23 January 1928
Dimensions: 359.5 / 348.1 x 55.2 x 14.8 ft
Tonnage: 3799 grt / 1479 nt / 845 dwt
Engines: 2 x srg steam turbines
Power Output: 1628 nhp / 8100 shp
Speed: 21 knots
Passengers: 1494 (B: 224 first and 158 second class)
First ref: September 1948

Pcs. Cost £222,521. Built for the London, Midland & Scottish Railway's service between Heysham and Belfast. (m/v) was in May 1928. Requisitioned in September 1939 for use as a troopship and later as a landing ship. Refitted as *Hospital Carrier no. 65* in June 1944. Resumed commercial services on 11 February 1946. Relieved on the P. Quay to HvH route during September / October 1948 and again in February 1951. Scrapped in 1956. Sister ships: *Duke of Lancaster (II), Duke of Rothesay (I).*

Duke of Lancaster (II); Relief ship
Built: by Wm. Denny & Bros., Dumbarton - yard no. 1193
Launched: 22 November 1927
Dimensions: 359.5 / 348.1 x 55.2 x 14.8 ft
Tonnage: 3794 grt / 1481 nt / 835 dwt
Engines: 2 x 2 sets srg turbines
Power Output: 8100 shp
Speed: 21 knots
Passengers: 1494 (B: 224 first and 158 second class)
First ref: April 1950

Pcs. Cost £221,083. Built for the London, Midland & Scottish Railway's service between Heysham and Belfast. (m/v) was in March 1928. Requisitioned in January 1944 and converted to *Hospital Carrier no. 56.* Resumed commercial services in mid December 1945. Relieved on the P. Quay to HvH route in April / May 1950. Scrapped in 1956. Sister ships: *Duke of Argyll (II), Duke of Rothesay (I).*

Duke of Lancaster (III); IMO: 5094496
Built: by Harland & Wolff Ltd., Belfast - yard no. 1540
Launched: 14 December 1955
Dimensions: 376.1 / 354.0 x 57.3 x 14.8 ft
Tonnage: 4797 grt / 2274 nt / 1064 dwt
Engines: 2 x Harland & Wolff srg turbines
Power Output: 10500 shp
Speed: 21 knots
Passengers: 1800 (B: 240 first and 214 second class)

Pcs. Cost £1,526,123. Built for the BTC for service between Heysham and Belfast. (m/v) was in August 1956. Space for 39 cars.. Seen at P. Quay during 1962 and 1963 whilst on extended cruising duties to Holland and France. Rebuilt in 1970 at Harland & Wolff and converted to a stern loading car ferry. 4450 grt / 1962 nt / 836 dwt. Pass: 1400 (B;299). Space for 105 cars and moved to service from Holyhead to Dun Laoghaire. Sold on 21 January 1979 to Empirewise Ltd of Liverpool and moved to lay up at Llanerch-y-Mormot, Mostyn. Left to languish there after plans for a static restaurant and attraction failed. Still in situ.

Duke of Rothesay (I); Trooping Services
Built: by Wm. Denny & Bros. Ltd., Dumbarton - yard no. 1195
Launched: 22 March 1928
Dimensions: 359.5 / 348.1 x 55.2. x 14.9 ft
Tonnage: 3805 grt / 1457 nt / 845 dwt
Engines: 2 x srg steam turbines
Power Output: 1628 nhp / 8100 shp
Speed: 21 knots
First ref: 7 August 1945

Pcs. Cost £222,187. Built for the London, Midland & Scottish Railway's service between Heysham and Belfast. Passengers: 1506. (702 First & 804 Third class) (B: 225 First & 158 Third class). (m/v) was in July 1928. Requisitioned in September 1943 for use as a landing ship. Refitted as *Hospital Carrier no. 62* in spring 1944 and then as a troopship in 1945. Served on trooping duties between P. Quay and HvH from 7 August 1945 to 14 September 1946. Resumed commercial services on 11 July 1947. Relieved on the P. Quay to HvH route in 1949. Arrived at Milford Haven on 18 January 1957 for breaking up. Sister ships: *Duke of Lancaster (II), Duke of Argyll (II).*

Duke of York; BR; IMO: 5423099
Built: by Harland & Wolff Ltd., Belfast - yard no. 951
Launched: 7 March 1935
Dimensions: 350.0 / 339.2 x 52.2 x 14.7 ft
Tonnage: 3759 grt / 1468 nt / 748 dwt
Engines: 2 x 2 sets srg turbines
Power Output: 1494 nhp / 8260 shp
Speed: 21 knots
Passengers: 1500 (B:139 First & 240 Tourist / Third class)
First ref: 31 July 1945 Parkeston Quay to Hook of Holland trooping for BAOR

Pcms. Originally built for the LMS Railway's Heysham to Belfast route. (m/v) was in June 1935. Passengers: 389 First & 1111 Third. Served during WW2 as a troopship, landing ship and, from 1942, as *H.M.S. Wellington.* Sailed as a troopship between P. Quay and Hook of Holland from 31 July 1945 until 14 November 1946. Refitted in 1947 with revised accommodation. Passengers: 1506 (380 First & 1126 Second). (B: 129 First & 206 Second class). Could carry 19 cars. Transferred to the P. Quay - HvH route on 31 May 1948 as long term cover for the loss of the *Prague.* Further refitted at Harland & Wolff in 1950/51 and converted to a single funnelled oil burner. Tonnage: 4190 grt / 1904 nt. Power Output: 8260 shp.. Passengers: 675 (B: 360 First & 160 Second class). Following a collision with *Haiti Victory* on 6th May 1953 she was refitted at Palmers Yard and given a new 90 ft bow that extended her length by about 7 ft. to 358.7 ft oa / 346.7 ft. Tonnage: 4325 grt / 1980 nt. Displaced by the *Avalon* and sold in August 1963 to Chandris Line of Greece and re-named *York.* Sent for refit into a 380 passenger cruise ship at Smith's Dock, North Shields. Re-named *Fantasia* and made her first cruise from her base at Venice on 15 March 1964. Sold for scrap in 1975 to Prodronos Sariktzis of Piraeus and broken up in May 1976.

Earl Granville; Chartered; IMO: 7310258
Built: by Jos L Meyer Schiffswerft, Papenburg Ems, Germany - yard no. 570
Launched: 17 March 1973
Dimensions: 109.15 x 17.25 x 4.70 m
Tonnage: 4477 grt / 1982 nt / 994 dwt
Engines: 2 x Pielstick-Crossley 12 cyl diesels type 12PC2VMK5
Power Output: 8240 kw
Speed: 19½ knots
Passengers: 1200 (B: 170)
First ref: January 1989

Pcms ro-ro. Launched as *Viking 4* for Rederi Ab Sally of Mariehamn, Finland. Engines: 2 x Smit-Bolnes diesels type V314HDK. Power Output: 10200 kw. Passengers: 1200 (B: 280). Space for 265 cars and 26 trailers. Placed in service between Turku, Mariehamn and Stockholm. Sold in April 1980 to William & Glynn Industrial Leasing Ltd, London. Re-named *Earl Granville* on 21 August 1980 and chartered to Sealink UK Ltd in September 1980. Refitted and re-engined by Jos L Meyer, Papenburg. Revised accommodation. Space now for 200 cars. Sailed throughout the 1980s mainly from Portsmouth - Channels Islands / Cherbourg. Briefly served on the P. Quay to HvH route from 8 January to 19 January 1989. Sold in November 1990 to Agapitos Express Ferries of Piraeus and re-named *Express Olympia.* Sailed to various Greek islands out of Piraeus. Sold in November 1999 to Minoan Flying Dolphins of Piraeus. Sold in Indian breakers in April 2004, re-named *Express O* and arrived in Alang on 21 July 2005.

Earl William; Chartered; IMO: 6417047
Built: by Kaldnes Mekaniske Verksted A/S, Tonsberg, Norway - yard no. 160
Launched: 30 April 1964
Dimensions: 99.50 x 17.73 x 4.42 m
Tonnage: 3670 grt / 1784 nt / 1219 dwt
Engines: 2 x Pielstick-Lindholmens 12 cyl diesels type 12PC2V
Power Output: 7500 kw
Speed: 18½ knots
Passengers: 940 (B:300)
First ref: 11 May 1987

Pcms ro-ro. Launched for Otto Thoresen Shipping Co. A/S of Oslo as the *Viking II.* Entered service on 19 July 1964 between Southampton and Cherbourg / Le Havre. Was part of the combined Townsend Thoresen Car Ferries Ltd created in September 1968 until sold to Lloyds Leasing Ltd., London on 22 December 1976. Re-named *Earl William* for service with Sealink. Sailed mainly Portsmouth/ Weymouth to Channel Islands. Transferred to Sea Containers Ltd on 27 July 1984. Chartered by HMG Home Office in May 1987 as a floating detention centre at Harwich. Arrived 11 May. Broke away from moorings in hurricane on 16 October 1987. Charter ended in November 1987. Opened a new Sealink BF service between Liverpool and Dun Laoghaire from 25 April 1988 until January 1990. Sold on 5 April 1992 to Ardonis Shipping Co., Valetta, Malta and re-named *Wiliam.* Operated between Italy and Greece as *Pearl William* until sold on 10 April 1996 to P & L Ferries Shipping Co. of Valetta and re-named *Mar Julia.* Sold in 1997 to Lucky Shipping sa, Kingstown, St. Vincent and re-named *Cesme Stern.* Sold in 2000 to Windward Lines, Kingstown and re-named *Windward II.* Sold in December 2006 to Treasure Queen Tours and re-built as the hotel ship *Ocean Pearl* sited in Trinidad & Tobago.

Empire Parkeston; Trooping Services
Built: by Cammell Laird & Co. Ltd., Birkenhead - yard no. 964
Launched: 17 January 1930
Dimensions: 385.0 / 366.0 x 57.0 x 16.5 ft
Tonnage: 6893 grt / 3072 nt / 5579 dwt
Engines: 2 x Parsons srg turbines
Power Output: 19300 ihp / 14500 shp
Speed: 22¼ knots
First ref: 4 April 1947

Pcms. Built as the *Prince Henry* for the Canadian National Steamship Co. and its British Columbia coast service. Cost $2.5m. Passengers: 404 (334 First & 70 Third class). (m/v) was on 3 July 1930 from Vancouver to Alaska. Transferred to American east coast in 1932 and sold to Clarke Steamship Co. of Quebec in 1938 for $500,000. Was re-named *North Star* and sailed between Miami and the Caribbean and from Montreal to New York. Sold on 11 March 1940 to Royal Canadian Navy for $800,000 and re-named *Prince Henry.* Refitted by Canadian Vickers of Montreal into an armed merchant cruiser at a cost of $815,000. Commissioned as *HMCS Prince Henry* on 4 December 1940. Sent to Vancouver on 6 March 1943 for conversion to a troop landing ship for D-Day operations carrying 8 landing craft and 444 troops. Paid off by the R.C. Navy on 15 April 1945 whilst being refitted in London's East India Dock following which she was loaned to the Royal Navy in May 1945 for use as the accommodation ship *HMS Prince Henry.* Bought by MOWT for $500,000 (£125,000) in 1946 and converted to troopship *Empire Parkeston.* Was fitted with 813 dormitory bunks and 182 cabins. Served on the P. Quay to HvH trooping service, under the management of General Steam Navigation Co., from 4 April 1947 to 25 September 1961 when the service closed. Arrived at the yard of Lotti SpA, La Spezia, Italy on 20 February 1962 for scrapping.

Empire Wansbeck; Trooping Services; IMO: 5106536
Built: by Danziger Werft in 1939 / Staalskisvaerft, Odense in 1943
Launched: 1940
Dimensions: 336.4 / 323.1 x 45 .6 x 18.0 ft
Tonnage: 3374 grt
Engines: 1 x MAN 6 cyl diesel
Power Output: 4800 bhp
Speed: 16 knots
First ref: 17 December 1945

Cms. Was originally intended to be a refrigerated fruit ship for Norddeutsche Lloyd. Was completed in Copenhagen and then seized in August 1943 to became the German minelayer *Linz* with a ships compliment of 212 men and a capacity for 340 mines. Post war she was acquired by MOWT on 1 December 1945 and refitted into a troopship, operating under the management of Ellerman's Wilson Line, with 700 dormitory bunks plus cabin berths for 150 officers and families. Was later modified to take 1050 passengers. Served on trooping duties between P. Quay and HvH from 17 December 1945 until the service closed on 26 September 1961. Sold in 1962 to Kavounides Shipping Co Ltd of Piraeus, re-named *Esperos* and in 1964 was converted to being a passenger ferry sailing between Venice and Rhodes. Tonnage: 3964 grt. Passengers: 591 (116 First, 175 Second, 100 Tourist & 200 Dormitory class). Later became a one class 500 passenger cruiseship. Sold in March 1980 for scrapping at Gandia, Spain.

Engeland; SMZ
Built: by Fairfield Shipbuilding & Eng. Co. Ltd., Govan, Scotland - yard no. 314
Launched: 23 December 1886
Dimensions: 286.5 x 35.3 x 16.6 ft
Tonnage: 1648 grt / 829 nt / 1529 dwt
Engines: Fairfield c.o. 2 cyl 60" & 104" - 84"
Power Output: 826 nhp
Speed: 17 knots
Passengers: 700
First ref: June 1887 Flushing to Queenborough (m/v)

Pcps. Built for the new 1887 dayboat service and served until 1910 when replaced by *Oranje Nassau.* Scrapped at Hendrik-ido-Ambacht in 1911. Sister ships: *Duitschland, Nederland*

England (I); DFDS
Built: by A/S Helsingors Jernskibs-og Maskinbyggeri, Ellsinore - yard no. 204
Launched: 14 January 1932
Dimensions: 324.2 / 304.0 x 44.0 x 18.2 ft
Tonnage: 2767 grt / 1543 nt / 1715 dwt
Engines: 2 x B&W 6 cyl diesels type 6150-MFX
Power Output: 545 nhp / 3200 bhp
Speed: 15½ knots
Passengers: 190 (108 First & 82 Third class)
First ref: 23 April 1932 Esbjerg to Parkeston Quay (m/v)

Pcms. Cost Dkr 2,259,884. In service between Esbjerg and P. Quay until September 1939. Laid up in Copenhagen between July 1940 and 19 January 1944, then used as the German barrack ship *Grenadier.* Bombed by Allies on 27 August 1944 whilst in Kiel for repairs and destroyed beyond repair. Later arrived under tow in Flensburg on 3 June 1950 and then towed to Odense in July 1950 for scrapping by H.J. Hansen of Odense. Sister ships: *Parkeston, Jylland, Esbjerg (II).*

England (II); DFDS; IMO: 6403278
Built: by Helsingor Skibsvaerft og Maskinbyggeri A/S, Ellsinore - yard no. 369
Launched: 10 December 1963
Dimensions: 459.7 / 410.4 x 63.5 x 18.2 ft
Tonnage: 8117 grt / 4277 nt / 1451 dwt
Engines: 2 x B&W 10 cyl diesels type 1050-VT2BF-110
Power Output: 14000 bhp / 10304 kw
Speed: 21 knots
Passengers: 475 (467 - 155 First, 244 Second & 68 Deck class)
First ref: 11 June 1964 Esbjerg to Parkeston Quay (m/v)

Pcms ro-ro. The North Sea's first drive-on drive-off car ferry. Space for 100 cars. First arrival at P. Quay was on 3 June 1964 for berthing trials. Utilised for low season cruises from Copenhagen to the West Indies or West Africa between 1966 and 1970. Rebuilt in early 1971 at Aalborg Werft A/S with extra berths, now 566. Further rebuilt in 1974 with more berths, now 634, and car capacity raised from 100 to 120. Transferred to Esbjerg to Newcastle / Faroes service in July 1974 and then on various Esbjerg or Copenhagen routes until 1982. Rebuilt in 1977, car capacity now 145. Re-appeared on Esbjerg to P. Quay route from 30 November 1976 to 21 December 1976, 6 to 20 March 1977 and 28 October 1979 to 25 November

1979. Sold on 16 September 1983 to Cunard and sailed until June 1985 ferrying construction workers between Cape Town and the Falkland Islands. Laid up at Birkenhead until sold in 1986 to Start Point Investments S.A. of Panama and re-named *America XIII*. Sailed on 23 December 1986 for Jeddah. Re-named *Ena* in 1987 and then *Europa* in 1988. Sold for scrap in March 2001 but sank in the Red Sea in May 2001 en-route to Alang, India.

Eos; DFDS
Built: by Wm. Simons & Co., London Works, Renfrew - yard no. 220
Launched: 30 April 1881
Dimensions: 228.5 / 219.0 x 29.6 x 17.0 ft
Tonnage: 838 grt / 444 nt / 920 dwt
Engines: Simons c.o. 2 cyl 26" & 54" - 48"
Power Output: 775 ihp
Speed: 10 knots
Passengers: 52 (12 First & 40 Third class)
First ref: 1904

Pcs. Variously seen at P. Quay up until 1914. First delivered to the Clyde Shipping Co., Glasgow in May 1881. Purchased by DFDS on 1 December 1899 for Dkr 150,000. Other names: Delivered as *Aranmore* (1881) then re-named *Eos* (1889). Lost after losing contact with a WW1 convoy on 27 February 1918 en-route to Copenhagen.

Epping; River Services
Built: 1914 by Vosper & Co., Portsmouth
Dimensions: 50.4 x 12.1 x 4.5 ft
Tonnage: 22.1 grt / 11.8 nt
Engines: 1 x semi-diesel Kromhout hot bulb ignition
Power Output: 35 bhp
Speed: 8 knots
Passengers: 125
First ref: May 1914

Pms. Cost £1,157. Single screw wooden harbour ferry sailing between Harwich, Shotley Gate and Ipswich. Requisitioned in 1914-18 for harbour duties and again on 29 August 1939 by MOWT for Admiralty service. Acquired by HM Government on 11 December 1942 Sold to private owner in 1962.

Esbern Snare; DFDS
Built: Built: by A/S Burmeister & Wain's Maskin-og Skibsbyggeri, Copenhagen -yard no. 90
Launched: 1875
Dimensions: 170.0 x 23.0 x 12.0 ft
Tonnage: 480 grt/ 295 nt / 434 dwt
Engines: B&W c.o 4 cyl (2) 16½" & (2) 34" - 20"
Power Output: 350 ihp
Speed: 9½ knots
Passengers: Nil
First ref: 1904 Esbjerg to Parkeston Quay

Cs. First delivered to H. Puggaard & Hage, Nakskov on 9 September 1875. Purchased by DFDS on 19 February 1876 for Dkr 300,000 for services to Newcastle and Leith. Rebuilt in 1877. Tonnage: 405 grt / 254 nt / 392 dwt. On the Esbjerg to P. Quay service 1904 to 1907. First ship to berth at P. Quay's new 1907 extension. Sold on 5 March 1926 to Hans Petersen of Copenhagen and by 24 September 1927 had been scrapped.

Esbjerg (I); DFDS
Built: by Cunliffe & Dunlop, Port Glasgow - yard no. 85
Launched: 5 November 1872
Dimensions: 182.5 / 174.5 x 26.5 x 12.7 ft
Tonnage: 485 grt / 296 nt / 534 dwt
Engines: Cunliffe & Dunlop c.o. 2 cyl 23¼" & 40¼" - 28"
Power Output: 71 nhp / 300 ihp
Speed: 8½ knots
Passengers: 23 (4 First & 19 Third class)
First ref: 5 June 1880 arrival at Harwich from Esbjerg

Cs. Cost £13,250. Delivered in December 1872 to A/S Esbjerg Dampskibsselskab and on 6 October 1873 was the first ship to arrive at the newly built port of Esbjerg - loaded with rails for the Jutland railway. Purchased by DFDS on 5 January 1876 and put on the Esbjerg to Thameshaven route. Transferred to Harwich route in 1880 and then to P. Quay until early 1883. Was re-named *Esbern Snare* in 1928. Collided with *Carl* on 14 February 1930 in the Elbe river and sank. Later raised and sold to Leth & Co., Hamburg for £950 and scrapped in March 1930.

Esbjerg (II); DFDS
Built: by A/S Helsingors Jernskibs-og Maskinbyggeri, Ellsinore - yard no. 186
Launched: 23 January 1929
Dimensions: 324.0 / 304.0 x 44.0 x 17.8 ft
Tonnage: 2762 grt / 1553 nt / 1620 dwt
Engines: 2 x B&W 6 cyl diesels type 6150-MFX
Power Output: 545 nhp / 3200 bhp
Speed: 15½ knots
Passengers: 220 (132 First & 88 Third class)
First ref: 25 April 1929 Esbjerg to Parkeston Quay (m/v)

Pcms. Cost Dkr 2,772,505. In service between Esbjerg and P. Quay until 6 September 1939 having completed 801 crossings. Was laid up in Copenhagen between April 1940 and 20 January 1944, then used as the German target ship and refugee carrier *Kurassier*. Abandoned by German Navy on 5 June 1945. Hit a mine off Stevns and sank on 25 July 1945 whilst a Danish crew were returning her to Copenhagen. Raised on 1 August 1946 and sold as a wreck in July 1947. Towed to Valencia, Spain in August 1947 and rebuilt for Cia. Trasmediterranea S.A. of Valencia who re-named her *Ciudad De Ibiza*. Sold for £15,000 in November 1978 to D. Ricardo Villanova & Cia. of Valencia for scrapping. Sister ships: *Parkeston, Jylland, England (I)*.

Essex (II); River Services
Built: 1896 by Earle's Shipbuilding & Eng. Co. Ltd., Hull
Dimensions: 175.5 x 23.1 x 7.2 ft
Tonnage: 297 grt / 126 nt
Engines: Earles compound diagonal 2 cyl 24" & 48" - 42"
Power Output: 160 nhp
Speed: 10 knots
Passengers: 450

Pps. Built for the GER. Sold in December 1913 to Henry Cooney of Westcliffe-on-Sea for service between Southend and Sheerness. Sold in May 1916 to Goole & Hull S.P.Co., Goole. Sold in 1918 to Hellenic Mediterranean Black Sea Co. of Piraeus and re-named *Acropolis* in 1920. Scrapped in the 1930s. Sister ship: *Suffolk*

Essex Ferry; BR; IMO: 5106653
Built: by John Brown & Co. Ltd., Clydebank - yard no. 694
Launched: 24 October 1956
Dimensions: 399.8 / 387.5 x 61.3 / 58.6 x 13.0 ft
Tonnage: 3242 grt / 1502 nt / 1987 dwt
Engines: 2 x John Brown Sulzer 6 cyl diesels
Power Output: 2680 hp
Speed: 13½ knots
Passengers: 12 (B: 12 First class)
First ref: 15 January 1957 Harwich to Zeebrugge (m/v) for BR.

Cms tf. Launched by Mrs C.K. Bird. Crew of 34. Fitted with 1132 feet of rail track with space for 38 continental wagons. Similar to the *Suffolk Ferry* but additionally fitted with a travelling crane that ran above the rail tracks in order to transport box containers to Antwerp or Rotterdam. Withdrawn from service in December 1981 and laid up. Further laid up in R. Blackwater from 17 December 1982 until 28 April 1983 when she left to arrive at Medway Secondary Metals at Bloor's Wharf, Rainham, on 29 April for conversion to a floating pontoon to assist in the salvage of the capsized oil rig *Alexander Kielland*. Re-named *Essex Ferry Pontoon* and scrapped in late 1983.

Estoril; UECC; IMO: 7359761
Built: 1974 by Ateliers & Chantiers du Havre, Le Havre, France
Dimensions: 100.46 x 15.90 x 4.00 m o.a.
Tonnage: 1592 grt / 734 nt / 1350 dwt
Speed: 14 knots
Stowage area: 5913 sq.m. on 6 levels
Trade car capacity: 610

Cms cc. Previously known as *Amage* until re-named *Estoril* in 1985. Arrived at Aliaga on 13 August 2001 for scrapping.

Expres; DFDS
Built: by Flensburger Schiffbau-Gesellschaft, Flensburg - yard no. 38
Launched: 25 March 1881
Dimensions: 217.5 / 208.4 x 27.3 x 14.0 ft
Tonnage: 654 grt / 380 nt / 640 dwt
Engines: s.o. 2 cyl 32½" & 60" - 36"
Power Output: 670 ihp
Speed: 11½ knots
Passengers: 18 (10 First & 8 Second class)
First ref: 1888 Esbjerg to Parkeston Quay

Cs. First delivered to A/S Nordjyllands Dampskibsselskab of Aalborg on 14 May 1881. Purchased by DFDS on 27 December 1883 for sailing mainly to Newcastle and then between Esbjerg and P. Quay from 1888 to 1897. Fitted with a refrigeration plant in 1897. Sold on 19 September 1929 for scrapping to J. Carlbom in Karlshamn for £2,100.

Fano; DFDS
Built: by M. Pearse & Co., Stockton-on-Tees - yard no. 119
Launched: 18 September 1872
Dimensions: 225.0 x 28.0 x 16.9 ft
Tonnage: 860 grt / 555 nt / 900 dwt
Engines: Blair & Co., Stockton-on-Tees c.o. 2 cyl 28" & 56.5" - 36"
Power Output: 500 ihp
Speed: 10 knots
Passengers: 49 (24 First & 25 Second class)
First ref: 1890

Cs. Seen at P. Quay during the 1890s. First delivered to Norddeutscher Lloyd, Bremen in 1872. Purchased by DFDS on 31 May 1890 for Dkr 99,823. Sold on 27 July 1897 to Chargeurs Algeriens Reunis, Algier. Other names: Delivered as *Strauss* (1872) then *Fano* (1890), *Rhone et Saone* (1897) and *Kabylie* (1913). Lost by grounding and wrecked off La Rochelle on 2 January 1915.

Federal Lakes; Fednav / Canada Maritime; IMO: 7324390
Built: Seaway Marine & Industrial, St. Catharines, Canada.
Launched: 1973
Dimensions: 202.10 x 22.90 x 9.30 m
Tonnage: 15005 grt
Engines: 2 x Pielstick diesels
Power Output: 13428 kw
Speed: 19 knots
First ref: 1987

Cms. General purpose deep sea ro-ro and cargo ship. Scheduled for service between P. Quay and the Canadian Great Lakes / USA eastern seaboard. Other names: Launched as *Avon Forest*, then re-named *Federal Lakes* (1985) and *Cape Lambert* (1988). Last owner: USA Government. Sister ship: *Federal Seaway*

Federal Seaway; Fednav / Canada Maritime; IMO: 7216854
Built: Seaway Marine & Industrial, St. Catharines, Canada.
Launched: 1972
Dimensions: 202.10 x 22.90 x 9.30 m
Tonnage: 15036 grt
Engines: 2 x Pielstick diesels
Power Output: 13428 kw
Speed: 19 knots
First ref: June 1987

Cms. General purpose deep sea ro-ro and cargo ship. Briefly seen at P. Quay on services to the Canadian Great Lakes and the USA eastern seaboard. Other names: Launched as *Laurentian Forest*, then re-named *Grand Encounter*, (), *Federal Seaway ()* and *Cape Lobos* (1988). Last owner: USA Government. Sister ship: *Federal Lakes*

Felixstowe; GER
Built: by Hawthorn's & Co. Ltd., Leith - yard no. 147
Launched: 11 May 1918
Dimensions: 215.1 x 33.2 x 16.0 ft
Tonnage: 882 grt / 354 nt / 754 dwt
Engines: Hawthorn's Tr. exp. 21", 33" & 54" - 36"
Power Output: 248 nhp
Speed: 12 knots
Passengers: Nil
First ref: 23 April 1919 Parkeston Quay to Rotterdam (m/v)

Cs. Cost £70,049. First post war new build delivered to the GER. Requisitioned in June 1940 and then again in August 1941 when she was re-named *H.M.S. Colchester*. Returned to service as *Felixstowe* in 1946. Sold on 18 October 1950 to Limerick Steamship Co. Ltd. and left P. Quay for a refit in Emden, Germany. Re-named *Kylemore*. Scrapped at Hendrick-ido-Ambacht, Rotterdam in November 1957.

Ficaria (I); DFDS
Built: Lobnitz & Co., Ltd., Renfrew - yard no. 451
Launched: 7 September 1896
Dimensions: 279.7 / 268.5 x 34.0 x 17.2 ft
Tonnage: 1530 grt / 672 nt / 1120 dwt
Engines: Lobnitz Tr. exp. 24", 40" & 64" - 42"
Power Output: 265 nhp / 2500 ihp
Speed: 14 knots
Passengers: 59 (39 First & 20 Deck class)
First ref: 1909 Esbjerg to Parkeston Quay

Pcs. (m/v) was on 22 October 1896 from Copenhagen to Newcastle. Moved to the service to Hull in 1906 and then onto the Esbjerg to P. Quay / Grimsby routes between 1909 and August 1914. Survived WW1 and sailed from Copenhagen to Danzig before returning to the Esbjerg to P. Quay route in 1923 until September 1931 when she was then laid up in Copenhagen. Sold on 22 November 1934 to Hughes Bolckow Shipbreaking Co. Ltd. of Blyth for £3,200. Scrapped in December 1934. Sister ship: *Primula*.

Ficaria (II); DFDS; IMO: 5114557
Built: by Helsingor Skibsvaerft og Maskinbyggeri A/S, Elsinore - yard no. 305
Launched: 10 August 1951
Dimensions: 101.10 / 93.00 x 13.97 x 5.59 m
Tonnage: 1811 grt / 855 nt / 2428 dwt
Engines: 1 x B&W 8 cyl diesel type 850-VF-90
Power Output: 2550 bhp
Speed: 14½ knots
Passengers: 6
First ref: early 1950s.

Rcms. Cost: Dkr 8.125m. Sold on 28 April 1972 to Sweet Lines Inc., Cebu. Other names: *Sweet Lord* (1972) and *Sweet Land* (1974). Lost by stranding off Maricaban Island on 5 July 1981. Sister ship: *Primula (II)*

Fichtelberg; Chartered; IMO: 7383451
Built: by Kristiansands Mekaniske Verksted, Kristiansand, Norway - yard no. 222
Launched: 24 January 1975
Dimensions: 137.55 x 20.60 x 7.17 m
Tonnage: 8055 grt / 2935 nt / 7597 dwt
Engines: 2 x Pielstick 12 cyl diesel
Power Output: 8825 kw
Speed: 18½ knots
Passengers: 12

Cms. Space for 170 teus. Sailed between P. Quay and Hamburg for DFDS in 1983 when chartered to Tor Line. Launched as *Tor Caledonia* and sold in 1975 to Veb Deutfracht Seereederei of Rostock. Other names: *Spirit of Dublin* (1991), *Norcliff* (1992), *Dana Minerva* (1994), *Seahawk* (1996), *Cetam Victoriae* (2002), *Aegean Sun* (2003) and *Archagelos* (2006). Arrived at Alang, India on 19 May 2012 for scrapping.

Flora; DFDS
Built: by A/S Burmeister & Wain's Maskin-og Skibsbyggeri, Copenhagen - yard no. 270
Launched: 7 September 1909
Dimensions: 262.9 / 253.4 x 34.5 x 16.1 ft
Tonnage: 1218 grt / 664 nt / 1173 dwt
Engines: B&W Tr. exp 21", 35" & 60" - 39"
Power Output: 1550 ihp
Speed: 13 knots
Passengers: 12
First ref: 1920

Cs. Cost: Dkr 618,000. Served on various North

Sea routes, including P. Quay, until 1939. Other names: *Flora II* (1940). Lost on 2 August 1942 when sunk by German submarine U254 off Iceland.

Frejr; DFDS
Built: by Lobnitz & Co., Renfrew - yard no. 226
Launched: February 1883
Dimensions: 173.2 / 164.3 x 26.3 x 13.7 ft
Tonnage: 473 grt / 291 nt / 532 dwt
Engines: Lobnitz c.o. 2 cyl 24" & 44" - 30"
Power Output: 400 ihp
Speed: 9 knots
Passengers: 46
First ref: 1900

Pcs. Served on various North Sea routes, including P. Quay, until 1924. First delivered to A/S Randers d.s. of Randers in February 1883. Purchased by DFDS on 17 May 1900 for Dkr 140,000. Sold on 5 March 1926 to Hans Petersen of Copenhagen for scrapping.

Frigga; DFDS
Built: by Frederikshavns Vaerft & Flydedok A/S, Frederikshavn - yard no. 172
Launched: 20 June 1922
Dimensions: 276.5 / 235.0 x 35.5 x 16.4 ft
Tonnage: 1095 grt / 571 nt / 1488 dwt
Engines: Frederikshavns Vaerft Tr. exp 18", 30" & 50" - 36"
Power Output: 800 ihp
Speed: 11 knots
Passengers: 12
First ref: 1922

Cs. Cost: Dkr 1.9m. Made infrequent visits to P. Quay until 1939. Requisitioned during WW2 and returned to DFDS service in 1945. Was the first DFDS cargo ship to arrive at P. Quay post war. Lost by hitting a stray mine in the North Sea on 27 November 1950.

Gabriele Wehr; Chartered; IMO: 7720477
Built: by Rickmans Werft GmbH, Bremerhaven, Germany - yard no. 391
Launched: 14 March 1978
Dimensions: 108.31 x 17.43 x 5.23 m
Tonnage: 1599 grt / 2866 dwt
Engines: 2 x MAK 8 cyl diesels
Power Output: 4413 kw
Speed: 15½ knots
Passengers: 12
First ref: 1985

Cms ro-ro. Space for 71 trailers. Chartered by DFDS in 1985 for service between P. Quay and Hamburg. Other names: *Tor Anglia* (1982), *Gabriele Wehr* (1985), *Sari* (1992), *Gabriele Wehr* (1993), *Flanders Way* (2001) and *Ranine* (2009).

Gannet; GSNCo
Built: by M. Pearse & Co., Stockton-on-Tees - yard no 175
Launched: 1 September 1879
Dimensions: 245.2 x 33.0 ft
Tonnage: 1246 grt / 804 nt
Engines: Blair & Co. Ltd, Stockton-on-Tees c.o. 2 cyl
Power Output: 150 nhp
Speed: 9 knots
First ref: 1890s

Pcs. Seen on the GSNCo. P. Quay to Hamburg route. Was sunk and raised in 1902. On 7 July 1916, whilst on a cargo sailing from Rotterdam to London, she hit a mine laid by UC6. She sank 5 miles e.n.e. of the Shipwash light vessel with the loss of 8 lives.

Georg; DFDS
Built: by Norddeutsche Schiffbau-Actien-Gesellschaft, Kiel-Gaarden - yard no. 66
Launched: May 1875
Dimensions: 218.2 / 210.0 x 28.3 x 15.1 ft
Tonnage: 788 grt / 490 nt / 945 dwt
Engines: Schweffel & Howaldt, Kiel c.o. 2 cyl 30" & 56" - 36"
Power Output: 600 ihp
Speed: 10 knots
Passengers: 12
First ref: early 1900s.

Cs. Operated on the Esbjerg to P. Quay route. First delivered to Theo Koch of Copenhagen in May 1875 for service to Newcastle. Purchased by DFDS on 3 May 1880 for Dkr 370,000. Sold on 25 February 1924 to Schubert & Krohn of Dortmund for scrapping. Sister ship: *Olga*

Gerlena; Railfreight; IMO: 7361764
Built: by J.J. Sietas Schiffswerft, Hamburg, Germany - yard no. 693
Launched: 21 December 1973
Dimensions: 81.39 / 78.82 x 13.42 x 4.89 m
Tonnage: 2130 grt / 2503 dwt
Engines: 1 x Alpha A/S 16 cyl diesel type 16V23L-VO.
Power Output: 2000 hp / 1471 kw
Speed: 13½ knots

Cms lo-lo. Space for 165 teus. Seen on Freightliner's P. Quay to Zeebrugge container service which operated from 3 January 1989 until 1994. Other names: *Thunar* (1975), *Osteland* (1976), *Achat* (1982), *Gerlena* (1989) and *Manila* (1998). Last owner: Bronze Shipping Holding, Miami, Florida.

Germania; H.J. Perlbach
Built: 1856 by J. Laing of Sunderland
Dimensions: 213.2 x 27.6 ft
Tonnage: 681 grt / 439 nt
Engines: Humphreys & Pearson of Hull c.o. 2 cyl 27" & 52" - 33"
Power Output: 110 hp
First ref: mid 1880s

Pcs. Served on H.J. Perlbach's P. Quay to Hamburg route. Previously known as the *Sylph*.

Goodwood; UECC; IMO: 7347720
Built: 1974 by Ateliers & Chantiers du Havre, Le Havre, France
Dimensions: 100.46 x 15.90 x 4.00 m o.a.
Tonnage: 1592 grt / 734 nt / 1350 dwt
Speed: 14 knots
Stowage area: 5913 sq.m. on 6 levels
Trade car capacity: 610

Cms cc. Arrived at Aliaga on 28 May 2003 for scrapping

Great Yarmouth; GER
Built: by Jones Bros., London
Launched: June 1866
Dimensions: 199.9 x 28.4 x 17.0 ft
Tonnage: 731 grt / 491 nt
Engines: R & W Hawthorn c.o. 2 cyl 25" & 48" - 30"
Power Output: 100 nhp
Speed: 10 knots
First ref: August 1866

Pcs. Delivered August 1866 and built for GER as a 'London coaster' i.e. she operated a feeder service between London and Harwich for goods and passengers using the Harwich steamers. Also ran a coastal service as far as Kings Lynn. In 1872 she was sold to T.G. Beatley of London on account of not having enough passenger accommodation but was chartered back for 3 months in 1876 when the GER had a temporary shortage of ships. Sold again in 1880 to R.B. Fenwick & J. Reay, Newcastle and used in the coal trade from Gateshead. Stranded and wrecked in Gulf of Bothnia in September 1887.

Hainault; River Services
Built: 1914 by Vosper & Co., Portsmouth
Dimensions: 50.5 x 12.8 x 4.5 ft
Tonnage: 21.59 grt / 11.07 nt
Engines: 1 x semi-diesel Kromhout hot bulb ignition
Power Output: 35 bhp
Speed: 8¼ knots
Passengers: 125
First ref: June 1914

Pms. Cost £1.157. Single screw wooden harbour ferry built for the GER. Sailed on Harwich to Shotley Gate service with the *Pinmill*. Also to Ipswich. Requisitioned in 1914-18 and 1939-45 for harbour duties. Sold in 1962 for use as a houseboat though now rotting at Pin Mill on the River Orwell.

Hamburg; DFDS; IMO: 7400778
Built: by Werft Nobiskrug GmbH, Rendsburg, Germany - yard no.685
Launched: 4 October 1975
Dimensions: 156.42 / 135.79 x 23.47 x 6.65 m
Tonnage: 13141 grt / 6757 nt / 2999 dwt.
Engines: 2 x Stork Werkspoor 20 cyl diesel type 20TM410
Power Output: 24000 bhp
Speed: 22½ knots
Passengers: 1035 (B:862).
First ref: 4 April 1987 Hamburg to Parkeston Quay

Pcms ro-ro. Built for Jahre Line of Sandefjord, Norway and launched as the *Kronprins Harald*. Tonnage: 12752 grt / 6492 nt / 2999 dwt. Passengers: 960 (B:619). (m/v) was on 2 April 1976 for Jahre Line between Oslo and Kiel. Sold on 27 February 1987 to DFDS Seacruises Ltd., Nassau, Bahamas. Emerged after refit as *Hamburg* on 3 April 1987. Space for 400 cars or 45 trailers. On 8 November 1989 was severely damaged with three passengers killed after collision with *Nordic Stream*. Sent to Blohm & Voss, Hamburg for repairs and back in service on 22 December 1989. Re-named *Admiral of Scandinavia* on 21 May 1997. Route from P. Quay to Hamburg changed to Cuxhaven on 2 March 2002. Sold to Access Ferries, Panama on 11 July 2002, left P. Quay on 13 November 2002 and re-named *Caribbean Express* for service between Puerto Rico and Santo Domingo. Variously owned by Caribbean interests until sold for scrapping in Alang, India arriving on 25 January 2011.

Harwich; GER
Built: by Messrs Simpson & Co., Pimlico, London
Launched: Delivered May 1864
Dimensions: 215.0 x 27.1 x 14.0 ft
Tonnage: 750 grt / 550 nt / 613 dwt
Engines: Simpson & Co. s.o. 2 cly 55" - 66"
Power Output: 220 nhp / 980 hp
Speed: 10 knots
Passengers: Nil
First ref: 9 August 1864 Harwich to Rotterdam (m/v)

Cps. Launched as a cattle and cargo paddle steamer. Fitted with 50 berths in 1865 later raised to 80 in 1871. In 1884 she was rebuilt and re-boilered by Earle's Co. Ltd of Hull as a 763 grt twin screw passenger and cargo steamer. Fitted with a new 155 nhp Earle's 4 cly compound engine 22" & 42" - 27" and space for 110 passengers. In 1889, as the accommodation was now too small, she was converted to a cattle carrier and delivered on 5 March 1889 as the first cattle only ship on the Harwich to Rotterdam route. In October 1907 she was sold for scrap in Holland. Sister ship: *Rotterdam*.

Haslemere; Relief ship
Built: by D & W Henderson Ltd., Glasgow - yard no. 719
Launched: 22 May 1925
Dimensions: 230.0 x 35.7 x 12.8 ft o.a.
Tonnage: 756 grt / 305 nt / 500 dwt
Engines: 2 x Tr. exp.
Power Output: 165 nhp / 1850 ihp
Speed: 15 knots
Passengers: 12

Cs. Built for the Southern Railway Co. with 32,000 cu. ft. of cargo space plus 20 horse stalls or 76 cattle. Sailed from Southampton to Channel Islands / St. Malo. Relieved on the P. Quay to Rotterdam / Antwerp cargo service in the 1950s. Arrived at Rotterdam on 29 August 1959 for scrapping, later demolished at Utrecht. One of nine near sister ships including *Hythe* and *Ringwood*.

Hawk; GSNCo.
Built: 1876
Dimensions: 200.2 x 27.3 ft
Tonnage: 648 grt / 375 nt
Power Output: 140 nhp
First ref: 29 March 1888 arrival at Parkeston Quay from Hamburg.

Pcs. Served on the GSNCo. P. Quay to Hamburg route. Stranded and condemned in 1897

Hebe; DFDS
Built: by A/S Kjobenhavns Flydedok og Skibsvaerft, Copenhagen - yard no. 103
Launched: 21 September 1912
Dimensions: 242.0 / 230.0 x 33.9 x 14.6 ft
Tonnage: 957 grt / 441 nt / 917 dwt
Engines: Kjobenhavns Flydedok Tr. exp 19.5", 32" & 53" - 36"
Power Output: 1100 ihp
Speed: 12 knots
Passengers: 30 (14 First & 16 third class)
First ref: early 1910s

Pcs. Cost: Dkr 553,750. Briefly served on the P. Quay to Esbjerg route until 1922. Variously requisitioned during WW2 and returned to DFDS service in 1945. Other names: *Hebe I* (1940), *Sainte Sylvia* (1940), *Hebe II* (1942) and *Hebe* (1945). Sold on 19 February 1959 to Eisen und Metal KG Lehr & Co. of Hamburg for scrapping. Sister ship: *Diana (I)*

Hengest; DFDS
Built: by Lobnitz, Coulborn & Co., Renfrew - yard no. 159
Launched: 25 August 1876
Dimensions: 219.0 / 209.0 x 27.5 x 15.9 ft
Tonnage: 750 grt / 464 nt / 925 dwt
Engines: Lobnitz Coulborn c.o. 2 cyl 27" & 54" - 42"
Power Output: 600 ihp
Speed: 9½ knots
Passengers: 6 (6 First class)
First ref: early 1900s.

Cs. Made 94 sailings between P. Quay and Esbjerg. First delivered to A/S Det Jydsk-Engelske d.s.. Aarhus in September 1876. Purchased by DFDS on 17 May 1900. Sold on 5 March 1926 to Hans Petersen of Copenhagen for scrapping.

Hero; DFDS
Built: by Robb Caledon Shipbuilders Ltd., Leith - yard no.511
Launched: 2 June 1972
Dimensions: 114.53 / 104.50 x 19.00 x 5.86 m
Tonnage: 3375 grt / 1079 nt / 3634 dwt
Engines: 2 x Pielstick 10 cyl diesel type 10PC2V
Power Output: 10000 bhp
Speed: 17 knots
Passengers: 12
First ref: January 1973 Esbjerg - Grimsby / Parkeston Quay (m/v)

Cms ro-ro. A near sister ship to the *Surrey* owned jointly by Ellerman Wilson Line Ltd, Hull and DFDS (UK) Ltd, Hull. Lengthened at Amsterdamsche Dragoon-Maatschappij N.V. in 1976. Dimensions: 132.75 / 122.72 x 19.00 x 6.00 m. Tonnage: 4493 grt / 1844 nt / 5754 dwt. Capacity raised from original 170 teus to 235 teus. Lost by sinking during a storm on 13 November 1977 en-route from Esbjerg to Grimsby with the loss of one life.

Hibernia; Relief ship; IMO: 5150111
Built: by Harland & Wolff Ltd., Belfast - yard no. 1367
Launched: 1949
Dimensions: 121.10 x 17.15 x 4.52 m
Tonnage: 5284 grt / 2849 nt / 815 dwt
Engines: 2 x B&W - Harland & Wolff 8 cyl diesel
Power Output: 7982 kw
Speed: 15 knots
Passengers: 2000 (B: 357)
First ref: 25 October 1968

Built for BTC for service between Holyhead and Dun Laoghaire. (m/v) was on 14 April 1949. Relieved on the P. Quay to HvH service in October 1968. Sold on 1 December 1976 to Agapitos Bros. of Piraeus and re-named *Express Apollon*. Sold for scrapping in 1980 and arrived at Solid Steel Traders of Darukhana, India on 12 January 1981.

Hirondelle; GSNCo.
Built: by Gourlay Bros & Co., Dundee - yard no. 143
Launched: 7 May 1890
Dimensions: 268.0 x 37.5 x 19.0 ft
Tonnage: 1607 grt / 817 nt
Engines: 3 cyl Tr. exp.
Power Output: 371 nhp

Speed: 14 knots
Passengers: 145 (70 First, 50 Second & 25 Third class)
First ref: June 1890

Pcs. Built for GSNCo's London to Bordeaux service. She sailed from P. Quay to Gravesend on 14 June 1890 whilst undertaking her trials. First served on the P. Quay to Hamburg route in 1905. Prior to WW1 she was sailing London to Leith. Requisitioned in 1914 as a supply ship until returning to commercial duties after 1915. On 25 April 1917, whilst sailing from London to Bordeaux, she was torpedoed by German submarine UC36 and sank 13 miles s.e. of Belle Isle in the Bay of Biscay. No loss of life.

Hockenheim; UECC; IMO: 7424475
Built: 1976 in Ateliers & Chantiers du Havre, Le Havre, France
Dimensions: 105.50 x 15.90 x 4.15 m o.a.
Tonnage: 1591 grt / 801 nt / 1350 dwt
Speed: 14½ knots
Stowage area: 6053 sq.m. on 6 levels
Trade car capacity: 650

Cms cc. Previously known as *Hunaudieres* until re-named *Hockenheim* in 1987. Arrived at Aliaga on 22 February 2002 for scrapping

Hythe; Relief ship
Built: by D & W Henderson Ltd., Glasgow - yard no. 706
Launched: 24 April 1925
Dimensions: 230.0 x 35.7 x 12.8 ft oa
Tonnage: 688 grt / 267 nt / 483 dwt
Engines: 2 x Tr. exp.
Power Output: 165 nhp / 1850 ihp
Speed: 15 knots
Passengers: Nil

Cs. Built for the Southern Railway Co. with 33,000 cu. ft. of cargo space plus 20 horse stalls. Initially sailed from Dover / Folkestone to Calais / Boulogne but later transferred to Southampton. Relieved on the P. Quay to Rotterdam / Antwerp cargo service in the 1950s. Scrapped on 31 January 1956 at Dover. One of nine near sister ships including *Haslemere* and *Ringwood*.

Indianapolis; UECC; IMO: 7901722
Built: 1980 by Astillero Barreras, Vigo, Spain
Dimensions: 88.78 x 17.01 x 4.75 m o.a.
Tonnage: 1414 grt / 761 nt / 1956 dwt
Speed: 13 knots
Stowage area: 5474 sq.m. on 7 levels
Trade car capacity: 570

Cms cc. Scrapped.

Ipswich; GER
Built: by Earle's Shipbuilding & Eng. Co. Ltd., Hull - yard no. 256
Launched: 21 May 1883
Dimensions: 260.2 x 31.3 x 15.0 ft
Tonnage: 1037 grt / 435 nt / 820 dwt.
Engines: Earle's 2 sets comp. 2 cyl 30" & 57" - 36"
Power Output: 270 nhp / 2000 ihp
Speed: 14½ knots
Passengers: 440 (B: 84 First & 42 Second class)
First ref: 23 October 1883 Parkeston Quay to Antwerp (m/v)

Pcs. Re-boilered in 1895 and sold to J. Constant of London in 1905. Sold in 1908 to Shah Steam Navigation Co, Bombay. Scrapped in May 1909. Sister ship: *Norwich*.

Ipswich (I); River Services
Built: 1864 by James Ash, Cubitt Town, London.
Dimensions: 120.3 x 15.0 x 6.9 ft
Tonnage: 87 tons

Pps. The first river steamer built for the Great Eastern Railway. Fitted with a simple oscillating single cylinder engine, 40 nhp, and space for 150 passengers. Replaced the *Cardinal Wolsey*, Was transferred to the Lowestoft Railway & Harbour Co in 1873. Scrapped in 1881. Sister ship: *Stour (I)*.

Isle of Ely; BR; IMO: 5164980
Built: by Goole Shipbuilding & Repairing Co. Ltd., Goole - yard no. 512
Launched: 18 July 1958
Dimensions: 241.8 / 226.0 x 37.0 x 13.2 ft
Tonnage: 866 grt / 278 nt / 935 dwt
Engines: Ruston & Hornsby Ltd 8 cyl diesel type VOXM
Power Output: 1806 bhp
Speed: 13½ knots
Passengers: Nil
First ref: 27 October 1958 Parkeston Quay to Rotterdam (m/v)

Cms. General purpose cargo ship with 89,171 cu.ft. of hold space and the first BR ship at P. Quay to offer a unit load / box container freight service. Capacity of 42 'B' type box containers. Left on 5 May 1968 for conversion to a cellular container ship at J. Readheads, South Shields. Withdrawn from P. Quay in 1971. Sailed on Irish Sea and Channel Island services until laid up at Barrow in November 1975. Sold in 1976 to Pounds Marine Shipping Ltd., Havant. Between 1978 and 1982 was owned by various interests in Panama. re-named *Spice Island* in 1978 then *Spice Island Girl* in 1979. Laid up in Portsmouth in March 1982. Sold for scrapping in 1984 and broken up in December 1986 by Jacques Bakker in Bruges, Belgium. Sister ship: *Colchester*.

Jacaranda; Chartered
Built: by De Haan & Oerlemans Shipbuilders, Heusden - yard no. 264
Launched: 2 April 1952
Dimensions: 209.3 / 191.9 x 32.0 x 11.9 ft
Tonnage: 499 grt / 232 nt / 870 dwt
Engines: 1 x Werkspoor 8 cyl TMAS 338
Power Output: 800 bhp
Speed: 12 knots
Passengers: Nil
First ref: 1962 Rotterdam to Parkeston Quay

Cms. Cargo ship built for Society Eiram III of Rotterdam. Managed by Hudig & Pieters who took the ship over in February 1961. Chartered for service between P. Quay and Rotterdam from spring 1962 to 31st December 1963. Sold in January 1968 to S. Harakoglou, Piraeus and re-named *Ios II*. Sold in December 1970 to Jacaranda Lines s.a., Piraeus and re-named *Starshine*. Lost, with all 17 crew, presumed sunk in a storm after leaving Mogadishu for United Arab Emirates on 28 July 1971.

Jan Becker; Bell Line; IMO: 8707771
Built: 1987 by J.J. Sietas Schiffswerft, Hamburg, Germany - yard no. 966
Dimensions: 94.50 / 87.81 x 15.90 x 5.05 m
Tonnage: 2749 grt / 1110 nt / 3178 dwt
Engines: 1 x Wartsila diesel type 6R32D
Power Output: 1353 hp / 995 kw
Speed: 14 knots
First ref: 11 November 1987 Rozenburg to P. Quay

Cms lo-lo. Space for 262 teus. Launched on 21 September 1987. One of 5 Sietas Type 122 feeder ships. Inaugurated Bell Line's Rotterdam (Rozenburg) to P. Quay service on 11 November 1987. Other names: Re-named *Triton Loga* (1998), *Mosa* (2006) and *Dan Supporter* (2007). Last owner: Hs Schiffahrt, Haren Ems, Germany. Sister ships: *Amazone, Angela Jurgens, Jan Kahrs* and *Otto Becker*.

Jan Kahrs Bell Line IMO: 8815308
Built: 1988 by J.J. Sietas Schiffswerft, Hamburg, Germany - yard no. 1000
Dimensions: 94.50 / 87.81 x 15.90 x 5.05 m
Tonnage: 2749 grt / 1110 nt / 3150 dwt
Engines: 1 x Wartsila diesel type 6R32D
Power Output: 1353 hp / 995 kw
Speed: 14 knots
First ref: January 1989 Rozenburg to P. Quay

Cms lo-lo. Space for 262 teus. One of 5 Sietas Type 122 feeder ships. Re-named *Jan Caribe* in 1998. Last owner: Hyde Shipping, Medley, Florida. Sister ships: *Amazone, Jan Becker, Angela Jurgens* and *Otto Becker*.

Jarama UECC IMO: 7805980
Built: 1980 by Astillero Barreras, Vigo, Spain
Dimensions: 88.78 x 17.01 x 4.75 m o.a.
Tonnage: 1414 grt / 762 nt / 1955 dwt
Speed: 13 knots
Stowage area: 5474 sq.m. on 7 levels
Trade car capacity: 570

Cms cc. Scrapped.

J.C. Jacobsen DFDS
Built: by A/S Burmeister & Wain's Maskin-og Skibsbyggeri, Copenhagen - yard no. 156
Launched: 16 November 1889
Dimensions: 228.5 / 218.0 x 31.0 x 17.0 ft
Tonnage: 1227 grt / 887 nt / 1478 dwt
Engines: B&W Tr. exp 16.5", 27" & 45" - 33"
Power Output: 620 ihp
Speed: 10¼ knots
Passengers: 12
First ref: mid 1930s.

Cs. Cost: Dkr 400,000. Occasionally seen at P. Quay. Lost by springing a leak and sinking in bad weather in the North Sea on 4 February 1947.

J.C. la Cour; DFDS
Built: by A/S Helsingors Jernskibs-og Maskinbyggeri, Ellsinore - yard no. 84
Launched: 6 October 1900
Dimensions: 282.0 / 270.0 x 36.5 x 15.4 ft
Tonnage: 1615 grt / 673 nt / 955 dwt
Engines: Hels. J.&M. Tr. exp. 31", 53" & 84" - 42"
Power Output: 457 nhp / 3600 ihp
Speed: 15¼ knots
Passengers: 112 (76 First & 36 Third class)
First ref: 13 August 1901 Esbjerg to Parkeston Quay (m/v)

Pcs. Cost Dkr 934,907. In service between Esbjerg and P. Quay until August 1914. Transferred during WW1 to other routes from Denmark to the UK, mainly Hull, otherwise laid up. Resumed the Esbjerg to P. Quay route between 29 October 1919 and 13 December 1921 and then again from 28 May 1923 until 5 September 1931. In total made 919 sailings between the two ports. Sold for scrap on 13 October 1933 to Hughes Bolckow Shipbreaking Co. of Blyth for £3,250. Demolished by Bartram & Sons Ltd of Sunderland.

John O'Groat; Chartered
Built: by Gourlay Bros. & Co., Dundee
Launched: 1877
Dimensions: 174.8 x 24.8 x 12.9 ft
Tonnage: 388 grt
Engines: 2 cyl c.o. 28" & 52" - 33"
Power Output: 116 nhp
First ref: 8 December 1888 Parkeston Quay to Rotterdam

Pcs. Chartered by the GER from John McCallum & Co. of Scotland for use between P. Quay and Rotterdam from 8 December 1888 until 9 August 1889. She took over from an earlier charter by the GER of the 338 grt *Corsican* (Pcs) between 18 December 1887 and 1 December 1888.

Jupiter (Black Watch); Fred Olsen; IMO: 6609834
Built: by Lubecker Flender-Werke, Lubeck, Germany - yard no. 560
Launched: 5 March 1966
Dimensions: 464.7 x 65.7 x 20.0 ft
Tonnage: 9499 grt / 5503 nt / 3425 dwt
Engines: 2 x Crossley Pielstick 18 cyl diesels type 18PC2V
Power Output: 12489 kw
Speed: 23 knots
Passengers: 587 (B: 151 First & 376 Tourist)
First ref: May 1977 arrival at Parkeston Quay from Kristiansand

Pcms ro-ro. Built jointly for Fred Olsen & Co of Kristiansand and Det Bergenske Dampskipsselskab / Bergen Lines of Norway. (m/v) was in October 1966 operating as Fred Olsen's *Black Watch* on winter cruises with 350 passengers to Canary Islands. In summer she became Bergen Line's *Jupiter* as a car ferry between Newcastle and Bergen. From May 1977 she was used on the summer season P. Quay to Kristiansand / Oslo service and again each summer until the route closed in September 1981. Variously an off season cruise ship and later chartered to DFDS for summer services out of Newcastle. Sold August 1986 to Norway Lines as *Jupiter*. Sold in May 1990 to Marlines of Limassol, Cyprus and renamed *Crown M*. Sailed mainly between Ancona, Patras and Heraklion until laid up in Eleusis Bay, Greece in September 1997. Renamed *Byblos* in 2000 and *Crown* in 2005. Sold in July 2008 for scrapping in India. Sister ship: *Black Prince / Venus*

Jylland; DFDS
Built: by A/S Helsingors Jernskibs-og Maskinbyggeri, Ellsinore - yard no. 176
Launched: 10 April 1926
Dimensions: 324.0 / 304.0 x 44.0 x 17.8 ft
Tonnage: 2762 grt / 1559 nt / 1620 dwt
Engines: 2 x B&W 6 cyl diesels type 6150-MFX
Power Output: 545 nhp / 3200 bhp
Speed: 15½ knots
Passengers: 220 (132 First & 88 Third class)
First ref: 26 June 1926 Esbjerg to Parkeston Quay (m/v)

Pcms. Cost Dkr 2,883,112. In service between Esbjerg and P. Quay until September 1939 having made 801 sailings. Laid up in Copenhagen between July 1940 and 19 January 1944, then used as the German barrack ship *Musketeer*. Bombed in Allied air attack on 3 May 1945 off Travemunde whilst carrying 800 refugees. Sank whilst under tow. Sister ships: *Parkeston, Esbjerg (II), England (I)*.

Karen Oltmann; Railfreight; IMO: 7528556
Built: 1977 by J.J. Sietas Schiffswerft, Hamburg, Germany
Dimensions: 97 x 16 x 6.9 m
Tonnage: 3622 grt / 5766 dwt
First ref: 3 January 1989

Cms lo-lo. Inaugurated Freightliner's new P. Quay to Zeebrugge service on 3 January 1989 sailing opposite the *Petuja*. Other names: *Nederland (1978), Karen Oltmann* (1985), *Geranta* (1989), *Gracechurch Star* (1989), *Geranta* (1991), *Ub Panther* (1994), *Godewind* (1997), *Tai Mar* (2005), *Rose S* (2006), *Touareg* (2008), *Olympic A* (2012) and *Princess Maria* (2012). Last owner: Al Maria Maritime, Belize City.

Kasan; DFDS
Built: by A/S Burmeister & Wain's Maskin-og Skibsbyggeri, Copenhagen - yard no. 122
Launched: 7 April 1883
Dimensions: 246.0 / 235.0 x 30.0 x 17.0 ft
Tonnage: 1132 grt / 734 nt / 1266 dwt
Engines: B&W compound 4 cyl (2) 24" & (2) 48" - 32"
Power Output: 750 ihp
Speed: 10¼ knots
Passengers: 16
First ref: 1907

Cs. Up until 1925 she made 67 sailings between P. Quay and Esbjerg. In 1887 was the first Danish ship to be fitted with an onboard refrigeration plant. Sold on 5 March 1926 to Hans Petersen, Copenhagen and re-named *Prins Hamlet*. Later sold on 2 February 1935 to Henry Andersen of Copenhagen and scrapped.

Kilkenny (Frinton); GER
Built: by Clyde Shipbuilding & Eng. Co. Ltd., Port Glasgow - yard no. 254
Launched: 30 December 1902
Dimensions: 269.7 x 36.2 x 16.3 ft
Tonnage: 1419 grt / 1596 dwt
Engines: Clyde Sh. & Eng. Tr. exp. 26", 43" & 69" - 42"
Power Output: 542 nhp
Speed: 15 knots
Passengers: 154 First class & Steerage
First ref: 13 November 1919 Parkeston Quay to Antwerp

Pcs. Built for the City of Dublin Steam Packet Company's route between Dublin and Liverpool. Purchased by GER in August 1917. After civilian and war duties was refitted and put into service at P. Quay in November 1919 and as the re-named *Frinton* from December 1919. Sold on 29 July

1929 to Inglesi Bros., Greece sailing between Piraeus and Brindisi. Later sold to Samos Steam Navigation Co and re-named *Samos* sailing out of Venice, later resuming the name *Frinton*. Was lost as a war casualty by being bombed off Megara on 22 April 1941.

Killarney; Chartered
Built: by Scott Sinclair & Co., Greenock
Launched: 14 July 1856
Dimensions: 148.5 x 21.9 ft
Tonnage: 281 grt / 191 nt
Power Output: 85nhp
First ref;- January 1864

Pcps. Chartered by the ECR from H.T. Watson of Goole from 19 January 1864 to 6 March 1864

Klintholm; DFDS; IMO: 5190161
Built: by Frederikshavns Vaerft & Flydedok A/S, Frederikshavn - yard no. 215
Launched: 15 November 1949
Dimensions: 66.70 60.96 x 10.03 x 4.41 m
Tonnage: 965 grt / 466 nt / 1255 dwt
Engines: 1 x Atlas-Polar 5 cyl diesel type N555M
Power Output: 580 bhp
Speed: 10 knots
Passengers: 2
First ref: late 1950s

Cms. Cost: Dkr 2.1m. Sold on 21 December 1965 to Greek interests in Piraeus. Other names: *Dimitrios* (1965) and *Cornilia* (1979. Was beached and abandoned on 2 April 1982 off Gythion, Greece. Beached for scrapping in July 1983 by G. Molaris at Gythion.

Koldinghuus; DFDS
Built: by Lobnitz & Co., Renfrew - yard no. 227
Launched: 24 April 1883
Dimensions: 269.1 x 39.4 ft
Tonnage: 1057 grt / 610 nt / 450 dwt
Engines: Lobnitz c.o. 4 cyl (2) 32" & (2) 58" - 90"
Power Output: 400 hp / 1600 ihp
Speed: 12½ knots
Passengers: 118 (48 First & 70 Deck class)
First ref: 19 July 1883 Esbjerg to Parkeston Quay (m/v)

Pcps. Cost £37,200. In service between Esbjerg and P. Quay until 1887 and then from 1889 to 1903 making a total of 572 sailings. Stranded off Fano on 5 January 1903. Towed away for use as a storage hulk *Depotskib I*. On 2 August 1906 was sold to Petersen & Albeck, Copenhagen and then to interests in Hamburg for scrapping.

Kong Haakon; DFDS
Built: by A/S Burmeister & Wain's Maskin-og Skibsbyggeri, Copenhagen - yard no. 251
Launched: 22 June 1906
Dimensions: 287.3 / 273.0 x 37.9 x 16.9 ft
Tonnage: 1761 grt / 871 nt / 1201 dwt
Engines: B&W Tr. exp 4 cyl 25½", 42½" & (2) 51" - 42"
Power Output: 2450 ihp
Speed: 15 knots
Passengers: 336 (134 First, 68 Second & 134 Deck class)
First ref: 8 November 1921

Pcs. Cost: Dkr 909,000. Built for the Copenhagen to Stettin and Oslo service. (m/v) was in August 1906. Refitted at Kiel in September 1921 for service on the North Sea. In service between P. Quay and Esbjerg from November 1921 until September 1926, alternating with service between Copenhagen and Oslo, and then again between 1931 and 1936. Sold on 27 September 1938 to Parma Laeva A/S, Parma and re-named *Vironia*. Struck a mine and sank off Kap Juminda on 28 August 1941. Sister ship: *Dronning Maud*.

Koningin Beatrix; SMZ; IMO: 8416308
Built: by Van de Giessen-de Noord, Krimpen a/d Ijssel, Holland, yard no. 935
Launched: 9 November 1985
Dimensions: 530 6 / 481.0 x 90.55 x 20.3 ft
Tonnage: 31189 grt / 15170 nt / 3060 dwt
Engines: 4 x MAN Augsburg 8 cyl diesels type 8L 40/45
Power Output: 25600 hp / 19360 kW
Speed: 21 knots
Passengers: 2100 (B: 1296)
First ref: 22 April 1986 Hook of Holland to Parkeston Quay (m/v)

Pcms ro-ro. Launched by H.M. Koningin Beatrix. Space for 485 cars or 220 cars and 76 trailers. Sailed on P. Quay to HvH route for SMZ until route was rebranded Crown Line in January 1989. Sold to Stena Ab, Gothenburg on 1 September 1989. Continued on HvH route until 2 June 1997. Moved to Fishguard to Rosslare route in June 1997 until 12 March 2003. Re-named *Stena Baltica* on 13 March and put onto the Karlskrona, Sweden to Gdynia Poland route. Rebuilt at Remontowa, Gdansk in spring 2005 and returned to route until 27 June 2011. Dimensions: 164.71 x 27.60 x 6.30 m. Tonnage: 31910 grt / 13080 nt / 4272 dwt. Passengers: 1200 (B: 1000) 524 cars. Lane metres increased from 1000 to 1800. Laid up in Landskrona and Lysekil until sold on 24 January 2013 to Snav Spa, Italy. Re-named *Snav Adriatico* for service out of Naples.

Koningin Emma; SMZ
Built: by Koninklijke Maatschappij De Schelde, Vlissingen, Holland - yard no. 209
Launched: 14 January 1939
Dimensions: 380.0 / 350.2 x 47.0 x 13.5 ft
Tonnage: 4135 grt / 2100 nt
Engines: 2 x De Schelde Sulzer 10 cyl diesels
Power Output: 1824 nhp / 12600 shp
Speed: 21½ knots
Passengers: 1800 (B: 90)
First ref: 4 June 1939 Flushing to Parkeston Quay (m/v)

Pcms. Launched by Queen Wilhelmina as the first diesel vessel built for SMZ. Day boat fitted with only 90 berths, space for 35 cars and a crew of 58. Escaped to England in May 1940. Requisitioned by the Royal Navy and re-named in 1941 as *H.M.S. Queen Emma*. Had an extensive wartime career before returning to SMZ in April 1946. Re-named *Koningin Emma* and refitted for civilian use for 1423 passengers with 203 First and 94 Second class berths. Re-profiled with a smaller funnel and a higher bridge. Back in service at P. Quay in 1948, chartered in March to BR as cover for the *Prague*, then in summer to Batavier Line between Rotterdam and London. Relegated to reserve ship upon arrival of *Koningin Wilhelmina* in 1960. Was towed to Jos De Smed, Antwerp on 18 December 1968 for breaking up. Sister ship: *Prinses Beatrix*

Koningin Fabiola; RMT; IMO: 5192963
Built: by J. Boel et Fils S.A., Tamise, Belgium - yard no.1391
Launched: 20 November 1961
Dimensions: 383.4 / 362.9 x 52.4 x 12.5 ft
Tonnage: 3057 grt / 1317 nt / 411 dwt
Engines: 2 x Sulzer 12 cyl diesels type 12NH51
Power Output: 9600 bhp / 7162 kw
Speed: 22 knots
Passengers: 850 (B:124)
First ref: late 1960s

Pcms ro-ro. (m/v) was on 10 June 1962 from Ostend to Dover. Capacity for 160 cars or 142 cars and 5 lorries. Served on this route until 15 June 1983. Underwent berthing trials at P. Quay on 19 September 1967. Utilised as a relief ship from P. Quay to HvH in summer 1970. Sold in February 1985 to Ionian Navigation Co. Ltd., Valleta, Malta, re-named *Olympia* and then again as *Lydia*. Variously sailed on routes out of Greece. Sold to Illyria Ferries in December 1995 and re-named *Ephesus* for services between Italy, Greece and Turkey. Re-named *Bergama* in 1996. Sold to Illyria lines in 1997, then chartered to Anatolia Ferries in 1998 and re-named *Bosporus*. Laid up in Cesme in 2000 and sold for scrapping in 2004. Arrived at Aliaga, Turkey on 11 March 2004.

Koningin Juliana; SMZ; IMO: 6808806
Built: by Cammell Laird & Co. Ltd., Birkenhead - yard no. 1331
Launched: 2 February 1968
Dimensions: 429.5 / 381.5 x 67.2 x 16.3 ft
Tonnage: 6682 grt / 3475 nt / 1290 dwt
Engines: 4 x MAN Augsburg 9 cyl diesels type R9V40/54
Power Output: 19560 hp
Speed: 21 knots
Passengers: 1200 by day / 750 by night (B: 267 First & 270 Second class))
First ref: 17 October 1968 Hook of Holland to Parkeston Quay (m/v)

Pcms. Launched by Madame A. van Roijen, wife of Dutch Ambassador. Built for a new integrated ro-ro service in partnership with the *St. George* that finally commenced on 8 November 1968. Space for 220 cars or 80 cars and 32 lorries. Sold in 1985 to Mr. Tromp of Leiden, re-named *Holland Trade Ship* amidst abortive plans for use as an exhibition ship for Dutch goods. Resold in September 1985 to Nav. Archipelago Maddalenino S.p.a. and re-named *Moby Prince* for service between Naples and Cagliari. Destroyed in a fireball after striking the oil tanker *Agip Abruzzo* on 11 April 1991 when leaving Livorno in thick fog. Of the 142 onboard the *Moby Prince*, only 1 survived. Wreck removed in June 1998 and arrived in Aliaga, Turkey on 22 July 1998 for scrapping.

Koningin Regentes; SMZ
Built: by Fairfield Shipbuilding & Eng. Co. Ltd., Govan, Scotland - yard no. 385
Launched: 9 July 1895
Dimensions: 320.0 x 35.8 x 16.0 ft
Tonnage: 1947 grt / 835 nt
Engines: Fairfield Tr. exp. 51", 75" & 112" - 78"
Power Output: 1350 nhp / 9000 hp
Speed: 21 knots
Passengers: 244 (180 First & 64 Second class)
First ref: Autumn 1895 Flushing to Queenborough (m/v)

Pcps. On 6 June 1918 whilst sailing as a hospital ship en route from Rotterdam to Boston (Lincs) she was torpedoed by U107 and sank 21 miles east of the Leman Lightship. Sister ships: *Koningin Wilhelmina, Prins Hendrik (II)*

Koningin Wilhelmina (I); SMZ
Built: by Fairfield Shipbuilding & Eng. Co. Ltd., Govan, Scotland - yard no. 384
Launched: 23 May 1895
Dimensions: 320.0 x 35.8 x 16.0 ft
Tonnage: 1943 grt / 885 nt
Engines: Fairfield Tr. exp. 51", 75" & 112" - 78"
Power Output: 1350 nhp / 9000 hp
Speed: 21 knots
Passengers: 244 (180 First & 64 Second class)
First ref: Autumn 1895 Flushing to Queenborough (m/v)

Pcps. One of three ships built in response to the improved 1894 GER service to Hook of Holland. All converted to being day boats in 1910. On 31 July 1916 whilst en route from Flushing to Tilbury she hit a mine and sank 2 miles off the North Hinder Lightship. Sister ships: *Koningin Regentes, Prins Hendrik (II)*

Koningin Wilhelmina (II); SMZ; IMO: 5192987
Built: by N.V. Scheepswerf & Machinefabriek 'De Merwede', Hardinxveld-Giessendam - yard no. 548
Launched: 30 May 1959
Dimensions: 394.7 / 361.8 x 53.5 x 14.8 ft
Tonnage: 6228 grt / 2727 nt / 732 dwt
Engines: 2 x MAN Augsburg 12 cyl diesels
Power Output: 15600 hp
Speed: 23½ knots
Passengers: 1600 (B: 21 First & 196 Second class)
First ref: 7 February 1960 Hook of Holland to Parkeston Quay (m/v)

Pcms. Launched by H.M. Queen Juliana. Built as a passenger only ship with hold space for 50 cars. Withdrawn from P. Quay to HvH service on 28 June 1978 and laid up in Flushing. Sold to C. Ventouris & Sons of Greece and left on 10 December 1978 for conversion in Piraeus to ro-ro ferry. Re-named *Captain Constantinos* and sailed between Syros, Tinos and Mykonos. Re-named *Panagia Tinoy* in 1981, sold to AK Ventouris in 1987 and transferred to Ventouris Sea Lines in 1990 who re-named her *Artemis*. Sold to Minoan Cruises of Piraeus in 1996 for cruises from Heraklion - Rethymnon - Agios Nikolaos and Santorini. Sold on 30 April 2001 to Vickie Navigation, San Lorenzo, Honduras and re-named *Temis*. Arrived in Alang, India on 14 May 2001 for scrapping.

Kronen; DFDS
Built: by Kochums Mekaniska Verkstads A/B. Malmo - yard no. 30
Launched: 12 October 1881
Dimensions: 171.7 / 166.0 x 25.1 x 13.1 ft
Tonnage: 458 grt / 262 nt / 500 dwt
Engines: Kochums c.o. 2 cyl 25.2" & 44" - 29.6"
Power Output: 450 ihp
Speed: 9 knots
Passengers: 30 (6 First & 24 Deck class)
First ref: late 1880s

Cs. Briefly seen on the Esbjerg to P. Quay route as her main route was to Newcastle. First delivered to Niels Nielsen of Nykjobing on 18 March 1882. Purchased by DFDS on 4 April 1887 for Dkr 200,000. Sank on 4 October 1899 off the Tyne Pier, Newcastle following a collision with the *Blythville*.

Kronprins Frederik; DFDS; IMO: 5196983
Built: by A/S Helsingors Jernskibs-og Maskinbyggeri, Ellsinore - yard no. 262
Launched: 20 June 1940
Dimensions: 375.5 / 348.5 x 49.7 x 18.6 ft
Tonnage: 3895 grt / 2284 nt / 1720 dwt
Engines: 2 x B&W 10 cyl diesel type 1050-VF-90
Power Output: 8500 ihp / 7100 bhp
Speed: 20¼ knots
Passengers: 358 (143 First, 159 Second & 56 Deck class)
First ref: 5 June 1946 Esbjerg to Parkeston Quay (m/v)

Pcms. Cost Dkr 5.66m. Ordered in 1939 but construction was curtailed because of WW2. Laid up in Copenhagen until completed in March 1946. Space for 33 cars. First arrival at P. Quay was on 27 May 1946 for berthing trials. Suffered severe fire damage on 19 April 1953 whilst alongside at P. Quay. Subsequently sank at her berth. Re-floated on 26 August and towed away in September to Elsinore for a rebuild. Returned to service with first sailing from P. Quay to Esbjerg on 7 May 1954. Displaced onto the Esbjerg to Newcastle service as from 26 June 1964. Refitted in 1965 with bow thrusters and anti roll tanks for services from Esbjerg to Faroe Islands and Iceland. Laid up in July 1974, sold on 10 March 1976 to Arab Navigation Co. of Suez and re-named *Patra*. Was lost to fire and sinking 50 miles off Jeddah on 24 December 1976 with loss of 102 lives. Sister ship: *Kronprinsesse Ingrid*.

Kronprinsesse Ingrid; DFDS; IMO: 5197016
Built: by Helsingor Skibsvaerft og Maskinbyggeri A/S, Ellsinore - yard no. 289
Launched: 16 January 1948
Dimensions: 375.5 / 348.5 x 49.6 x 18.5 ft
Tonnage: 3968 grt / 2292 nt / 1967 dwt
Engines: 2 x B&W 10 cyl diesels type 1050-VF-90
Power Output: 8500 ihp / 7100 bhp
Speed: 20½ knots
Passengers: 334 (148 First, 146 Second & 40 Deck class)
First ref: 13 June 1949 Esbjerg to Parkeston Quay (m/v)

Pcms. Cost Dkr 12.9m. Space for 35 cars. Often utilised for off season sailings between Copenhagen and Oslo or, during the mid 1960s, for low season cruises between Copenhagen and the Mediterranean. Displaced from P. Quay onto the seasonal Esbjerg to Newcastle service as from 23 June 1967. Sold 28 May 1969 to Rederi-og Handelsselskabat Montana A/S of Copenhagen and re-named *Copenhagen*, sailing Copenhagen to Halmstad. Sold 3 November 1969 to Costas Spyrou Latsis of Piraeus and re-named *Mimika L*, sailing around Greek Islands from Piraeus. Sold in 1978 to Astir Shipping Enterprises Co. Ltd., of Piraeus and re-named *Alkyon*. Laid up in October 1983 at Piraeus and later scrapped in Karachi by Talha & Haroon in June 1985. Sister ship: *Kronprins Frederik*.

Kursk; DFDS
Built: by A/S Burmeister & Wain's Maskin-og Skibsbyggeri, Copenhagen - yard no. 116
Launched: 30 April 1881
Dimensions: 246.0 / 235.0 x 30.1 x 16.0 ft

Tonnage: 1131 grt / 731 nt / 1266 dwt
Engines: B&W c.o. 4 cyl (2) 24" & (2) 48" - 32"
Power Output: 750 ihp
Speed: 8½ knots
Passengers: 20 (16 First & 4 Second class)
First ref: early 1880s

Cs. Made only the occasional visit to P. Quay as she was mainly used between the Baltic and the Mediterranean. Lost with all hands in a storm off Vlissingen on 26 August 1912 whilst sailing between Antwerp and St. Petersburg.

Lady of Mann; Trooping Services; IMO: 5201893
Built: by Vickers Armstrong Ltd., Barrow - yard no. 660
Launched: 4 March 1930
Dimensions: 371.0 x 50.2 x 12.8 ft
Tonnage: 3104 grt / 1258 nt
Engines: srg steam turbine
Power Output: 12700 ihp
Speed: 23 knots
First ref: 13 January 1945

Pcs. Built for the Isle of Man Steam Packet Co. for service between Heysham and Douglas. Passengers: 2873. (m/v) was on 28 June 1930. Requisitioned for use as a troopship in September 1939. Served on trooping duties between P. Quay and Calais from 13 January 1945 until February 1945. Paid off in March 1946, refitted in May and resumed original commercial service on 15 June 1946. On 31 December 1971 she arrived at Arnott Young's of Dalmuir for scrapping.

Lady Tyler; GER
Built: by T. & W. Smith, North Shields.
Launched: 1880
Dimensions: 261.0 x 30.2 x 13.8 ft
Tonnage: 951 grt / 421 nt / 802 dwt
Engines: R & W Hawthorn c.o. 6 cyl (2) 33" & (4) 44" - 60"
Power Output: 340 nhp / 1700 ihp
Speed: 13 knots
Passengers: 709
First ref: 29 May 1880 Harwich to Rotterdam (m/v)

Pcps. Fitted with compound surface condensing steeple engines and electric light. Underwent sea trials on 4 May 1880. Sold to Earle's Co. Ltd. of Hull in 1893 and re-named *Artemis*. Was replaced by the *Chelmsford*. Sold for scrap in November 1955 after having survived as a coal hulk at Gravesend since 1900.

Laird's Isle; Trooping Services
Built: by Wm Denny & Bros, Dumbarton - yard no. 937
Launched: 1 April 1911
Dimensions: 323.0 / 316.0 x 41.0 x 14.2 ft
Tonnage: 1674 grt / 649 nt
Engines: 3 sets Parson's steam turbines, direct drive
Power Output: 850 nhp / 8100 ihp
Speed: 20½ knots
First Ref: 4 January 1945

Pcms. Cost £85,106. Launched as the South Eastern & Chatham Railway's *Riviera* for service between Dover and Calais. Triple screwed. (m/v) was on 8 June 1911. Saw service during WW1 as a seaplane carrier. Purchased by Burns and Laird Lines on 18 November 1932 and re-named *Laird's Isle* in 1933 for service between Ardrossan and Belfast. Commissioned as *HMS Lairds Isle* on 15 September 1939 as an armed boarding vessel and then in 1944 as a landing ship. Served on trooping duties between P. Quay and Calais from 4 January 1945 to 13 January 1945. Paid off in July 1946 following trooping duties between Tilbury and Ostend and between Southampton and Le Havre. Resumed original commercial service on 29 July 1946. Scrapped in October 1957 at Troon by West of Scotland Shipbreaking Co.

Landguard (I); LNER
Built: by William Simons & Co., Renfrew - yard no. 356
Launched: 29 September 1898
Dimensions: 190.0 x 30.0 x 12.4 ft o.a.
Tonnage: 691 grt / 264 nt
Engines: 3 cyl Tr. exp.
Power Output: 950 ihp
First ref: 1935

Entered service as a coal fired hopper barge. Launched as the *Thames Conservancy Hopper no. 3* for use by the Conservators of the River Thames. Was re-named *Port of London Authority Hopper no. 3* in 1909. Requisitioned by the Admiralty in January 1917 for use as the oil carrier *RFA Barkol*. After service as far afield as Scotland she was released in 1920 and returned to service with the PLA. Sold in 1929 to the Ipswich Dock Commission and re-named *Landguard*. Purchased by the LNER in 1935 at a cost of £6,367 for use as a grab dredging hopper based at Harwich. Normal dredging depth was 30 feet with a maximum of 60 feet. The working outreach of the grab was 30 feet with a safe lift of 6.5 tons discharging into her own hold of 650 cubic yards capacity. Scrapped in May 1957 in Bruges by Jacques Bakker & Zonen.

Landguard (II); BR; IMO: 5203140
Built: by Goole Shipbuilding & Repairing Co. Ltd., Goole - yard no. 520
Launched: 5 October 1959
Dimensions: 158.0 / 145.0 x 35.6 x 12.9 ft
Tonnage: 674 grt / 737 dwt
Engines: 1 x Ruston & Hornby 6 cyl diesel
Power Output: 382 kw
First ref: March 1960

Built for BR as a motor powered grab dredger. Fitted with a 12 ton slewing grab and a hold of 500 cubic metres / 650 tons capacity. In service at Harwich and P. Quay from March 1960 until 1990.

Lapwing; GSNCo.
Built: 1879
Tonnage: 1215 grt
First ref: 1890s

Pcs. Seen on the GSNCo. P. Quay to Hamburg route. Sold in 1910 to an Egyptian company

Le Castellet; UECC; IMO: 8020044
Built: 1982 by Ateliers & Chanters La Rochelle Pallice, La Rochelle, France
Dimensions: 116.50 x 18.00 x 5.30 m o.a.
Tonnage: 1600 grt / 841 nt / 2400 dwt
Speed: 15 knots
Stowage area: 7402 sq.m. on 6 levels
Trade car capacity: 897

Cms cc. Scrapped

Lemnos; DFDS
Built: by Helsingor Skibsvaerft og Maskinbyggeri A/S, Elsinore - yard no. 286
Launched: 16 March 1948
Dimensions: 331.2 / 305.0 x 43.2 x 18.4 ft
Tonnage: 1768 grt / 919 nt / 2675 dwt
Engines: 1 x B&W 8 cyl diesel type 850-VF-90
Power Output: 2550 bhp
Speed: 14½ knots
Passengers: 12
First ref: late 1950s.

Cms. Cost: Dkr 4.8m. Occasional service between P. Quay and Esbjerg. Sold on 4 April 1968 to Associated Levant Lines Ltd of Beirut and re-named *Beiteddine*. Lost by grounding in Bejaia Roads following an onboard fire on 5 September 1973. Sister ship: *Melos*.

Lolland; DFDS
Built: by H. McIntyre & Co. Merksworth Yard, Paisley - yard no. 84
Launched: 31 January 1882
Dimensions: 178.0 / 173.6 x 26.5 x 13.4 ft
Tonnage: 493 grt / 284 nt / 584 dwt
Engines: Hutson & Corbett, Glasgow c.o. 2 cyl 24" & 48" - 30"
Power Output: 420 ihp
Speed: 10 knots
Passengers: 5
First ref: late 1880s.

Cs. Occasional service between P. Quay and Esbjerg. First delivered to G. Bottern of Nakskov on 7 March 1882. Purchased by DFDS on 4 January 1883. Lost through capsize and sinking in the North Sea on 1 September 1909.

London; Chartered
Built: in Glasgow for Maples & Morris, Newhaven
Launched: 1853
Dimensions: 194.0 x 21.0 x 12 ft
Tonnage: 341 grt / 192 nt
Engines: s.o 1 cyl
Power Output: 120 hp
First ref: April 1857 Harwich to Rotterdam

Pcps. Built for service between Brighton, Newhaven and Dieppe. Chartered for services between Harwich and Rotterdam by the London, Harwich & Continental Steam Packet Co. on 25 April 1857 and then by the Harwich Steam Packet Co. from 1 July 1857 to 7 January 1858 though the last sailing was on 26 December 1857. Made a total of 47 sailings. Chartered by the ECR during 1858 in an unsuccessful attempt to resurrect a service to Rotterdam.

Lutterworth; GCR
Built: by Earle's Shipbuilding & Eng. Co. Ltd., Hull
Launched: 8 April 1891
Dimensions: 240.6 x 32.0 x 14.8 ft
Tonnage: 1002 grt / 495 nt
Engines: Earle's Tr. exp. 22", 35" & 57" - 42"
Power Output: 249 nhp
Speed: 12½ knots
Passengers: 410 (B:50 First & 360 Emigrant class)
First ref: November 1918 repatriation sailings between Parkeston Quay and Rotterdam.

Pcs. The *Lutterworth*, along with the *Leicester* in June 1891, were the second pair of four ships ordered by the Manchester, Sheffield & Lincolnshire Railway for their Grimsby to Hamburg service but built instead by Earle's of Hull. Had the same technical details but with slightly different accommodation. Transferred to GCR on 1 August 1897 with the *Lutterworth* being placed on the Rotterdam service. Both were requisitioned on 12 October 1914 as store carriers. The *Leicester* was mined and sunk on 12 February 1916 but post war the *Lutterworth* was engaged in repatriation work between P. Quay and Rotterdam from November 1918 up until 7 November 1919 and then returned to the GCR on 14 November. Sold in 1932 to British & Irish Steam Packet Co. and later scrapped by T.W. Ward at Preston in 1933. Sister ship: *Leicester* (See also *Nottingham* and *Staveley*)

Lynn Trader; Chartered
Built: by W.J. Yarwood & Sons Ltd., Northwick - yard no. 287
Launched: 11 December 1926
Dimensions: 130.4 x 23.4 x 9.5 ft
Tonnage: 327 grt / 122 nt
Engines: 1 x Yarwood Tr. exp.
Power Output: 53 nhp
Speed: 8 knots
First ref: February 1946

Cs. Delivered as *Vivonia* to H. Leetham & Sons Ltd. of York. Acquired by GSNCo. in March 1929 and re-named *Goldfinch*. Transferred to the Great Yarmouth Shipping Co on 31 December 1931 and in 1936 was re-named *Lynn Trader*. Chartered by the LNER in February and March 1946 to resume a post war cargo service between P. Quay and Rotterdam.
Sold to A.H. Tucker of Cardiff in 1951 for conversion to a dredger. Re-named *Imogen*. Scrapped in June 1964 by Haulbowline Industries Ltd of Cork.

Magnolia; DFDS; IMO: 5217165
Built: by A/S Aarhus Flydedok & Maskinkompagni, Aarhus - yard no. 118
Launched: 29 November 1962
Dimensions: 106.85 / 98.00 x 15.10 x 5.85 m
Tonnage: 2359 grt / 1122 nt / 2830 dwt
Engines: 1 x B&W 6 cyl diesel type 650-VTBF-110
Power Output: 3450 bhp
Speed: 15½ knots
Passengers: 4
First ref: 1967

Rcms. Cost: Dkr 15.7m. Seen on the P. Quay to Esbjerg route in the late 1960s. Sold on 29 January 1974 to Ben Shipping Ltd., Singapore. Other names: *C. Ranee* (1974) and *Al Gilani* (1976). Scrapped in October 1987 by Shri Ram Shipbreakers of Bombay. Sister ship: *Petunia*.

Malines; GER
Built: by High Walker yard of Armstrong, Whitworth & Co., Newcastle - yard no. 972
Launched: 6 January 1921
Dimensions: 337.0 / 320.6 x 43.1 x 17.8 ft
Tonnage: 2969 grt / 1257 nt / 2384 dwt
Engines: 2 x 2 John Brown Curtis srg turbines
Power Output: 1476 nhp / 10500 shp
Speed: 21 knots
Passengers: 1680 (B: 263 First & 87 Second class)
First ref: 21 March 1922 Parkeston Quay to Antwerp (m/v)

Pcs. Last ship built for the GER. Engines built by Wallsend Slipway & Eng. Co Ltd., Newcastle. Requisitioned in May 1940 after having assisted with evacuation work in Rotterdam. Served in the Mediterranean and was hit by aerial torpedo and beached off Port Said on 22 July 1942. Towed back to England in 1945 and scrapped in April 1948 by Clayton & Davie Ltd at Dunston-on-Tyne. Sister ships: *Antwerp, Bruges*

Manxman (I); Trooping Services
Built: by Vickers, Sons & Maxim Ltd., Barrow-in-Furness - yard no. 315
Launched: 15 June 1904
Dimensions: 341.0 / 334.0 x 43.0 x 13.8 ft
Tonnage: 2174 grt / 835 nt / 589 dwt
Engines: 3 Parsons steam turbine
Power Output: 10000 ihp / 6300 shp
Speed: 22½ knots
Passengers: 2020 (1155 First & 865 Third class)
First ref: 16 March 1946

Pcs. Initially served on the Midland Railway Co.'s route between Heysham and Belfast and then on 1 June 1905 inaugurated a new service between Heysham and Douglas. Triple screwed. Requisitioned by the Admiralty for use as a seaplane carrier in 1916. Acquired by Isle of Man Steam Packet Co. in March 1920 for their Liverpool to Douglas route. Requisitioned in September 1939 as a troop carrier. Commissioned on 29 May 1942 as *HMS Caduceus* and paid off on 23 January 1945. Reverted to *Manxman* and served on trooping duties between Tilbury and Ostend from 15 September 1945 before moving to the P. Quay and HvH trooping service on 16 March 1946 until 24 February 1949. Immediately thereafter she left P. Quay at 10.00 am on 25 February 1949 bound for Barrow Docks. On 9 August 1949 she was towed to Preston for breaking up.

Margrethe; DFDS
Built: by A/S Helsingors Skibs-og Maskinbyggeri, Elsinore - yard no. 144
Launched: 13 June 1914
Dimensions: 300.0 / 285.0 x 40.4 x 19.8 ft
Tonnage: 2441 grt / 1490 nt / 2725 dwt
Engines: Helsingors Skibs Tr. exp 22", 36" & 60" - 42"
Power Output: 1500 ihp
Speed: 12 knots
Passengers: 88 (10 First & 78 Second class)
First ref: 1925

Pcs. Cost: Dkr 1.005m. Seen on the P. Quay to Esbjerg route only until 1926 having made just 8 sailings. Other names: Originally launched as *Moskov* (1914) and re-named *Margrethe* in 1925. Sold on 19 February 1959 to Eisen und Metal KG Lehr & Co. of Hamburg for scrapping.

Marocco; DFDS
Built: by A/S Helsingors Jernskibs-og Maskinbyggeri, Elsinore - yard no. 232
Launched: 17 December 1935
Dimensions: 288.1 / 270.0 x 40.2 x 18.3 ft
Tonnage: 1684 grt / 925 nt / 2306 dwt
Engines: 1 x B&W 5 cyl diesel type 550-VF-90
Power Output: 1600 bhp
Speed: 12½ knots
Passengers: 12
First ref: late 1940s.

Cms. Cost: Dkr 1,313,286. Seen on the P. Quay to Esbjerg route. Sold on 22 June 1966 to Greek interests based in Piraeus. Other names: *Santa*

Cruz (1966) and *Dimitra M* (1971). Scrapped in Greece in November 1978. Sister ship: *Tunis*.

Marylebone; GCR
Built: by Cammell Laird & Co. Ltd., Birkenhead - yard no. 670
Launched: 21 April 1906
Dimensions: 270.2 x 41.1 x 20.3 ft
Tonnage: 1972 grt / 522 nt
Engines: 3 x Cammell Laird & Co. Ltd. turbines - direct drive
Power Output: 960 nhp
Speed: 18 knots
Passengers: 398 (B:74 First, 24 Second and 300 Emigrant class)
First ref: December 1918 Tilbury to Antwerp

Pcs. Built for GCR as a triple screw turbine steamer for the Grimsby to Rotterdam service. Moved to the Hamburg route and in July 1911 was re-engined by Earle's of Hull. Fitted with a new 398 nhp Earle's triple expansion engine, 23½", 38" & 62" - 42", a single screw making 13 knots and made single funnelled by the removal of the one forward. During WW1 she remained in commercial service based at Tilbury and was chartered post war by the GER for sailings to Antwerp. Passengers: 12. Was the first post war British steamer to return to Antwerp on 17 December 1918. Was the first post war commercial arrival at P. Quay, from Antwerp, on 21 January 1919. After her last trip from Antwerp on 30 September 1919 she was returned to the GCR on 2 October. Sold in 1933 to Greek interests and variously re-named *Velos*, *Arafat* and then *Velos* until broken up in Italy in 1938. Sister ship: *Immingham* which was not seen at P. Quay.

Mecklenburg (I); SMZ
Built: by Fairfield Shipbuilding & Eng. Co. Ltd., Govan, Scotland - yard no. 463
Launched: 25 October 1909
Dimensions: 349.8 x 42.7 x 16.4 ft
Tonnage: 2885 grt / 1120 nt / 2405 dwt
Engines: Fairfield Tr. exp. 8 cyl in 2 sets 28", 43½" & (2) 49" - 33"
Power Output: 1130 nhp / 10000 ihp
Speed: 22 knots
Passengers: (B: 246 First & 110 Second class)
First ref: April 1910 Flushing to Queenborough (m/v)

Pcs. On 27 February 1916 whilst en route from Tilbury to Flushing she hit a mine and sank south east of the Galloper Lightship. Sister ships: *Prinses Juliana (I)*, *Oranje Nassau*.

Mecklenburg (II); SMZ
Built: Built: by Koninklijke Maatschappij De Schelde, Vlissingen, Holland - yard no. 170
Launched: 18 March 1922
Dimensions: 350.4 x 42.7 x 16.4 ft
Tonnage: 2907 grt / 1122 nt / 2407 dwt
Engines: Fairfield Tr. exp. 8 cyl in 2 sets 28", 43½" & (2) 49" - 33"
Power Output: 1130 nhp
Speed: 22 knots
Passengers: 377 (267 First & 110 Second class)
First ref: 19 July 1922 Flushing to Folkestone (m/v)

Pcs. Built under the same circumstances as *Prinses Juliana (II)*. Transferred to the new SMZ Flushing to P. Quay route in January 1927. Escaped to England in May 1940 and used as a Royal Dutch Navy depot ship at Portsmouth until 1941. Later converted to landing ship and was present at Dunkirk. Post war she operated a service on behalf of the Dutch Government between Tilbury / P. Quay and Rotterdam from 21 November 1945 to 4 April 1946, (P. Quay from 9 January 1946). Converted to oil burning in 1946 and on 14 June 1947 she re-instated SMZ day boat service from P. Quay but to HvH instead of Flushing. Sailed on a summer season Flushing to Folkestone route between 1949 and 1952. Scrapped in 1960 at Van Heyghen Freres in Ghent. Sister ship: *Prinses Juliana (II)*

Melos; DFDS
Built: by Frederikshavns Vaerft & Flydedok A/S, Frederikshavn - yard no. 214
Launched: 20 May 1948
Dimensions: 331.2 / 305.0 x 43.2 x 18.3 ft
Tonnage: 1767 grt / 918 nt / 2675 dwt
Engines: 1 x B&W 8 cyl diesel type 850-VF-90
Power Output: 2550 bhp
Speed: 14½ knots
Passengers:12
First ref: late 1950s.

Cms. Occasionally seen on the P. Quay to Esbjerg route. Sold on 16 April 1968 to Associated Levant Lines Ltd of Beirut. Other names: *Bouar* (1968) and *Nouran* (1978). Scrapped at Gadani Beach, Pakistan on 20 May 1981. Sister ship: *Lemnos*.

Mercandian Transporter; Chartered; IMO: 7637307
Built: by Frederikshavn Vaerft A/S. Frederikshavn, Denmark - yard no. 376
Launched: 18 February 1978
Dimensions: 105.62 / 96.0 x 19.23 x 4.97 m
Tonnage: 1599 grt / 863 nt / 3708 dwt
Engines: 1 x MAK 12 cyl diesel type 12M453AK
Power Output: 4500 hp / 3310 kw
Speed: 15 knots
Passengers: Nil
First ref: 1981

cms ro-ro. Space for 200 teus. Delivered as *Mercandian Transporter* to K/S Merc-Scandia XXII of Copenhagen in 1978. Chartered in 1981 by DFDS for service between P. Quay and Esbjerg. Collided with and wrecked a quayside crane at P. Quay on 14 August 1981. Other names: *Transporter II* (1984) and *Mercandian Transporter II* (1986). Sold on 13 January 1987 to Sea Malta Co Ltd of Valetta and re-named *Pinto*. Sold on 3 December 1998 to Yantai Ferry Co., China, converted to a passenger ferry and re-named *Sheng Lu*. Lost by sinking after an onboard fire on 17 October 1999 30 n.miles off Dalian. Loss of 2 lives with 300 saved.

Mercandian Universe; Chartered; IMO: 8400036
Built: by Frederikshavn Vaerft A/S. Frederikshavn, Denmark - yard no. 418
Launched: 21 February 1986
Dimensions: 160.51 x 20.76 x 6.73 m
Tonnage: 15375 grt / 6022 nt / 9200 dwt
Engines: 1 x MAK 8 cyl diesel
Power Output: 6660 kw
Speed: 15 knots
Passengers: Nil
First ref: January 1989

Cms ro-ro. Space for 2191 lane metres of freight and briefly chartered by Sealink BF during January 1989 for use on the P. Quay to HvH service. Other names: *Seaboard Universe* (1992), *Crowley Universe* (1999) and *Maestro Universe* (2008).

Meteor; Cruise ship
Built: by Blohm & Voss, Hamburg - yard no. 170
Launched: 15 March 1904
Dimensions: 346.1 / 299.2 x 44.3 x 18.4 ft
Tonnage: 3718 grt / 1883 nt / 1500 dwt
Engines: 2 x Blohm & Voss Tr. exp.
Power Output: 235 nhp / 1550 ihp
Speed: 12 knots
Passengers: 411 (B: 283 First & 128 Third class)
First ref: summer 1921 cruising to Norway

Ps. Built for Hamburg America Line of Hamburg and considered as being the first ship purpose built for cruising. Designed in the clipper style complete with bowsprit. (m/v) was on 3 June 1904 from Hamburg to Norway. Requisitioned by German Navy in August 1914 for use as accommodation ship. Acquired by Britain in May 1919 as a war reparation and utilised on repatriation work by H.M. Government. Sold to Bergen Line in March 1921 reverting to use as a cruise ship to the North Cape. In June 1922 was registered in Bergen for 250 passengers. Rebuilt in 1935 at Laksevag Passengers: 205. Continued cruising until outbreak of WW2. Captured by German Navy on 7 May 1940 whilst in Bergen and used as a hospital ship. Re-named *Rostock* in March 1942, then *Meteor II* on 28 May 1942. Sunk by Russian aircraft on 9 March 1945 in Pillau harbour.

Meteor (III); Cruise ship; IMO: 5233535
Built: by Aalborg Vaerft, Aalborg, Denmark - yard no. 104
Launched: 6 May 1954
Dimensions: 296.7 / 282.5 x 45.1 x 15.7 ft
Tonnage: 2856 grt / 650 nt / 640 dwt
Engines: 1 x B&W 9 cyl diesel type 9-50VBF-90
Power Output: 5000 hp / 3730 kw
Speed: 18 knots
Passengers: 200 (B:90 First & 110 Second class)

Pcms. Ordered by Bergen Line as a replacement for the Stella Polaris. Initially used on the Norwegian Hurtigruten and from Bergen to Newcastle / Rotterdam but from the summer of 1955 until the early 1960s she was further based at P. Quay for seasonal cruises to the North Cape and Svalbard. Sold in 1970 to Meteor Cruises of Bergen. Severely damaged by fire in Vancouver on 22 May 1971 with the loss of 32 lives. Sold in October 1971 to Epirotiki Lines of Piraeus, Greece and rebuilt as the Neptune. Tonnage: 2402 grt / 1003 nt / 640 dwt. Passengers: 206 (B:206). Cruised the Mediterranean and North Cape until 1995. Laid up until arriving at Aliaga, Turkey on 2 March 2002 for scrapping.

M.G. Melchior; DFDS
Built: by A/S Burmeister & Wain's Maskin-og Skibsbyggeri, Copenhagen - yard no. 136
Launched: 8 August 1885
Dimensions: 230.0 / 220.0 x 30.0 x 15.0 ft
Tonnage: 1064 grt / 672 nt / 889 dwt
Engines: B&W c.o. 2 cyl 33" & 60" - 36"
Power Output: 1350 ihp
Speed: 12 knots
Passengers: 300 (110 First, 30 Second & 160 Deck class)
First ref: 22 January 1902

Pcs. Cost: Dkr 442,000. Briefly served on the P. Quay to Esbjerg route from January 1902 until 10 March 1902. Sold on 1 September 1947 to J. Asmussens of Aalborg. Other names: *Astrea* (1948). Broken up by the Aarhus Flydedok & Maskinkompagni A/S in February 1950.

Minerva; H.J. Perlbach
Built: 1863 by M. Samuelson of Hull
Dimensions: 191.9 x 27.1 ft
Tonnage: 702 grt / 537 nt
Engines: Jansen & Schmilimsky of Hamburg c.o. 2 cyl 25" & 43" - 30"
Power Output: 100 hp
First ref: mid 1880s

Pcs. In 1892 there were reports concerning Messrs Perlbach involvement in the emigrant trade, mainly of Jews, between Hamburg and London. Although other companies were transporting vast numbers of emigrants en-route to America, via Hull and then by train to Liverpool, the *Minerva* was mentioned as an example of the London trade. Down below conditions on board were described in horrendous detail with people being treated like cattle. Dark, cramped and unsanitary conditions were all that was offered in return for a single fare of around 16 shillings for an adult, 8 shillings for a child, and with no provision of either food nor bedding. The passage took between 40 and 60 hours and required two nights on board. The ship arrived in London either at Tilbury, the Upper Pool or St. Katherine's Docks. It was considered that conditions on board the *Minerva* were no different to those on board other ships that sailed from Hamburg to other English ports, i.e. 'miserably insufficient'.

Minsk; DFDS
Built: by Palmer Bros & Co, Jarrow - yard no. 67
Launched: 11 February 1858
Dimensions: 197.5 x 25.6 x 16.0 ft
Tonnage: 688 grt / 519 nt / 700 dwt
Engines: Day, Summers & Co. Southampton c.o. 2 cyl 26" & 52" - 36"
Power Output: 450 ihp
Speed: 8¼ knots
Passengers: 30 (12 First & 18 Second class)
First ref: early 1880s

Cs. Seen on the P. Quay to Esbjerg route during the 1880s. First delivered to Norddeutscher Lloyd, Bremen in 1858. Purchased by DFDS on 3 December 1881 for £6.000. Sold on 2 July 1898 to H. Haslum of Moss. Other names: Delivered as *Schwan* (1858) them re-named *Minsk* (1881).

Scrapped in Moss in March 1905. Sister ships: *Romney*, *Charkow*, *Tula*.

Montlhery; UECC; IMO: 8006878
Built: 1982 by Ateliers & Chanters La Rochelle Pallice, La Rochelle, France
Dimensions: 116.50 x 18.00 x 5.30 m o.a.
Tonnage: 1600 grt / 841 nt / 2400 dwt
Speed: 15 knots
Stowage area: 7402 sq.m. on 6 levels
Trade car capacity: 897

Cms cc. Scrapped.

Munich (St. Denis); GER
Built: by John Brown & Co. Ltd., Clydebank - yard no. 384
Launched: 26 August 1908
Dimensions: 343.0 / 331.2 x 43.2 x 17.8 ft
Tonnage: 2410 grt / 1019 nt / 1503 dwt
Engines: 3 x Parsons turbines - direct drive
Power Output: 1325 nhp / 8961 ihp
Speed: 20 knots
Passengers: (B: 320 First & 130 Second class)
First ref: 16 November 1908 Parkeston Quay to Hook of Holland (m/v)

Pcs. Launched by Miss Lawson, daughter of company Director. Triple screwed. Requisitioned in October 1914, re-named *St.Denis* in October 1915 for use as a hospital ship. Released in October 1919. Scuttled in Rotterdam on 12 May 1940 whilst on evacuation work. Raised on 1 November 1940 and used by Germans as training ship *Barbara*. Returned to LNER in 1945 but remained in Kiel as accommodation ship until 1949. In February 1950 was towed to Sunderland for scrapping by T. Young & Sons, arrived 2 March. Sister ships: *Copenhagen*, *St. Petersburg*.

Naesborg; Chartered; IMO: 7504524
Built: by Ab Lodose Varv., Lodose - yard no. 169
Launched: 11 May 1977
Dimensions: 162.11 x 18.01 x 6.60 m
Tonnage: 11591 grt / 3556 nt / 8538 dwt
Engines: 2 x Zgoda Sulzer diesels type 8ZL40/48
Power Output: 7650 kw
Speed: 17¼ knots
Passengers: 12
First Ref: March 1989

Cms ro-ro. Space for 1589 lane metres of freight. Briefly chartered by Tor Line A.B., Helsingborg in 1989 for service between Gothenburg and Immingham / P. Quay. Other names: Launched as *Kafrifol* (1977), then *Linne* (1982), *Naesborg* (1988), *Dana Corona* (1990), *Naesborg* (1991), *Attika* (1993), *Euromagique* (1995) and *Magi* (2003). Scrapped in Alang, India in 2003.

Nassau; Chartered
Built: by N.V. Scheepswerf & Machinefabriek 'De Merwede', Hardinxveld-Giessendam - yard no. 601
Launched: 18 November 1970
Dimensions: 76.82 (66.53) x 13.06 x 4.13 m
Tonnage: 658 grt / 419 nt / 1600 dwt
Engines: 1 x MWM 6 cyl diesel
Power Output: 1800 bhp / 1343 kw
Speed: 13 knots
Passengers: Nil
First ref: Autumn 1972

Cms lo-lo. Ordered as *Craigavon* for Dietrich Sander Bereederungs Gmbh. of Kiel but launched as *Kieler Forde*. Re-named *Nassau* in 1972 and chartered by SMZ from autumn 1972 until December 1973 for container ship service between P. Quay and Rotterdam. Sold in 1982 to Vacation Line B.V., Rotterdam who rebuilt her in Harlingen as a cruise ship for 250 passengers. Re-named *Vacationer*. Tonnage: 2430 grt / 2047 nt / 1680 dwt. Sold in 1986 to Cariba Corp., Rotterdam and re-named *Carib Vacationer*. Sold in 1986 to Exploitatie Maatsch Kuminaine, Willemstad, Dutch Antilles. Sold in 1993 to Cariva Inc., Willemstad. No details beyond 2009 when she was still in service.

Naxos; DFDS; IMO: 5248188
Built: by Frederikshavns Vaerft & Flydedok A/S, Frederikshavn - yard no. 221
Launched: 18 November 1954
Dimensions: 101.15 / 93.00 x 13.64 x 5.60 m

Tonnage: 1799 grt / 913 nt / 2652 dwt
Engines: 1 x B&W 8 cyl diesel type 850-VF-90
Power Output: 2550 bhp
Speed: 14½ knots
Passengers: 12
First ref: 1967

Cs. Seen on the P. Quay to Esbjerg route. Sold on 27 November 1969 to Compamia Naviera Odisen s.a., Piraeus. Other names: *Ulysses Ogygia* (1970), *Calypso* (1971), *Manuella Pride* (1973) and *Hoe Hing* (1974). Arrived for scrapping by Thai Steel & Iron Corp., Bangkok on 14 September 1983.

Nederland; SMZ
Built: by Fairfield Shipbuilding & Eng. Co. Ltd., Govan, Scotland - yard no. 315
Launched: 1 March 1887
Dimensions: 286.5 x 35.3 x 16.6 ft
Tonnage: 1660 grt / 871 nt / 1531 dwt
Engines: Fairfield c.o. 2 cyl 60" & 104" - 84"
Power Output: 826 nhp
Speed: 17 knots
Passengers: 700
First ref: June 1887 Flushing to Queenborough (m/v)

Cps. Built for the new 1887 dayboat service and served until 1910 when replaced by *Mecklenburg (I)*. Scrapped at Hendrik-ido-Ambacht in 1910. Sister ships: *Duitschland, Engeland.*

Newmarket; GER
Built: by Earle's Shipbuilding & Eng. Co. Ltd., Hull - yard no. 534
Launched: 11 July 1907
Dimensions: 245.0 x 31.3 x 15.2 ft
Tonnage: 833 grt / 192 nt / 721 dwt
Engines: Earle's Tr. exp. 6 cyl in 2 sets 15½", 25¼" & 41" - 36"
Power Output: 202 nhp / 2000 ihp
Speed: 14 knots
Passengers: Nil
First ref: August 1907 Parkeston Quay to Rotterdam (m/v)

Cs. Requisitioned in October 1914. Sunk by UC38 off Nikaria Island, Aegean Sea on 16 July 1917. Sister ship: *Clacton.*

N.J. Fjord; DFDS
Built: by Lobnitz & Co., Renfrew - yard no. 445
Launched: 14 May 1896
Dimensions: 268.5 / 258.6 x 34.0 x 16.0 ft
Tonnage: 1425 grt / 653 nt / 900 dwt
Engines: Lobnitz Tr. exp. 24", 40" & 64" - 42"
Power Output: 265 nhp / 2500 ihp
Speed: 15 knots
Passengers: 347 (74 First & 273 Deck class)
First ref: 15 July 1896 Esbjerg to Parkeston Quay (m/v)

Pcs. Cost £43,600. On the Esbjerg to P. Quay service until August 1914. Transferred during WW1 to other routes from Denmark to the UK, mainly Leith, until 1916. On 5 April 1917 was captured and sunk by the Germans some 40 miles off Fano whilst en route from Blyth to Odense.

Nidaros; DFDS
Built: by Lobnitz & Co., Renfrew - yard no. 341
Launched: 11 December 1889
Dimensions: 186.2 / 177.0 x 29.0 x 14.7 ft
Tonnage: 859 grt / 478 nt / 700 dwt
Engines: Helsingor J&M Tr. exp 18", 30" & 48" - 36"
Power Output: 875 ihp
Speed: 11 knots
Passengers: 144 (44 First, 18 Second & 82 Deck class)
First ref: 1894

Pcs. Cost: Dkr 338,040. Variously seen on the P. Quay to Esbjerg route, mainly between 1894 and 1914 and then again from 1920 to 1925. Lengthened in 1904 - Dimensions: 227.0 / 218.0 x 29.0 x 15.6 ft. Tonnage: 1024 grt / 610 nt / 840 dwt. Sold on 5 October 1937 to Danziger Werft & Eisenbahnwerkstatten AG., Danzig for scrapping.

Norfolk; Chartered
Built: by Ditchburn and Mare, Blackwall, London
Launched: 1846
Dimensions: 151 feet long
Tonnage: 147 nt
Power Output: 120 nhp
First ref: 6 November 1863 Harwich to Rotterdam

Pcps. Chartered by the GER from Cuncliffe & Watson of Goole from 28 October 1863 to 23 November 1864 and from 1 January 1865 to 26 February 1865.

Norfolk (I); River Services
Built: 1882 by the Thames Ironworks Co. Ltd., Victoria Dock, London.
Dimensions: 140.0 x 17.5 x 6.7 ft
Tonnage: 114 tons
Engines: T.A. Young of London s.o. 1 cyl 30" - 33"
Power Output: 50 nhp

Pps. Built for the GER. Sold in 1896 to T.W. Woods of Liverpool. Sold in 1897 to Eastham Ferry Pleasure Gardens and Hotel Co. and re-named *Onyx.*

Norfolk (II); River Services
Built: 1900 by Gourlay Bros. & Co., Dundee - yard no. 194
Dimensions: 184.0 x 24.1 x 7.0 ft
Tonnage: 295 grt / 163 nt
Engines: Gourlay compound diagonal 2 cyl 23½" & 45" - 45"
Power Output: 86 nhp

Pps. Built for the GER. Launched 25 April 1900 as a single funnel version of *Essex (II)*. Sold in 1931 to Dutch owners and later broken up in Holland.

Norfolk Ferry; BR; IMO: 5255985
Built: by John Brown & Co. Ltd., Clydebank - yard no. 661
Launched: 8 March 1951
Dimensions: 397.6 / 380.0 x 61.5 / 58.5 x 13.0 ft
Tonnage: 3157 grt / 1408 nt / 1986 dwt
Engines: 2 x John Brown Sulzer 6 cyl diesels
Power Output: 2821 shp
Speed: 13½ knots
Passengers: 12 (B: 12 First class)
First ref: July 1951 Harwich to Zeebrugge (m/v)

Cms tf. Launched by Madame Delory, wife of Director-General of Belgian National Railways and Chairman of SBA Ferryboats. Fitted with 1126 feet of rail track with space for 38 continental wagons. Near sister ship to the *Suffolk Ferry* and similarly served the Zeebrugge route. Opened a new Harwich to Dunkirk service on 2 October 1967. Withdrawn in October 1981 and laid up in the River Blackwater from January 1982. Towed by tug *Banckerk* to be scrapped by Vianen bei Marel B.V. at Ouderkerk where she arrived on 17 April 1983.

Normannia; Relief ship; IMO: 5256408
Built: by Wm. Denny & Bros., Dumbarton - yard no.1454
Launched: 19 July 1951
Dimensions: 309.2 / 299.1 x 48.2 x 12.5 ft
Tonnage: 3543 grt / 1912 nt
Engines: 2 x Pametrada direct drive turbines
Power Output: 8000 shp
Speed: 19 knots
Passengers: 1410 (780 First & 680 Third class) (B: 325)

Built for the BTC Southern Region for services between Southampton and Le Havre. (m/v) was on 3 March 1952. Relieved on the P. Quay to HvH service in September / October 1953. Rebuilt in 1962 at Hebburn as a car ferry for 111 cars. Tonnage: 2217 grt / 717 nt. Passengers: 500 and transferred to Dover. Was laid up at P. Quay on 17 September 1968 during which time she made one trip to HvH on 25 October 1968. Overhauled by the P. Quay workshops in December 1968. Sold in June 1978 for service with Red Sea Ferries, Dubai but later arrived in Gijon, Spain on 6 December 1978 for scrapping.

Northern Ice; Reever Line; IMO: 5060859
Built: in 1960 by HDW, Kiel, Germany - yard no. 1112
Tonnage: 4100 grt / 4271 dwt
First ref: late 1973

rcms. Refrigerated general purpose cargo ship that sailed on deep sea routes from P. Quay's Fishers Terminal. Other names: Launched as *Cap Valiente.* Re-named *Cacique Yanquetruz* in 1970, then *Northern Ice* in 1973. Arrived for scrapping at Gadani Beach, Pakistan as *Falcon* on 14 March 1982.

Norwich; GER
Built: by Earle's Shipbuilding & Eng. Co. Ltd., Hull - yard no. 255
Launched: 6 March 1883
Dimensions: 260.2 x 31.3 x 15.0 ft
Tonnage: 1037 grt / 437 nt / 816 dwt
Engines: Earle's 2 sets comp. 2 cyl 30" & 57" - 36"
Power Output: 270 nhp / 2000 ihp
Speed: 14½ knots
Passengers: 440 (B: 84 First & 42 Second class)
First ref: 24 July 1883 Parkeston Quay to Antwerp (m/v)

Pcs. The GER's first twin screw steamer. Re-boilered in 1897 and sold in 1905 to Queenstown Dry Dock Shipbuilding & Eng. Co. Ltd. Sold in 1911 to J. Dos Santos Silva, Cape Verde Islands and re-named *Fortuna.* Sold in 1913 to Continental Trading Co., New York and re-named *Evelyn.* Sold in 1915 to Cuneo Importing Co. Inc., New York and re-named *Neptune.* Variously operated throughout Central and South America before sinking off the U.S.A. in March 1921. Sister ship: *Ipswich.*

Nottingham (Notts); GCR
Built: by C.S. Swan & Hunter, Ltd., Newcastle - yard no. 164
Launched: 13 March 1891
Dimensions: 240.2 x 32.0 x 15.2 ft
Tonnage: 1033 grt / 492 nt
Engines: Wallsend Slipway & Eng. Co., Tr. exp. 27", 35" & 57" - 42"
Power Output: 248 nhp / 1450 ihp
Speed: 12½ knots
Passengers: 360 (B:30 First & 330 Emigrant class)
First ref: November 1918 Tilbury to Rotterdam

Pcs. The *Nottingham*, along with the *Staveley*, were built as the first pair of four ships ordered by the Manchester, Sheffield & Lincolnshire Railway for their Grimsby to Hamburg service. Both were transferred to GCR on 1 August 1897 with the *Nottingham* being placed on the Rotterdam service. The *Nottingham* was requisitioned on 12 October 1914 as a store carrier and renamed *Notts.* In November 1918 she was loaned to the GER as a cargo ship between Tilbury and Rotterdam. Passengers: 12. Re-opened P. Quay to Rotterdam service on 1 March 1919 until making her last trip from Rotterdam on 29 July 1919. Returned to GCR on 1 August and reverted to *Nottingham.* Scrapped at Inverkeithing in October 1935. Sister ship: *Staveley.*

Olga; DFDS
Built: by Norddeutsche Schiffbau-Actien-Gesellschaft, Kiel-Gaarden - yard no. 65
Launched: June 1875
Dimensions: 218.2 / 210.0 x 28.3 x 15.1 ft
Tonnage: 787 grt / 492 nt / 925 dwt
Engines: Schweffel & Howaldt, Kiel c.o. 2 cyl 30" & 56" - 36"
Power Output: 600 ihp
Speed: 10½ knots
Passengers: 12
First ref: 1895

Cs. Seen on the P. Quay to Esbjerg route up until 1904. First delivered to Theo Kock of Copenhagen in June 1875. Purchased by DFDS on 3 May 1880 for Dkr 370,000. Sold on 25 February 1924 to Schubert & Krohn of Dortmund for scrapping. Sister ship: *Georg.*

Oranje Nassau; SMZ
Built: by Fairfield Shipbuilding & Eng. Co. Ltd., Govan, Scotland - yard no. 462
Launched: 3 July 1909
Dimensions: 349.7 x 42.7 x 16.4 ft
Tonnage: 2885 grt / 1121 nt / 2405 dwt
Engines: Fairfield Tr. exp. 8 cyl in 2 sets 28", 43½" & (2) 49" - 33"
Power Output: 1130 nhp / 10000 ihp
Speed: 22 knots
Passengers: (B: 246 First & 110 Second class)
First ref: April 1910 Flushing to Queenborough (m/v)

Pcs. On 23 June 1919 re-opened the night service from Flushing to Folkestone. On 1 January 1927 she inaugurated the new SMZ P. Quay to Flushing day service. In May 1940 escaped to England and used as a Royal Dutch Navy depot ship in Holyhead. Post war was used as a troopship on behalf of the Dutch Government between Rotterdam and Tilbury / P. Quay from 27 August 1945 until 29 June 1946. (P. Quay from 25 April 1946). On 29 July 1946 joined the Hook of Holland to P. Quay night boat service. Relegated to relief ship in May 1947 and chartered to Batavier Line during the summers of 1949 to 1952. On 12 July 1954 arrived at Hendrick-ido-Ambacht for scrapping. Sister ships: *Prinses Juliana (I), Mecklenburg (I)*

Orion; River Services
Built: 1841 by Read & Page of Ipswich
Dimensions: 160.1 x 21.5 x 9.6 ft
Tonnage: 222 grt

Pps. Coastal steamer. Space for 500 passengers. 100 nhp engine. Jointly owned by Read & Page of Ipswich, Alexander Ltd of Ipswich and Lloyd & Easter of London who sailed her between Ipswich and London. Owned by Kemp & Laidley of Fleetwood in June 1845, by T. Fletcher of Goole in June 1850 and by J. Fletcher of Goole in October 1850. Bought by P. Bruff in 1852 and sailed in conjunction with EUR. She was sold to the ECR in July 1854 who re-sold her in 1859. Made six trips from Harwich to Antwerp for the ECR in summer 1855.

Ortolan (I); GSNCo
Built: by Caledon Shipbuilding & Engineering Co. Ltd., Dundee - yard no. 165
Launched: 1902
Dimensions: 275.5 x 40.4 ft
Tonnage: 1727 grt
Speed: 13 knots

Pcs. Seen on the GSNCo. P. Quay to Hamburg route. Sunk 100 miles wsw of Bishop Rock by U82 on 14 June 1917 whilst en-route from Palermo to London with cargo. Three lives lost.

Orwell (I); River Services
Built: 1839 by Ditchburn and Mare, Blackwall, London.
Dimensions: 144.0 x 21.2 x 9.7 ft
Tonnage: 220 grt

Pps. Coastal steamer. Fitted with 80 nhp engine and built for the Ipswich Steam Navigation Company. Chartered for the EUR / ECR demonstration trip to Holland on 17 June 1846. Sold in May 1853 to Alfred Cobbold when the ISNC was liquidated. Sold in June 1854 to the Eastern Counties Railway who re-sold her on 8 August 1857 together with the *Pearl.*

Orwell (II); River Services
Built: 1873 by Lewis & Stockwell, London.
Dimensions: 125.5 x 17.5 x 6.9 ft
Tonnage: 114 grt
Engines: John Penn & Son s.o. 2 cyl 30" - 33"
Power Output: 52 nhp

Pps. Re-boilered in 1880 and scrapped in 1890. Sister ship: *Stour (II)*

Otto Becker; Railfreight; IMO: 8818879
Built: 1989 by J.J. Sietas Schiffswerft, Hamburg, Germany - yard no. 935
Dimensions: 94.5 x 15.9 x 5.0 m
Tonnage: 2749 grt / 1110 nt / 3146 dwt
Engines: 1 x Wartsila diesel type 6R32D
Power Output: 1353 hp / 995 kw
Speed: 14¼ knots

Cms lo-lo. Space for 262 teus. One of 5 Sietas Type 122 feeder ships. Re-named *Maria Schepers* in 2001. Last owner: Hs Schiffahrt, Haren Ems, Germany. Sister ships: *Amazone, Jan Becker, Angela Jurgens* and *Jan Kahrs.*

Pacific; GER
Built: by C. Lungley, Deptford, London
Launched: 1864
Dimensions: 235.5 x 26.6 x 11.5 ft
Tonnage: 712 grt / 515 nt / 507 dwt
Engines: C. Lungley s.o. 2 cyl 48" - 54"
Power Output: 170 nhp / 700 hp
Speed: 10 knots
Passengers: 400
First ref: March 1865 Harwich to Rotterdam

Pcps. Acquired by the GER on 23 February 1865 without a change of name. In using 20 tons of coal less per week and with 2 less seafarers on board she was cheaper to operate than either the *Avalon* or *Ravensbury*. However she was too slow for passenger work and in 1887 was sold for scrap.

Parkeston; DFDS
Built: by A/S Helsingors Jernskibs-og Maskinbyggeri, Elsinore - yard no. 173
Launched: 31 January 1925
Dimensions: 324.0 / 304.0 x 44.0 x 17.8 ft
Tonnage: 2762 grt / 1572 nt / 1670 dwt
Engines: 2 x B&W 6 cyl diesels type 6150-MFX
Power Output: 545 nhp / 3254 bhp
Speed: 15½ knots
Passengers: 212 (124 First & 88 Third class)
First ref: 8 August 1925 Esbjerg to Parkeston Quay (m/v)

Cms. Cost Dkr 3,344,407. Built as DFDS's first diesel powered vessel and one of four sister ships all of which could carry up to 20 cars. In service between Esbjerg and P. Quay until the outbreak of WW2 in September 1939. Laid up in Copenhagen between April 1940 and 20 January 1944, then used as the German depot ship *Pioneer*. Returned to DFDS on 27 July 1945 as the only one of the sister ships to survive. Re-named *Parkeston* and re-opened the Esbjerg to P. Quay route on 6 December 1945 and remained on this route until 31 July 1949. Transferred to a Copenhagen to Newcastle service but briefly returned to P. Quay between 23 June and 15 September 1953 as cover for the fire damaged *Kronprins Frederik*. Passenger capacity raised to 274 in 1952. Sailed between Esbjerg and Newcastle until September 1963 with occasional trips between Esbjerg and P. Quay in 1954 and 1955, her last at P. Quay being 19 March 1955. Made a total of 1,263 sailings on the route. Sold on 18 September 1964 to A/S Aker Mek of Oslo for £65,000, re-named *Aker 2* and used as accommodation ship for shipyard workers. Sold in August 1975 for scrapping by P Bergsoe & Son A/S of Glostrup. Demolished in Masnedo. Sister ships: *Jylland, Esbjerg (II), England (I).*

Patricia; Thule Line
Built: by Stabilimento Tecnico, Trieste. Italy - yard no. 334
Launched: 1901
Dimensions: 344.0 x 43.0 x 20.5 ft
Tonnage: 2981 grt
Engines: 3 cyl Tr. exp.
Power Output: 5000 ihp
Speed: 16½ knots
Passengers: 302 (76 First & 226 Third class)
First ref: late 1921 arrival at Parkeston Quay from Gothenburg

Pcs. Built as *Mongolia* for Chinese Eastern Railway Co., Vladivostok, Russia for service between Vladivostok and Shanghai. Sold to Government of Western Australia in 1910, re-named *Western Australia*.. Requisitioned in 1915 as ambulance carrier and then as a troopship out of Britain. Sold to Swedish Lloyd in April 1919 and re-named *Patricia*. Following a major refit inaugurated a Gothenburg to Newcastle emigrant service with the *Saga* before transferring to the Gothenburg to London service on 21 July 1920. Passengers: 572 (116 First, 434 Second & 22 Third class). Sold in May 1929 to United Baltic Corporation, London and re-named *Baltavia*. In service between London and the Baltic until sold for scrap in February 1935 by J. Cashmore of Newport.

Paula; Freightliner; IMO: 8509844
Built: 1985 by J.J. Sietas Schiffswerft, Hamburg, Germany - yard no. 972
Dimensions: 87.89 x 12.81 x 4.61
Tonnage: 2561 grt / 3705 dwt
Speed: 11½ knots

Cms lo-lo. Space for 153 teus. Launched as 999 grt. Other names: *Simon B* (2006) and *Maple* (2008). Last owner: Rana Shipping, Istanbul, Turkey.

Pearl; River Services
Built: 1835 by Fletcher & Furnell, Blackwall, London.
Dimensions: 138.5 x 15.5 x 8.3 ft
Tonnage: 137 tons

Pps. Coastal steamer. Built for the Gravesend and Milton Shipping Co. and the Diamond Steam Packet Co.. Sold in 1850 to W. Robertson of Pembroke Dock for a route between Bristol, Tenby and Pembroke. Purchased in 1852 from Milford Haven by P. Bruff. Sold to the ECR in June 1854. Sold in August 1857 together with the *Orwell*, the deal raising £850.

Peregrine (II); GSNCo.
Built: by W.B. Thompson & Co, Dundee - yard no. 115
Launched: 12 May 1892
Dimensions: 279.8 x 38.1 x 16.1 ft
Tonnage: 1681 grt
Engines: 2 sets of 3 cyl Tr. exp.
Power Output: 455 nhp
Speed: 16 knots
Passengers: 250
First ref: Summer 1892 between Parkeston Quay and Hamburg

Pcs. Requisitioned in 1914 as a supply ship until 22 November 1915. Thereafter returned to GSN Co. for service between P. Quay and Rotterdam. Out ran a German submarine on 8 February 1917. Was lost on 29 December 1917 after running aground on the Longsand near the Sunk light vessel. She was sailing from Rotterdam to London and all of her 92 passengers and crew were rescued by the Walton lifeboat

Petuja; Railfreight; IMO: 8609606
Built: 1986 by J.J. Sietas Schiffswerft, Hamburg, Germany - yard no. 984
Dimensions: 87.99 x 13.03 x 4.68 m
Tonnage: 2673 grt / 3004 dwt
Speed: 12½ knots
First ref: 3 January 1989

Cms lo-lo. Space for 198 teus. Launched on 1 December 1986 as 1009 grt. Inaugurated Freightliner's new P. Quay to Zeebrugge service on 3 January 1989 sailing opposite the *Karen Oltmann*. Other names: *Domalde* (1994), *Dyggve* (1995), *Nedgard* (2001) and *Nedland* (2010). Last owner: Vg Shipping, Turku, Finland.

Petunia; DFDS; IMO: 5276678
Built: by Aalborg Vaerft A/S, Aalborg - yard no. 139
Launched: 27 July 1962
Dimensions: 106.89 / 98.00 x 15.10 x 5.85 m
Tonnage: 2383 grt / 1139 nt / 2830 dwt
Engines: 1 x B&W 6 cyl diesel type 650-VTBF-110
Power Output: 3450 bhp
Speed: 15½ knots
Passengers: 4
First ref: mid 1960s

Rcms. Cost: Dkr 15.7m. Seen on the P. Quay to Esbjerg route. Sold on 17 December 1973 to Ben Shipping Co. Ltd., Singapore. Other names: *C.Joyce* (1973), *Kalimantan Fortune* (1976), *Frio Dolphin* (1977), *Snowfrost* (1979) and *Iguana* (1985). Arrived for scrapping by Pacifia Enterprises, Gadani Beach, Pakistan on 26 April 1986. Sister ship: *Magnolia*.

Pinmill; River Services
Built: 1910 by the Whitstable Shipping Co., Herne, Kent.
Dimensions: 40.3 x 10.0 x 3.7 ft
Tonnage: 11.17 grt / 7.6 nt
Engines: 2 cyl paraffin
Power Output: 20 ihp
Speed: 9 knots
First ref: 22 July 1912

Pms. Fitted out at Dan Marine Motor Eng Co Ltd., Ipswich. Cost £425. Certified to carry no more than 80 workmen though as the vessel was under 15 tons she was not required by the Merchant Shipping Act to have a Certificate of Registry. Inaugurated the Harwich to Felixstowe service on 22 July 1912 with a passenger certificate that was not to exceed 80 workmen. Re-engined in 1918. Engines: 1 x semi-diesel Kromhout hot bulb ignition. Requisitioned in 1914-18 for harbour duties and again on 2nd July 1940 by MOWT for Admiralty service. Acquired by HM Government on 11 December 1942. Relegated to being a workboat upon the arrival of the *Brightlingsea*. Was given a new funnel and 4 cyl Kelvin engine in 1967. Survived to become a part of the Sealink fleet. Sold in 1988 to the Ipswich Maritime Trust and ran leisure trips from Ipswich. Fitted with a 3 cyl 35 hp Lister engine. Sold in May 2005 to the Iron Wharf Boatyard, Faversham, intention being to convert into a cruiser for the Gloucester and Sharpness Canal.

Prague; LNER
Built: by John Brown & Co. Ltd., Clydebank - yard no. 528
Launched: 18 November 1929
Dimensions: 366.0 / 350.8 x 50.1 x 15.3 ft
Tonnage: 4220 grt / 1988 nt / 3028 dwt
Engines: 2 x 2 John Brown Curtis srg turbines
Power Output: 1520 nhp / 11500 shp
Speed: 21 knots
Passengers: 708 (B: 427 First & 126 Second class)
First ref: 1 March 1930 Parkeston Quay to Hook of Holland (m/v)

Pcs. Requisitioned in December 1939 as a troopship and later converted to a hospital ship in May 1944. Re-named *Hospital Carrier No. 61*. Returned to P. Quay and re-opened the HvH service on 14 November 1945 having been refitted to 520 berths - (132 First, 22 Second & 366 Bunk class). On 14 March 1948 she was destroyed by a fire whilst being refitted at John Brown's yard. Arrived at Barrow on 14 September 1948 for scrapping by T.W. Ward. Sister ships: *Vienna (II), Amsterdam (II).*

Primula (I); DFDS
Built: by Lobnitz & Co., Ltd., Renfrew - yard no. 452
Launched: 5 November 1896
Dimensions: 279.7 / 268.5 x 34.0 x 17.2 ft
Tonnage: 1524 grt / 676 nt / 1103 dwt
Engines: Lobnitz Tr. exp. 24", 40" & 64" - 42"
Power Output: 265 nhp / 2500 ihp
Speed: 14 knots
Passengers: 257 (72 First & 185 Third class)
First ref: 19 December 1896 Esbjerg to Parkeston Quay (m/v)

Pcs. Cost £43,700. Her maiden voyage was just the one round trip between Esbjerg and P. Quay. Thereafter she mainly sailed between Copenhagen and Newcastle / Grimsby. She re-appeared on the Esbjerg to P. Quay service between Spring 1903 and August 1914. Transferred during WW1 to other routes to the UK, mainly Hull and Newcastle. Re-appeared on Esbjerg to P. Quay route from 3 December to 18 December 1923. In total made 342 route crossings. Re-fitted in 1924 with refurbished passenger accommodation. Sold on 7 February 1938 to Clayton & Davie, Dunston-on-Tyne for scrapping. Sister ship: *Ficaria*.

Primula (II); DFDS
Built: by Helsingor Skibsvaerft og Maskinbyggeri A/S, Elsinore - yard no. 309
Launched: 15 May 1952
Dimensions: 101.10 / 93.00 x 13.97 x 5.59 m
Tonnage: 1812 grt / 855 nt / 2401 dwt
Engines: 1 x B&W 8 cyl diesel type 850-VF-90
Power Output: 2550 bhp
Speed: 14½ knots
Passengers: 6
First ref: August 1954

Rcms. Cost: Dkr 8.5m. Sailed on the P. Quay to Esbjerg route until November 1969 making 130 sailings. Sold on 18 April 1972 to Sweet Lines Inc., Cebu City. Other names: *Sweet Love* (1972). Sold for scrapping in March 1985 at Phil-Asia Shipbreaking in Btanga, Philippines. Sister ship: *Ficaria (II).*

Prince; River Services
Built: 1852 by Harvey & Son, Ipswich.
Dimensions: 108.0 x 13.3 x 7.1 ft
Tonnage: 72 tons

Pps. Built for the EUR, registered to P. Bruff. Fitted with simple oscillating single cylinder engine, 36 nhp, and space for 125 passengers. Sold to the ECR in June 1854, owned by the GER in 1862. Broken up in 1869.

Prince Albert; River Services
Built: 1842 by Walker, Newcastle-on-Tyne.
Dimensions: 154.3 x 18.5 x 10.3 ft
Tonnage: 202 grt

Pps. Coastal steamer. Purchased by P. Bruff from London owners in 1853 and sold to the ECR in July 1854. Re-sold by the ECR in 1855 for £1,000.

Prince of Wales; Chartered
Built: by Tod & McGregor, Glasgow - yard no. 2
Launched: 1842
Dimensions: 159.6 x 24.6 x 13.5 ft
Tonnage: 500 grt / 313 nt
Power Output: 250nhp
First ref: 16 December 1863 Harwich to Rotterdam

Pcps. Chartered by the ECR from F. Kemp & Co. of Fleetwood from 16 December 1863 to 15 January 1864 and from 4 May 1864 to 5 January 1865.

Princess Alice; Chartered
Built: by Tod & McGregor, Glasgow - yard no 36
Launched: 1843
Dimensions: 164.7 x 27.3 x 13.9 ft
Tonnage: 433 grt / 257 nt
Power Output: 150 hp
First ref: 29 January 1864 Harwich to Rotterdam

Pcps. Engines: s.o. 2 cyl. Chartered by the ECR from F. Kemp & Co. of Fleetwood from 29 January 1864 to 28 October 1864.

Princess of Wales; GER
Built: by London & Glasgow Eng. & Iron Shipbuilding Co., Govan, Glasgow - yard no. 203
Launched: 4 February 1878
Dimensions: 265.5 x 30.4 x 14.2 ft
Tonnage: 1098 grt / 468 nt / 798 dwt
Engines: London & Glasgow s.o. 2 cyl 68" - 84"
Power Output: 400 nhp / 1800 ihp
Speed: 14 knots
Passengers: 579 (B: 110 First & 77 Second class)
First ref: 6 July 1878 Harwich to Rotterdam (m/v)

Pcps. Initially put onto the Rotterdam route but later sailed to Antwerp. Was replaced by the *Berlin* in 1894 and then on 16 May 1895 sold to J.S. Turnbull of Manchester and scrapped in 1896.

Princesse Astrid; RMT; IMO: 6813320
Built: by J. Boel et Fils S.A., Tamise, Belgium - yard no.1440
Launched: 2 February 1968
Dimensions: 384.5 / 363.0 x 52.5 x 12.5 ft
Tonnage: 3188 grt / 1519 nt / 485 dwt
Engines: 2 x Sulzer 12 cyl diesels
Power Output: 9600 bhp / 7061 kw
Speed: 22 knots
Passengers: 850 (B: 135)
First ref: late 1960s

Pcms ro-ro. Built for the RMT route between Ostend and Dover. (m/v) was on 15 August 1968. Capacity equal to 173 cars. Sailed on the Ostend to P. Quay route between 1968 and 1972. Sold to Ventouris Group, Piraeus in July 1983. Refitted and re-named *Bari Express* in 1984. Tonnage: 3397 grt / 1919 nt / 592 dwt. Passengers: 1800. Cars: 180. Sold in October 1998 to Agapitos Express Ferries, Piraeus and re-named *Express Hermes*. Sold to Minoan Flying Dolphin / Hellas Ferries, Greece on 8 November 1999. Sold in September 2003 for scrapping at Alang, India where she arrived 20 October 2003 as *Express Erme*. Sister ship: *Roi Baudouin*

Prins Hamlet (I) (Prinz Hamlet (I)); Prins Line;

IMO: 6604470
Built: by Crichton Vulcan Oy, Turku, Finland - yard no. 1133
Launched: 17 December 1965
Dimensions: 134.32 x 20.11 x 5.50 m
Tonnage: 7658 grt / 4614 nt / 1808 dwt
Engines: 2 x Wartsila-Sulzer 8 cyl diesels type 8RD56
Power Output: 14000 bhp / 10298 kw
Speed: 21 knots
Passengers: 824 (B: 444)
First Ref: 23 May 1966 Bremerhaven to Parkeston Quay (m/v) for Lion Ferry

Pcms ro-ro. Cost £3m. Built for Lion Ferry and was the first ro-ro passenger ship to berth at P. Quay. Space for 268 cars or 26 lorries. Rebuilt at Gotaverken, Gothenburg in November 1966 with extra accommodation. Tonnage: 8687gt / 4614 nt / 1808 dwt. Passengers: 1100 (B: 684). Space reduced for 165 cars or 16 lorries. Chartered to American International Travel Services for trans-Atlantic cruising January to May 1968 and September 1968 to May 1969. Sold to Hadag, Hamburg and re-named *Prinz Hamlet* on 29 May 1969 for Prinzenlinien (Prins Ferries) new route from Hamburg to Harwich Navyard Dock. First arrival at Harwich Navyard on 1 June 1969. Sold to CGTM in November 1970 and re-named *Roussillon* to sail from Marseille to Tunis / Corsica. Sold to Dane Line, Greece in January 1980 and re-named *Kamiros* to sail between Piraeus and Rhodes. Further sold to Ascot Seatrade Corp., Malta in October 1997 as *Thessaloniki*, to Anez Shipping in July 2000 as *Queen Calliope* and then to Iska Metal Gemi Sokum, Turkey as *Opi* for scrapping at Alang, India in June 2002.

Prins Hamlet (2); Prins Line; IMO: 7320332
Built: by Werft Nobiskrug GmbH, Rendsburg, Germany - yard no. 679
Launched: 26 May 1973
Dimensions: 118.83 / 107.85 x 18.55 x 5.00 m
Tonnage: 5830 grt / 3036 nt / 1127 dwt
Engines: 4 x Stork Werkspoor 6 cyl diesels type 6TM410
Power Output: 16000 bhp / 11700 kw
Speed: 22½ knots
Passengers: 1034 (B: 570)
First Ref: 12 November 1973 Hamburg to Harwich Navyard Dock (m/v) for Prins Line.

Pcms ro-ro. Space for 225 cars. Switched UK port from Harwich Navyard to P. Quay on 2 May 1979. Continued to sail between Hamburg and P. Quay until displaced by the *Hamburg* on 4 April 1987. Sold to DFDS A/S, Copenhagen on 4 May 1987, re-named *Prins Hamlet* and placed on services from Newcastle to Esbjerg / Gothenburg. Sold to Stena Roro Line Ltd, Nassau, Bahamas on 30 September 1988 and re-named *Stena Baltica*. Chartered to Polferries, Kolobrzeg in November 1988 for service between Ystad and Swinoujscie as the *Nieborow* then sold to Polferries in November 1989. Sold to Adriatic Lines SA, Monaco in October 2002. In service as *Sveti Stefan II* between Bar and Bari since 26 January 2003.

Prins Hendrik (I); SMZ
Built: by John Elder & Co., Govan, Glasgow - yard no. 232
Launched: 25 March 1880
Dimensions: 278.7 x 35.0 x 16.5 ft
Tonnage: 1573 grt / 814 nt
Engines: J. Elder c.o. 2 cyl 60" & 104" - 84"
Power Output: 638 nhp / 3500 hp
Speed: 16 knots
Passengers: 300 by day, 240 by night (B: 150 First class)
First ref: 1880 Flushing to Queenborough (m/v)

Pcps. Laid up in 1895 when replaced by new *Prins Hendrik (II)*. Little used as a spare ship until sold in August 1902 to Gebruder Specht of Bremen for scrapping. Sister ships: *Prinses Marie, Prinses Elisabeth, Willem Prins van Oranje*

Prins Hendrik (II); SMZ
Built: by Fairfield Shipbuilding & Eng. Co. Ltd., Govan, Scotland - yard no. 386
Launched: 22 August 1895
Dimensions: 320.0 x 35.8 x 16.0 ft
Tonnage: 1945 grt / 835 nt
Engines: Fairfield Tr. exp. 51", 75" & 112" - 78"
Power Output: 1350 nhp / 9000 hp
Speed: 21 knots
Passengers: 244 (180 First & 64 Second class)
First ref: Autumn 1895 Flushing to Queenborough (m/v)

Pcps. Re-opened a post war day boat service on 31 January 1919 from Flushing to Gravesend. In November 1922 was scrapped by Diederichsen in Bremen. Sister ships: *Koningin Wilhelmina, Koningin Regentes*

Prins Oberon; Prins Line; IMO: 7011515
Built: by Werft Nobiskrug GmbH, Rendsburg, Germany - yard no. 663
Launched: 21 February 1970
Dimensions: 134.02 x 21.04 x 4.92 m oa
Tonnage: 7993 grt / 4321 nt / 1778 dwt
Engines: 2 x OEW Pielstick 16 cyl diesels type 16PC2V400
Power Output: 16000 bhp / 11936 kw
Speed: 22 knots
Passengers: 1040 (B: 702)
First Ref: 8 June 1970 Bremerhaven to Harwich Navyard Dock (m/v) for Prins Line.

Pcms ro-ro. Space for 238 cars or 30 lorries. Sold to Deutche Leasing AG, Bremen on 30 September 1978 and re-named *Prinz Oberon*. Switched UK port from Harwich Navyard to P. Quay on 1 May 1979. Chartered to SMZ from 11 February to 11 March 1983 and to Sealink from 12 March to 10 June 1983 for the P. Quay to Hook of Holland service. Sold to DFDS Deutschland, Hamburg in 30 November 1983, variously utilised including Cuxhaven / P. Quay / Gothenburg from 23 June to 19 August 1984. Sold to Swedish interests in November 1984 and converted to the cruise ship *Nordic Sun*. Re-named *Cruise Muhibah* when sold to PNSL, Malaysia in April 1986. Chartered to B&I Line in December 1989 and re-named *Munster*. In May 1993 chartered to New Olympic Ferries Ltd of Cyprus and re-named *Ambassador*. Became *Ambassador II* in June 1994 when chartered to Cotunav, Tunisia. Variously chartered in the Baltic or Mediterranean until laid up in Southampton in April 1997. Sold to Sterling Shipping One, Monrovia and converted to 1,400 passenger casino ship. Operated out of Port Canaveral, Florida from 1999 until laid up in July 2008. Later sold for scrapping in January 2011 at New Orleans.

Prinses Astrid; Trooping Services; IMO: 5607130
Built: by S.A. Cockerill-Ougree, Hoboken, Antwerp. Belgium.
Launched: 20 July 1929
Dimensions: 347.0 x 46.2 x 22.8 ft
Tonnage: 2950 grt / 1331 nt
Engines: 2 x srg turbines
Power Output: 2779 nhp / 15400 ihp
Speed: 23½ knots
First ref: 17 January 1945

Pcs. Built for Belgian Marine service between Ostend and Dover. Passengers: 1425. (m/v) was on 24 April 1930. Requisitioned for use as an assault ship and re-named *HMS Prinses Astrid* on 26 May 1941. Served on trooping duties between P. Quay and Calais from 17 January 1945 to 12 February 1945. Paid off on 10 April 1945 and served on trooping duties between Dover and Ostend / Calais. Resumed commercial service on 7 October 1946. Lost by hitting a mine 4 miles west of Dunkirk on 21 June 1949. Sister ship: *Prinses Josephine Charlotte*

Prinses Beatrix (I); SMZ
Built: by Koninklijke Maatschappij De Schelde, Vlissingen, Holland - yard no. 210
Launched: 25 March 1939
Dimensions: 380. 0 / 350.2 x 47.0 x 13.5 ft
Tonnage: 4135 grt / 2100 nt
Engines: 2 x De Schelde Sulzer 10 cyl diesels
Power Output: 1824 nhp / 12600 shp
Speed: 21½ knots
Passengers: 1800 (B: 90)
First ref: 3 July 1939 Flushing to Parkeston Quay (m/v)

Pcms. Launched by Prins Bernhard. Day boat with only 90 berths, space for 35 cars and a crew of 58. Escaped to England in May 1940. Requisitioned by the Royal Navy and re-named in 1941 as *H.M.S. Prinses Beatrix*. Had an extensive wartime career very similar to her sister ship *H.M.S. Queen Emma*. Paid off on 13 April 1946, reverting to *Prinses Beatrix*, and used as a Dutch Government troopship between Rotterdam and P. Quay from 3 July 1946 until 28 September 1946. Returned to SMZ, re-named *Prinses Beatrix* and refitted for civilian use and similarly re-profiled with a smaller funnel and a higher bridge. Entered service between P. Quay and HvH on 31 May 1948. Replaced by *Koningin Juliana (II)* in 1968 and towed on 19 December 1968 to Jos De Smed, Antwerp for breaking up. Sister ship: *Koningin Emma*.

Prinses Beatrix (II); SMZ; IMO: 7637149
Built: by Scheepswerf Verolme, Heusden - yard no. 959
Launched: 14 January 1978
Dimensions: 429.8 / 392.1 x 72.2 x 16.4 ft
Tonnage: 9356 grt / 4862 nt / 1887 dwt
Engines: 4 x Stork Werkspoor 8 cyl diesels type 8TM410LL
Power Output: 22000 hp / 16182 kw
Speed: 21 knots
Passengers: 1500 by day / 1024 by night (B: 278 First & 294 Second class)
First ref: 29 June 1978 Hook of Holland to Parkeston Quay (m/v)

Pcms ro-ro. Launched by HRH Prinses Beatrix for SMZ. Space for 320 cars or 12 cars and 44 trailers. Sold on 1 October 1985 to Societe Economique Mixte D'Armement Naval Du Calvados, Morlaix - (Brittany Ferries) and chartered back to SMZ until May 1986. Re-named *Duc de Normandie* on 1 May 1986 during a refit in Rotterdam for service between Caen and Portsmouth as from 5 June 1986. Moved to sail between Roscoff and Plymouth from 10 July 2002 to 30 September 2004. Thereafter laid up in Caen and then Gdansk before being sold in March 2005 to Trans Europe Ferries, Limassol, Cyprus and re-named *Wisteria*. Rebuilt in Oostende and chartered to Ferrimaroc, Morocco. In service between Almeria and Nador from 30 March to October 2005, then between Ostend and Ramsgate from 7 November until again being chartered in January 2006 to Acciona Trasmediterranea / Ferrimaroc, Spain for service mainly between Almeria and Nador. Sold 9 April 2013 to Nizhniy Shipping Ltd, Portoz, Slovenia and re-named *Vronskiy*. In service between Algeciras and Tanger Med in Morocco.

Prinses Elisabeth; SMZ
Built: by John Elder & Co., Govan, Glasgow - yard no. 215
Launched: 10 December 1877
Dimensions: 278.2 x 34.8 x 16.1 ft
Tonnage: 1545 grt / 810 nt
Engines: J. Elder c.o. 2 cyl 60" & 104" - 84"
Power Output: 600 nhp / 3500 hp
Speed: 16 knots
Passengers: 300 by day, 240 by night
First ref: 5 April 1878 Flushing to Queenborough (m/v)

Pcps. Chartered in 1896 to Albert Ballin of Hamburg and re-named *Prinzess Elisabeth*. Sold in December 1898 to G.O. Wallenberg, re-named *Princess Elisabeth* and put on route Stettin to Stockholm with sistership *Prinses Marie*. Sold again in 1900 to Rederi ab Sverige Kontintenten, re-named *Svea* for the Trelleborg and Sassnitz route. Sold in 1909 and scrapped in Stettin in 1910. Sister ships: *Prinses Marie, Prins Hendrk, Willem Prins van Oranje*

Prinses Josephine Charlotte (I); Trooping Services; IMO: 5607387
Built: by S.A. Cockerill-Ougree, Hoboken, Antwerp. Belgium
Launched: 28 June 1930
Dimensions: 347.0 x 46.2 x 22.8 ft
Tonnage: 2950 grt / 1331 nt
Engines: 2 x srg turbines
Power Output: 2779 nhp / 15400 ihp
Speed: 23½ knots
First ref: 5 January 1945

Pcs. Built for Belgian Marine service between Ostend and Dover. Passengers: 1425. (m/v) was on 19 January 1931. Requisitioned for use as a landing ship and re-named *HMS Prinses Josephine Charlotte* on 16 May 1941. Served on trooping duties between P. Quay and Calais from 5 January 1945 to 26 February 1945. Paid off on 10 October 1945 following trooping duties between Tilbury / Dover and Ostend. Resumed commercial service until broken up in Belgium in 1950. Sister ship: *Prinses Astrid*

Prinses Josephine Charlotte (II); RMT; IMO: 5285356
Built: by John Cockerill S.A., Hoboken, Belgium - yard no.731
Launched: October 1948
Dimensions: 373.0 / 357.0 x 53.6 x 12.4 ft
Tonnage: 2572 grt / 1197 nt / 819 dwt
Engines: 2 x Sulzer 10 cyl diesels
Power Output: 5670 kw
Speed: 22 knots
Passengers: 700
First ref: late 1960s

Pcms. Launched as the *Car Ferry* with capacity for 110 cars. (m/v) was on 3 June 1949 from Ostend to Dover and she entered commercial service on 17 June 1949. Re-named *Prinses Josephine Charlotte* (II) in 1952. Finished service on 15 March 1974. Sold on 8 March 1976 to Blanca Compania Naviera s.a., Panama and re-named *Leto*. Sold in 1977 to G. Kousouniadis of Piraeus and re-named *Athens Express* for service between Greece and eastern Mediterranean. Scrapped at Eleusis Bay in June 1984.

Prinses Juliana (I); SMZ
Built: by Fairfield Shipbuilding & Eng. Co. Ltd., Govan, Scotland - yard no. 461
Launched: 22 May 1909
Dimensions: 349.6 x 42.7 x 16.4 ft
Tonnage: 2885 grt / 1133 nt / 2405 dwt
Engines: Fairfield Tr. exp. 8 cyl in 2 sets 28", 43½" & (2) 49" - 33"
Power Output: 1130 nhp / 10000 ihp
Speed: 22 knots
Passengers: (B: 246 First & 110 Second class)
First ref: April 1910 Flushing to Queenborough (m/v)

Pcs. One of three ships built in response to an improved 1908 GER service to Hook of Holland. Due to their increased draught the Flushing service was transferred to Folkestone in 1911. On 1 February 1916 whilst en route from Flushing to Tilbury she hit a mine near the Sunk Lightship. She managed to beach at Felixstowe but broke up in gales on 29 March 1916. Sister ships: *Oranje Nassau, Mecklenburg (I)*

Prinses Juliana (II); SMZ
Built: Built: by Koninklijke Maatschappij De Schelde, Vlissingen, Holland - yard no. 171
Launched: 13 March 1920
Dimensions: 350.4 x 42.7 x 16.4 ft
Tonnage: 2908 grt / 1122 nt / 2407 dwt
Engines: Fairfield Tr. exp. 8 cyl in 2 sets 28", 43½" & (2) 49" - 33"
Power Output: 1130 nhp
Speed: 22 knots
Passengers: 377 (267 First & 110 Second class)
First ref: 15 August 1920 Flushing to Folkestone (m/v)

Pcs. Was to have been built at Fairfields but a lack of yard capacity saw her built in Holland using the same plans as for the *Prinses Juliana (I)*. Transferred to the Flushing to P. Quay route in 1927. On 29 June 1935 she collided with DFDS vessel *Esbjerg* off Harwich. On 12 May 1940, whilst ferrying troops from Flushing to Ijmuiden, she was bombed and beached north of HvH. On 24 June she broke in two. Sister ship: *Mecklenburg (II)*

Prinses Marie; SMZ
Built: by John Elder & Co., Govan, Glasgow - yard no. 214
Launched: 24 October 1877
Dimensions: 278.2 x 35.1 x 16.1 ft

Tonnage: 1566 grt / 791 nt
Engines: J. Elder c.o. 2 cyl 60" & 104" - 84"
Power Output: 826 nhp / 3500 hp
Speed: 16 knots
Passengers: 300 by day, 240 by night
First ref: 28 March 1878 Flushing to Queenborough (m/v)

Pcps. The first ship built for SMZ. In regular use until 5 December 1895 when she became the reserve ship. Chartered in 1896 to Albert Ballin of Hamburg and re-named *Prinzess Marie*. Sold in August 1899 to Stettin Dampfschiff Ges., re-named *Germania* and put on route Stettin to Stockholm with sistership *Prinses Elisabeth*. In 1902 was sold for scrapping in Stettin. Sister ships: *Prinses Elisabeth, Prins Hendrik, Willem Prins van Oranje*

Prinz Hamlet (II) (Vikingfjord); Prins Line; IMO: 6922341
Built: by Jos L. Meyer Verft Papenburg, Ems, Germany - yard no. 545
Launched: 31 May 1969
Dimensions: 108.11 x 17.42 x 4.75 m
Tonnage: 3777 grt / 2108 nt / 1000 dwt
Engines: 2 x MAN 12 cyl diesels type V6V40/54
Power Output: 13400 bhp / 9997 kw
Speed: 18½ knots
Passengers: 650 (B: 364)
First ref: 20 March 1970 arrival at Harwich Navyard Dock from Hamburg for Prins Line.

Pcms ro-ro. Built for Partenreederei Nordlandfahre, Hamburg as the *Vikingfjord* for service between Cuxhaven, Stavanger and Bergen. (m/v) was on 11 August 1969. Space for 156 cars or 14 lorries. Chartered in Spring 1970 as overhaul cover for *Prinz Hamlet (I)* between Hamburg and Harwich Navyard. Chartered to Fred Olsen from 1 July to 30 September 1970 to sail between Kristiansand and P. Quay / Amsterdam. First arrival on 4 July. Chartered to Hadag, Hamburg in November 1970 to sail as *Prinz Hamlet (II)* between Hamburg and Harwich Navyard. First arrival on 15 November. Displaced by *Prinz Hamlet (2)* in November 1973. Sold to Comanav, Morocco in 1974 and re-named *Agadir*. Sailed between Tangier and Sete. Sold to Fragline, Cyprus in 1986 and re-named *Ouranos*. Sailed between Patras and Brindisi via Corfu. In May 1999 sold to Portuguese interests and re-named *Golfinho Azul* for Acor Line. Sold as *Golf* for scrapping in India in January 2007.

Ravensbury; GER
Built: by Messrs J. & W. Dudgeon, Poplar, London
Launched: Delivered 14 November 1865
Dimensions: 239.8 x 27.1 x 14.0 ft
Tonnage: 666 grt / 484 nt
Engines: J & W Dudgeon s.o. 2 cyl 54" - 54"
Power Output: 220 nhp
Speed: 14 knots
Passengers: 483
First ref: November 1865 Harwich to Rotterdam

Pcps. On 5 March 1870, whilst approaching Rotterdam, she ran aground. All passengers and crew were safely evacuated. By 8 March she had disappeared into the River Maas to become the first GER ship to be lost in service. Built to same cost and design as Sister ship: *Avalon (II)*.

Regina Maris; Cruise ship; IMO: 6603012
Built: by Lubecker Flender-Werke AG, Germany - yard no. 558
Launched: 14 December 1965
Dimensions: 400.1 x 55.4 x 18.9 ft
Tonnage: 5813 grt / 2974 nt / 1150 dwt
Engines: 2 x MAN 10 cyl diesels type G10V-52/74MA
Power Output: 8050 hp / 6002 kw
Speed: 20 knots
Passengers: 276
First ref: mid 1970s

Pms. Built for Lubeck Linie as a European based cruise ship with a small car deck for 25 cars. Made occasional visits to P. Quay in the mid 1970s. Sold in 1976 to Canadian interests based in Halifax and re-named *Mercator One*. Sold in 1979 to Peter Dielmann of Neustadt, Germany and re-named *Frankfurt* though later resumed the name of *Regina Maris* for cruising in Singapore and Canada. Sold to J.S. Latsis of Piraeus, Greece in 1983 and in 1985 was converted into the luxury yacht *Alexander*. Passengers: 12. Converted again in 1997. Tonnage: 5933 grt / 1779 nt / 1243 dwt. Passengers: 53. and sold to Madere Ltd, London. Laid up in 2009.

Rhodri Mawr; BR; IMO: 7019220
Built: by Verolme Cork Dockyard Ltd., Cobh - yard no. 810
Launched: 6 May 1970
Dimensions: 351.9 / 324.8 x 57.0 x 13.5 ft
Tonnage: 4098 grt / 1882 nt / 3150 dwt
Engines: 2 x Mirrlees Blackstone 6 cyl diesels type KLSSGMR
Power Output: 4200 bhp / 3090 kw
Speed: 14½ knots
Passengers: Nil
First ref: December 1975 Parkeston Quay to Zeebrugge / Dunkirk

Cms lo-lo. Introduction into service similarly delayed as per *Brian Boroime*. Space for 184 teus. 18 crew. Sailed from Heysham to Belfast / Dublin before first sailing from Holyhead on 31 January 1972. Transferred to assist between P. Quay and Dunkirk / Zeebrugge from 29 December 1975 to 12 October 1978. Displaced by *Brathay Fisher* and returned to Irish Sea until her last sailing from Dublin to Holyhead on 20 December 1989. Sold in 1990 to Satinwave Shipping Co, Cyprus. Re-named *Peliner* in January 1990 for Sarlis Container Services around the eastern Mediterranean. Sold in 1993 to Softwave Shipping, Cyprus. Re-named *Destiny* in September 2004. Sold in 2010 to Yoska Management, Constantza, Romania, re-named *Yamm* for service between Constantza and Istanbul. Still in service. Sister ship: *Brian Boroime*.

Rhone; DFDS
Built: by A/S Kjobenhavns Flydedok og Skibsvaerft, Copenhagen - yard no. 128
Launched: 18 November 1915
Dimensions: 246.9 / 235.0 x 35.5 x 16.6 ft
Tonnage: 1064 grt / 567 nt / 1718 dwt
Engines: Kjobenhavns Flydedok Tr. exp 18", 28.5" & 48 - 33"
Power Output: 800 ihp
Speed: 10½ knots
Passengers: 10
First ref: early 1920s

Cs. Cost: Dkr 442,000. Seen on the P. Quay to Esbjerg route in the 1920s. Lost by sinking by German submarine U14 in the North Sea on 16 February 1940.

Riberhuus; DFDS
Built: by Gourlay Bros. & Co., Dundee - yard no. 67
Launched: 20 May 1875
Dimensions: 190.7 x 25.9 x 13.2 ft o.a.
Tonnage: 615 grt / 407 nt / 525 dwt
Engines: Gourlay's c.o. 2 cyl 32" & 56" - 54"
Power Output: 150 nhp / 500 ihp
Speed: 9½ knots
Passengers: 28 (28 First class)
First ref: 4 June 1880 arrival at Harwich from Esbjerg.

Cps. (m/v) was on 24 June 1875 from Esbjerg to Thameshaven. First arrival at Parkeston Quay was on 22 September 1882. Re-engined and converted to screw steamer in 1883/84 by Lobnitz & Co., Renfrew. Dimensions: 206.5 / 200.0 x 27.0 x 13.5 ft Tonnage: 592 grt / 362 nt / 530 dwt. Engines: Lobnitz c.o. 2 cyl 27" & 50" - 36". Power Output: 125 nhp / 580 ihp. Left the P. Quay route in mid 1900s. Sold 28 December 1918 to A/S Triton of Aalborg. Sank after colliding with *Westwood* on 1 November 1920 off St. Nazaire. Re-floated but condemned on 4 January 1921.

Richard Young; (Brandon); GER
Built: by Messrs J. & W. Dudgeon, Poplar, London
Launched: 1871
Dimensions: 239.8 x 27.0 x 13.5 ft
Tonnage: 668 grt / 305 nt / 582 dwt
Engines: J & W Dudgeon s.o. 2 cyl 54" - 54"
Power Output: 220 nhp / 950 ihp
Speed: 14 knots
Passengers:
First ref: November 1871 Harwich to Rotterdam

Pcps. Noted for being the first sea going ship to pass through the New Waterway on 9 March 1872. In March 1889 she was converted to a cattle carrier, Then in 1890 was further converted by Earle's Co. Ltd. of Hull into a single screw steamer for 607 passengers. Fitted with new 168 nhp Earle's triple expansion engines 20½", 32" & 54" - 33" and boilers. Re-entered service when re-named *Brandon*. Tonnage: 718 grt / 405 nt / 571 dwt and 12 knots. Used as relief ship until sold for scrap at Wilton's of Rotterdam in July 1905.

Ringwood; Relief Ship
Built: by D & W Henderson Ltd., Glasgow - yard no. 730
Launched: 13 April 1926
Dimensions: 230.0 x 35.7 x 12.8 ft o.a.
Tonnage: 755 grt / 304 nt / 500 dwt
Engines: 2 x Tr. exp.
Power Output: 165 nhp / 1850 ihp
Speed: 15 knots
Passengers: 12

Cs. Built for the Southern Railway Co. with 32,000 cu. ft. of cargo space plus 4 horse stalls or 100 cattle. Sailed from Southampton to Channel Islands / Le Havre / St. Malo. Relieved on the P. Quay to Rotterdam / Antwerp cargo service in the 1950s. Scrapped in December 1959 at Nieuw Lekkerkerk. One of nine near sister ships including *Hythe* and *Haslemere*.

River Queen; River Services
Built: 1839 by Ditchburn and Mare, Blackwall, London.
Dimensions: 98.3 x 13.2 x 6.5 ft
Tonnage: 67 grt

Pps. Built for the Ipswich Steam Navigation Company. Fitted with a simple oscillating single cylinder engine and space for 150 passengers. Sailed between Ipswich and Harwich in arrangement with the Eastern Union Railway. Took part in the celebrations for the opening of the EUR line from Ipswich to Colchester on 15 June 1846. Sold in May 1853 to Alfred Cobbold when the ISNC was liquidated. Owned by the ECR in September 1854 though still registered to Alfred Cobbold. Broken up in 1861.

Roi Baudouin; RMT; IMO: 6510851
Built: by N.V. Cockerill Yards Hoboken, Belgium - yard no.828
Launched: 13 February 1965
Dimensions: 383.9 / 362.9 x 52.5 x 12.5 ft
Tonnage: 3241grt / 1762 nt / 477 dwt
Engines: 2 x Sulzer 12 cyl diesels
Power Output: 9600 bhp / 7061 kw
Speed: 22 knots
Passengers: 850 (B: 124)
First ref: 29 May 1968 arrival at Parkeston Quay from Ostend

Pcms ro-ro. (m/v) was on 13 June 1965 from Ostend to Dover. Capacity for 160 cars or 120 cars and 5 lorries. Underwent berthing trials at P. Quay on 10 May 1968. Inaugurated an all year round service between Ostend and P. Quay from May 1968 and was the principal ship on this route. Service changed to being summer season only from 1970 onwards. Underwent a refit at Schiedam, Holland from December 1972 to April 1973. Tonnage: 3023 grt / 1762 nt / 477 dwt. Passengers:1700 (B:104). Cars: 190. Closed the P. Quay to Ostend route on 10 September 1973. Resumed Ostend to Dover service until July 1982, then chartered to Sealink for cross channel services from Dover and Folkestone. Sold to Ventouris Group, Piraeus on 15 April 1983 and re-named *Georgios Express* in July. Rebuilt in Piraeus in August 1983. Tonnage: 3023 grt / 1318 nt / 809 dwt. Served mainly Piraeus to Greek island routes until being laid up in Eleusis in 2001 awaiting sale. Eventually left for scrapping in Aliaga in March 2009. Sister ship: *Princesse Astrid*.

Roland; H.J. Perlbach
Built: 1855 by T.D. Marshall of South Shields
Dimensions: 187.2 x 29.0 ft
Tonnage: 617 grt / 458 nt
Engines: Humphreys & Pearson of Hull c.o. 2 cyl 26" & 48" - 30"
Power Output: 95 hp
First ref: 1884

Pcs. Once registered to the North of Europe Steam Navigation Co. in 1858. She was sold to H.J. Perlbach on 26 February 1861 by J. Lever of London as the *Propeller* and re-named the *Roland*. Sailed out of Hamburg mainly to Hull, Antwerp, Le Havre and Rotterdam before first arriving at P. Quay in autumn 1884. Made 20 visits that year rising to 30 in 1885. Last seen at P. Quay in 1887.

Romira; Chartered; IMO: 7627962
Built: by Ishikawajima Ship & Chemical Plant Co, Tokyo, Japan - yard no. 491
Launched: 30 November 1977
Dimensions: 122.94 x 21.04 x 4.76 m
Tonnage: 2625 grt / 1018 nt / 3522 dwt
Engines: 2 x Stork Werkspoor diesels type 12SW280
Power Output: 5880 kw
Speed: 16 knots
Passengers: 12
First ref: November 1984

Cms ro-ro. Space for 1100 lane metres of freight. Chartered by DFDS in 1984 for service between P. Quay and Hamburg, then again in spring 1985 between P. Quay and Hamburg / Esbjerg. Other names: Launched as *Admiral Atlantic* (1977) then re-named *Romira* (1984), *Duke of Flanders* (1986), *Maersk Flanders* (1990), *Maersk Friesland* (1999), *Friesland* (2000), *Magallanes* (2000) and *Evangelistas* (2007).

Romny; DFDS
Built: by Palmer Bros & Co, Jarrow - yard no. 65
Launched: 22 September 1857
Dimensions: 197.5 x 25.6 x 16.0 ft
Tonnage: 692 grt / 510 nt / 720 dwt
Engines: Day, Summers & Co. Southampton c.o. 2 cyl 26" & 52" - 36"
Power Output: 450 ihp
Speed: 9 knots
Passengers: 26 (14 First & 12 Second class)
First ref: late 1880s

Cs. Seen on the P. Quay to Esbjerg route. First delivered to Norddeutscher Lloyd, Bremen in October 1857 as the *Adler*. Purchased by DFDS on 10 December 1881 for £5.000 and re-named *Romny*. Sold on 24 March 1898 to A. Lodders, Riga. Broken up in Boulogne in February 1909. Sister ships: *Charkow, Minsk, Tula*.

Rosita Maria; Railfreight; IMO: 7605873
Built: 1977 by J.J. Sietas Schiffswerft, Hamburg, Germany - yard no. 810
Dimensions: 92 x 14 x 4.6 m
Tonnage: 2316 grt / 3403 dwt
Speed: 14 knots

Cms lo-lo. Space for 262 teus. Launched as 999 grt. Other names: *Rosita* (2002), *Axiom 2* (2009) and *Rania (*2012). Last owner: Bia shipping, Constantza, Romania.

Rota; DFDS
Built: by Deutsche Werke A.G. Kiel - yard no. 171
Launched: 20 October 1923
Dimensions: 241.0 / 230.0 x 33.9 x 14.6 ft
Tonnage: 840 grt / 418 nt / 1030 dwt
Engines: Deutsche Werke Tr. exp 19.75", 32.25" & 52.4" - 35"
Power Output: 1100 ihp
Speed: 12 knots
Passengers: 12
First ref: 1947

Cs. Cost: Dkr 760,000. Seen on the P. Quay to Esbjerg route in 1947 and then again in 1958. Sold on 19 February 1962 to Petersen & Albeck A/S of Copenhagen for scrapping.

Rotterdam (Peterborough); GER
Built: by Messrs Simpson & Co., Pimlico, London
Launched: Delivered August 1864
Dimensions: 215.0 x 27.1 x 14.0 ft
Tonnage: 757 grt / 557 nt / 613 dwt
Engines: Simpson & Co. s.o. 2 cyl 55" - 66"
Power Output: 220 nhp / 1060 hp
Speed: 10 knots

Passengers: Nil
First ref: 14 November 1864 Harwich to Rotterdam (m/v)

Cps. Launched as a cattle and cargo paddle steamer. Fitted with 50 berths in 1865 later raised to 80 in 1871. In 1887 she was rebuilt and re-boilered by Earle's Co. Ltd. of Hull as a 822 grt twin screw passenger and cargo steamer. Fitted with a new 168 nhp Earle's 4 cyl compound engine 22" & 44" - 27" and space for 108 passengers. Re-entered service when re-named *Peterborough*. Usually used as relief ship until sold in 1908 for scrap. Sister ship: *Harwich*.

Royal Ulsterman; Trooping Services
Built: by Harland & Wolff Ltd., Belfast - yard no. 963
Launched: 10 March 1936
Dimensions: 339.5 / 328.0 x 47.7 x 14.0 ft
Tonnage: 3250 grt
Engines: 2 x diesels
Power Output: 7500 bhp
Speed: 16 knots
First ref: 31 July 1945

Pcms Built for Burns & Laird Lines Ltd service between Glasgow and Belfast. (m/v) was on 15 June 1936. Requisitioned in April 1940 for use as a stores and personnel carrier. Served on trooping duties between P. Quay and HvH from 31 July 1945 to 16 November 1945. Paid off on 20 December 1945 and resumed commercial service on 27 September 1946 until 30 December 1967. Sold to Cammell Laird shipbuilders on 29 March 1968 for use as an accommodation ship, re-named *Cammell Laird*, until sold again in April 1968 to Mediterranean Link Lines and re-named *Sourion*. Sank after hitting a mine in Beirut on 3 March 1973 and later broken up in Perama on 10 September 1973.

Rynstroom; IMO: 6600852
Built: by Arnhemsche Scheepsbouw Mij, Arnhem, Holland - yard no. 438
Launched: 1966
Dimensions: 80.80 x 10.83 x 3.36 m
Tonnage: 554 grt
Engines: 1 x MAN 16 cyl diesel type V8V30/45
Power Output: 1800 hp / 1324 kw
Speed: 14 knots
First ref: 1969

Cms cc. Built as the ro-ro carrier *Rijnstroom* for the Hollandsche Stoomboot Maatschappij of Amsterdam to sail between Amsterdam and Shoreham. Sailed between P. Quay and Amsterdam importing Ford cars in 1969. Re-named *Car Express* in 1976. Converted to a livestock carrier in 1977. Tonnage: 1512 grt / 453 nt / 931 dwt. Other names: *Brahman Express* (1981) and *Eaga Rapid Trader I* (1996). Last owner: Eaga Ship Management, Manila, Philippines.

Saga; Thule Line
Built: by Swan Hunter & Wigham Richardson, Neptune Yard, Tyneside - yard no. 812
Launched: 21 April 1909
Dimensions: 322.4 x 46.2 x 19.5 ft
Tonnage: 2943 grt / 1552 nt / 2980 dwt
Engines: 3 cyl Tr. exp.
Power Output: 4000 ihp
Speed: 15 knots
Passengers: 170 (85 First, 55 Second & 30 Steerage class)
First ref: 16 May 1910 arrival at Parkeston Quay from Gothenburg

Pcs. Entered service between Gothenburg and London Tilbury in June 1909. Transferred to Swedish Lloyd in January 1916. Chartered to Moore McCormack Line for passenger service between New York and Rio de Janeiro. Returned to Sweden in 1919 and opened Gothenburg to Newcastle route. Sold in September 1929 to Compagnie Generale Transatlantique and re-named *Mayenne*. Seized by Italy in 1942, re-named *Fabriano* and lost to being torpedoed on 11 May 1943.

Saga Star; Chartered; IMO: 7931997
Built: by Fartygsentreprenader Ab., Kalmar - yard no. 153
Launched: January 1981
Dimensions: 147.0 x 24.0 x 6.26 m
Tonnage: 8226 grt / 2786 nt / 5492 dwt
Engines: 4 x Lindholmen Pielstick 8 cyl diesels type 8PC2-5L
Power Output: 15300 kw
Speed: 19 knots
Passengers: 80
First ref: October 1988

Cms ro-ro. Space for 1408 lane metres of freight. Briefly in service between P. Quay and Bremerhaven when chartered by DFDS from October 1988 until February 1989. Other names: Was built in sections throughout 1981 and first delivered as the *Saga Star* for TT-Saga Line in December 1981. Re-named *Girolata* (1989), *Saga Star* (1993), *Dieppe* (2002), and *Baltivia* (2006). Still in service. Last owner: Polska Zegluga Baltyska, Kolobrzeg, Poland.

Saint-Germain; SNCF; IMO: 5305895
Built: by Helsingor Skibs og Mask, A/S, Elsinore - yard no. 303
Launched: 1951
Dimensions: 379.8 / 367.0 x 60.5 x 13.5 ft
Tonnage: 3400 grt / 1400 nt
Engines: 2 x B&W 9 cyl diesels
Power Output: 6400 bhp
Speed: 18½ knots
Passengers: 850
First ref: 31 March 1985

Cms tf. Only seen the once whilst undergoing berthing trials at Harwich train ferry terminal. Operated on the Dover to Dunkirk train ferry service with space for 36 rail wagons or 8 rail sleeping cars or 135 cars. Other names: *Germain* (1988). Arrived at Alang, India on 11 August 1988 for scrapping.

Schulau; Railfreight; IMO: 7723687
Built: 1978 by J.J. Sietas Schiffswerft, Hamburg, Germany.
Dimensions: 73 x 13 x 3.2 m
Tonnage: 1678 grt / 1964 dwt

Cms lo-lo. Other names: *Minchen D* (1999) and *Solveig K* (2008). Last owner: Konig Reederei, Rostock, Germany.

Seafowl; Chartered; IMO: 7500736
Built: by Soc. Nouvelle des At & Ch. Du Havre, Le Havre, France - yard no. 239
Launched: July 1977
Dimensions: 109.77 x 17.53 x 5.23 m
Tonnage: 1576 grt / 780 nt / 2743 dwt
Engines: 2 x MAK diesels type 9M453AK
Power Output: 4855 kw
Speed: 15 knots
Passengers: 12
First Ref: September 1989

Cms ro-ro. Space for 672 lane metres of freight or 61 trailers. Briefly chartered by Cobelfret in September 1969 for a new ro-ro service between P. Quay and Zeebrugge. Other names: Launched as *Cap Lardier* (1977) then *Gyptis* (1983), *Seafowl* (1987), *Libeccio* (1992) and *Cap Canoille* (1992).

Sea Freightliner I; BR; IMO: 6803416
Built: by John Readhead & Sons Ltd., South Shields - yard no. 621
Launched: 2 December 1967
Dimensions: 388.5 / 366.0 x 53.0 x 14.5 ft
Tonnage: 4034 grt / 2108 nt / 3293 dwt
Engines: 2 x Mirrlees National diesels type KLSSGMR6
Power Output: 3780 bhp
Speed: 13½ knots
Passengers: Nil
First ref: 17 May 1968 Parkeston Quay to Zeebrugge (m/v)

Cms lo-lo. Built for BR as Britain's first cellular container ship and opened Britain's first short sea container terminal at P. Quay. Space for 218 teus. 18 crew. Served on the routes to Zeebrugge and Dunkirk until the services closed in December 1985. Suffered a major fire on board whilst in Holyhead dry dock on 12 July 1980. Out of service until 27 October 1980. Laid up in the River Stour until towed to the River Blackwater on 30 July 1986. Left from there on 9 February 1987 for Falmouth and then for Naples loaded with cargo. In March 1987 she sailed to China via Colombo loaded with electrical cables. Sailed on to Kaohsiung in Taiwan where she arrived on 4 May 1987 for scrapping. Sister ship: *Sea Freightliner II*

Sea Freightliner II; BR; IMO: 6812352
Built: by John Readhead & Sons Ltd., South Shields - yard no. 622
Launched: 15 March 1968
Dimensions: 388.5 / 366.0 x 53.0 x 14.5 ft
Tonnage: 4034 grt / 2108 nt / 3293 dwt
Engines: 2 x Mirrlees National diesels type KLSSGMR6
Power Output: 3780 bhp
Speed: 13½ knots
Passengers: Nil
First ref: 18 June 1968 Parkeston Quay to Rotterdam (m/v)

Cms lo-lo. As per *Sea Freightliner I* was built for BR's short sea container terminal at P. Quay. Space for 218 teus. 18 crew. Served on the routes to Zeebrugge and Dunkirk until the services closed in December 1985. Laid up in the Stour until towed to the Blackwater on 1 August 1986. Left on 26 September 1986 for Tilbury and then Naples loaded with empty containers. She left Naples on 8 October 1986 for Pakistan loaded with scrap pipe. Arrived at Karachi on 2 January 1987 and was beached for scrapping. Sister ship: *Sea Freightliner*.

Seamew; GSNCo.
Built: by Palmer's Shipbuilding & Iron Co. Ltd, Jarrow - yard no. 593
Launched: 26 May 1888
Dimensions: 260.0 x 36 6 x 17.3 ft
Tonnage: 1505 grt / 765 nt
Engines: Tr. exp 31", 50" & 76" - 45"
Power Output: 580 nhp
Passengers: 200 (100 First class)
First ref: mid 1890s

Pcs. Built for GSNCo's London to Leith service in July 1888. Joined the P. Quay to Hamburg service during the 1890's. In 1899 a single saloon fare to Hamburg was £1.10s.0d. Sold in 1914 to J. McDowell, Piraeus and re-named *Daphne*. Sold in 1919 to Hellenic Co., Piraeus and re-named *Dafni*. Sold in 1924 to Istiklal- I Bahri Sirketi, Istanbul and re-named *Ismet Pasa*. Eventually broken up in Istanbul in 1929.

Sheringham; LNER
Built: by Earle's Shipbuilding & Eng. Co. Ltd., Hull - yard no. 669
Launched: 14 August 1926
Dimensions: 265.0 / 255.0 x 36.1 x 14.8 ft
Tonnage: 1088 grt / 429 nt / 950 dwt
Engines: Earle's Tr. exp. 22", 35" & 60" - 39"
Power Output: 379 nhp / 2352 ihp
Speed: 14 knots
Passengers: Nil
First ref: 15 September 1926 Parkeston Quay to Rotterdam (m/v)

Cs. First LNER ship built for service at P. Quay and the last built for there by Earle's of Hull. In 1940 was transferred to GWR Weymouth services and requisitioned in July 1940 for use as a military stores and cargo ship around the Irish Sea. Resumed service between P. Quay and Rotterdam on 23 March 1946 until October 1958. Sold in December 1958 for scrapping by Van Huyghen Freres of Ghent.

Skyros; DFDS; IMO: 5331612
Built: by Frederikshavn Vaerft & Tordok A/S, Frederikshavn - yard no. 232
Launched: 13 April 1962
Dimensions: 110.41 / 100.00 x 15.50 x 6.10 m
Tonnage: 2661 grt / 1286 nt / 3317 dwt
Engines: 1 x B&W 6 cyl diesel type 650-VTBF-110
Power Output: 3450 bhp
Speed: 15¼ knots
Passengers: 12
First ref: February 1972

Cms. Cost: Dkr 13.3m. Seen at P. Quay only between February and April 1972, last leaving for Esbjerg on 23 April as DFDS's last conventional freight ship sailing from the UK. Sold on 6 December 1973 to Associated Levant Lines, Beirut. Other names: *Beryte* (1973), *Wing Ko* (1984) and *Asian Express* (1992). Broken up in March 1995 by Rajeev Shipbreakers in Alang.

Somerset; DFDS; IMO: 6703343
Built: by Helsingor Skibsvaerft og Maskinbyggeri A/S, Ellsinore - yard no.380
Launched: 20 October 1966
Dimensions: 111.60 / 101.00 x 16.99 x 4.93 m
Tonnage: 2245 grt / 587 nt / 2195 dwt
Engines: 4 x B&W 10 cyl diesels type 1026-MTBF-40V
Power Output: 6600 bhp
Speed: 18 knots
Passengers: Nil
First ref: December 1967 Esbjerg to Parkeston Quay

Cms ro-ro. Cost Dkr 20,762,648. The first DFDS cargo ship equipped for both bow and stern loading. Space for 113 trailers. (m/v) was on 31 December 1966 from Hamburg to Grimsby. Top deck container crane added at Elsinore in September 1969. Lengthened at Frederikshavn Verft & Tordok A/S in November 1972. Dimensions: 124.19 / 113.59 x 16.99 x 4.93 m. Tonnage: 2603 grt / 740 nt / 2947 dwt. Trailer capacity now 135. Variously used throughout the North Sea from 1967 until 1981 including periods on the Esbjerg to P. Quay service. Also Hamburg to P. Quay in 1980 and 1981. Sold on 24 July 1981 jointly to Scandinavian Livestock Carriers Inc and DFDS Monrovia. Converted to carry livestock, re-named *Purcell Livestock* and chartered to Purcell Export Ltd. Other names: *Livestock* (1982), *Fastock* (1984) and *Aphrodite* (1987). Sold in 1991 to Olympic Mediterranean Cruises Shipping Co, Piraeus and then in 1994 to Jay Shipping Corp. of St. Vincent and Grenada. Sold in 1995 to A. Sleiman & Co, Lebanon and re-named *Zaher V*. In service between Puerto Cabello, Venezuela and Vila do Conde Belem, Brazil. Sister ship: *Stafford*

Speedlink Vanguard; BR; IMO: 7325576
Built: by A Vuyk & Zonen Scheepswerven B.V., Capelle d'Ijssel, Holland - yard no. 864
Launched: 16 June 1973
Dimensions: 469.8 / 423.5 x 60.7 x 16.8 ft o.a.
Tonnage: 3320 grt / 1893 nt / 4100 dwt
Engines: 2 x Werkspoor Amsterdam 6 cyl diesels type 6TM410
Power Output: 7200 bhp / 5296 kw
Speed: 18 knots
Passengers: 36
First ref: 21 August 1980 Harwich to Zeebrugge for BR.

Cms tf. Launched as *Stena Shipper*, a multi-purpose freight ship built for Stena Ab, Gothenburg. Dimensions: 378.1 x 53.6 x 19.4 ft. Tonnage: 2638 grt / 798 nt / 3816 dwt. Passengers: 12. First entered service as the *Union Wellington* when chartered to Union Steamship Co of New Zealand. Lengthened by almost 90 feet in 1976 by Howaldtswerke Deutsche Werft AG, Kiel. Then chartered to Arghiris Line, Piraeus as the *Alpha Express*. Registered to Stena Cargo Line Ltd, Bermuda in 1980 as *Stena Shipper* and converted to a twin deck train ferry at Smith's Dock, Middlesbrough with capacity for 32 continental rail wagons on main deck and 24 on top deck. Otherwise 40 x 40 ft vehicles on main deck only. Emerged as the *Speedlink Vanguard* and chartered to Sealink UK Ltd, London. Collided with *European Gateway* on 19 December 1982 off Felixstowe leading to the loss of six lives. Closed the Harwich to Zeebrugge train ferry service on 30 January 1987. Re-named *Caribe Express*, *Stena Shipper* and *Kirk Shipper* before being chartered to Truckline Ferries in June 1989 as *Normandie Shipper*. Sailed Poole to Cherbourg and then Portsmouth to Caen until October 1995. Sold to Adecon Shipping, Bahamas in October 1999 and re-named *Bonavista*. Sold to Kyst-link, Bahamas in July 2001 and re-named *Boa Vista* for services between Denmark and Norway. Sold in June 2004 to Kittilsen Shipping, Panama. In service for Thraki

Med Ro-Ro in September 2006 between Volos, Greece and Izmir, Turkey. Volos then being the port used by the former *European Gateway*. Sold to Thraki Shipping, Panama, re-named *Birlik 1*. Seen at P. Quay in December 2007 en-route from Gdansk to Turkey. In service between Zonguldak and Skadovsk in 2008. Scrapped at Aliaga, Turkey in June 2013.

St. Andrew; Trooping Services
Built: by Cammell Laird & Co. Ltd., Birkenhead - yard no. 981.
Launched: 1932
Dimensions: 336.0 x 49.0 x 14.2 ft o.a.
Tonnage: 3035 grt / 1322 nt / 710 dwt
Engines: 2 x srg turbines
Power Output: 1590 nhp / 8400 shp
Speed: 21 knots
First ref: 18 August 1945

Pcs. Built for the Great Western Railway's service from Fishguard to Rosslare. Passengers: 1300 (966 First and 334 Third class) (B: 242 First and 100 Third class). Requisitioned on 11 September 1939 and converted to *Hospital Carrier no. 24*. Served on trooping duties between P. Quay and HvH from 18 August 1945 to 24 July 1946. Resumed original commercial service on 24 May 1947. Arrived in Antwerp on 24 June 1967 for breaking up.

St. David (III); Relief ship
Built: by Cammell Laird & Co. Ltd., Birkenhead - yard no.1182
Launched: 6 February 1947
Dimensions: 321.0 / 306.5 x 48.0 x 13.2 ft o.a.
Tonnage: 3352 grt / 1352 nt / 364 dwt
Engines: 2 x 2 sets Parsons srg turbines
Power Output: 8500 hp
Speed: 20¾ knots
Passengers: 1300 (B: 251 First & 102 Second class)
First ref: January 1950

Pcs. Built for the Fishguard & Rosslare Rly & Harbour Co. (m/v) was in July 1947. Relieved on the P. Quay to HvH service in January / February 1950 and again in April / May 1951. Rebuilt in 1964 as a car ferry for Irish sea service. Sold in January 1971 to Chandris Cruises in Piraeus and re-named *Holyhead*. Plans for conversion to a cruise ship were dropped and she was later scrapped in Greece in 1979.

St. Edmund; BR; IMO: 7340710
Built: by Cammell Laird Shipbuilders Ltd., Birkenhead - yard no. 1361
Launched: 14 November 1973
Dimensions: 430.0 / 392.1 x 74.2 x 17.0 ft
Tonnage: 8987 grt / 4697 nt / 1830 dwt
Engines: 4 x Stork Werkspoor 8 cyl diesels type TM410
Power Output: 20400 bhp
Speed: 21 knots
Passengers: 1400 by day, 1000 by night (B: 273 First & 398 Second class)
First ref: 19 January 1975 Parkeston Quay to Hook of Holland (m/v)

Pcms ro-ro. Cost £7.5m. Named on 13 November 1973 by Mrs Caroline Marsh, wife of BRB Chairman but due to bad weather was launched on 14 November. Space for 296 cars or 148 cars and 40 lorries. Requisitioned by the Ministry of Defence on 12 May 1982 for conversion to a troopship in response to the Falkland Islands invasion. Left Devonport after refit on 20 May to join the Task Force and arrived at Port Stanley on 17 June. Thereafter used as accommodation and transport ship. Sold to M.O.D. on 16 February 1983 for £7.75m whilst returning from the Falklands to Tyne Shiprepairers, Wallsend. Re-named *H.M.S. Keren* on 1 April 1983, decommissioned a few days later as *m.v. Keren* and returned to the Falklands. Sold in January 1986 to Cenargo Navigation Ltd, Nassau and re-named *Scirocco*. Variously chartered to Mediterranean operators, eg Tirrenia in 1986, Comanav and Trasmediterranea in 1987 and Cotunav in 1988. Chartered to British Channel Island Ferries as the *Rozel* between Poole and Guernsey / Jersey from 21 February 1989 until 18 January 1992. Resumed the name *Scirocco* on 19 January 1992 and again chartered for work in the Mediterranean. eg Trasmediterranea in 1992, FerriMaroc and Comanav in 1993, Cotunav in 1994 and then for FerriMaroc until June 2003. Sold to El Salam Maritime, Cairo, Egypt in April 2004 and re-named *Santa Catherine I*. Further chartered to Comanav in 2004 and Algeria Ferries in 2005. Towards the end of 2005 she sailed from Suez as a pilgrim ship. On 30 May 2006 was re-named *Sara 3* for use as a pilgrim ship between Jeddah and Sawakin. Laid up in 2008 until sold in June 2009 for breaking up in India.

St. George (1); GER
Built: by Cammell Laird & Co. Ltd., Birkenhead - yard no. 665
Launched: 13 January 1906
Dimensions: 364.0 / 352.0 x 41.1 x 15.0 ft
Tonnage: 2456 grt / 1012 nt / 420 dwt
Engines: 3 Parsons turbines - direct drive
Power Output: 10000 shp
Speed: 20 knots
Passengers: 498 (B:220 First & 100 Second class)
First ref: April 1920 Parkeston Quay to Hook of Holland

Pcs. Originally built for the Fishguard & Rosslare Railways and Harbours Co. (part of the GWR) as one of four triple screw sister ships, (*St. Patrick, St. David* and *St. Andrew*) with accommodation for 1000 passengers, 562 First / 438 Second, with berths for over 400 in First and some in Second class. Entered GWR service on 13 September 1906. Sold in May 1913 to Canadian Pacific Railway Co. for service across Bay of Fundy between Digby and St. John. Requisitioned in 1915 for use in 1917 as a hospital ship. Purchased by GER in June 1919 who reduced her original capacity to 498 passengers and 320 berths. Sold in October 1929 for scrapping at Hughes Bolckow of Blyth.

St. George (II); BR; IMO: 6810897
Built: by Swan Hunter & Tyneside Shipbuilders, - yard no. 2029
Launched: 28 February 1968
Dimensions: 420.0 / 378.0 x 67.5 x 16.5 ft
Tonnage: 7356 grt / 3869 nt / 1036 dwt
Engines: 4 x Ruston & Hornsby 9 cyl diesels type 9AO
Power Output: 18000 bhp
Speed: 21 knots
Passengers: 1200 by day 750 by night (B: 261 First & 304 Second class)
First ref: 17 July 1968 Parkeston Quay to Hook of Holland (m/v)

Pcms ro-ro. Cost £3m. Launched by Mrs. H. Johnson, wife of the Chairman of BRB, as the first BR ro-ro ship at P. Quay. Space for 220 cars or 32 lorries and 80 cars. Relegated to relief ship in 1975. Displaced in June 1983 and sent to Immingham on 20 September 1983 for repairs to main engines. Laid up in the river Fal until sold on 18 September 1984 to Psatha Navigation Co. Ltd, Limassol, Cyprus, re-named *Patra Express* and put into service in March 1985 for Ventouris Lines between Patras and Bari. Main engines replaced with 2 Wartsila Vasa diesels type 16V32 in 1988. Power Output: 16120 bhp. Speed: 19½ knots. February 1990 saw abortive plans by British Iberian Lines to buy her for a service between Poole and Bilbao as the *Maiden Castle*. Instead she was sold to Sea Escape, Miami on 10 February 1990 and left Piraeus for Immingham, via Hull, to be rebuilt as a casino ship by Humber Ship Repair Ltd. Initially re-named *Scandinavian Sky II* she left Immingham on 16 August as the *Scandinavian Dawn* to sail for *Sea Escape* from 27 October 1990 to 31 August 1996 on one day cruises between Fort Lauderdale and Freeport, Bahamas. Was chartered to Discovery Cruises in September 1996 who re-named her *Discovery Dawn* and then bought her in February 1997. Re-named *Island Dawn* in April 1998 for a failed venture as a floating casino in New York. Laid up until October 1999 before operating day cruises out of Port Isabel, Texas. Chartered to Viva Gaming & Resorts in July 2000 and re-named *Texas Treasure* for cruises out of Corpus Christi, Texas. On 20 February 2003 she moved to Port Aransas, Texas. In May 2008 she was docked in the Bahamas with a faulty alternator that proved too expensive to repair. Was subsequently sold for breaking up in Alang, India in July 2008.

St. Helier; Trooping Services
Built: by John Brown & Co. Ltd., Clydebank - yard no. 510
Launched: 23 March 1925
Dimensions: 291.2 / 282.1 x 42.5 x 13.1 ft
Tonnage: 1949grt / 789 nt / 371 dwt
Engines: 2 x 2 sets Parsons srg turbines
Power Output: 4350 bhp
Speed: 18 knots
First ref: 15 November 1945

Pcs. Cost £140,244. Built for the Great Western Railway's Weymouth to Channel Islands service. Passengers: 1004 (B:140 First and 120 Third class). (m/v) was in June 1925. Refitted in 1937 with more cabins. Passengers: 950 (B:209 First and 130 Third class). Requisitioned in autumn 1939 for services as a troopship, thereafter as *HMS St. Helier* on 9 February 1941. Was paid off on 14 August 1945. First arrived at P. Quay on 15 November 1945 and served on trooping duties between P. Quay and HvH from 18 November 1945 to 15 March 1946. Resumed original commercial service on 16 June 1946. Sold in December 1960 for scrapping by Jos de Smelt of Antwerp.

St. Nicholas; Sealink British Ferries; IMO: 7901772
Built: by Gotaverken Arendal, Gothenburg - yard no. 909
Launched: 22 May 1981
Dimensions: 488.8 / 429.8 x 91.9 x 20.1 ft
Tonnage: 17043 grt / 7859 nt / 3315 dwt
Engines: 4 x Nohab Wartsila Vasa diesels type 12V32A
Power Output: 20600 hp / 15360 kw
Speed: 20½ knots
Passengers: 2100 (B: 401 First & 660 Second class)
First ref: 10 June 1983 Parkeston Quay to Hook of Holland

Pcms ro-ro. Launched as 'yard no. 909' for Rederi Ab Goteborg - Frederikshavn Linjen (GFL) trading as Sessan Line. (m/v) was on 3 June 1982 as the 14,368 grt *Princessan Birgita*. Passengers: 2100 (B:616). Space for 700 cars or 70 lorries. Chartered to Sealink BF from 28 February 1983 for three years. Rebuilt as night ferry at Cityvarvet, Gothenburg with reduced space for 460 cars or 52 lorries. Re-named *St. Nicholas*. Sold in June 1983 to Hill Samuel Trading Ltd., London and then to various UK interests until Paxro Ltd, Nassau in 1988. Sold to Rederi Ab Gotland, Visby in December 1989 for US$57.7m. Re-named *Stena Normandy* in January 1991. Last trip on the P. Quay to HvH route was 19 June 1991. On 28 June 1991 she opened a new route from Southampton to Cherbourg until 29 November 1996. January 1997 saw her chartered to Hansatee Oy, Tallinn, re-named *Normandy* and from 23 April until 30 December 1997 was in service between Tallinn - Helsinki. Chartered to Irish Ferries, Dublin and put in service on 19 February 1998 between Pembroke and Rosslare. Sold to Irish Continental Ferries, Dublin on 10 November 1999 and refitted in Poland. Re-entered service in March mainly from Rosslare to Cherbourg until 4 November 2007. Sold on 28 January 2008 to Equinox Offshore Accommodation Ltd. Singapore and chartered to Ferrimaroc of Morocco for summer season between Almeira and Nador. Arrived Singapore on 19 October 2008 for conversion to the offshore Accommodation and Repair Vessel *ARV2*. After being laid up with no work on conversion she was sold in September 2012 for scrapping in India. Arrived at Alang on 30 November 2012.

St. Patrick (II); Chartered; IMO: 7310260
Built: by J.J. Sietas Schiffswerft, Hamburg, Germany - yard no. 702
Launched: 17 March 1973
Dimensions: 125.22 x 21.53 x 5.27 m
Tonnage: 7984 grt / 4319 nt / 1325 dwt
Engines: 2 x Stork Werkspoor diesels type 16TM410
Power Output: 15445 kw
Speed: 21½ knots
Passengers: 1500 (B:330)
First Ref: March 1985

Pcms ro-ro. Briefly chartered by DFDS in March 1985 for services from P. Quay to Hamburg and Cuxhaven. Also in September 1985 between P. Quay and Hamburg. First delivered to Viking Line in July 1973 as the *Aurella*. Purchased by Irish Continental Line in January 1982 and re-named *St. Patrick (II)*. Other names: *Ville de Sete*. *City of Cork*. Sold in 2002 to CTMA of Canada and sailing as *C.T.M.A. Vacancier*. Still in service.

St. Petersburg (Archangel); GER
Built: by John Brown & Co. Ltd., Clydebank - yard no. 397
Launched: 25 April 1910
Dimensions: 343.0 / 331.2 x 43.2 x 17.8 ft
Tonnage: 2448 grt / 1039 nt / 1502 dwt
Engines: 3 Parsons Turbines - direct drive
Power Output: 1325 nhp / 10197 ihp
Speed: 20 knots
Passengers: (B: 320 First & 130 Second class)
First ref: 7 July 1910 Parkeston Quay to Hook of Holland (m/v)

Pcs. Launched by Miss Green. Triple screwed. Requisitioned in October 1914. Re-named *Archangel* in May 1915. Requisitioned again in November 1939. Sunk by being bombed off Aberdeen on 16 May 1941. Sister ships: *Copenhagen, Munich*.

Stad Breda; SMZ
Built: by Caird & Co., Greenock
Launched: 22 May 1863
Dimensions: 228.6 x 26.3 x 14.1 ft
Tonnage: 604 grt / 295 nt
Engines: Caird s.o. 2 cyl 58" - 69"
Power Output: 250 nhp
Speed: 14 knots
Passengers: 390 (140 First & 250 Third class)
First ref: July 1875 Flushing to Sheerness

Pcps. Originally built as the *Snaefell (I)* for Isle of Man Steam Packet Co.. Acquired by SMZ as a former blockade runner in 1875 for £15,500 who re-named her *Stad Breda*. Used as a reserve vessel until sold in 1888 for scrapping in Flushing.

Stad Middleburg; SMZ
Built: by Quiggin & Co., Liverpool
Launched: 1865
Dimensions: 275.0 x 33.1 x 15.7 ft
Tonnage: 1622 grt / 905 nt
Engines: Jack of Liverpool s.o. 2 cyl 64" - 78"
Power Output: 300 nhp / 1200 hp
Speed: 13 knots
Passengers: 200 (150 First & 50 Second class)
First ref: 26 July 1875 Flushing to Sheerness

Pcps. Originally built as the American Civil War blockade runner *Southern*. Acquired by SMZ in 1875 who converted her to a passenger steamer and re-named *Stad Middleburg*. Was the first to visit Queenborough on 19 May 1875 with guests for inaugural celebrations. Further re-named in 1881 as *Aurora* and used as reserve ship. Sold in 1888 for breaking up in 1889. Sister ship: *Stad Vlissingen*.

Stad Vlissingen; SMZ
Built: by Quiggin & Co., Liverpool
Launched: 1865
Dimensions: 275.0 x 33.1 x 15.7 ft
Tonnage: 1622 grt / 905 nt
Engines: Jack of Liverpool s.o. 2 cyl 64" - 78"
Power Output: 300 nhp / 1200 hp
Speed: 13 knots
Passengers: 200 (150 First & 50 Second class)
First ref: July 1875 Flushing to Sheerness

Pcps. Originally built as the American Civil War blockade runner *Northern*. Acquired by SMZ in 1875 who converted her to a passenger steamer and re-named *Stad Vlissingen*. Grounded at Nieuivestins off Flushing in 1879 and broke in two. Sister ship: *Stad Middleburg*.

Stafford; DFDS; IMO: 6708252
Built: by Helsingor Skibsvaerft og Maskinbyggeri A/S, Ellsinore - yard no.381
Launched: 24 January 1967

Dimensions: 111.60 / 101.00 x 16.99 x 4.93 m
Tonnage: 2245 grt / 587 nt / 2195 dwt
Engines: 4 x B&W 10 cyl diesels type 1026-MTBF-40V
Power Output: 6600 bhp
Speed: 18 knots
Passengers: Nil
First ref: 8 June 1967 Esbjerg to Parkeston Quay (m/v)

Cms ro-ro. Space for 113 trailers. Top deck container crane added at Elsinore in October 1969. Lengthened at Frederikshavn Verft & Tordok A/S in January 1973. Dimensions: 124.19 / 113.59 x 17.00 x 4.93 m. Tonnage: 2602 grt / 740 nt / 2947 dwt. Trailer capacity now 135. Variously used throughout the North Sea from 1967 until 1983 including periods on the Esbjerg to P. Quay service. Also Hamburg to P. Quay between 1980 and 1983 and Bremerhaven to P. Quay in 1983. Was re-named *Dana Gloria* on 30 January 1984. Sold to Tzmar Voyage Ltd, Limassol in November 1984 and in December was re-named *Voyager*. Briefly seen again at P. Quay in January 1985. Converted to a passenger car ferry in 1985. Tonnage: 3956 grt. Passengers: 400 (B:400). Sold to Cross Med Maritime Co, Piraeus and re-named *Monaco* in 1985 for service between Patras and Brindisi, then as *Sitia* in 1988 between Piraeus and Crete. Became a cruise ship in America as the *Tropic Star* in June 1991, *Pacific Star* in May 1993, *Aegaion Star* in April 1995 and *New York Fortune I* in November 1997. Returned to Greece as *Atlantis* in April 2002, then to Miami as *Island Breeze* on 14 September 2007. Refitted as a casino ship in 2008. Sister ship: *Somerset*.

Staveley; GCR
Built: by C.S. Swan & Hunter, Ltd., Newcastle - yard no. 166
Launched: 1 May 1891
Dimensions: 240.7 x 32.0 x 15.2 ft
Tonnage: 1034 grt / 494 nt
Engines: Richardson's, Westgarth & Co., Tr. exp. 22", 35" & 57" - 42"
Power Output: 244 nhp
Speed: 12½ knots
Passengers: 360 (B:30 First & 330 Emigrant class)
First ref: July 1916 Parkeston Quay to Rotterdam for GER

Pcs. Ordered by the Manchester, Sheffield & Lincolnshire Railway for their Grimsby to Hamburg service. Transferred to GCR on 1 August 1897. Requisitioned in October 1914 until 8 July 1916 after which she was loaned to GER for services between Tilbury / P. Quay and Holland. Passengers: 12. Placed on P. Quay to Rotterdam route on 5 March 1919. Her last trip was from Antwerp on 30 August 1919. Returned to GCR on 1 September. Sold in 1932 to British & Irish Steam Packet Co. and re-named *Lady Glen*. Scrapped at Preston in August 1933. Sister ship: *Nottingham* (See also *Lutterworth*)

Stella Polaris; Cruise ship; IMO: 5340431
Built: by Ab Gotaverken, Gothenburg - yard no. 400
Launched: 11 September 1926
Dimensions: 389.3 / 360.5 x 50.5 x 17.0 ft
Tonnage: 5208 grt / 2250 dwt
Engines: 2 x B&W 8 cyl diesels
Power Output: 5250 bhp
Speed: 16 knots
Passengers: 200 (B:200 First class)
First ref: summer 1927 cruise ship to Norway

Pms. Launched by Miss Lillie Lehmkuhl, daughter of Bergen Line MD. Designed in the clipper style complete with bowsprit and built specifically for cruising. Extreme length of 428 feet and crew of 130. (m/v) was on 26 February 1927 from Gothenburg to Tilbury and then onto the Mediterranean. Her annual round the world cruises westward from New York would finish at P. Quay. Laid up in Oslo on 1 September 1939. Moved to Bergen but later captured by the Germans on 30 October 1940. Intermittently used as a hotel ship for U-boat crews until 1 September 1943 and thereafter used as a troopship. Returned to Bergen Line on 7 November 1945 and given an extensive refit at Gotaverken, Gothenburg lasting until 1 June 1946. Passengers: 189. Resumed cruising in August 1946 from New York and the Caribbean. Re-appeared at P. Quay in 1947 though she sailed between Bergen and Newcastle during the summer. Sold in October 1951 to Rederi Ab Clipper of Malmo and refitted. First cruise with Clipper Line was on 10 December 1951 across the Atlantic but no more round the world voyages. Refitted in October 1953 by AG Weser of Bremen. Passengers: 155. Was further refitted until one in October 1968 at Kockums, Malmo reduced passenger numbers still further to 70 and crew to 100. Sold on 23 October 1969 to International House Co. Ltd of Tokyo. Left Lisbon on 28 October to become a floating hotel and restaurant, anchored in Kisho Nishiura, Japan as *Floating Restaurant Scandinavia*. Sold in August 2006 to Petro-Fast Ab of Sweden for use as a hotel and restaurant in Stockholm. Whilst under tow to China she sank on 2 September 2006 around 280 n.miles s.w. of Tokyo.

Stena Britannica; Chartered; IMO: 7528623
Built: by Hyundai Heavy Industries Co Ltd., Ulsan, South Korea - yard no. 648
Launched: 13 January 1978
Dimensions: 155.99 x 22.71 x 7.22 m
Tonnage: 5466 grt / 2485 nt / 8811 dwt
Engines: 2 x Pielstick 12 cyl diesels type 12PC2-5V-400V
Power Output: 11475 kw
Speed: 17 knots
Passengers: 12
First Ref: 1986

Cms ro-ro. Briefly in service with Stena Portlink between P. Quay and Esbjerg. Other names: Launched as *Stena Project* (1978), then *Atlantic Project* (1978), *Merzario Hispania* (1981), *Stena Hispania* (1983), *Kotka Violet* (1984) and *Stena Hispania* (1985). Re-named *Stena Britannica* on 8 January 1986 and fitted with an extra freight deck - now 2100 lane metres or 562 teus. Later re-named *Bore Britannica* (1988) and *Finnforest* (1996). Scrapped in July 2011 in Turkey.

Stena Gothica; Chartered; IMO: 7528609
Built: by Hyundai Heavy Industries Co Ltd., Ulsan, South Korea - yard no. 646
Launched: 26 August 1977
Dimensions: 155.99 x 22.97 x 7.22 m
Tonnage: 5466 grt / 2485 nt / 8811 dwt
Engines: 2 x Pielstick 12 cyl diesels type 12PC2-5V-400V
Power Output: 11475 kw
Speed: 17 knots
Passengers: 12
First Ref: December 1985

Cms ro-ro. Space for 2100 lane metres of freight or 562 teus. In service with Stena Portlink between P. Quay and Esbjerg until 1986. Launched as *Stena Prosper* for Stena Container Line Ltd. Other names: *Atlantic Prosper* (1978), *Merzario Ionia* (1981) and *Stena Ionia* (1982). Sold to Rederi Ab Concordia of Gothenburg on 27 December 1985 when re-named *Stena Gothica*. Later became *Bore Gothica* (1988) and *Finnbirch* (1996). Sank in a storm off Gotland on 1 November 2006 with the loss of two crew.

Stena Sailer; Chartered; IMO: 7365069
Built: by Verolme Cork Dockyards Ltd, Cork, Ireland - yard no. 874
Launched: 12 September 1974
Dimensions: 119,00 x 16.20 x 4.20 m
Tonnage: 2353 grt / 2495 dwt
Engines: 4 x British Polar diesels type SF112VS-F
Power Output: 6030 kw
Speed: 17 knots
Passengers: 12
First ref: January 1982

Cms ro-ro. Space for 432 lane metres of freight. Chartered by Sealink UK Ltd from January 1982 to June 1982 for service between P. Quay and HvH. Also on the P. Quay to HvH service from June 1986 to end of August 1986 for Sealink BF. Other names: Launched as *Dundalk* for B&I Line and later re-named *Stena Sailer* (1980), *St. Cybi* (1988), *Wind Cybi* (1991) and *Theseus* (1992). Scrapped in May 2006 at Aliaga, Turkey.

Stockport; GCR
Built: by Earle's Shipbuilding & Eng. Co. Ltd., Hull - yard no. 577
Launched: 15 May 1911
Dimensions: 276.0 / 265.0 x 36.0 x 17.4 ft
Tonnage: 1637 grt / 832 nt
Engines: Earle's Tr. exp. 22", 35" & 60" - 42"
Power Output: 309 nhp / 1912 ihp
Speed: 13 knots
Passengers: 450 (B:140 First, 10 Second and 300 Emigrant class)
First ref: November 1918 repatriation sailings between Parkeston Quay and Rotterdam. Returned to the GCR on 12 November 1919.

Pcs. Details as per *Dewsbury*. Also requisitioned in WW2 as a convoy rescue ship but was lost by having been torpedoed in the North Atlantic in February 1943.

Storebelt; DFDS
Built: by Lobnitz, Coulborn & Co., Renfrew - yard no. 176
Launched: 10 December 1879
Dimensions: 198.5 / 188.7 x 27.0 x 13.7 ft
Tonnage: 589 grt / 328 nt / 540 dwt
Engines: Lobnitz c.o. 2 cyl 32" & 60" - 36"
Power Output: 710 ihp
Speed: 10 knots
Passengers: 12
First ref: late 1890s

Cs. Seen on the P. Quay to Esbjerg route. First delivered to G Bottern of Nakskov in February 1880. Purchased by DFDS on 4 January 1883. Sold on 23 March 1922 to Mezz & Bleckwehl of Hamburg for scrapping.

Stour (I); River Services
Built: 1864 in Poplar, London.
Dimensions: 120.5 x 15.0 x 6.9 ft
Tonnage: 87 tons

Pps. Fitted with a simple oscillating single cylinder engine, 40 nhp, and space for 150 passengers. Replaced the *River Queen*. Sold in 1878 and replaced by *Stour (II)*. Sister ship: *Ipswich (I)*

Stour (II); River Services
Built: 1878 by the Thames Ironworks Co. Ltd., Victoria Dock, London.
Dimensions: 125.0 x 17.6 x 6.8 ft
Tonnage: 112 tons
Engines: T.A. Young of London s.o. 2 cyl 23½" - 27"
Power Output: 30 nhp

Pps. Replaced *Stour (I)*. Sold in 1900 to Thames Steamboat Co (1897) Ltd. for Thames river service. Scrapped in 1908. Sister ship: *Orwell*

Suffolk; DFDS; IMO: 6610522
Built: by Cantieri Navale Felszegi S.p.A.. Trieste - yard no.81
Launched: 30 October 1965
Dimensions: 79.22 / 70.00 x 14.25 x 3.73 m
Tonnage: 999 grt / 424 nt / 1072 dwt
Engines: 1 MAK 10 cyl diesel type 10MZU582AK
Power Output: 2200 bhp
Speed: 14 knots
Passengers: Nil
First ref: January 1968 Esbjerg to Parkeston Quay

Cms ro-ro. Cost Dkr 7m. The first DFDS cargo ship equipped with a bow visor. Launched as *Forenede* and re-named *Suffolk* on 11 May 1966. Capacity of 50 teus. (m/v) was on 13 May 1966 from Copenhagen to Felixstowe. First seen at P. Quay in January 1968 and then at various times until December 1977. Lengthened between 1 September and 14 October 1969 at Boele's Scheepswerven en Machinefabriek N.V., Bolnes, Holland. Dimensions: 94.19 / 84.99 x 14.25 x 3.73 m. Tonnage: 1211 grt / 568 nt / 1471 dwt. Capacity now 85 teus. Sold on 31 December 1979 to Abdull Jaleel Musa A. Samkari Trading & Shipping Establishment, Jeddah and re-named *Nawaf*. Sold in 1982 to Najd Marine Corp. Jeddah. Damaged in a collision off Jeddah on 28 December 1988 and sunk. Sister ship: *Sussex*

Suffolk (I); River Services
Built: 1881 by the Thames Ironworks Co. Ltd., Victoria Dock, London.

Pps. A 90 ton vessel that was only in service with the GER for two years. Sold in 1883 to Messrs G.P. Bidder and H. Harrison. Sold abroad in 1884.

Suffolk (II); River Services
Built: 1895 by Earle's Shipbuilding & Eng. Co. Ltd., Hull - yard no. 395
Dimensions: 165.3 x 21.2 x 7.0 ft
Tonnage: 245 grt / 104 nt
Engines: Earles compound diagonal 2 cyl 24" & 46" - 42"
Power Output: 90 nhp
Speed: 10 knots
Passengers: 450

Pps. Launched for the GER on 13 May 1895 for service between Ipswich, Harwich and Felixstowe. Also sailed on excursions to Felixstowe and Great Yarmouth. Requisitioned in 1914-18 as picket ship. Re-opened the local pre-war services on 26 May 1919. Sold in 1930 to Dutch owners and broken up in Holland in 1931. Sister ship: *Essex (I)*

Suffolk Ferry; LNER; IMO: 5343160
Built: by John Brown & Co. Ltd., Clydebank - yard no. 638
Launched: 7 May 1947
Dimensions: 404.5 / 380.0 x 61.5 / 58.5 x 12.1 ft
Tonnage: 3134 grt / 1427 nt / 1977 dwt
Engines: 2 x John Brown Sulzer 6 cyl diesels
Power Output: 386 nhp / 3200 ihp
Speed: 13½ knots
Passengers: 12 (B: 12 First class)
First ref: 3 September 1947 Harwich to Zeebrugge (m/v) for LNER.

Cms tf. Launched by Mrs. A. Bibby, wife of LNER Steamship Committee Chairman. Crew of 29. Fitted with 1126 feet of rail track with space for 38 continental wagons. Initial instability problems corrected at Palmers of Hebburn in December 1947 where one central rudder was changed for twin rudders. Remained in service until July 1980 having sailed over 1 million miles. Sold for scrap in August 1980, left under tow from tug *Engeland* on 25 November and was broken up by Boelwerf N.V. of Antwerp in April 1981.

Surrey; DFDS; IMO: 6920159
Built: by Helsingor Skibsvaerft og Maskinbyggeri A/S, Ellsinore - yard no.388
Launched: 14 May 1969
Dimensions: 114.50 / 105.00 x 19.00 x 5.78 m
Tonnage: 3375 grt / 1079 nt / 3647 dwt
Engines: 2 x B&W 8 cyl diesels type 8S45HU
Power Output: 8800 bhp
Speed: 17½ knots
Passengers: 12
First ref: November 1970 arrival at Parkeston Quay from Esbjerg

Cms ro-ro. Cost Dkr 29m. (m/v) was on 2 September 1969 from Esbjerg to Grimsby. Space for 87 x 12m trailers. Lengthened at Amsterdamsche Droogdok - Maatschappij N.V. in spring 1975. Dimensions: 132.70 / 123.25 x 19.00 x 5.82 m. Tonnage: 4061 grt / 1665 nt / 5436 dwt. Capacity now 128 x 12m trailers. Variously used throughout the North Sea, mostly to Grimsby, and then between Esbjerg to P. Quay from 1972 onwards. Also Hamburg to P. Quay from 1980 to 1982 and again from 1984 to 1988 plus Bremerhaven to P. Quay in 1988. Sold to Ellerman Wilson Line Ltd, Hull and DFDS (UK) Ltd, Hull on 10 May 1979. Sold to DFDS A/S in August 1981. Sold to A.K. Ventouris, Pireus, Greece in 1992 for services in eastern Mediterranean and re-named *Patra*. Converted to passenger and car ferry in 1993 and re-named *Anna V*. Passengers: 740 (B:140), 420 cars. Sold to Priority Shipping Ltd, Kingstown, St. Vincent in April 1997 and re-named *Jupiter*, then sold to Perco Shipping, Kingstown in 1999. Arrested in Brindisi in June 2000, laid up and later broken up in India in April 2005 having been re-named *Pit*.

Sussex; DFDS; IMO: 6609303
Built: by Cantieri Navale Felszegi S.p.A.. Trieste - yard no.82
Launched: 19 February 1966
Dimensions: 94.19 / 84.99 x 14.25 x 3.73 m
Tonnage: 1211 grt / 568 nt / 1471 dwt.
Engines: 1 MAK 10 cyl diesel type 10MZU582AK
Power Output: 2200 bhp
Speed: 14 knots
Passengers: Nil
First ref: December 1969 Esbjerg to Parkeston Quay

Cms ro-ro. Cost Dkr 7.6m. Launched as *United* and re-named *Sussex* on 29 August 1966. Dimensions: 79.20 / 70.00 x 14.25 x 3.70m. Tonnage: 999 grt / 424 nt / 1069 dwt. Capacity of 50 teus. (m/v) was on 6 September 1966 from Copenhagen to Antwerp. Details the same as for Sister ship: *Suffolk* except lengthening at Boele's Scheepswerven was between 14 October and 29 November 1969. Capacity now 85 teus First seen at P. Quay in December 1969 and then at infrequent intervals until January 1977. Likewise sold to Samkari Trading in December 1979, re-named *Sattam,* and then sold to Najd Marine Corp. in 1982.

Tara; Arrow Line; IMO: 5222421
Built: in 1957 by Fincantieri Trieste, Italy
Tonnage: 7441 grt / 10933 dwt
First ref: November 1973

rcms. Refrigerated general purpose cargo ship that sailed on deep sea routes from P. Quay's Fishers Terminal. Other names: Launched as *Maria Angela Martinoli.* Sold to Preekookeanska Plovidba in 1966 when re-named *Tara.* Re-named *Tarka* in 1982 and arrived in Bombay for scrapping on 9 April 1982.

Thomas Wehr; Chartered; IMO: 7613404
Built: by Rickmans Werft GmbH, Bremerhaven, Germany - yard no. 388
Launched: 18 January 1977
Dimensions: 108.30 x 17.43 x 5.20 m
Tonnage: 1599 grt / 2900 dwt
Engines: 2 x MAK 8 cyl diesels type 8M453
Power Output: 4410 kw
Speed: 17½ knots
Passengers: 12
First Ref: March 1985

Cms ro-ro. Space for 1148 lane metres of freight. In March 1985 she was briefly chartered by DFDS and temporarily re-named *Dana Germania* for service between P. Quay and Esbjerg / Hamburg. Other names: Launched as *Thomas Wehr* (1977), delivered as *Wacro Express,* then *Thomas Wehr* (1978), *Tor Neerlandia* (1982), *Dana Germania* (1985), *Thomas Wehr* (1985), *Mana* (1993), *Santa Maria* (1993), *Fuldatal* (1993), *Hornlink* (1994), *Thomas Wehr* (1994), *Anglian Way* (2001), *Taurine* (2009) and *Lider Samsun* (2010).

Thule; Thule Line
Built: by Wigham Richardson Ltd., Neptune Yard, Low Walker, Tyneside - yard no. 272
Launched: 29 February 1892
Dimensions: 282.4 x 37.7 x 15.7 ft
Tonnage: 1914 grt
Engines: 3 cyl Tr. exp.
Power Output: 2760 ihp
Speed: 14 knots
Passengers: 75 (50 First & 25 Second class)
First ref: 9 May 1910 arrival at Parkeston Quay from Gothenburg

Pcs. Entered service between Gothenburg and London Tilbury. Transferred to Swedish Lloyd in January 1916. Rebuilt in 1920 with an enlarged superstructure, boat deck and new bridge. Resumed Gothenburg to P. Quay / London service in 1920 until 1921. Sold in December 1925 to Villain & Fassio soc.anon. Italia di Mercantile and re-named *Franca Fassio* for service between Genoa and Barcelona. Chartered to Tirrenia Co, Italy in 1935. Lost to being torpedoed by Royal Navy submarine Triton on 4 October 1940 off Capo Noli.

Thy; DFDS
Built: by Burmeister & Wain, Copenhagen - yard no. 51
Launched: May 1869
Dimensions: 150.0 / 140.0 x 20.5 x 7.0 ft
Tonnage: 266 grt / 180 nt / 118 dwt
Engines: B&W c.o. 4 cyl (2)15" & (2)30" - 20"
Power Output: 250 ihp
Speed: 9 knots
Passengers: 210 Deck class
First ref: early 1880s

Pcs. Briefly seen on the P. Quay to Esbjerg route. Sold on 1 February 1922 to Petersen & Albeck of Copenhagen for scrapping.

Thyra; DFDS
Built: by Frederikshavns Vaerft & Flydedok A/S, Frederikshavn - yard no. 173
Launched: 6 December 1922
Dimensions: 276.5 / 235.0 x 35.5 x 16.4 ft
Tonnage: 1088 grt / 560 nt / 1535 dwt
Engines: 1 x Atlas of Copenhagen steam turbine
Power Output: 915 ihp
Speed: 10 knots
Passengers: 12
First ref: mid 1940s

Cs. Cost: Dkr 1.9m. Seen on the P. Quay to Esbjerg route. Other names: *Thyra II* (1940) and *Thyra* (1945). Sold on 8 February 1957 to Eisen und Metall KG Lehr & Co. of Hamburg for scrapping.

Tjaldur; DFDS
Built: by Murdoch & Murray, Port Glasgow - yard no. 158
Launched: 26 March 1898
Dimensions: 206.7 / 198.0 x 29.9 x 12.4 ft
Tonnage: 795 grt / 433 nt / 622 dwt
Engines: Rankin & Blackmore, Greenock Tr. exp 18", 29" & 47" - 33"
Power Output: 800 ihp
Speed: 10 knots
Passengers: 353 (31 First, 22 Second & 300 Deck class)
First ref: 1923

Pcs. Seen on the P. Quay to Esbjerg route. First delivered to A. Schaumann of Nikolaistad in April 1898 as the *Vega.* Purchased by DFDS on 4 May 1904 and re-named *Tjaldur.* Sold on 21 June 1939 to Constantin Atychides of Panama and re-named *Dora.* Sunk by the Royal Navy off Tunis on 21 December 1942.

Tor Britannia; DFDS; IMO: 7361312
Built: by Flender Werft A.G., Lubeck - yard no.607
Launched: 10 October 1974
Dimensions: 182.35 / 163.00 x 23.60 x 6.30 m
Tonnage: 14905 grt / 7933 nt / 3335 dwt
Engines: 4 x Pielstick 12 cyl diesels type 12PC3V
Power Output: 45600 bhp / 33540 kw
Speed: 24½ knots
Passengers: 1357 (B:845)
First ref: April 1983 arrival at Parkeston Quay from Gothenburg

Pcms ro-ro. Cost £13m. Originally built for Rederi AB Salenia, Salenrederierna AB and Rederi AB Transatlantic, Gothenburg, each owning a third share. (m/v) was on 21 May 1975 for Tor Line between Gothenburg and Amsterdam / Felixstowe. Space for 440 cars. Briefly re-named *Scandinavian Star* on 2 November 1981 after being sold to Scandinavian Seaways (Bahamas) Ltd for cruising between Freeport and Florida. Laid up then sold on 26 March 1982 to DFDS, resumed the name of *Tor Britannia* and put on original services from Gothenburg. UK port switched from Felixstowe to P. Quay on 1 April 1983. Rebuilt at Blohm & Voss, Hamburg between 8 November 1990 and 11 January 1991. Re-named *Prince of Scandinavia* on 20 November 1990. Tonnage: 15730 grt / 8119 nt / 2459 dwt. Passengers: 1543 (B:1213). 375 cars or 150 cars and 70 teus. Sold to Moby Lines Spa, Italy on 24 October 2003 and re-named *Moby Drea.* In service from May 2004 between Livorno and Olbia and from May 2007 between Genoa and Porto Torres. Still in service. Sister ship: *Tor Scandinavia.*

Tor Finlandia; Chartered; IMO: 7369039
Built: by Framnaes Mekaniske Verksted, Sandefjord, Norway - yard no. 182
Launched: November 1973
Dimensions: 136.80 x 21.06 x 7.10 m
Tonnage: 4128 grt / 1619 nt / 7480 dwt
Engines: 2 x Pielstick-Lindholmen 12 cyl diesel
Power Output: 8825 kw
Speed: 18½ knots
Passengers: 12

Cms. Space for 246 teus. Sailed between P. Quay and Hamburg for DFDS in 1983 when chartered to Tor Line. Other names: *Baltic Wasa* (1984), *Ocean Link* (1984), *Assi Scan Link* (1992), *Acacia* (2004) and *Aegean Sky* (2007). Arrived at Alang, India in October 2010 for scrapping.

Tor Scandinavia; DFDS; IMO: 7361324
Built: by Flender Werft A.G., Lubeck - yard no.608
Launched: 4 November 1975
Dimensions: 182.35 / 163.00 x 23.60 x 6.30 m
Tonnage: 14893 grt / 7964 nt / 3335 dwt
Engines: 4 x Pielstick 12 cyl diesels type 12PC3V
Power Output: 45600 bhp / 33540 kw
Speed: 24½ knots
Passengers: 1357 (B:845)
First ref: 1 April 1983 arrival at Parkeston Quay from Gothenburg

Pcms ro-ro. Originally built for Rederi AB Salenia, Salenrederierna AB and Rederi AB Transatlantic, Gothenburg, each owning a third share. (m/v) was on 15 April 1976 for Tor Line between Gothenburg and Amsterdam / Felixstowe. Space for 440 cars. Sold to DFDS Esbjerg on 1 December 1981. Chartered as a floating exhibition ship, *Worldwide Expo,* between 25 October 1982 and 25 February 1983 in the far east and Singapore. UK port switched from Felixstowe to P. Quay on 1 April 1983. Sold to K/S Difko, Esbjerg on 19 December 1983. In service Gothenburg / Esbjerg to P. Quay from 1984. Damaged by arson fire on 25 September 1989 en-route from Gothenburg to P. Quay with the loss of two lives. Sold back to DFDS on 14 January 1991. Rebuilt at Blohm & Voss, Hamburg between 17 January and 11 March 1991. Re-named *Princess of Scandinavia* on 22 February 1991. Tonnage: 15730 grt / 8119 nt / 2427 dwt. Passengers: 1543 (B:1213) 375 cars or 150 cars and 70 teus. Sold to Moby Lines, Italy on 6 September 2006 and re-named *Moby Otta.* In service from May 2007 between Genoa and Porto Torres. Still in service. Sister ship: *Tor Britannia*

Train Ferry No. 1 (Essex Ferry); LNER
Built: by Sir W.G. Armstrong, Whitworth & Co. Ltd., Low Walker, Newcastle - yard no. 921
Launched: 3 August 1917
Dimensions: 363.5 / 350.6 x 61.5 / 58.7 x 9.5 ft
Tonnage: 2683 grt / 1533 nt / 960 dwt
Engines: Wallsend Slipway & Eng. Co. Tr. exp. 6 cyl in 2 sets 18", 29" & 47" - 27"
Power Output: 403 nhp / 3200 ihp
Speed: 12 knots
Passengers: Nil
First ref: 17 July 1924 Harwich to Zeebrugge for GETFL.

Cs tf. One of three train ferries built for the British Military Authorities (BMA) in WW1 to transport supplies to France. Total order cost of £560,000. First sailed Richborough to Calais on 10 February 1918. Bought by the LNER controlled Great Eastern Train Ferries Ltd (GETFL) to inaugurate a new Harwich to Zeebrugge service as from 24 April 1924. Fitted with 1080 feet of rail track with space for 54 loaded 12-ton wagons. Requisitioned on 24 September 1939 as a transport ship. Served out WW2 variously re-named from October 1940 onwards as *Iris / H.M.S. Iris / H.M.S. Princess Iris.* Sold to HM Government in January 1942. Repurchased by LNER for £33,334 in May 1946 and resumed Harwich service on 16 August 1946 having been re-named *Essex Ferry.* Tonnage: 2755 grt / 1065 nt / 1250 dwt and with 1018 feet of track. Replaced in 1956 by a new *Essex Ferry* and was re-named *Essex Ferry II* before being broken up at T.W. Ward's in Grays in 1957.
Sister ships: *Train Ferry No. 2, Train Ferry No. 3.*

Train Ferry No. 2; LNER
Built: by Sir W.G. Armstrong, Whitworth & Co. Ltd., Low Walker, Newcastle - yard no. 922
Launched: 12 September 1917
Dimensions: 363.5 / 350.5 x 61.5 / 58.7 x 9.5 ft
Tonnage: 2678 grt / 1533 nt / 960 dwt
Engines: Wallsend Slipway & Eng. Co. Tr. exp. 6 cyl in 2 sets 18", 29" & 47" - 27"
Power Output: 403 nhp / 3200 ihp
Speed: 12 knots
Passengers: Nil
First ref: 24 April 1924 Harwich to Zeebrugge for GETFL.

Cs tf. As per *Train Ferry No. 1.* First sailed Richborough to Calais on 10 February 1918. Requisitioned on 24 September 1939 and used as a transport ship until being shelled and sunk at St. Valery-en-Caux, near Le Havre, on 13 June 1940. Sister ships: *Train Ferry No. 1, Train Ferry No. 3.*

Train Ferry No. 3; LNER
Built: by Fairfield Shipbuilding & Eng. Co. Ltd., Govan, Scotland - yard no. 540
Launched: 12 September 1917
Dimensions: 363.5 / 350.6 x 61.5 / 58.6 x 9.5 ft
Tonnage: 2672 grt / 1533 nt / 960 dwt
Engines: Fairfield Tr. exp. 6 cyl in 2 sets 18", 29" & 47" - 27"
Power Output: 410 nhp / 3220 ihp
Speed: 12 knots
Passengers: Nil
First ref: 25 April 1924 Harwich to Zeebrugge for GETFL.

Cs tf. As per *Train Ferry No. 1.* First sailed Southampton to Dieppe in December 1917. Opened Harwich to Calais route on 8 November 1931. Requisitioned on 11 October 1939 as a transport ship. Served from October 1940 onwards as *Daffodil / H.M.S. Daffodil.* Sold to HM Government in January 1942. Was mined and sunk off Dieppe on 17 March 1945. Sister ships: *Train Ferry No. 1, Train Ferry No. 2.*

Transcontainer 1; SNCF; IMO: 6904478
Built: by Const. Nav. & Ind. de la Mediterranee, La Seyne, France - yard no. 1381
Launched: 30 November 1968
Dimensions: 341.3 / 314.9 x 61.3 x 15.4 ft
Tonnage: 2760 grt / 759 nt / 1829 dwt
Engines: 2 x MotorenWerk Mannheim 8 cyl diesels
Power Output: 4400 bhp / 3236 kw
Speed: 16 knots
Passengers: 36
First ref: 13 March 1969 arrival at Parkeston Quay from Dunkirk (m/v)

Cms ro-ro / lo-lo. Twin deck dual mode container and ro-ro freight ship. Space for 192 containers. Sailed between Dunkirk and P. Quay as a container ship from March 1969 until August 1974. Converted in October 1974 for use as a train ferry but instead was transferred to serve as a freight ship between Dunkirk and Felixstowe from 8 January 1975 until April 1984. Sold in 1986 to Pireo Cia. Nav, S.A., Piraeus. Sold in 1991 to Corporation Trans. S.A., Panama for use as a passenger ferry, *Nour 1,* in Jordan. Sold in 1995 to Kassimeris Arab Bridge, Panama and re-named *Niobe 1.* Later sold in 1995 to Rainbow Lines for service in eastern Mediterranean. Arrived at Alang on 27 December 2000 and scrapped.

Trapezitza; Chartered; IMO: 7806099
Built: by Kochums Varv AB, Malmo, Sweden - yard no. 568
Launched: 13 October 1979
Dimensions: 163.51 / 150.76 x 23.00 x 7.92 m
Tonnage: 8920 grt / 3802 nt / 10500 dwt
Engines: 2 x Sulzer diesels type 7RLA56
Power Output: 17720 hp / 13038 kw
Speed: 18 knots
Passengers: 175 (B:175)
First Ref: September 1988

Cms ro-ro. Space for 2250 lane metres of freight. Equivalent to 175 x 12m trailers or 880 teus. Chartered in September 1988 by DFDS for one month's service between P. Quay and Helsingborg. Other names: Launched as *Ariadne,* then *Soca*

(1980), *Trapezitza* (1981), *Fantasia* (1988), *Channel Seaway* (1989), *Fiesta* (1990), *SeaFrance Cezanne* (1996) and *Western Light* (2011). Arrived at Alang, India in November 2011 for scrapping.

Trondhjem; DFDS
Built: by A/S Helsingors Jernskibs-og Maskinbyggeri, Elsinore - yard no. 168
Launched: 16 December 1922
Dimensions: 242.2 / 230.0 x 35.0 x 16.5 ft
Tonnage: 1399 grt / 826 nt / 1525 dwt
Engines: Helsingors J&M Tr. exp 18", 30" & 50" - 36"
Power Output: 900 ihp
Speed: 11 knots
Passengers: 52 (26 First, 16 Second & 10 Deck class)
First ref: March 1948

Pcs. Cost: Dkr 1,619,659. Made 111 crossings between P. Quay and Esbjerg up until 1963. Refitted in 1946 - Tonnage: 1398 grt / 791 nt / 1385 dwt. Passengers: 24. 1958: Passengers: 12. Sold on 13 August 1963 to Brugse Scheepssloperij N.V. Belgium for scrapping. Sister ship: *Bergenhus*

Tula; DFDS
Built: by Palmer Bros & Co, Jarrow - yard no. 68
Launched: 4 December 1857
Dimensions: 197.5 x 25.6 x 16.0 ft
Tonnage: 695 grt / 521 nt
Engines: Day, Summers & Co. Southampton c.o. 2 cyl 26" & 52" - 36"
Power Output: 450 ihp
Speed: 9 knots
Passengers: 25 (16 First & 9 Second class)
First ref: early 1880s

Cs. Seen on the P. Quay to Esbjerg route. First delivered to Norddeutscher Lloyd, Bremen in January 1858 as the *Schwalbe*. Purchased by DFDS on 10 December 1881 for £5.000 and re-named *Tula*. Sank at a quay in Copenhagen on 21 December 1896, raised and then sold to R. Neugebauer of Hamburg for scrap on 28 February 1897. Sister ships: *Romney, Charkow, Minsk.*

Tunis; DFDS
Built: by A/S Helsingors Jernskibs-og Maskinbyggeri, Elsinore - yard no. 231
Launched: 8 November 1935
Dimensions: 288.1 / 270.0 x 40.2 x 18.3 ft
Tonnage: 1690 grt / 917 nt / 2220 dwt
Engines: 1 x B&W 5 cyl diesel type 550-VF-90
Power Output: 1600 bhp
Speed: 12½ knots
Passengers: 12
First ref: late 1940s

Cms. Cost: Dkr 1,313,037. Seen on the P. Quay to Esbjerg route. Other names: *Aquila* (1941), *AK-47 Aquila* (1941), *Bonanza* (1945), *Tunis* (1946), *Maria T* (1966) and *Mathios* (1972). Scrapped in Greece in August 1978. Sister ship: *Marocco.*

Tyr; DFDS
Built: by Lindholmens Mek.Werkstad, Gothenburg - yard no. 342
Launched: June 1890
Dimensions: 182.0 / 175.0 x 27.0 x 13.2 ft
Tonnage: 526 grt / 315 nt / 627 dwt
Engines: Motala Mek Tr. exp 15", 24" & 40" - 26"
Power Output: 600 ihp
Speed: 10 knots
Passengers: 12
First ref: 1897

Cs. First delivered to A/S Randers d.s. in June 1890. Chartered by DFDS from 20 January 1897 to 19 April 1897 for North Sea service including P. Quay to Esbjerg. Purchased by DFDS on 17 May 1900. Variously seen throughout the North Sea, including P. Quay to Esbjerg, between 1902 and 1950. Sold on 13 January 1951 to H.J. Hansen of Odense for scrapping.

Tzarevetz; Chartered; IMO: 7814462
Built: by Kochums Varv AB, Malmo, Sweden - yard no. 569
Launched: 1 December 1979
Dimensions: 163.51 / 150.76 x 23.00 x 7.92 m
Tonnage: 8920 grt / 3802 nt / 10500 dwt
Engines: 2 x Sulzer diesels type 7RLA56
Power Output: 17720 hp / 13038 kw
Speed: 18 knots
Passengers: 175 (B:175)
First ref: September 1988

Cms ro-ro. Space for 2250 lane metres of freight. Equivalent to 175 x 12m trailers or 880 teus. Chartered in September 1988 by DFDS for one month's service between P. Quay and Bremerhaven. Other names: Launched as *Scandinavia*, then *Tzarevetz* (1982), *Fiesta* (1988), *Fantasia* (1990), *Stena Fantasia* (1990), *P&OSL Canterbury* (1998), *PO Canterbury* (2002), *Alkmini A* (2004) and *Wawel* (2004). Last owners: Polska Zegluga Baltycka, Kolobrzeg, Poland.

Ulster Monarch; Trooping Services
Built: by Harland & Wolff Ltd., Belfast - yard no. 635
Launched: 24 January 1929
Dimensions: 358.9 x 46.0 x 14.9 ft
Tonnage: 3735 grt / 1781 nt / 828 dwt
Engines: 2 x B&W 10 cyl diesels
Power Output: 7500 bhp
Speed: 18 knots
First ref: 1 August 1945

Pcms. Built for Belfast Steamship Co. service between Belfast and Liverpool. (m/v) was on 11 June 1929. Requisitioned as a troopship on 7 September 1939 and later commissioned as *HMS Ulster Monarch* on 5 October 1940. Served on trooping duties between P. Quay and HvH from 1 August 1945 to 16 August 1945. Paid off on 1 October 1945, refitted and resumed commercial service in mid August 1946. Sold for scrap in October 1966, arriving at Van Heyghen Freres, Ghent on 8 December 1966.

Union; DFDS
Built: by Lobnitz, Coulborn & Co., Renfrew - yard no. 149
Launched: 5 May 1875
Dimensions: 197.0 / 188.7 x 25.7 x 13.3 ft
Tonnage: 542 grt / 292 nt / 497 dwt
Engines: B&W compound tandem 4 cyl (2)20" & (2)40" - 36"
Power Output: 450 ihp
Speed: 10 knots
Passengers: 7
First ref: late 1880s

Cs. Seen on the P. Quay to Esbjerg route in the late 1880s and also between 1920 and 1923. First delivered to A/S Nordjyllands d.s. of Aalborg in 1875. Purchased by DFDS on 27 December 1883 for Dkr 250,000. Sold on 25 February 1924 to Schubert & Krohn of Dortmund for scrapping.

Uranus; H.J. Perlbach
Built: 1870 by T & W Smith, North Shields
Dimensions: 216.0 x 30.3 ft
Tonnage: 926 grt / 696 nt
Engines: G. Clark of Sunderland s.o. 2 cyl 40" - 30"
First ref: mid 1880s

Pcs. Sailed between P. Quay and Hamburg in the mid to late 1880s. Formerly known as *Bamborough*.

Valdemar; DFDS
Built: by Andrew Leslie & Co., Hebburn, Newcastle-on-Tyne - yard no. 80
Launched: November 1866
Dimensions: 219.1 / 209.0 x 28.1 x 16.3 ft
Tonnage: 821 grt / 578 nt / 890 dwt
Engines: Thompson, Boyd & Co, Newcastle-upon-Tyne c.o. 2 cyl 25" & 48" - 30"
Power Output: 350 ihp
Speed: 9 knots
Passengers: 5
First ref: mid 1900s

Cs. Seen on the P. Quay to Esbjerg route. Originally ordered by the Anglo Danish and Baltic S.N.Co. Ltd which was taken over by DFDS on 1 January 1867. Purchased on 15 February 1867 for £16,800. Grounded off the island of Rauna, Norway on 27 November 1908 and the wreck later sold.

Vidar; DFDS
Built: by A/S Burmeister & Wain's Maskin-og Skibsbyggeri, Copenhagen - yard no. 301
Launched: 27 February 1915
Dimensions: 267.0 / 252.0 x 36.7 x 17.2 ft
Tonnage: 1353 grt / 720 nt / 1493 dwt
Engines: B&W Tr. exp 22", 36" & 60" - 42"
Power Output: 1650 ihp
Speed: 12 knots
Passengers: 31 (31 First class)
First ref: early 1920s.

Pcs. Cost: Dkr 740,000. Seen on the P. Quay to Esbjerg route. Lost by sinking by German submarine U21 in the North Sea on 31 January 1940.

Vienna (I) (Roulers); GER
Built: by Earle's Shipbuilding & Eng. Co. Ltd., Hull - yard no. 387
Launched: 18 July 1894
Dimensions: 302.4 x 36.0 x 16.2 ft
Tonnage: 1753 grt / 550 nt / 1131 dwt
Engines: Earle's Tr. exp 6 cyl in 2 sets 26", 39½" & 61" - 36"
Power Output: 447 nhp / 5800 ihp
Speed: 18 knots
Passengers: 780 (B: 218 First & 120 Second class)
First ref: 25 October 1894 Parkeston Quay to Hook of Holland (m/v)

Pcs. Requistioned in August 1914. Re-named *Roulers* in August 1919. Placed on the new P. Quay to Zeebrugge service in 1921. Sold for scrap on 23 March 1930. Sister ships: *Berlin, Amsterdam (I).*

Vienna (II); LNER
Built: by John Brown & Co. Ltd., Clydebank - yard no. 527
Launched: 10 April 1929
Dimensions: 366.0 / 350.8 x 50.1 x 15.3 ft
Tonnage: 4227 grt / 1985 nt / 3028 dwt
Engines: 2 x 2 John Brown Curtis srg turbines
Power Output: 1520 nhp / 11500 shp
Speed: 21 knots
Passengers: 708 (B: 427 First & 126 Second class)
First ref: 15 July 1929 Parkeston Quay to Hook of Holland (m/v)

Pcs. Additionally operated as a summer season cruise ship during the 1930s. Requisitioned in December 1939 and served out the war in the Mediterranean. Returned to P. Quay and from 1 August 1945 served as a BAOR troop ship, under LNER management, until 2 July 1960. Left P. Quay on 2 September 1960 under tow for breaking up at Van Huyghen Freres of Ghent. Sister ships: *Prague, Amsterdam (II).*

Viking III; Prins Line; IMO: 6511128
Built: by Orenstein-Koppel und Lubecker Mach A/G, Lubeck, Germany - yard no. 618
Launched: 10 March 1965
Dimensions: 99.50 / 90.02 x 18.32 x 4.42 m
Tonnage: 3824 grt / 1823 nt / 1199 dwt
Engines: 2 x Pielstick-Lindholmens 12 cyl diesels type 12PC2V400
Power Output: 10200 bhp / 7500 kw
Speed: 18½ knots
Passengers: 940 (B: 284)
First Ref: 19 September 1966 Bremerhaven to Parkeston Quay for Lion Ferry.

Pcns ro-ro. Built for Otto Thoresen A/S, Oslo, Norway for service with Thoresen Car Ferries Ltd. between Southampton and Cherbourg / Le Havre. Space for 180 cars or 17 lorries. (m/v) was on 25 June 1965 from Southampton to Cherbourg. Chartered to Lion Ferry, Halmstad for off season sailings from Bremerhaven to P. Quay between 1966 and 1968 before opening a new route from Bremerhaven to Harwich Navyard Dock on 1 January 1969. Left Lion Ferry charter on 31 May 1969. Resumed services from Southampton and later chartered as a car ferry within the UK and Scandinavia. Sold to Da-No Linjen A/S, Oslo in 1982 and renamed *Terje Vigen*. Sold to Rederi Narko A/S, Askim in 1986 and re-named *Scandinavia*. Sold to Europe Cruise Line A/S, Bergen in 1990 and chartered to Vasa Line in Finland as the *Fenno Star*. Sold to Koncern Vaerft A/S, Sandefjord in 1992 and re-named *Sandefjord* for Scandi Line. Became the *Sagafjord* when sold to Saga Linie A/S, Fredrikstad in 2003 and then the *Gabriel Scott* in 2005 when sold to Gabriel Scott Rederi A/S, Kristiansand. Still in service as the *Red Star 1* sailing between Brindisi and Vlore for Panamanian interests since 2007.

Vistula; DFDS
Built: by A/S Burmeister & Wain's Maskin-og Skibsbyggeri, Copenhagen - yard no. 583
Launched: 10 April 1930
Dimensions: 234.2 / 220.0 x 35.7 x 13.1ft
Tonnage: 1250 grt / 753 nt / 425 dwt
Engines: 1 x B&W 6 cyl diesel type 650-MTF-90
Power Output: 1375 bhp
Speed: 13 knots
Passengers: 261 (45 First & 216 Third class)
First ref: 1936.

Pcms. Cost: Dkr 1.115m. Made just two arrivals at P. Quay, in August and September 1936, in conjunction with publicity organised by DFDS and the Danish Bacon Co. During February and March 1946 was used as a troopship between HvH and Tilbury. Sold on 20 April 1966 to Laiva O/Y Polar of Helsinki. Other names: *Wurzburg* (1944), *Vistula* (1945), *Polar* (1966) and *Stella Polar* (1968). Sold on 11 December 1969 to Jos. Boel & Fils, Tamise for scrapping.

Willem Prins van Oranje; SMZ
Built: by John Elder & Co., Govan, Glasgow - yard no. 278
Launched: 26 April 1883
Dimensions: 278.9 x 35.1 x 16.5 ft
Tonnage: 1573 grt / 865 nt
Engines: J. Elder c.o. 2 cyl 60" & 104" - 84"
Power Output: 787 nhp / 4000 hp
Speed: 17 knots
Passengers: 300 by day, 240 by night (B: 150 First class)
First ref: 12 July 1883 Flushing to Queenborough (m/v)

Pcps. Replaced by *Prinses Juliana* in 1909 and on 10 September 1909 arrived for scrapping at Hendrik-ido-Ambacht. Sister ships: *Prinses Elisabeth, Prinses Marie, Prins Hendrk.*

Winston Churchill; DFDS; IMO: 6718233
Built: by Cantieri Navale del Tirreno e Riuniti S.p.A., Rio Trigoso, Genova - yard no.277
Launched: 25 April 1967
Dimensions: 461.5 / 410.4 x 67.4 x 19.4 ft
Tonnage: 8658 grt / 4488 nt / 1790 dwt
Engines: 2 x B&W 10 cyl diesels type 1050-VT2BF-110
Power Output: 14000 bhp
Speed: 21 knots
Passengers: 462 (124 First, 274 Second & 64 Deck class)
First ref: 2 June 1967 Parkeston Quay to Esbjerg (m/v)

Pcms ro-ro. Cost Dkr 51m. Space for 180 cars. First arrival at P. Quay was on 29 May 1967 for berthing trials. Refitted at Helsingor in 1971 as a one class ship with increased accommodation. Passengers: 757 (B:641 in 232 cabins & 116 couchettes). In service between Esbjerg and P. Quay until 22 May 1978 and then displaced onto Esbjerg to Newcastle service on 4 June 1978. Also sailed Gothenburg to Newcastle and Esbjerg to Faroes until 1991. Re-appeared at P. Quay each May from 1979 to 1983 as relief ship. Sold to Mols Linien A/S of Esbjerg on 26 December 1985 but re-purchased on 27 August 1986. From May 1987 to September 1991 undertook early and late season North Cape and Baltic cruises. Briefly in service between Esbjerg and P. Quay as a freight ship from 15 to 26 January 1993. Sold on 4 July 1996 to Emerald Empress Holdings Ltd, Kingstown and re-named *Mayan Empress*. Sold 1 May 2003 to Weesham Shipping in Dubai and then for breaking up at Alang, India where she arrived on 22 January 2004.

Woodcock; GSNCo.
Built: 1906 by Gourlay Bros & Co., Dundee - yard no. 221
Tonnage: 1673 grt

Engines: Tr. Exp
Speed: 16 knots
Passengers: 56 (44 First and 12 Second class)
First ref: late 1900s

Pcs. Seen on the P. Quay to Hamburg route. Sold in 1925 to Italian interests.

Wrexham; GCR
Built: by Sir Raylton Dixon & Co. Ltd., Cleveland Dock, Middlesborough - yard no. 494
Launched: 1 December 1902
Dimensions: 239.9 x 35.3 x 20.8 ft
Tonnage: 1432 grt / 818 nt / 1000 dwt
Engines: Richardson's, Westgarth & Co., Tr. exp. 22", 35" & 59" - 39"
Power Output: 217 nhp / 1700 ihp
Speed: 12½ knots
Passengers: 189 (B:24 First, 28 Second & 137 Emigrant class)
First ref: December 1914 Parkeston Quay to Rotterdam

Pcs. Originally built as *Nord II*, one of three sister ships, for the Angyfartygs Aktieb Nord of Helsinki and delivered on 23 January 1903. Bought by the GCR on 8 March 1905, re-named *Wrexham* and put on their Grimsby to Rottcrdam / Antwcrp services. Loaned to GER for services between Tilbury / P. Quay and Rotterdam as from 2 December 1914. Last sailing was from Rotterdam to P. Quay in October 1916. Requisitioned in November 1916 as an armaments carrier. Ran aground and sank on 19 June 1918 near Chavanga in Gulf of Archangel.

Yarmouth; GER
Built: by Gourlay Bros. & Co., Dundee - yard no. 208
Launched: 18 March 1903
Dimensions: 245.3 x 31.3 x 15.3 ft
Tonnage: 806 grt / 218 nt / 702 dwt
Engines: Gourlay's Tr. exp. 6 cyl in 2 sets 15½", 25¼" & 41" - 36"
Power Output: 201 nhp
Speed: 14 knots
Passengers: Nil
First ref: June 1903 Parkeston Quay to Rotterdam

Pcs. Last seen on 27 October 1908 listing heavily near the Outer Gabbard light vessel. Sank with the loss of 22 lives. Sister ship: *Cromer*

Zealous; GER
Built: by Messrs J. & W. Dudgeon, Cubitt Town, London
Launched: 24 May 1864
Dimensions: 245.0 / 230.0 x 27.1 x 11.8 ft
Tonnage: 613 grt / 455 nt / 499 dwt
Engines: J & W Dudgeon s.o. 2 cyl 54" - 30"
Power Output: 220 nhp / 950 hp
Speed: 10 knots
Passengers: 150
First ref: 8 July 1864 Harwich to Rotterdam (m/v)

Pcps. Launched by Miss Goodson. Inaugurated the Harwich to Antwerp service on 1 August 1864. Rebuilt in 1873 for carrying cargo as well as passengers. Sold for scrap in 1887. Sister ship: *Avalon (I)*.

Zeeland; Chartered; IMO: 7230599
Built: by Ateliers & Chantiers du Havre, France - yard no. 212
Launched: 23 October 1972
Dimensions: 420.3 x 65.6 x 18.0 ft o.a.
Tonnage: 6801 grt / 3370 nt / 1202 dwt
Engines: 4 x Stork Werkspoor 8 cyl diesels type 8TM410
Power Output: 20400 hp / 15014 kw
Speed: 21 knots
Passengers: 1500 (B: 544)
First ref: 2 April 1984 Hook of Holland to Parkeston Quay

Pcms ro-ro. Built for A/S Larvik - Frederikshavnferjen, Norway as the *Peter Wessel*. First in service with Larvik Line between Larvik - Frederikshavn on 19 August 1973. Sold in 1984 to Admiral Shipping (Nassau) Ltd, Bahamas. Chartered by SMZ on 30 March 1984 for two years and re-named *Zeeland*. Space for 300 cars or 32 cars and 32 x 15m trailers. Went off charter on 25 March 1986 having meanwhile been sold to Stena AB, Gothenburg in November 1985. Re-named *Stena Nordica* for service between Moss, Frederikshavn and Gothenburg. Sold 23 November 1988 to Jadrolinija of Yugoslavia and re-named *Marko Polo* for service in 1989 between Italy and Greece. Variously chartered to TT-Line in 1992, Olympic Ferries in 1993 and Comanav in 1994. Still in service between Ancona and Split.

Credits

My sources of information have ranged from that which has been published before to a snippet of detail found hidden away on the internet. To those responsible for work that included material relevant to this subject I offer my grateful appreciation and trust that it be readily accepted. Within such an eclectic collection of material I have woven a variety of official detail from documentation and other reports not known to have been published before.

My intention throughout was to show that there was more to Harwich than just the prestigious 'Harwich to the Hook of Holland route', a route fully accounted for in the Ferry Publications book, *Harwich - Hook of Holland 1893-2010*, and my initial reference was '100 Years of Parkeston Quay and its Ships' by Philip Cone. My sincere thanks therefore go to Philip for allowing me to use his material as also do they go to Robert Clow for permission to include items from amongst his extensive collection of historic railway and shipping memorabilia, to Jerzy Sweiszkowski for the use of his research into the early days of the railway ships and the troopships, to Stephen Gooch for providing a source of photographs and material relating to DFDS and to David Cobley for the loan of material covering the early years of the railway's activities and on into the 1930s.

My final thanks go to Colin Crawford, a former Parkeston Quay Shipping and Port Manager, for kindly agreeing to write the foreword and to Miles Cowsill of Ferry Publications and Ian Smith of Camrose Media for having turned my volume of dry text into such a readable end result.